Travaux
d'Humanisme et Renaissance

N° CCCXXII

MALCOLM SMITH

November 15th 1941 - October 26th 1994

MALCOLM SMITH

RENAISSANCE STUDIES

ARTICLES 1966-1994

Introduced
by

M.A. SCREECH and MICHAEL HEATH

Edited
by

RUTH CALDER

LIBRAIRIE DROZ S.A.
11, rue Massot
GENÈVE
1999

ISBN: 2-600-00281-2
ISSN: 0082-6081

CONTENTS

FOREWORD

The death of a scholar in the flower of his age is more than a personal sadness. How much more would he have written if he had lived; and how many more young people would he have led into the intricate ways of scholarship.

A scholar is remembered for two things: for his direct influence on his students (and on his colleagues); and for his writings. There was no doubt in Malcolm Smith's mind which came first. He was a born teacher. He loved teaching. He was seldom happier than when he had a group sitting round a table with a *Ronsard*, a *Du Bellay* or a *Montaigne* open before them. He had a flair for awakening dormant curiosity wherever he saw it. He could make Ronsard come alive as few others can. He was a profoundly poetic man, with a love for the rhythms of Ronsard and a passion for the roots and achievements of Humanist poetry, in French first, but in Latin and English too. Seeing how much he wrote, it is a surprise to realise that for him, scholarship came second. First came a determination to awaken in his students an interest in the text and an appreciation of it. Only then did he fan the flames of scholarly curiosity in the young, bringing them to see it as a means of deepening a truer appreciation of the beauty and significance of what they read. He delighted in Ronsard's love poetry; it was often through those sonnets that he led his students on to other things: he never doubted though that the greatness of the *Prince des poëtes* was especially to be appreciated in the more doctrinal and combative verse, in the *Hymnes* and in the *Discours*.

That Ronsard was a committed Roman Catholic was an added attraction, for Malcolm Smith was a firm and serene believer in that faith. Was that partly an off-shoot of his Irish roots? He was at once a very English Londoner and a man gently aware of the Irish origins of his family. It was typical that, when he wanted to find out at first hand what life was like in Ulster, he got on his bike and cycled all over the north of the island, criss-crossing the frontier and, even more important, criss-crossing the multiple and complex cultural divides. He stayed in boarding-house after boarding-house, listening, joking and questioning, delighting in being a Lon-doner called Smith whom nobody could 'place'. He came back with a degree of optimism.

Montaigne appealed to him also partly for the allegiance shown in the *Essais*, and in real life, to the *Eglise catholique, apostolique, et Romaine*. Like many a Renaissance scholar he was intrigued that the questioning by so many influential writers and thinkers in the first half of the sixteenth century did not lead to an even wider rejection of the Church of Rome. French intellectuals did not all leave it in droves. He attributed that in part to the influence of Ronsard and Montaigne, who showed that the old religion could be intellectually respectable and satisfying.

Malcolm Smith wrote to Cardinals and to the Vatican Library in the hope of unearthing documents touching on the religion of Montaigne, and especially on the process by which Montaigne made his way into the *Index Librorum Prohibitorum*. He found it hard to believe that a few bundles of papers were not to be found sculling about somewhere, misplaced and unrecognised.

That did not mean that Malcolm Smith lived and studied with blinkers on his eyes and mind. He had a special weakness for the Protestant epic poets, especially for Du Bartas; and he studied everything which, in the Renaissance, savoured of œcumenical understanding, of concord, of tolerance, or of political realism in matters of religion.

Everyone who knew him will have his own treasured memories. I remember first the gangling young man with the mischievous grin who first came to me in the early sixties after studying Renaissance literature for his B.A. at U.C.L. with D.P. Walker. (He got a first-class degree.) Walker's rejection of even the remotest possibility of there being any truth whatsoever in any form of Christianity never stopped that scholar from attaching a central importance to the role of theology and religious controversy in the history of ideas and of literature. That was enough for Malcolm.

Malcolm would tumble into my room in U.C.L., papers spewing out of what I remember as an old army gas-mask case; a bunch of British Museum slips was often in his hand. We would discuss the books he was reading and ways of finding others to read. At that time I discovered his passion for cycling – something very much rarer in England than in France. I had suggested that there was something to look up in Lucca. I brought up the subject again a few weeks later: he had already cycled there from London, looked up the material and, if my memory is right, found it disappointing. Later, as his interest grew wider and deeper, he cycled to countless libraries at home and abroad. I like to think of the surprise many librarians must have experienced when that learned young man, dressed for the bicycle, came smiling into their holy of holies to pore over the rarest of their books and to make new discoveries.

In those early days he had already studied a rare *Ronsard* in Manchester. (He had cycled there of course from Leeds or London.) He realised that no less an authority than Isidore Silver did not know of its existence. He wrote to him, so starting off a warm and friendly correspondence. Isidore Silver, with the perspicacity of the generous older scholar, recognised Malcolm as his natural successor.

Malcolm found, he said, a warm welcome everywhere. Certainly his enthusiasm was infectious. The wife of a great and learned book collector once told me that she suspected her husband wanted to be like him. Certainly I have met students who consciously modelled themselves on him, throwing themselves into their studies with something of his energy and delight. He had little time for pomposity, and no time whatsoever for jargon and for wilful or pretentious obscurity.

His doctoral thesis on Ronsard won the admiration of his examiners. Frances Yates was especially impressed and judged Malcolm to be a Warburg man by nature. And indeed Malcolm shared in her conception of cultural history, which owed so much to Ernst Gombrich and his team – a team unique in being led by learned exiles from Nazi and Fascist oppression, yet already flourishing in London and extending its roots. Out of that thesis was born our standard edition of the *Discours des misères de ce temps*.

[X]

Malcolm's first post was in Leeds, in the department led by Professor Philip Thody, who appreciated him as a scholar and a man, affording him every encouragement and sharing in a valued friendship. From Leeds Malcolm went to Bedford College in London – cycling down from Leeds for the interview – where once again the head of his department, Professor Felix Leakey, gave him encouragement, friendship, and the means of establishing himself in London as a scholar to be taken notice of. When Malcolm died I received many letters from those who knew him: none was more appreciative and warmer than that of Felix Leakey: under his ægis Malcolm had really found his wings.

Amongst many invitations he was able to take up were visiting professorships to Western Ontario and Cornell. Malcolm was sought after for numerous colloquies, not least by neo-Latinists. When Bedford College made a shot-gun marriage with Royal Holloway, forming what was then known as Royal Holloway and Bedford New College, he was the man elected to become the head of its French Department. His colleagues found it an inspired election, ensuring for the combined department the distinction that it deserved.

Then Malcolm's whole life suddenly changed. He was sawing off a limb of a tree in his garden when he slipped. His foot caught in a branch. The fall was awkward, and serious in its effects. From then on he walked with a slight limp. And his serious cycling days were over. For a while he was depressed. Even his scholarship suffered, though not his teaching nor his effective leading of his department. For a few months even his infectious smile became rarer. But not for long. He remained as keen as ever on cycling, fighting for cycle-paths in the country and cycle-routes in London. But those legendary trips were over. Yet his scholarly fire, his enthusiasm, and his grin soon returned.

It was at this period too that he launched himself into what were then the new mysteries of word-processing. He became a computer wizard, playing a major role in building up his college's very successful desk-top publishers, Runnymede Books.

As article followed article, as book followed book, his colleagues confidently awaited that special bloom that great scholars break into in their fifties. And then the blow fell. Stomach pains were wrongly diagnosed as something minor. Too late he was found to have cancer. He knew that there was no cure and that he had a year or so to live. Not more. He went on working, keeping to the time on his contracts and seeing one book come out within days of his death.

In his illness he was nursed by all the members of his close-knit family, especially by his brother Gavin and his French sister-in-law Marie-Neige. He bore his painful illness with little outward change of character. He was serene, witty, and jokingly resigned. He continued to jest even about his cancer. Malcolm was no prude. He had more than an affinity with Rabelais, another of his special authors. His sense of fun remained with him to the end, in the intervals between pain. There is no doubt that his faith remained his sheet anchor. He was truly supported by his family and by the Roman Catholic chaplain of his College, Robert Hamilton. No one could have done more.

It was always a pleasure to spend time with Malcolm. To spend some hours with him in those last days was a privilege. So too was to talk to him on the telephone. He arranged his funeral service – finding something to grin about even in that. He chose his hymns and arranged for friends to read not only from Scripture but from his favourite Renaissance authors, and, at their gentle insistence, from his own works. He sent for his Latin dictionary to check the inscription on his tombstone. ('Only Latin will do!') And all that without rancour or gloom. He died on the twenty-sixth of October, 1994. He was nearly fifty-three.

Malcolm's achievements as a scholar are witnessed to by this collection of some of his articles, and by the bibliography of his works given in the appendix. They need no puffing. Malcolm worked in the best tradition of humanist scholarship. Shoddy work puzzled him. Pretentious obscurity and jargon both irritated and amused him. His Socratic questioning of a participant in a colloquy who was devoted to such things became a legend amongst those who witnessed it or heard of it. (Such tales lose nothing in the telling.)

As editor, exegete, and historian of ideas he has left his very personal mark on Renaissance scholarship – not least on Ronsard studies; on Montaigne studies; on our understanding of Joachim Du Bellay; on Renaissance religious controversy, and on Renaissance attempts at tolerance and concord.

As a man, he was lovable.

M.A. Screech

The feast of William Law,
mystic and non-juror,
1997
Wolfson College, Oxford

MALCOLM SMITH'S WRITINGS

[This survey is designed, in part, to put the articles into context; figures in **bold** refer to the numbering of the articles in this volume.]

*

*   *

Qui veut guerir de l'ignorance, il faut la confesser.

Montaigne found inspiration in quoting his cherished Latin poets; Malcolm Smith found inspiration in quoting Montaigne. This Socratic confession opens Malcolm's essay on Montaigne's lost writings (**17**), which are characteristically arranged 'in the ascending order in which they arouse my curiosity'. The well-spring of Malcolm's scholarship was indeed curiosity, and from it flowed the stream of books, editions and articles listed in the bibliography. They record his ceaseless dialogue with some of the subtlest minds of the French Renaissance, and his eagerness to explore the results through a further dialogue with his modern audience.

Malcolm tried to satisfy his and our curiosity in three particular fields: bibliography, allegory, and biography. Many of his articles stemmed from a polite reluctance to accept unquestioningly the word of bibliographers or commentators; how often he found that a careless or incomplete reference concealed some unsuspected gem which would enrich the history of a text, the context of an allusion, or the by-ways of a life. In editing and annotating he insisted on testing all assumptions for himself, applying a rigorous, almost forensic, standard of proof. He acknowledged that the unveiling of allegory is a chancy business, but reduced the risks by immersing himself in the essential detail, developing an instinctive sensitivity to the proclivities of an author, to the intellectual, political and theological climate, and to the contemporary theory and practice of allegory (see **6**). Though aware of the modern fashion for downgrading the author, he persisted resolutely in discerning the presence of a vibrant and approachable human personality behind every work he studied.

Malcolm's doctoral thesis, completed in 1967 and on deposit in the London University Library at Senate House, is entitled 'Political and religious controversy in the work of Ronsard, with special reference to the *Discours des miseres*'. Something of its textual and historical richness may be glimpsed in articles **2** and **4**. The political and theological implications of literary texts preoccupied him throughout his career and, with poignant symmetry, he returned to many of the issues raised by his thesis in the posthumously-published *Ronsard and Du Bellay versus Bèze: Allusiveness in Renaissance Literary Texts.*

The findings of his thesis led eventually to the definitive edition of Ronsard's *Discours des misères* published in 1979. It is an archetypal Smith performance, as he disentangles the complicated history of these originally ephemeral texts (cf. **1** and **3**), elucidates their veiled allusions and, above all, illuminates the context of Ronsard's declamations by adopting the style of a Renaissance commentator – his model, explicitly, was Marc-Antoine Muret's delicious commentary on Ronsard's *Amours*. Significantly, this was the first edition of the *Discours* to supply the essential references to Calvin, Bèze and other opponents of Ronsard (cf. **20**), as Malcolm strove to emulate the poet's own doomed attempt to be impartial. The edition underlines Malcolm's knack of locating and analysing 'lost' or previously unknown editions of Ronsard's works (**5, 7, 8, 13, 14** and **19**), though in a wryly despairing public lecture (**15**) he confessed that there was still much to do. His finds were often located in out-of-the-way municipal archives and ecclesiastical libraries, from Lichfield to Lucca, though he turned up many a *trouvaille* even in the British Library and the Bibliothèque Nationale. His extraordinary bibliographical expertise was, however, a treasure to be shared rather than jealously hoarded. Send him an offprint and in a few days back would come the note of thanks together with a few diffident but devastatingly pertinent suggestions for further reading!

Even before the *Discours*, Malcolm had published his edition of the *Sonnets pour Helene* (1970). Applying the same principles, he provided the 'Muret edition' of this collection, using dense footnotes to establish the historical, cultural and poetic context of this most complex of sonnet cycles. With characteristic intertextual expertise, he also identified, more distinctly than his predecessors, the factitious nature of this cycle, as Ronsard, the consummate professional poet, is shown judiciously recycling old material to produce a supremely literary but scarcely autobiographical *roman d'amour*.

Similarly, Malcolm's study of Joachim Du Bellay's *Regrets*, published in 1974, shows parts of the collection in a new light, with closer affinities to the Juvenalian style than had previously been supposed. Malcolm reasserted the important role of topicality in much Renaissance poetry by identifying the specific targets of certain sonnets. Even if, as he admitted, all such unmasking of 'veiled victims' risks being conjectural, his study cogently portrays the relations between Du Bellay and his patrons, and argues eloquently that social and literary history are kindred disciplines which can and should be mutually enriching. Not least, it broaches the neglected question of Du Bellay's religious outlook. Malcolm returned to this theme with an ingenious reading of Du Bellay's enigmatic *Songe* in the last edition he published, a parallel text of the *Antiquitez de Rome* and *Songe*, with translations by Edmund Spenser. Typically, Malcolm commented on the textual discrepancies not to expose Spenser's deficiencies as a linguist, but to illuminate his qualities as a poet. The brief introduction evokes Joachim's appeal, to which Malcolm had increasingly succumbed: his inimitable subtlety, inspired allusiveness, nimble wit, and above all his timeless humanity.

The essay of 1974 was accompanied by editions of Du Bellay's little-known *Xenia* and of a Latin elegy, with translation, addressed to the principal 'victim' of the *Regrets*, the cardinal of Lorraine. The editions reflected Malcolm's growing interest in neo-Latin literature, fired by his bibliographical (and topographical) investigations of Du Bellay's disregarded Latin poetry (**9** and **10**). His enthusiasm is conveyed in a series of sparkling contributions (**11**, **19** and **24**) to the triennial congresses of the International Association for Neo-Latin Studies.

Malcolm's two books on Montaigne also reflect a developing empathy with a writer whom he had at first approached with some awe. *Montaigne and the Roman Censors* (1981) is probably his most revealing excursion into intellectual biography, combining erudition and judicious speculation to illuminate an almost unexplored episode. Montaigne's encounter with the Inquisition (which itself appears in an unexpected light) had fascinating repercussions upon the text of the *Essais*, as Montaigne reacted, far from obsequiously, to the reservations of Rome. An intriguing study of the interplay between the *Journal de voyage* and the *Essais* leads to a reassessment of Montaigne's theological competence and of his relations with the Church. This was, incidentally, the first book in which Malcolm, with no visible reluctance, conceded that his readers' grasp of languages might not match his own. A codicil was added to its discussion of Fortune in the article on Montaigne's (veiled) attack on Machiavelli (**18**).

Montaigne and Religious Freedom (1991), whose closing passage was read at Malcolm's memorial service, is the most wide-ranging and personal of his books, as its subtitle, *The Dawn of Pluralism*, may suggest. It covers not only a lengthy period, from the embryonic toleration policy of 1560 to the Edict of Nantes, but also a timeless and universal theme (see **16** on Montaigne and Tacitus). By studying the moral struggles of Montaigne and his predecessors, Malcolm was able to highlight the unchanging intellectual foundations on which religious freedom and indeed all freedoms rest. The fundamental questions concerning political action, characterised by Montaigne as the conflict between the *utile* and the *honneste*, are posed – with a gentle reminder that none was inapplicable to the Britain in which the book was being written. But alongside the great themes Malcolm pursued his characteristic decipherment of fleeting allusion; from his study of Montaigne's relations with the contemporary Establishment, the essayist emerges, as he does from the *Roman Censors*, as a man of stronger convictions than is sometimes allowed.

In its broad sweep this book takes in such lesser-known but attractive figures as Michel de l'Hospital, Paul de Foix (**26**, **27**) and above all Montaigne's mentor, and another of Malcolm's belated discoveries, Estienne de La Boëtie. Malcolm undertook to fill the gap left by one of Montaigne's 'lost writings', the complete edition of La Boëtie's *Œuvres* that was apparently published at about the time of Montaigne's death. Two of La Boëtie's works had not appeared in Montaigne's extant 1571 edition, nor in the *Essais* in 1580, presumably because Montaigne feared that their publication would be exploited by opponents of reconciliation. Malcolm repaired the omission by editing the *Memoire sur la pacification des troubles* (1983) and *De la Servitude volontaire* (1987); a typically quirky yet helpful English translation of the latter appeared the following year from Malcolm's own imprint, Runnymede Books. The *Memoire*, maltreated by its only previous editor, and virtually ignored since, benefits from Malcolm's theological expertise as well as from his unmatched study of its political context. The *Servitude volontaire*, a work both more familiar and more often traduced, is rescued from the insobriety of previous commentators and editors. Textual and contextual scholarship is accompanied once more by

[XV]

plausible speculation, here on potentially subversive allusions to the contemporary French monarchy; Malcolm had sketched the theme in a public lecture (22) and was to expand upon it in the English edition of the *Servitude volontaire*. Above all, he threw into relief the intellectual kinship, so often underrated, between La Boëtie and Montaigne. At the time of writing, we await the consummation of a long-cherished project: Malcolm's work on an edition of the complete works of Estienne de La Boëtie is shortly to appear, fittingly embedded in the Pléiade edition of Montaigne.

It will be noticed that Malcolm never produced the 'big book', the would-be definitive study of some author or movement. Humility, perhaps, an admission of Socratic ignorance. Or, more likely, a sense that there can be no definitive studies. Malcolm's method was frequently accumulative (see for example 10 and 21), as unsatisfied curiosity led him further and deeper into a topic. At his death, one vast project was left incomplete and perhaps literally interminable. He gave the loose title 'The World of Estienne Dolet' to a huge assemblage of dossiers, notes and files packed with information on all those – very numerous and some very obscure – who were in some way connected with Dolet. A few glimpses of the material have appeared (23 and 24), but a mass of rare and fascinating information awaits some resourceful scholar.

*
* *

One of Malcolm's favourite chapters of Montaigne was *De l'art de conférer*. Malcolm's was a life filled with *conférence*: dialogue with family and friends, with colleagues and students, with the past and the present, with his readers and with his chosen writers. Towards the end Malcolm invited friends to choose a gift from among his books. I have before me his teaching copy of *Les Regrets* and a reprint of Cotgrave's *Dictionarie of the French and English Tongues* – which he had snatched from under my nose in a book sale years before. They are a sorry sight, dog-eared, disbound, the pages blackened by scribbled annotation. Yet more than anything they represent the man and the scholar who, like Montaigne, would have gone on, talking, arguing, laughing with his books, for as long as there were paper and ink in the world...

Michael Heath

King's College London
16 April 1997

TABULA GRATULATORIA

Professor Dominic BAKER-SMITH, University of Amsterdam
M. Jean Paul BARBIER, Musée Barbier-Mueller, Genève
Dr Jean BARRON, Royal Holloway, University of London
Dr Jennifer BRITNELL, University of Durham
Dr Sally BURCH, University College London
Dr Andrew CALDER, University College London
Dr Ruth CALDER, University College London
Professor Terence CAVE, St John's College, Oxford
Mr Harry COCKERHAM, Royal Holloway, University of London
Professor Richard COOPER, Brasenose College, Oxford
Ms Jacqueline DOYLE, Bedford College, University of London
Mr Clive FRANKISH, University of Manchester
Professor Michael FREEMAN, University of Bristol
The Revd Robert HAMILTON, Roman Catholic Chaplain, Royal Holloway, University of London
Professor Michael HEATH, King's College London
Dr Edward HUGHES, Royal Holloway, University of London
Professor Felix LEAKEY, Emeritus Professor of French, Bedford College, University of London
Mr Paul LEAKEY, Ely
Dr John LEWIS, The Queen's University of Belfast
Monica McCANN, Ely (Malcolm Smith's sister)
Abbé Germain MARC'HADOUR, Amicale Thomas More, Angers
Dr Wendy MERCER, University College London
Dr Letizia PANIZZA, Royal Holloway, University of London
Professor Malcolm QUAINTON, University of Lancaster
Miss Anne REEVE, University College London
The Revd Professor M.A. SCREECH, Wolfson College, Oxford
Mr Douglas SMITH, London (Malcolm Smith's father)
Mr Graham SMITH, Crowborough, E. Sussex (Malcolm Smith's brother)
Mrs Irene SMITH, Crowborough, E. Sussex
Mr Gavin SMITH, Hailsham, E. Sussex (Malcolm Smith's brother)
Mrs Marie-Neige SMITH, Hailsham, E. Sussex
Mr Lionel SWAIN, Royal Holloway, University of London

Professor Isamu TAKATA, Président de la Société des Amis de Ronsard du Japon
Professor J.B. TRAPP, The Warburg Institute
Dr Ruth WEBB, Bristol
Dr Gwyneth WILKIE, University College London

St CHRISTOPHER'S CATHOLIC CYCLING CLUB
VANGUARD CYCLING CLUB
La SOCIÉTÉ DES AMIS DE RONSARD DU JAPON
The Department of French, ROYAL HOLLOWAY, University of London
The Department of French, UNIVERSITY COLLEGE LONDON
The Department of French, UNIVERSITY OF LEEDS
The WARBURG INSTITUTE, University of London

ACKNOWLEDGEMENTS

All publications in which Malcolm Smith's articles first appeared have been informed of our project to republish the articles which form this collection. We are most grateful to the following, who have specifically replied, for permission to reproduce material:

- The Helen Dwight Reid Educational Foundation, Heldref Publications, Washington DC (for article 6)
- W. Fink Verlag (for article 11)
- *Moreana* (for article 12)
- *Revue de Littérature Comparée* (for articles 10 and 21)
- *The Sixteenth Century Journal* (for article 27)

Should any copyright be inadvertently infringed, we duly apologise.

AN EARLY EDITION OF A *DISCOURS* BY RONSARD

The purpose of this article is to determine the circumstances of composition and publication of Ronsard's *Prière à Dieu pour la victoire* and to republish for the first time the original text of this important *Discours*.[1]

Ronsard is known to have published in 1569 two important poems dealing with events of the third civil war. To celebrate the victory of the royal army at Jarnac (13 March 1569) he published the *Chant triomphal pour jouer sur la lyre. Sur l'insigne victoire qu'il a pleu à Dieu donner à Monseigneur, Frere du Roy* (XV, 61-66).[2] This poem appeared in the *Sixiesme livre des Poëmes* in 1569, and subsequently in the third (1571) and fourth (1573) editions of Ronsard's *Œuvres*. In the fifth edition of the *Œuvres*, it appeared under a different title: *Hymne sur la victoire obtenue à Moncontour par Monseigneur d'Anjou, à present Roy de France.* It was never included in the *Discours*, doubtless because, unlike the *Discours*, it was written "*pour jouer sur la lyre.*" We shall refer to it henceforth by its opening line, "*Tel qu'un petit aigle sort.*"

The second poem known to have been published in 1569 is *L'Hydre deffaict ou la Louange de Monseigneur le duc d'Anjou, frere du Roy* (XV, 377-387). This poem was written after the royal victory at Montcontour (3 October 1569) and appeared in a collection of Latin, Greek and French poetry dealing with the war.[3] It did not appear in the *Œuvres* until the fifth edition (1578), where it was included in the *Discours*.

The third civil war ended in 1570 with the Edict of Saint-Germain (8 August), but in the fifth edition of his *Œuvres*, in 1578, Ronsard published among the *Discours* two more poems dealing with this war. The first, a *Priere à Dieu pour la victoire* (XVII, 401-408) we shall refer to by its opening words, "*Donne Seigneur.*" The other is entitled *Les Elemens ennemis de l'Hydre* (XVII, 408-411). The fifth edition of 1578 provides what has hitherto been the earliest known text of each poem.[4]

But it is known that both these poems were written in 1569. This is evident from their content and, in the case of "*Donne*

---

[1] I am at present working on a Ph. D. thesis for London University, entitled "Political and religious controversy in the work of Ronsard, with particular reference to the *Discours des misères*". The material in this article will be included in it.

[2] *Œuvres complètes*, éd. crit. par P. Laumonier, Paris, STFM. All references unless otherwise indicated are to this edition.

[3] *Paeanes sive Hymni in triplicem victoriam, felicitate Caroli IX, Galliarum Regis invectissimi, & Henrici fratis, Ducis Andegavensis virtute partam.* Joanne Aurato poeta regis, & aliis doctis poëtis autoribus. Lutetiae. Joannes Charron, 1569, in-4, Bibl. Nat. Yc 1204. (Details from XV, 377, n. 2).

[4] For "*Donne Seigneur*" see XVII, 401, and P. de RONSARD, *Discours des misères de ce temps*, ed. J. Baillou, Paris, 1949, p. 53. For *Les Elemens ennemis de l'Hydre*: XVII, 408, and Baillou, p. 54.

Seigneur ", is confirmed by the testimony of Amadis Jamyn. Jamyn, in a poem to Charles IX, dealt with the prophetic function of poets and cited the case of Ronsard :

> Trois jours devant ceste heureuse journée
> Que la bataille en Poictou fut donnée
> Pres Moncontour : vous sçavez qu'en ses vers
> Il predisoit, que sur les champs ouvers
> Les ennemis au milieu de la guerre
> Plat estandus devoyent mordre la terre
> Ensanglantez, renversez, poudroyez... [1]

Jamyn's words are an echo of the opening lines of " *Donne Seigneur.*" It would therefore appear that Ronsard's poem was already written by 30 September 1569.

One cannot however be certain that it was already in the hands of the printer by that date, although there are reasons to believe this may be so. The very nature of the *Discours* demanded their immediate publication. They are polemical poems, intended to influence public opinion in given circumstances. Ronsard may have liked to spend nine years licking an ode into shape—*nonum prematur in annum* (cf. *Ôdes, Au lecteur*, I, 46)—but a *Discours* written in 1569 was meant to be published before 1578 !

We can now state that " *Donne Seigneur* " was indeed first published in 1569. Both the British Museum and the Bibliothèque Nationale possess copies of a work containing the poem. It is entitled, *Chant triumphal sur la victoire obtenuë par le Roy, à l'encontre des rebelles & ennemys de sa Majesté*. Premierement faict en françoys, et depuis mis en latin par Antoine Valet Medecin. A Paris, chez Gervais Mallot, 1569, in-4º, 8 ff. ; B.M. 11474. h. 27 (12) ; B. Nat., Rés. Ye 1136 ; Inv. Yc 1759.[2]

The circumstances of publication were as follows. On 7 September 1569 Coligny raised the siege of Poitiers [3] (there are allusions in the text of " *Donne Seigneur* " to the relief of Poitiers). Coligny then offered battle, but the royal army refused. Coligny was forced to accept battle in unfavourable conditions at Montcontour and suffered a heavy defeat (3 October). There are no references in the text of " *Donne Seigneur* " to Montcontour. However, the content suggests that a battle was imminent and the poem is more than a mere

---

[1] *Les Œuvres poetiques d'Amadis Jamyn*. Au Roy de France et de Pologne, Paris, M. D. LXXV, B. M. 11474. h. 17, 42vo. The reference to this poem is given in XVII, 401, n. 2.

[2] The pamphlet contains the following pieces :
Extraict du privilège du roy (verso of title-page) ;
Observandiss. P. F. Iacobo Hugoni, D. Th. Par. Regio. Ecclesiast. Mecœnatique suo beneficentiss. Anto. Valetius (2ro) ;
Chant triumphal pour la victoire obtenue, et continuation d'icelle (2vo-7vo) ;
Idem totidem versibus expressum. Anto. Valetio Iunianensi Authore (3ro-8ro).
De Antonio Valetio Franciscus Amboysius Lutetianus (8vo).
Ronsard's text and Valet's Latin translation therefore face each other.
Manuscript notes in each of the Bibliothèque Nationale's copies point out that the date 1569 has been altered in the one case to 1571 and in the other to 1572. According to A. E. Picot, *Les Français italianisants au XVIe siècle*, 2 v., Paris, 1906, 1907, II, 82-83 there exists in fact an edition of 1572. If we find it, and it has variant readings, we shall publish a list of them.

[3] E. Lavisse, *Histoire de France*, 9 v., Paris, 1903-1911, 6, i (by J. H. Mariéjol), p. 110-111.

execration of an enemy before battle: it is essentially a prayer for
victory. In the circumstances of its composition, some such title
as *Prière à Dieu pour la victoire* would have been appropriate. We
may assume that a topical poem such as this would have been passed
on to the printer without delay, still before Montcontour. However,
within a day or two, the prayed-for victory materialised. Pamphlet
literature has to be topical so, although in substance the poem was
still a " prayer ", its title was altered to take account of the new
situation: Ronsard's *Priere à Dieu pour la victoire* became a *Chant
triumphal sur la victoire* [Poitiers] *et continuation d'icelle* [Mont-
contour]. The title given in the privilege (dated 9 November) which
was granted to Antoine Valet is *Chant Triumphal, sur la victoire &
continuation d'icelle, par luy faict Latin*. The title of the original
edition of " *Donne Seigneur* " is thus more up-to-date than the
content.

That the printer supplied the makeshift title is the more probable
in that Ronsard had already applied the title *Chant triomphal* earlier
in the year to " *Tel qu'un petit aigle sort.*" Moreover, when he
included " *Donne Seigneur* " in the *Œuvres* in 1578, he adopted a
" new " title—perhaps his original one—*Prière à Dieu pour la victoire*.
None of the variants introduced in 1578 is attributable to any desire
to make the " new " title fit: it was perfectly apt in the first place,
and is probably the one Ronsard originally supplied.[1]

Nowhere in the 1569 pamphlet is Ronsard mentioned by name as
the author of " *Donne Seigneur* " (the anonymous publication of
this poem explains of course its not having been examined by Ronsard
scholars). The omission of Ronsard's name does not necessarily
mean that this 1569 edition was published without his approval.
He had published anonymously before and without detriment to his
renown. He did not put his name to the *Livret de folastries* but he
was recognised as its author.[2] Later he acknowledged authorship
by including most of the *Folastries* in the *Œuvres*.[3] The earliest
editions of one of the *Discours*, the *Remonstrance au peuple de France*,
were published anonymously but the identity of the author was
undoubtedly widely known, and in 1564 Ronsard acknowledged
authorship.[4] The anonymous publication of " *Donne Seigneur* " is
doubtless simply due to reluctance on the part of Ronsard to become
involved in controversy in the same way as he had during the first
civil war. Controversial literature in the style of the early *Discours*
had been forbidden [5] and in his poetry of the third civil war Ronsard

---

[1] As we saw above, the title of " *Tel qu'un petit aigle sort* " was altered in 1578.
The change in title from *Chant* to *Hymne* is no doubt connected with the placing of the
poem at this date among the *Hymnes*. But it is surprising that a poem written in
celebration of Jarnac should now be called an *Hymne sur la victoire obtenue à Moncontour*.
Perhaps Ronsard was confusing this poem with " *Donne Seigneur* " which, as we now
know, was originally offered to the public as a eulogy of Montcontour and which,
like "*Tel qu'un petit aigle sort* ", bore the title of *Chant triomphal*.

[2] P. LAUMONIER, *Ronsard poète lyrique*, 2e éd., Paris, 1923, p. 103.

[3] His *Exhortation au camp du roy* was also anonymous at first: IX, 1.

[4] See Baillou's edition of the *Discours des misères* (cited above), p. 51.

[5] In his preface to the *Trois livres du Recueil des nouvelles poësies* (1563) Ronsard
wrote:
Toutesfois sans le commandement des plus Grands qui ont expressement deffendu
les libelles, je les eusse vivement grattez où il leur demange, car, Dieu mercy, nous avons
bons & amples memoires de la vie de ces deux compaignons: mais dorenavant je me
tairay pour obeyr à ceux qui ont puissance sur ma main, & sur ma volonté. (XII, 16-17).

restricts the element of religious controversy and personal acrimony.

Although Ronsard did not put his name to the first edition of " *Donne Seigneur* ", the pamphlet contains more than a hint at his authorship. In the first place, the wording of the title heavily underlines the fact that Antoine Valet is responsible only for the Latin translation : the poem has been " *Premierement* faict en françoys, *et depuis* mis en latin par Antoine Valet Medecin ". In his dedicatory poem to Hugo, Valet stresses that he is not the author, and, albeit in conventional terms, praises highly the unnamed author :

> Tum sacer hæc Vates oracula mente reponens,
>   Doctiloqui Vates gloria prima chori,
> Auratos residis nervos testudinis urget :
>   Et Gallis aptat Galla trophaea sonis.
> Huius ego captus mira dulcedine cantus,
>   Effinxi Latiis Gallica metra modis.

But it is the poem by François d'Amboise which reveals the truth for all who have ears to hear. It is presented as a eulogy of Valet, but the greater part of it consists in transparent and flattering allusions to Ronsard. This all suggests that the publication had Ronsard's approval.

As in the case of poems which he had previously published anonymously, Ronsard counted on avowing his authorship of " *Donne Seigneur* " at the opportune time. This may explain why the privilege granted to Valet and the printer, Mallot, is for only two years' duration : Ronsard no doubt hoped to include the poem in editions of his *Œuvres*. In fact, like *L'Hydre deffaict* and *Les elemens ennemis de l'Hydre* it does not appear in the third and fourth editions.[1] However, by 1575, Ronsard no longer felt any desire to veil his authorship of " *Donne Seigneur.*" As we have seen, Jamyn identified him as the author in that year. From 1578 onwards, it is found in every edition of the *Œuvres*.

The 1569 text of " *Donne Seigneur* " which we now present shows signs of hasty composition : Ronsard's expression is occasionally inelegant and imprecise. A study of the subsequent texts shows that these weaknesses have often been eliminated (e.g. at lines 9, 11, 21, 55, 66, 89, 106 and 130-131 - 1569 numbering). On the other hand, the original edition is in places more blunt and vivid than the later ones (e.g. lines 17, 40, 42 and 123). The interest of the *Discours* lies precisely in the fact that they were written in the heat of a battle which was being waged *par livres* as well as *par armes* ; it is the original, polemical document, the creature of the events it describes, which has most to offer Ronsard scholars and historians of the civil wars.[2]

Leeds   M. C. SMITH.

---

[1] The explanation given by the editor of the critical edition for the absence of " *Donne Seigneur* " and *Les Elemens ennemis* from collected editions prior to that of 1578 is that the prayer of the one and the prediction of the other were frustrated by Coligny's ability to rebuild his army and conclude the advantageous treaty of Saint-Germain (XVII, 411, n. 3).

[2] Is there an earlier edition of *Les Elemens ennemis de l'Hydre*? It may well have been published in circumstances similar to those outlined above.

[4]

Chant triumphal pour la victoire obtenue, et continuation d'icelle [2 Vᵒ]

DONNE SEIGNEUR, que nostre ennemy vienne
Mesurer, mort, les rives de la Vienne,
Et que sanglant de mille coups persé,
Dessus la pouldre il tombe renversé
5   Auprès des siens au milieu de la guerre :
Et de ses dents puisse mordre la terre
Plat estendu, comme un Pin esbranché,
Qu'un charpentier de son long a couché :
Au prochain bord qu'il trenche, & qu'il decouppe,
10   Pour le tourner en quarreaux d'une pouppe :
Ou pour en faire une charrüe, affin
Qu'une s'en aille, errante en son chemin,
Fendre la mer, que le vent accompagne :
Et l'autre fende une large campagne.
15   Au Pin tombé soit pareil l'ennemy,
Sans pied, sans teste, amoncellé parmy
Un grand monceau de morts, & de carnage,
Ayant pour tombe un sablonneux rivage.
DONNE SEIGNEUR, que l'avare Germain,
20   Et Reistres fiers puissent sentir la main
Du jeune Duc, occis de mort cruelle :
Si qu'un tout seul n'apporte la nouvelle   [3 Vᵒ]
En son pays, que le Rhin va lavant :
Et que leur nom se perde dans le vent :
25   Eux, & leur race : & que leur renommée
S'esvanouisse ainsi que la fumée.
Que leurs corps soient accablez de cent coups,
Proye des chiens, des corbeaux, & des loups.
O tout puissant, donne que nostre Prince
30   Sans compagnon maistrise sa province :
Et que pompeux en haute majesté,
Soit sur un char en triomphe porté
Dedans Paris : & sans misericorde
Traine lié l'ennemy d'une corde,
35   Bien loing derriere en son char attaché.
Punition de son grave peché :

Variants: We give the variant readings of the 1578 edition. Minor differences in punctuation and spelling have been ignored.

6. morde la dure terre,

8. de travers a couché

9-13. Au prochain bord, puis le fer de decouppe / Pour le tourner en forme d'une pouppe, / Ou de charue, à fin que l'un des deux / Aille voguer par les chemins venteux, / Que la tormente & la mort accompagne,

16. Sans bras, sans teste,

17. Le plus espais d'un charongneux carnage,

20. Ces Reistres

21-23. si qu'une mort cruelle / Face qu'un seul n'en conte la nouvelle / En ce pays

24-28. Et que leur nom se perde en nostre vent, / Et qu'à jamais leur morte renommée / S'esvanouisse ainsi qu'une fumée, / Et que leurs corps accablez de cent coups / Soient le disner des corbeaux & des loups.

31-33. Et que pompeux de brave majesté / Entre à Paris en triomphe porté, / Et que sans grace & sans misericorde

35. à son char attaché,

[5]

D'avoir osé d'une vaine entreprinse
France esbranler, son Prince, & son Eglise :
Qui ne se peut esbranler nullement,
40   Car un seul Christ en est le fondement.
      DONNE, SEIGNEUR, que la belle Touraine
Ne sente plus l'avarice Germaine :
Et que noz fruicts, noz jardins, noz vergers,
Qu'aux laboureurs les champs non mensongers,
45   Trompent les mains de la jeunesse blonde,
Que le Danube abbreuve de son onde :
Et les nourrist superbes & felons,
Comme les filz des ourseaux Aquilons :
Qui vont soufflant à leurs fieres venües   [4 Vo]
50   Loing devant eux les legions des nües.
Balais de l'air, qui serainent soudain
Du ciel d'azur les voutes & le sein.
      DONNE, SEIGNEUR, que l'infidelle armée
Soit par soymesme en un rien consumée :
55   Et que l'un l'autre il se puisse tüer,
Sans les souffrir si longuement süer
Sous le harnois : que tout à coup ils meurent,
Et de leurs pas les places ne demeurent.
Comme il advint dedans le champ de Mars,
60   Lors que les dents conceurent des soldars :
Dents de serpens, qui leur forme changerent
En la moisson de guerriers, qui chargerent
Les champs d'espieux, de dards, & de pavois,
De traicts poinctus, de haches, de harnois.
65   Mais se tüants eux mesmes de leur dextre,
Un seul les veit vivre, mourir & naistre.
      O SEIGNEUR Dieu, ma priere adviendra.
Ta dextre main le glaive aigu prendra
Pour nous, Seigneur, ains que Phœbus s'abbaisse
70   Tout haletant au sein de son hostesse.
Ou bien, Seigneur, si l'ennemy poursuit
Tant le combat, qu'on se batte de nuict,
l'Aube vermeille au large sein d'yvoire
Puisse en naissant annoncer la victoire.
75   Et moy, qui suis le moindre des François,
D'estomach foible, & de petite voix,   [5 Vo]
Je chanteray de ce Duc la louange :
Affin, Seigneur, que toute terre estrange

38-40.   Forcer le Ciel, nostre Prince, & l'Eglise / Que Dieu bastit d'un fondement tresseur : / Aussi son bras en est le defenseur.

41-45.   Donne, Seigneur, que la chance incertaine / Ne tombe point sur noz champs de Touraine, / Que noz raisins, noz bleds & noz vergers / Aux laboureurs ne soient point mensongers, / Trompant les mains de la jeunesse blonde

51-52.   Comme ceux-cy soufflent en notre sein / Un camp armé de pestes & de fein.

54.   en son sang consumée :

55-58.   Qu'elle se puisse elle mesme tuer, / Ou bien du Ciel qu'il te plaise ruer / Ton feu sur elle, & que toute elle meure / Si que d'un seul la trace ne demeure :

60-66.   *Contracted to* Quand la moisson Colchide de soudars / Nasquit de terre en armes herissée, Que mesme jour vit naistre & trespassée.

68-69.   Ta gauche main son Egide prendra, / Le fer ta dextre, ains que Phœbus s'abaisse

72.   qu'on le veinque de nuit,

Craigne la France, & ne passe son bord :
80   Ou le passant, le pris en soit la mort.
Sans remporter de Gaule, qui surmonte
Tous les haineux, qu'ont la vergogne & honte,
Le deshonneur de ce [*sic*] prendre à ce Roy,
Qui doit donner à tous autres la loy.
85   Monarque grand, à qui la destinée
Beaucoup de terre en partage a donnée.
    Vive ce Roy, & vivent ses guerriers,
Qui de Poictiers remportent cent lauriers
Dessus le front : non selon la coustume
90   Des courtisans, par l'otieuse plume,
Le lict, l'amour : mais bien par la vertu,
Soing, & travail, par un rampar batu,
Et rebatu de ces foudres humaines :
Par veille & fain, par soulcis & par peines :
95   Et qui nous ont par leur sang acheté
D'un cueur hardy la doulce liberté.
    BORNE le cours, l'entreprinse & l'audace
Des ennemis, qu'une si foible place
A faict froisser, briser & trebuscher,
100   Comm'une nef se rompt contr'un rocher :
Qui retournoit de Carpathe, ou d'Ægée :
Joyeuse au port, de lingots d'or chargée : [1]
Mais en voulant dedans le havre entrer,
Un grand rocher elle vient rencontrer,   [6 V°]
105   Où son thresor respand sur le rivage :
Que le fort vent, que le vent, que l'orage
N'avoyent sceu rompre. Ainsi cest Admiral
Ayant passé maint travail, & maint mal,
Perte de gents, & perte de muraille,
110   Une premiere & seconde bataille,
S'est venu rompre en cent mille quartiers
Entre les murs bien foibles de Poictiers.
Où ses cheveux, qui par aage grisonnent,
Vaincus font place aux joües que [*sic*] cottonnent
115   De jeune barbe, & qui à peine encor
Font blondoyer leurs mentons d'un poil d'or.
    CUEUR genereux, hoste d'une belle ame.
On dit bien vray, Fortune est une femme,
Qui aime mieulx les jeunes, que les vieulx :
120   Les jeunes sont tousjours victorieux :

---

[1] Line 102 is missing and has been restored according to the text of 1578.

81-86. *suppressed. Between 80 and 87, insertion of the following couplet, which begins the new paragraph:* Vivent, Seigneur, noz terres fortunées, / A qui tu as tes Fleurs-de-liz données.

88-89. les lauriers, / Lauriers gaignez, non selon la coutume

104-107. Par un destin elle vient rencontrer / Un grand rocher qui la froisse au rivage, / Perdant son bien, que la mer, que l'orage / N'avoit sceu rompre :

112. Contre les murs

113-116. Là ses cheveux, qui par l'âge grisonnent, / Donnerent place aux Princes, qui cottonnent / D'un jeune poil leurs mentons, & encor / Ne sont crespez que de petits fils d'or.

117. Cœurs genereux, hostes d'une belle ame,

Et la Fortune aime mieulx la jeunesse,
Qu'une grisonne, & peu forte vieillesse.
  DONNE, SEIGNEUR, que ce grand Duc d'Anjou,
Frere du Roy, mette dessous le jou
125 Ses ennemis, & tous ceulx de son frere,
Imitateur des vertus de son pere.
Imitateur de ces Ducs Angevins,
Princes & Rois, qui haultains & divins,
Plantans le feu de France, & de l'Horraine,
130 Ont possedé la ville à la Seraine,
Laissant son nom mourant dessus la mer, [7 Vº]
Qui ville & rive en son nom feit armer.
Qui desdaignans ces petites conquestes,
Jusques au ciel esleverent leurs testes.
135 Et mesprisans la mer & les dangers,
Terres, labeurs, & peuples estrangers,
Conquirent seuls d'un hault cueur magnanime
Nicée, Tyr, Sydon, Hierosolyme,
Toute Judée : où Jesus autrefois
140 Pour noz pechez ensanglanta sa croix.
  DONNE, SEIGNEUR, que tout cecy advienne.
Que l'ennemy aux rives de la Vienne
Tombe sanglant, de mille coups persé,
Dessus la pouldre en son long renversé
145 Aupres des siens, au milieu de la guerre :
Et de ses dents puisse mordre la terre,
Comm'insensé, de voir tous ses desseins
Comme fumée eschapper de ses mains.

121-122. *Expanded to* Tousjours le chaut surmonte la froidure, / Du gay Printemps plaisante est la verdure, / Et le Soleil en naissant est plus beau / Que le couchant qui se panche au tombeau.

123-125. *Expanded to* Donne, Seigneur, que ceste barbe tendre / Puisse à la grise une vergongne apprendre, / Et qu'au seul bruit de ce grand Duc d'Anjou / Les ennemis ployent dessous le jou, / Imitateur de l'esprit de son frere,

128-134. *Contracted to* Princes guerriers, qui hautains & divins, / N'estimans point les petites conquestes, / Jusques au ciel ont eslevé les testes,

136. Terres, travaux,

137-139. Conquirent seuls d'une force asseurée / Tyr & Sidon, Nicée & Cesarée, Et la cité où Jesus autrefois

141. que mon souhait avienne,

146. morde la dure terre,

148. Vent & fumée eschapper de ses mains.

De Antonio Valetio Franciscus Amboysius Lutetianus

        Homeri tuba, Pindarique Franci
        Vocalis lyra, Cynthio favente, &
        Toto Francigenum approbante cœtu,
        Audax per truculenta bella Martis,
5   Per heroïca facta Francionis,
        Per præconia Regis, & per hymnos,
        Per rura ac elegos Ovidianos,
        Hetruscique iocos leves Petrarchæ,
        Per suspiria mollicella, perque
10   Thebanos, nova metra, dithyrambos,
        Et per tramitis aggerem Calabri,
        Cursu præpete ad ætherem volavit.
        Nunc isto labra percitus furore,
        Quo Latonius afflat ora vatum,
15   Vates haud viridi piger senecta
        Devotis precibus Deum fatigat,
        Fortuna ut miseros beet : superbis
        Inconstans abeat : iuvetque Gallos.
        Hos versus Clarium undiquaque totum
20   Spirantes, cecinit Poëta Francæ
        Quos Princeps citharæ, VALETUS unus,
        Lumen Pœoniae, Poëticæque
        Phœbi delicium, & novem sororum,
        Argiva & Latia madens Minerva,
25   Adstrinxit Latiæ modis camœnæ,
        Mutans carmina Gallicis Latina.
        Tydides Lemovix Ulysse, at illo
        Dignus Vindovicæus est Ulysses.
        Vates dignus uterque utroque Vate.
30   Dignus VINDONICUS suo VALETO :
        DIGNUS VINDONICO suo VALETUS.

[9]

RONSARD AND QUEEN ELIZABETH I

The subject of this article is Ronsard's book entitled *Elegies, Mascarades et Bergerie,* dedicated to queen Elizabeth of England. I hope to show in the first two sections of this article how Ronsard came to write the poems dedicated to queen Elizabeth, Robert Dudley and William Cecil and, in the second two sections, to show how he modified the texts of these poems when political and religious circumstances changed.[1]

1. POLITICAL PROPAGANDA

The *Elegies, Mascarades et Bergerie* appeared in 1565. The book opens with a dedicatory letter in prose headed *A la Majesté de la Royne d'Angleterre* (XIII, 33-36) [2], and it includes notably the three following poems : *Elegie à la majesté de la Royne d'Angleterre* (XIII, 39-62) ; *Elegie à mylord Robert Du-Dle* [that is, Dudley] *conte de l'Encestre* [that is, Leicester] (XIII, 63-74) ; *Au seigneur Cecille Secretaire de la Royne d'Angleterre* (XIII, 159-170).

It is at first surprising that Ronsard should praise Elizabeth and her privy councillors. Relations between France and England had recently been strained, for a number of reasons. Among these reasons were the claim of Mary Stuart and her husband Francis II to the English throne (1559), and the English intervention in the first French civil war on behalf of the Reformers (1562) [3]. Ronsard had

---

[1] I am at present working on a Ph. D. thesis for London University. Its title is " Political and religious controversy in the work of Ronsard with special reference to the *Discours des miseres* ". The material in this article will be included in it.

[2] All references to the works of Ronsard, unless otherwise indicated, are to the edition by Laumonier published by the *Société des Textes Français modernes*, Paris.

[3] For the claim of Mary Stuart, see J. E. PHILLIPS, *Images of a queen, Mary Stuart in sixteenth-century literature*, Berkeley and Los Angeles, 1964, p. 18-19. Mary's claim to England was based on the fact that " Her father, James V of Scotland, was the son of Margaret Tudor, who in turn was a daughter of the first of the Tudors, Henry VII " (*ibid.*, p. 10). Before her marriage to Francis, Mary signed a secret agreement whereby Scotland and any rights she had to England were made over to France in the event of her death without issue (*ibid.*) French opinion had been almost unanimously in favour of the marriage (*ibid.*, p. 3-4, 12-18). On their accession to the throne of France (10 July, 1559) Francis and Mary " [...] openly proclaimed their right to the throne of England as well " (*ibid.*, p. 19). According to C. READ, *Mr. Secretary Cecil and Queen Elizabeth*, London, 1955, p. 125, the claim had been made on behalf of Mary by Henry II immediately on the death of Mary Tudor.

For the English support of the French Reformers, see E. LAVISSE, *Histoire de France depuis les origines jusqu'à la Révolution*, t. 6, i, Paris, 1904, by J. H. Mariéjol, p. 67-69.

Other causes of hostility between England and France included the French occupation of Calais (6 January 1558), an event which was celebrated by very many French

[10]

expressed support for the French position in both these matters:
he had endorsed the claim of Mary Stuart [4], and he had deplored the
English occupation of Normandy [5].

However, part of the purpose of the *Elegies, Mascarades et Bergerie*
is to help dispel the prevalent anglophobia. By 1565, the political
situation had changed radically. The English army had been driven
out of Normandy amidst popular rejoicing in France [6], and Catherine
de Medici had negotiated with England the advantageous treaty of
Troyes (11 April, 1564) [7]. Catherine now hoped to consolidate the
new-found friendship with France by marrying her son Charles to
Elizabeth [8]. Obviously, it was desirable to acclimatize public opinion
to the change in policy, and Catherine turned to Ronsard for help.

Ronsard was at the time one of the most influential propagandists
writing in French. A large part of his poetry, especially since 1558,
had taken the form of commentary on political events, and his reputation as a propagandist had been established by his polemical poems

---

writers (cf. G. Ascoli, *La Grande-Bretagne devant l'opinion française*, 3v., Paris, 1927-
1930, I, p. 85-87); the clash in Scotland in 1560 (January-April: see Lavisse, *op. cit.*,
p. 21); and the suspected implication of England in the Amboise conspiracy (March
1560 : William Cecil "... contradicted the current rumour that the Queen had had a
hand in it "—cf. C. Read, *op. cit.*, p. 165—but Elizabeth appears in fact to have financed
the operation—cf. L. Romier, *La Conjuration d'Amboise, l'aurore sanglant de la liberté
de conscience, le règne et la mort de François II*, Paris, 1923, p. 73-76).

[4] Ronsard's endorsement of Mary's claim is found in IX, 138. In the *Epitre à Charles
cardinal de Lorraine* (1556) he had written about Mary without making the claim to
England (VIII, 329) and he did so later in *Le Tombeau de Marguerite de France* (XVII,
76, l. 256). Mary's claim was supported also by Joachim Du Bellay and Michel de l'Hospital (see J. E. Phillips, *op. cit.*, p. 19 and note 40).

[5] In the *Continuation du discours des miseres* (XI, 54):
        L'autre jour en pensant que ceste pauvre terre
        S'en alloit (ô malheur) la proye d'Angleterre, [...]
        M'apparut tristement l'idole de la France
and in the *Responce aux injures* (XI, 148):
        Si tous les Predicans eussent vescu ainsi, [...]
        [...] les blonds nourissons de la froide Angleterre
        N'eussent passé la mer achetant nostre terre.
The elegy to Elizabeth contains a warning to the warlike English (" Contentés vous,
enfans, de vostre terre [...] ", XIII, 56-57).

[6] Cf. F. Charbonnier, *La poésie française et les guerres de religion (1560-1574)*, Paris,
1919, p. 256-257.

[7] Lavisse, *ibid.*, p. 78. There is an echo of the prevailing hostility towards England
in a *Chant d'allegresse* by Jean Passerat written for Charles IX's entry into Troyes :
        Puisse CHARLES un jour l'aiant conquis en guerre
        A son frere donner le sceptre d'Angleterre
(" *Chant d'allegresse pour l'entrée de Charles IX de ce nom roy de France en sa ville de
Troïe*, Paris, G. Buon, 1564; in-4 de 8 feuilles ". The quotation, and these bibliographical details, are taken from the edition of Passerat by P. Blanchemain, 2v., Paris,
1880, II, p. 180, 196).

[8] " [...] à l'issue des conférences de Bayonne, Paul de Foix, notre ambassadeur, que
connaissait Ronsard, a demandé la main de la reine d'Angleterre pour Charles IX "
(P. Champion, *Ronsard et son temps*, Paris, 1925, p. 217-218). According to Read
(*op. cit.*, p. 328), " The hint [that a marriage be considered] came from her [Elizabeth],
the proposal from Catherine de Medicis ". He says (note 12), " Probably Elizabeth
herself had started the ball rolling with one of her not too subtle hints. That was the
story which De Foix told later to De Silva, Cal[endar of] S[tate] P[apers], Spanish,
1558-1567, 443 ". Paul de Foix, the French ambassador in London, conducted negotiations with Cecil on the subject of the marriage (*ibid.*, p. 328). Cecil " insisted in his
interviews with De Foix that she did not intend to marry Leicester or any other Englishman ". Cecil gave some objections to the marriage but " did not shut the door ". The
negotiations were very confidential and went on for about six months (*ibid.*).

of the first civil war, which were later to be grouped under the collective title *Discours des miseres de ce temps* [9]. His renown extended beyond France at this time, and with a justifiable pride he recalled the fact several times [10]. Some foreign governments were now informed about Ronsard's activities [11], and the English government was among them [12]. Now that Catherine needed a propagandist it was natural she should turn to Ronsard, and in his book Ronsard discreetly and dutifully prepares French and English readers for the imminent royal marriage [13].

In the *Elegies, Mascarades et Bergerie* Ronsard lays stress on his position as an official poet. He carefully points out that in dedicating the book to Elizabeth, he is performing a service for Catherine de Medici. In the dedicatory letter, he tells Elizabeth: "... je ne puis faire service plus agreable à la Royne ma maistresse que vous honorer de ce livre" (XIII, 35), and the book has been published "par son commandement" (XIII, 36) [14]. The reason he stresses this point may simply be that Ronsard did not wish to be thought of as an anglophile. Be this as it may, the official nature of the assignment made it an attractive one for Ronsard. The Pléiade believed that poetry

---

[9] For the 1558-1559 poems, see the whole of volume IX; for the influence of the *Discours des miseres*, see below, note 38.

[10] For example, in the *Responce aux injures* (XI, 118):
Tu es faible pour moy, si je veux escrimer
Du baston qui me fait par l'Europe estimer
and in the *Epistre* preceding the *Trois livres du recueil de nouvelles poesies* (XII, 23):
"Quant à moy je seray tousjours bien ayse de vous mettre en caprice & en cervel, & vous faire crucifier vous mesme par une envie qui vous ronge le cœur, de me voir estimé des peuples estrangers & de ceux de ma nation".

[11] The Spanish ambassador in France, Chantonay, wrote on 23 November 1563 that *Pantagruel* and the Reformers' replies to Ronsard had been read to the young king: "Y por instruirle bien leen le delante con gran pesar desu preçeptor un libro de disparates que se llama *Pantagruel*, hecho por un hombre anabaptista, lleno de mill burlas de la religion, y por impio ha sido dias ha condenado por la Sorbona; assimismo le han leydo ciertos escriptos que un herege ha hecho contra un poeta françes catholico que sellama Ronsart. Donde se tratan mill opprobrios contra la religion". (J. PLATTARD, "'Pantagruel' lu au Louvre, devant le roi Charles IX en 1563", *Revue des Etudes rabelaisiennes*, 9, 1911, p. 442-443. Plattard does not believe the story, but it is possible that Ronsard was referring to such an occurrence when he wrote—XI, 113—"Je ne fais point de doute que ta malice ne se soit maintesfois efforcée de vouloir soubs couleur de belles parolles irriter les Princes & Seigneurs contre moy, interpretant faucement mes escris"; cf. XII, 14 and note 2).
For the story that pope Pius V thanked Ronsard for writing the *Discours des miseres*, see C. BINET, *La vie de P. de Ronsard*, ed. P. Laumonier, Paris, 1910, p. 24, 152.

[12] On 10 February, 1565 the English ambassador, Sir Thomas Smith, wrote to Cecil sending "the news of Ronsard, the archpoet of France, sent him from Paris" (*Calendar of State Papers, Foreign Series, Elizabeth, 1564-1565*, no. 980, par. 7). Later, Smith sent Cecil a copy of Ronsard's book deploring the cardinal of Lorraine's meanness towards him, *Le Proces* (*ibid.*, no. 1090, par. 5, 10 April, 1565).

[13] XIII, 119 (*Bergerie*, ll. 861-864); 166 (elegy to Cecil, ll. 127-130). The French language was widely known in England: see K. LAMBLEY, *The teaching and cultivation of the French language in England during Tudor and Stuart times*, Manchester, London, etc., 1920, especially p. 61-85, "The French language at court and among the nobility". Elizabeth herself knew French well (*ibid.*, p. 73-74).

[14] That the publication was ordered by Catherine has been emphasised, rightly, by Laumonier, XIII, x, cf. xx; J. HERITIER, *Catherine de Médicis*, Paris, 1959, p. 314.

should appeal to monarchs [15], and Ronsard already had a reputation as poet of princes [16]. The Reformers had however tried to dislodge him from this position [17], so he was doubtless very pleased to be able to dedicate the *Elegies, Mascarades et Bergerie* to one queen, at the request of another. In the elegy to Dudley, he describes himself as a " chantre de tant de Rois " (XIII, 73). He hopes his book will be favourably received at the English Court and to this end he praises the French ambassador to England (XIII, 150-158), who in fact sent the book to Cecil with a request in Ronsard's name that it be presented to the queen [18]. The same motive doubtless underlies his praise of

---

[15] In an ode to Du Bellay, Ronsard wrote :
   Seule en France est nostre Lire
   Qui les fredons sache elire
   Pour les Princes rejouir.
(I, 111 : cf. I, 123-124, 127, 137 ; II, 156 ; III, 159 ; V, 264 ; VII, 33 ; XII, 176. For Du Bellay's view, cf. the edition of his *Œuvres poétiques* by H. Chamard (Société des Textes français modernes), VI, 247 : " [...] ce n'est une des moindres felicitez dont les hommes se puissent vanter, que d'avoir peu en quelque liberal exercice faire chose agrëable aux Princes ").

[16] See, for example, the beginning of an *Eloge de la paix à Pierre de Ronsard* by Guillaume des Autels (published in his *Remonstrance au peuple Françoys, de son devoir en ce temps, envers la majesté du roy. A laquelle sont adjoustez troys Eloges, De la paix, De la trefure, & De la guerre.* Paris, 1559, B. Nat. Rés. Ye. 982, 8vº) and Du Bellay, *Regrets*, XVI and XIX.

[17] They insinuated that Ronsard had calumniated the prince of Condé (see *Response aux calomnies contenues au Discours & Suyte du Discours sur les Miseres de ce temps, Faits par Messire Pierre Ronsard, jadis Poëte, & maintenant Prebstre. La premiere par A. Zamariel : Les deux aultres par B. de Mont-Dieu, s.l., M.D.LXIII, B.M. C. 125.d.6 (2), g iiiʳᵒ⁻ᵛᵒ ; Seconde response de F. de la Baronie à messire Pierre de Ronsard Prestre-Gentilhomme Vandomois Evesque futur. Plus le Temple de Ronsard où la Legende de sa vie est briefvement descrite, s.l., M.D.LXIII, B.M. C.125.d.6 (3), B iʳᵒ, F ivvº).* Much of Ronsard's *Responce aux injures* (XI, 109-179) is devoted to a refutation of this charge.

[18] *Calendar of State Papers, Foreign Series, Elizabeth, 1564-1565,* no. 1411 : a letter of 23 August, 1565, from Paul de Foix to Cecil. I am grateful to the Keeper of Public Records for permission to publish a transcription of the letter. The transcription is as follows :
Paulus Fuxius Regis Galliæ in Anglia legatus D. Guillelmo Cecilio Angliæ primicerio salutem. Nescio, vir optime, an insito quodam & ingenito laudis & gloriæ studio fiat, ut Socratis dictum illud verissimum mihi videatur, τον λιβανωτον τοις θεοις, τὸν δὲ ἐπαινον τοις αγαθοις ἀπονέμειν δει. Adeo enim sentio me inflammari honoris cupiditate, ut & bonorum iacturam, corporisque infirmam valetudinem vel minimo dedecore & infamia leviora esse ducam : tantopereque capior hominum doctorum & proë borum de me rectis iudiciis, ut omnia præ illis contemnam. Eodem modo non dubito tibi homini multis & magnis meo quidem iudicio laudibus abundanti literatoris præconio commendari voluptati esse. nam optimi quique maxime gloria ducuntur. Ei vero quod dici solet, eos qui laudant si præter modum id faciant odio haberi, in eo qui ad te mittitur poeta, nihil loci relinquitur, cum id intra modum fecerit. Eum tu non solum natura & mentis viribus, sed etiam doctrina & arte tantopere valere scito, ut unus omnes qui ante se gallice scripserunt longo post se intervallo reliquerit, & futuris omnem assequendi spem ademerit. Nam tanta in eo inest poetici illius divini spiritus vis, ut quæ ab Homero & Pindaro & aliis præclaris græcis dicta sunt dum usurpat, plerumque meliora faciat. Itaque ne littera quidem ulla ab eo proficiscitur quæ non sit scriptione maximopere digna, geniumque quodam inclusum habeat, quæ illam vitæ immortalitati consacret. Accedit eidem generis nobilitas & vitae dignitas, quæ efficiunt ut non leve præconium, sed grave testimonium omnibus quos commendavit impertitum ab eo videatur. Quocirca ex animi mei sententia factum est, ut Reginam vestram (quam ego quotidianis sermonibus in astra efferre soleo) & vos duo, quorum unius humanitatem morumque suavitatem, alterius fidem & integritatem tantopere amo, suis scriptis ornarit. quibus mihi piam & æternam pacem concordiamque suavem & salutarem denunciare inter nostra regna videtur. Nam Poëtas (quos Ennius sanctos appellat) divino quodam furore impulsos futura canere arbitror. Cæterum hæc scripsi libentius, & ut ei qui me laudarit aliquo simile reponerem, & quod existimarim tam egregium scriptorem tibi tam erudito & sapienti viro iure commendari debere. Igitur te ex omnibus unum deligere maxime

Elizabeth's two most powerful privy councillors [19]. When he celebrates Dudley (he is said to be the only Frenchman to have done so [20]), it is almost certainly because Ronsard knew Dudley had been a candidate for Elizabeth's hand [21]. When he praises Cecil it is because he knew Cecil was among the first privy councillors Elizabeth appointed [22], and perhaps also knew that the request for the book to be presented to Elizabeth would pass through his hands. It appears that Ronsard did in fact succeed in winning the favour of the English queen, so much so that she compared his writings to a diamond and sent him one [23]. Ronsard celebrated the " Princesses d'autres nations ", he tells us, " [...] tant pour envoyer (selon ma petite puissance) les honneurs des Françoys aux peuples voysins, que pour faire connoistre mon nom aux Royaumes estrangers " [24].

In the *Elegies, Mascarades et Bergerie*, Ronsard shows a considerable knowledge of English affairs. To enable Ronsard to write poems in praise of the English Court it seems that Catherine made available to him information possessed by ambassadors to England. Certainly, Ronsard was informed by people who had visited the English Court [25]. He praises both Dudley and Cecil for their courtesy towards foreign-

---

volui, quem rogarem ut librum, qui in Reginæ nomine apparuit, quemque hoc tabellario Ronsardus ad eam misit offerres ; quod arbitrarer eum per te magis gratum & acceptum suæ Maiestati futurum. Vale. Londini. 10 Calend. Septembr. 1565.

[19] " [...] From this time [October 1562] forward until peace was restored with France the triumvirate which determined and dictated English policy was the Queen herself and Lord Robert Dudley and William Cecil " (READ, *op. cit.*, p. 252).

[20] The statement is made by J. H. GREW, *Elisabeth d'Angleterre dans la littérature française*, Paris, 1932, p. 52. In E. J. MACINTIRE, " French influence on the beginnings of English classicism ", *Publications of the Modern Languages Association of America*, 26, 1911, p. 496-527, there is an unsupported reference to " Leicester's publicly avowed admiration of Ronsard " (p. 500). A. H. UPHAM affirmed that " Ronsard appears to have been a close friend of the Earl of Leicester ", but this conclusion is based only on Ronsard's praise of him as ' l'ornement des Anglois ' (*The French influence in English Literature from the accession of Elizabeth to the Restoration*, New York, 1911, p. 47). Ronsard's name is not found in the index to E. ROSENBERG, *Leicester, patron of letters*, New York, 1955.

[21] See READ, *op. cit.*, chapter x, " Elizabeth and Dudley ", p. 198-217. " The story was picked up by the Venetian ambassador in Spain [in 1559], and was presently common talk in the capitals of Europe " (p. 198). Ronsard heard the rumour in Paris which predicted
> [...] qu'un Anglois si fortuné sera
> Que sa maistresse un jour l'espousera. (XIII, 274).

[22] XIII, 161-162 ; cf. READ, *op. cit.*, p. 119.

[23] BINET, *op. cit.*, p. 28, l. 42 : " Il fut tant admiré par la Royne d'Angleterre, qui lisoit ordinairement ses escrits, qu'elle les voulut comparer à un diamant d'excellente valeur qu'elle luy envoya ". This passage is first found in the 1597 edition of Binet.

[24] XIII, 35. For Ronsard's influence outside France, see I. SILVER, " Ronsard in European literature : a synoptic view of scholarly publications ", *Bibliothèque d'Humanisme et Renaissance*, 16, 1954, p. 241-254.

[25] The elegy to Elizabeth begins (XIII, 39) :
> Mon cœur esmeu de merveille se serre,
> Voyant venir un Françoys d'Angleterre,
> Lors qu'il discourt combien vostre beauté
> Donne de lustre à vostre Royauté.

ers [26]. That Ronsard's informant was an ambassador is suggested by
a passage in the elegy to Dudley [27] as well as by the inclusion in
Elegies, Mascarades et Bergerie of the poem to the ambassador Paul de
Foix. Another ambassador to England, Michel de Castelnau, seigneur
de Mauvissière, features in the publication (XIII, 212-214) : Ronsard
had recently dedicated the third book of the *Nouvelles poësies* (1564 :
XII, 244) to him. At all events, Ronsard had good informants : the
portraits of Elizabeth, Dudley and Cecil are fairly detailed ones.
Ronsard knows, for example, that Cecil is interested in his ancestry [28],
is a humanist [29], was among the first called into the queen's Privy
Council [30], and has a learned wife [31].

In the *Elegies, Mascarades et Bergerie*, the poet of princes praises
Mary Stuart. Ronsard had praised her frequently, especially between 1558 and 1561 [32]. But it is doubtful whether Mary's " yeux plai-
sans " were the principal motive for his flattering remarks. Mary was
the niece of the cardinal of Lorraine, and between 1558 and 1560
Ronsard had been cultivating the patronage of the cardinal. In 1564-
1565, Ronsard lives up to his position as poet of princes by again
praising Mary [33] : but after this date he has virtually nothing to say

---

[26] The praise of Cecil is found at XIII, 162, the praise of Dudley at XIII, 72. The
compliment to Dudley is somewhat two-edged :
> Nul mieux que toy l'estranger ne caresse,
> Qui doucement par ta grace se laisse
> Prendre & gaigner, ainsi que le poisson
> Sans y penser se prend à l'hameçon.

[27] XIII, 72-73 :
> Nul mieux que toy d'un visage accointable,
> Et d'un parler courtois & amiable,
> Pour de ta Royne illustrer la grandeur,
> Ne fait caresse à un Ambassadeur,
> De quelque part qu'en Angleterre il vienne,
> Et que ta grace amy ne le retienne :
> Aussy es tu la facture des Dieux.

[28] In the *Dictionary of National Biography*, vol. 9, London, 1887, A. JESSOP writes
of Cecil (p. 406) : " Though immense pains were taken to construct a long pedigree of
the family by no less a person than Camden the antiquary, and though Cecil himself
spared no effort to prove his descent from an ancient stock of noble personages, it has
hitherto proved impossible, and probably will always remain so, to trace the origin of
the family further back than the great statesman's grandfather, David Cecil ". " He
had made large collections in heraldry and genealogy, with which studies he was much
interested " (*ibid.*, p. 411). For more detail, cf. O. BARRON, *ed.*, *Northamptonshire
Families* (*The Victoria History of the counties of England*, Genealogical volume), London,
1906, p. 21-23, 25-29.

[29] JESSOP, *ibid.* : " [...] he was a lover of books and of learned men, and a student to
the last ".

[30] See note 22, above.

[31] READ, *op. cit.*, p. 34-35 quotes contemporary judgements on Mildred Cooke, who
was Cecil's second wife.

[32] See P. LAUMONIER, " Ronsard et l'Ecosse ", *Revue de littérature comparée*, 4, 1924,
p. 408-428, especially p. 416-421.

[33] The *Bergerie* (written in March or April 1564, according to Laumonier, XIII, 75,
note 1) is dedicated to Mary and contains praise of Elizabeth and of Mary (ll. 823-824 ;
XIII, 118-119) ; see also an *Elegie* (XIV, 152-159) dealing with Mary, and an *Elegie à la
Royne*. This latter poem was written to accompany the copy of the *Elegies, Mascarades
et Bergerie* sent to her (XIV, 177-180). Mary is also praised in the *Elegie à la majesté
de la Royne d'Angleterre* (XIII, 44).

about her until 1578 [34]. Similarly, he has nothing to say about the cardinal of Lorraine after 1560 except that he has failed to reward him for services rendered [35]. Laumonier explained Ronsard's silence on Mary Stuart as imposed by the Court, and said his outraged indignation over her treatment by Elizabeth was repressed until it finally exploded in the 1578 sonnet [36]. It is more probable that Ronsard was simply disinclined to go on writing eulogies of a princess who had long since left France and whose uncle had shown a philistine insensitivity to Ronsard's tributes to him and his family. Be this as it may, the 1564-1565 praise of Mary confirms our impression that Ronsard saw himself then as the poet of princes [37].

* * *

2. THE RELIGIOUS ISSUE

There is a second reason why the publication of the *Elegies, Mascarades et Bergerie* is apt to surprise readers. Ronsard was a Roman Catholic, and the English government officially rejected the papal supremacy. Ronsard had recently published a series of polemical pamphlets which establish him as one of the greatest popular controvertists of the Catholic Reformation [38]. Queen Elizabeth, on

[34] In *Le Tombeau de Marguerite de France* (1575) he wrote that when Francis II died, he left " sa jeune espousée en plainte douloureuse " (XVII, 76).

[35] In *Le Proces*, Ronsard gives a list of his poems written for the cardinal, and adds a complaint :

Et toutesfois, Seigneur, apres que ce Ronsard
A despendu pour vous son labeur & son art
A vous rendre immortel, pour toute recompense
Un autre a pris le fruit de sa vaine esperance,
Vous ne l'ignorant point : car par vostre moyen
Le mettant en oubly un autre a eu son bien :
Il vous en advertist & vous en feit requeste,
Il tendit les filets, un autre en prit la queste.   (XIII, 24).

[36] *Art. cit.*, p. 423 : " C'est que Catherine de Médicis avait un puissant intérèt à rester en bons termes avec Elisabeth, se flattant de lui faire épouser un de ses fils, soit Charles IX, soit Henri III, soit même François d'Anjou. Ronsard, poète de la Cour, qui en 1564, nous l'avons vu, avait célébré Elisabeth en même temps que Marie Stuart, dut garder un silence prudent et rester neutre dans la grande querelle des deux reines, quelle que fût son opinion. Un beau jour, cependant, son indignation, trop longtemps contenue, éclata, et, dédiant à Marie Stuart tout un livre de ses *Poèmes* en 1578, il le fit précéder de ce sonnet chevaleresque, où le sentiment condamne les raisons de la politique et va jusqu'à l'appel aux armes ". For this sonnet, see below, p. 109-110.

[37] In an *Elegie à la royne*, written to accompany the copy of *Elegies, Mascarades et Bergerie* sent to Mary Stuart, Ronsard wrote (XIV, 178) :

[...] quelquefois mes vers vous elisez
Entre un millier, dont je tressaute d'aise,
Brave de faire un œuvre qui vous plaise :
Car je ne veux en ce monde choisir
Plus grand honneur que vous donner plaisir.

[38] The importance of Ronsard's religious controversial writing is illustrated by the volume of replies by Protestants. Ronsard listed these replies, XII, 10 ; cf. F. CHAR-BONNIER, *Pamphlets Protestants contre Ronsard (1560-1577)* (Bibliothèque littéraire de la Renaissance, nouv. sér., 11), Paris, 1923. These pamphlets contain grudging tributes to

100 M. C. SMITH

the other hand, had, in virtue of the 1559 Act of Supremacy, assumed
the title of " the only supreme governor of this realm, [...] as well in
all spiritual or ecclesiastical things or causes, as temporal [...] " [39],
and had deprived the bishops who had with one exception refused to
swear allegiance to her as supreme governor of the Church [40].

It is difficult to estimate how much Ronsard knew about the
English religious situation, but it is unlikely that he could have
pleaded complete ignorance. It has been said that in the early years
of Elizabeth's reign, French people knew little about her religious
policies [41], but this conclusion needs re-examining. It may well be
true of the general public, but at least some French people were
acquainted with the situation in England. The French Reformers
in Geneva knew of the great expectations of their exiled English
brethren who had left the city on the accession of Elizabeth to return
home [42]. Calvin himself had dedicated an edition of his *Commentarii
in Isaiam* to Elizabeth in 1559 and had exhorted her to restore the
Reformed religion in England [43]. Popular Protestant literature in
French in the early years of Elizabeth's reign speaks of the new

---

Ronsard's influence : the author of the *Seconde responce*—see above, note 17—says that
in defending " la Prestrise ", " Il a plus fait luy seul que toute la Sorbonne " (C ii^{ro}),
and speaks of Ronsard's " faveur envers le peuple bas " (G iiiv^o). The influence of the
Discours was commented on by a number of contemporaries, including Du Perron in
his *Oraison funebre* for Ronsard : " [...] ce grand Ronsard prenant en main les armes de sa
profession, c'est à dire, le papier et la plume, afin de combatre ces nouveaux escrivains,
s'aida si à propos d'une science profane, comme la sienne, pour la defence de l'Eglise,
et apporta si heureusement les richesses et les tresors d'Egypte en la terre saincte, que
l'on recogneut incontinent que toute l'elegance et la douceur des lettres n'estoit pas de
leur costé, comme ils pretendoient " (*Œuvres complètes de Ronsard*, ed. H. Vaganay,
7 v., Paris, 1923-1924, VII, 33).

[39] Cf. C. S. MEYER, *Elizabeth I and the religious settlement of 1559*, Saint Louis, 1960,
p. 38-39. According to READ, *op. cit.*, p. 133, " Cecil, more than anyone else except
Elizabeth herself, was responsible for the Elizabethan religious settlement ".

[40] Cf. MEYER, *op. cit.*, p. 75-76. The exception is Anthony Kitchin of Llandaff.

[41] " Vers 1560, la personnalité d'Elisabeth s'imposait à l'attention des Français.
Non qu'ils fussent exactement informés de ses grandes entreprises, notamment de l'orga-
nisation rapide d'une Eglise à la tête de laquelle elle se plaçait " (ASCOLI, *op. cit.*, p. 104).

[42] See C. MARTIN, *Les protestants anglais réfugiés à Genève au temps de Calvin, 1555-
1560, leur Eglise, leurs écrits*, Genève, 1915, chapter vi, " La fin de l'Eglise ", p. 255-264.
On the death of Mary Tudor, exiles returned to England from all over the continent.
Martin quotes (p. 258) an entry in the " Registres du Conseil " for 24 January 1559 :
" Les dictz Anglois et leurs ministres ont presenté supplication au nom de plusieurs
ministres et autres d'entre eulx, proposans qu'il a pleu à Dieu mettre la parolle de Dieu
en leur pays et liberté d'enseigner, à quoy ils se veulent employer et se retirer avec congé
et licence, remercians aussi du bon recueuil qu'ilz ont heu icy et quilz demeureront à
jamais obligez à ceste Seigneurie. Arresté qu'on leur donne congé et s'ilz en veulent
lettres leur soient faites en bonne forme ". For biographies of the exiles, see C. H.
GARRETT, *The Marian exiles, a study in the origins of Elizabethan Puritanism*, Cambridge,
1938.

[43] *Ioannis Calvini Commentarii in Isaiam prophetam. Nunc demum ab ipso Authore
recogniti, locupletati, magnoque labore & cura expoliti*, Genevae, apud Io. Crispinum,
M.D.LIX, B.M. C.24.c.10. Calvin also called the attention of the English ambassador
in Paris to Gabriel de Saconay's edition (1561) of Henry VIII's *Assertio*. This edition
contains a preface affirming that Elizabeth is illegitimate and that Mary Stuart's claim
to England is justified. See PHILLIPS, *op. cit.*, p. 23-24. Elizabeth protested frequently
and vigorously, and the book was withdrawn. For the text of the letter of the ambassador Throckmorton to Calvin, thanking him for drawing his attention to this publication,
see H. de la FERRIERE, *Le seizième siècle et les Valois*, Paris, 1879, p. 62.

situation in warm terms [44]. Many works of French Reformers were translated into English in these years [45], and a French Reformed Church was established in London [46].

The early Elizabethan policies were also made known in France by the Catholic controvertist Osorius. Osorius, whom Montaigne described as " le meilleur historien Latin de noz siecles " [47], published his *Epistola ad Elizabetham*, and a French translation of it, in 1563 [48]. The partial suppression of the old religion in England is due, Osorius says, to Elizabeth's privy councillors; the partial retention of the old religion is due to the " clemence, douceur, pieté & probité " of Elizabeth herself [49]. William Cecil arranged for the publication of a reply to " Osorius's slanderous epistle " [50].

Finally, the English religious policies were well known to French people close to government circles and especially to French ambassadors in England [51]. Ronsard, as we saw, was probably informed by

---

[44] See, for example, the *Balade du pape malade* (published originally in *Deux chansons spirituelles* [...], Lyon, 1562), in A. de MONTAIGLON, *Recueil de poésies françoises des XVe et XVIe siècles*, t. VIII, Paris, 1857, p. 275 :
Pres de mourir je suis, quoy que l'on die,
Tant petit est l'espoir de mon support ;
Car l'Escossois, l'Anglois, la Germanie,
M'ont tous laissé, sans qu'ilz ayent remort ;
Flamans, François, Espagnolz, sont d'accord
De me laisser, et n'y puis recourir.
See, too, the Colloquies of Mathurin Cordier, quoted (after the edition of 1593) by MARTIN, *op. cit.*, p. 258-259 : " Dis-tu que l'Evangile est maintenant en Angleterre ?— C'est une chose certaine.—Et que l'idolàtrie en est chassée ?—Entièrement.—O bonnes nouvelles plaisantes à ouyr !—Ains très plaisantes ".

[45] Some of them are listed in J. H. M. SALMON, *The French religious wars in English political thought*, Oxford, 1959, p. 171-180 : " Appendix A, A list of French works published in England 1560-1598 ".

[46] This Church was set up in 1560 with Des Gallars as the pastor. See F. de SCHICKLER, *Les Eglises du refuge en Angleterre*, 3 v., Paris, 1892, I, p. 79-136 (chapter iii, " L'Eglise de Nicolas des Gallars ").

[47] *Essais*, I, xiv, p. 68 in the edition by " Les textes français ", Paris, 1946-1948.

[48] There were several editions of the Latin text : Venetiis, 1563 (B. Nat. *E368 (4) ; B.M.3936.cc.6) ; Parisiis, 1563 (B. Nat. Mz.4106 ; B.M. G. 5925) ; Lovanii, 1563 (B.M. 3901.d.22). The French edition is the following : J. OSORIO DA FONSECA, *Les graves et sainctes remonstrances de l'Empereur Ferdinand, à nostre sainct pere le Pape, Pie, quatriesme de ce nom, sur le faict du Concile de Trente, & des choses proposées en iceluy. Avec une brieve exhortation dudict Seigneur Empereur, addressée, à Monsieur le Cardinal de Lorraine, sur les mesmes affaires. Plus, une bien longue & docte Epistre, escrite par certain personnage Portugallois, homme de grandes lettres, & envoyée à Ma-Dame Elizabeth, Royne d'Angleterre, qui contient un beau & elegant discours, sur les choses du monde, & notamment sur le gouvernement politique des Royaumes, Republiques, & Empires, & restablissement de l'ancienne Religion, selon la doctrine catholique des sainctz Peres de l'Eglise de Dieu, Le tout traduict de Latin en François*, Paris, chez Nicolas Chesnau, 1563, B.M.1360.c.3 ; also B. Nat., B 5440 and Mz. 4313.

[49] 35vo.

[50] See C. READ, " William Cecil and Elizabethan public relations, in *Elizabethan government and society. Essays presented to Sir John Neale*, London, 1961, p. 21-55 who quotes (p. 26) from a letter of Cecil to Sir Thomas Smith in France (November, 1563), asking whether it will be possible to have the reply to Osorius printed in France.

[51] If Muret's eulogy can be believed, Paul de Foix was left in no doubt about the religious orientation of England while he was ambassador : " Illud vero commemoratione dignissimum, quod quamdiu in Anglia fuit, nullum unquam diem intermisit, quin, quamlibet fremente Regina, sacrosanctum Missae sacrificium domi suæ celebrari iusserit : ad quod clam avide conveniebat ac concurrebat, magna et Anglorum et exterorum Catholicorum multitudo, quos ille fovebat, consolabatur, protegebat, quorum

ambassadors. We do not know whether they told him about the religious situation, but the balance of probability is that Ronsard knew in which direction the English government was moving in religious matters [52].

Did Ronsard therefore have qualms of conscience about praising Elizabeth? This is unlikely for three reasons. The first is that the early Elizabethan policy was explicable to a great extent in terms of political opportunism. Elizabeth was trying to steer a middle course. The new owners of confiscated church property had an interest in maintaining the breach with Rome [53]. On the other hand, a thoroughgoing enforcement of Protestant worship on a Calvinistic pattern would have abruptly provoked English Catholics and provided France with a pretext for enforcing the claims of Mary Stuart. In the sixteenth century, political opportunism could lead to flexible religious policies. Ronsard knew this well. Henry II had but recently obtained the military alliance of Lutheran German princes: it was only when the treaty of Cateau-Cambresis enabled him to dispense with their help that he was completely free to persecute the French Reformers, " cette infâme canaille luthérienne " [54]. In England, a political wind of change might blow at any moment. There was little evidence that Elizabeth was personnally committed to the cause of the Reformers. After all, she had heard John Knox's trumpet blast against government by women, and had not been amused [55].

---

omnium arx, portus, præsidium, perfugium erat: a quibus non tantum mala multa imminentia depulit, sed effecit etiam, ut multa damna, quæ eis data erant, restituerentur. Ob quæ merita, ubi primum ex Anglia revertit, in sanctius atque interius Regis consilium adlectus est " (*Marci Antonii Mureti* [...] *Orationes quattuor* [...], Ingolstadii, M.D.XXCV, B.M.1090.i.8 (6), p. 31-32).

[52] Ronsard may have been informed about the Edwardian phase of the Anglican Reformation by Nicolas Denisot, who had been employed in England as tutor of the Seymour sisters (cf. M. A. HARRIS's study of *L'Amant resuscité de la mort d'amour*. Ph. D. thesis for the University of Birmingham, typescript). Among the poems contributed by Ronsard to the *Tombeau* of Marguerite of Valois (III, 37-85) is an ode dedicated to the Seymour sisters (III, 41-49) in which Ronsard pays tribute to Denisot's merits as a teacher.

[53] Under Mary, " The Reformation sat as yet lightly on most Englishmen's minds, but the nobility, gentry and yeomanry who had invested in those lands were not prepared to disgorge them, and their self-interest saved protestantism in England " (G. R. ELTON, *England under the Tudors*, London, 1957, p. 216).

[54] For Henry II's relations with German Protestant princes, see LAVISSE, *op. cit.*, t. V, ii (by H. LEMONNIER, Paris, 1904), p. 145-146, 157, 166. According to J. LECLER, *Histoire de la tolérance au siècle de la Réforme*, 2 v., Paris, 1955, II, p. 27, Henry II was exasperated by the growth of the French Reformed Church and by the intercession of German Protestants on its behalf. In the summer of 1558 he exclaimed: ". Je jure que si je peux régler mes affaires extérieures, je ferai courir par les rues le sang et les têtes de cette infâme canaille luthérienne ". Ronsard refers to Henry II's activities on behalf of the German princes in the *Hymne du roy Henri II*, ll. 585-628 (VIII, 36-38).

[55] Calvin did not endorse the views expressed in John Knox's *First blast of the trumpet against the monstruous regiment of women* and, on the accession of Elizabeth, Hotman congratulated him for his restraint (cf. R.M. KINGDON, *Geneva and the coming of the wars of religion in France, 1553-1563*, Genève, 1956, p. 89) but the publication contributed to Elizabeth's hostility to the Genevan Reformers, as Beza himself admitted (*Correspondance*, t. II, ed. F. Aubert, H. Meylan and A. Dufour, Genève, 1962, p. 128, note 12).

The second reason why Ronsard could praise Elizabeth with an easy conscience is that for some time there was in France doubt about the precise doctrinal status of the Elizabethan settlement itself. The Elizabethan *Book of Common Prayer* had made a favourable impression on conciliatory Catholics in France, notably the cardinal of Lorraine [56]. In fact, John Jewel's *Apologia ecclesiae anglicanae* was produced largely for a French audience and, according to the English ambassador in France, was well received by the Roman Catholics [57]. It was clear that the Elizabethan Anglican Church and the French Reformed Church were not the same. Moreover, the English settlement had been introduced, as the French ambassador Castelnau put it, " fort subtilement sans aucun remuëment ny altercation " [58].

Finally, Ronsard could praise Elizabeth for her personal qualities without offering an opinion on her religious policies; this in fact is the course he adopts. Similarly, his praise of Cecil and Dudley concerns their learning and wisdom. Whether or not he knew that Cecil was urging the queen to adopt an anti-Roman policy, Ronsard certainly does not praise him for this ! He does not deal with religion in any of the three poems. Elsewhere in the collection dedicated to Elizabeth he makes it plain that his religious views have not chang-

---

[56] " Paul de Foix, returning from a diplomatic mission in England, had brought back a French translation of the Common Prayer which had commended itself very much to the middle-party Catholics. It was ' less repugnant to the papists '—in Throckmorton's words—' than any form used in Germany '. A few influential but unfortunately anonymous churchmen advised Throckmorton to have an apology for the book composed [...] " (H. O. EVENNETT, *The cardinal of Lorraine and the Council of Trent, a study in the Counter-reformation*, Cambridge, 1930, p. 403-404. He also says (p. 417) : " [...] the Cardinal was pla⁴nly not so much out of harmony with the liberal spirits at Court who were bestowing their compliments upon the Anglican liturgy about this time "). Cf. J. H. POLLEN, *The English Catholics in the reign of Elizabeth, a study of their politics, civil life and government, 1558-1580*. London, 1920, p. 99-100 : " Moreover, Elizabeth was now priding herself on the reception of her liturgy by the *politiques* of Catherine de Medici, and alleging that the Pope himself might approve of it, or perhaps had already done so ". He states (p. 101) that the pope certainly had not approved it.

[57] See J. E. BOOTY, *John Jewel as apologist of the Church of England*, London, 1963 and especially chapter ii, " Jewel, Cecil, and the birth of the ' Apologia ' ", p. 36-57. The *Apologia* was received in Paris by 24 January, 1562 (p. 49). Two days later Throckmorton wrote to Cecil saying the papists were satisfied by the book, but that the calvinists were not (p. 50). The book was spread throughout Europe (p. 55) and, according to Jewel, was translated into many European languages, including French, and was discussed at Trent (p. 56). For the ensuing controversy, see chapter iii, " The great controversy : the personal encounter of Jewel and Harding ", p. 58-82.

[58] *Les Memoires de Messire Michel de Castelnau, seigneur de Mauvissiere* [&c.]. *Ausquelles sont traictées les choses plus remarquables qu'il a veuës & negotiées en France, Angleterre, & Escosse, soubs les Rois François II & Charles IX tant en temps de paix qu'en temps de guerre.* Paris, chez Claude Chappelet, M.DC.XXI, p. 62. Elizabeth was reluctant to make martyrs. In 1563, when the penalties for recusancy were increased, the queen gave instructions that the oath of royal supremacy was not to be tendered a second time (which would put a recusant in danger of death) without archbishop Parker's written mandate (J. E. NEALE, *Elizabeth I and her parliaments, 1559-1581*, 2v., I, London, 1953, p. 121). In 1564, a sizeable minority of Justices of the Peace was able to express hostility to the religious changes (cf. A. L. ROWSE, *The England of Elizabeth, the structure of Society*, London, 1950, p. 439). The acts of Supremacy and Uniformity were not rigidly enforced, and Roman Catholics attended the universities until the ' eighties (cf. A. C. SOUTHERN, *Elizabethan recusant prose 1559-1582*, London, 1950, p. 21-22).

ed [59]. There seems little reason to conclude, therefore, as several scholars have done, that Ronsard had to be constrained to celebrate the " heretic " queen ; and it is certain that the Inquisition would have had no cause to sink its teeth into him [60].

The book of *Elegies, Mascarades et Bergerie*, then, is a work of political propaganda. The religious issue, in 1565, is not a dominant factor in anglo-French relations.

* * *

3. MARY QUEEN OF SCOTS

Between 1565 and 1578, when the fifth collected edition of his works appeared, Ronsard's opinion of Elizabeth and her privy councillors changed. His opinion in these years is influenced by the English government's treatment of Mary Stuart. The purpose of this section of the article is to establish what was being said about Mary in France during these years.

Mary's marriage to Darnley on 29 July, 1565, antagonised Elizabeth [61], and it was in that year that Thomas Jeney wrote the first attack on Mary [62], possibly at the instigation of the English government [63]. At the time he wrote against Mary, Jeney was a Protestant,

---

[59] In the *Bergerie* he deplores the recent vandalism of the Reformers (ll. 341-346 ; XIII, 93), gratefully acknowledges Philip II's intervention in the French civil war (ll. 811-822 ; XIII, 117) and refers to the pope as " le grand Pasteur de tant d'ames chrestiennes " (l. 869 ; XIII, 120).

[60] " Il doit servir la politique royale : au moment où notre gouvernement projette une alliance franco-anglaise, renforcée par un mariage, Ronsard flatte l'hérétique Elisabeth, vante ses qualités physiques et morales, célèbre les mérites de son favori Leicester et de son ministre Cecil, et s'efforce de convaincre les Anglais de la paix et de la prospérité qui règnent en France. " (R. LEBEGUE, *Ronsard, l'homme et l'œuvre*, Paris, 1950, p. 97-98.) Similarly, Laumonier is surprised at Ronsard writing the elegy to Cecil : " [...] le seul fait de l'avoir écrit a de quoi nous étonner, vu le rôle qu'il [Ronsard] venait de jouer en face des réformés français ; c'est que, en 1564, Catherine de Medicis tenait à se concilier, coûte que coûte, les bonnes grâces de la Cour anglaise " (XIII, 159, note 1). It is said that " If Ronsard had ever fallen into the hands of the Inquisition, he would also [i.e. like Giordano Bruno, who had called Elizabeth " diva "] have been hard put to it to account for his extravagant praise of Elizabeth " (F. A. YATES, *The French Academies of the sixteenth century*, London, 1947, p. 232, note 1) : maybe, but some English Roman Catholic martyrs were just as " extravagant " in their praise of the queen as Ronsard was.

[61] Because " Darnley had a claim to the English throne almost as strong as that of Mary herself "—PHILLIPS, *op. cit.*, p. 27. The marriage also antagonized the Scottish Protestants, because Darnley was a Catholic.

[62] " The attack was launched in 1565, the year of the Darnley marriage, with a poem by one Thomas Jeney entitled ' Maister Randolphes Phantasey : a breffe calgulacion of the procedinges in Scotlande from the first of Julie to the Last of Decembre '. The poem purports to be an account by Thomas Randolph, Elizabeth's ambassador in Scotland, of a dream in which the true circumstances and consequences of the Darnley marriage were revealed to him by the Queen of Scots herself. The theme of the poem is the tragic mistake that Mary made in choosing a husband in accordance with the dictates not of her reason and wisdom, but of her lustful passions " (*ibid.*, p. 34).

[63] Mary complained to Elizabeth, thinking that Randolph himself was the author. " As a matter of fact, although Randolph was probably innocent of the authorship, Elizabeth's government may have indeed instigated the poem, for Jeney was in Scotland

and the identification of the Protestant cause with Elizabeth, and of the Catholic cause with Mary, is implicit in his work [64]. Thomas Jeney lived for a while in France [65] : he translated Ronsard's *Discours des miseres* into English [66].

Other people wrote for and against Mary [67], and particularly after her alleged connivence at the murder of Darnley (9 February, 1567) and her almost immediate marriage to Bothwell (15 May, 1567). By August 1567, she had been deposed [68]. The deposition was defended by propagandists on the grounds of her private life. Her public image suffered in France : among her detractors was Michel de l'Hospital, who had earlier been one of her admirers [69]. Again, there is a tendency for Mary's cause to be identified with that of the Roman Catholic faith [70].

---

at the time in the employ of Sir William Cecil, Elizabeth's principal councilor. Moreover, in a dedicatory epistle to Randolph, Jeney admits that he 'compiled this tragedy' because 'some of my countrymen entreated me to write what I saw which chiefly by their procurement I have done ' " (*ibid.*, p. 36).

[64] Jeney does not refer directly to Mary's religion, but " He reiterates the charge that she has forsaken the sage and honest counsel of Murray and his group—all supporters of Protestantism—to follow the lusts and ambitions of the Catholic Lord Darnley. He also makes frequent reference to the influence of the brothers Guise on Mary's conduct " (*ibid.*, p. 35-36).

[65] Cf. the article " Jenye, Thomas (*fl.* 1565-1583) " by J. CRANSTOUN in the *Dictionary of National Biography*. On 13 July, 1567, Jeney wrote to Cecil about an attempt he was making to secure the escape from France to England of the earl of Moray. He dedicated his translation of Ronsard's *Discours* to Sir Henry Norris, the English ambassador in France.

[66] *A discours of the present troobles in Fraunce, and the miseries of this tyme*, compyled by Peter Ronsard, gentilman of Vandome, and dedicated unto the quene mother, translated in to English by Thomas Jeney, gentilman. Printed at Anduerpe, 1568. See SOUTHERN, *op. cit.*, p. 335, footnote, and 434-435. According to A. F. ALLISON and D. M. ROGERS, " A catalogue of Catholic books in English printed abroad or secretly in England, 1558-1640 ", *Biographical Studies*, 3, 1956, " The translation is, in fact, a Protestant one ". I have not examined the translation, but this statement is surprising. A copy of it was among a collection of books " putt furth in this realme or beyonde the seas for Defense of papistrye " found in the library of John Stowe on 21 February, 1569 (see *A transcript of the Registers of the Company of Stationers of London, 1554-1640*, ed. E. Arber, vol. 1, London, 1875, p. 393-394). Eight days after the confiscation of this collection the queen issued a proclamation stating that seditious books had been disseminated, and warning people to desist from the " use or dealing with any such seditious bookes, made or translated by any person, contayning matter derogatorie to the soveraigne estate of her Majestie, or impugning the orders and rites established by lawe for Christian religion and devine service within this Realme, or otherwise styrring and nourishing matter tending to sedition [...] " (*ibid.*, p. 430).

[67] For two works favourable to Mary published in 1566, see PHILLIPS, *op. cit.*, p. 38-40. One is the *Proditionis ab aliquot Scotiae Parduellibus Adversus Serenissimam suam Reginam non ita pridem perpetratae brevis et simplex narratio*, published at Louvain (cf. *ibid.*, note 35), and the other is Peter Frarin's *An Oration against the Unlawful Insurrections of the Protestantes of our time, under pretence to Refourme Religion*, published at Antwerp. The latter work probably had editions in Latin, French and Dutch (cf. *ibid.*, note 36).

[68] PHILLIPS, *op. cit.*, p. 40.

[69] See PHILLIPS, *op. cit.*, p. 45 and note 48.

[70] Perhaps because she was the niece of the cardinal of Lorraine. The author of a book entitled *Advertissement sur le pourparlé, qu'on dit de Paix, entre le Roy & ses rebelles. Avec son Contrepoison*, s.l., 1568, B. M. 8052. aa. 24, rejoiced that the Protestant religion was established in England and in Scotland : " Elle commande en Escosse, avec le piteux & tragique evenement de celle qui en estoit Royne : & le tout pour avoir esté trop addonnée à la part & au conseil de son oncle : laquelle toutefois Dieu vueille par sa misericorde bien consoler, & fortifier en toute patience, & recognoissance de son devoir " (L ii v°).

Mary also features in the French literature on the revolt of the English northern earls (November 1569). This event aroused considerable interest in France : Elizabeth had supported French Protestant rebels in the third civil war in France [71] : Ronsard had deplored the fact [72]. She was now faced with a rebellion of English Catholics [73]. Reports of this event were published in France and the writer of one of them, who mentions ' le piteux & deplorable estat de la Royne d'Ecosse ' and presents the demands of the Catholic earls, suggests that in the event of civil war in England, foreign intervention might be necessary [74]. The English government tried to have this particular pamphlet suppressed in France, and Cecil wrote a reply to it [75]. The cause of Mary is becoming identified with that of those English Catholics who used political action to defend their religion.

In 1571, after the arrest of Norfolk for plotting to release, marry and enthrone Mary Stuart, the English government actively though surreptitiously propagated Buchanan's famous tract against Mary, his *De Maria Scotorum regina, totaque eius contra regem coniuratione* [76]. This has been described as " the fountainhead of all later attacks on the Scottish Queen's character and conduct " [77]. It

---

[71] For her intervention in the first civil war, see above. Cecil had urged her to support the Reformers in the second war, but she had refused (cf. READ, *op. cit.*, p. 392-395). For her surreptitious aid in the third, see *ibid.*, p. 419-420.

[72] In *Les Elemens ennemis de l'Hydre* : XVII, 409.

[73] For a convenient historical outline of the rebellion, and a survey of the contemporary English literature of the rebellion, see J. K. LOWERS, *Mirrors for rebels, a study of polemical literature relating to the Northern Rebellion, 1569* (University of California Publications, English Studies, 6), Berkeley and Los Angeles, 1953.

[74] This work is the *Discours des troubles nouvellement advenuz au Royaume d'Angleterre, au moys d'Octobre 1569. Avec une declaration, faicte par le Comte de Nortumberland & autres grands Seigneurs d'Angleterre*, Lyon, M.D.LXX (B. Nat. Nc 154 ; University of Leeds, Anglo-French Collection). The pamphlet deals with Mary Stuart on p. 14-17. It contains no direct appeal to the French government to intervene : PHILLIPS (*op. cit.*, p. 93) appears to be mistaken on this point. There is, however, a broad hint that foreign aid will be called upon in the event of " seditions " in England : [...] " les Anglois auront meilleur besoin d'aide des estrangiers, que non pas d'envoyer gens hors leur pays pour nous faire la guerre " (p. 13).
Other works dealing with the revolt are the following : *Continuation des choses plus celebres & memorables advenues en Angleterre, Escosse & Irlande, depuis le moys d'Octobre M.D.LXIX. Jusques au XXV. jour de Decembre ensuyvant & dernier passé. Aussi comment le Regent d'Escosse fut dernierement occis*, Lyon, M.D.LXX, B. Nat., Nc 155 ; *Petit discours sur une lettre responsive de l'empereur Maximilian au roy, 1568. Plus une copie de la conspiration de deux Comtes d'Angleterre contre leur Royne, sous ombre de la religion, & de l'arrest de ladite Dame Royne contre lesdits Comtes*, Imprimé nouvellement, s.l., M.D.LXX, B. Nat. Lb [33]257. For this last publication, see E. DROZ, *L'imprimerie à La Rochelle, 1 : Barthélemy Berton, 1563-1573* (Travaux d'Humanisme et Renaissance, 34), Genève, 1960, p. 95.

[75] *Ibid.* Phillips says " Burghley " wrote a reply, although according to C. READ, *Lord Burghley and Queen Elizabeth*, London, 1960, p. 33, Cecil did not become lord Burghley until 25 February 1571. READ, *art. cit.*, p. 32, writes : " Early in 1570 a book was published in France defending the action of the northern rebels. Cecil attempted a reply to it, under the title, ' Copy of a letter from a gentleman in England to his cousin, a Student in Paris '. We have a manuscript of it in Cecil's hand. It was a poor effort and Cecil never finished it. "

[76] For the bibliographical details, see PHILLIPS, *op. cit.*, p. 253, note 31.

[77] *Ibid.*, p. 61.

was printed in London, before 1 November 1571, and with it there appeared a Latin essay entitled *Actio contra Mariam*, by Thomas Wilson, and " three of the more incriminating Casket Letters " [78]. The English ambassador distributed the book in France, and " said it did much to discredit her cause " [79]. A French translation was inspired by Cecil, who had by now become Lord Burghley, and the Casket Letters were published with it [80].

Although little is known about Ronsard's opinion of Mary's adversary Buchanan [81], we have an account of his views on the love poems supposedly written by Mary to Bothwell, which form part of the Casket Letters. Brantôme tells us that he and Ronsard read them together, and came to the conclusion that they were forgeries, on the grounds that they were " trop grossiers et mal polis pour estre sortis de sa belle boutique " [82]. This was the argument regularly put forward by supporters of Mary [83].

---

[78] Cf. *ibid.*, p. 62.

[79] READ, *Burghley*, p. 64 ; cf. PHILLIPS, *op. cit.*, p. 67-68. Phillips notes that an English agent reported to Burghley from France that Buchanan's book on Mary had " made the matter so plain that they were ashamed to defend her that fain would " (p. 68). For further evidence of official English encouragement of " unauthorized " publications against Mary in France, see *ibid.*, p. 252, note 22 (1572) and p. 59 and note 21 (1583-1584).

[80] " Finally, Cecil himself arranged for a French translation that appeared with an Edinburgh imprint, but actually was produced at the great French Huguenot center of La Rochelle "—*ibid.*, p. 63. The book is not mentioned in any of the three volumes of *L'imprimerie à La Rochelle* (Travaux d'Humanisme et Renaissance, 34), Genève, 1960. The translation, which is by " a Huguenot lawyer named Camuz (or Cumez) "—PHILLIPS, *op. cit.*, p. 63, note 34—is entitled *Histoire de Marie Royne d'Escosse, touchant la conjuration faicte contre le Roy, & l'adultere commis avec le Comte de Bothuel, histoire vrayement tragique*, traduicte de Latin en François, Edimbourg, 1572. The copy I used is in the Anglo-French Collection of the Library of the University of Leeds. The Casket Letters are included, 61vo-77ro ; among them are eleven sonnets in French (two of which have one line missing) and a sextet, 74ro-77ro. For a discussion of these poems, see E. I. BANNERMAN, *Les influences françaises en Ecosse au temps de Marie Stuart*, Besançon, 1929, p. 135-139.

[81] I. SILVER, *art. cit.* writes (p. 247-248) : " Although Buchanan's correspondence contains no allusion to Ronsard, and although there is no mention of the poet either in the brief autobiography that the humanist wrote not long before his death in 1582, or in his extant verse, we may safely assume that Buchanan, who reckoned among his friends Adrien Turnèbe and Henri Estienne, knew and was not unknown to Ronsard. We possess, in fact, the testimony of Jacques-Auguste de Thou that the French poet knew Buchanan and held him in high esteem ". The relevant passage of De Thou is given by P. de NOLHAC, *Ronsard et l'humanisme* (Bibliothèque de l'École des Hautes Etudes, Sciences historiques et philologiques, Fasc. 227), Paris, 1921, p. 144. Du Bellay praises Buchanan in *Les Regrets*, sonnet 187.

[82] P. de Bourdeille seigneur de BRANTOME, *Œuvres complètes*, ed. L. Lalanne, 11v., Paris, 1864-1882, VII, 406-407 :
" Surtout elle [Mary] aimoit la poésie et les poëtes, mais sur tous M. de Ronsard, M. du Belay, et M. de Maisonfleur, qui ont faict de belles poésies et élégies pour elle, et mesmes sur son partement de la France, que j'ay veu souvent lire à elle-mesmes en France et en Escosse, les larmes à l'œil et les souspirs au cœur.
Elle se mesloit d'estre poëte, et composoit des vers, dont j'en ay veu aucuns de beaux et très-bien faicts, et nullement ressemblans à ceux qu'on luy a mis à sus avoir faict sur l'amour du comte de Baudouel : ils sont trop grossiers et mal polis pour estre sortis de sa belle boutique. M. de Ronsard estoit bien de mon opinion en cela, ainsy que nous en discourions un jour, et que nous les lisions. Elle en composoit bien de plus beaux et de plus gentils, et promptement, comme je l'ay veue souvent qu'elle se retiroit en son cabinet, et sortoit aussitost pour nous en monstrer à aucuns honnestes gens que nous estions là. "

[83] John Lesley's argument was that " epistles of such coarse obscenity could never have been written by one so wise, so virtuous, and so refined as the Queen of Scots "

An important reply to Buchanan's publication is *L'innocence de la tres illustre tres-chaste, et debonnaire princesse, Madame Marie Royne d'Escosse* [84]. It was accompanied by a *Discours contre les conspirations pretendues estre faites sur l'estat d'Angleterre, avec les responces à* [sic] *celuy qui deffend la cause & innocence de la tre-illustre royne d'Escosse traduit d'Anglois en François l'an 1572*. In both these works the device of sparing Elizabeth by blaming her privy councillors is adopted [85]. Moreover, the prefatory *Advertissement au lecteur* is largely an indictment of two " Sinons " : they recall the crafty Greek by their very names, " L'un commençant avec la premiere syllabe du nom de Sinon et l'autre finissant avec les dernieres lettres du mesme " [86]. This is an attack on Cecil (whose name was often spelt ' Sisil ' and is usually still so pronounced) and Nicholas Bacon : these two privy councillors, and not the queen, are responsible for the introduction of " leur monstrueuse teste de la religion nouvelle " [87]. In the *Discours contre les conspirations* Cecil again comes under attack personally [88]. The device of blaming the privy councillors for government policy, and exonerating the queen, is a very important one. Elizabeth herself appears to have encouraged its use [89]. The French ambassador Castelnau thought it was a trick [90], but contemporary English Catholics gave Elizabeth the benefit of the doubt, and used the device habitually [91].

In the following years, Mary Stuart became a focal point in the cold war which opposed the Catholic and Protestant factions in Europe. The pamphlet war was fought with particular bitterness in France. After 1572, French tracts denounced Mary's claim to England as intolerable on the grounds of her religion and her connection with

---

(PHILLIPS, *op. cit.*, p. 90). This argument was later applied explicitly by Robert Turner to " the love poem ostensibly addressed by her to Bothwell and found in the casket along with the notorious letters " (*ibid.*, p. 187 : in fact, as we have seen, there were several love poems).

[84] S.l., 1572, B.M. 600. d. 19. See PHILLIPS, *op. cit.*, p. 96-97.

[85] In *L'innocence*, 62ro, and in the *Discours contre les conspirations*, 17vo-18ro.

[86] A vvo.

[87] *Advertissement*, A viiro.

[88] Marginal notes refer to Cecil : " C'est vu des tours de Sicile " (18ro[or rather 16ro]), and " Un trait Sicilien imputant à autrui la propre cruauté " (26vo).

[89] In 1571, she spoke of the Treasons bill, which was part of the government's response to the Northern Rebellion, in the following terms : " In this Parliament it was showed us of a bill devised of for our safety against treasons, whereof, when we had the sight, it liked us not. Nevertheless, being persuaded by our Council of the necessity thereof, and that it was for our safety, we were contented the same should proceed " (NEALE, *op. cit.*, p. 225-226). cf. Machiavelli, *il principe*, XIX.

[90] " Elle avoit un conseil qu'elle rendoit responsable de toutes les violences de son règne, elle feignoit de combattre quelque fois avec lui pour la défense de la bonne foy [...] et protestoit tousjours pour le bon party " (GREW, *op. cit.*, p. 21-22, quoting CASTELNAU, *Memoires*, ed. J. Léonard, Bruxelles, 1731, I, p. 560).

[91] " Like the rest of their contemporaries, they were king-worshippers to excess, and it was natural for them to excuse their sovereign by laying the whole blame for the heresy on her ministers " (POLLEN, *op. cit.*, p. 12).

the Guises and not, as formerly, on the grounds of her personal character [92]. Reformers called on the French government to make an alliance with England and the Protestant powers [93]. Roman Catholics, as we have seen and will see again, called on the government to help Mary Stuart. By 1578, the attitude of French Catholics towards the English government had become decidedly cool [94].

This prevailing attitude of Roman Catholics is reflected in the 1578 edition of Ronsard's *Œuvres*. Since the appearance in 1565 of the book of *Elegies, Mascarades et Bergerie*, the poems to Elizabeth, Dudley and Cecil had reappeared in the three subsequent editions of Ronsard's works with only minor modifications, dictated by aesthetic considerations ; and they had reappeared with substantially the same titles [95]. In the 1578 edition the titles of the " English " poems are altered, and drastically, as follows : the *Elegie à la Majesté de la Royne d'Angleterre* becomes a mere *Discours* ; the *Elegie à mylord Robert Du-Dlé conte de l'Encestre* is now simply an *Elegie* ; and the elegy *Au seigneur Cecille Secretaire de la Royne d'Angleterre* which in 1567 had become an *Elegie au S. Secille Anglois* is now, similarly, nothing more than an *Elegie*. The alterations to the content of these poems seem to be aesthetic, not political. The praise of Elizabeth and her privy councillors remains. However, the amendments to the titles of the poems suggest that Ronsard was less anxious than in the past to be known as a panegyrist of the English Court.

This conclusion is confirmed by the treatment of Mary Stuart in this edition. A sonnet to her dating from the time of her first husband Francis is suppressed, perhaps because it contains her claim to the

---

[92] This is the conclusion of PHILLIPS, *op. cit.*, p. 74. Besides their antipathy towards her on religious grounds, the French Reformers had a political motive for hostility towards Mary. The deposition of Mary on the grounds of her allegedly shameless personal life illustrated their contention that, in certain circumstances, the subject can legitimately resist the " tyranny " of the monarch : see, for example, [Th. de Bèze] *Du droit des magistrats sur leurs subjets. Traitté tres-necessaire en ce temps, pour advertir de leur devoir, tant les Magistrats que les Subjets : publié par ceux de Magdebourg l'an MDL : & maintenant reveu & augmenté de plusieurs raisons & exemples*, s.l., 1574, B.M.878 f.3 (2), p. 40, and *Resolution claire et facile sur la question tant de fois faite de la prise des armes par les inferieurs*, Reims, 1577. B.M. 1193 c.5, p. 64-65.

[93] One writer thinks that such an alliance could include the queen of Scotland (which Mary no longer was), and would be of advantage to French Catholics (*Articles contenans la requeste presentée au Roy par les deputez des Eglises reformées du païs de Languedoc & autres lieux circonvoisins, assemblez par le commandement de sa Majesté. Item une autre requeste à luy presentée par les gens du tiers Estat du pays de Provence. Avec response d'iceluy à icelles. Aussi une response du Seigneur Comte Louys de Nansau, aux advertissemens à luy donnez par le Roy*. A Basle, par Pierre de Ray, M.D.LXXIIII, B.M.3900.a.1 p. 24).

[94] The number of English Catholic refugees in France was increasing rapidly. On 29 October 1577, Poulet wrote to Burghley from Paris : " It is pitiful to see the number of young English gentlemen repaired hither for matter of religion, whereof some have been here of good continuance, others are come out of the Low Countries to avoid the troubles there. God grant them better knowledge of His truth, and dutiful mind towards her Majesty " (*Calendar of State Papers, Foreign Series, Elizabeth, 1577-1578*, no. 388). For this emigration, see J. A. BOSSY's study of *Elizabethan catholicism, the link with France*, Ph.D. thesis for the University of Cambridge, 160, typescipt, p. 30-143.

[95] The only title to be altered was that of the elegy to Cecil, as noted below.

throne of England, a claim which had by now become an embarass-
ment to her [96]. More important, however, is the inclusion of a sonnet
at the beginning of the second book of *Poemes*, dedicated to Mary.
This sonnet is worth quoting in full :

> Encores que la mer de bien loin nous separe,
> Si est-ce que l'esclair de vostre beau Soleil,
> De vostre œil qui n'a point au monde de pareil,
> Jamais loin de mon cœur par le temps ne s'esgare.
> Royne, qui enfermez une Royne si rare,
> Adoucissez vostre ire, & changez de conseil :
> Le Soleil se levant et allant en sommeil
> Ne voit point en la terre un acte si barbare.
> Peuple, vous forlignez (aux armes nonchalant)
> De vos ayeux Renault, Lancelot & Rolant,
> Qui prenoient d'un grand cœur pour les Dames querelle,
> Les gardoient, les sauvoient où vous n'avez, François,
> Ny osé regarder ny toucher le harnois
> Pour oster de servage une Royne si belle.   (XVII, 378-379).

Whether Ronsard really was in favour of a war against England to
liberate Mary Stuart, as he implies in the tercets, is not known. But
he deplores the detention of Mary Stuart and, in common with most
Catholic pamphleteers, blames Elizabeth's Privy Council and urges her
to get rid of it [97].

Ronsard deals with the situation with a certain restraint. He
only expresses his view explicitly in one sonnet. The reason for this
restraint may well be a diplomatic one. The duke of Alençon had long
been a candidate for Elizabeth's hand, and still was [98]. Ronsard
did not wish to embarass him [99]. Nevertheless, Ronsard's attitude
towards Elizabeth and her Privy Council, reflecting French Catholic
opinion, is hardening.

* * *

---

[96] X, 68. The author of the *Discours contre les conspirations* had exonerated Mary of
ever pursuing the throne of England : " [...] il n'y a preuve, ny ombre seule d'icelle, par
laquelle on puisse monstrer que la Royne d'Escosse ayt jamais querellé ny poursuyvy
la couronne de vostre royne, & ny a homme qui le sçache simplement par ouyr dire, si
ce n'est en la conjonction des armoires d'Angleterre, & d'Escosse dressées en quelques
escus par l'expres commandement du roy de France Françoys second espoux de la sus-
ditte royne d'Escosse, en quelque tryomphe fait en France, il y a treize ans & davantage : & lesquelles armoires ceste illustre Princesse peut plus à droit, & loisiblement
porter que autre qui vive, eu esgard au sang d'où elle est sortie, & la consanguinité &
parenté qu'elle à [*sic*] avec la maison d'Angleterre, fors tant seulement les enfantz,
legitimes sortis du Roy Henry vostre Prince ". If anyone is to blame for making the
claim, it is Francis. (*Discours contre les conspirations*, 14ro). Ronsard had also asserted
Mary's claim to the English throne in a *Chant de liesse* written on the occasion of the
Cateau-Cambresis treaty and dedicated to Henri II (IX, 138) : this poem was not
suppressed until 1584.

[97] This is the probable meaning of the phrase " changez de conseil ". GREW, *op. cit.*,
p. 55 interprets the phrase in this sense. Ronsard's sonnet was first published in 1578
and not, as Grew implies, in 1583.

[98] For the marriage negotiations, see READ, *Burghley*, chapter xii, p. 203-234, " The
Alençon courtship, 1579-1581 ".

[99] Alençon visited Ronsard's home shortly after negotiating the Beaulieu treaty
(the " Paix de Monsieur ", 1576), and Ronsard wrote five sonnets to him on this occasion (XVII, 341-346 : see also XVII, 79, note 4).

4. DUDLEY AND CECIL

The controversy over Mary Stuart continued to rage. Soon after the appearance of the fifth edition of Ronsard's *Œuvres*, Buchanan attacked Mary again in his *De iure regni apud Scotos* [100], and Adam Blackwood replied with his *Pro regibus apologia* : a French translation of this work was also published [101]. Ronsard may have known Blackwood's work : his biographer Crittonius was Blackwood's son-in-law [102]. At all events, it is certain that Ronsard's sympathy for Mary continued undiminished. Mary, for her part, read Ronsard's poetry eagerly even during her captivity (" ne se pouvoit souler de lire ses vers sur tous autres ", says Binet [103]). Moreover, in 1583, she rewarded him handsomely for his praise of her [104] : this date is significant, as we shall see.

Another issue which influenced French judgements on the English government during the early ' eighties was the treatment of Roman Catholics in England [105]. The English government mistrusted Catholics, for many of them hoped to enforce the deposition pronounced on Elizabeth by pope Pius V in 1570. The clash between the Catholics

---

[100] Edinburgi [or rather, London], 1580 : cf. PHILLIPS, *op. cit.*, p. 256, note 54. For this work, and Blackwood's reply, see also C. H. HAY, " George Buchanan et Adam Blackwood ", *Bibliothèque d'Humanisme et Renaissance*, 8, 1946, p. 156-171. Montaigne knew these two books : see *ibid.*, p. 161 and *Essais*, III, vii, *ed. cit.*, p. 192-193.

[101] *Apologie des rois, contre le dialogue de Buchanan*—see PHILLIPS, p. 274, note 77.

[102] Cf. ASCOLI, *op. cit.*, p. 205 and PHILLIPS, *op. cit.*, p. 146.

[103] BINET, *op. cit.*, p. 28, ll. 45-46. This quotation is from a passage which first appears in the 1597 edition.

[104] BINET, *op. cit.*, p. 28-29 : " [...] l'an 1583 elle luy fit present d'un buffet de deux mil escus qu'elle luy envoya par le sieur de Nau son Secretaire, avec une inscription sur un vase qui estoit elabouré en forme de rocher, representant le Parnasse, et un Pegasse au dessus. L'inscription portoit ces mots : A RONSARD L'APOLLON DE LA SOURCE DES MUSES ". The passage first appears in the 1597 edition of Binet. Mary's generosity towards Ronsard is also mentioned by Crittonius in his *Laudatio funebris* (cf. BINET, *ibid.*, p. 177, note to l. 34).

[105] Not much literature on the situation was published before the jesuit mission. There is a passing reference to the situation in M. de LAUNOY and H. PENNETIER, *La declaration et refutation des fausses suppositions, et perverses applications d'aucunes sentences des sainctes Ecritures, desquelles les Ministres se sont servis en ce dernier temps, à diviser la Chrétienté*, A Paris, chez Jean du Carroy, 1578, B.M. 3900. aaa.24 (1), 211vo (numbered 2011) : " Mais que dirons nous de l'Ecosse & de l'Angleterre ? Combien en a on fait mourir, & combien en a on chassé & banny à cause de l'ancienne doctrine & religion Catholique ? Il s'en trouvera plus, depuis vingt cinq ans, que de Calvinistes, depuis cinquante : tellement qu'en toutes sortes le nombre des martyrs de l'Eglise Catholique surmonte celuy des sectes nouvellement elevées. Par ainsi les Calvinistes n'ont dequoy se prevalloir en cette article ". A marginal note opposite this passage reads " Persecution en Ecosse & Angleterre contre les Catholiques ". The authors go on to distinguish between the Calvinists, who suffered because they were " Schismatiques tumultueux, heretiques & imposteurs, perturbateurs du repos de la vraye Eglise, & unité d'icelle ", and Catholics, who suffered and are suffering for maintaining the old, apostolic religion.
Another early work is entitled *Acta quaedam insignia anglica ad Catholicam religionem pertinentia*. Ex Seminario Rhemensi allata, in Latinum conversa Ioanne Antonio Guarnerio Canon. Bergom. interprete, Bergomi, M.D.LXXX, B. Nat., Nf 286. The fate of priests of the Douai seminary who went to England is mentioned, B^{ro} : " Ex eo numero, qui in Seminario versatur, hoc ipso anno MDLXXVIII quinque in Anglia, qui eo traiecerant, comprehensi sunt. ex iis unus tantum ab Haereticis est interemptus : reliqui in vincula coniecti ".

and the government came to a head with the abandonment of the
projected marriage between Elizabeth and Alençon [106], and especially
with the mission in England of jesuits, which began in 1580. This
mission was compromised from the start by the political activities of
other Catholics [107]. In the 1581 Parliament, a measure was enacted
which provided for a traitor's death for anyone who " withdrew the
Queen's subjects from their natural obedience, or converted them
for that intent to the Romish religion " [108].

This legislation opened the door to persecution of priests as such,
and although the English government carefully maintained that it
was not prosecuting on the grounds of religion [109], continental readers
were repeatedly assured that English Catholics were being persecuted
for their religion : " [...] il ne leur est laissé que crainte, que servitude,
rien de libre, rien d'entier, non pas la voix, non pas la conscience ny
seulement le sentiment et pensée de Dieu & des choses divines : Car
la violence est telle, qu'il faut parler avec et comme les autres [110]. "
The case of Edmund Campion and his companions offered excellent
ammunition to the Catholic pamphleteers [111].

---

[106] Various attempts had been made during the negotiations for the marriage to
secure an alleviation of the lot of English Catholics. However, Alençon himself had not
pressed the point. See J. A. Bossy, " English Catholics and the French marriage,
1577-1581 ", *Recusant History*, 5, 1959, p. 2-16.

[107] " Political " Catholics included the rebellious northern earls, the duke of Norfolk
and his fellow-conspirators, John Leslie (see Phillips, *op. cit.*, p. 104) and cardinal
William Allen (see G. Mattingly, " William Allen and Catholic propaganda in England ", *Aspects de la propagande religieuse*, Travaux d'Humanisme et Renaissance,
28, Genève, 1957, p. 325-339). Plots against Elizabeth were indeed rife in the ' eighties :
the Throckmorton plot (1583), the Parry plot (1584), and the Babington plot (1586)
(Mary Stuart knew of and approved at least two of these : cf. Phillips, *op. cit.*, p. 74-
75).

[108] Neale, *op. cit.*, p. 388. Cf *ibid.*, p. 370 : " [...] in converting Englishmen back to
Catholicism, the priests were in fact creating potential enemies of the Protestant State,
on whose aid the Enterprise [of Catholic monarchs to depose Elizabeth by force] would
count if and when it was launched ".

[109] This point was made by Cecil in *The execution of justice in England*, (1583), a
work which appeared also in Latin, French and Dutch translations (1584) : cf. Read,
art. cit., p. 37-38. On 18 January 1584 Stafford wrote to Walsingham from Paris claiming to have had some success in refuting the widely-held belief that Englishmen were
being executed for their religion (*Calendar of State Papers, Foreign Series, Elizabeth,
July 1583-July 1584*, no. 376, p. 317).

[110] *Epistre de la persecution meue en Angleterre*, Paris, 1582, B.M. 1368. c. 8, p. 8.
This work is a translation, by Matthieu de Launoy, of Robert Persons's *De persecutione
anglicana, epistola*, [Rouen], 1581 : see Southern, *op. cit.*, p. 504 ; cf. p. 319-322. The
claim that the persecution was a religious one was repeatedly made : see also T. Stapleton, *Speculum pravitatis haereticae, per orationes quodlibeticas sex ad oculum demons-
tratae*, Duaci, ex officina I. Bogardi, 1580, B. Nat. H. 10045, 126r° ; *Discours des cruautez
et tirannyes qua* [sic] *faict la royne d'Angleterre, à l'endroict des Catholecques* [sic], *Anglois,
Espagnolz, François, & prestres Catholicques, qui soutenoient la foy & le tourmant qui
l'ont* [sic] *soufert avec les noms & surnoms d'iceux. Plus y est adjousté la mort d'Edouard
Hance Prestre Anglois & le martyre qui la* [sic] *soufert*, Paris, Jouste la coppie imprimée
à Londres par Pierre le Sage Imprimeur, s.d., B. Nat. Nf 297 (Ascoli *op. cit.*, p. 155
note 3 dates this work at 1582-1583), Ciiiv° ; *Duo edicta Elizabethæ reginæ Angliæ contra
sacerdotes Societatis Jesu, & alumnos seminariorum* [...] *Una cum Apologia doctissimi
viri D. Gulielmi Alani pro iisdem sacerdotibus societatis Jesu, & aliis seminariorum
Alumnis* ; [...] *Additur eiusdem Gulielmi Alani piissima admonitio & consolatio vere
Christiana ad afflictos Catholicos Angliae*, Augustae Trevirorum, M.D.LXXXIII,
(B.M.860.b.9 and B. Nat. Nf 289), p. 21, 22, 48.

[111] Edmund Campion secured from pope Gregory XIII a postponement or cancella-
tion of the deposition of Elizabeth (the meaning of the papal letter is disputed, see

These pamphleteers had a very good hearing in France, for there had long been widespread popular impatience with Reformers' demands for liberty of conscience, and the news from England showed that Catholics were not given freedom of conscience in countries where they were not in power. [112] Pamphlets on England were made available in French very rapidly, and made a great impact. The *Histoire* of Campion's execution was available in Paris within five weeks of the event [113], and the book was vigorously propagated, as Cobham made

---

READ, *Burghley*, p. 253 and note 82). He returned to England in June 1580 and, when asked about the motives for his return, replied that his mission was to " administer the sacraments of the Catholic religion, to preach, and to teach people the way of salvation. He could not, and would not, get involved in the affairs of the sovereign " (*Vita et martyrium Edmundi Campiani, diligenter collecta ex variis scriptis, tam Anglicis quam Latinis* [...] in *Concertatio Ecclesiæ Catholicæ in Anglia, adversus Calvinopapistas & Puritanos, a paucis annis singulari studio quorundam hominum doctrina & sanctitate illustrium renovata.* Augustae Trevirorum, apud Emundum Hatotum, An.1583, B.M. 860.b.9, p. 159 : "affirmat [...] sibi nec demandatum aliud, nec aliud esse propositum, quam ut Catholicæ religionis Sacramenta administret, conciones habeat, ac populum pro virili viam salutis edoceat ; seque nec posse, nec velle Principis regnique negotiis implicare "). He evaded capture for thirteen months. During this time he published his *Epistola ad Reginæ Angliæ Consiliarios* (*Concertatio*, p. 17-22). This is Campion's " brag ", or " challenge ". In this work he affirms that his mission is a religious one (par. 3) and that he has been forbidden to involve himself in politics (par. 4), and invites the Privy Council to allow a disputation (par. 5) which the queen might grace with her presence (par. 7). He also published his *Ten Reasons* (*Rationes decem: quibus fretus certamen adversariis obtulit in causa fidei, idem Edmundus Campianus allegatæ ad clarissimos viros Anglos Academicos ab ipso auctore latine editæ*: this work is found in the *Concertatio*, p. 27-78). He was finally betrayed, tortured and, on 1 December 1581, hanged.

Jean Bodin, who was in England conducting negotiations for the projected marriage of Alençon and Elizabeth, was asked by Robert Persons to intervene on behalf of the Catholics. According to Persons, Bodin " answered perversely, as he was a politike, and as some thinke worse, saying that he came to treate matters of marriage, and not of Religion " (T. H. CLANCY, *Papist pamphleteers, the Allen-Persons party and the political thought of the Counter-Reformation in England, 1572-1615*, Chicago, 1964, p. 170-171). But in the 1586 Latin edition of his *Republic*, Bodin inserted a statement that the prince must not use force in matters of religion, and claims to have put this point to Elizabeth in connection with the Campion case : " Haec mea fuit ad Elizabetham Anglorum Reginam et ad optimates ac Senatores oratio, cum de Campiano Jesuita deque catholicis questiones capitales haberentur " (quoted *ibid.*, p. 226, note 29).

Campion's *Rationes decem* were translated into French by Pierre Madur and published in 1584 : *Les dix raisons, pour lesquelles M. Edmond Campian, de la Compagnie de JESUS, s'est faict fort d'entreprendre la dispute pour la religion Catholique contre les adversaires d'icelle*, Lyon, par Jean Pillehotte, 1584, B.M. C.37.a.13 (2). Agrippa d'Aubigné read Campion's *Rationes decem*, but the book did not convert him to the Roman faith (see P.-F. GEISENDORF, " Trois chroniqueurs devant la propagande ", *Aspects de la propagande religieuse*, Travaux d'Humanisme et Renaissance, 28, Genève, 1957, p. 405). Marc-Antoine Muret, however, described the book as a " Libellum aureum, vere digito Dei scriptum " (E. CAMPION, *Ten reasons* [...], ed. J. H. P[ollen], London, 1914, p. 1, 26).

[112] Cf. John HAY, *Demandes faictes aux ministres d'Escosse: Touchant la religion Chrestienne*, Lyon, 1583, p. 135 : " Puisque vous faictes tant de cas de la liberté de conscience, et preuvez que personne ne doit estre contraint, pourquoy en Escosse, Angleterre, Geneve, et par tout ou vous estes les plus forts, ne permettez vous le libre exercice de la religion Chretienne, comme vous voulez avoir presche partout ? " This work is accompanied, on p. 182-183, by extracts from Ronsard's *Responce aux injures* (ll. 1091-1104 ; XI, 171-172) and his *Continuation du discours des miseres* (ll. 351-364, 369-372 ; XI, 55-56).

[113] *L'histoire de la mort que le R. P. Campion prestre de la compagnie du nom de Jesus, & autres ont souffert en Angleterre pour la foy Catholique & Romaine le premier jour de Decembre, 1581.* Traduict d'Anglois en François. A Paris, chez Guillaume Chaudiere, 1582, B.M. 698.b.39. It was published by 4 January 1582 and sent by Cobham to Walsingham from Paris the following day (cf. *Calendar of State Papers, Foreign Series, Elizabeth, January 1581—April 1582*, nos. 491, 493). SOUTHERN, *op. cit.*, p. 273, footnote, describes the *Histoire* as " the earliest published version " of Alfield's *True report* (see note 117) : in fact, the two works are quite distinct.

clear in a letter from Paris to Walsingham : " I sent you a small book of the death of Campion. They have been crying these books in the streets with outcries, naming them to be cruelties used by the Queen in England [114]. " The effect of such publications is illustrated by a comment by the English ambassador in France. On 18 January 1584, in a letter to Walsingham, Stafford wrote : " [...] it is generally put into men's heads that they are only executed in England for conscience and not for treason [115]. "

A feature of these publications is that their tone is conciliatory towards Elizabeth, but often hostile towards her Privy Council. The author of the *Epistre de la persecution meue en Angleterre* maintains that the legislation providing for a traitor's death for religious offenders has been devised by the queen's councillors who wanted her to believe that the Catholic religion is a danger to her crown [116]. And the author of one of the poems printed with *A true report of the death and martyrdom of M. Campion* [...] summarized the prevailing opinion when he wrote, " Your secret foes do misenforme your grace [117]. " Among these " secret foes " were Dudley and Cecil : and when French people read, as they often did in these years, of the queen's evil Council, these names would have sprung most readily to mind. [118]

---

[114] *Ibid.*, no. 508. Cobham also tells of his apparently successful attempt to have the book suppressed. The letter is dated 14 January 1582.

[115] *Ibid.*, *July 1583-July 1584*, no. 376, p. 317.

[116] P. 19-20 ; see also p. 122-123.

[117] *A True report of the death and martyrdome of M. Campion*, s.l., s.d., B.M. G.11658, E ii^ro (for this work, and the attribution to Thomas Alfield, see SOUTHERN, *op. cit.*, p. 279-283, 376-379). There may well have been some justification for this interpretation of events. According to READ, *Burghley*, p. 237, " [...] after Arundel's death in 1580, all of the Privy council except Sir James Croft were much more anti-Catholic than Elizabeth ". See also p. 238.

[118] English exiles in Paris regarded Dudley as their worst enemy : " In their view Leicester was not only responsible for the collapse of plans for Norfolk to marry Mary Stuart in 1569, but he had become, after an early flirtation with the Catholics, their bitterest opponent in the Council and the patron of the Puritans. As such he had led the opposition to the French match in 1579-1580. When those plans were foiled some Catholic courtiers who had favoured the match went into exile in France. *Leicester's Commonwealth* came from this circle... " (CLANCY, *op. cit.*, p. 24-25). The *Epistre de la persecution* tells how Dudley responded to Catholics' requests for a disputation by iniquitously granting one in which a Protestant minister, after being praised by those of his own side, put the case for Catholicism (p. 82-84). For Dudley's activities as a patron of anti-Catholic writers, see ROSENBERG, *op. cit.*, chapter vi, p. 184-229, " Puritans and their works " and chapter vii, p. 230-277, " Anti-Catholic propaganda ".
Cecil was becoming known in France at this time as one of the queen's influential Protestant privy councillors. Belleforest, in *Les Grandes annales et histoire generale de France, des le regne de Philippe de Valois jusques à Henri III, à present heureusement regnant*, tome second, Paris, chez Gabriel Buon, M.D.LXXIX, B.M.595.k.13, affirms (1601ro) that at Elizabeth's accession " le commun peuple " and certain lords were Catholic, and adds : " voire y avoit il plusieurs des Gouverneurs qui estoient Catholiques, mais non ceux qui se tenoient aupres de la Royne. Or ceux qui gouvernaient ceste Royne estoient [...] le Secretaire Sisil (qui a esté le plus autorisé) qui souloit servir le Roy Edouard de Secretaire [...] " He says it is Elizabeth's Privy Council that has made her suspect the English Catholics of political intrigue and ill-treat them (1601vo). Cf. JEAN BERNARD, *Discours des plus mémorables faicts des roys & grands seigneurs d'Angleterre depuis cinq cens ans avec les généalogies des roynes d'Angleterre et d'Ecosse*, Paris, G. Mallot, 1579, B. Nat. Na 16, 62 ^vo : " Plusieurs Princes, Seigneurs & Chevaliers se retirerent des le commencement de son regne à cause de la religion Catholique : d'autant que le conseil de la Royne embrassoit les opinions des protestans : Les Seigneurs

In 1584, Ronsard published the sixth collected edition of his works. Its content reflects the increasing hostility of French Catholics and supporters of Mary Stuart towards the English government. Ronsard has changed the texts of the " English " poems. The changes are subtle, but they are more far-reaching than those made in 1578.

In the 1578 edition of the *Œuvres*, the 1565 *Elegie à la Majesté de la Royne d'Angleterre* had been renamed, simply, *Discours*. Now, in 1584, the same *Discours* becomes a *Discours à tres illustre et tres-vertueuse Princesse, Elizabeth, Royne d'Angleterre*. We shall shortly discuss the meaning of this change. Meanwhile, certain alterations to the content of the poem should be noted [119]. Many passages in praise of Elizabeth are suppressed (ll. 13-112 ; 117-126 ; 447-454 ; 489-518). The effect of these suppressions is to give greater prominence to passages in praise of Mary Stuart (ll. 113-116) and of Catherine de Medici (ll. 473-488) [120].

The *Elegie* to Dudley is transormed into a *Discours à elle mesme* [i.e. Elizabeth]. *Les Paroles que dist Merlin, le Prophete Anglois, esmerveillé de voir Artus en sa jeunesse accomply de toutes vertus.* Since Laumonier has observed that in the 1584 version of this work, Ronsard carefully cuts out all mention of Dudley (XIII, 63, note 1), it is only necessary to note this profound modification before passing to the 1584 version of the *Elegie* to Cecil.

The alterations to this work are less obvious but just as significant. The earlier versions were eulogies of the queen of England's minister. The 1584 version manifestly is not. If it is read as though it were, it is incomprehensible, and this is why Ronsard's alterations have puzzled one of the greatest of modern Ronsard scholars, leading him, in fact, into real error [121].

---

ayans faveur & credit pres ceste Dame, & qui furent choysis de son privé conseil, furent [...] le Secretaire Sisil [...] " Cf. NEALE, *op. cit.*, p. 391 : " Failing any direct evidence, it looks as if we might assume that Burghley was in favour of a measure planned to eradicate Catholicism from England by making life intolerable even for its peaceful and loyal adherents ". READ, *Burghley*, p. 247, says that " The evidence at hand gives little support to " this conclusion, but admits that Burghley came close to such a position later.

[119] Alterations attribuable only to aesthetic considerations have been ignored. As has been shown (H. NAÏS, " A propos des corrections de Ronsard dans ses œuvres complètes ", *Bibliothèque d'Humanisme et Renaissance*, 20, 1958, p. 405-420) Ronsard eliminated some commonplaces and repetitions when he revised his work. This possibly explains the suppression of some of the lines of the poem to Elizabeth (ll. 5-12, 179-182, 305-308, 333-344, and perhaps 447-454). Moreover, towards the end of his life, Ronsard expressed the view that elegies should be short (Cohen edition, Bibliothèque de la Pléiade, 1950, II, p. 647). This possibly explains the suppression of parts of the " English " poems, but the interest lies in *which* parts are suppressed.

[120] The praise of Elizabeth and certain unspecified " grands Mylords " in the *Bergerie* (ll. 823-864 ; XIII, 118-119) is left intact ; Catherine and especially Mary Stuart are associated with Elizabeth in this passage.

[121] Laumonier (XIII, 159, note 1) does not point out that in 1584 Ronsard stopped praising Cecil, and it is clear that he has not noticed the fact. He offered the following explanation of the words " ton Prince ", which occur in a variant of 1584 : " Pour la variante des vers 57-78, Marcassus note que " ton Prince c'est le roi d'Angleterre ; grave erreur, car en 1584 l'Angleterre n'avoit pas de roi. Je conjecture que Ronsard

The first versions of this poem include a pun on Cecil's name. Ronsard had playfully made the Englishman a native of Sicily (XIII, 160). When, therefore, the 1584 title of the poem is found to be *Discours à Cecille Sicilien*, this is hardly surprising. However, a close scrutiny of the text of the poem reveals that in 1584 Ronsard is no longer celebrating Elizabeth's privy councillor at all! Ronsard has meticulously cut out all mention of England and its queen, and the poem now reads as a eulogy of a Sicilian, not an Englishman. The following list of alterations to the 1578 text will make this clear:

Ll. 29-31 :

1578 :
        Non pour autant que la Muse latine,
        Angloise, et Grecque a mis en ta poitrine
        Je ne sçay quoy de grand et de parfait [...]

1584 :
        Non pour autant que la Muse latine,
        La Muse Grecque ont mis en ta poitrine
        Je ne sçay quoy de grand et de parfait [...]

Ll. 35-50 :

1578 :   These lines are inalienably associated with Cecil and England. They contain, notably, references to Cecil's role in the government, to *his queen's* appreciation of him, to his judgement and to his learned wife.

1584 : These lines are suppressed.

Ll. 55-78 :

1578 : You are happy, not on account of your virtues,
        Mais pour autant que tu vois de plus pres
        Que nous la grace, & les yeux, & les traiz
        De la beauté de ta Royne si belle,
        Que rien n'est beau en son isle aupres d'elle [...]

(The rest of these lines deal with Cecil's happy contemplation of his queen).

1584 :
        Mais pour autant que tu vois de plus pres
        Que nous le port & les yeux & les traicts
        De la splendeur de ton Prince, qui passe
        L'Honneur d'honneur et les Graces de grace.

The rest of the passage is suppressed.

Ll. 127-130 :

1578 :
        [...] le nostre [roi], à qui les Cieux amis
        Ont de grands dons des naissance promis,
        Pour joindre un jour par fidelle alliance
        Vostre Angleterre avecques nostre France.

---

entendait par là le comte d'Essex, amant de la reine Elisabeth, et même, disait-on, son fils naturel, qui prétendait avoir des droits à sa succession " (XIII, 163, note 2). In fact, " ton Prince " is the king of Sicily.

1584 :   [...] le nostre, à qui les Cieux amis
Ont de grands dons des naissance promis,
Pour joindre un jour par fidelle alliance
Vostre Sicille avecques nostre France.

Ll. 197-200 (The subject is Jupiter) :

1578 :   Mais, par sur tous les Princes de la terre,
Ayma la France, Espagne & Angleterre,
Les couronna de gloire & de bon heur,
Et jusque au Ciel en envoya l'honneur.

1584 :   Mais par sur tous sa faveur est monstrée
Dessus la France, Espagne & *ta contrée*,
Qu'il couronna de gloire & de bon-heur,
Et jusqu'au ciel en envoya l'honneur.

The following lines are added, and they can only refer to Sicily, as Laumonier points out :

Sacré berceau de Ceres la tresbelle
Qui nourrist tout de sa grasse mamelle :
Tesmoins en sont Archimede, & celuy
Qui courtizan avoit un double estuy,
L'un plein de vent & l'autre de finance,
Et ce pasteur qui fut des son enfance
En Arcadie, & sur Menale vit
Pan qui fleutoit, dont le son le ravit.

Ll. 210-212 (the subject is " ton nom ") :

1578 :   ... A fait ta gloire abondante & fertile,
T'a fait du peuple & des grands favorit,
Aussi es-tu de ta Royne l'esprit.

1584 :   A fait ta gloire abondante & fertille,
T'a fait du peuple & des grands bien-aimé,
Tant vaut l'honneur quand il est renommé.

Ll. 213-216 :

1578 :   Non seulement ta vive renommée,
N'est chichement de ta Mer enfermée,
Mais franchissant l'Ocean des Anglois,
S'est apparüe au grand peuple Gaulois [...]

1584 :   Non seulement ta vive renommée,
N'est chichement de ta Mer enfermée,
Mais franchissant *le rempart Sicilois*
S'est apparüe au grand peuple Gaulois [...]

Thus, no less than seven references to England or to the queen have been removed, and there is nothing to tell the reader of the 1584 text that the Cecil in question has anything to do with England. The subject of this version is a Sicilian gentleman. This is why Ronsard speaks to " Cecille " of " la splendeur de ton Prince " : this " Prince ", incidentally, was Phillip II of Spain, king of Sicily ! [122]

It is now clear that when he revised his works for the sixth collected edition, Ronsard eliminated all praise of the privy councillors of queen Elizabeth. It is apparent that Ronsard's work, as in 1578, reflects the attitude of his Catholic compatriots. This conclusion is all the more reasonable when we observe that, just as attacks on English policy were normally directed at the Council and not at the queen, so Ronsard, while eliminating his praise of Dudley and Cecil, retains much of his praise of Elizabeth. In fact he gives the elegy to the queen the enhanced title of *Discours à tres illustre et tres-vertueuse Princesse, Elizabeth, Royne d'Angleterre*. He was still proud to be the poet of princes [123]. This change pinpoints the contrast between the treatment of the queen and that of her councillors. In 1584, the position of panegyrist of Dudley and Cecil was, for a Catholic Frenchman, untenable.

As for Mary queen of Scots, we have already seen that in the 1584 version of the elegy to Elizabeth she has a more prominent part than in the original. In addition, the second book of *Poemes*, dedicated in 1578 to Mary Stuart and headed by the 1578 sonnet, has now become the first, and following the sonnet, Ronsard has grouped all the poems about Mary Stuart which are retained in this edition, and which had previously been dispersed in his works [124]. Mary thus has a very much more prominent place in the 1584 edition than in any of the previous ones.

Thus Ronsard's attitude evolved, and in step with French Catholic opinion. Praise of Elizabeth, Dudley and Cecil in 1565 ; a more reserved praise in 1578 ; and in 1584, continued praise of Elizabeth, but suppression of poems to her councillors.

Between 1584 and his death, Ronsard's opinion on these matters knew no change. In 1584, he had compared Elizabeth and Mary to the sun :

On voit ensemble en lumiere pareils
Dedans une Isle esclairer deux Soleils.

In the posthumous edition, a poignant couplet is added :

---

[122] Ronsard had praised Philip as king of Sicily : IX, 139.

[123] He may have been anxious to assert this title, in view of the growing prestige of rival poets like Du Bartas : cf. Cohen edition, II, 947 :
Ils ont menty, d'Aurat, ceux qui le veulent dire,
Que Ronsard, *dont la Muse a contenté les Rois*,
Soit moins que le Bartas, & qu'il ait par sa voix
Rendu ce tesmoignage ennemi de sa lire.

[124] XVII, 378 and Cohen edition, II, 290. In 1584, Ronsard suppressed an outmoded ode to Mary (" O belle et plus que belle et agreable Aurore ", VII, 306), and all of the *Inscriptions*, two of which (IX, 196-197) were dedicated to Mary.

> Ou bien on voit deux flames esclairantes
> De mesme feu, mais de sort differantes.   (XIII, 44).

The poet of princes was thus able to retain to the end his praise of both queens : his death in December 1585 spared him the dilemma that would have arisen with the execution of the queen of Scots.

Leeds.   M. C. SMITH.

ASPECTS DE LA BIBLIOGRAPHIE
DES ÉDITIONS ANCIENNES DE RONSARD

Communication de M. Malcolm C. SMITH
(*Université de Leeds*)

au XXIe Congrès de l'Association, le 23 juillet 1969.

Ronsard, on le sait bien, était très jaloux de la paternité de ses œuvres. Jacques Davy du Perron, un des nombreux biographes du poète, nous a laissé une anecdote assez révélatrice à ce sujet. On aurait suggéré un jour à Ronsard — c'est probablement Du Perron lui-même qui a fait la suggestion — qu'il fît des coupures dans ses poèmes pour éliminer des longueurs, et même qu'il retranchât certains poèmes lors de la préparation des éditions de ses œuvres complètes. Ronsard avait justement l'habitude de faire cela, mais il n'entendait pas qu'un autre lui donnât un tel conseil. « Mon bon amy », aurait-il répondu, « il fâche bien à un Pere de couper les bras à ses enfans » (1).

Ronsard était donc très conscient de ses devoirs paternels. De façon générale, il a fait son possible pour sauvegarder la vie et l'immortalité de ses « enfans ». D'ordinaire, un poème

---

(1) V. J. D. Du Perron et J. A. De Thou, *Perronina et Thuana ou Pensées Judicieuses, bons mots, rencontres agreables & observations curieuses du Cardinal du Perron et de M. le Président de Thou, Conseiller d'État*, Cologne, M. DC. XCIV, art. « Ronsard », p. 333.

de Ronsard, ou un recueil de poèmes, paraissait pour la première fois en édition séparée. Par la suite, dans la plupart des cas, il recueillait soigneusement ces poèmes et les faisait entrer dans l'une ou l'autre des éditions des œuvres complètes. Et la grande majorité des poèmes que Ronsard n'a pas recueillis de la sorte ont été découverts par les chercheurs. Dans le tome XVIII de la magnifique édition critique de Ronsard, on trouve la liste — heureusement très courte — des œuvres de Ronsard qui restent à découvrir (2).

Or, si nous possédons désormais le texte à peu près complet des *Œuvres* de Ronsard, nous sommes toujours très loin d'avoir établi la bibliographie définitive des différents recueils où ses œuvres ont paru à l'époque. Car les enfants de Ronsard paraissent un peu partout dans les livres du XVIe siècle. Dans plusieurs cas, on trouve du Ronsard dans un livre publié sous le nom d'un autre auteur : Ronsard a souvent placé ses enfants chez autrui, quitte à les reprendre lors de la préparation d'une édition complète de ses œuvres. Il arrive également qu'un auteur peu scrupuleux enlève à Ronsard l'un ou l'autre de ses « fils ». N'importe quel livre du XVIe siècle est donc susceptible de receler un poème de Ronsard. C'est pourquoi l'établissement d'une bibliographie ronsardienne, même approximativement complète, serait, comme la composition d'un bon poème épique au XVIe siècle, une « œuvre de laborieuse longueur et quasi de la vie d'un homme ». Dans cette communication, je me contente de signaler certaines éditions de ses poèmes et certains tirages qui sont conservés dans les bibliothèques anglaises, et dont l'existence n'est pas notée dans l'apparat critique de la grande édition Laumonier.

Certains des livres qu'on va passer en revue possèdent une valeur pour l'établissement du texte du poète, et on devrait en tenir compte dans la révision de l'édition critique. Certains autres, qui ne nous éclairent guère sur le texte de Ronsard, n'en possèdent pas moins un intérêt historique

---

(2) P. DE RONSARD, *Œuvres complètes*, éd. crit. par P. Laumonnier, révisée et complétée par I. Silver et R. Lebègue (Société des Textes Français Modernes), Paris, t. XVIII (1967), p. 522-529.

comme témoins de la diffusion de ce même texte. Je présente ces livres à peu près dans l'ordre chronologique de la publication des éditions princeps.

Un très précieux livre ronsardien est entré récemment au British Museum. Il s'agit d'un exemplaire du rarissime *Second livre des meslanges*. Ce livre n'existe pas à la Bibliothèque Nationale, et le *Catalogue d'une collection unique des éditions originales de Ronsard*, dressé par Seymour de Ricci pour la librairie londonienne Maggs Brothers en 1926, mentionne seulement trois exemplaires, dont deux avaient disparu. C'est l'exemplaire que possédaient les Maggs Brothers que Laumonier a utilisé pour la préparation de l'édition critique. Cet exemplaire est daté de 1559, et porte la marque de Robert Mangnier. Or Laumonier savait, grâce au *Manuel du libraire* de Brunet, qu'il existait un tirage portant la marque de Vincent Sertenas. Bien que Laumonier n'ait pas vu un exemplaire du tirage Sertenas, il a bien résumé les rapports qui ont dû lier les deux libraires :

> [...] il arrivait [...] que le libraire pourvu d'un privilège (V. Sertenas dans le cas qui nous occupe) s'arrangeait avec un confrère pour lui céder un certain nombre d'exemplaires et le droit d'y apposer sa marque propre et son adresse (3).

Or, voici enfin un exemplaire du tirage Sertenas qui est entré au British Museum. Une rapide comparaison de ce tirage Sertenas avec le texte de l'édition Laumonier m'a persuadé que les différences qui séparent les deux tirages sont minimes. J'ai seulement trouvé certaines variantes d'orthographe, de mise en page et de guillemettage. Il n'en reste pas moins très utile de pouvoir consulter un tirage longtemps perdu de cet ouvrage, et il est également rassurant de savoir qu'un exemplaire de l'édition originale de cette publication importante est désormais accessible aux chercheurs. Je signale que c'est seulement dans le supplément du catalogue du British Museum, supplément sur fiches et qui se consulte

---

(3) RONSARD, *Œuvres complètes*, éd. cit., t. X, p. V, n. 3.

sur place, que l'on trouvera ce *Second livre des meslanges* (4).

L'utilité du British Museum dans le domaine des recherches bibliographiques ronsardiennes ne se limite pas aux éditions rarissimes du poète qu'il possède. En effet cette bibliothèque renferme un catalogue sur fiches des livres imprimés conservés dans les bibliothèques des cathédrales anglaises et dans les châteaux qui appartiennent au *National Trust*, et ce catalogue a permis une autre découverte. Il s'agit du livre des *Elegies, Mascarades et Bergerie*, dont un exemplaire se trouve dans la bibliothèque de la cathédrale de Peterborough. Livre rarissime : on en trouve un autre exemplaire à la Bibliothèque Nationale : un autre était mentionné dans le catalogue Maggs. Point d'exemplaire au British Museum, ni, à ma connaissance, dans aucune autre bibliothèque anglaise.

Outre la rareté de ce livre, il y avait une autre raison de vouloir consulter l'exemplaire de Peterborough. C'est que je savais qu'il devait exister quelque part un exemplaire somptueux de ce livre. Quand les *Elégies, Mascarades et Bergerie* parurent, en 1565, un exemplaire fut offert par l'ambassadeur de France, Paul de Foix, au secrétaire de la reine Elisabeth, qui devait transmettre le livre à la reine d'Angleterre. A cette occasion, Paul de Foix a adressé une lettre latine, très élogieuse à l'égard de Ronsard, au secrétaire Cecil. La lettre se trouve actuellement à Londres, dans le Public Record Office. Mais on avait vainement cherché le précieux exemplaire du livre lui-même. Or, c'est précisément à côté de Peterborough que le secrétaire Cecil habitait.

Flatteuse espérance ! Mais, après ma visite à Peterborough, je cherche toujours l'exemplaire des *Elégies, Mascarades et Bergerie* offert par Ronsard à la reine d'Angleterre. Je ne puis pas croire qu'il ait osé lui offrir un exemplaire aussi ordinaire que celui de la cathédrale de Peterborough, Si je me rappelle bien, cet exemplaire n'a même pas été épargné par les vers !

(4) Un autre exemplaire du tirage Sertenas est passé en vente à Londres, chez Sotheby, le 19 décembre 1962.

Malgré cette déception, le voyage à Peterborough ne fut point inutile. J'ai pu constater qu'il existe des variantes entre l'exemplaire que j'y ai consulté et celui que Laumonier a dû utiliser à la Bibliothèque Nationale. Il arrive que l'exemplaire de Peterborough nous offre de meilleures leçons que celles de Laumonier et que les corrections que l'on pourra apporter au texte suggèrent des corrections aux notes historiques de Laumonier.

Prenons par exemple un passage de la lettre-préface, en prose. Dans le texte Laumonier, Ronsard affirme, au sujet des reines Élisabeth et Catherine de Médicis que

> les dames sont parvenues, les unes par qui doivent naistre, les autres par vertu au sommet de tout supreme commandement.

Selon Laumonier, l'expression plutôt obscure « les unes par qui doivent naistre » s'applique à Catherine de Médicis, et les mots « les autres par vertu » désignent Élisabeth : dans une note, il explique que « l'antithèse est certaine entre les Reines procréatrices comme Catherine, et celles qui, comme Élisabeth, se vantent de rester vierges. » Mais à cette époque il n'était nullement certain qu'Élisabeth ne serait pas une « reine procréatrice ». Ronsard se permettait même d'exprimer le vœu — dans ce même recueil précisément — qu'elle le fût. Car au moment où les *Elégies, Mascarades et Bergerie* paraissaient, des pourparlers se poursuivaient en vue d'un mariage de la reine Elisabeth et du roi Charles IX. Le recueil de Ronsard était une œuvre de propagande, destinée à préparer la voie à ce mariage (5).

L'exemplaire de Peterborough des *Elégies, Mascarades et Bergerie* nous offre un texte plus correct et qui rend superflue une note erronée. On lit, dans cet exemplaire :

> ... les dames sont parvenues, les unes par race [c'est-à-dire, non pas Catherine, mais Élisabeth : car en Angleterre on admettait le droit de succession des femmes], les autres par vertu [c'est-à-dire, selon toute vraisemblance, Catherine] au sommet de tout supreme commandement.

(5) Cf. mon article, « Ronsard and Queen Elizabeth I », *Bibliothèque d'Humanisme et Renaissance*, XXIX, 1967 (p. 93-119), p. 94-95 et les notes 8 et 13.

Il y a maintes autres variantes dans l'exemplaire de Peter-borough, dont on devrait tenir compte désormais dans la révision du texte des *Elégies, Mascarades et Bergerie*.

Dans le recueil dont nous venons de parler, Ronsard a publié, pour la première fois, paraît-il, sa traduction d'un hymne chrétien latin qui s'appelle le *Te Deum laudamus*. Les seules autres éditions anciennes de ce poème mentionnées dans l'édition critique de Laumonier sont celles des *Œuvres complètes* de Ronsard, où il entre dans la section des *Discours des miseres*. C'est que, dans la préparation de son édition, Laumonier a volontairement écarté les éditions « sans valeur critique ». Le principe est incontestable si l'on vise seulement l'établissement du texte de Ronsard. Il est intéressant pourtant de constater que dans le cas du *Te Deum*, les éditions « sans valeur critique » sont probablement assez nombreuses. Ce poème entre dans certains recueils dont on trouve des exemplaires dans le British Museum. C'est ainsi qu'on le trouve publié comme une sorte d'appendice dans un livre intitulé *La conqueste, et recouvrement du marquisat de Salusse en Piedmont, faite par le Roy de France*, qui fut publié à Lyon, « Pour Anthoine Prat, en sa Boutique au Palais », en 1580. Le *Te Deum* de Ronsard figure également dans le recueil de poèmes religieux publié par Etienne de Maisonfleur sous le titre de *Cantiques*. Ce recueil, qui regroupe des œuvres d'auteurs catholiques et réformés, a été édité plusieurs fois, et le poème de Ronsard se trouve dans les éditions de 1586, 1587, 1591 et 1602. L'existence de ces éditions du *Te Deum* suggère que ce texte a eu un plus grand rayonnement que l'on n'avait supposé jusqu'ici.

Au cours de la même année qui a vu paraître le recueil des *Elégies, Mascarades et Bergerie* — c'est-à-dire en 1565 —, Ronsard a publié à Paris et à Lyon son poème contre le cardinal de Lorraine. Dans ce poème, Ronsard établit une sorte de catalogue des poèmes qu'il avait écrits autrefois à la louange du cardinal et des membres de sa famille, et il porte plainte contre le cardinal, qui ne l'a pas dédommagé de ses services. La pièce, en effet, s'intitule *Le Proces*. Malgré le millésime de 1565, la composition de ce poème doit remonter, comme

le constate Laumonier, à une date bien antérieure, probablement 1561. On peut préciser, je crois, la raison du retard
dans la publication de cette plaquette. C'est que, vers 1561,
le cardinal de Lorraine était violemment attaqué par les propagandistes réformés, et Ronsard, qui reprochait précisément
aux Réformés leurs « libelles & placars », n'a guère voulu y
ajouter son réquisitoire contre le cardinal. Une deuxième
petite remarque au sujet du *Proces*, c'est que le gouvernement anglais se serait intéressé aux démêlés du prince des poètes
avec le prince de l'Église. L'ambassadeur d'Angleterre à
Paris a envoyé un exemplaire du *Proces* au secrétaire Cecil.
La dépêche de l'ambassadeur est datée du 10 avril 1565, et
cette date constitue donc un *terminus ad quem* pour la publication de la première édition du poème (6).

Or, le British Museum possède un exemplaire d'une réimpression lyonnaise de cet opuscule. La réimpression est datée
de 1569, et porte la marque de Jean Gerard. Laumonier
mentionnait cet exemplaire dans son *Tableau chronologique
des œuvres de Ronsard*, mais il ne l'a pas rappelé dans son édition critique. A vrai dire, la réimpression en elle-même est
d'un intérêt restreint. Elle reproduit, dans l'ensemble, jusqu'aux coquilles des éditions antérieures. Tout au plus ai-je
trouvé deux variantes significatives, et dans les deux cas on
a le droit de préférer les leçons des éditions antérieures (7).
Mais il est piquant de constater qu'au moment précis où Ronsard renouvelait sa polémique avec les Réformés, en 1569,
son réquisitoire contre un grand personnage catholique paraissait de nouveau, peut-être à l'insu du poète.

En 1569 donc, voilà Ronsard replongé dans la controverse
avec les Réformés. Controverse politique plutôt que religieuse, à cette date. Ses poèmes sont des exécrations des
armées des protestants, et des chants de réjouissance inspirés

---

(6) V. *Calendar of State Papers, Foreign Series, Elizabeth*, 1564-65,
n° 1090, 10 avril 1565. Une autre dépêche de l'ambassadeur d'Angleterre
permet de préciser la date de publication du poème *Les nues*, qui a dû
paraître avant le 10 février 1565 (V. *ibid.*, n° 980, 10 février 1565).
(7) Au vers 104 on lit dans la réimpression, « De l'Anglois, deliberé un
divin Truchement » ; et au vers 266, « Affin de vous gaigner, puis consultant l'affaire ».

par les victoires des catholiques. Par exemple, il a publié, dans le *Sixiesme livre des poèmes*, un *Chant triomphal pour jouer sur la lyre, Sur l'insigne victoire qu'il a pleu à Dieu donner à Monseigneur, Frere du Roy*. Par la suite, ce poème a reparu dans les éditions successives des œuvres complètes de Ronsard. Je rappelle que, à côté de ces éditions, ce poème a été maintes fois réédité dans les recueils musicaux publiés par Adrian le Roy et Robert Ballard. Ce texte a donc reparu, avec la musique, en 1572, 1573, 1575 et 1580. Ces éditions témoignent encore du rayonnement du texte de Ronsard (8).

Ronsard a publié plusieurs autres poèmes contre les Réformés en 1569. Le cas de la *Priere à Dieu pour la victoire*, publiée d'abord sous le voile de l'anonymat, est particulièrement significatif pour la bibliographie ronsardienne. Un exemplaire de l'édition originale de ce texte, édition qui est restée longtemps inconnue, est conservé au British Museum : il y a trois exemplaires de cette édition à la Bibliothèque Nationale. Si je reviens sur ce que j'ai écrit au sujet de ce livre, c'est dans l'espoir de provoquer une nouvelle découverte.

Il faut d'abord rappeler sommairement les circonstances dans lesquelles cette *Priere à Dieu* a vu le jour. On sait que les *Discours* de Ronsard — et cette *Priere* se range parmi ceux-là — sont des œuvres à la fois d'information et de propagande. Ces œuvres sont inspirées par l'actualité religieuse et politique dont elles sont une narration et un commentaire. Ces poèmes, qui ont été publiés primitivement sous forme de plaquettes, sont donc, sous bien des rapports, des précurseurs des journaux modernes. La composition et la publication de ces ouvrages suivent obligatoirement de très près l'événement. Ronsard nous signale qu'il a écrit la très longue *Remonstrance au peuple de France* en trois jours, et une remarque d'Amadis Jamyn suggère que Ronsard aurait composé en une seule journée la *Priere à Dieu pour la victoire*. Dans le cas de la plupart de ces poèmes, Ronsard a dû passer son manuscrit à l'imprimeur aussitôt le poème achevé. L'im-

(8) V. G. THIBAULT et L. PERCEAU, *Bibliographie des poésies de P. de Ronsard mises en musique au XVIe siècle* (Publications de la Société Française de Musicologie), Paris, 1941, nos 53, 57, 69, 107.

primeur, pour sa part, n'a guère tardé à le publier. Ensuite, au moment de faire entrer ces poèmes dans les diverses éditions de ses œuvres complètes, Ronsard les a revus. Mais c'est le document original qui intéresse surtout l'historien.

Or, la *Priere à Dieu pour la victoire* fut écrite, selon Amadis Jamyn, trois jours avant la bataille de Moncontour, c'est-à-dire le 30 septembre 1569. Ronsard a dû transmettre son manuscrit aussitôt à l'imprimeur. Le 3 octobre, la bataille survient, et c'est une victoire des troupes catholiques. Et voilà que l'imprimeur a entre les mains une *Priere à Dieu pour la victoire* qui, bien sûr, n'est plus actuelle. Qu'est-ce qu'il fait ? Il publie tel quel le texte de Ronsard, mais il apporte une petite modification au titre. La *Priere à Dieu pour la victoire* devient, dans les mains de l'imprimeur, un *Chant triumphal sur la victoire* (9). Métamorphose rentable, sans doute. Le poème était publié sans nom d'auteur, mais Ronsard revendiqua la paternité de ce fils en le recueillant dans ses œuvres complètes en 1578. C'est la connaissance du texte de 1578 qui a permis la restitution à Ronsard de ce fils dont la naissance remonte à 1569 et qu'il n'a d'abord pas voulu avouer comme sien.

Or, il reste une découverte analogue à faire. En cette même année 1569, Ronsard a écrit contre les Réformés deux poèmes qui consistent en une comparaison entre l'armée des Réformés et l'un des monstres tués par Hercule. Ces deux poèmes ont pour titres *L'Hydre deffaict* et *Les elements ennemis de l'Hydre*. Le texte de 1569 du premier est connu depuis longtemps, mais le poème des *Elemens ennemis de l'Hydre* ne nous est connu que par l'édition de 1578 des œuvres complètes. Je cite le début du poème, selon cette dernière édition :

> Non seulement les hommes ont fait teste
> A ceste horrible, abominable beste,
> A ce serpent qui de grandeur eust bien
> Esté la peur du bras Tyrinthien [= Hercule] ;
> Mais l'air glueux d'une espesse gelée
> Et d'une neige en la pluye meslée
> Et d'un long froid de glaces renfermé
> S'est contre luy cruellement armé.

(9) J'en ai réimprimé le texte dans la *Bibliothèque d'Humanisme et Renaissance*, XXVIII (1966), p. 686-689.

6

Espérons que quelque chercheur retrouvera une version plus ancienne de ce texte.

Je termine cette communication en évoquant brièvement une des éditions anciennes des œuvres complètes de Ronsard. Il s'agit de celle de 1587, la première édition posthume, qui est en train d'être rééditée avec tout le soin souhaitable par M. Silver. Cette édition nous offre une belle leçon de bibliographie. Jusqu'à tout récemment, on n'en connaissait qu'un seul exemplaire complet, celui de la Bibliothèque Nationale. J'en ai trouvé un deuxième à Manchester, dans la John Rylands Library (10). M. D. Wilson a préparé une notice bibliographique au sujet de cet exemplaire de Manchester, et dans cette notice, qui doit paraître dans un prochain numéro de *French Studies*, M. Wilson énumère d'autres exemplaires partiels de cette édition. Selon le catalogue des bibliothèques des cathédrales anglaises, la cathédrale de Lichfield posséderait la plupart des tomes de cette édition. Mais il y a plus. Dans un compte rendu de l'édition de M. Silver paru dans le *Times Literary Supplement* du 12 septembre 1968, il est fait état d'un troisième exemplaire complet : c'est celui de la vente Chadeau, de 1865. D'ailleurs, j'ai consulté récemment le catalogue de la bibliothèque Robert Hoe, et voilà encore un exemplaire complet, le quatrième, de l'édition de 1587. Un cinquième exemplaire complet est passé en vente à Londres, chez Sotheby, le 3 août 1917, et un autre exemplaire, également complet, le numéro six, figure dans la deuxième partie du catalogue de la bibliothèque de M. le comte de Lignerolles (1894).

Dans les recherches ronsardiennes, le bibliographe n'est donc point celui qui sait, il est assurément celui qui cherche.

Malcolm C. SMITH.

---

(10) La John Rylands Library possède également plusieurs des biographies anciennes de Ronsard. Mrs D. Dial prépare actuellement à l'Université de Leeds une thèse qui sera une édition de ces biographies.

RONSARD AND THE WORD *PURITAN*

The invention of the word *puritain* has often been credited to Pierre de Ronsard. This word is ascribed to him, and its invention dated at 1562, in F. MACKENZIE's *Les relations de l'Angleterre et de la France d'après le vocabulaire*;[1] A. DAUZAT, J. DUBOIS and H. MITTERAND's *Nouveau dictionnaire étymologique et historique*, Paris, 1964; E. BLOCH and W. von WARTBURG's *Dictionnaire étymologique de la langue francaise*, 4e. éd., Paris, 1964; P. ROBERT's *Dictionnaire alphabétique et analogique de la langue francaise*; and in W. von WARTBURG's *Französisches Etymologisches Wörterbuch*, 18. Band, *Anglizismen*, Basel, 1967. All of these authorities cite the English word *puritan* as a model for Ronsard's word,[2] and all of them give 1562 as the year of its first appearance, thus positing the existence by 1562 of the word in its English form.

Ronsard has however also been credited with providing the model for the English word. The earliest verifiable example of the word which the *Oxford English Dictionary* gives dates only from 1572. The *Oxford English Dictionary*, in fact, points out that *puritan* is antedated by Ronsard's *puritain*, which it dates at 1564; and Lee, in *The French Renaissance in England*, implied that Ronsard used the word in 1563, and stated: "The word 'Puritan' would seem to have been used familiarly in French before it was generally accepted in English."[3]

* * *

It may seem at first sight a little odd that a word like *puritan* should owe its creation to a Frenchman and odder still that its invention should be credited to Ronsard. But the prince of poets, known today (though not in his lifetime) primarily as an author of love poetry, did involve himself in religious controversies. His politico-religious *Discours des miseres de ce temps*, a series of poems

---

[1] See vol. I, *Les infiltrations de la langue et de l'esprit anglais, Anglicismes français*, Paris, 1939, p. 62-63. The reference to this work, and to several of the dictionaries cited in this article, was very kindly given to me by Professor T. E. Hope.

[2] The *Französisches Etymologisches Wörterbuch* states: "E. puritan ist eine latinisierende ablt. von e. pure 'rein'. Der erste englische beleg ist von 1572, also später als der beleg bei Ronsard, weswegen die vermutung geäussert worden ist, das wort sei im fr. gebildet worden und von da ins engl. übergegangen. Doch berechtigt der kleine zeitliche unterschied nicht zu diesem an sich unwahrscheinlichen schluss, umsoweniger als die vereinzelung des wortes im fr. zeigt, dass dieser beleg nur auf einer momentanen und individuellen übernahme aus dem e. beruht." Mackenzie says however that the word was "peut-être créé en France," and Robert suggests that the French word may alternatively be based on *puritas*. The word is not given in E. BONNAFFÉ's *Dictionnaire étymologique et historique des anglicismes*, Paris, 1920.

[3] See S. LEE, *The French Renaissance in England*, Oxford, 1910, p. 193, note 3.

written in vindication of the Roman Catholic faith and published mainly in 1562 and 1563 during the first civil war, enjoyed a massive influence: it is in a text of one of these poems, the *Continuation du discours des miseres*, that the word *puritain* is found.

Ronsard moreover was a prolific inventor of new words.[4] He practised more vigorously than any other French poet of the Renaissance the principles of lexicographical innovation which Du Bellay expounded in the second book of the *Deffence et illustration de la langue françoyse*. Ronsard indeed claimed to have inspired Du Bellay to write this treatise [5] and he echoed many of its precepts in his own *Abbregé de l'Art poëtique françois* of 1565.[6] And in a work of personal apologia written against the Reformers in 1563, the *Responce aux injures et calomnies, de je ne sçay quels Predicans, & Ministres de Geneve*, he claimed to have vastly enriched his native tongue:

> Je vy que des François le langage trop bas
> Se trainoit sans vertu, sans ordre, ny compas:
> Adonques pour hausser ma langue maternelle,
> Indonté du labeur, je travaillé pour elle,
> Je fis des mots nouveaux, je rapellay les vieux:
> Si bien que son renom je poussay jusqu'aux cieux [...] [7]

It is plausible that Ronsard also enriched other languages than French. It was for him a matter of patriotic pride that the French language, and his own poetry, should be known outside France. He declared, in the *Abbregé de l'Art poëtique françois*, that "[...] les Princes ne doivent estre moins curieux d'agrandir les bornes de leur empire, que d'estendre leur langage par toutes nations." [8] Claude Binet, in a eulogy of Ronsard published shortly after the poet's death, attributed grateful words to Henri III:

> Il [*sc.* Ronsard] fut l'un des premiers qui de gloire allumé
> Fit passer mon langage aux nations estranges. [9]

It is well known that Ronsard's poetry was widely appreciated outside France, especially perhaps in England.[10]

Despite his involvement in religious controversy, and despite his lexicographical inventiveness, Ronsard almost certainly was not the first man to use *puritain*. This word is indeed found in his *Conti-*

---

[4] See L. MELLERIO's still valuable *Lexique de Ronsard précédé d'une Etude sur son vocabulaire, son orthographe et sa syntaxe*, Paris, 1895; and especially C. MARTY-LAVEAUX's *La Pléiade francoise. Appendice. La langue de la Pléiade*, 2 t., Paris, 1896, 1898.

[5] See the beautiful and historically very interesting passage in the *Elegie à Loïs des Masures Tournisien* in which Ronsard tells how the ghost of Du Bellay appears to him: it is found in the *Œuvres complètes*, éd. P. Laumonier, Paris, Société des Textes Français Modernes, X, p. 367. All quotations from the work of Ronsard in this article are taken from this edition.

[6] This manifesto, written in prose, is found in Laumonier's S.T.F.M. edition, XIV, p. 3-38.

[7] *Ibid.*, XI, p. 167.

[8] *Ibid.*, XIV, p. 11-12.

[9] *Ibid.*, XVIII, p. 122.

[10] See I. SILVER, "Ronsard in European literature: a synoptic view of scholarly publications," *Bibliothèque d'Humanisme et Renaissance*, XVI, 1954, p. 241-254 (an analysis of the influence of Ronsard on the literature of England, Scotland, Germany, Belgium and Holland, Italy and Poland) and H. M. RICHMOND, "Ronsard and the English Renaissance," *Comparative Literature Studies*, Urbana, 1970, p. 141-160.

nuation du discours des miseres in a passage in which he castigates the Reformers for the variety of their beliefs :

> Les Apostres jadis preschoient tous d'un accord,
> Entre vous aujourdhuy ne regne que discord :
> Les uns sont Zvingliens, les autres Lutheristes,
> Les autres Puritains, Quintins, Anabaptistes,
> Les autres de Calvin vont adorant les pas,
> L'un est predestiné, & l'autre ne l'est pas,
> Et l'autre enrage apres l'erreur Muncerienne,
> Et bien tost s'ouvrira l'escole Beszienne. [11]

It is true that the *Continuation du discours des miseres* was first published in 1562 (and not, as Lee presumably thought, in 1563 or, as the writer of the entry in the *Oxford English Dictionary* must have imagined, in 1564).   But the passage just cited is a revised version of the original text.   And this particular revised version did not appear until 1587 !   The word *puritain* is not found in any of the earlier versions of the text.   By 1587 the word was in common use in English, and it had certainly also been used considerably earlier than 1587 in French.   I have been unable to find any other, earlier example of its use by the prince of poets, and it seems safe to say that Ronsard did not invent it.[12]

* * *

Who did first use the French word *puritain*?   Examples cited by lexicographers are few and relatively late.   It is quite possible that the puritans were known in France around 1580 for their strident opposition to the projected marriage of queen Elizabeth and the duke of Alençon.   But the earliest example of use of the word that I have found dates only from 1582.   It was in that year that Hierosme Bolsec published his satirical biography of Theodore Beza and in this work, in a passage curiously reminiscent of the extract from Ronsard which we have just examined, he castigated the Reformers for the diversity of their opinions : among the many heretical sects, says Bolsec, is that of the English and Irish puritans, who emerged from the sewers of hell two or three years ago.[13]   In 1587, the word

---

[11] See Laumonier's S.T.F.M. edition, XI, p. 49-50.

[12] The erroneous attribution to Ronsard of *puritain* is traceable to Blanchemain's edition of Ronsard.   The *Französisches Etymologisches Wörterbuch* refers for Ronsard's use of *puritain* to an extract from the *Continuation du discours des miseres* quoted from Blanchemain's edition by A. DARMESTETER and A. HATZFELD in *Le seizième siècle en France* (Paris, 1893, II, p. 231).   Lee (see above, note 3) also used Blanchemain's edition, but he does not give a reference for the passage in which *puritain* occurs, and confounds it with a passage in the *Responce aux injures* : the former poem is dated by Blanchemain (again, erroneously, for 1562) at 1563 (see VII, p. 9, n. 1).   The inadequacies of Blanchemain's edition were fully demonstrated by Laumonier in the introduction to his S.T.F.M. edition (see I, p. v-x).

[13] Though Bolsec's argument is similar to Ronsard's, it is less temperately expressed. Of the Reformers, he wrote :

is found, as we saw, in Ronsard's *Continuation du discours des miseres*, and in the following year it is encountered in a work by the Scottish jesuit John Hay, published in French. The puritans, says Hay, may be identified not with the Anglicans but with the Calvinist Reformers: "Car il est certain qu'entre les Calvinistes Puritains, & les Evesques, ou (pour mieux dire) ceux, qui contre tout droit, se sont usurpez les Sieges des Evesques en Angleterre, il y a grand different, & haine mortelle." [14]

* * *

Ronsard's use of *puritain* is of considerable historical interest. The poet was continually revising his polemical politico-religious verse in the light of current events, for literature of this kind had to be topical, just as modern journalism does. In the original version of the *Continuation du discours des miseres*, published in 1562, the relevant lines of the passage cited above read as follows:

> Les uns sont Zvingliens, les autres Lutheristes,
> Œcolompadiens, Quintins, Anabaptistes [...]

The puritans were obviously more topical in France in 1587 than the followers of Œcolampadius! The reason for this interest in the English radical Reformers is that when, in 1584, the death of the duke of Alençon made the Reformer Henri of Navarre the heir to the French throne, French Roman Catholics looked more keenly at the religious situation in England: they read accounts of the trials and grim executions of English Roman Catholics, and these accounts were accompanied by warnings of the intolerance of heretic

---

     Aucuns sont Lutheriens, autres huss[i]tes : autres Vuingletistes : autres Zuingliens, autres Œcolenpadiens : autres Melanctoniens : autres Donatistes : autres Anabaptistes : autres Calvinistes. Outre lesquels despuis deux ou trois ans en çà, se sont levez en Angleterre, Ibernie, les Puritains sortis des cloaques d'enfer : & sont tous differens en opinions, cerimonies, & traditions, voire de affections contraires & interieurement ennemis, chacun estimans sa secte plus parfaicte que les autres : Combien qu'en une chose ils sont accordans, c'est de contredire, resister, & destruire la superiorité & dignité de tous temps ordonné, & baillée de Dieu aux prelats & pasteurs de l'Eglise, selon l'institution divine.
     (Histoire de la vie, mœurs, doctrine, et deportements de Theodore de Beze, dit le Spectable, grand Ministre de Geneve, selon que lon a peu voir & cognoistre jusqu'à maintenant, en attendant que luy mesme, si bon luy semble, y adjouste le reste, A Paris, chez Guillaume Chaudiere, M.D.LXXXII, B.M. 1193 h 30 (10), 10ro).
     [14] See *L'Antimoine, aux response, que Th. de Beze faict à trente sept demandes de deux cents & six, proposées aux ministres d'Escosse, par M. Ian Hay de la Compagnie de Iesus* [...], Tournon, M.D.XXCVIII, B.M. 1008 a 8 (1), p. 276-277.
     According to Paul Barbier's manuscript *French dictionary : materials for a dictionary of the French language*, c. 1920-1947 (Brotherton Library, University of Leeds, MS. 270) the word occurs in a *Sommaire discours du notable martyre de deux venerables prestres et deux hommes lais, advenu en l'Université d'Oxonio* [...] [Lyon, Jean Patrasson], 1590, p. 19 : "Et puis, on les posa sur les murailles du vieux chasteau, auquel lieu les ministres puritains balafroyent à coups de cousteaux leurs glourieuses faces [...]". I am very grateful to Professor C. P. Barbier for permission to quote from this most impressive compilation which deserves to be much more widely known.
     The examples of *puritain* given by E. Huguet in his *Dictionnaire de la langue française du seizième siècle* are not dated by him, but they are all relatively late. In chronological order, and with Huguet's bibliographical information corrected and expanded, they are found in the following works : [P. Charron,] *Les trois veritez contre les Athées, Idolatres, Iuifs, Mahumetans, Heretiques, & Schismatiques. Le tout traicté en trois livres*, Bourdeaus, M.D.XCIII, B.M. 851 f 15, pp. 317-318, 488 ; François de Sales, *Œuvres*, édition complète, publiée par les soins des religieuses de la Visitation du 1er monastère d'Annecy, 2v., Annecy, 1892, p. 317 (according to the editors, the *Controverses*, in which *puritain* occurs, were written between 1594 and 1598: see I, xlix) ; P. Le Loyer, *Discours, et histoires des spectres, visions et apparitions des esprits, anges, demons, et ames, se monstrans visibles aux hommes. Divisez en huict livres* [...], Paris, M.DCV, B.M. 719 i 9, p. 328, 809. I did not find the word *puritain* in Le Loyer's *IIII Livres des spectres ou apparitions et visions d'esprits* [...], Angers, 1586, B.M. 719 f 6.

monarchs.[15]   It is significant that John Hay identified the Calvinist Reformers not with the Anglicans, whose religion had in the early days of the reign of Elizabeth been favourably commented on by French Roman Catholics,[16] but with the dreaded puritans !   In revising the earlier text of the *Continuation du discours des miseres*, and introducing a reference to the puritans, Ronsard is reflecting the contemporary interest of Frenchmen in the English religious situation.[17]

*   *

*

Who did invent the word *puritan* ?   Was the word a *calque* based on the καθαροί thus discrediting contemporary religious thinkers by linking them with the long-condemned Novatian heresy ? [18]   Or did it derive from some popular preacher's derision of the Reformers' claims to preach the word of God "purely ?"   Or from satire of the ostentatious piety with which the Reformers were often reproached (by Du Bellay, Ronsard and Jodelle among others) ?   Like many another epithet of a religious group, it appears to have been coined by an adversary of the movement : and now that the attribution to Ronsard has been shown to be unsound, it seems on the whole likely that the word was first used in its English form.

Leeds.   Malcolm SMITH.

---

[15] This literature seems to have been widely disseminated, and to have been very influential : see my article on "Ronsard and queen Elizabeth I", *Bibliothèque d'Humanisme et Renaissance*, XXIX. 1967, p. 93-119 and especially p. 111-114.

[16] See "Ronsard and queen Elizabeth I", p. 103 and notes 56, 57 and 58.

[17] Ronsard's sensitivity to the English political and religious situation was quite acute.   I have tried to show, in "Ronsard and queen Elizabeth I" how, shortly after writing in defence of the Roman Catholic faith, Ronsard came to compose poems in praise of queen Elizabeth, Robert Dudley and William Cecil ; and how, in 1584, he drastically altered the texts of these poems, influenced, no doubt, by reports of the treatment of Roman Catholics in the 1580's in England and by the continued detention of Mary queen of Scots.
Ronsard died in December 1585 and the 1587 text of his complete works was prepared by his literary executors, Claude Binet and Jean Galland, on the basis of the poet's own revision of the 1584 edition.   Ronsard's own interest in the affairs of England suggests that it was he, and not his editors, who introduced into his work the reference to the puritans.   Binet and Galland are moreover generally accepted to have respected scrupulously the poet's text (see C. GUÉPIN, "Les éditions de Ronsard," *Le Portique*, IV, 1946, pp. 129-143 and particularly p. 136-140 ; I. SILVER's edition of *Les œuvres de Pierre de Ronsard, texte de 1587*, 8 v., Chicago, London, Paris, Toronto, 1966-1970, and especially the same scholar's sensitive and illuminating introduction to volume XVIII of the S.T.F.M. edition of Ronsard).

[18] This suggestion is found in the *Oxford English Dictionary* and is taken up by M. M. KNAPPEN in *Tudor puritanism, a chapter in the history of idealism*, Gloucester, Mass., 1963 : see the discussion headed "Terminology" (Appendix II, p. 487-493). None of the books about puritans which I have looked at seems to deal with Ronsard's alleged invention of the word, but I have learned a great deal about the early days of puritanism, and pleasurably, from the following : P. COLLINSON, *The Elizabethan puritan movement*, London, 1967 ; E. H. EMERSON, *English puritanism from John Hooper to John Milton*, Durham, N.C., 1968 ; C.H. GARRETT, *The Marian exiles, a study in the origins of Elizabethan puritanism*, Cambridge, 1938 ; C. H. GEORGE and K. GEORGE, *The protestant mind of the English Reformation, 1570-1640*, Princeton, N.J., 1961 ; W. HALLER, *The rise of puritanism*, New York, 1938 ; C. HILL, *Society and puritanism in pre-revolutionary England*, London, 1964 ; D.J. McGINN, *The Admonition controversy*, New Brunswick, 1949 ; P. McGRATH, *Papists and puritans under Elizabeth I*, London, (1967) ; I. MORGAN, *The Godly preachers of the Elizabethan church*, London, 1965 ; A. F. S. PEARSON, *Thomas Cartwright and Elizabethan puritanism, 1535-1603*, Cambridge, 1925 ; H. C. PORTER, *Puritanism in Tudor England* (History in depth), London and Basingstoke, (1970) ; and B. R. WHITE, *The English separatist tradition from the Marian martyrs to the Pilgrim Fathers* (Oxford theological monographs), London, 1971.

THE FIRST EDITION OF RONSARD'S *RECUEIL DES NOUVELLES POËSIES*

Ronsard's *Recueil des nouvelles Poësies* was first published in 1564 : in that year three versions at least of the text appeared, and they can be placed in chronological order : "A," the first edition, has hitherto only been fleetingly glimpsed by scholars, has never been collated with any other edition, and all trace of it has long since been lost ; "B," a later text, has also been lost, but Alfred Pereire was able to collate it with "C," a version which is later still and which has on its titlepage the words "Seconde edition." A copy of "C," which has long been the only one of these three texts available to scholars, is preserved in the Bibliothèque de l'Institut in Paris, and another is in the Bibliothèque Nationale. The present note is about the discovery of a copy of "A" : I shall give a full list of textual variants and thereby make the original 1564 text available to scholars for the first time.

In 1564 Ronsard published a composite volume containing in its original version four distinct pamphlets :

1 (*a*) *Le premier livre du Recueil des nouvelles Poësies de P. de Ronsard Gentilhomme Vandomois. Lesquelles n'ont encores esté par cy devant imprimées. Ensemble une epistre par laquelle succintement il respond à ses calomniateurs.* A Paris, Pour Gabriel Buon, au clos Bruneau à l'enseigne S. Claude. 1564. Avec Privilege du Roy.

This titlepage (fol. 1ro) is followed in this pamphlet only by the *Epistre* in which Ronsard writes against the Reformers who had attacked him (fol. 2ro-10vo) and by a sonnet dedicating "ce livret" to Ysabeau de La Tour (10vo). The "livret" which follows this dedication forms a second and separate part of the volume as a whole.

1 (*b*) *Les quatre saisons de l'an, aveques une Eglogue, une Elegie, l'Adonis et l'Orphée. Par P. de Ronsard, Gentilhomme Vandomois.* A Paris, chez Gabriel Buon, au clos Bruneau, à l'enseigne S. Claude. 1563. Avec Privilege du Roy.

This pamphlet consists of 46 folios, including the titlepage and two lots of pages numbered 21-24 (the last folio is thus numbered 42). Its date suggests it may have been published separately before being included in the *Recueil des nouvelles Poësies*. Clearly, *Les quatre saisons de l'an* and the poems published with it are intended to form the first book of the *Recueil des nouvelles Poësies* announced on the titlepage of 1 (*a*) and in the sonnet to Ysabeau de La Tour.

2. *Le second livre du Recueil des nouvelles Poësies de P. de Ronsard Gentilhomme Vandomois. Lesquelles n'ont encores esté par cy devant imprimées.* A H. Luillier Seigneur de Maisonfleur, Gentilhomme servant de leurs Magestez. A Paris, Pour Gabriel Buon, au clos Bruneau à l'enseigne S. Claude. 1564. Avec Privilege du Roy.

This pamphlet with its titlepage occupies 38 folios (the last one is incorrectly numbered 39).

3. *Le troisieme livre du Recueil des nouvelles Poësies de P. de Ronsard Gentilhomme Vandomois. Lesquelles n'ont encores esté par cy devant imprimées.* A M. de Castelnau, Seigneur de Mauvissiere Gentilhomme, servant de Monsieur. A Paris, Pour Gabriel Buon, au clos Bruneau à l'enseigne S. Claude. 1564. Avec Privilege du Roy.

This pamphlet with its titlepage occupies 24 folios.

The existence of this first, composite edition "A" has been known about for a long time and descriptions of it similar to the one given above have been published before. But no editor of Ronsard has been able to actually use a copy in preparing an edition. Paul Laumonier saw a copy fleetingly : a bookseller allowed him to see this "rarissime édition tant convoitée" and to confirm its rarity and importance, but he was unable to copy the text and the book was sold to an individual at a price no public library could afford.[1] Alfred Pereire also had brief access to the original text but was only able to "prendre quelques notes" : however, he was able also to consult at much greater leisure an intermediate version, published after "A" and before "C." It was Messrs Maggs Brothers of London who allowed Pereire to use this intermediate text "B" and collate it with "C." [2]

When Laumonier came to edit these poems for the twelfth volume of his critical edition, he had not been able to locate another copy of the original edition, and was obliged to reproduce the text of "C." But he did not think this mattered very much :

> Quant au texte même, j'ai adopté celui de la seconde édition, à défaut du princeps, que je n'avais pu copier en 1919 ; il doit, d'ailleurs, en différer très peu, à part les variantes que j'ai signalées d'après A. Pereire dans l'apparat critique, et d'après Suz. Brunet dans les Additions.

The variants which Laumonier took from Pereire, and they are very few, are all ones which the latter scholar found in the "B" text. The material which Laumonier owes to Mlle Suzanne Brunet consists in "[...] quelques variantes qu'elle avait collationnées sur le texte princeps des Nouvelles Poesies chez les libraires Maggs", but it is conceivable that it was also the intermediate text "B" that Mlle Brunet collated with "C" : this would explain why her list of variants is so short.[3]

Although Laumonier put a good face on the absence of the original text he may well have suspected that its discovery would have considerably enriched his edition. For Pereire, who had also seen the original edition briefly, had hinted that it contains numerous variants : "Pour [l'édition originale] la plupart des éléments de comparaison nous manquent, lorsqu'il s'agit du texte." [4] M. Raymond Lebègue,

---

[1] See P. LAUMONIER, "Une double découverte bibliographique à propos d'un recueil de vers de Ronsard," *Revue du seizième siècle*, VIJ, 1920, p. 160-167 and Laumonier's introduction to volume XII of his critical edition of Ronsard (Société des Textes Français Modernes), p. vi-viii.

[2] See A. PEREIRE, "A propos d'une édition originale rarissime de Ronsard", *Bulletin du Bibliophile*, 1934, p. 253-264.

[3] See vol. XII of LAUMONIER's critical edition of Ronsard, p. viii. The variants from Pereire are on p. 13, 16, 100 and 103. Those from Mlle. Brunet are on p. 305 : the spelling in the variants she supplied differs from that of "A" and the "A" text has variants which she did not give adjacent to variants which she did give. These facts suggest either that Mlle. Brunet only had access to "B" or that she was able to consult "A" but not make a thorough collation of it : this latter hypothesis is more probable since it would explain why she was able to state that lines 211-250 of the *Eglogue* in the first book of the *Recueil* were added in "B."

[4] PEREIRE, *article cited*, p. 257, note 1.

in an introductory note in the eighteenth volume of the critical edition, appealed for information on the whereabouts of the original edition, no doubt because he suspected—as indeed he told me in a letter a few weeks ago—that the original version contained variants which Laumonier had not included in his edition.[5]

Three years ago, in preparation for a forthcoming edition of Ronsard's *Discours des miseres*, I had photocopies made of several pamphlets which are preserved in the Houghton Library of Harvard University : among those photocopies was one of that *Epistre* which was first published in the *Recueil des nouvelles Poësies* but which was also later included among the *Discours des miseres* in some early editions of Ronsard's complete works. It is only in the last few weeks that I have checked the text of this copy of the *Epistre,* and found that it is the text of the original edition "A." I immediately asked the Houghton Library to photocopy the whole book, and have now been able to collate the whole of "A" and Laumonier's edition of "C." Laumonier's suggestion that the original text was unlikely to be very different from the text he used is not borne out by this collation.

The two items in the *Recueil des nouvelles Poësies* in which the divergencies between the original edition and Laumonier's text are most numerous are the *Epistre* and the *Eglogue* in the first book. The changes to the *Epistre* are particularly interesting historically : the fact that Ronsard took the trouble to revise even a prose tract against the Reformers within a very short while of its original appearance is an indication of the degree of his commitment to this polemic. The content of the alterations is interesting, too : in the later edition "C" Ronsard added to the list of pamphlets against him and, most interestingly, included new veiled references to the identity of his antagonists.[6]

The *Epistre* is not the only part of the *Recueil des nouvelles Poësies* in which Ronsard engages in controversy with the Reformers : I have tried to show (in an article to be published elsewhere soon) that a whole poem in the collection, the *Hymne de l'Hyver,* consists in a detailed allegorical commentary on the contemporary political and religious situation. Other poems in the *Recueil des nouvelles Poësies* may well be allegorical denunciations of the Reformers : the study of topical meanings in Ronsard's mythological poems is as yet in its infancy.

The first edition of the *Recueil des nouvelles Poësies* shows signs of having been published in haste : for example, the presentation of *Les quatre saisons de l'an* obscures the position of that group of poems as the first book of the *Recueil.* The fact that the *Recueil* is to a considerable extent part of Ronsard's polemic with the Reformers could explain why it was hastily published : for polemical literature has to be topical. The later version "C" is more tidy than "A," having a general titlepage (*Les trois livres du Recueil des nouvelles Poësies*), no individual titlepage for *Les quatre saisons de l'an,* continuous page numbering and only one privilege whereas "A" has four.

Many of the differences between the original text and that reprinted by Laumonier could not be given without republishing the whole book : there are very numerous variants in paragraph division, spel-

---

[5] M. Lebègue is, with Mr. Isidore Silver, revising and finishing Laumonier's critical edition. The appeal for information about the *Recueil des nouvelles Poësies* is in volume XVIII, p. xiii.

[6] See the variants listed below, lines 146, 275-277, 403-404 and 438 respectively.

ling and punctuation. However, the integral original text of the *Epistre* will shortly be available in my edition of the *Discours des miseres,* and that of the hymns of the seasons will appear, should he decide to use it, in M. Albert Py's forthcoming edition of the *Hymnes.* But the variants which are of most interest to Ronsard scholars are undoubtedly the textual ones, and they are published here for the first time since 1564.

Ithaca, N.Y.   Malcolm SMITH.

The passages italicized are the ones in which the original text "A" differs from that of "C" as published by Laumonier. Laumonier's critical apparatus includes fragments of the "B" text as given by Pereire and he has "Additions" which may be from either "A" or "B" (see note 3 above). The date 1564 in Laumonier's critical apparatus also accompanies readings of "C" which he considered erroneous and which he rejected in favour of readings found in subsequent editions of the complete works. Where these readings are also found in "A" and I also consider them erroneous I have not mentioned them here. Where they are found in "A" and I do not consider them erroneous I have noted my opinion here. Where they are not found in "A" I have given the "A" text. Where "A" has errors not found in Laumonier's edition, I mention them here. It is thus possible to reconstitute the whole of the "A" text on the basis of Laumonier's edition and the material given here. Laumonier does not state whether he based his edition on the copy of the "C" text in the Bibliothèque de l'Institut or on that in the Bibliothèque Nationale, but he only notes one very minor textual discrepancy between the two (see XII, p. 250). Pereire noted only "quelques différences typographiques" between these two copies (see the article cited, p. 262, note 1). The page numbers refer to volume XII of Laumonier's critical edition.

Page 2, Privilege : the words "donné à S. Germain en Laye, le XX. jour de septembre, l'an mil cinq cens soixante" are lacking ; the imprimatur has the words " faire imprimer, *Le Premier livre* du recueil," and lacks the words "Et ce."

P. 7, l. 88-91 : par la grace de Dieu, *imprimée en mon cerveau,* tellement que j'ay pris pour devise ces deux vers que dit Horace de l'homme constant & *vertueux.*

P. 8, l. 107 : lacks the word "honneste."

P. 10, l. 146 : lacks the words "une autre tierce responce."

P. 10, l. 152 : lacks the word "leur."

P. 11, l. 171 : *suyvant* maintenant ce party (Laumonier may conceivably have mis-transcribed the text).

P. 13, l. 204-206 : qui l'avois *aymé, festié & chery: ny* de fait

P. 16, l. 275-277 : Mais puis *lecteur que mes calomniateurs* l'ont voulu

P. 16, l. 279-280 : plaisir de *les voir* agitez

P. 16, l. 281-286 : Toutesfois sans *l'expres mandement des plus grands j'eusse chatouillé ces nouveaux rimasseurs encores un peu,* mais dorenavant

P. 17, l. 289 : lacks the word "espointées."

P. 19, l. 341 : & *nom* de Perce (misprint).

P. 20, l. 366 : tu faux encores à la fable, *& m'esbahis comme tu es si ignorant.* Hesiode ne dit

P. 20, l. 380 : je pourray seurement dire *desormais*

P. 21, l. 383-384 : te monstrer qu'en te voulant moquer *que* tu as dit

P. 21, l. 390 : ouy dire *que les estoilles s'enyvrassent sinon à toy,* qui les veux

P. 21, l. 392 : scavent *bien* si je mens ou non

P. 21, l. 393 : lacks the word "pauvres."

P. 21, l. 403-404 : lacks the words "& en celle de l'ignorant Drogueur."

P. 22, l. 406 : Achevons *le* deux (misprint).

P. 22, l. 430 : laisse *point* de me luire

P. 23, l. 434 : honneur *que* de te respondre

P. 23, l. 435-448 blasmant les *hommes* dont l'honneur ne peut estre blessé par leur *miserable* caquet. Si tu as envie de faire le Charlatan, *tu le pourras faire tout seul, quant* à moy je seray tousjours bien ayse de *te* mettre en caprice & en cervel, & *te* faire crucifier *toymesme* par une envie qui *te* ronge le cœur, de me voir estimé des peuples estrangers & de ceux de ma nation ("C" is much longer).

Between page 24 and 25 : titlepage *Les quatre saisons de l'an* [...] and, on the verso of the titlepage, *Extraict du privilege du Roy*, which has the text printed by Laumonier in v. XI, p. 14 of the critical edition, followed by : *Ledict Ronsard a permis à Gabriel Buon d'imprimer ou faire imprimer, Les quatre saisons de l'An, aveques une Eglogue, une Elegie, l'Adonis & l'Orphee jusques au terme de six ans, finis & accomplis, à commancer du jour que ledict livre sera achevé d'imprimer.*

P. 32, l. 90 : Et le fist derechef amoureux denir (misprint).

P. 35, title : *L'*Hymne de l'esté

P. 36, l. 27 : Qui *sens* se remuer, gist le long d'un sentier, (misprint).

P. 41, l. 128 : *Mis* si tost que le ciel de flames se rougist, (misprint).

P. 43, l. 165 : Toutesfois *ell' embrasse*, ell' le touche, & le baise,

P. 44, l. 185 : Et comme elle sentoit *une* amour la plus forte,

P. 45, l. 221 : *Perruque* de rayons, qui sers de longue guide

P. 46, title : *L'*Hymne de l'autonne

P. 52, l. 116 : Adonque elle appelle, & luy dist tels propos (misprint).

P. 54, l. 174 : Depuis le bas des flancs *jusque au* haut des esselles :

P. 59, l. 284 : Cherchant de tous costés son frere *ny* trouva (misprint).

P. 61, l. 326 : Pour *en parer* son chef, puis alla voir sa mere.

P. 61, l. 327 : *Le* palais magnifique où Nature habitoit, (Laumonier's text is perhaps a mistranscription).

P. 65, l. 410 : Je n'eus onques *au cœur*, & tant plus je m'essaye

P. 66, l. 439 : Il la monte en son char en *grande* majesté

P. 68, title : *L'*Hymne de l'hyver (but the title of the first of these poems is "Hymne du printemps," without the article).

P. 70, l. 31 : Quand je *le* porte es mains, au front, ou sur la robe,

P. 79, l. 229 : Comme un foudre emporté *desur* l'asile du vent,

P. 79, note 3 : est *dedans* les Argonautes

P. 80, note 3 : violence des *vers* (a misprint). Vix nunc obsistitur illis *Cum sua quisque regat diverso flamina tractu Quin laniant mundum tanta est discordia fratrum.*

P. 85, l. 394 : Qu'*il* viennent au grenier d'usure redoublés

P. 87-108 : The *Hymne de l'hyver* is followed by the *Eglogue* and after this comes the *Elegie au seigneur Baillon.*

P. 88, l. 10 : Decouppé par morceaux, & par *tanues* roüelles, (a different misprint from that mentioned by Laumonier).

[56]

P. 90, l. 61 : Qui les Antres *avoient* pour maisons tapissées, (misprint).

P. 91, l. 82 : Mais tant plus est suivy *moins il* se laisse prendre,

P. 93, l. 5 : De là vous deviendrés plus grasses & plus belles, (no misprint).

P. 94, l. 23 : Nous sommes arrivés *dedans* l'Antre sacré

P. 95, l. 35-36 :

> *Me combatent chés moy, mais l'effroyable* peur
> *Se campe la premiere, &* veinq toujours mon cueur.

P. 96, l. 41-65, instead of these twenty-five lines, the nine which follow :

> *Et bien que la saison de ce plaisant Autonne*
> *Qui de chault & de froid ensemble s'assaisonne,*
> *Comme un Printemps soit douce, & que la vive ardeur*
> *De l'Esté ja passé, & la proche froideur*
> *De l'Hyver ne defend que l'herbe ne verdoye,*
> *   Bien que le bon Bachus dedans sa cuve ondoye,*
> *Boullonnant escumant, ayant les pieds tachés*
> *Les mains & tout le front de raisins écachés:*
> *   Si est-ce que cela* non plus ne me contente,

P. 97, l. 68 : *Souflé* dessus les fleurs la neige & les glaçons,

P. 97, l. 73 : Qui *tous sçavent* joüer des douces Cornemuses,

P. 99, l. 110 : Tous deux nous menerons nos beufs *en* pastourage,

P. 100, l. 138-141 :

> Me rebaiser *le sein,* la bouche, & les oreilles,
> *Me rompre ma chemise, & me taster le* sein,
> Que j'aurois & d'œillets & de roses tout plein,
> Pour *getter sur le* tien, qui meintenant pommelle,

P. 101, l. 155-156 :

> Or *à Dieu* Marion, ma chanson & le jour,
> *Je suis las de chanter, & non lassé d'*Amour.

P. 102, l. 165 : *Voicy le propre jour, ce me semble, & l'*année,

P. 102, l. 179-180 :

> M'a choisy pour amy : hyer mesme *Caton,*
> *Qui a les yeux brunets, & poignant le teton,*

P. 102, l. 184 : Aveque son present *se donne à toy* aussy,

P. 103, l. 191 : Les buissons porteront *des* œillets rougissans,

P. 103, l. 196-199 :

> *A la ligne tiré, qu'*un rude sauvageau,
> D'Autant qu'*une Chevre est plus qu'un Chevreau pelue,*
> *D'autant qu'un fille est des amans mieux voulue*
> *Qu'une vefve: & d'autant que l'Aurore* qui luit

P. 103, l. 201 : D'autant ma Janeton dessur *toutes* pucelle,

P. 104-106, l. 211-250 are lacking.

P. 106, l. 261 : De l'ardeur du Soleil *non plus* je me soucye,

P. 107, l. 273 : Ne *repose* jamais, & jamais ne s'alente,

P. 108, l. 291 : Que les vers me sont doux, voyre autant que *les* yeux,

P. 110, l. 22-23 :

> Avant que leur *beauté* par le chaut ne se passe.
> Bref ce jeune pasteur est tout *gaillard &* beau

P. 111, l. 46 : Et la rend comme il veut joyeuse *ou* offencée.

P. 116, l. 145 : Ayant la hache au poing, luy fis lascher la prise (no misprint).

P. 116, l. 154 : Dessoubs un *Pastoureau* si vilement s'abaisse : (there is perhaps an error in Laumonier's critical apparatus).

P. 123, l. 310 : Dittes *leurs* que d'odeurs son corps ne se peut oindre,

P. 135, l. 205 : Ses cheveux sont plus courts *qui* de coustume : & somme (misprint).

P. 136, l. 230 : Dont le cueur n'est flechy par la *priere* humaine.

P. 137, l. 244 : Et je croy qu'icy bas *il est* aussi de vous :

P. 139, l. 290 : Et mal caut, je *jette* sur elle ma lumiere,

P. 141, l. 338 : Reveille la vertu & ton cueur magnanime, (not necessarily a misprint).

Between pages 144 and 145, titlepage: *Le second livre* [. . .]

P. 149, l. 50 : Et des mains & des pieds & de *nerfs* il s'efforce

P. 151, l. 89 : J'approche & *le* decouppe, & comme je m'arreste, (misprint).

P. 159, l. 203 : Si je tenois un jour de sur l'herbe *ma mye*

P. 160, l. 233 : Seul je ne sens d'*amour* les fleches trop cruelles, (Laumonier may have mistranscribed the text).

P. 161, l. 240 : Aguestes le tropeau qui par l'herbe me suyt (no misprint).

P. 163, l. 270 : Qui passent en douceur les douceurs *de* avettes : (misprint).

P. 164, l. 27 : Tournent *leur* lumieres belles,

P. 167, l. 71 : *Que* me tient (no misprint).

P. 182, l. 209 : *Presque* un seul Montluc esloigné d'avarice (misprint).

P. 191, l. 45 : Sur le haut de sa coche *où* je voudrois reluire (misprint).

P. 196, l. 47 : Ny *prés* ny bois son *malheur* ne console,

P. 198, l. 84 : Errer ainsi que Déle : & que tu *eusses* (misprint).

P. 202, l. 50 : misprint in Laumonier's edition : "& *et* si belle."

P. 206, l. 18 : *Au doux labeur* de la Muse,

P. 209, l. 24 : D'avoir un jour de *leur* maux delivrance :

P. 213, l. 134 : De moy *c*'est fait le Seigneur & le Roy, (misprint).

P. 227, l. 83 : Ou si vostre bel œil ne faisoient leur devoir, (no misprint).

P. 233, l. 75 : Car si c'est bien aymer toujours penser en *elle*

P. 233, l. 77 : Ne songer ne *penser* & ne rever sinon

P. 236, l. 131 : Qui par armes *on* fait aux autres peuples honte : (misprint).

P. 236, l. 144 : *Es* bien ny des thresors : mais en la suffisance,

P. 237, l. 164 : Je vaincray le Destin d'*un* amour importune, (misprint).

P. 241, l. 33 : Ou *dedans* son bouclier, une recognoissance,

P. 243 : at the end of *Le second livre* is an *Extraict du privilege du Roy* identical to that printed in *Le premier livre*, including even the words, "faire imprimer, Le premier livre."

Between pages 243 and 244, titlepage, *Le troisieme livre* [. . .]

P. 248, l. 49 : *Pour emmener* mon cueur *avecques* luy pour vous voir ("avecques" is doubtless a misprint for "avec").

P. 249, l. 77 : Je sens par leur *discords* deux effets dedans moy,

P. 250, l. 103 : *Autonne* les raisins & l'Yver la froidure :

P. 253, l. 54 : Dont *d'un chacun gaignés* l'affection :

P. 254, l. 63 : Qui fuit le jour, & *dans* l'ame grossiere (misprint).

P. 256, title : *Discours amoureux* (only).

P. 262, l. 122 : Et que *tes volontés* estoient soubs le tombeau.

P. 265, l. 177 : Il me plaist bien encor mon *cueur* te descouvrir, (Laumonier's assumption that this is a misprint is gratuitous).

P. 266, l. 205 : *Dans ces* vergers de Cypre à Mars son bien chery,

P. 269, l. 289 : Dessoubs la grand *forests* des Myrthes ombrageux, (misprint).

P. 273, l. 391 : Ce pendant *tes* parens qui trespassé le virent (misprint).

P. 276, l. 470 : Et ne nous *laisse* rien sinon que le regret (misprint).

P. 280, l. 56 : *Se* monde fut conduit sans prevoyance aucune. (misprint.)

P. 283, l. 128 : misprint in Laumonier.

P. 285, l. 23 : Comme *une* image fait de bronze ou de metal,

P. 290, l. 143 : Et la rechante aux vens, & *ce* dit bien heureux (misprint).

P. 291, l. 154 : S'impriment dans l'esprit *de nouveau ramassés.*

P. 299, l. 7 : A moy qui le Soldat *aux combats* animé,

P. 302, *Extraict du privilege du Roy*, identical to that of *Le premier livre* except that, this time, the imprimatur has the words, "faire imprimer Le Troisième livre."

P.S. Since I wrote this article, M. Raymond Lebègue has checked Laumonier's text against the copy of "C" in the Bibliothèque de l'Institut and has very kindly sent me his findings : "Il faut corriger le texte fautif de Laumonier : lire, p. 11, l.171, suyvant ; p. 61, v. 327, Le palais ; p. 88, v. 10, apparat critique, tanues ; p. 136, v. 230, la priere humaine (donc supprimer l'apparat critique) ; p. 227, v. 83, supprimer l'apparat critique. Mais Laumonier me semble avoir raison de corriger *elle* par *celle*, p. 233, v. 75 ; p. 249, v. 77, la seconde édition porte, comme la première, discords."

THE HIDDEN MEANING OF RONSARD'S
HYMNE DE L'HYVER

Malcolm C. Smith

---

1. *The advantages of "veiling"*

RONSARD SEVERAL TIMES EXPRESSED the view that the proper way
for a poet to communicate truths is not by expounding them
directly, but by enveloping them in a veil of fiction. [1] The notion
that the literal sense of the fictions of the poets conceals a deeper
edifying moral meaning was frequently propagated and well
understood in Ronsard's time and earlier. [2] The advantages of the
poetic use of untruths to convey deeper moral truth are considerable. A first advantage is that veiling the truth in fiction has a
very venerable tradition, and to write that way is to join the
company of illustrious classical authors: Ronsard stresses in
the *Hymne de l'Hyver* that when he veils his message in fables,
he is following the example of Hesiod and Homer (ll. 70-80). [3]

---

[1] A masterly article by I. Silver includes a survey of Ronsard's
statements on this subject: see "Ronsard's Theory of Allegory: The
Antinomy between Myth and Truth," *Kentucky Romance Quarterly*, XVIII
(1971), 363-407, especially pp. 383-394.

[2] See especially the article cited above and the studies there mentioned. In addition, I have learned much on the subject from H. Rahner,
Greek Myths and Christian Mystery (London, 1963); D. P. Walker, *The
Ancient Theology, Studies in Christian Platonism from the Fifteenth to
the Eighteenth Century* (Ithaca, 1972), especially chapter I, "Orpheus the
theologian," pp. 22-41; G. Demerson, *La Mythologie classique dans
l'œuvre lyrique de la Pléiade*, Travaux d'Humanisme et Renaissance, 119
(Genève, 1972); T. Cave, "Ronsard's mythological universe," in *Ronsard
the Poet*, ed. T. Cave (London, 1973), pp. 159-208; and on the use to
which allegories were put, F. A. Yates, *The French Academies of the
Sixteenth Century*, Studies of the Warburg Institute, 15 (London, 1947),
especially chapter XI, "The Academies and court entertainments: the
Ballet comique de la Reine," pp. 236-274.

[3] This *Hymne* is found in volume XII of Paul Laumonier's critical

Secondly, a veiled message is psychologically easy to accept, since the reader is invited to discern moral truth for himself rather than being presented with dogmatic assertions. Thirdly, the message becomes an object of awe: Ronsard insisted that "veiling" is a divine invention designed to prevent sacred mysteries being too easily understood and consequently despised.[4] Fourthly, an esoteric communication incites interest and curiosity: Ronsard said that this is one reason why he veiled his message,

> A fin que le vulgaire ait desir de chercher
> La couverte beauté dont il n'ose approcher.   (ll. 77-78)

Fifthly, an appealing fable can bring moral truth within the intellectual reach of simple folk, as Ronsard pointed out in the *Abbregé de l'Art poëtique françois*:

Car la Poësie n'estoit au premier aage qu'une Theologie allegoricque, pour faire entrer au cerveau des hommes grossiers par fables plaisantes & colorées les secretz qu'ilz ne pouvoyent comprendre, quand trop ouvertement on leur descouvroit la verité.   (XIV, 4)

A sixth advantage is that a poem with more than one level of meaning can be enjoyed on the literal level alone even if the deeper meanings are not discerned. A seventh benefit is that the veil of allegory can conceal allusive references to matters which in a given social climate it would not have been politic to discuss openly. Finally, allegorical poems may refer to contemporary events but at the same time the moral truths which they offer transcend the ephemeral and appeal to an eternal audience.

The fact that Ronsard was certainly aware of many of these advantages of allegory, and perhaps aware of all of them, makes it at least probable that veiled meanings are to be discerned in his own poetry.

---

edition, pp. 68-86. All references here to Ronsard's work are to this edition.

[4] Ronsard made this point in an *Elegie à J. Grevin* of 1561 (XIV, 196), in the *Hymne de l'Hyver* (XII, 71-72) and in a *Discours à Monsieur de Cheverny*, first published in 1584 (XVIII 96-97). Louis Le Caron attributed this view to Ronsard in *Les Dialogues* (Paris, 1556; B. M. 8409 e 1, 132vo).

2. *Discerning the hidden sense*

Ronsard does not content himself with pointing out advantages of veiling: he gives several examples of ways in which fables of antiquity which he uses in his own poetry may be interpreted morally. His earliest expositions of such hidden meanings may have been prompted by criticisms of the "paganism" of his early poetry. [5] These earliest explanations are found in the *Hymnes* of 1555 and 1556: in the *Hercule chrestien* (the most famous case), Ronsard tries to show that the legends of Hercules are simply prophecies of events in the life of Christ (VIII, 207-223). But Ronsard gives explanations of many other fables. The torments of the mythological underworld, he claims in the *Hymne de la Philosophie,* represent the restlessness of the greedy or ambitious man (VIII, 100). [6] The names of the pagan gods, he maintains in the *Hymne de la Justice,* simply depict the various aspects of the nature of the one true God:

> Car Jupiter, Pallas, Apollon, sont les noms
> Que le seul DIEU reçoit en meintes nations
> Pour ses divers effectz que l'on ne peut comprendre,
> Si par mille surnoms on ne les fait entendre.   (VIII, 69) [7]

The fable of the Harpies who spoil Phineas's food is not just an intriguing story: it is, Ronsard explains in the *Hymne de Calaïs, et de Zethes,* a warning to monarchs against the depredations of greedy courtiers (VIII, 291).

It is not only in the *Hymnes* of 1555 and 1556 that Ronsard gives explanations of fables. In *Le Pin,* a poem published in 1569, he claims that the story of Atys, who castrated himself to join the

[5] Some of the attacks on Ronsard's "paganism" are surveyed by M. Raymond, *L'Influence de Ronsard sur la poésie française (1550-1585),* nouv. éd., Travaux d'Humanisme et Renaissance, 73 (Genève, 1965), I, 329-357.

[6] A likely source for this is a passage in Lucretius' *De rerum natura,* III, 978-1023. A survey of passages in which Ronsard interprets the torments described in classical mythology as representations of guilt and remorse is found in I. Silver, "Ronsard's Ethical Thought," *Bibliothèque d'Humanisme et Renaissance,* XXIV (1962), 88-92.

[7] Ronsard made the same point later in the *Abbregé de l'Art poëtique françois* (XIV, 6) and in the posthumously published preface to the *Franciade* (XVI, 345). The argument has a very venerable tradition: see especially the chapter by D. P. Walker cited in n. 2 above.

devotees of Cybele, teaches that a philosopher must cut himself off from worldly pleasures to cultivate philosophy (XV, 178-185). Ronsard's contemporary biographer Binet cites allegorical interpretations of the *Franciade* of 1572, which he says Ronsard pointed out to him; [8] and Ronsard himself notes in an *Epistre au lecteur* that in this epic "comme presque en tous autres Poëtes," Juno represents "... une maligne necessité qui contredit souvent aux vertueux" (XVI, 10). A final example: in a *Discours à Monsieur de Cheverny,* first published in 1584, Ronsard recalls that Jupiter chose two privy councilors, Minos and Tantalus: Tantalus rashly revealed Jupiter's secrets to men and was thrust into the underworld. Minos however was discreet and reliable. That story, says Ronsard, is not literally true: it must be interpreted as a commentary on the relationship between a monarch and his servants (XVIII, 97-98). [9]

The purpose of fables was not to bury the truth but to propagate it. The fictional veil does conceal the body of doctrine, but it also indicates its shape. That Ronsard sometimes actually shows how some poems of his may be interpreted allegorically proves that those poems at least have such meanings. Moreover, it is virtually certain that veiled meanings exist in a great many poems in which Ronsard does not refer to the theory of "veiling" at all. [10] After all, the New Testament has very many parables but only exceptionally is a given parable accompanied by an explanation of its hidden sense. The essence of such teaching is that it demands the sensitive participation of the recipient of the message, and if the author were to give more than occasional necessary guidelines he would defeat his whole object. Ronsard then was at pains to educate his reader to discern hidden meanings.

[8] C. Binet, *La Vie de P. de Ronsard,* ed. P. Laumonier (Paris, 1910), p. 41 (variant C). A contemporary Reformer interpreted parts of this poem as a veiled attack upon the Court: see below, n. 26.

[9] The whole poem (pp. 96-105) is interesting for Ronsard's adaptation of fables. Ronsard hints that Cheverny, to whom the poem is dedicated, is represented by Minos and the king by Jupiter. One wonders, therefore, whether Tantalus designates any individual!

[10] See the list which I. Silver has published in "Ronsard's Theory of Allegory," p. 394, n. 124, and his more detailed survey of some passages, pp. 394-403.

3. *The background to the* Hymne de l'Hyver

The theory and practice of veiling belongs with a particular kind of poetry. One need not in general look for veiled meanings in the polemical *Discours* against the Reformers in which Ronsard overtly engages in political and religious controversy: in these poems (which, in so far as they are not "fictional," are not in the strict traditional sense "poems" at all), Ronsard's use of fables is sparse, and the meaning almost invariably clear. In the *Hymnes*, on the other hand, the fictional content is considerable, the sense often arcane, and as we have already seen, statements about "veiling" and examples of its use are quite commonly found. In the *Hymne de l'Hyver*, an edifying mythological story about an abortive revolt against Jupiter's authority, Ronsard expounds the theory of veiled meanings and says that this poem has such meanings. Obviously, he was anxious that the concealed meaning should be discerned. But he does not say what that meaning is, so the poem evidently contains material which Ronsard was reluctant to convey openly. The poet's contemporaries would have seen the message and understood the need for it to be veiled. For the modern reader, some exploration of the circumstances of the poem's composition is necessary.

Ronsard published the *Hymne de l'Hyver* in the autumn of 1563 (XII, vi-viii). The first civil war had recently ended, and in April 1563, Ronsard had written a long reply to accusations which Reformers had made against him when he defended the Roman Catholic cause before and during the war: this reply bears the title *Responce aux injures et calomnies, de je ne sçay quels Predicans, & Ministres de Geneve* (XI, 109-179). But the *Responce aux injures* had not silenced Ronsard's adversaries, and he defended himself again in a long *Epistre au lecteur par laquelle succinctement l'Autheur respond à ses calomniateurs* (XII, 3-24). This *Epistre* serves as a preface to the *Recueil de nouvelles poësies*, where it is immediately followed by the four *Hymnes* on the seasons. It is helpful here to summarize the *Epistre*, since it reveals some of Ronsard's main preoccupations and is his own introduction to the *Recueil de nouvelles poësies*.

(i) This book, the *Recueil de nouvelles poësies*, contains, says Ronsard, *nouvelles compositions, toutes differentes de stille et d'argument de celles que durant les troubles j'avois mises en lumiere.* The poems (he adds) which I published during the civil wars were *un peu mordantes . . . & faites contre la modestie de mon naturel.*

(ii)   But I had to write those polemical poems to show the Reformers who wrote against me that they are merely *jeunes aprantis.* Perhaps I am boastful, but my achievements are something to boast about.

(iii)   There are two kinds of poetry, and I can claim to have eclipsed my adversaries in both : that is, *Quand j'ay voulu escrire de Dieu* and *Quand j'ay voulu parler des choses plus humaines & plus basses, de l'amour, de la victoire des Roys . . .*

(iv)   I write in praise of eminent men if they are virtuous, and certainly not, as my enemies have suggested, because I am anyone's hireling.

(v)   I am content with my lot, following the ideal of constancy praised by Horace :

> Si fractus illabatur orbis
> Impavidum ferient ruinae. [11]

(vi)   I know I have made a lot of poetasters jealous of my renown — but their proliferating attacks upon me are a *tesmoignage de ma vertu.*

(vii)   Some of my adversaries are sincere Reformers writing with a good conscience. Others are atheists who shelter in the fold of the Reformers. *Je ne puis approuver ces meschantes ames* [the atheists], *& loue grandement ceux* [the Reformers] *qui sont fermes en leur religion.*

(viii)   The poetasters have implied, but falsely, that I spoke disrespectfully of princes and noblemen.

(ix)   I would write against some of my adversaries were I not restrained by *le commandement des plus Grands qui ont expressement deffendu les libelles . . .; dorenavant je me tairay pour obeyr à ceux qui ont puissance sur ma main, & sur ma volonté.*

[11] *Carmina,* III, iii, 7-8.

Clearly, therefore, at the time he published his *Recueil de nouvelles poësies,* Ronsard was still deeply concerned with issues raised in his polemic with the Reformers: in the *Epistre* which presents his "new" and "different" poems, he is at pains to refute allegations that the Reformers have made. "But now," he says, "contentious literature has been forbidden and I will refrain from such writing."

This highly combative *Epistre* is followed by the four *Hymnes* on the seasons. These mythological poems certainly bear out Ronsard's claim that he is writing a different kind of poetry from his recent polemical pamphlets. Nevertheless, echoes of his recent controversies may be discerned in the *Hymne de l'Esté* where (ll. 7-20) he berates his mediocre disciples (cf. *Responce aux injures,* ll. 1035-1045) and in the *Hymne de l'Automne* where (ll. 1-76) he stresses that his poetry is divinely inspired, that he loves the simple life and that he has no great wealth (cf. *Responce aux injures,* ll. 847-898, 531-541, 968-974). But it is in the fourth and last of the "seasonal" *Hymnes* that most echoes are to be found.

4. *Ronsard's preliminary remarks in the* Hymne de l'Hyver

The *Hymne de l'Hyver* contains an introductory section (ll. 1-80) and a narration (ll. 81-398) of Winter's revolt against Jupiter. The introductory section has some thinly veiled and relatively mild references to Ronsard's recent controversies. Ronsard affirms that he is a respected and venerated poet. Loved by monarchs and revered by the people, dreaded by his enemies, he is a philosopher armed with virtue. Leaves torn from his laurel crown by young and disloyal disciples wither at once (ll. 1-42). Philosophy, Ronsard continues (ll. 43-80), is of two kinds, that which explores divine mysteries and that which is concerned with human affairs. The findings of philosophy are presented to the people in a veiled manner, so that truth will inspire both curiosity and respect. This *Hymne* is written in the same way.

Certain elements in this introductory section call for explanation. Lines 15-16 ("Il est soudain aymé des seigneurs & des Princes, / Il marche venerable au milieu des provinces") are probably Ronsard's reply to the Reformers' charge that he had slandered their leader, Prince Condé (and thereby incurred the wrath of a government now bent on promoting reconciliation).[12] Ronsard's assertion of his own constancy and self-assurance (ll. 21-26) is a clear echo of passages in the *Epistre* (ll. 77-93; cf. 251-256, 281). The attack on "Ces jeunes aprentis deloyaux à leur maistre" (l. 27) is directed almost certainly at Jacques Grévin, a young poet whose early work had been commended by Ronsard but who, it seems, had recently published the most scurrilous of the attacks upon him: the actual phrase *jeunes aprantis* is found also in the *Epistre* (l. 14, and cf. l. 118).[13] Ronsard's statement that leaves plucked from his laurel crown die instantly is almost certainly a deprecation of pamphlets against him, especially the *Palinodies,* skillful adaptations of his own text published by the Reformers under his name.[14] Ronsard had very recently, in the *Responce aux injures* (ll. 13-16, 59-62, 1035-1042) and in the *Epistre* (ll. 312-319), attacked his adversaries' plagiarism of him. The distinction between divine science (ll. 43-58) and human science (ll. 59-70) echoes the *Remonstrance au peuple de France* published late in 1562 (XI, ll. 143-166) and the *Epistre* (ll. 30-50): Ronsard, like other Roman Catholic writers including Montaigne, sought to establish that divine revelation is not subject to refutation by human reason.

5. *The fable of Winter*

The narrative section of the *Hymne de l'Hyver* presents a fable, which may be summarized as follows. After Winter is born, he is shown to Jupiter who derides this hideous infant and throws him out of heaven. He eventually lands in Thrace, where Boreas cares

---

[12] Cf. the *Epistre* analyzed above, ll. 233-245, and the *Responce aux injures,* ll. 1059-1090; see also the *Continuation du discours des miseres,* XI, ll. 293-306, and the *Remonstrance au peuple de France,* XI, ll. 611-640, 677-710, 733-758.

[13] The attack on Ronsard has the title, *Le Temple de Ronsard où la legende de sa vie est briefvement descrite,* and Grévin is almost certainly the author of it: see F. Charbonnier, *La Poésie française et les guerres de religion (1560-1574)* (Genève, 1970), pp. 96-97, and L. Pinvert, *Jacques Grévin (1538-1570), Etude biographique et littéraire* (Paris, 1899), pp. 320-335.

[14] The *Palinodies,* adaptations of the *Elegie à Guillaume des Autels* and of the *Discours des miseres,* have been published by F. Charbonnier, *Pamphlets protestants contre Ronsard (1560-1577),* Bibliothèque littéraire de la Renaissance, nouv. sér., 11 (Paris, 1923), 24-59.

for him and goads him to make war on Jupiter (ll. 81-118). Boreas, in a harangue to Winter, appeals to his pride, mentions the allies who can be enlisted, and deplores Jupiter's errors in promoting the wrong gods to important jobs (ll. 119-158). Boreas's envoys enlist allies including the monsters of the underworld and the Titans. They assemble and camp in a cloud. The stars warn the gods, and Jupiter has his army assembled: it is attacked and almost defeated (ll. 159-234), Jupiter bribes Night to delay her course and to ask Sleep to overwhelm Winter. Night does this and Mercury captures Winter and brings him in chains to Jupiter (ll. 235-306). Juno persuades Jupiter to be merciful to Winter. A peace treaty is announced, and Winter is invited to Juno's banquet: the plates have engravings of Jupiter's past victories over the Titans. Jupiter declares that it is for the sake of peace that he is releasing Winter and allowing him to live on Earth (ll. 307-398).

It is much more difficult to interpret this fable than the thinly veiled autobiographical statements of the early part of the *Hymne*. But there are clues to the meaning. At the beginning of this story, Winter, when presented to Jupiter, is dressed in a lamb's clothing. Such apparel belongs, according to a well-known biblical text, to wolves and false prophets: Ronsard had used biblical, pastoral imagery against the Reformers before. [15] Is Winter then an allegorical portrayal of the Reformed Church? The description of him which follows (ll. 95-99) — "rechigné, pensif, & solitaire" — is certainly comparable to Ronsard's repeated caricatures of the ministers of the Reformed Church (cf., for example, *Remonstrance*, ll. 195-204).

The identification of Winter with the Reformed Church is now given very strong confirmation by a key passage (ll. 119-158) which echoes the theme, language and structure of Ronsard's account, in the *Remonstrance au peuple de France* (ll. 269-312), of the genesis of the Reformed Church. In each of these passages (too long, unfortunately, to be cited here, but readily accessible), Ronsard presents a tempter (the monster Opinion in the *Remonstrance* and Boreas in the *Hymne de l'Hyver*) who seduces his victim (respectively Luther and Winter) by exploiting his pride and ambition (*Remonstrance*, ll. 272-276; *Hymne de l'Hyver*, ll. 119-123), by citing powerful allies who can be mustered (*Re-*

---

[15] The warning against wolves in lamb's clothing is in *Mt.* VII, 15. For Ronsard's use of biblical imagery, see the *Remonstrance*, ll. 425-426, 443-446.

monstrance, ll. 304-306; *Hymne de l'Hyver,* l. 124) and by offering specious motives for revolt (ll. 227-286 and 131-135 respectively). The motives for rebellion which Boreas gives Winter tally with those which Ronsard listed in his overt poems against the Reformation and elsewhere. Thus, Boreas points out to Winter that Jupiter gives top jobs in heaven to the wrong gods, and favors foreigners to the detriment of his own kith and kin (ll. 131-135). [16] Boreas's speech to Winter ends, as Opinion's speech to Luther also had, with an exhortation to militancy (ll. 144-158; cf. *Remonstrance,* ll. 295-312).

The sequel to the temptation in the *Hymne de l'Hyver* also echoes the *Remonstrance au peuple.* Boreas raises allies in all quarters (ll. 159-180), just as the revolt of Luther led to uproar in all countries (*Remonstrance,* ll. 323-336 and cf. *Discours des miseres,* XI, ll. 155-158). Among these allies of Winter are the Titans: these rebels against Jupiter had often been used by Ronsard and other Roman Catholics as symbols of the Reformers. [17] Battle is joined, and Winter and his allies almost defeat Jupiter's forces, commanded by Mars. Mars may represent the recently assassinated Duke of Guise, one of the leaders of the royal army during the civil war, who had very frequently been compared by poets to Mars on account of his military prowess, most notably after his capture of Calais in 1558. [18] Ronsard may be suggesting here that it is futile to attempt to defeat the Reformed Church by force, an opinion which he had eloquently advanced in 1560, before the war, in his *Elegie à Guillaume des Autels,* and one which accorded with the postwar policy of reconciliation adopted by the government. [19]

When military force fails to quell the rebellion, Jupiter adopts another strategy which is much more intelligent and successful:

---

[16] Cf. *Remonstrance,* ll. 407-414, and the *Compleinte à la Royne mere du Roy* (XII, 181, ll. 179-184). Interestingly, Ronsard was never content merely to condemn the Reformers: each of his three principal refutations of their teaching is accompanied by an analysis of the ills which gave rise to the Reformation (see the *Elegie à Guillaume des Autels* of 1560, the *Remonstrance,* and the *Responce aux injures*).

[17] See F. Joukovsky-Micha, "La guerre des dieux et des géants chez les poètes français du seizième siècle (1500-1585)," *Bibliothèque d'Humanisme et Renaissance,* XXIX (1967), 71-73.

[18] See G. Demerson, *La Mythologie classique,* pp. 533-534.

[19] Ronsard's endorsement of this policy is perhaps indicated also in the greeting to Winter with which the *Hymne de l'Hyver* ends.

Winter is overwhelmed by Sleep. This may allude to the government's success in inducing Prince Condé to sign a peace treaty which inhibited the growth of the Reformed Church. [20] And Mercury leads Winter, in chains, to Jupiter. Mercury may well designate the brother of the Duke of Guise, the Cardinal of Lorraine, who had frequently been compared by poets to Mercury on account of his eloquence, an eloquence which, according to many contemporaries, including Ronsard, kept many people within the fold of the traditional Church. [21] Then, in a patent reference to government policy, Ronsard has Juno, whom in earlier poems he had identified with Catherine de Médicis, [22] beseech Jupiter to treat the defeated rebels with moderation: "Laisse les moy gaigner par douce courtoisie" (l. 324). Peace is therefore agreed upon: a reference to the recent agreement between the government and the Reformers. [23] Ronsard wrote several poems about rebellion against Jupiter and in almost all of them the defeated rebels are severely punished. The very unusual twist given to the story in the *Hymne de l'Hyver,* in which Winter and his cohorts are treated exactly as the government was treating the defeated Reformers, strongly confirms the impression that the poem is allegorical.

But Ronsard is quick to add that peace with the Reformers does not mean capitulation to them. At the banquet which celebrates peace, the vessels used remind the feasters of Jupiter's

[20] See E. Lavisse, *Histoire de France depuis les origines jusqu'à la Révolution,* VI, i, by J. H. Mariéjol (Paris, 1904), 73-75.

[21] For comparisons of the Cardinal of Lorraine to Mercury, see Ronsard's *Hymne du treschrestien roy de France Henry II. de ce nom* (VIII, 27-28), and Demerson, *op. cit.,* pp. 533-534. Ronsard praises the Cardinal's preaching in the *Hymne de Charles de Lorraine* (IX, 47-48), and in the *Elegie à Guillaume des Autels* (X, 361). For other tributes to his preaching, see H. O. Evennett, *The Cardinal of Lorraine and the Council of Trent, A Study in the Counter-Reformation* (Cambridge, 1930), pp. 18-20, 113, 229, 307.

[22] Ronsard identifies Catherine de Médicis and Juno in an ode *A la Roine* (VII, 36), and in the *Hymne du treschrestien roy de France Henry II. de ce nom* (VIII, 30). He was not the only poet to do so: see Demerson, *op. cit.,* pp. 533, 534, 537, n. 83. In fact, the most notable persons at Court were each conventionally identified with some god: see E. Bourciez, *Les Mœurs polies et la littérature de cour sous Henri II* (Paris, 1886), II, ii, "L'Olympe nouveau," pp. 176-202.

[23] The "Edit de Pacification d'Amboise" is dated 19 March 1563: see Lavisse, *op. cit.,* p. 74.

past victories over the Titans: a tacit reminder to the pardoned rebels of the fate that may await any subsequent insurrection. Ronsard is saying that the Reformers, who have defied the traditional Church and the government by starting the civil war, have not been exonerated but have been forgiven by an act of mercy on the part of Catherine de Médicis.

6. *The poet of princes*

This poem gives a revealing insight into Ronsard's relations with the government. It is dedicated to Jacques Bourdin, a secretary of state who had negotiated the capitulation of some of the Reformers' mercenaries and was shortly to be employed by the government in peace talks with the English. [24] The *Hymne de l'Hyver,* reflecting as it does the official policy of reconciliation, may well have been published with the support of the government, especially as the prefatory *Epistre* has a deferential bow towards the "plus Grands qui … ont puissance sur ma main, & sur ma volonté." Ronsard's polemical poems, too, had probably enjoyed official approval: the individual poem titled *Discours des miseres de ce temps,* published in 1562, had been dedicated to Catherine de Médicis. The polemical poems had contained overt and occasionally virulent denunciations of the Reformers: the *Hymne de l'Hyver,* on the other hand, is allegorical, restrained and, without obsequiousness, conciliatory. The use of the allegorical method here admirably reflects the changed political situation. Ronsard is setting out firm and easily intelligible comment on contemporary events, and at the same time avoiding vituperative polemic which, as he pointed out in the *Epistre,* had been forbidden by the government. Obviously, the poet of princes had to reflect the changing policies of princes with sensitivity and skill. The government's practice of *détente* was very shortly to extend to foreign policy, and Ronsard was to respond by writing poems in praise of Queen Elizabeth I and her ministers — poems which themselves were later to be drastically altered in response to changing situations. [25]

---

[24] See N. M. Sutherland, *The French Secretaries of State in the Age of Catherine de Medici* (London, 1962), pp. 134, 143.

[25] See my article, "Ronsard and Queen Elizabeth I," *Bibliothèque d'Humanisme et Renaissance,* XXIX (1967), 93-119.

Indeed, one of these latter poems in praise of a minister of Elizabeth provides an interesting epilogue to our analysis of the *Hymne de l'Hyver*. In the *Elegie à seigneur Cecille*, Ronsard writes at the prompting of the French government, and again writes allegorically, urging forgiveness for the defeated Giants who clearly designate the defeated French Reformers — who had enjoyed English assistance. In this poem Ronsard adopts the same conciliatory stance towards England as he had in the *Hymne de l'Hyver* towards the French Reformers. Here again, however, he avoids obsequiousness by the strong implicit hint to Elizabeth's chief minister that assistance to French rebels is not appreciated by the French government (XIII, 159-170).

7. *Criteria for the interpretation of fables*

Clearly, if the *Hymne de l'Hyver* has the meanings suggested here, then there may be a great many poems by Ronsard containing allegorical references to contemporary situations. A Reformer interpreted parts of his *Franciade* of 1572 as a veiled attack upon Charles IX and Catherine de Médicis. [26] The existence of this contemporary interpretation of parts of the *Franciade* reminds us that a wealth of contemporary political meaning may lie beneath the literal sense of many of Ronsard's poems. At the same time, the dubiousness of this particular interpretation serves as a warning to be circumspect. Speculation in this domain must be governed by a feeling for the intellectual climate, a familiarity with Ronsard's statements on the theory and practice of allegory, an awareness of the poet's personal convictions and of the controversies he was engaged in, a knowledge of the vicissitudes of the contemporary political and religious climate, a close scrutiny of individual poems and a sensitivity to possible relationships between one poem and another.

THE SOCIETY FOR THE HUMANITIES
CORNELL UNIVERSITY

---

[26] This interpretation is found in a dialogue by Nicolas Barnaud with the title, *Le Reveille-Matin des François et de leurs voisins, composé par Eusebe Philadelphe, cosmopolite*, published in 1573: see F. Charbonnier, *La Poésie française*, pp. 353-359, and K. Cameron, "Ronsard and Book IV of the *Franciade*," *Bibliothèque d'Humanisme et Renaissance*, XXXII (1970), 395-406.

A "LOST" PROTESTANT PAMPHLET AGAINST RONSARD

Ronsard considered that the numerous and highly vituperative pamphlets which the Reformers directed against him during and immediately after the first civil war were a most eloquent tribute to his prowess as a controversialist, and that posterity would look on them as such. In the *Epistre* which accompanied the *Recueil des nouvelles poësies* which he published in 1564, he wrote:

[...] je ne veux laisser à la postérité plus grand tesmoignage de ma vertu que les injures edentées, que ces poëtastres vomissent contre moy. Et pour une mesdisance je leur conseille d'en dire deux, trois, quatre, cinq, six, dix, vingt, trente, cent, mille, & autant qu'il en pourroit en toutes les caques des harangeres de petit Pont. [1]

Their mere existence in large numbers is indeed an implicit tribute to Ronsard. Moreover, these pamphlets contain occasional explicit testimony to the influence of his polemical poems: one Reformer acknowledges that Ronsard enjoys a "faveur envers le peuple bas" and another concedes that he has done more to refute the Reformers than all the theologians had been able to do: "Il a plus fait luy seul que toute la Sorbonne." [2] These pamphlets are also a key to the meaning of some specific passages in Ronsard's own poems, notably his very witty *Responce aux injures et calomnies de je ne sçay quels Predicans & Ministres de Geneve*. And some of the Reformers' invectives possess an intrinsic interest, notably *Le Temple de Ronsard où la legende de sa vie est briefvement descrite*, for its vigorous scurrility, and the *Apologie ou deffence d'un homme chrestien pour imposer silence aus sottes reprehensions de M. Pierre Ronsard* [...] for its clever deployment of erudition. A complete edition of these pamphlets, which were published in 1563 and 1564, has long been considered desirable: Edouard Tricotel suggested in 1875 that they should be edited by Blanchemain, [3] and Charbonnier suggested they be incor-

---

[1] This quotation is from the critical edition of Ronsard by Paul LAUMONIER (Société des Textes Français Modernes), XII, p. 9.

[2] These quotations are from *La polémique protestante contre Ronsard*, édition des textes avec introduction et notes par Jacques Pineaux (S.T.F.M.), Paris, 1973, p. 391 and 350 respectively.

[3] See E. TRICOTEL, "Un pamphlet latin contre Ronsard," *Bulletin du Bibliophile*, 1875 (p. 57-80), p. 59.

porated in Laumonier's critical edition of Ronsard. [4] Most of them have in fact been republished over the last hundred years or so (and some of them several times) but now they have been assembled by Jacques Pineaux in two volumes. M. Pineaux's very useful edition is prefaced by an admirably succinct introduction dealing in turn with the authorship of the various pamphlets, the views of the Reformers on contested issues, their charges against Ronsard, their opinions on the nature of poetry and the lives of the various authors of the pamphlets. [5]

One point which M. Pineaux does not touch upon and which could have been usefully examined is the genesis of Ronsard's dispute with the Reformers. This polemic did not appear out of nowhere during the first civil war : it had been simmering long before. Many Reformers (and indeed some members of his own faith) had from the beginning of Ronsard's career denounced him for writing poetry which they considered to be pagan or licentious or both. Very soon after the publication of Ronsard's *Odes* in 1550, Theodore Beza derided these poems in the preface to his *Abraham sacrifiant*, suggesting that Ronsard and other poets would be better employed writing religious verse. [6] And throughout the 1550s a succession of writers had appealed to Ronsard to devote himself to edifying subjects. Ronsard made many concessions to these critics : in some of the *Hymnes* of 1555 and 1556, for example, he spelled out the moral meanings which can be discerned beneath the literal meanings of the fables of the pagan poets ; and from 1558 onwards a considerable proportion of his poetry was christian in tone. But the objections continued unabated and finally, in his *Elegie à Loïs des Masures* of 1560, Ronsard gave vent to his indignation at this stream of hostile criticism. [7] Those Reformers therefore who in the pamphlets of 1563 and 1564 reproach Ronsard for the paganism and licentiousness which they discern in his poetry are following in a tradition, and repeating objections which Ronsard had long since done much to meet. It is helpful, when reading the texts collected by M. Pineaux, to bear in mind the long history of antipathy between Ronsard and his critics.

Another aspect of M. Pineaux's edition which calls for comment is his attribution of the various pamphlets. He attributes the *Remonstrance à la Royne* to André de Rivaudeau largely on the grounds that

---

[4] See F. CHARBONNIER, *Pamphlets protestants contre Ronsard (1560-1577)* (Bibliothèque Littéraire de la Renaissance), Paris, 1923, p. 1.

[5] See note 2 above. Earlier studies containing Reformers' invectives against Ronsard are the following : Blanchemain's edition of Ronsard's complete works (vol. VII, Paris, 1866, p. 87-94) ; F. FLEURET and L. PERCEAU, *Les satires françaises du XVIe siècle*, 2 v., Paris 1922, I, p. 84-96 ; A. DE ROCHAMBEAU, *La famille de Ronsart, recherches généalogiques, historiques et littéraires sur P. de Ronsard et sa famille*, Paris, 1868, p. 137-138, 142-172 ; E. TRICOTEL, "Vers satiriques contre Ronsard," *L'amateur d'autographes*, X 1872, p. 1-7 ; the same author's article cited above in note 3 ; C. READ, "Les défenses de Zamariel, de B. de Mont-Dieu et de F. La Baronie contre Pierre Ronsard," *Bulletin de la Société de l'Histoire du Protestantisme Français*, XXXVII, 1888, p. 578-602, 636-657 ; the same author's "Une réplique à Ronsard sur la réponse par lui faite aux défenses de Zamariel, Mont-Dieu et la Baronie, contre ses calomnies (1563)," published in the same *Bulletin*, XXXVIII, 1889, p. 130-140 ; P. PERDRIZET's *Ronsard et la Réforme*, Nancy, 1902, p. 149-163 ; and, most important of all, the book by Charbonnier cited in note 4 above.

[6] See Théodore DE BÈZE, *Abraham sacrifiant*, ed. K. Cameron, K. M. Hall & F. Higman (Textes Littéraires Français), Genève, 1967, p. 47-48.

[7] Many criticisms of Ronsard's "paganism" are cited by M. Raymond in *L'influence de Ronsard sur la poésie française (1550-1585)*, nouv. éd. (Travaux d'Humanisme et Renaissance, 73), Genève, 1965, chap xiii, "La doctrine de Ronsard et les poètes chrétiens", I, p. 329-357. The denunciations were much more numerous however than even M. Raymond's study indicates : I hope to publish some of them in due course and to show how Ronsard responded to such criticisms.

several passages in it have analogues, quite close it is true, in texts by
Rivaudeau. It would be legitimate to infer from the existence of
these analogues that the author of the *Remonstrance à la Royne* may
have read Rivaudeau, but it is not legitimate to infer from this that
he is Rivaudeau. M. Pineaux's reasons for attributing the *Réplique
de Lescaldin* to Bernard de Montméja seem to be that the initials of
the pseudonym "D. M. Lescaldin" may stand for "de Montméja"
and that the surname "fait songer à Escaldun (ou Escaldunac), nom
national des Basques" and Montméja may have had relations who
were Basques. This attribution seems very speculative. M. Pineaux's
rejection of the traditional view that Jacques Grévin collaborated in
the composition of *Le Temple de Ronsard où la legende de sa vie est
briefvement descrite* and his attribution of it to Florent Chrestien also
seems questionable. The evidence he gives is that Chrestien claimed
to have written about Ronsard's life and to have satirically "canonized"
him. But M. Pineaux's own quotations indicate only that Chrestien
may have had a hand in composing the *Temple* — or indeed in composing some other satirical biography of Ronsard which may be among
the many lost pamphlets against the poet : these quotations do not
exclude the possibility that Grévin collaborated in composing the
Temple, or even that he wrote it all. Ronsard's own attack on a
"jeune drogueur, de qui la vie ne sera pas mauvaise descrite" does
indeed seem, as Laumonier pointed out, to designate Grévin and to
echo the full title of the *Temple* : Ronsard moreover purged his works
of all references to Grévin and there is no reason to disbelieve the
statement in Binet's life of Ronsard that this purge was prompted
by the fact that Grévin helped write the *Temple*. It is worth noting,
incidentally, that Grévin attempted, in a passage of his *Response aux
calmonies de Guymara* of 1564, to exculpate himself of slandering
Ronsard — but the passage is so ambivalently worded (Grévin denies
writing certain of the works against Ronsard, while making no mention
of the *Temple*) that it only confirms that Grévin was in fact suspected
of having written against the poet. [8]

The list Ronsard gave of the pamphlets against him and
Charbonnier's bibliography of them make it plain that many still
remain to be rediscovered. [9] The text given here is of a pamphlet
which M. Pineaux was not able to locate : to the best of my knowledge
it is published here for the first time since 1563. Its titlepage reads as
follows :

REMONSTRANCE SUR LA DIVERSITÉ DES POËTES *de nostre temps,*
dont les uns s'addonnent à vérité, les autres à vanité.
Nouvellement imprimé, 1563.

This pamphlet is in the Houghton Library of Harvard University,
catalogued under "Ronsard," and the shelf mark is FC5 R6697
Sz 563rb. Although Ronsard's name is nowhere mentioned, he is
clearly the victim of this *Remonstrance*. It is, as the following summary
shows, in the tradition of those invectives which, even before
Ronsard's main controversy with the Reformers, reproached him on
the grounds of the allegedly pagan and licentious nature of his poetry.

---

[8] See PINEAUX's edition of the pamphlets, p. 99-102, 224-230 and 302-304 and
L. PINVERT, *Jacques Grévin (1538-1570), études biographique et littéraire*, Paris 1899,
p. 333.
[9] Ronsard's list is found in the critical edition, XII, p. 10 and Charbonnier's bibliography is in the book cited in note 4 above.

Lines 1 - 46 : Painters and poets both possess the ability to present their fictions in alluring colours.

47-90 : Among the ancient poets are some who offer "bonne discipline," "sentences notables" and "histoires memorables," while others purvey "fables, vanités, discours d'amour immondes." Similarly, some modern poets write divine songs in praise of God, others imitate the pagans.

91-136 : The christian poet feeds his mind on the holy scriptures, invokes God in his writing, looks to the holy Spirit to inspire him. He deplores idle chatter and deceit, is chaste in heart, word and life, adores one God, names the pagan gods only when he must and then without honouring them.

137-234 : The profane poet on the other hand consorts with vicious companions or goes to Mass to hear "un tas de beaux fatras de l'Eglise Romaine". He gives pre-eminence to the numerous gods of the pagans, since one god, according to him, could not govern everything. If the pagan gods do not hear his prayer, he appeals to the saints. He attributes the function of Providence to Destiny and Fortune, claims to have invented a new language (a reference to Ronsard's *Responce aux injures*, lines 1017-1026), and has a heart devoted to idleness.

235-282 : The followers of Epicurus and Zeno, when taught by saint Paul, could not understand his teaching and derided it : similarly, our poet, mocking what he cannot understand, rejects "la religion contraire à la Romaine"—but for the sake of appearances writes that a king must be virtuous (a reference to Ronsard's *Institution pour l'adolescence du Roy*), and that the church must be cleaned up.

283-330 : He has to flatter the pope and prelates to secure benefices to pay for his vices : pagans like him should be shunned.

331-422 : These spurious christians prop up the tottering edifice which the pope has designed, the Mass : but a gentle breeze is now blowing away this sordid building.

423-490 : As the Mass gets swept away, all error disappears with it. Reformers' literature gets disseminated (an interesting list of titles is given), the voice of the gospel is heard everywhere, the primitive state of the church is restored, and henceforth only one kind of poet will exist, the christian kind.

Ithaca, N. Y.   Malcolm C. SMITH

REMONSTRANCE
SUR LA DIVERSITE DES
Poëtes de nostre temps,
dont les uns s'addon-
nent à verité, les
autres à va-
nité.

Aucuns ont egalé les Poëtes & Peintres,
Parce qu'egalement ils traittent choses feintes,
Et qu'une liberté de farder toute chose,
Ou de la controuver, à tous deux se propose.
5   Le Peintre saura bien sur un tableau moysi
Estendre un beau pourtrait dans son cerveau choisi,
D'une chose pourrie en faire une nouvelle,
D'une defigurée en former une belle.
Ce n'est rien tout cela, il fait bien encor' mais,
10 Il fait mille animaux qui ne furent jamais.
Bref en ce spacieux terroir de controuver
Luy mesme ne sauroit ses forces esprouver,
Et si de ses coleurs les forces il sondoit,
Son esprit & son sens dans un gouffre fondroit.   [A 2 vo]
15   Son subjet & son fard divaguent comme l'onde,
Sans se pouvoir bourner dans le creux de ce monde.
Car par dessus les cieux voltige son audace,
Voulant de l'Eternel tantost peindre la face,
Tantost de Paradis la situation,
20 Puis descend en Enfer, lieu d'habitation
De Satan & des siens, & en fait pourtraiture :
Somme tout ce qu'il veut il depeint & figure.
    Les Poëtes aussi de leur part font de mesme,
Quand l'eguillon les poingt de leur fureur supreme.
25 Ils forgent des discours du creu de leurs cerveaux,
Et par leur plaisant fard nous les font trouver beaux.
Fables, inventions, vanitez, menteries,
Sont fruicts de leur labeur & de leurs metteries.
Leurs puantes amours, & leurs putains infames,
30 Semblent par leurs beaux vers pures & chastes femmes.
S'ils veulent appliquer leurs plumes à louange,
Ils feront transformer soudain le diable en ange.
Et si leur cueur chagrin à mesdire les mord,
Un ange ils descriront plus hideux que la mort.
35   Le compas de leurs vers decoulant par l'aureille,
Lié par motz dorez d'une grace pareille,
Leur couleur azuré, & leur hardie frase,
Donnent à leur subjet plaisant lustre & emfase.
Mais si ces beaux attours on oste de leurs vers,
40 Et que leurs dits à clair dedans & à l'envers   [A 3]
On voye de sens coy, incontinent le ris
Se rompra, d'avoir pris pour un beuf la souris.
Lors on egalera telle œuvre deffardée,
Au vil tableau qui a son image effacée.
45 Lors un front tout rideux avec un laid minoir
Apparoistra honteux sur un visage noir.

      Cependant toutesfois tous Poëtes n'ont pas
      Leur haut style accroupy sur ces inegaux pas.
      L'eage des vieux ayeulx en a porté des braves,
50   Qui en style pareil ont traitté choses graves,
      Qui ont des bonnes meurs enseigné la doctrine,
      Entremeslé leurs vers de bonne discipline,
      Leurs escris parsemé de sentences notables,
      Et qui ont poursuivy histoires memorables.
55   Comme en un beau verger au Printemps florissant
      L'aveille ça & là s'esgaye, en repaissant
      Les douces fleurs, naissans dessus la cheveleure
      Que la terre produit pour nostre nourriture :
      Des bonnes elle succe, avec son hameçon,
60   L'odorante liqueur, & saute la poyson
      Des plantes dont la fleur le froit venin respire :
      Ainsi dedans les bons Poëtes faut eslire
      Ce que sert pour chacun rendre meillieur ou sage,
      Et le tout appliquer à vertueux usage.
65   Mais il faut rejetter de ceux là les escris,
      Qui de folle fureur ayans leurs sens espris,
      N'ont rien puysé dedans leurs caballines ondes,
      Que fables, vanités, discours d'amours immondes.   [A 3ᵛᵒ]
      Noz ans si precieux ne nous sont pas donnez
70   Pour à leurs livres vains sans fruict estre addonnez.
      Le Seigneur qui nous doüe & d'esprit & de sens,
      Ne veut pas que si mal nous prodigeons noz ans.
      Ses dons il nous despart pour tout honneur luy rendre,
      Et à nostre prochain la main promptement tendre.
75   Or comme le vieux temps, doré d'un beau langage,
      Ses Poëtes livroit de bien divers partage,
      Car l'un pour son subjet choisissoit vanité,
      Et l'autre pour son lot embrassoit verité :
      Ainsi en nostre temps, riche de bons esprits,
80   Noz Poëtes ont fait bien differens escris.
      Les uns ont employé leurs doux & graves sons
      A louer l'Eternel, par divines chansons.
      Les autres imitans des vieux Payens les traces,
      Ont leurs vains argumens orné de belles graces.
85   Les uns veulent avoir leur liberté bournée,
      Et les autres la leur retiennent desbourdée.
      Ceux là traittent subjets qui nourrissent leurs ames,
      Ceux ci vont pourrissant en leurs objets infames
      Et pour te faire voir à l'œil leur difference,
90   Voy cy de leurs pourtraits la vive conference.
          Le Poëte Chrestien remply d'un sacré zele,
      En premier lieu se range en la trouppe fidelle.
      Il sert à Dieu vivant par tous les exercices
      De sa Religion, ennemye des vices.   [A 4]
95   Les nerfz de son esprit il tend en la lecture,
      Savourant le doux goust de la sainte Escriture.
      Fait servir à ce but les profanes autheurs,
      Et de la primitive Eglise les Docteurs.
      L'anchre de son salut, & sa justice seure,
100   En un seul Jesus Christ, non aillieurs, il asseure.
      S'il fait discours tissus par mesure ou en prose,
      Le nom du tout puissant il invoque & prepose,

Son esprit & son corps, & toute son essence,
Il tient & recognoit de sa toutepuissance.
105 Tous ses bons mouvemens & ses bonnes pensées,
Luy sont du saint Esprit estincelles sacrées.
Tout ce qu'il fait de bien, qu'il dit, ou qu'il escrit,
Luy sont dons precieux d'iceluy mesme Esprit.
Il recognoit de là les sciences humaines
110 Yssir, comme surgeons de celestes fontaines,
Icelles fait servir à sa profession,
Cheminant rondement en sa vocation.
Celuy qui tous ses biens luy moyenne & procure,
C'est Christ, restaurateur de l'humaine nature.
115 Il croit la providence, & que le souverain
Donne aux siens bien & mal, pour leur bien, de sa main.
Tous vains propos sans fruict, qui n'ont point d'edifice,
Et toute menterie, il repute pour vice,
Il est chaste de cœur, chaste en parole & vie,
120 Ne celebre qu'un Dieu, auquel seul il se fie.
Les noms des Dieux payens, parce que cela touche   [A 4vo]
L'honneur du Dieu vivant, il n'a point en sa bouche.
Et si à les nommer son propos le contraint,
Du moins avec honneur ne les nommera point.
125 Il n'a moins en horreur Apollon, Mars, Mercure,
Et telz autres faux dieux, de Satan geniture,
Que leur pere, par eux qui tonna des oracles,
Abusant les humains, comme par faux miracles.
Son esbat & plaisir sont chansons & cantiques,
130 Qui resonent de Dieu les honneurs autentiques.
Les tapis verdoyans de terre, & ses delices,
Luy font parmy les champs prendre maintz exercices.
Donnant tousjours louange au Pere de nature,
Qui sa force & bonté monstre en sa creature.
135 Bref les traces qu'il suit, la voye où il chemine,
Tesmoignent de son cœur une saine doctrine.
   Le Poëte profane est de contraire sorte :
L'assemblée où il va sont ceux de sa cohorte,
Qui pour rassasier leurs gousiers indomptez,
140 Ou bien pour assouvir leurs sales volontez,
S'assemblent en un lieu propre pour cest affaire.
Ou s'ils veulent les bons Catholicz contrefaire,
Ils s'en vont au monstier voir des bragardes Messes,
Dont ils paissent leur yeux, comme de leurs deesses.
145 Ou ils vont pour esbat ouyr, apres gousté,
Des Vespres que l'on dit le chant regringoutté.
Mais qui leur fait trouver ceste Messe si bonne ?
Le jeu du gobelet, qui leur Musique entonne.
Et puis joyeusement cependant le temps passe,   [B]
150 En avisant jouër le jeu de passe-passe.
Qui leur fait applaudir à l'invention vaine
D'un tas de beaux fatras de l'Eglise Romaine ?
Parce que tout cela est emprompt des Poëtes,
Desquels ils ont les dieux & les meurs en leurs testes.
155   Ce Poëte reclame en chacune matiere
Un Dieu particulier, de vertu peculiere.
Aux villes, aux fauxbourgs, aux bois, champs, & villages,
A la guerre, aux mestiers, aux arts, aux labourages,

160 Il donne dieux à part à tous, car il luy semble
Qu'un seul Dieu ne pourroit tout gouverner ensemble.
En recit belliqueux le Dieu des exercites
Marchera dessous Mars, à forces bien petites.
Si la victoire aux uns par glaive se despart,
Le Dieu victorieux n'y aura point de part.
165 Quelque cas composé de veine singuliere,
Ne sera pas infus du pere de lumiere.
Il en donra l'honneur à Minerve ou Mercure,
Ou à quelque autre Dieu de semblable facture.
Si, comme Solomon, il demande sagesse,
170 Vers Apollon tout droit il prendra son adresse.
S'il veut des biens avoir & riche devenir,
Il monte à Juppiter, pour ses dons obtenir.
Et s'il veut se veautrer en quelque turpitude,
Venus est son recours, son port, & son estude.
175 Pour le mal eschevir, ou le bien recevoir,
Il a dieux à foyson de special pouvoir.
Et si ces dieux ireux n'exaucent ses prieres,
Il trouvera de saints fort amples formilieres.
Et comme de tels dieux sont pleines ses paroles,
180 Son cœur est attourné aussi d'autant d'idoles.
De transporter l'honneur, où son cœur se propose,
Du Dieu fort & jaloux, ce luy est peu de chose.
Bref le grand Dieu vivant il tient en moindre estime,
Que le moindre des dieux que son cerveau machine.
185 Les langues, le sçavoir, l'engin, luy sont infus
Des neuf seurs, de Pallas, des Graces, de Phœbus.
De Bacchus il reçoit la liqueur qui l'enteste,
De Ceres la moisson. Il fait de tous la feste,
Soit en les perfumant d'encens & sacrifices,
190 Ou par vœus leur offrant de ses fruicts les primices.
Si ce n'est à ces dieux qu'il fait un tel hommage,
Au moins c'est à ces saints de mesme parentage.
Les Pontifes Romains, peres de tous les deux,
Forgent les saints ainsi comme ils faisoyent les dieux.
195 Ce Poëte empiegé aux fillets & aux toilles
De Clotho & ses seurs, & au flus des estoilles,
Machine en son cerveau ses Destins & Fortune,
Roulans tout l'univers que le ciel environne.
Il met dessous les pieds de l'aveugle deesse
200 Tout le monde & son bien, & l'invoque sans cesse.
Les causes des effets que ses sens poëtiques
Ne peuvent percevoir, luy sont Destins Stoiques.
Mais de Dieu tout puissant qui tout gouverne à point
Par sa mer de sagesse, il ne se souvient point.
205 Son titanique orgueil luy met en la cervelle,
De bastir derechef une Babel nouvelle.
Là regnant au milieu de ses confus ouvrages,
Il fait des mots nouveaux, & des nouveaux langages.
Les vieux il fait mouvoir, par inique puissance,
210 De son fief, & d'iceux passer recognoissance.
En façon que tous ceux qui ont l'art & le sens
De sçavoir bien parler, luy en doivent le cens.
Il remesle Chaos en sa masse premiere,
Mettant l'obscurité aveques la lumiere :

[B ᵛᵒ]

[B 2]

215 Et croit, tant il est fier, que son œuvre parfaitte,
    Par dessus le Soleil il haussera la teste.
        Son cueur qui va bouillant d'affection diverse,
    Parmy ses quatre humeurs à la nage traverse,
    Les reschauffant si fort, que la part plus liquide,
220 Exhalant en fumée, abandonne l'aride.
    Ceste exhalation luy monte en la cervelle,
    Et se meut par le cours de la Lune nouvelle.
    C'est là de ses humeurs la pure Entelechie,
    Qui l'esleve au sommet de toute frenesie.
225   L'autre humeur mybruslée au fond du cueur domine,
    C'est celle qui le fait de nature canine,
    Enflé, presompteux, & qui plustost s'attache
    Au vestement tout pur, qu'au sale & plein de tache.
        Mais ce cueur flottoyant en ceste lie humide,
230 Demeure cependant de pur sang du tout vuide,
    Qui le fait au labeur degenereux & lasche,
    Amy d'oysiveté, qui jamais ne le fache.   [B 2ᵛᵒ]
    En elle il se complait, il se baigne & promeine,
    Elle est de ses plaisirs le comble & la fontaine.
235   Comme les sectateurs d'Epicure & Zenon,
    Captoyent le vent du peuple & son fumeux renom,
    En raillant & bavant de vertu magnifique,
    A l'ombre des jardins & du triste portique,
    Ne faisans cependant que disputer & braire,
240 De ce qu'ils ne sçavoyent ny enseigner ny faire
    Dont saint Paul indigné, de leur sagesse folle
    Leur monstre les erreurs, & les meine à l'escolle
    Pour cognoistre le Dieu, qui dessus leur autel
    Leur estoit incognu, estre Dieu immortel,
245 Lequel n'habite point és temples faits des mains,
    Et n'est representé par ouvrages humains,
    Qui d'un sang a creé des hommes le lignage,
    Qui tout gouverne à poinct par sa conduite sage,
    Nous dresse à verité, nous pique à repentance,
250 A fin qu'au jugement par sa juste sentence
    Ne soyons condamnez, quand sa voix tonnera,
    Qui les mortz des tombeaux resusciter fera.
    Mais ces cerveaux fumeux, par raison naturelle
    Ne pouvans concevoir une doctrine telle,
255 Se moquoyent de l'Apostre, & l'assailloyent d'outrage,
    Et son presche blasmoyent de furieuse rage,
    Comme contrariant à la Philosophie
    D'Epicure & Zenon laquelle ils ont suyvie.
        Ainsi nostre Poëte, en qui raison repose,
260 Et comme en sa maison dedans luy se tient close,   [B 3]
    (Car il le croit ainsi) voyant que l'Aristote,
    L'Homere, le Platon, pleins de sçavoir si docte,
    Et son esprit aigu (qui sillogize & cherche
    La raison de la Foy, & de ce que lon presche)
265 Ne peuvent du tout rien y cognoistre & comprendre,
    Il se moque & reprend ce qu'il ne peut entendre,
    Blasmant la pureté, & la doctrine saine
    De la Religion contraire à la Romaine.
        Cependant neantmoins pour se laver la gorge
270 D'honnesteté, par foys il fabrique en sa forge

Disputes & propos d'honneur & de vertu,
Comment un Prince doit en estre revestu,
Comment on doit purger la saincte mere eglise,
Ostant les plus grossiers abus de la prestrise.
275 Et tels autres propos de semblable farine,
Criblez de gros en gros à la large estamine.
Mais tenant ce langage il resemble au tragique,
Qui en jouant un Roy est grave & magnifique,
Pompeux, & eslevé en gestes & parolle,
280 Mais à la fin du jeu qu'il est à bout de rolle,
Il n'a pas un seul traict royal en sa personne,
Vil homme & mesprisé, qui [sic] tout vice environne.
    Pour vivre à son souhait, en plaisirs & delices,
Il cherche les moyens d'avoir des Benefices.
285 Et d'autant que tousjours tel butin se rameine
Du Pape, & des prelats de l'Eglise Romaine,
Il les flatte & cherit, les dore & amadoüe,
Et comme or precieux il prise leur gadoüe.
Il abbaye en mastin contre l'Eglise pure,   [B 3//]
290 Eglise renversant l'autre pleine d'ordure.
O que si tu estois, verité, riche & grasse,
Maints Poëtes gaillars te suyvroyent à la trace.
    Sa conversation est epicurienne,
Et son souverain bien volupté terrienne.
295 De son aveugle Dieu il cherche les esbas,
Il veut tousjours avoir le ventre plein & gras.
Son large & long gousier, entonnoir de sa panse,
Estant dompté, il quiert le lict, le bal, la dance.
Si un prestre a deceu finement quelque femme,
300 A raconter le fait il recree son ame :
Mais si en ses discours l'adultere n'a place,
Le conte est sans rizée, & n'a ny goust ny grace.
Les cartes & les dez, les masques, & propos
D'amour, luy font passer toute nuict sans repos.
305 Puis il dort l'endemain jusques à son repas,
Estant levé de table il reprend ses esbas,
Faisant de ses plaisirs tousjours ainsi la ronde,
Voyla quel est le train qu'il demeine en ce monde.
    Si Rome & ses Catons florissoyent derechef,
310 Telz galans n'oseroyent chez eux monstrer le chef.
Et si France logeoit severe discipline,
Elle voumiroit hors leurs meurs & leur doctrine.
Ja le temps nous promet, & monstre une esperance
De voir ces garnemens enflez d'outrecuidance
315 Huez & dechassez, comme corruption
Des esprits & des meurs de nostre nation.   [B 4]
    Comme le laboureur en reant sa couture,
De son champ plantureux repurge toute ordure,
Arrache le chardon & la ronce espineuse :
320 Ainsi faut rejetter le Poëte & la Muse,
Qui n'a que vanité souz une frase belle,
Et qui gaste l'esprit en chatouillant l'aureille.
    Fuyez o fuyez donc, Ames de Dieu choisies,
Ces resveurs transpercez de folles fantasies,
325 Qui en leurs vers fardez d'un attinté langage
N'ont rien que vanité, qu'erreur, qu'amour volage.

Qui ont pour seul objet leur lubrique deesse,
Et son aveugle filz, peste de la jeunesse.
Les dieux, les meurs & traiz des Payens ils ensuyvent,
330 Ils parlent avec eux, comme ils parlent ils vivent.
Ils captent cependant de Chrestiens le renom,
Et se veulent coiffer par masque de ce nom.
Les uns en revestant l'habit qu'un prestre porte,
Et les autres un froc, les autres d'autre sorte.
335 Mais d'eux tous en un poinct s'accorde le courage,
C'est de bien soustenir leur grand' piece d'ouvrage,
Ce bastiment bragard, ce parangon d'autesse,
Ce cher & beau thresor, qu'on appelle la Messe.
C'est là c'est là le but où leur esprit s'arreste,
340 Monstrans par là qu'ils ont des saintetez en teste.
Sus Poëtes gaillars, pleins d'esprit & proesse,
Tenez bon, & prestez l'espaule à vostre Messe,
Assemblez ses suppostz qui sont de vostre brigue.   [B 4ᵛᵒ]
Elle panche deça, empoignez une bigue
345 Pour soustenir son poidz, à fin qu'elle ne verse.
Mettez de ce costé pour l'appuyer une herse.
Ha qu'est ce que je voy ! le fondement on mine,
Ayez des pillotis, usez de contremine,
Pour engouffrer dans terre & du tout arracher
350 Ces maudits Huguenots, qui vous viennent fascher.
Ce sont eux qui ont mis vostre Messe en ce poinct,
Ils sont tousjours apres, & ne cesseront point,
Jusqu'è tant qu'elle soit du tout mise par terre.
Mais non, ne faites plus aux fidelles la guerre,
355 Recoignoissez plustost que Dieu leur party tient,
Qu'il les a soustenu & tousjours les soustient,
Qu'il veut faire par eux retentir sa Parole,
Despuis le bout de l'un jusques à l'autre pole.
Et n'y a, tant soit grande, aucune force humaine,
360 Qui s'opposant à Dieu ne se treuve estre vaine.
Addonnez voz esprits à sa Parole entendre,
Et ne vous bandez plus pour la Messe defendre.
Car elle anneantit de Christ le benefice,
Se subrogeant au lieu de son seul sacrifice.
365 C'est une invention de ce Pape Romain,
Qu'il a par cinq cens ans ravaudé de sa main.
Ces ans là estoyent pleins de tenebres obscures,
Aussi est l'œuvre g[r]osse & ramassé d'ordures.
Comme quelque masson ignare du compas,
370 De la regle & l'esquiar, & du plomb qui pend bas,
Qui pas un seul reglet en son cerveau ne treuve
De l'art ingenieux que nous descrit Vitruve,   [C]
Voulant pour son chef d'œuvre une maison bastir,
Sur un sablon bourbeux commence à despartir
375 Les traces des paroys, qui ceindront l'edifice.
Les angles & les flancz opposez droit en lice
Il projette inegaux, creusant son fondement
En lieu tout limoneux d'un pied tant seulement.
Puis à son tombereau ses deux asnes attelle,
380 Et s'en va aux charniers, pleins de poyson mortelle.
Ramassant des corbeaux & des loups la pasture,
Puis des secretz infectz puise la pourriture,

Les voerres assemble & les fumiers en tas,
Des esgoutz & retraits broye son mourtier gras.
385 Puis commence à bastir sa grossiere besoigne,
Accoule de ce glus la fiente & charoigne,
Joignant quelque morceau de pierre par dedans,
Et se travaille apres par plusieurs siecles d'ans.
Ayant muré ses pans, il s'en vient au couvert,
390 Qu'il fait de papier blanc, noir, rouge, gris & verd.
Son paroy ondoyant, qui de tout costé panche,
Il plastrit tout autour de belle nege & blanche.
Il esleve au frontail une idole en rond peinte,
L'adore & la cherit comme une chose sainte.
395 Son chef d'œuvre parfait, il l'accroit de joyaux,
Puis en fait le manoir des avares corbeaux.
    Mais un doux Aquilon, qui du pole prend source
En temps obscur & froid, poursuit si bien sa course,
Qu'il remet l'air à clair, & dissipe les nues,   [C ᵛᵒ]
400 Qui s'en revont és creux des montaignes cornues.
Lors nous sommes joyeux de revoir la lumiere
Du Soleil, & r'avoir nostre clarté premiere.
Lors sa chaleur empreint ceste heureuse saison,
Pour avoir de tous fruicts abondance & foyson.
405 Cependant la maison de nege revestue
Deteste ce Soleil qui par trop s'esvertue,
Ne peut souffrir ses raiz ny sa vertu profonde,
Qui, peu s'en faut, la font en un abisme fondre.
Ce serain Aquilon la fait trembler, de mesme
410 Qu'une feuille d'Autonne en un orage extreme.
Les corbeaux rapineux, en leurs enroüez sons,
Vont tandis croassant leurs funebres chansons,
Volent entour leur nid, où leurs œufz soloyent pondre,
Pour d'haut en bas le voir abismer & confondre.
415 Et si ceste clarté & cest Aquilon dure,
Le nid & les oyseaux tomberont en peu d'heure.
    Vostre Messe, Papaux, semble ceste maison,
Voz prestres ces corbeaux, le Pape est le masson
Qui jadis la bastit d'erreurs & de blasphemes.
420 Le souffle vigoreux & les rayons supremes
De Dieu dissiperont Pape, Prestres, & Messe,
A clin d'œil, qui cherront tous au vas de detresse.
    Devinez maintenant si la Messe succombe
Que deviendra le reste ? Il faudra que tout tombe.
425 Voz braves marmousetz d'haut en bas sauteront,
Les pauvres trespassez plus rostis ne seront
Es brasiers flamboyans de vostre Purgatoire.   [C 2]
Les marchans coronnez ne tiendront plus leur foire,
Et ne vendront le chant, le baizer, les paroles,
430 Le son, ny le regard de leurs braves Idoles.
Les temples, de leur gaing detestables boutiques,
Seront tout desolez, & eux & leurs traffiques.
Ils lairront leurs beguins, ils couvriront leur teste,
A fin de ne monstrer la marque de la Beste.
435 Nostre salut, qui est enclos & limité
En Christ, ne sera plus par œuvres merité.
Le liberal Arbitre à servir se prendra,
Le Moyne, ventre oyseux, travailleur deviendra.

Les jours ne seront plus, l'un maigre l'autre gras,
440 L'un saoul l'autre affamé, ains iront de compas,
Prenant de soubre main egale nourriture.
Le mariage saint, la couche sans souillure
(Seul loysible moyen pour revenger des ans
Le pere qui renaist en ses tendres enfans)
445 Fera renouveller la vieille Loy Poppœe,
Honorant le mary & sa maison peuplée.
La priere & l'honneur qui aux saintz se desvoye,
A Dieu fort & jaloux redressera sa voye.
Et mille & mille erreurs dont la doctrine est pleine,
450 Avec dix mille abus, de l'Eglise Romaine
Auront, pour retourner à Rome, leur congé,
Et revoir l'Antechrist qui les avoit forgé.
    Le petit garsonneau qui se treuve à la porte
Du temple quand l'on sort, pour vendre ce qu'il porte,
455 Lors criera tout haut en la trouppe amassée,   [C 2ᵛᵒ]
L'abus du gobelet, la Marmite versée,
Le rasoir des rasez, le Ian blanc du cyboire,
L'accord & union d'Enfer & Purgatoire,
Le trespas de la Messe, Indulgences papales,
460 La dispense des vœus, les vertus cardinales,
La desolation du Pape & sa vermine,
Les adieux des fratres & de leur maigre mine,
Bref il gazouillera mille petis livretz,
Qui monstrent les abus descouvers & secretz.
465   L'autre porteur qui a de livres pleine caisse,
Criera haut & clair, Confession de Besze,
Le nouveau Testament, les Pseaumes tout completz,
La Bible figurée & mise par versetz,
Les œuvres de Calvin, de Viret, de Luther,
470 De Martyr, Bullinger, de Muscule & Bucer,
De Zvingle & Melancthon, d'Oecolampade & Brance,
Qui voleront par tout ce Royaume de France.
    Alors retentira aux champs & en la ville,
En public & privé, la voix de l'Evangile.
475 Et l'estat & les meurs de l'Eglise premiere
Seront mis en avant, pour exemple & lumiere.
Chacun s'adonnera & en prose & en vers,
A celebrer celuy qui regit l'univers.
Noz Poëtes seront alors tous d'une sorte,
480 Et ne chanteront plus que la puissance haute.
En divers argumens sonnera leur voix d'Ange,
Les faits de l'Eternel, sa gloire & sa louange.
Ils lairront folle amour, vanité, fiction,   [C 3]
Et viseront au but d'edification.
485   O Seigneur qui nous vois de ta sainte demeure,
Haste toy, & nous fais la grace de voir l'heure,
Que ça bas nous puissions voir ce siecle doré,
Auquel tu seras seul des hommes adoré,
Lesquels de toutes pars te chanteront louanges
490 En terre, comme és cieux font tes bien-heureux Anges.

AD POETAS
PROFANOS

    Qui populos legum sacro rexere superbos
Imperio quondam, atque animos domuere feroces,
Quique suas sanctis auxerunt moribus urbes,
Sæpe suos procul extorres fecere Poëtas.
5   Nempe solent rari, sinuoso tramite & æstu,
Per maria & scopulos & tot discrimina, veræ
Virtutis sacros infessi ambire recessus.
Quin sua tegminibus pars mulcet pectora opacis,
Solliciti tantum latas explere lacunas
10 Latrantis stomachi, ast ad cætera munia prorsus
Ignavi, & nimium fragiles, operumque perosi,
Et soliti exemplis operosos frangere cives.
    Ecce redit prisca, qualis sub consule, forma
Roma vetus, redeunt Censores, & venerandæ   [C 3ᵛᵒ]
15 Sacrarum legum Tabulæ, redit ipse Lycurgus.
CAROLUS æthereo missus de sydere nimbo,
Aurea virtutis divinæ secla reducit,
Purgat & errorem pelagus, populosque reformat.
Dejicite exuvias nudum nomenque Poëtae,
20 Et si qua est pietas animis, si restat & ulla
Relligio, summum dociles audite Tonantem,
Invisi qui sunt vani, & qui vana loquuntur,
Quosque superstitio fictorum falsa deorum
Raptat, & æterni rapientes Patris honores,
25 In quos extensa vibrat sua fulmina dextra.
Aut si nulla tenet vestrum reverentia pectus
Numinis, este tamen, vestra vel vindice Musa,
Et patriæ & vobis vestrisque parentibus æqui.

FIN.

NOTES ET DOCUMENTS

THE FIRST EDITION OF RONSARD'S
ESTREINES AU ROY HENRY III

A few months after Henry III's accession to the throne Ronsard presented to him a poem with the title *Estreines au roy Henry III*. This poem is important for two main reasons. The first is that in it Ronsard spells out what he hopes his relationship with the new monarch will be. He cannot, he says, be an obsequious courtier and the king ought not to expect him to act like one. He is like a noble and spirited warhorse who has served his royal master well: a good master would now see that he is well cared for in his old age, would remember his past services at Montcontour and at Jarnac and would earn the warm affection of his old charger. After recalling thus how he had praised Henry in 1569 during the third civil war, Ronsard explicitly appeals to the king for patronage.

A second and more significant reason why this poem is important is that in it Ronsard mentions his project of writing satire. He asks the king to protect him for, as Joachim du Bellay had explained, writing satire was a hazardous enterprise [1]. In the *Estreines*, Ronsard touches on two reasons for wanting to write satire. The first is the over-abundance of love poetry: the proliferation of mediocre but admired love poetry was in fact threatening Ronsard's pre-eminence as a poet, and the growing prestige of Desportes was soon to goad him into publishing the *Sonnets pour Helene*. His other reason for writing satire was what he saw around him at court and in the nation at large: in this poem he gives a panorama of potential objects of satire. No doubt his desire to castigate the overweening, the racketeers and the indolent courtiers was inspired by a sense of grievance: Ronsard had, as he recalls in this poem, served three French monarchs, yet still had to appeal for patronage, while many parasites lived affluently off the community. In his last years, Ronsard wrote much satire: some of it is quite devastating, but it is not among the better-known parts of his *œuvre*. [2]

Ronsard published the *Estreines* for the first time in 1575. [3] The original version has not been republished since 1575 because it has

---

[1] See E. Courbet's edition of Du Bellay's *Poésies françaises et latines* (2 v., Paris, 1918), I, pp. 462-463. Du Bellay had carefully secured the protection of Henry II before publishing *Les Regrets*: see P. de Nolhac's edition of the poet's *Lettres* (Paris, 1883), pp. 44-45.

[2] Ronsard's satire has been discussed by R. Lebègue in « Ronsard poète officiel » (*Studi in onore di V. Lugli e D. Valeri*, Collani di varia critica, XVI, 2 v., Venezia, 1961, II, pp. 573-587) and by I. Silver in "Pierre de Ronsard, panegyrist, pensioner and satirist of the French court" (*The Romanic Review*, XLV, 1954, pp. 89-108).

[3] See Laumonier's critical edition (Société des Textes Français Modernes), XVII p. 85, n. 1.

not hitherto been available. The only editor of Ronsard who had at one time an opportunity of reprinting this original version was Prosper Blanchemain who between 1857 and 1867 published eight volumes which he called Ronsard's *Œuvres complètes*. When he published the poem he did not know that it had originally appeared in 1575. In his edition he put the date 1578 in brackets after the poem and this would lead any unsuspecting reader to suppose that Blanchemain's text is that of the 1578 edition of Ronsard's *Œuvres*. But Blanchemain's text is not a reproduction of any one of the early versions : the apparatus in Laumonier's critical edition makes it plain that Blanchemain has here, as in many other places, published a hybrid text, and that this one is based mainly on the 1587 edition but with elements of both the 1578 and 1584 texts. It was not until after he had published this text that Blanchemain found a copy of the original version. He found it in the library of his friend baron Jérôme Pichon : this copy had belonged, Blanchemain states, to Jacques-Auguste de Thou. A very cursory glance revealed to Blanchemain that the original version contains eight more lines than the 1578 and subsequent texts, so in the last volume of his edition he published those eight lines.[4] No other editor of Ronsard has had access to a copy of the original edition and Laumonier could only reproduce the fragment which Blanchemain had published.

A copy of the original edition is to be found in the British Library (formerly the "British Museum Library"). It is printed at the end of the following pamphlet :

Le Tombeau de tresillustre Princesse Marguerite de France, Duchesse de Savoye. Ensemble celuy de tresauguste & tresaincte memoire François premier de ce nom, & de Messieurs ses enfans. Par P. de Ronsard Gentilhomme Vandomois. A Paris, Chez Gabriel Buon [...], 1575, C39.g.20 (9).

A note in pencil on the titlepage of this copy adds, after "Messieurs ses enfans", the words " & Etrennes au Roy Henry III". Interestingly, this is almost certainly the copy which belonged to baron Pichon, since it has impressed in gold on its covers the arms of Jacques-Auguste de Thou and his second wife. Blanchemain thought the *Estreines* which follow the *Tombeau* form a separate pamphlet. But it seems certain, for three reasons, that both works were published together : (i) a statement by Ronsard following the *Extraict du privilege du Roy* (both are found on the verso of the titlepage of the *Tombeau*) authorizes Gabriel Buon to print "[...] Le tombeau de Marguerite de France, Duchesse de Savoye : Ensemble celuy de tresauguste & tresaincte memoire, François premier de ce nom, & de Messieurs ses enfans, & les Estreines presentées au Roy, par ledict de Ronsard [...]" ; (ii) the *Estreines* has no separate titlepage and (iii) the signatures (though not the folio numbers) follow successively from the *Tombeau*.

In spelling, capitalization and punctuation the original edition differs considerably from the text of 1578 and the subsequent variants published in volume XVII of Laumonier's critical edition, and there are also some differences in the paragraph divisions. Moreover, there are interesting differences in the text itself and they are not confined to the eight lines (105-112) which Ronsard suppressed in 1578 and

---

[4] See Blanchemain's edition, III, pp. 283-288 for the hybrid text, VIII, p. 88 for the description of baron Pichon's copy of the original edition and VII, p. 306 for the eight lines of the original text.

which Blanchemain reproduced (inaccurately, alas !). In the original edition, Ronsard addresses the king in lines 47-48 as follows :

> Vostre vouloir soit faict sans m'en donner martel,
> Le mien est d'obeir & sera tousjours tel.

In 1578, Ronsard altered these very uncharacteristically obsequious lines to read as follows :

> Je resve ! vostre main me doit faire sentir
> Qu'au service des Rois n'a point de repentir.

The original reading of line 54 ("Ou il fault de doux mots les oreilles luy paistre") is much better than the 1578 version ("Ou il faut de *deux* mots les oreilles luy paistre") and Ronsard reverted in 1584 and 1587 to something more like the original ("Ou faut de doux propos les oreilles luy paistre"). In 1578 Ronsard made six other alterations to his original text. They are as follows : line 15, Je ne *sçaurois mentir*, je ne puis embrasser ; line 29, Et couvert de sueur, d'escume et de *poudriere* ; line 34, Son bon maistre le loge au *plus haut* de l'estable ; line 46, Sinon à vous *le blasme* et à moy le dommage ; line 65, *Mais je ne puis sans vous !* sans vostre faveur Sire ; line 91, Si quelque *viloteur* aux Princes devisant.

London.   Malcolm C. Smith.

LE TOMBEAV
DE TRESILLVSTRE
PRINCESSE MARGVERITE
DE FRANCE, DVCHESSE
DE SAVOYE.

Enfemble celuy de trefaugufte & treffaincte memoire, F R A N ç O I s premier de ce nom,
& de Meffieurs fes enfans.

Par P, de Ronfard Gentilhomme Vandomois.

A PARIS,

*Chez Gabriel Buon, au cloz Bruneau, à l'enfeigne
fainct Claude.*

1 5 7 5.

Auec priuilege du Roy.

[90]

I

ESTREINES

AV ROY HENRY

III. ENVOYEES A SA MAIESTE

AV MOIS DE DECEMBRE.

V o v s race de Roys Prince de tant
    de Princes,
Qui tenez deſſous vous deux ſi grã-
    des prouinces,
Qui par toute l'Europe eſclairez
    tout ainſi
Qu'vn beau ſoleil d'eſté de flam-
mes eſclarcy,
Que l'eſtranger admire & le ſuiect honore,
Et dont la maieſté noſtre ſiecle redore.
A vous qui auez tout, ie ne ſçauroïs donner
    Preſent, tant ſoit-il grand, qui vous puiſſe eſtrener,
    La terre eſt preſque voſtre, & dans le ciel vous mettre
    Ie ne ſuis pas vn Dieu, ie ne puis le promettre,
    C'eſt à faire au flateur: ie vous puis mon meſtier
    Promettre ſeulement, de l'encre & du papier.
Ie ne ſuis Courtizan ny vendeur de fumées
    Ie n'ay d'ambition les veines allumées,

D

Ie ne puis deguifer,ie ne puis embraſſer
Genoux,ny baiſer mains,ny ſuyure,ny preſſer,
Adorer,bonneter,ie ſuis trop fantaſtique,
Mon humeur d'Eſcolier,ma liberté ruſtique
Me deuroient excuſer, ſi la ſimplicité
Trouuoit auiourd'huy place entre la vanité.
C'eſt à vous mon grand Prince à ſuporter ma faute,
Et me louër d'auoir l'ame ſuperbe & haute
Et l'eſprit non ſeruil,comme ayant de Henry
De Charles,de François trente ans eſté nourry.
Vn gentil Cheualier qui aime de nature
A nourrir des harats, ſil treuue d'auanture
Vn courſier genereux qui courant des premiers
Couronne ſon ſeigneur de palme & de lauriers,
Et couuert de ſueur d'eſcume & de pouſſiere
Raporte à la maiſon le prix de la carriere.
Quand ſes membres ſont froids debiles & perclus,
Que vieilleſſe l'aſſault,que vieil il ne court plus,
N'ayant rien du paſſé que la monſtre honorable,
Son bon maiſtre le loge au hault coing de l'eſtable,
Luy donne auoine & foin,ſoigneux de le penſer,
Et d'auoir bien ſeruy le faict recompenſer :
L'appelle par ſon nom,& ſi quelqu'vn arriue,
Dict:voyez ce cheual qui d'aleine pouſſiue
Et d'ahan maintenant bat ſes flancs à l'entour,
I'eſtois monté deſſus au camp de Moncontour,
Ie l'auois à Gernac:mais tout en fin ſe change:
Et lors le vieil courſier qui entend ſa louange,

2

Hanniſſant & frapant la terre ſe ſoubs-rit,
Et beniſt ſon ſeigneur qui ſi bien le nourit.
Vous aurez enuers moy(ſ'il vous plaiſt)tel courage
Sinon à vous la faute & à moy le dommage :
Voſtre vouloir ſoit faict ſans m'en donner martel,
Le mien eſt d'obeir & ſera touſiours tel.
Mais ie ſuis importun, la perſonne importune
Ne rencontre iamaisvne bonne fortune,
Laiſſons faire au deſtin qui nous donne la loy,
Le deſtin de grand Duc vous a faict vn grand Roy:
Puis il ne fault iamais ou parler à ſon maiſtre,
Ou il fault de doux mots les oreilles luy paiſtre.
SIRE, voicy le mois où le peuple Romain
Qui tenoit tout le monde enclos dedans la main,
Donnoit aux ſeruiteurs,par maniere de rire
Congé de raconter tout ce qu'ils vouloient dire:
Donnez moy(ſ'il vous plaiſt)vn ſemblable congé,
I'ay la langue de rongne & le palais mangé,
Il fault que ie la frotte,ou il fault que ie meure,
Tant le mal grateleux me demange à toute heure.
Puis voicy le Printemps où ſe purge vn chacun,
Il fault que mon humeur ſe purge ſur quelqu'vn
Hé! ie ne puis ſans vous!ſans voſtre faueur SIRE
Ie n'oze enuenimer ma langue à la Satyre.
Si eſt-ce que la rage & l'vlcere chancreux
Me tient de compoſer:le mal eſt dangereux
Et ne plaiſt pas à tous:mais ſi ie vous puis plaire
Il me plaiſt,vous plaiſant,d'eſcrire & de deſplaire.
                                   D ij

ESTREINES

Qui bons dieux n'escriroit voyant ce temps içy!
  Quand Apollon n'auroit mes chansons en soucy,
  Quand ma langue seroit sans Muses & muette,
  Encores par despit ie deuiendrois Poëte.
C'est trop chanté d'amour & en trop de façon,
  La France ne cognoist que ce mauuais garson
  Que ses traicts que ses feux:il fault qu'vne autre **voye**
  Par sentiers incogneus sur Parnasse m'enuoye,
  Pour me serrer le front brauement attaché
  D'vn laurier,d'autre main non encores touché.
Apres que vostre esprit & voz mains diligentes
  Seront lasses du faix des affaires vrgentes
  Aux heures de plaisir vous pourrez vostre esprit
  Esbatre quelquefois en lisant mon escript.
S'il y a quelque braue ou mutin qui se fasche
  Et qui entre ses dents des menasses remasche
  Pour se voir ou de biens ou de faueur desdit,
  Si vn plus qu'il ne doibt veult monter en credit,
  Si quelcun en faueur de sa faueur abuse,
  S'il faict le Courtizan & s'arme d'vne ruze,
  Si quelque vilotier aux princes deuisant
  Contrefait le boufon le fat ou le plaisant ,
  Si noz Prelats de Cour ne vont à leurs Eglises,
  Si quelque trafiqueur qui vit de marchandises
  Veult gouuerner l'estat faisant de l'entendu,
  Si quelcun vient crier qu'il a tout despendu
  En Poloigne,& qu'il braue enflé d'vn tel voyage,
  Et pour le sien accroistre à tous face dommage,

AV ROY. 5

Si plus quelque valet de quelque bas meftier
Veult par force acquerir tous les biens d'vn cartier,
Si plus noz vieux corbeaux gourmandent voz finances
Si plus on fe deftruit d'habits & de defpenfes,
Et fi quelque affamé nouuellement venu
Veult manger en vn iour tout voftre reuenu,
Si quelque Dameret fe farde ou fe déguife,
S'il porte vne putain, au lieu d'vne chemife,
Atifé gaudronné, au colet empoizé,
La cappe retrouffée, & le cheueil frizé.
Si plus ie voy porter ces larges verdugades,
La coiffeure éhontée, & ces ratepenades,
Ces cheueux empruntez d'vn page ou d'vn garfon :
Si plus des eftrangers quelcun fuit la façon :
Qu'il craigne ma fureur: d'vne encre la plus noire
Ie luy veux engrauer les faicts de fon hiftoire
D'vn long traict fur le front, puis aille où il pourra
Toufiours entre les yeux ce traict luy demourra.
Ie feray comme vn ours que le peuple éguillonne
Qui renuerfe la tourbe & mord toute perfonne
De grand ny de petit ne me donnant foucy
Si l'œuure vous agrée, & qu'il vous plaife ainfi.
I'ay trop long temps fuyuy le meftier Heroïque,
Lyrique, Elegiaq': ie feray Satyrique
Difois-ie à voftre frere, à Charles mon feigneur
Charles qui fut mon tout mon bien & mon honneur.
Ce bon Prince en m'oyant fe prenoit à foubsrire
Me prioit, m'enhortoit, me commandoit d'efcrire,

D iij

D'eſtre tout Satyrique inſtamment me preſſoit:
Lors tout enflé d'eſpoir qui de vent me paiſſoit
Armé de ſa faueur, ie promettois de l'eſtre
Ce pendant i'ay perdu ma Satyre & mon maiſtre.
A Dieu Charles à Dieu ſommeilles en repos
Ce pendant que tu dors ie ſuyuray mon propos.
Il n'y a ny Rubarbe, Agaric, ny racine
    Qui puiſſe mieux purger la malade poictrine
    De quelque patient fieureux ou furieux,
    Que faict vne Satyre vn cerueau vitieux,
    Pourueu qu'on la deſtrampe à la mode d'Horace,
    Et non de Iuuenal, qui trop aigrement paſſe:
    Il fault la preparer ſi douce & ſi à point
    Qu'à l'heure qu'on l'aualle on ne la ſente point,
    Et que le moqueur ſoit à moquer ſi adeſtre,
    Que le moqué ſ'en rie & ne penſe pas l'eſtre.
O Prince mon ſupport heureux & malheureux,
    Heureux d'auoir l'eſprit ſi vif & genereux,
    Et malheureux d'auoir dés la premiere entrée
    Voſtre France rebelle en armes rencontrée,
    D'ouyr de tous coſtez reſonner le harnois,
    Violer la iuſtice & meſpriſer les loix,
    Et preſque tout l'eſtat tumber à la renuerſe
    Par vne deſtinée à la France peruerſe.
Receuez, ſ'il vous plaiſt, d'vn viſage ſerain
    Et d'vn front deridé mon eſcrit, que la main
    De la muſe a dicté ceſte nouuelle année,
    Pour en vous eſtrenant ſe reuoir eſtrenée.

[96]

4.

Ne la mefprifez pas bien que foyez yſſu
   D'vne race & d'vn fang de tant de Roys conceu,
   Et ne fermez aux vers l'oreille inexorable,
   Minerue autant que Mars vous rendra venerable.
Homme ne penfez eſtre heureufement parfaiᴄt,
   De mefme peau que nous nature vous a faiᴄt,
   Dieu tout feul eſt heureux noſtre nature humaine
   Mifere fur mifere en naiſſant nous ameine,
   Et ne fault f'efbaïr fi nous auons icy
   Pour partage eternel la peine & le foucy.
On diᴄt que Promethée en poitriſſant l'argille
   Dont il feiſt des humains l'eſſence trop fragile
   Pour donner origine à noz premiers malheurs,
   En lieu d'eau la trempa de fueurs & de pleurs:
   Car plus l'homme eſt heureux plus fortune l'efpie,
   A telle qualité nous trainons noſtre vie :
   Mais c'eſt trop babillé, il fe fault depefcher
   Souuent en voulant plaire on ne faiᴄt que fafcher.
Quand Hercule ou Atlas ont chargé fur l'efchine
   De ce grand vniuers la pefante machine
   Que de col & de teſte & de bras bien nerueux
   Se bandent fous le faix qui tumberoit fans eux.
Si quelque fafcheux fot arriuoit d'auenture
   Qui vint les amufer d'vne longue efcriture,
   Ou d'vn maigre difcours foit en profe ou en vers,
   Offenferoit-il pas contre tout l'vniuers?
   Malin i'offenferois contre toute la France
   Dont vous portez le faix dés voſtre ieune enfance,

S'importun i'amuſois voſtre diuin eſprit
(Aux affaires bandé)par vn faſcheux eſcrit.
Dieu ne demande pas(car Dieu rien ne demande)
    Qu'on charge ſes autels d'vne peſante offrande
    Il n'aime que le cueur:il regarde au vouloir
    La ſeule volonté l'offrande faict valoir:
Ainſi ſuyuant de Dieu la diuine nature
    Vous prendrez mon vouloir & non mon eſcriture.

F I N.

10 MA 70

AN EARLY EDITION OF JOACHIM DU BELLAY'S
VERONIS IN FONTEM SUI NOMINIS

Joachim Du Bellay is the author of three collections of Latin poems. The first of these to appear was the *Poematum libri quatuor* of 1558. This is perhaps the best-known collection: the *libri quatuor* of the title contain respectively elegies, epigrams, love poems and epitaphs. Among the elegies is an attractive poem titled *Veronis in fontem sui nominis*: this elegy, which tells the story of the transformation of the nymph Veronis into a stream bearing her name, is the subject of this article. The second collection is the *Tumulus Henrici Secundi* of 1559: it contains notably an epitaph of Henry II in French and Latin versions, and an elegy dedicated to the cardinal of Lorraine which is interesting especially for its defence of poetry. The third collection, the *Xenia seu Illustrium quorundam Nominum Allusiones*, contains epigrams in which the poet discerns characteristics of famous contemporaries in the supposed etymologies of their names, together with an autobiographical elegy dedicated to Jean de Morel.[1] Many of the poems published in these three collections appeared also in books by some of Du Bellay's contemporaries: Michel de l'Hospital,[2] Girolamo della Rovere,[3] Carolus Utenhovius[4] and George Buchanan;[5] a few short poems, mostly commendatory,

---

[1] The *Poematum libri quatuor* can be read in E. Courbet's edition of Du Bellay's *Poésies françaises et latines* (2 v., Paris, 1918, I, p. 419-535). Of Du Bellays's second collection of Latin poems, the epitaph of Henry II is in Chamard's edition of the *Œuvres poétiques* (VI, p. 75-102) and the elegy to the cardinal of Lorraine is in my book on *Joachim Du Bellay's veiled victim* (Genève, 1974, p. 75-88). The whole of the third collection, the *Xenia*, is in *Joachim Du Bellay's veiled victim* (p. 89-124).

[2] Michel de l'Hospital's book, published anonymously, is titled *Amplissimi cuiusdam viri Epistola ad illustriss. principem Francisc. Lotaringum ducem Guisianum: cui addita est Elegia Ioach. Bellaii, cum aliquot eiusdem Epigrammatis* (Paris, 1558) (see H. CHAMARD, "Bibliographie des éditions de Joachim Du Bellay", *Bulletin du Bibliophile*, 1949, no. 24).

[3] See GIROLAMO DELLA ROVERE's *Les deux Sermons Funebres es obseques & enterrement du feu Roy Treschrestien Henri deuxieme de ce nom* [...], Paris, M.D.LIX, B.L. 10660 dd 30, A ii[ro] and Aii[vo]. Mr David Hartley kindly drew my attention to this publication.

[4] See *Epitaphium in mortem Herrici Gallorum Regis Christianissimi, eius nominis secundi, per Carolum Utenhovium Gandavensem, & alios, duodecim linguis* [...], Paris, M.D.LX (B.L. 1213 m 10 (2)), C i[ro], E ii[vo], E iii[vo] (with a prose letter to Utenhovius at C iv[vo]).
One of the items by Du Bellay in this collection has not to my knowledge been reprinted since 1560. It is the tribute to a Latin poem on the death of Henry II by Jean de Morel's eleven-year-old daughter Camille (C i[ro]):
Quid mirum hos versus nostram cecinisse Camillam?
Carolus Utenhovus nempe magister erat.

[5] See BUCHANAN's *Franciscanus & fratres, Quibus accessere varia eiusdem & aliorum Poëmata* [...], 3 parts, Basileæ Rauracorum, [1568] (B.L. 1213 g 10), I, p. 132-133; II, p. 94, 173-174, 174-175; and the third part contains some of the *Xenia*.

appeared in books by other authors;[6] and the *Antonii Minarii Tumulus* appeared originally on a single sheet.[7] But apart from the three main collections, no separate book of Du Bellay's Latin poems is now known to be extant.

However, Pierre de Nolhac discovered that Du Bellay hoped to publish separately his *Veronis in fontem sui nominis.* Nolhac's discovery is based on a letter by the poet to Jean de Morel which he found among Morel's documents in Munich. The letter, as published by Nolhac, reads as follows:

> Monsieur et frère,
>
> N'ayant pour ceste heure la commodité de vous aller veoyr, pour une despesche qui me tient empesché il y a ja troys iours, je me suys advisé de vous saluer de ce petit mot et vous envoyer une coppie de la transformation de la nymphe Veronis en la fontaine de Veron, que je vous prye veoir et, si la trouvez digne de sortir dehors de nos mains, la faire mettre en estampe de nostre Mᵉ Simon, pour puys apprès en faire ung beau present à Monsʳ de Nevers, que j'appelle Jacques Spifame, m'estant bien au vray informé si c'est ou Jehan ou Jacques ou quelque autre nom.
>
> J'espere vous veoyr demain de quelque heure, et ce pendant je me recommanderay de bien bon cœur à vostre bonne grace, priant Dieu vous donner la sienne.
>
> De vostre maison au cloistre.
>
> Vostre obéissant et meilleur frère à vous faire service,
>
> DUBELLAY.

Nolhac knew of no separate edition of *Veronis* unfortunately and stated that the poem is found only in the collected Latin works, by which he meant the *Poematum libri quatuor.*[8]

Nolhac was mistaken in this belief. A separate edition of *Veronis* did appear. A copy of it is in the Houghton Library of Harvard University. The titlepage of Du Bellay's pamphlet reads as follows:

> Veronis in fontem sui nominis. Ad Iacobum Spifamium
> Episcopum Nivernensem. Ioachimo Bellaio authore.
> Excudebat Senonibus AEgid. Richeboesius, M.D.LVIII.

On the titlepage is a signature which reads "Franciscus Rassius Noëns Chirurgus Paris[iensis]. 1561." On the verso of the titlepage is a letter headed *Ioach. Bellaio Poetae & Oratori clariss. Joan. Penonius Senon. s.* This is followed (p. 3-6) by the text of *Veronis*

---

[6] See my "Joachim Du Bellay's renown as a Latin poet," due to appear in the *Proceedings of the Second International Congress of Neo-Latin Studies*, Amsterdam, 1973.

[7] See Du BELLAY's *Œuvres poétiques*, ed. Chamard, VI, p. xii and 103-109.

[8] Nolhac gave the text in "Documents nouveaux sur la Pléiade: Ronsard, Du Bellay," *Revue d'Histoire Littéraire de la France*, VI, 1899 (p. 351-361), p. 360-361. It is unfortunate that this letter is not dated.

Du Bellay's letter seems to imply the "Mᵉ Simon" he mentions has some link with printers. He may be Henry Simon, who was among the editors of Jodelle's poetry, and whom Jodelle extolled for having helped him—in what way is unknown—to introduce classical-style drama in France: see E. BALMAS, *Un poeta del rinascimento francese, Etienne Jodelle*, Firenze, 1962, p. 177-179, 657-663.

Du Bellay's relationship with Jean de Morel was very cordial: see H. CHAMARD, *Joachim Du Bellay, 1552-1560* (Lille, 1900, p. 390-392). Several letters from Du Bellay to Morel are extant (see Du BELLAY's *Lettres*, ed. P. de Nolhac, Paris, 1883, or Y. BELLENGER's *Du Bellay: ses "Regrets" qu'il fit dans Rome*, Paris, 1975, p. 416-425). An important autobiographical elegy which Du Bellay dedicated to Morel can be read in *Joachim Du Bellay's veiled victim* (see note 1 above), p. 115-124.

with, on an unnumbered final page, a two-line eulogy of Du Bellay by Jean Berger.[9]

The discovery of this copy of *Veronis* led to the finding of a second copy. Seeking information about the printer, Gilles Richeboys, I was led by Albert Kolb's *Bibliographie des französischen Buches in 16. Jahrhundert* to an article by Félix Chandenier in the *Bulletin de la Société Archéologique de Sens*.[10] Chandenier had evidently seen a copy of the pamphlet (indeed, he reproduced the printer's device from the titlepage), and he stated that the poem had been published in 1866 in the *Annuaire de l'Yonne*. Indeed, an unsigned note in that review, titled "La fontaine de Véron, poésie par J. Du Bellay, Sens, 1558" (p. 104-107), gives the text of the poem, and states at the end that the original is in the library at Auxerre. After remarkably persistent research in a byzantine collection of catalogues, the library staff there found the copy for me. A signature on the titlepage reads "Taveaulx." The Auxerre copy is identical to the Harvard copy, except that the second line of Berger's tribute to Du Bellay begins "Veronen" not "Veronem."

The *Annuaire de l'Yonne* is not among the more widely-available periodicals (to the best of my knowledge no copy of the 1866 volume exists in Britain) and it is perhaps not surprising that despite the appearance of this short (and rather fanciful) unsigned note in 1866, the existence of Du Bellay's pamphlet appears to have been forgotten. Henri Chamard seems not to have known it existed, and there is no reference to the separate *Veronis*, or to either of the old articles which mentioned it, in Margaret Brady Wells's list of studies on Du Bellay.[11]

The version of *Veronis* in this pamphlet differs textually and in other ways from that found in the *Poematum libri quatuor* and it is therefore important to establish whether Du Bellay himself is responsible for the text. In 1558, Du Bellay began having his poems

---

[9] The call number of the pamphlet is *FC5 D8517 558v. Its early owner, Rasse Des Neux, was a keen collector of tracts. Madame J. Veyrin-Forrer published an interesting article on him ("Un collectionneur peu connu, François Rasse Des Neux, chirurgien parisien," in *Studia bibliographica in honorem Herman de la Fontaine Verwey*, Amstelodami, 1966, p. 389-417). He owned also a copy of Du Bellay's *Antonii Minarii tumulus* (see *Œuvres poétiques*, ed. Chamard, VI, p. XII).

On the verso of the titlepage a manuscript note reads "Harvard College Library. Gift of Carleton R. Richmond. June 13, 1951."

[10] See KOLB's *Bibliographie* [. . .] (Wiesbaden, 1966), p. 384. Chandenier's article is titled "Gilles Richeboys, deuxième imprimeur sénonais (1556-1565)" and it appeared in the 1916 volume of the *Bulletin* (no. 30 ; p. 198-289) : his discussion of *Veronis* is on p. 267-269.

In his article, Chandenier stated that a copy of the pamphlet edition of *Veronis* "[. . .] avait été recueilli par M. Th. Tarbé et se trouve au tome IX de la Bibliothèque d'un Sénonais" (p. 267). An exhaustive and vain search for a publication titled *Bibliothèque d'un Sénonais* has convinced me that no such publication exists, and that Chandenier may have been referring to the volume of tracts and manuscripts in which the Auxerre copy referred to below was inserted.

Richeboys was no mean printer. On p. 200-201 of his article, Chandenier cited glowing and interesting tributes to the quality of his work.

[11] Du Bellay's pamphlet is not mentioned in Chamard's "Bibliographie des éditions de Joachim Du Bellay" (see note 2 above). Margaret Brady Wells's compilation is titled *Du Bellay, a bibliography* (Research bibliographies and checklists, London, 1974).

An entry in A. CIORANESCU's *Bibliographie de la littérature française du seizième siècle* (Paris, 1959, no. 8345) refers, under "Du Bellay," to "I. B. Veronis in fontem carmen. Sens, 1558, 8o." This perfunctory entry looks as though it derives from some earlier bibliographical compilation. Cioranescu may in turn be the source of an identical entry in the *Répertoire bibliographique des livres imprimés en France au seizième siècle*, 145, Sens, by J. BETZ (Bibliotheca Bibliographica Aureliana, XXXIII, Baden-Baden, 1970, p. 71). Neither Cioranescu nor Betz gave the location of any copy.

published by the Paris printer Fédéric Morel and his commitment
to Fédéric Morel was to become a strong one.[12]   In a letter dated
31 July 1559, Du Bellay denounced pirated editions of his works
and declared that he had taken legal action against publishers of
such editions who had been fined and obliged to pay compensation.[13]
There is therefore a *prima facie* case against the authenticity of texts
of poems by Du Bellay published in or after 1558 by any other printer
than Fédéric Morel.[14]   This would certainly apply to poems which
appeared in the *Poematum libri quatuor*, for Morel was awarded sole
rights on this publication.   The note on the verso of the titlepage
in Morel's edition of the *Poematum libri quatuor* is quite explicit:

PRIVILEGII SENTENTIA.

Cautum est auctoritate Henrici. II. Francorum Regis, ne quis alius præter Federi-
cum Morellum, hosce Ioachimi Bellaii Poëmatum libros ante sexennium ab hac prima
editione, excudat, neve vendat. Qui secus fecerit libris & pœna in sanctione æstimata
mulctabitur. Datum apud Aquae bellae fontem, die Martii tertio. An. M.D.LVII. Ex
mandato regio, I. Avansonio, Regi ab intimis Consiliis, Præsente, subsignatum,
DUTHIER[15].

Since *Veronis* forms part of the *Poematum libri quatuor*, its separate
appearance in pamphlet form would appear at first sight to have
been unauthorized.
    However, a letter from Penon to Du Bellay published as a preface
to the pamphlet sheds further light on the publication.[16]   In this
letter, Penon admits that he published *Veronis* without Du Bellay's
explicit approval, and concedes that perhaps he ought not to have
done this ("[...] fortasse te inconsulto non fuit faciundum").   But,
implicity forestalling the possible objections of Du Bellay and his
authorized printer, Penon recalls that Du Bellay had given him the
copy of the poem; he affirms that the text of *Veronis* has in any
case already become well-known; he hints that the opportunity of

---

[12] See especially J. DUMOULIN, *Vie et œuvres de Fédéric Morel imprimeur à Paris
depuis 1557 jusqu'à 1583*, Paris, 1901, p. 27-45; also J. W. Jolliffe, "Fédéric Morel and
the works of Du Bellay," *Bibliothèque d'Humanisme et Renaissance*, XXII, 1960,
p. 359-361 and "Further notes on Du Bellay," *Bibliothèque d'Humanisme et Renaissance*,
XXVIII, 1966 (p. 112-122), 3, 'The uniform edition of Du Bellay's works,' p. 119-121.

[13] See DU BELLAY's *Lettres*, ed. Nolhac, p. 44. The letter is addressed to cardinal
Jean Du Bellay.

[14] Some pirated editions are listed in Chamard's "Bibliographie" (see note 2
above): no. 19, 20 and 37.

[15] This text is taken from the British Library's copy (1213 m 11). Courbet did not
give the text in his edition of the *Poésies françaises et latines* (see note 1 above).

[16] Penon, who was a lawyer, had a hand in the publication of legal books, notably
the *Coustumes du Bailliage de Sens* published by Richeboys in 1556. He was described
by a contemporary as an "homme de vif esprit, de lectres et de diligence, mais de contradiction, maling et factieux" and was, to say the least, well-disposed towards the
Reformers. He was a friend of Jacques Spifame, bishop of Nevers, to whom *Veronis*
is dedicated. See CHANDENIER's article on Richeboys (cf. note 10 above), p. 209-212,
216-225, 233, 256-257 and 279-280.
    Interestingly, the printer (Richeboys), the editor (Penon) and the dedicatee
(Spifame) of Du Bellay's pamphlet were all sympathetic (at least) towards the Reformed
Church. Richeboys, like many another printer, joined the Reformed Church and in
April 1562, as Chandenier records (p. 284-289), he and his pregnant wife were murdered
by sectarian assassins. Spifame fled to Geneva in February 1559; he was executed
there in March 1566 on conviction for adultery and forgery, though his real crime was
apparently treason (see A. DELMAS, "Le procès et la mort de Jacques Spifame,"
Bibliothèque d'Humanisme et Renaissance, V, 1944, p. 105-137). Du Bellay himself, on
the other hand, was a convinced member of the traditional church: see *Joachim Du
Bellay's veiled victim* (cf. note 1 above), p. 46-57.

personally presenting a printed copy of *Veronis* to Jacques Spifame, to whom Du Bellay had himself dedicated the poem, was too good to miss ; and finally, he expresses the hope that his recently established friendship with Du Bellay will as a result of his action in publishing the poem, be strengthened. The cordial tone of Penon's note certainly tends to dissipate doubt about the authenticity of the text he published. Moreover, Du Bellay's letter to Morel makes it clear both that Du Bellay intended to publish *Veronis* separately and that he wanted a copy of the separate *Veronis* to be presented to Spifame. It therefore seems probable that Penon's pamphlet was at least tacitly authorized by the poet. The authenticity of the text is strongly indicated by Penon's categorical statement that he received the poem from Du Bellay himself.

Given that the text published by Penon is authentic, it is desirable to establish whether it was published before or after the *Poematum libri quatuor*. In the foreword to the pamphlet Penon states that having received the text from Du Bellay in Paris he returned to Sens on 1 August and the pamphlet seems to have been published very soon after, for the foreword is dated 1 September 1558. The *Poematum libri quatuor* have a *privilegium* dated 3 March 1557 (1558 n.s.) but since (at least in the British Library's copy) they are prefaced by a letter from François Olivier to Jean Morel dated 29 August 1558, they cannot have been published before that date (unless of course an earlier issue appeared without Olivier's letter).[17] There is no further dated material in either publication which might indicate which of them appeared first ; and Du Bellay's letter to Jean de Morel dealing with the projected separate edition of *Veronis* (cited at the beginning of this article) is unfortunately not dated. But I would guess that the pamphlet appeared first, since in his foreword Penon states that he has undertaken to present *Veronis* "καθ' ἄπερ βιβλίδιον excussam," and this seems to imply that it had not previously been printed. His statement in the same sentence that the poem has already become well-known ("per [...] manus & ora doctorum omnium volitantem") must refer to its diffusion in manuscript copies as he would not have admitted that he had pirated an existing authorized printed edition. It is not possible to say which version was written first.

The pamphlet version of *Veronis* can therefore be regarded as authentic and as being probably the first printed edition. Where there are differences between the text in the pamphlet and that in the British Library's copy of the *Poematum libri quatuor* (shelfmark 1213 m 11, 13vo-15ro), the latter reads as follows : differences in the text in line 28, "Cui *Thetys genitrix*, Oceanusque parens" ; line 58, "Illic *tam* longæ meta reperta fugæ" ; and lines 69-70, "*Dura silex Cererem rapido demittit* ab orbe, / Quodque opus est amnis, *fontis & illud* opus" ; differences in spelling, line 2, edita ; line 33, colleis ; line 50, fontes ; line 81, Cygni and line 86, Spiffamique ; differences in punctuation in line 10, comma after Solaque ; lines 19 and 31, colon at end ; line 21, full stop after volat ; line 23, colon after demens ; lines 28 and 38, full stop at end ; line 47, commas after effugies and dixit, no comma at end, no brackets ; line 53, comma at end ; line 54, no comma ; line 57, full stop after requievimus ; line 62, full stop after surgit ; lines 63, 73 and 79, colons at end ; line 65,

---

[17] Olivier's letter, and an English translation, are in *Joachim Du Bellay's veiled victim*, p. 2, 10.

colon after magis. The text in the *Poematum libri quatuor* does not
have the proper names in lines 57, 83 and 86 in capitals, and in line 55
alpeisque begins with a lower-case "a". The word improbus in line
37 is not abbreviated. The *Poematum libri quatuor* are in italic, not
Roman type.[18]

Penon's reference to "Veronidem [...] per [...] manus & ora
doctorum omnium volitantem" is an interesting tribute to the
success which this beautiful poem enjoyed. The fact of its separate
appearance in pamphlet form is further evidence of its popularity.
Other tributes to this poem are not wanting. On the strength of
this poem Jean Berger likened Du Bellay to Ovid in the couplet
published at the end of the poem. Scévole de Sainte-Marthe the
Elder was to declare that *Veronis* was among Du Bellay's most
admired productions:

[...] carmen de Veronide & lusus de puellæ raptu, nec pauca summæ argutiae summique
leporis epigrammata suos merito laudatores invenere, quorum iudicio, ut vix ullum in
carmine Gallico parem habet, sic paucissimos in latino superiores[19].

Guillaume Colletet, in his *Vie de Joachim Du Bellay*, also included
it in his short-list of Du Bellay's best Latin poems.[20] And Girolamo
Ghilini, the author of a *Teatro d'huomini letterati*, included it in his
short-list—though implying that *Les Antiquitez de Rome* and *Les
Regrets* were Du Bellay's best poems.[21] Henri Chamard, unwittingly
echoing Jean Berger, opined that this elegy "pourrait être signée
d'Ovide."[22]

To conclude, it may be helpful to lay to rest a ghost conjured up
by Chamard on the basis of the letter from Du Bellay to Morel
which was cited at the beginning of this article. Du Bellay there
declared that he was sending Jean de Morel "une coppie de la transformation de la nymphe Veronis en la fontaine de Veron." Chamard
inferred from this that after writing *Veronis* in Latin, Du Bellay
composed a "transformation" of the poem into French which is not
now extant.[23] Chamard's reading of the letter is ingenious but
wrong: Du Bellay's words refer simply to the subject of *Veronis*
itself, the transformation of the nymph into the stream named
after her! It is of course conceivable that Du Bellay composed a

---

[18] Janus Gruterus reproduced the *Poematum libri quatuor* text in his *Delitiae C.
Poetarum Gallorum*, Pars prima, M.D.C. IX (B.L. 1213 a 3), p. 406-409 but with the
readings "Quem mirere magis" in line 65 and "murmure *collem*" in line 71, and the
word *erat* missing in line 34. Courbet reproduced the *Poematum libri quatuor* text
with minor changes in punctuation (see *Poésies françaises et latines*, I, p. 447-450).

[19] *Opera*, 2 parts, Lutetiae, M.DC.XVI (B.L. 1213 l 15), II, p. 63-64.

[20] Colletet's biography of the poet has been published by Y. Bellenger in *Du
Bellay: ses "Regrets" qu'il fit dans Rome* (Paris, 1975 : p. 269-301), and Colletet's praise
of the Latin poems is in p. 281-282.

[21] Published in Venice in 1647, the book (in two parts; B.L. 617 k 14) contains
the following appraisal of Du Bellay's work (II, p. 116):
Si vedono del suo bell'ingegno stampate alcune Opere, parte in verso, e parte in
prose, cioè, Carmen de Veronide: Lusus de Puellae raptu: Epigrammata: Collapsa
vetustae Urbis Monumenta [that is, *Les Antiquitez de Rome*]: Corrupti Aulae N. mores,
totaque Aulicorum gens aculeatis ubique Epigrammatis aptissime depicta, & ad oculos
posita [that is, *Les Regrets*]; i quali due ultimi componimenti da lui fatti in Roma,
sono, e per le materie, e per l'eloquenza, e soavità dello stile veramente aurei.

[22] Chamard included two other poems in this judgement, namely *In vitae quietoris
commendationem* and *Patriae desiderium*: see *Joachim Du Bellay* [...] (cf. note 8
above), p. 360 and note 4.

[23] References to Chamard in this paragraph derive from *Joachim Du Bellay* [...],
p. 360-361 and notes.

French version of *Veronis* but the letter to Jean de Morel does not at all imply this. A French *Veronis* is entirely a conjecture and in fact a weak one: given the fame of the Latin *Veronis*, any French version would surely have attracted the attention of Guillaume Aubert, the early editor of Du Bellay's complete works, or of some early commentator. Moreover, Chamard's misreading of the letter to Jean de Morel seems to have led him towards a further dubious statement: that, in those cases where Du Bellay published both a Latin and a French version of the same poem, the Latin text was composed first.[24] Chamard gave this view a certain currency by reiterating it several times in his edition of Du Bellay's *Œuvres poétiques*: but, based as it is on a misinterpretation of Du Bellay's letter, it is no more than a guess.

London.   Malcolm C. Smith.

PS. The stream which Du Bellay wrote about, the "fontaine de Véron," emerges from a hill to the east of the lane which goes from Rosoy to Véron, six miles south of Sens. The stream runs directly into a large metal tank, then through a wash-house, under the road and through a cress-farm. However idyllic the spot was in Du Bellay's day, it is now quite unremarkable. Local people seem rather amused that it inspired a poem by Du Bellay!

---

[24] The only evidence Chamard cites for this view is an unsupported statement by C. A. Sainte-Beuve (*Nouveaux Lundis*, 13 v., Paris, 1870, XIII, p. 343).

VERONIS
IN FONTEM
SVI NOMI-
NIS,

Ad Iacobum Spifamium Epifcopum
Niuernenfem.

IOACHIMO BELLAIO
AVTHORĚ.

EXCVDEBAT SENONIBVS
AEGID. RICHEBOESIVS,
M. D. LVIII.

Trunifcus Raffins Aocins
Chirurgus parg. 156t.

VERONIS IN
FONTEM SVI NO-
MINIS,

AD

Iacobum SPIFAMIVM *Episcopum*
Niuernensem.

ERONA genitrice olim,
Phœboque parente,
Benâci ad ripas ædita
Nympha fui.
Nympha decus Latii, qua
non formosior vlla
Formosas visa est inter
Hamadryadas.
Veronis mihi nomen erat, Veronidis ardor
Silueftres vffit, capripedéfque Deos.
Quos tamen elufi connubia noftra petentes,
Nec mea lafciuus pectora læfit amor.
Nam mihi virginei placuit laus vna pudoris,
Soláque quam colui, cafta Diana fuit.
Multa meis iaculis præda eft deiecta, meúmque

A. ii.

IOACH. BELLAIO POETAE
& Oratori clariff. Ioan. Penonius Senon. s.

QVM ad Calendas Augufti cum Io. RICHERIO Senonum Præ-
fide meritiffimo abs te Lutetiæ accepta Veronide, Senones rediiffem,
venit Typographus, méque tuam vt ille typis excuderet Veronidem
rogauit, & obtinuit. Atque commodum euénit vt tum tem-
poris hâc iter ad Regiam faceret SPIFAMIVS, Niuernéfis Epifcopus, vir (vt
tu ipfe fcis) ordinis fui ἐξαίρετος. Cui quû nafcentem adhuc Veronidem feu gen-
tilem addixiffes, non alienum ab officio meo fore exiftimaui, fi iam adolefcen-
tem, péfque manus & ora doctorum omnium volitantem fifterem, ipfamque
pro tabella, καὶ καθ' ἀπη βιβλίδιον excuffam, hoc adiecto corollario SPIFAMIO
repræfentarem. Quod tametfi fortaffe te inconfulto non fuit faciundum,
fpero tamen (quæ tua eft humanitas) nihil hinc tuæ erga me beneuolentiæ
conuulfum iri, quin potius magnam inde recéns initæ amicitiæ futuram
acceffionem. Quod vt facias te etiam atque etiam oro & obteftor, Bene vale
doctiff. Bellai, Senonib. Calend. Septemb. M. D. LVIII.

IOACH. BELLAII IN

Inscriptum spoliis robora nomen habent.
Sed dum forte è sequor celeris vestigia ceruæ,
Dúnque leuis crineis ventilat aura meos,
Me pater aspexit vitreo Benácus ab antro,
Continuo flammis incaluitque nouis.
Ergo Deus visámque cupit, sequirúrque cupitam,
Præcipiti fugio nota per arua pede.
Non amnes, montesq; fugan, non saxa morantur,
Tardius è neruo missa sagitta volat.
Nec minus ille volat, magnú est certamen vtrinq;:
Me timor, ast illum feruidus vrget amor.
Quem fugis? ah demens! sævú sic cerua leoném,
Crudelem mitis sic fugit agna lupum.
Non ego cornigeri natus de sanguine Fauni,
Nec sum lasciuo de grege capripedum.
Me quódam Hesperiis genuit pater Adria canpis,
Cui genitrix Tethys, Oceanúsque parens,
Hunc tibi do socerú. non est leue numé aquarum:
Benácus coniux nec tibi turpis erit.
Sic ait, & rapidis præceps volat ocyor Euris,
Effugio celeri per iuga summa gradu.
Iámque per aërios colles, campósque patentes
Ventum erat vndosi littus ad Eridani.
Tum mihi decurrit toto de corpore sudor,
Spiritus & grauior tum mihi membra quatit.
Etiam iámq; magis fessam premit improb⁹ hostis,

FONT. VERON.

Iámque meas afflat proximus ore comas
Virginis ô miserere tuæ, Latonia virgo,
Si colui numen Nympha pudica tuum.
Vix ea finieram, totúmque liquescere corpus
Cœpit, & ex Nympha lympha repente fui.
Me tamen ille capit, votóque potitus inani
Stringit, at ex manibus protinus effugio.
In venásque abeo magnæ per viscera terræ:
Lusit amatorem sic Arethusa suum.
Non tamen effugies (dixit) liquidúsque repente,
Persequitur nostram sævus vt ante fugam.
Sed grauior, cursúmque trahens maioribus vndis
Inuitus fonteis reppetit ipse suos.
Nec minus interea (vireis timor addit eunti)
Sub terram celeri labimur vnda pede.
Quáque licet, patrios tuto iam tramite campos
Linquimus, & latii rura inimica soli.
Linquimus Allobrogú montes, Alpéisq; niuosas,
Tangimus & fines, Gallia pulchra, tuos.
Finibus & SENONVM fessæ requieuimus, illic,
Illic tum longæ meta reperta fugæ.
Paruus erat molli deiectus tramite cliuus,
Hunc subter viridi gramine floret ager.
Illic herbofo paulatim cespite campus
In tumulum surgit, hâc via aperta mihi est.
Hinc nouus egredior salientis riuulus vndæ,

A. iii.

AD

IOACHIMVM
BELLAIVM.

QVI Metamorphofeon tria quinq; volumina fcripfit,
Veronem voluit te ceciniffe Deam.

Io. Bergerii Senonenfis.

IOAC. BELL. IN FON. VERON.

Hîc cælum nobis contigit, atque folum.
Quin mirête magis, latè porrectus in orbem
Fons fcatet, atque imo vortice torquet aquas.
Hinc furit emiffus finuofo è gurgite riuus,
Limofúfque fluit, duráque faxa creat.
Trita Ceres filicis crebro decurrit ab orbe,
Quódq; opus eft annis, hoc quoq; fontis opus.
Inde per herbofum trepidanti murmure callem
Noftra fuum timidè lympha recurrit iter.
Atque iterum liquido fub terram mergitur anne,
Nunc quoque virginei cura pudoris ineft.
Aureus eft fundus nobis, argentea lympha,
Purpureo circum flore renidet humus.
Et circum in viridi crepitantis margine riui
Intexunt denfas lenta falicta comas.
Hîc volucres liquidas mulcent concentibus auras,
Hîc faciunt fomnos murmura blanda leueis.
Hîc cantant niuei per prata recentia Cycni,
Hinc pafti referunt vbera tenta greges.
PACCIADES Nymphæ, Satyri, Driadéfq; puellæ
Hîc agitant lætos nocte filente choros.
Alternífque canunt diuini fontis honores,
SPIFAMIQVE fui nomen in aftra ferunt.
Qui pecus immundû noftris procul arcet abvndis,
Et facri fontis me iubet effe Deam.

[109]

LOOKING FOR ROME IN ROME :
JANUS VITALIS AND HIS DISCIPLES

(I) Introduction.

A very famous epigram by Janus Vitalis addresses the reader
as though he were a visitor who has come to Rome to see the great
ancient city but is unable to find Rome in the midst of Rome, since
all is ruins. For the destiny of Rome was to conquer all the world
and to fulfil this destiny she conquered even herself. Only the
Tiber remains : showing that while great monuments perish,
things in constant movement endure.

The first objective of this article is to make available the text
and variant readings of Vitalis's beautiful poem. The other
objectives are : to bring together the texts of translations and
adaptations of Vitalis's poem, and thereby to show the development
of a tradition ; to stress the link between Renaissance vernacular
literatures and the Latin literature of the same era — for to know
Vitalis's fine poem and the fame it enjoyed is to appreciate the
self-confidence which Du Bellay, for example, displayed in emulating it ; to recall (explicitly here and in the rest of the article implicitly) that a spirit of emulation was one of the mainsprings of
poetic creativity in the Renaissance ; and to recall that Renaissance poetry appeals not only in a general way to an eternal audience
but also, often, in a particular way to the audience of its own day :
much Renaissance poetry is born of a dialogue in the author's mind
(perhaps largely a subconscious dialogue) between moral verities
which are of their nature eternal and the exigencies of a historical
moment. In the conclusion to this article I shall return to this
last point.

(II) The attraction of the ruins.

Janus Vitalis's poem, which we shall examine soon, is a meditation
on the ruins of Rome. It is a model poem in a great tradition.

Ancient pagan writers had evoked ruins to suggest the destructiveness of time, the power of divine retribution, the need for literary renown as a means of immortality, and the fragility of human endeavour. Christian theologians and poets added to this a perception of the hand of God at work in the destruction of great cities. The ancient pagans used Troy as their prime example, while ancient Christian authors cited biblical examples of destroyed cities. Later, the Fathers of the Church, notably Jerome and Augustine, pondered on the fall of Rome. Jerome was the more anguished, and reflected that *in una urbe totus orbis interiit*. Augustine, more optimistically, offered the thought (which Joachim Du Bellay expresses differently in the *Antiquitez de Rome*) that *si non manet civitas quae nos carnaliter genuit, manet quae nos spiritualiter genuit*[1]. Renaissance authors, too, wrote often and eloquently about ruins, especially those of Rome. Petrarch, for example, contrasted the ruins of Rome with the glories of the past ; and Erasmus reflected in the *Ciceronianus*, published in 1528, that « (...) Roma Roma non est, nihil aliud habens praeter ruinas ruderaque priscae calamitatis cicatrices ac vestigia »[2].

The theme of the ruins of Rome was often closely associated with other topoi expressing transience : with the " ubi sunt " device, whereby an author would rhetorically ask what has become of splendid cities and great men of the past ; with reflections on vanity which often echo the book of *Ecclesiastes* ; and with Fortuna, the blindfold goddess who spins men around on her " furious fickle wheel ". Sometimes, as indeed in this epigram by Vitalis, more than one of these themes are brought together in a single poem[3].

I am very grateful to Professor James Hutton of Cornell University and Dr D. P. Walker of the Warburg Institute who read the typescript of this article and made helpful comments. This article was written in the course of a very happy year as a Junior Postdoctoral Fellow in the Society for the Humanities at Cornell University.

1. See C. GARAUD's admirable article, « Remarques sur le thème des ruines dans la littérature chrétienne », *Phenix*, XX, 1966, p. 148-158. The quotations from Jerome and Augustine are found, with references, on p. 154. Cf. DU BELLAY'S *Antiquitez de Rome*, sonnets 8 and 18.

2. See W. S. HECKSHER, *Die Romruinen, Die geistigen Voraussetzungen ihrer Wertung im Mittelalter und in der Renaissance*, Dissertation, Würzburg, 1936, p. 17-29 (for Petrarch), and ERASMUS, *Opera omnia*, I, ii, Amsterdam, 1971, p. 694. See also A. GRAF, *Roma nella memoria e nelle imaginazioni del medio evo*, Torino, 1915 (a very useful book : see especially pages 25-29 and 39-42) ; M. A. CARO, *La canción a las ruinas de Italica del licenciado Rodrigo Caro*, ed. J.M. Rivas Sacconi, Bogotá, 1947 (an unjustly neglected book) ; W. REHM, *Der Untergang Roms im abendländischen Denken*, Darmstadt, 1966 (see especially VII, « Zur Enstehung des Dekadenzbegriffs in Frankreich », p. 82-92) ; F. JOUKOVSKY, *La Gloire dans la poésie française et néolatine du XVIe siècle*, Genève, 1969 (especially p. 37-40, 95-96 and 307-312) ; B. W. WARDROPPER, « The Poetry of Ruins in the Golden Age », *Revista hispanica moderna*, XXXV, 1969, p. 295-305 ; and A. ROBICHOU-STRETZ, *La Vision de l'histoire dans l'œuvre de la Pléiade*, Paris, 1973, VI, « La Vision tragique de l'histoire et la chute de Rome », p. 201-204.

3. For the « ubi sunt » device, see especially E. GILSON, *Les Idées et les lettres* (Essais d'Art et de Philosophie), 2e éd., Paris, 1955, « De la Bible à François

(III) Janus Vitalis.

Janus Vitalis is now a little-known figure, so it seems appropriate to recall the salient facts in his life. The following account is taken from Antonio Mongitore's *Bibliotheca Sicula* :

> Janus Vitalis of Palermo was a priest, of noble family, a theologian, and a most renowned poet. He was given the name Joannes, but changed it to Janus [...] At a very early age he moved to Italy, and lived for a good while at Naples and longer still at Rome [...] He devoted his lively mind principally to the Muses, composed songs in Latin of such richness, charm and polish that they were acclaimed by men of learning, and won for himself immortal renown. He was an especial favourite of Leo X, an erudite man well-versed in literature [...] He lived long in Rome, enjoying great fame and widespread veneration, and he had many close links with the principal men of letters of his day, including Lilius Gregorius Giraldus and Joannes Pierius Valerianus. Valerianus had an almost brotherly love for him and praised his most distinguished mind, his gentle, civilized manners, and his singular honesty. I think he eventually died in Rome about 1560[4].

Vitalis seems to have been remembered most for his epigram on Rome. It was often praised, for example by Estienne Pasquier. Pasquier, in a letter to La Croix du Maine, urged the bibliographer to be selective in compiling his *Bibliothèque* :

> [...] Car pour avoir fait courir quelque chanson, sonnet, ou épigramme, celà ne me semble digne d'en faire grand compte, s'il n'estoit superlatif en son espece.

And, anticipating Boileau's aphorism about a good sonnet, Pasquier immediately singled out Vitalis's poem as the paragon :

> Parce qu'il y a bien difference entre bien faire un epigramme ou un livre : & toutefois il peult avenir qu'un epigramme bien fait tel que celuy de Vitalis pour la ville de Rome, se parangonnera à un livre[5].

Why, among the very numerous poems on the ruins of Rome, was Vitalis's epigram so successful ? There are several factors in its

---

Villon », p. 9-38 ; for the vanity theme, see T. C. CAVE, *Devotional Poetry in France, c.* 1570-1613, Cambridge, England, 1969, p. 147-156 ; on Fortuna, the literature is vast, but a good starting point is H. R. PATCH'S *The Goddess Fortuna in Mediaeval Literature*, Cambridge, Mass., 1927.

4. *Bibliotheca Sicula*, vol. I, 1707 (British Library 616 m 10), p. 305-306. Some contemporary eulogies of Vitalis were collected by Vincenzo AURIA (who died in 1710) to form a biography of Vitalis. This biography, which has remained in manuscript in Palermo, is referred to by G. TUMINELLO in his « Giano Vitale, umanista del secolo XVI » (*Archivo Storico Siciliano*, nuova serie, VIII, Palermo, 1883, p. 1-94). Tuminello mentions (p. 2-4) an edition of Vitalis's *Opera* published in Palermo in 1816 by Gregorio SPECIALE, but says that it is very defective. Vitalis is given only a passing mention by Girolamo TIRABOSCHI in his *Storia della letteratura italiana* (vol. 25, Milano, 1834, p. 34).

5. *Les Lettres*, Paris, M. D. LXXXVI (British Library 636 i 21), 278vo. Vitalis is not included in LA CROIX DU MAINE's *Bibliothèque* (Paris, 1584, British Library C75 g 2) : this lists only authors who wrote in French.

excellence : its involvement of the reader as the main protagonist, its demands upon his imagination, its brilliant synthesis of visual description and moral reflection, its spectacularly graphic elements (like the picture of the skeleton breathing threats), its almost miraculous conciseness and, above all perhaps, its author's acute sense of paradox, seen in the opening lines (" looking for Rome in Rome "), in the middle of the poem (" Rome conquered Rome ") and in the conclusion (" firm things collapse, fleeting things remain "). The text of Vitalis and its analogues given in this article will be numbered consecutively.

1. *JANUS VITALIS.* This epigram was published in *Iani Vitalis Panormitani sacrosanctae Romanae Ecclesiae Elogia*, a collection which appeared probably in 1552 or early in 1553.

> Qui Romam in media quaeris novus advena Roma,
>   Et Roman in Roma vix reperis media :
> Adspice murorum moles, praeruptaque saxa,
>   Obrutaque horrenti vasta theatra situ.
> Haec sunt Roma. Viden' velut ipsa cadavera tantae
>   Urbis adhuc spirent imperiosa minas ?
> Vicit ut haec mundum, nisa est se vincere : vicit,
>   A se non victum ne quid in orbe foret,
> Nunc victa in Roma, Roma illa invicta sepulta est ;
>   Atque eadem victrix, victaque Roma fuit.
> Albula Romani restabat nominis index,
>   Quia fugit ille [sic] citis non rediturus aquis.
> Disce hinc quid possit fortuna ; immota labascunt,
>   Et, quae perpetuo sunt agitata, manent[6].

6. For the dating of the *Romanae Ecclesiae Elogia*, see Tumminello, « Giano Vitale (...) » (cf. note 4 above), p. 58-59. I have not been able to consult a copy of the *Romanae Ecclesiae Elogia* and have reproduced the text as published by Tumminello (p. 59-60) who took it from G. Speciale's edition of Vitalis : *Iani Francisci Vitalis Rubimontii Panormitani Opera cura, studio et magnis sumptibus ex antiquis editionibus undique conquisitis accuratissime descripta*, Panormi, 1816.
    The epigram appeared also in the following works, and with the variant readings given :
(a) *Antonii Terminii Contursini Lucani, Iunii Albini Terminii senioris, Molsae, Bernardini Rotae equitis Neapolitani, et aliorum illustrium poetarum Carmina,* Venetiis, M.D.LIIII (Bibliothèque Nationale, Paris, Yc 7964), 64ro. The text (which in this edition is headed « Incerti ») is as above, except as follows : line 2, Et *Romae* in Roma *nil* reperis media ; line 7, *visa* est se vincere ; line 11, Romani *restat nunc* nominis ; line 12, *Quin etiam rapidis fertur in aequor* aquis. Line 14 reads perpetuo *sint* agitata but I take *sint* to be a misprint : all other editions give *sunt*.   This 1554 text seems better than the earlier one published by Tumminello.
(b) *Theodori Bezae Vezelii Poematum editio secunda, ab eo recognita. Item, ex Georgio Buchanano aliisque variis insignibus poetis excerpta Carmina, praesertimque epigrammata,* M.D.LXIX, excudebat Henr[icus] Steph[anus] (British Library 677 b 23 (1)), p. 191-192.   The text is that of (a) except that line 7 has *nisa* est se vincere.
(c) R. Gherus [*i.e.* Janus Gruterus], *Delitiae CC. Italorum poetarum, huius superiorisque aevi illustrium* [Frankfurt], M.D.CVIII (British Library 238 i 1-4), vol. 2, p. 1433 and (d) Bottari's *Carmina illustrium poetarum Italorum* (see poem 2 below), vol. 11, p. 375. In both cases the text lacks lines 7-8 and has the follo-

(iv) Latin analogues of Vitalis's poem.

The remainder of this article is concerned with the tradition Vitalis founded[7]. I start with two Latin analogues. The first

wing variants from the 1554 text : line 9 (of the 1554 text), *victrix Roma illa sepulta est* ; line 12, *Qui quoque nunc rapidis*.

(e) Philippus CAMERARIUS, *Operae horarum subcisivarum, sive Meditationes historicae* [...] *Centuria tertia*, Francofurti, M.DC.IX, British Library 1197 c 7, p. 240-241 and (f) the 1625 edition of the same work, British Library 1433 c 1 (3), p. 230. Both give the text of (a), ascribed to « quidam nobilis Poeta », except line 4, *Obsitaque ingenti* ; line 6, adhuc *spirant* ; line 7, *nixa* est se vincere.

(g) the 1610 translation by Simon GOULART of Camerarius's book : *Les Meditations historiques* [...], Lion, British Library 1195 k 16, III, p. 266, text of (e) and (f), ascribed to Vitalis ; and (h) the translation by François de ROSSET published in the same year : *Les Heures desrobées* [...], Paris, British Library 1197 b 7, p. 433-434, text of (e) and (f) (except line 10 has Atque *cadens* victrix), ascribed to « un excellent Poëte ». Both these books give also Du Bellay's poem.

(i) A. WARGOCKI, *O Rzymie poganskim i chrześcianskim*, Kraków, 1610, p. 56-57, The text given in this book, as reproduced by Graciotti (see below, note 7 : p. 123), presents the following variants from the 1554 text : line 4, Obrutaque *ingenti* ; line 6, adhuc *spirant* ; line 7, *nixa* est se vincere ; line 9, nunc *eadem in victa* Roma illa invicta sepulta est.

(j) Franciscus SWEERTIUS, *Selectae christianae orbis Deliciae ex Urbibus, Templis, Bibliothecis, et aliunde*, Coloniae Agrippinae, M.DC.XXV (British Library 604 b 18), p. 14. The text differs from (a) as follows : line 9, in Roma *victrix* invicta ; line 12, *Quaeque* etiam rapidis.

(k) P. LABBÉ, *Thesaurus epitaphiorum veterum ac recentium* [...], Parisiis, M.DC. LXVI (British Library 11405 bb 18), p. 467. The text, described as « omnium in ore vagantium », differs from (a) as follows ; line 4, *vasto* theatra situ ; line 9, *victrix Roma illa* sepulta est ; line 12, *Quaeque etiam rapidis in mare fertur* aquis.

(l) Joachim DU BELLAY, *Œuvres françoises*, éd. C. Marty-Laveaux (La Pléiade françoise), 2v., Paris, 1866, 67, II, p. 553-554, note 2, where the text is given as found in a manuscript in the Bibliothèque impériale. The poem is headed *De Roma incerti authoris* and has the following departures from the 1554 text : line 4, Obrutaque *ingenti* ; line 5, velut *alta* cadavera ; line 6, adhuc *spirant* ; line 7, *nixa* est se vincere ; line 11, restat *tum* nominis.

See also poem 18 below. A manuscript in Coimbra gives in line 3 « Aspice pendentes moles exesaque saxa » (see A. da COSTA RAMALHO, « Um epigrama em latim imitado por varios », *Humanitas*, Coimbra, N.S. I, 1952, p. 55-60 and N.S. II-III, 1953-54, p. 55-64.

7. Studies which mention one or more derivatives of Vitalis's epigram are the following : a note signed « EIRIONNACH », « Quevedo's sonnet on Rome », *Notes and Queries*, II, IX, 1866, p. 253, 448 ; J. Vianey, « *Les Antiquitez de Rome* : leurs sources latines et italiennes », *Bulletin italien*, I, 1901 (p. 187-189), p. 187 ; L. Léger, « Un petit problème de littérature comparée », *Académie des Inscriptions et Belles-Lettres, Comptes-rendus*, 1918, p. 123-126 ; H. G. Ward, « A Spanish quotation in Boswell's ' Johnson ' », *Notes and Queries*, 156, 1929, p. 111-112 ; M. R. Lida, « Para las fuentes de Quevedo », *Revista de Filología hispanica*, I, 1939 (p. 369-375), p. 370-371 ; L. Aragon, *Les Yeux d'Elsa*, Londres, 1943, p. XIII, footnote ; V. L. Saulnier, « Commentaires sur les *Antiquitez de Rome* », *Bibliothèque d'Humanisme et Renaissance*, XII, 1950 (p. 114-143), p. 132-133 ; S. Graciotti, « La fortuna di una elegia di Giano Vitale, o le rovine di Roma nella poesia polacca », *Aevum*, XXXIV, 1960, p. 122-136 ; R. Mortier, *La Poétique des ruines en France, ses origines, ses variations de la Renaissance à Victor Hugo*, Genève, 1974, p. 46-56. See also the studies by M. A. Caro and Costa Ramalho mentioned above (notes 2 and 6 respectively) and a thesis by M. D. Quainton (see note 9 below).

Besides the poems cited in this article, which are all substantially derived from Vitalis directly or indirectly, I have found many poems which include elements taken from Vitalis. Examples are a poem by Ioannes METELLUS SEQUANUS given by Sweertius (see previous note : p. 15), and two sonnets by GRÉVIN in addition to poem n° 6 below (see E. TRICOTEL, « Sonnets inédits de Grévin sur Rome », *Bulletin du Bibliophile*, 1862, n° XXII and GRÉVIN's *Théatre complet et poésies choisies*, ed. L. Pinvert, Paris, 1922, p. 341).

of these, though clearly related to Vitalis's poem, differs from it in a number of respects : it may conceivably have been written before it though this is unlikely since no early author that I have read questions the originality of Vitalis's poem. This analogue has been attributed to Fulvius Cardulus and, in a different version, to Andreas Frusius.

2. *FULVIUS CARDULUS* (?) or *ANDREAS FRUSIUS* (?). *Carmina illustrium poetarum Italorum* (collected and edited by Giovanni Gaetano Bottari), Florentiae, M.DCCXIX-M.DCCXXVI, British Library 657 a 16-26, III, p. 250 (" Fulvii Carduli ") :

In urbem Romam

Languentem gressum paulisper siste viator,
    Et lege marmoreis carmina scripta notis.
Roma fui, quondam toto celeberrima mundo,
    Arte, situ, ingeniis, Marte, opibusque potens.
Sola triumphatum fraenavi legibus orbem :
    Paruit imperio terra, fretumque meo.
Impositae septem nituerunt montibus arces,
    Totque arcus, themae, templa, theatra, domus.
Prorsus eram felix, si non ruitura fuissem ;
    Et mihi ni cunctas sors rapuisset opes.

Roma, ego iam non sum : perii, propriisque ruinis
    Obruta sum : gremio condor & ipsa meo.
Relliquias quascumque vides, quae diruta cernis
    Moenia, splendoris sunt monumenta mei.
Frustra igitur Romam Romae nunc quaeris : abire
    Hinc licet : ah Romae Roma sepulta iacet.
Interea monitus, perituras ne strue moles :
    Exemplo poteris cautior esse meo.
Carpe viam, volui scires haec pauca : memento
    Ut meminisse mei, sic meminnisse tui[8].

The second Latin analogue, by Jean-Antoine de Baïf, clearly derives from Vitalis. But it is much less rich than the Sicilian's poem : lines 11-12 of Baïf's poem lack the sustained metaphor of Vitalis (*cadaver* and *sepulta*), the successful repetition (of forms of the word *vincere*) and the elegant chiasmus.

3. *JEAN ANTOINE DE BAÏF*, Carminum liber I, Lutetiae, M.D.LXXVII (British Library 843 b 14 (3)), 25 vo :

Tu cui per ipsam Roma quaeritur Romam,

---

8. The text which SWEERTIUS (*Deliciae*, p. 15-16) and LABBÉ (*Thesaurus epitaphiorum*, p. 471) (see note 6 above) attributed to FRUSIUS has the following variants : line 2, carmina *sculpta* ; line 4, *Marte, situ, ingenio, nobilitate* potens ; line 5, *Quippe triumphalis* fraenavi ; line 7, septem *micuerunt collibus* ; line 8, Theatra, *Viae* ; line 9, *peritura* fuissem ; line 10, Et *nisi tam multas* sors ; line 15, *tu* quaeris ; line 16, *Iam potes hinc*, Romae ; line 17 Interea *temere* perituras ; line 18, *Cautior exemplo cum potes* esse meo.

Et cui per ipsam Roma nulla iam Romam
Apparet, Hospes : Cerne saxa murorum
Exesa, vasto culmine obrutas moles,
Theatra, circos, ambulationesque
Thermasque & arcus pensiles triumphales,
Bellique iure temporisque destructa
Haec omnia : haec sunt Roma : in his iacet Roma.
Videsn' ut immane urbis hoc ruinosum
Adhuc cadaver imperii minas spirat ?
Devicit orbem seque postea vicit,
Ne quidquam in orbe non sibi foret victum.
Victamque Romam nunc se habet suum victa
Tandem sepulcrum Roma, quae stetit victrix.

(v) French imitations of Vitalis.

A very famous derivative of Vitalis's poem is that by Joachim du Bellay, published in 1558 in the *Antiquitez de Rome*.

A comparison between the texts of Vitalis and Du Bellay makes it plain that Du Bellay was imitating and emulating the Sicilian poet. Du Bellay, writing in French (and choosing ten-syllable lines for this sonnet, whereas half the *Antiquitez de Rome* are in twelve-syllable lines), has to sacrifice some of the substance of Vitalis's poem, for the French language was much less economical than the Latin : Ronsard wrote in the 1572 preface to his *Franciade* that thirty lines of Latin are the equivalent of more than sixty lines of French. Thus, Du Bellay has no equivalent for the words *horrenti situ*, and omits the notion of the skeleton breathing threats. While simplifying the poem, he makes the moral conclusions more explicit (for example in lines 5 and 8 of his sonnet) and his concluding paradox is especially well-expressed. To emulate a Latin poem successfully in as many lines of French is a virtuoso performance. It is an example of Du Bellay's successful practice of that process of imitation that he had advocated in the *Deffence et illustration de la langue françoyse* (I, VII)[9]. François Garasse, in *Les recherches des recherches & autres Œuvres de Me Estienne Pasquier* (...), cited Du Bellay's imitation of Vitalis's poem to support his proposition that the French language can produce good epigrams : « Quand il fut accommodé à la Françoise par Joachim du Belay, on l'estima beaucoup plus que devant pour la beauté de sa conclusion (...) »[10]. And Guillaume Colletet, in a section of *L'Art poétique* headed « Sonnets fameux en nostre

---

9. For a fuller, and excellent, comparison of the two texts see Malcolm D. QUAINTON's *Themes of flux and stability in the poetry of Ronsard and the Pléiade* (Ph. D. thesis, Exeter, 1974, vol. I, p. 144-149).

10. Paris, M.DCXXII, p. 543-544. Garasse attributed the original poem not to Vitalis but to « Casanova », presumably meaning M. Antonius CASANOVA. But I have not found it printed anywhere with the works of Casanova : in all the ancient editions which I have consulted it is either anonymous or attributed to Vitalis.

langue », wrote : « Son Sonnet des antiquitez de Rome (...) qui n'est à dire vray qu'une pure traduction d'une élegante Epigramme Latine de Janus Vitalis, éclata merveilleusement d'abord ; et ce d'autant plus, que la conclusion en est infiniment noble, et surprenante (...) ».[11]

4. *JOACHIM DU BELLAY, Les Regrets et autres œuvres poëtiques suivis des Antiquitez de Rome, Plus un songe ou Vision sur le mesme subject*, texte établi par J. Joliffe, introduit et commenté par M. A. Screech (Textes Littéraires Français), Genève, 1966.   The third sonnet in the *Antiquitez de Rome* reads :

       Nouveau venu qui cherches Rome en Rome,
           Et rien de Rome en Rome n'apperçois,
           Ces vieux palais, ces vieux arcz que tu vois,
           Et ces vieux murs, c'est ce que Rome on nomme.
       Voy quel orgueil, quelle ruine : & comme
           Celle qui mist le monde sous ses loix
           Pour donter tout, se donta quelquefois,
           Et devint proye au temps, qui tout consomme.
       Rome de Rome est le seul monument,
           Et Rome Rome a vaincu seulement.
           Le Tybre seul, qui vers la mer s'enfuit,
       Reste de Rome. O mondaine inconstance !
           Ce qui est ferme, est par le temps destruit,
           Et ce qui fuit, au temps fait resistance.

Another French imitation of Vitalis, that by Jean Doublet, is much less good than Du Bellay's.   Doublet's second line, for instance, loses the paradox of the original, since it can be read " straight ".   An abundance of padding dissipates Du Bellay's and Vitalis's conciseness : the most glaring example is perhaps in the last line which is just where padding ought not to be !   Lines 5-8 of Doublet illustrate a peril which Du Bellay sidestepped : a poet who tries to include in a French poem every detail of a Latin original risks prolixity.   Lines 13-16 lose or dilute Vitalis's chiasmus, antithesis and repetition.

5. *JEAN DOUBLET, Élégies, suivies des Épigrammes et Rimes diverses* (Cabinet du bibliophile, XI), Paris, 1871.   It is stated in the introduction that Doublet's *Elegies* were published in 1559, but the editor (whose name is not given) does not make clear whether the *Epigrammes*, which include the poem reproduced here, were also published at that time.   The following poem is found on p. 142-143 :

               Sur les ruines de Rome
               Tiré de l'épigramme latin

---

11. G. COLLETET, *L'Art poétique, I : Traitté de l'épigramme et Traitté du sonnet*, ed. P. A. Jannini (Textes Littéraires Français), Genève, 1965, p. 178.

> Estranger qui viens, bon homme,
>   A Rome pour Rome voir,
>   Et ne peus méme, dans Rome,
>   Rien de Rome apercevoir,
> Voi des murailles les masses,
>   Voi les marbres démolis
>   Et les grans desertes places
>   Des théatres abolis.
> Voi-la Rome : considere
>   Comme, morte qu'ell' soit or,
>   Sa charoigne brave et fiere
>   Semble menasser encor.
> Ell' a vaincu terre et onde,
>   Pui ell' s'est veincue aussi,
>   Afin qu'à veincre du monde
>   Ne lui restat rien ainsi.
> Or, sous ceste Romme esclave,
>   Rome la maistresse git,
>   Et l'asservie et la brave
>   Dorment en ce mesme lit.
> Le Tibre, d'entiere marque,
>   Reste seul au nom Romain,
>   Et encor, sous mainte barque,
>   A la mer file soudain,
> Voi combien peut la fortune :
>   Ce qui ne bougeoit vient bas,
>   Et ce qui n'a cesse aucune
>   Demeure, et ne se sert pas[12].

Jacques Grévin is a more interesting minor poet, remembered principally for his plays and for the invectives which he wrote against Ronsard when Ronsard defended the Roman Catholic faith. The sonnet given here clearly belongs to the tradition founded by Vitalis, but Grévin has introduced so much that is new that it is impossible to say whether he was imitating the Sicilian poet or Du Bellay.

6. *JACQUES GRÉVIN*. E. Tricotel, " Sonnets inédits de Grévin sur Rome ", *Bulletin du Bibliophile*, 1862, p. 1044-1061. There are twenty-four sonnets, and sonnet IV reads as follows :

> Arrivé dedans Rome en Rome je cherchois
> Rome qui fut jadis la merveille du monde ;
> Ne voyant cette Rome à nulle autre seconde,
> D'avoir perdu mes pas honteux je me faschois.

12. A note on p. 154 (wrongly numbered 254) says that the epigram imitated by Doublet is by Andrea Navagero, but no reference is given in support of this statement. Navagero did write a comparable poem *Ad urbem Patavium*, but the likeness is remote (see GRUTERUS's *Delitiae CC. Italorum poetarum*, vol. 2, p. 126-127).
    Doublet's poem was also published in *Annales poétiques, ou Almanach des Muses, depuis l'origine de la Poésie Françoise*, 40 v., 1778-1788 (British Library 242 d 39 — e 32), vol. 10, p. 69-70, but without the last two verses and with minor variants : line 10, *Quoique* morte ; line 11, *Que son ombre*, brave ; line 14, *Et puis* s'est ; line 18, *sa* maistresse ; line 20, *un* meme lit !

Du matin jusqu'au soir ça et là je marchois
Ores au Colisée, et ore à la Rotonde,
Ores monté bien haut regardant à la ronde,
De voir cette grand Rome en Rome je taschois.

Mais enfin je cognus que c'estoit grand folie,
Car Rome est dès longtemps en Rome ensevelie,
Et Rome n'est sinon un sépulchre apparent.

Qui va donc dedans Rome et cherche en cette sorte
Ressemble au chevaucheur qui toujours va courant
Et cherche en tous endroit le cheval qui le porte.

(vi) The devotional tradition.

Vitalis's poem is a compelling blend of description and reflection and it is scarcely surprising that authors of devotional poems, who so often used the visual as a starting-point for contemplation, assimilated his poem and published adaptations of it. Antoine de la Roche Chandieu, who published sometimes under the pseudonym of " Sadeel " and who incidentally was another Reformer who wrote against Ronsard, invokes the ruins to undermine man's earthly hopes : his poem was published in a collection of edifying verse, the *Octonaires suz la vanité et inconstance du monde*. Chandieu's *Octonaires* were translated into Latin by Joannes Jacomotus (Jean Jaquemot), and two versions of his translation are given here. It is not possible to deduce from these texts whether it is Vitalis or Du Bellay who is his model.

7 and 8. *JOANNES JACOMOTUS (JEAN JAQUEMOT)*, *Variorum poematium liber* (Geneva), M.D.CI (British Library 11712 b 36 (2)), includes *Octonaires de M. de Chandieu, suz la vanité & inconstance du monde* and on facing pages *De inconstantissima Mundi vanitate, ex octostichis Gallicis A. Sadeelis* (p. 94-133). There are fifty poems each in French and Latin. Number XXXII reads as follows (p. 118 and 119) :

L'estranger estonné regarde, & se pourmeine
Par les antiquités de la gloire Romaine :
Il void ses arcs rompus, & ses marbres luisans
Mutilés, massacrés par la fureur des ans :
Il void pendante en l'air une moussue pierre
Qui arme ses costés des longs bras du lierre :
Et qui est-ce, dit-il, qui icy bas se fonde,
Puis que le temps vainqueur trionfe de ce monde ?

Antiquam attonitus Romuleae videns
Gentis gloriam, opes, scriptaque marmora,
Arcus, & lapides aethere pendulos,
Quos muscus tenuis, quos hederae ambiunt
Circum bacciferae, quosque furentium
Annorum series invida diruit,

Vanas, hospes ait, quis stolide locat
Hic spes, tempus ubi cuncta domat vorax ?

9. *JOANNES JACOMOTUS (JEAN JAQUEMOT)*. The following poem is found in *Delitiae C. poetarum Gallorum, huius superiorisque aevi illustrium*, a compilation published by Janus Gruterus under the pseudonym of Ranutius Gherus (3v., (Frankfurt,) M.D.CIX, British Library G. 9605-7). Poems by Jacomotus are in volume II (p. 350-375), and this one is under the heading *De inconstantissima mundi vanitate, ex Gallicis Sadeelis* and is on p. 359 :

Antiqua priscae monstra superbiae
Gentis Quiritum, quum videt insolens
    Hospes, Colossos, porticus &
    Marmora cum Theatris, stupendos
Arcus, sequentum quae fuga temporum,
Imbres edaces, atque Aquilo impotens
    Deiecit & muscus, teguntque
    Nunc hederae simul obsoleta ;
Miratur immortalia si bona
Hic esse credant, tempore qui brevi
    Cernunt triumphatas opes, &
    Tot veteris monumenta saecli.

Two devotional poems filiated to Vitalis's epigram are by Simon Goulart. Goulart's sonnets are found in an anthology of poems by Reformers published to " resjouir ceux qui ont quelque crainte de Dieu " and to " inciter beaucoup d'excellens personnages qui suppriment trop long temps leurs doctes & sainctes poësies, de les mettre en avant ". In his dedicatory epistle to Frederick, Count Palatine of the Rhine and First Elector of the Empire, the editor, Philippe Depas, claims that the holy content of these poems will compensate for any lack of polish : « la saincteté de ces poemes-ci fera que les lecteurs ne s'arresteront pas du tout aux mots ni à la rime ». Such studied amateurishness, which was not uncommon among Reformers, may give poetry a certain unsophisticated charm, but this is a dubious substitute for the inspired professionalism of Du Bellay. Goulart is much less successful than Du Bellay in involving the reader : he lacks the concentration on essentials, the haunting images, the bewitching paradoxes ; and the concluding lines of these two sonnets by Goulart are so explicitly didactic they make both poems sound banal. A poet who exploits a well-known theme has to be in some way better than his predecessors to avoid seeming much inferior. Goulart, like Chandieu, uses the original themes so independently that it is impossible to say whether his model is Vitalis or Du Bellay.

10 and 11. *SIMON GOULART. Poëmes chrestiens de B. de Montmeja, & autres divers auteurs.* Recueillis et nouvellement mis en

lumière par Philippes Depas, (s.l.,) M.D.LXXIIII, Bibliothèque
Nationale, Paris, Rés. Ye 1825.   This anthology includes a series
of *Imitations chrestiennes* and a *Suite des imitations chrestiennes*
both ascribed to « S.G.S. » : these initials, according to T. C.
Cave (*Devotional Poetry* (...), p. 140 — see above, note 3), designate
Goulart.   The *Suite des imitations chrestiennes* comprises two books
of sonnets, and sonnets 13-16 of the second book are headed *Sur
les pourtraicts des antiquitez Romaines*.   Sonnets 15 and 16 (p. 182)
read as follows :

> Tout ce que Rome tient de sa gloire premiere,
> C'est le Tybre coulant. Ses palais arrangez,
> Ses Theatres, tombeaux, ont esté saccagez
> Par le feu devorant & l'espée meurtriere.
>   Le temps qui mange tout, laisse un peu de matiere
> Rude, vieille & rompue, & des piliers rongez
> De sa maligne dent : brief par luy sont changez
> Les beaux traits qu'avoit Rome en sa grandeur entiere.
>   Ce capitole grand qui tant ferme sembloit,
> Et sous qui l'univers fleschissoit & trembloit ;
> Presque tout ruiné, chet tous les jours en poudre.
>   O dieu, quels changemens ! ce qui ne semble rien,
> Ce qui coule & s'enfuit, brise du temps la foudre :
> Et toute grandeur tombe en ce val terrien.

>   Quand je pense aux palais, aux portiques, aux temples,
> Amphitheatres ronds, aux monts audacieux,
> Dont Rome se bravoit, quand le destin des cieux
> Rangeoit dessous sa main, rois & provinces amples.
>   Je m'escrie dans moy : puis qu'or tu ne contemples
> Qu'une ruine horrible, en l'œuvre industrieux
> Du burin qui combat le temps injurieux :
> Voy de la vanité mortelle les exemples.
>   Rome dompta le monde, & soy mesme donta.
> Alors que sa grandeur à son comble monta,
> Sa ruine survint. Ce que tu vois de reste
>   Aux humains va monstrant, que dedans la rondeur
> De ce grand univers, plus l'humaine grandeur
> Esleve haut son chef, plus sa ruine est preste.

(VII) The French civil wars.

   In 1562 France plunged into a long series of civil wars.   To express
their feelings French poets had no better literary models than earlier
poets' reflections on the self-destruction of Rome, no better model
than Vitalis's epigram and its derivatives.   The three sonnets
given here seem all to be based on Du Bellay's poem.   The conclusion to La Jessée's sonnet is based on the sixth sonnet of Du Bellay's
Antiquitez.

12. *JÉROME HENNEQUIN, Regrets sur les miseres advenues
à la France par les Guerres Civiles. Avec deux prieres à Dieu*, par

H. H. (Jérôme Hennequin) Parisien, Paris, M.D.LXIX, Bibliothèque Nationale, Paris, Rés. Ye 436.   The attribution to Hennequin is from the Bibliothèque Nationale's catalogue of printed
books.   Hennequin, frequently imitating Ronsard's *Discours des
miseres*, laments the civil wars and places the responsibility for
them on the Reformers.   The following sonnet is found at 4ᵛᵒ :

Toy estranger qui viens ici cercher la France,
Et rien de France, en France, esbahy n'aperçois,
Fors que ces vieux Palais, & ces murs que tu vois
De nouveau efforcez tomber en decadence.
Ce n'est des estrangiers la force ny puissance,
Que a faict ce mechef, ains ce sont ces François,
Qui dompterent hardis le monde quelque fois,
Auteurs de ce malheur, par leur sotte inconstance.
La France, de la France est le seul monument,
Et seulle France, France a vaincu seullement.
Le païs ruyné, les Églises bruslées,
    Sont le reste de France, ô par trop grand malheur.
O fortune inconstante, ô trop grand creve-cueur.
De voir par ses subjects les villes desolées.

13. *JEAN DE LA JESSÉE, Les premieres œuvres francoyses*,
Anvers, M.D.LXXXIII, British Library 839 h 25, 26, p. 179 :

Passant, qui par la France esmerveillé chemines,
La France n'est plus France : & ces champz depeuplez,
Ces Chasteaux demolis, ces murs demantelez,
Sont encor frais tesmoingz de ses noyses mutines.
Tu vois ce que les gentz loingtaines, & voysines,
Ne mirent onc à chef : où ses sugetz troublez
Debellantz tout, se sont à la fin debellez :
Ainsi l'heur des grandeurs cede au gast des ruines.
Le seul Françoys estoit son Seigneur, & son Roy,
Le seul Françoys estoit son exemple, & sa Loy :
Il devoit seul aussi se brasser ceste guerre.
    Car les Dieus ne vouloyent qu'autre pouvoir deffit
D'un pouvoir non-pareil, cil qui pareille fit
Sa hardiesse au Ciel, & sa force à la Terre.

14. *Sonnets sur la corruption et malice de ce temps*, [s.l.,] M.D.XCI,
Bibliothèque Nationale, Paris, Rés. p. Ye 381.   The tenth sonnet
(A ivᵛᵒ) reads :

Voyageur curieux, qui cherches France en France,
Et qui plus rien de France en France n'appercois,
Ces villes & ces forts qu'en ruine tu vois,
Ne sont plus que de France un petit d'apparance.
Quoy, tu es estonné, tu demeures en transe.
Elle, qui tout pouvoit asservir à ses Loix,
S'asservit elle-mesme & donte à ceste fois
Par combats intestins, se perdant à outrance.
Ores France de France est le vray monument.
Tu vois que France France a vaincu seulement,

Elle-mesme s'est pleuë à se couper la gorge.
O pitié ! ce n'est plus qu'un horrible desert,
Qui ore à l'estranger aveque honte sert
De fables & blasons qu'à bon droit il en forge.

(VIII) Polish, English and Spanish derivatives of Vitalis.

It is scarcely surprising that, at a time when the vernacular
literatures of Europe owed a lot not only to contemporary Latin
texts but also to each other, Vitalis's epigram found echoes not
just in Italy and France, but in other places too. The poem by
Sep Szarzynski is based, as Mr P. S. Ziaja kindly informed me,
on Vitalis's epigram. It was apparently not printed until 1601,
twenty years after Szarzynski's death[13]. Spenser's poem is
found in his translation of Du Bellay's *Antiquitez de Rome* : it
retains much of Du Bellay's original, though in line seven it
loses the idea that supreme power is necessarily self-destructive,
and in the conclusion the notion of *temps* (a deliberate and very
poignant echo, in Du Bellay, of line eight) is lost. The poems by
Thomas Heywood (d. 1650 ?) and William Browne (1590-c. 1645)
are translations of Vitalis. Quevedo's poem appears to be a fairly
free imitation of Vitalis : Samuel Johnson was to point out the
source when a companion of his cited Quevedo's poem[14].

15. *MIKOŁAJ SĘP SZARZYŃSKI*, *Rytmy abo wiersze polskie*,
opracowała i wstępem opatrzyła Jadwiga Sokołowska, Warszawa,
1957, p. 74 :

Epitafium Rzymowi

Ty, co Rzym wpośród Rzyma chcąc baczyć, pielgrzymie,
A wżdy baczyć nie możesz w samym Rzyma Rzymie,
Patrzaj na okrąg murów i w rum obrócone
Teatra i kościoły, i słupy stłuczone :
To są Rzym. Widzisz, jako miasta tak możnego
I trup szczęścia poważność wypuszcza pierwszego.
To miasto, świat zwalczywszy, i siebie zwalczyło,
By nic niezwalczonego od niego nie było.
Dziś w Rzymie zwyciężonym Rzym niezwyciężony
(To jest ciało w swym cieniu) leży pogrzebiony.
Wszytko się w nim zmieniło, sam trwa prócz odmiany
Tyber, z piaskiem do morza, co bieży, zmieszany.
Patrz, co Fortuna broi : to się popsowało,
Co było nieruchome ; trwa, co się ruchało.

16. *EDMUND SPENSER*, *Poetical works*, ed. J. C. Smith and

---

13. There is a survey of poems in Polish on the ruins of Rome in the article
by GRACIOTTI cited in note 7 above : Graciotti analyzes Szarzynski's poem on
pages 127-129 of his article.
14. See *Boswell's Life of Johnson* [& c.], ed. G. B. Hill and L. F. Powell, 6 v.,
III, Oxford, 1934, p. 250-251.

E. de Selincourt, London, New York & Toronto, 1966, includes
(p. 509-514) the *Ruines of Rome : by du Bellay*, originally published
in 1591 as part of the *Complaints, Containing sundrie small Poemes
of the Worlds Vanitie*. Spenser's translation of the third sonnet
(the italics are found in the text) reads :

> Thou stranger, which for *Rome* in *Rome* here seekest,
> And nought of *Rome* in *Rome* perceiv'st at all,
> These same olde walls, olde arches, which thou seest,
> Olde Palaces, is that which *Rome* men call.
> Behold what wreake, what ruine, and what wast,
> And how that she, which with her mightie powre
> Tam'd all the worlds, hath tam'd herselfe at last,
> The pray of time, which all things doth devowre.
> *Rome* now of *Rome* is th'onely funerall,
> And onely *Rome* of *Rome* hath victorie ;
> Ne ought save Tyber hastning to his fall
> Remaines of all : O worlds inconstancie.
> That which is firme doth flit and fall away,
> And that is flitting, doth abide and stay.

17. *THOMAS HEYWOOD, The Hierarchie of the blessed Angells.
Their Names, orders and Offices. The fall of Lucifer with his
Angells*, London, 1635, British Library 641 k 19 refers (p. 459) to
« an excellent Epigram composed by *Ianus Vitalis* », cites the
first four lines (1554 text), and gives the following translation :

> New Stranger to the City come,
> Who midst of Rome enquir'st for Rome,
> And midst of Rome canst nothing spye
> That lookes like Rome, cast backe thine eye ;
> Behold of walls the ruin'd mole,
> The broken stones not one left whole ;
> Vast Theatres and Structures high,
> That levell with the ground now lye.
> These now are Rome, and of that Towne
> Th'imperious Reliques still do frowne,
> And ev'n in their demolisht seat
> The Heav'ns above them seem to threat.
> As she the World did once subdue,
> Ev'n so her selfe she overthrew :
> Her hand in her owne bloud she'embru'd,
> Lest she should leave ought unsubdu'd :
> Vainquisht in Rome, Invict Rome now
> Intombed lies, as forc'd to bow.
> The same Rome (of the World the head)
> Is Vanquisher and Vanquished.
> The river Albula's the same,
> And still preserves the Roman name ;
> Which with a swift and speedy motion
> Is hourely hurry'd to the Ocean.
> Learne hence what Fortune can ; what's strong
> And seemeth fixt, endures not long :
> But more assurance may be layd
> On what is moving and unstayd.

18. *WILLIAM BROWNE, The poems*. ed. G. Goodwin (The Muses' Library), 2v., London & New York, 1894, includes, under the heading *In urbem Romam qualis est hodie*, the text of Vitalis's poem. The version given is that of Sweertius (see note 6 above) with variants (line 6, adhuc *spirant*; line 9, victrix *Roma illa sepulta est*; line 11, *nunc restat* nominis). Then comes the following (II, p. 300-301):

> On Rome as it is now
>
> Thou, who to look for Rome, to Rome art come,
> And in the midst of Rome find'st nought of Rome;
> Behold her heaps of walls, her structures rent,
> Her theatres overwhelm'd of vast extent;
> Those now are Rome. See how those ruins frown,
> And speak the threats yet of so brave a town.
> By Rome, as once the world, is Rome o'ercome,
> Lest ought on earth should not be quell'd by Rome:
> Now conqu'ring Rome doth conquer'd Rome inter;
> And she the vanquish'd is and vanquisher.
> To show us where she stood there rests alone
> Tiber; yet that too hastens to be gone.
>> Learn hence what fortune can. Towns glide away;
>> And rivers, which are still in motion, stay.

19. *FRANCISCO DE QUEVEDO, Obra poética*, ed. J. M. Bleuca, 3 v., Madrid, 1969-1971, I, p. 418:

> A Roma sepultada en sus ruinas.
>
> Buscas en Roma a Roma, ¡ oh, peregrino !,
> y en Roma misma a Roma no la hallas:
> cadáver son las que ostentó murallas,
> y tumba de sí proprio el Aventino.
> Yace donde reinaba el Palatino;
> y limadas del tiempo, las medallas
> más se muestran destrozo a las batallas
> de las edades que blasón latino.
> Sólo el Tibre quedó, cuya corriente,
> si ciudad la regó, ya, sepoltura,
> la llora con funesto son doliente.
> ¡ Oh, Roma !, en tu grandeza, en tu hermosura,
> huyó lo que era firme, y solamente
> lo fugitivo permanece y dura.

According to the editor, this sonnet appeared in print in *El Parnaso español* (...), Madrid, 1648 and in *El Parnaso español* (...), Zaragoza, 1649.

(IX) Conclusion.

The translations and adaptations of Vitalis's poem by so many different authors writing in such varied circumstances in the sixteenth and seventeenth centuries show how timeless his epigram is; and many poems of more recent date could be cited. For example, many of Vitalis's ideas were reproduced and developed by John Dyer in a long poem published in 1740 with the title *The Ruins of Rome* : Dyer implicitly acknowledged his indebtedness by reproducing on his titlepage an extract from Vitalis's epigram[15]. In 1758, Nicodemo Czeczel published a poem in Polish based apparently on Du Bellay's adaptation of Vitalis[16]. In the early nineteenth century, Charles-Julien Lioult de Chênedollé, a protégé of Madame de Staël and a friend of Chateaubriand, published an imitation of Quevedo's adaptation of Vitalis (Louis Aragon, to whom I owe the reference to Chênedollé, also drew on the tradition of Vitalis's epigram in his preface to *Les yeux d'Elsa*) ; the modern English and American translations of Vitalis's epigram and its derivatives are numerous (these include a rendering of Du Bellay's poem by Ezra Pound) ; and, interestingly, Quevedo's poem was put back into Latin by Miguel Antonio Caro who, it seems, did not know that Quevedo's poem had a Latin source[17]. Clearly the appeal of Vitalis's poem to poets and readers of poetry is an eternal one.

Besides its timeless attraction, good poetry very often has also, as I indicated at the beginning of this article, a particular appeal to the poet's own contemporaries. The poet will in some cases be giving a detailed commentary, either overt or allegorical, on contemporary cultural, social or political issues. But a poet can be topical without addressing himself to specific contemporary

15. The extract on the titlepage of DYER's pamphlet, which was published in London, consists in the four lines beginning « Aspice murorum moles ».
16. CZECZEL's poem is referred to by Graciotti in the article cited in note 7 above (p. 131). The text can be found in *Poezja Polskiego Oswiecenia, Antologia*, opracował Jan Kott, rysunki J. P. Norblina, Warszawa, 1954, [p. 49].
17. For CHÊNEDOLLÉ's text, first published in his *Études poétiques* of 1820, see his *Œuvres complètes*, précédées d'une notice par Sainte-Beuve, Paris, 1864 (p. 222-223). For the reference to ARAGON, see note 7 above. POUND's translation can be read in *The Translations of Ezra Pound*, ed. H. Kenner, London, 1953, p. 406. For CARO, see his *Versiones latinas*, edicion dirigida por Jose Manuel Rivas Sacconi, Bogota, 1951, p. 37.
See also : L. R. LIND, ed., *Latin Poetry in Verse Translation from the Beginnings to the Renaissance*, Boston, 1957, p. 384 (translation by J. V. CUNNINGHAM of Vitalis's poem) ; *Formal Spring, French Renaissance poems [...]* with translations by R. N. CURREY, London, New York & Toronto, 1950, p. 137 (translation of Du Bellay's poem) ; J. C. L. Simonde de Sismondi, *De la Littérature du Midi de l'Europe*, 4 t., Paris, 1813, IV, p. 90 (translation of Quevedo) ; the translation of Sismondi by Thomas ROSCOE (*Historical View of the Literature of the South of Europe*, 2nd ed., 2v., London, 1846, II, p. 361 : a translation of Quevedo perhaps done from Sismondi's French rendering) ; D. LARDNER, *The Cabinet Cyclopedia, Biography, Eminent Literary and Scientific Men of Italy, Spain and Portugal*, 3 v., London, 1835-37, III, p. 274 (a translation of Quevedo by one of the WIFFEN brothers) ; S. RESNICK & J. PASMANTIER, *An Anthology of Spanish Literature in English Translation*, London, 1958, p. 272 (translation by Felicia D. HEMANS of Quevedo) ; A. FLORES, ed., *An Anthology of Spanish Poetry from Garcilaso to Garcia Lorca in English Translation with Spanish Originals*, New York, 1961, p. 131 (translation by Kate FLORES of Quevedo). For a French translation of Quevedo, see R. BOUVIER, *Quevedo, Homme du diable, homme de Dieu*, Paris, 1929, p. 358.

issues : his work can be a response to the psychological needs of the men of his day. This was perhaps more often the case in the Renaissance than it is today, for in the Renaissance, poetry seems to have touched the hearts and minds of the masses. Meditative poems like those we have been examining are undoubtedly among the poems which appeal to the psyche of contemporaries.

To define precisely the psychological appeal that any particular poem or group of poems had at the time of publication is very difficult. My one suggestion about the contemporary appeal of Vitalis's tradition is prompted by the fact that well over half the poems cited in this article were produced by French authors during the period of the civil wars — several of them, indeed, as we have seen, refer specifically to the wars. It is distinctly possible that many of these adaptations of Vitalis's epigram are attempts to exorcise the insecurity of those historical moments by using a venerably traditional set of topoi to express that insecurity : to show that history and culture securely prove that man's earthly existence is intrinsically insecure.

Malcolm C. Smith.
Bedford College, London.

Malcolm C. Smith

JOACHIM DU BELLAY'S RENOWN
AS A LATIN POET

The aim of this paper is to draw attention to Joachim du Bellay's Latin poems which today are relatively little known. I shall examine first Du Bellay's reasons for writing poetry in Latin; secondly, the content of his three collections óf Latin poetry; thirdly, evidence for the success of certain individual poems; and finally, contemporary verdicts upon his Latin poetry.

It is a curious paradox that the man who most ardently defended vernacular poetry in the early days of the Pléiade was later to acquire renown as the author of three collections of Latin poetry. When, in 1558, Du Bellay published the first of these three collections, the P o e m a t u m l i b r i q u a t u o r , he seems, not surprisingly, to have felt that he owed his readers some explanation for his adoption of the Latin language. This adoption of Latin, he suggests, was motivated by a personal, almost capricious whim: though wedded to the French Muse, he mischievously declared, he had fallen in love with the Latin. [1] But there are other, much more plausible explanations. The most obvious one, perhaps, is that in writing these poems during his four-year stay in Rome, he was influenced by the G e n i u s l o c i . The occasion for his change of language, he implied in an epigram with the title "Cur intermissis gallicis latine scribat", was his journey to Rome in 1553. [2] When in Rome, one should, as he hinted in his famous elegy "Patriae desiderium", write as the Romans wrote:

> Hoc Latium poscit, Romae haec debita linguae
> Est opera, huc Genius compulit loci. [3]

In sonnet 10 of L e s R e g r e t s , Du Bellay specifies that he wrote Latin because nobody in Italy understood French. He was moreover in contact with Italian poets who wrote in Latin. [4] Besides, it appears that his employer in Rome, cardinal Jean du Bellay, himself no mean Latin poet, was encouraging him to write in Latin: Guillaume Colletet wrote in his V i e d e J o a c h i m d u B e l l a y that "(...) ce fut à l'imitation, et par le conseil du Cardinal du Bellay, son parent, qu'il composa des

vers latins". [5] One can readily understand the cardinal giving such encouragement: he must have been distinctly less embarrassed by Joachim's
P o e m a t u m   l i b r i   q u a t u o r than he was by L e s   R e g r e t s . [6]

A second reason for Du Bellay's adoption of Latin may well be a desire
to enhance his stature as a poet. His own success as a vernacular poet, and Ronsard's,
led to a proliferation of very mediocre French poetry, as Montaigne explained:

> Depuis que Ronsard et Du Bellay ont donné credit à
> nostre poësie Françoise, je ne vois si petit apprentis
> qui n'enfle des mots, qui ne renge les cadences à peu pres
> comme eux. P l u s   s o n a t   q u a m   v a l e t . Pour le vulgaire,
> il ne fut jamais tant de poëtes. [7]

Indeed, so numerous were third-rate poets that Etienne Pasquier declared: "(...) il se presentoit tant de petits avortons de Poesie, qu'il fut un
temps, que le peuple se voulant mocquer d'un homme, il l'appelloit Poete".
[8] Du Bellay himself was aware of the lack of public respect for poets,
and said it may owe something to "(...) la trop grande & indocte multi-
tude des escrivains, qui de jour en jour s'eleve en France, au grand deshonneur & abatardissement de nostre langue". [9] One of the works in the
P o e m a t u m   l i b r i   q u a t u o r , a witty epigram "In turbam poetarum Gallice scribentium", compares the teeming vernacular poetry
to the litter of a dog: the good will be kept, the weak swept away. [10] An
effective way to separate oneself from mediocre poets writing in French
was to write in a language which was more prestigious than French. And
even the author of the "Deffence et illustration de la langue françoyse"
acknowledged that Latin w a s more prestigious. In the preface to the
second edition of L ' O l i v e , of 1550, Du Bellay wrote: "(...) je ne
pouroy' & ne voudroy' nier, que si j'eusse ecrit en grec ou en latin,
ce ne m'eust esté un moyen plus expedié pour acquerir quelque degré
entre les doctes hommes de ce royaume". [11] That Du Bellay was proud
of his Latin poems and wanted them to be widely known is suggested by
several references to them in L e s   R e g r e t s . [12] Moreover, it is
distinctly possible that Du Bellay felt that Latin poetry was one sphere

in which he could eclipse Ronsard, and this suggestion is supported by
the fact that the first reference in L e s   R e g r e t s to the Latin poems
is precisely in a sonnet addressed to Ronsard and extolling Ronsard's
achievement as a poet writing in French. [13]

   The intrinsic advantages of the language of the humanists constitute
a third reason for Du Bellay's adoption of Latin. Latin gave access to
a more international audience than French poetry could yet reach. [14]
And Henri II's patriotically motivated poets, always seeking to eclipse
the ancient and modern Italians, strove for supremacy even in Latin poetry.
Michel de l'Hospital's Latin poetry, Du Bellay exclaimed in sonnet 67 of
L e s   R e g r e t s , excelled that of the Romans; and Dorat could emulate
the Greeks as well:

> Auratus Latiis pariter, Graiisque Camoenis
> Nostra aequans priscis secula temporibus (...) [15]

Dorat, for his part, paid tribute to Du Bellay's emulation of the Roman
poets, as we shall see. And if one wrote the language of the immortal
poets of Rome, one could aspire to share their undying renown. All that
remains alive of ancient Rome, Du Bellay points out in R o m a e d e s -
c r i p t i o , is the poetry of Virgil, of Ovid, of Tibullus and Catullus.
Now that he is in Rome, he prays to be allowed to uncover the springs of
their inspiration, to write Latin poetry which may be more durable than
French:

> Sit mihi fas Gallo vestros recludere fonteis,
>   Dum coeli Genio liberiore fruor.
> Hactenus & nostris incognita carmina Musis
>   Dicere, & insolito plectra movere sono.
> Hoc mihi cum patriis Latiae indulgete Camoenae,
>   Alteraque ingenii sit seges ista mei.
> Forte etiam vivent nostri monumenta laboris,
>   Caetera cum domino sunt peritura suo.
> Sola virum virtus coeli super ardua tollit
>   Virtutem coelo solaque Musa beat. [16]

Joachim du Bellay published three principal collections of Latin poetry:

(a) "Ioachimi Bellaii Andini Poematum libri quatuor". This collection, published in 1558 by Federic Morel in Paris, comprises E l e g i a e , V a r i a e p i g r a m m a t a , A m o r e s and T u m u l i . This is Du Bellay's best known collection of Latin poems: it includes, among the elegies, "Romae descriptio", "In vitae quietoris commendationem" and "Patriae desiderium". [17] The epigrams are varied indeed: two of them urge Ronsard to write an epic poem rather than love poetry; another warns of the dangers involved in writing satire; one extols the birth of Christ; several poems celebrate the French capture of Calais; and another pleads with the cardinal of Lorraine for patronage. The A m o r e s are professedly inspired by a Roman lady named Faustina; and the T u m u l i are epitaphs mainly of Italian and French personalities. Many of the poems in the P o e m a t u m l i b r i q u a t u o r have counterparts in Du Bellay's French poems. [18] The 1558 edition is the only known separate ancient edition and there is only one complete modern edition. [19]

(b) "Tumulus Henrici secundi Gallorum Regis Christianiss(imi). Idem Gallice totidem versibus expressum per eumdem. Accessit et eiusdem Elegia ad illustriss(imum) Principem Card(inalem) Lotharingum". The long epitaph of Henri II in its Latin and French versions appeared in 1559 and subsequently in 1561: it has been published, with some of the other poems found in this collection, by Chamard. [20] The 1559 edition contains also other Latin poems which Chamard did not publish, notably a long and interesting elegy to the cardinal of Lorraine which contains a defence of poetry and a plea for patronage. Those items in this T u m u l u s H e n r i c i s e c u n d i which Chamard did not publish are available in my book on J o a c h i m d u B e l l a y ' s v e i l e d v i c t i m . [21] The 1561 edition of the T u m u l u s H e n r i c i s e c u n d i contained also Du Bellay's Latin epitaphs on Antoine Minard, and these poems were published by Chamard. [22]

(c) "Xenia, seu Illustrium quorundam Nominum Allusiones". In these
short poems, published posthumously in 1569, Du Bellay cleverly discerns
qualities of famed contemporaries in the supposed etymologies of their
names. Many of these poems had been published the year before in a similar compilation by Carolus Utenhovius. The first modern edition of
Du Bellay's X e n i a can be found in my book on Du Bellay.

In addition to the poems in these three main collections, Du Bellay
wrote the following Latin poetry:

(a) six lines in praise of Louis Le Roy's translation of Plato's S y m p o -
s i u m , published with that translation in 1558;[23]

(b) a four-line poem in praise of Henri II's sister, published in 1559 in
the "Epithalame sur le mariage de (...) Philibert Emanuel duc de Savoye
et (...) Marguerite de France";[24]

(c) an eight-line poem in praise of Louise de Mailly, abbess of Caen, published by Aubert in his edition of Du Bellay;[25]

(d) two poems in praise of Adrien Turnèbe which are found in a 1660 edition of the latter's work;[26]

(e) a lament on the state of the church, extant in two manuscripts in which
the poem bears respectively the titles "Ecclesiae Querimonia" and "Sponse
Dei Querimonia".[27]

Du Bellay may also be the author of ten lines of Latin verse which were
published with his French translation of Turnèbe's D e n o v a c a p t a n -
d a e u t i l i t a t i s e l i t t e r i s r a t i o n e e p i s t o l a .[28]

An indication of the success of certain individual Latin poems of Du
Bellay is the frequency with which they were reprinted in collections
other than those of his own work. The poems on the capture of Calais
were particularly widely appreciated and one of them, "In reditum ducis
Guisiani", was published at least six times in books by other authors:
this is evidence not just of patriotic delight at the expulsion of the English
from French shores, but of admiration for Du Bellay's Latin poetry.[29]

Another poem which seems to have been widely appreciated was the epitaph "Cuiusdam iuvenis" which appeared among the T u m u l i in the
P o e m a t u m l i b r i q u a t u o r : this poem, inspired apparently
by one of Alciati's emblems, describes how Death and Cupid exchange
their weapons, Cupid bearing the scythe and Death the torch, with the result that a young man dies and an old man falls in love. It was cited by
Claude Mignault in his commentary on Alciati's emblems, [30] and it appeared
also, with the title "De morte et amore", in Abraham Fraunce's I n -
s i g n i u m , a r m o r u m , e m b l e m a t u m , h i e r o g l y p h y i -
c o r u m , et s y m b o l o r u m , q u a e ab I t a l i s IMPRESE
n o m i n a n t u r , e x p l i c a t i o . [31]

The verdicts which Du Bellay's contemporaries pronounced upon his
Latin poems were almost without exception glowing ones. Jean Dorat,
in a poem "Ad Ioachimum Bellaium, De eius reditu ab Italia", reassured the
nymphs of the Seine that when Joachim returned to France after rivalling the
ancient Latin poets he would still be able to write in French:

> Non quia cum veteris Romae contendit honore,
>   Peligno certans versibus ingenio:
> Idcirco patria est oblitus carmina voce [32]
>   Cantare, emeritus qualia cantat olor.

Another favourable verdict on Du Bellay's Latin verse, and a historically interesting one, is found in a poem by Carolus Utenhovius, a friend
and collaborator of Du Bellay, which serves as an epilogue to Du Bellay's
P o e m a t u m l i b r i q u a t u o r . Utenhovius pays tribute to the fact
that Du Bellay's poetry contains nothing obscene:

> Este procul tetrici, teneri procul este Poetae,
>   Quique canis Paphiae furta nefanda Deae.
> Nil nisi Bellaius bella canit arte politum,
>   Nil nisi concessos, legitimosque iocos.
> Illius in flammas, nul vel amoribus ardor,
>   Illius ignitus nullus in igne calor.
> Ecquid ab his rigidi teneros prohibetis alumnos? [33]
>   Hic nihil est pueros, quod vetet esse probos.

A fitting tribute, since Du Bellay himself appears to have thought - as against Catullus and Ronsard - that a poet's verse should be as chaste as he is. [34)]

Shortly after Du Bellay's death several volumes of epitaphs on him were published. These epitaphs offer evidence that he was equally re- nowned as a Latin and French poet. On the title-page of one pamphlet, L e s e p i t a p h e s s u r l e t r e s p a s d e J o a c h i m d u B e l l a y, he is described as a "Poete Latin & Francois", and one of the epitaphs in this volume, by Camille Morel, contains the following tribute:

> Dotibus ingenii linguae reparavit honorem
> Illae suae, Latiae restituitque decus. [35)]

Jacques Grévin's epitaph in the same volume pays tribute equally to the A m o r e s and the R o m a e d e s c r i p t i o, and to L e s R e g r e t s and L ' O l i v e . [36)] Another pamphlet, I n I o a c h i m u m B e l l a - i u m A n d i n u m p o e t a m c l a r i s s i m u m d o c t o r u m c a r m i n a e t t u m u l i, similarly has poems extolling his Latin and French poetry alike. One poem by Adrien Turnèbe has the following passage:

> Bellai (...)
> Quem Phoebus, comes & Camoena Phoebi
> Fontis Pierii rigavit unda:
> Et vincto pede fecit & soluto
> In lingua Latiaque Gallicaque,
> Et fandi Coryphaeon & canendi,
> Sic nos deseris (...) [37)]

A poem by Elie André offers a similar tribute:

> (...) operosa etiam Francis, Latiisque Camoenis
> Edideras gnavus iam monumenta duo. [38)]

Though his Latin verse was widely admired, some commentators thought his French poetry was better. Jacques-Auguste de Thou declared that Du Bellay was praised especially for L e s R e g r e t s , the D i v e r s j e u x r u s t i q u e s and his poems in praise of Margaret of France:

> (...) Tristia, quae ille, cum in familia agnati
> cardinalis Romae esset, fecit, ludi item rustici,
> et alia ad Margaritam, quae Philiberto Sabaudiae
> duci nupsit, collectanea praecipue laudantur: in
> Latinis, quae itidem Romae fecit, minus felix fuit. [39]

Scévole de Sainte-Marthe also thought Du Bellay's French poetry was better

than his Latin, and he gave an interesting explanation of the "superiority"

of the French poems:

> (...) Nam cum Romae profectus hortante Ioanne Bellaio
> Cardinale gentile suo ad Latina se convertisset, certe
> res illi paulo minori felicitate successit; homini
> videlicet levioribus assueto. Suus enim cuique linguae
> attributus est lepos, neque mollities illa sermonis
> quae idiomati Gallico propria & peculiaris est
> Romanae facundiae dignitatem gravitatemque ferre
> potest.

Sainte-Marthe immediately adds however that Du Bellay's Latin poems

have their admirers and that it is right that they should :

> Quanquam & carmen de Veronide & lusus de puellae
> raptu, nec pauca summae argutiae summique leporis
> epigrammata suos merito laudatores invenere, quorum
> iudicio ut vix ullum in carmine Gallico parem habet,
> sic paucissimos in latino superiores. [40]

Du Bellay's Latin work continued to be read long after his death. A

collection of gnomic verse compiled by Damasus Blyenburgius and pub-

lished in 1599 has several extracts. [41] The great majority of his Latin

poems were included in a compilation which Janus Gruterus edited and

published in 1609. [42] Vauquelin de la Fresnaye translated two of Du Bel-

lay's Latin poems into French. [43] English translations of some of them

appeared in 1637. [44] And in his V i e   d e   J o a c h i m   d u   B e l l a y ,

Guillaume Colletet included a particularly interesting tribute to the Latin

poems, declaring that Joachim had followed the example of Jean du Bellay

in writing Latin, and had far excelled him:

(...) Ceux qui ont une parfaite connaissance des
graces de cette langue, savent si le poëme qu'il fit
en faveur d'une dame italienne nommée Véronide, aussi
bien que celui qu'il fit sur le ravissement d'une
belle fille; comme cet autre encore, qu'il intitula
Tybiris ou le Tybre; celui de la Vie tranquille, son
P a t r i a e d e s i d e r i u m ou son désir de revoir la France,
et quelques autres encore de même trempe, sans parler
de ses épigrammes qui sont pour la plupart excellentes;
savent, dis-je, si ce sont des ouvrages d'un
esprit vulgaire, et s'ils ne se sentoient pas du doux
air du Tybre qu'il respiroit à Rome; aussi par là sa
réputation s'épandit si loin dans le monde qu'il n'y
eut guère d'homme ni plus connu, ni plus estimé de son
siècle. Les uns l'appelloient l'Ovide, les autres
l'Horace, et moi je l'appellerois volontiers tous les
deux ensemble, puisque son style tant latin que
françois a la douceur de l'un et la gravité de l'autre. [45]

The influence of Du Bellay's Latin poems seems to have been a durable
one: several of them were republished in the eighteenth century, [46] and
they were imitated, it seems, by Goethe. [47]

N O T E S

(1) See the witty epigram "Ad lectorem" in Du Bellay's P o é s i e s
    f r a n ç a i s e s e t l a t i n e s , ed. E. Courbet (2 v., Paris,
    1918), I, p. 453. For a discussion of the contemporary debate bet-
    ween partisans of French and Latin, see P. de NOLHAC, Ronsard et
    l'humanisme (Bibliothèque de l'Ecole des Hautes Etudes (...), Scien-
    ces historiques et philologiques, 227e fasc.), Paris, 1966, pp. 1-8
    and the works noted i b i d ., p. 2, n. 1.

(2) The epigram serves as a foreword to the P o e m a t u m l i b r i
    q u a t u o r (see P o é s i e s f r a n ç a i s e s e t l a t i n e s ,
    ed. Courbet, I, pp. 431-432).

(3) Ovid, he adds, was obliged to change his language when in exile: •
    see P o é s i e s f r a n ç a i s e s e t l a t i n e s , ed. Courbet, I,
    p. 447.

(4)   Du Bellay dedicated epigrams to Basilius Zanchius and Laurentius
        Gambara (see P o é s i e s   f r a n ç a i s e s   e t   l a t i n e s , ed.
        Courbet, I, pp. 455-456 and 457-458). Professor J. IJsewijn kind-
        ly reminded me of Du Bellay's contact with Italian poets.

(5)   This view appears to be founded on a passage, quoted in the last
        part of this study, in Scévole de Sainte-Marthe's eulogy of Du Bellay.
        Colletet's biography of Du Bellay was published by A. van Bever in
        his edition of Du Bellay's D i v e r s   j e u x   r u s t i q u e s (&c)
        (Paris, 1912): my quotation is from p. 33. Colletet paid tribute to
        Jean du Bellay's "vers latins dignes de la force de son génie et du
        suffrage de la posterité même" (o p .   c i t ., p. 15).

(6)   That the cardinal was disturbed (to put it mildly) by the satirical
        content of L e s   R e g r e t s is apparent from a long letter which
        Joachim wrote to him in defence of this collection: see P. de Nol-
        hac's edition of Du Bellay's L e t t r e s (Paris, 1883), pp. 41-52.

(7)   E s s a i s , I, xxvi: p. 44 in the edition by J. Plattard in L e s
        T e x t e s   F r a n ç a i s   series.

(8)   This quotation is from L e s   r e c h e r c h e s   d e   l a   F r a n c e
        (...) (Paris , M. DC. XI, B. M. 596. g. 4), Livre VI, ch. vii, "De
        la grande flotte de Poëtes que produisit le regne du Roy Henry
        deuxiesme, & de la nouvelle forme de Poësie par eux introduite"
        (pp. 738-748). See also a letter which the same author wrote to
        Ronsard (Pasquier, L e s   O e u v r e s (...), 2 v., Amsterdam,
        M. DCCXXIII, B. M. 1487. z. 2, II, col. 11-12).

(9) The quotation is from Du Bellay's O e u v r e s   p o é t i q u e s , ed.
        H. Chamard (S. T. F. M.), Paris, 6 v., 1908-1931, III, pp. 57-58:
        see also L a   D e f f e n c e   e t   i l l u s t r a t i o n   d e   l a   l a n -
        g u e   f r a n ç o y s e , ed. H. Chamard (S. T. F. M.), Paris, 1948,
        pp. 173-179.

(10)   See P o é s i e s   f r a n ç a i s e s   e t   l a t i n e s , ed. Courbet,
        I, pp. 459-460.

(11)   See O e u v r e s   p o é t i q u e s , ed. Chamard, I, pp. 11-12. He
        added, in this 1550 preface, that he could not, without vast effort,
        aspire to fame as a Latin poet.

(12)   See L e s   R e g r e t s , sonnets 10, 18 and 22.

(13)   I am grateful to Professor I. D. McFarlane for the suggestion that
        Du Bellay's Latin poetry was inspired by rivalry with Ronsard.

[137]

Ronsard wrote very little Latin poetry: it has been discussed by Nolhac in "Ronsard et l'humanisme " (see note 1 above), T r o i - s i è m e   p a r t i e , "Les écrits latins de Ronsard", pp. 244-270.

(14)   Ronsard's achievement in acquiring fame outside France for poems written in French lay in the future: see Nolhac, "Ronsard et l'humanisme", pp. 205-235 and I. Silver, "Ronsard in European literature: a synoptic view of scholarly publications" (Bibliothèque d'Humanisme et Renaissance, XVI, 1954, pp. 241-254).

(15)   P o é s i e s   f r a n ç a i s e s   e t   l a t i n e s , ed. Courbet, I, p. 443.

(16)   P o é s i e s   f r a n ç a i s e s   e t   l a t i n e s , ed. Courbet, I, p. 436.

(17)   See respectively P o é s i e s   f r a n ç a i s e s   e t   l a t i n e s , ed. Courbet, pp. 432-436, 442-443 and 445-447.

(18)   See H. Chamard , Joachim du Bellay, 1522-1560 (Travaux et Mémoires de l'Université de Lille, t. VIII, mém. no. 24), Lille, 1900, p. 360, n. 5.

(19)   The modern edition is P o é s i e   f r a n ç a i s e s   e t   l a t i n e s , ed. Courbet, I, pp. 419-535. Some of the Latin poems have also been published by M. Hervier in his edition of Du Bellay's P o ë s i e s (5 v., Bibliothèque des éditions Richelieu, 1954: notably vols. II, pp. 397-402, III, pp. 321-348 and IV, pp. 37-40, 412-416). The A m o - r e s (and a few other of the Latin poems) have been published, with translations, by T. Sandre, in L e s   A m o u r s   d e   F a u s t i n e , Amiens, 1923. Two older editions of some of Du Bellay's Latin poems are mentioned below, notes 39 and 42.

(20)   See Du Bellay's OE u v r e s   p o é t i q u e s , ed. Chamard, VI, pp. 77-93 and 98-101 for some of the poems published in the T u m u l u s   H e n r i c i   s e c u n d i .

(21)   This book has been published by Librairie Droz of Geneva in the E t u d e s   d e   P h i l o l o g i e   e t   d ' H i s t o i r e   series.

(22)   See OE u v r e s   p o é t i q u e s , ed. Chamard, VI, pp. 103-109.

(23)   The only modern edition of Du Bellay's poem is in the P o ë s i e s , ed. Hervier, III, p. 221. The text, as given by Hervier, reads as follows:

Regibus in toto majus nil nascitur orbe.
   Nil magis Augustum, nil propiusve deo.
Dum studet ad Gallos magnum transferre Platona,
   Quo nullum in terris grandius extat opus,
Scilicet ipse suo dignum se nomine reddit
   Regius, & magnis regibus aequa facit.

(24)   See OEuvres poétiques, ed. Chamard, V, p. 227.

(25)   See OEuvres poétiques, ed. Chamard, V, p. 340, n. 7.

(26)   See J. BOULANGER, "Des vers latins de du Bellay inconnus", Humanisme et Renaissance, IV, 1937, p. 208. The second is in fact an amplified version of a poem found in the Xenia (B.M. G.17778 (2), 12vo).

(27)   See J. ROUAULT, "Découverte d'un important inédit latin de Joachim du Bellay (1559)", Eurydice, Cahiers de poèmes et d'humanisme, 1933 (pages unnumbered).

(28)   Towards the end of his translation of Turnèbe's poem, Du Bellay inserts a denunciation of a historian who has gained fame for a book he has never actually written. No equivalent lines are found in the Latin version of this poem given in editions of Turnèbe's work. However, the volume containing Du Bellay's French translation, in which Turnèbe's text is also given, has these "missing" lines - which may well be by Du Bellay himself - in an appendix. See Du Bellay's OEuvres françoises (La Pléiade françoise), ed. C. Marty-Laveaux, 2 v., Paris, 1866, 1867, I, p. 508, n. 221 and OEuvres poétiques, ed. Chamard, VI, pp. 126-128 and p. 126, n. 4.

(29)   The locations of five of these copies are given in Joachim du Bellay's veiled victim, n. 67. The sixth location, which I have discovered since writing the book, is the following: Leodegarius a QUERCU (Léger du Chesne), Flores epigrammatum ex optimis quibusque authoribus excerpti, 2 t., Lutetiae, 1555, 1560, t. 2 (which has the separate title Farrago poematum (...)), 318vo.

(30)   See Poésies françaises et latines, ed. Courbet, I, p. 514 and Mignault's note to Emblem 154 (p. 546 in Omnia Andreae Alciati Emblemata (...), Antuerpiae, M.D.LXXXI (B.M. 12305.bb.37)). For an impressive list of poems on this theme, see J.G. Fucilla, "De morte et amore", Philological Quarterly, XIV, 1935, pp. 97-104.

(31)   Londini, 1558: B. M. C. 123. e. 25, N 2vo.

(32)   The quotation is from a poem "Ad Ioachimum Bellaium, De eius
        reditu ab Italia", found in George Buchanan's "Franciscanus &
        fratres, Quibus accessere varia eiusdem & aliorum Poëmata (...)",
        Basiliae Rauracorum, (1568), (B. M. 1213, g. 10), second part, pp.
        153-155: the lines cited are found on p. 155.

(33)   See P o é s i e s   f r a n ç a i s e s   e t   l a t i n e s , ed. Courbet,
        I, p. 534.

(34)   See the witty epigram "Ad Fabullam, cur amatoria non scribat",
        in P o é s i e s   f r a n ç a i s e s   e t   l a t i n e s , ed. Courbet,
        I, pp. 499-500. Ronsard had invoked Catullus's phrase (Nam castum
        esse decet pium poëtam / Ipsum, versiculos nihil necesse est": XVI,
        5-6) on the titlepage of his own L i v r e t   d e   F o l a s t r i e s   of
        1553 (V, p. 1 in Laumonier's critical edition of Ronsard), and Du
        Bellay's genial strictures about it may be an implicit deprecation
        of Ronsard's notorious book. The elegy to the cardinal of Lorraine
        which Du Bellay published in the T u m u l u s   H e n r i c i   s e -
        c u n d i   offers an eloquent statement of the proper role of the
        Muses: see lines 25-28 and 37-48 in my edition in J o a c h i m
        d u   B e l l a y ' s   v e i l e d   v i c t i m . When Guillaume Aubert
        published Du Bellay's complete works, he prefaced them with a
        letter to the king in which he urged poets to avoid writing "chose
        qui ne soit de bonne instruction, & de bon exemple: ou si quelque-
        fois ils s'esbatent en choses plus legeres, qu'à tout le moins ce
        soit avec telle modestie & temperance, que les chastes oreilles
        n'en puissent estre offensées ny corrompues: à fin que si le lecteur
        outre le plaisir n'en peut retirer aucun proufit, qu'à tout le moins
        il n'en reçoyve aucun dommage" (Joachim Du Bellay , L e s
        OE u v r e s   f r a n ç o i s e s (...), Paris, M. D. LXIX (B. M.
        1073. e. 15), a vi ^{ro}).

(35)   See "Epitaphium in mortem Henrici Gallorum regis christianissimi,
        eius nominis secundi, per Carolum Utenhovium et alios (...) plus
        Les epitaphes sur le trespas de Joachim du Bellay Angevin, Poete
        Latin & François", Paris, M. D. LX (B. M. 1213. m. 10 (21)); the
        quotation from Camille Morel's poem, a D i a l o g u s   featuring
        Jean Morel and his wife Antoinette de Loynes, is at F iii ^{vo}.

(36)   See P o u r   l e   t o m b e a u   d e   J o a c h i m   d u   B e l l a y ,
        O d e : G iii $^{ro-vo}$ in the same pamphlet.

(37)   The pamphlet was published in Paris in 1560 (B.M. 11408. f.53).
          Turnèbe's poem is the first in the pamphlet, and the passage quo-
          ted is at A ii^{ro} .

(38)   See the same pamphlet, A v^{vo}. The poem which follows, "Eiusdem
          ex P. Bembo", describes Du Bellay as F r a n c a e   L a u s , L a -
          t i a e q u e   l y r a e (A vi^{ro}).

(39)   H i s t o r i a r u m   s u i   t e m p o r i s (...) l i b r i
          C X X X V I I I , 7 tom., Londini, 1733 (B.M. 685.1.1), II, p.72.

(40)   See Scévole de Sainte - Marthe, Poemata et elogia, Collecta nunc
          in unum corpus, & ab auctore partim aucta, partim recognita, 2 parts,
          Augustoriti Pictonum, M.DC.VI (B.M. C65.bb15), second part,
          pp. 60-61. Sainte-Marthe expresses especial admiration for Du Bellay's
          A n t i q u i t e z   d e   R o m e and L e s   R e g r e t s . A transla-
          tion of these E l o g i a was published by Guillaume Colletet in 1644.

(41)   The title of the book is "Cento ethicus ex variis Poëtis hinc inde
          contextus" (Lugduni Batavorum, M.D.IC, B.M. 11408.aaa.58 (1))
          and the extracts from Du Bellay are on pages 95, 164-165 and
          182-183.

(42)   See Ranutius Gherus , p s e u d . (i.e. Janus Gruterus) Delitiae
          C. poetarum gallorum (...), pars prima, (Frankfort,) M.D.CIX,
          B.M. 1213.a.3, pp. 390-487.

(43)   Colletet pointed out that La Fresnaye's pastoral poems beginning
          "Quittez, ô Francois, qui chantez / D'amour la douceur la plus
          grande" and "Comme jadis, belle Delie" (L e s   d i v e r s e s
          p o é s i e s (..), ed. J. Travers, Caen, 1869-1870, II, pp. 486
          and 488) are translations of Latin poems by Du Bellay (see Colletet's
          V i e   d e   J o a c h i m   d u   B e l l a y in Du Bellay's D i v e r s
          j e u x   r u s t i q u e s (&c), ed. A. van Bever, Paris, 1912, p.58
          and notes 3 and 4).

(44)   Professor I.D. McFarlane kindly drew my attention to the fact that
          they appeared in a compilation by A.B. Wright . The book, which
          I have not been able to consult, bears the title D e l i t i a e   d e -
          l i t i a r u m .

(45)   See Du Bellay's D i v e r s   j e u x   r u s t i q u e s (&c), ed. A.
          van Bever, pp. 33-34.

(46)   See "Amoenitates poeticae, sive Theodori Bezae, Marci-Antonii
        Mureti, et Joannis Secundi Juvenilia: Tum Joannis Bonefonii Pan-
        charis: Joachimi Bellaii Amores, &c. &c.", Lugduni-Batavorum,
        M DCC LXXIX (B.M. 159.c.17). The poems from Du Bellay (not
        all of them from the A m o r e s) are on pages 355-389.

(47)   See J.ROUAULT, "Joachim du Bellay et Goethe, amoureux de Faustine,
        la belle romaine", E u r y d i c e , C a h i e r s d e p o è m e s
        e t d ' h u m a n i s m e , 1937, (pages unnumbered).

        A d d i t i o n :

        A Latin poem by Du Bellay in praise of Ronsard ("Undique in Oceanum
        volvant cum flumina lymphas") was published in the 1560 edition of
        Ronsard's complete works, and in subsequent editions (see Ronsard's
        O E u v r e s c o m p l è t e s , ed. P. Laumonier, S.T.F.M., X, p. 174).
        Many of Du Bellay's Latin poems appeared in Philippe Labbé's T h e -
        s a u r u s e p i t a p h i o r u m of 1666. Additional information on early
        editions of Du Bellay's Latin poetry is found in my article "An early
        edition of Joachim Du Bellay's V e r o n i s i n f o n t e m s u i n o m i -
        n i s " (B i b l i o t h è q u e d ' H u m a n i s m e e t R e n a i s s a n c e , 1977).

REFLECTIONS ON THE *FORTUNA* OF THOMAS MORE

This note supplements R.W. Gibson's *St. Thomas More : a preliminary bibliography of his works and of moreana to the year 1750* (New Haven and London, 1961). In writing it I place myself (as no doubt Gibson would place himself) among what Montaigne called *historiens fort simples,* those who *n'apportent que le soin et la diligence de ramasser tout ce qui vient à leur notice, et d'enregistrer à la bonne foy toutes choses sans chois et sans triage (Essais,* II, x). Montaigne commends such unambitious but faithful historians for providing an unadulterated fund of evidence on which others can base judgments : *C'est la matiere de l'histoire, nue et informe ; chacun en peut faire son profit autant qu'il a d'entendement.*

But the time has surely come for some historian to use the raw material so diligently collected by Gibson (and other scholars who have published supplementary information in *Moreana).* What is needed is a study of the *fortuna* of More's personality and of his thought, which would show in what ways his influence was felt at various times. Such a task requires a historian familiar with the personality of More and the issues he stood for, and able to discern the relative importance of various issues ; a historian, in short, of a type again conveniently described by Montaigne : *Les* [historiens] *bien excellens ont la suffisance de choisir ce qui est digne d'estre sceu, peuvent trier de deux rapports celuy qui est plus vraysemblable... Ils ont raison de prendre l'authorité de regler nostre creance à la leur ; mais certes cela n'appartient à guieres de gens.*

Since I have begun this note under the aegis of Montaigne, it is difficult not to comment on the conspicuous absence of that author from the Morean bibliography. It is hard to conceive that a man as catholic in his reading as Montaigne should not have known the then most famous English writer. This is especially the case as Montaigne had an interest in the religious affairs of England and (in the *Apologie de Raimond Sebond)* deplored the instability of religious policies in England. How, then, can the absence of More in the *Essais* be explained ? It is possible that some allusive reference to him has escaped the attention of commentators, or that Montaigne refrained from comment on More as his martyrdom was being widely exploited in a partisan way by propagandists of the League. Kinship between More and Montaigne is profound : both of them men of complete probity, both born with a gift for friendship, both equally socratic « citizens of the world » and delighting to hear opinions which challenged their own, both defenders of the rights of conscience while insistent that conscience has jurisdiction only over the individual, both committed Roman Catholics and prepared to stand by their commitment in the most perilous circumstances, both given to allusiveness and irony (to the confusion of humourless commentators).

But let us get back to the new material on More which is the object of this note. It includes some by quite famous authors. If it is possible to find as many significant new references to More without deliberately looking for such material, then it is probable that much remains to be discovered. I have not bothered to list here books which would merely supplement information already present in Gibson's book : for example Du Bartas' *Works* (ed. Holmes, Lyons and Linker, III, 141) ; the Italian edition of Giovio's *Elogia* (see the entry on Henry VIII) ; the 1555 edition of Leodegarius a Quercu's *Flores* ; Gruterus' *Delitiae poetarum Belgicorum,* and *Delitiae poetarum Italorum ;* the second edition of Beza's *Poemata* (containing, a little suprisingly, Vitalis' epigram on More's execution) ; Labbé's *Thesaurus epitaphiorum.* On the other hand, since authors in my list seem not to have been noted by More scholars, I have gone beyond the scope of Gibson's book and tried to give the essence of what each says about More. Unlike Gibson I have given references to good modern editions where available.

1. Jean de BORDES, *Maria Stuarta tragoedia,* written in 1589 and preserved in manuscript in the Morgan Library, New York City : see J.E. Phillips, « Jean de Bordes' « Maria Stuarta tragoedia » : the earliest-known drama on the queen of Scots », in *Essays critical and historical dedicated to L.B. Campbell,* Berkeley and Los Angeles, 1950, p. 43-62. In the play, Mary, as she is being led to execution, « again rejoices in this opportunity to die for her faith, as did More, Fisher, and other martyrs » (Phillips, p. 50).

2. Pierre de Bourdeille, seigneur de BRANTOME (c. 1540-1614) compares More to Michel de L'Hospital (c. 1504 - 1573), who is famous as Chancellor of France, as an architect of religious tolerance, and as a poet and patron of poets ; his comments on More's *Utopia* were quoted by Mical H. Schneider in *Moreana* 27-28 (1970), 108-9. The following quotation is from Brantôme's *OEuvres complètes,* éd. L. Lalanne (11 v., Paris, 1864-82), III, 315 :

J'ay ouy de ce temps faire comparaison de luy [L'Hospital] et de Thomas Morus, chancelier d'Angleterre, le plus grand qui fût jamais en ces pays, fors que l'un estoit fort catholique, et l'autre le tenoit-on huguenot, encor qu'il allast à la messe ; mais on disoit à la cour : « Dieu nous gard' de la messe de M. de l'Hospital ! »

3. *Calendar of letters and state papers relating to English affairs preserved in, or originally belonging to, the archives of Simancas,* IV, Elizabeth, 1587 - 1603, ed. M.A.S. Hume, p. 294-295. A translation is given of the concluding paragraphs of an exhortation to the soldiers of the Armada :

The saints of Heaven will go in our company, and particularly the holy patrons of Spain ; and those of England itself, who are persecuted by the heretics, and cry aloud to God for vengeance, will come out to meet us, as well as those who sacrificed their lives in establishing our holy faith in the land, and watered it with their blood. There we shall find awaiting us the aid of the blessed John Fisher, cardinal bishop of Rochester, of Thomas More....

4. Jean Calvin, *Commentaires sur le Prophete Isaïe, au roy d'Angleterre Edouard, sixiesme de ce nom,* Genève, 1552, B.L. 3166 e 2. In his commentary on chapter XXII of Isaiah (the oracle against Shebna), Calvin deplores the arrogance of people who seek to remain famous after their death by having memorials to them erected :

Or toutefois & quantes que je ly ce passage, un semblable exemple me vient principalement en memoire, d'autant qu'il convient à cestuy cy beaucoup plus que tous les autres : à savoir, de Thomas Morus, qui avoit un tel office que ce Sobna. Car comme on sait assez, il estoit chancelier du Roy d'Angleterre. Comme ainsi soit, que ce monsieur icy, fust fort grand ennemy de l'Evangile, & persecutast cruellement les fidelles à feu & à sang, il vouloit aussi par ce moyen se faire renommer, & aquerir bruit, & perpetuer la memoire de son impiété & cruauté entre les hommes. Parquoy, il fit engraver les louanges de ses vertuz en un fort beau sepulchre, qu'il avoit fait bastir magnifiquement. Et envoya à Basle, à Erasme (auquel il envoya pour present un hobin [that is, a horse]) son epitaphe, qu'il avoit luy mesme composé : à fin qu'Erasme le feit imprimer. Tant estoit il convoiteux de gloire, que durant sa vie, il vouloit donner commencement à sa renommée, & à ses louänges heroiques, lesquelles devoyent suyvre sa mort, comme il esperoit. Or la principale de toutes ses louänges, c'estoit qu'il estoit grand persecuteur des Lutheriens, c'est à dire, des fidelles. Mais qu'est-il advenu ? Il fut accusé de trahison, il fut condamné : & pour le faire bref, il eut la teste trenchée. Ainsi, son sepulchre fut un gibbet. Voudrions-nous des jugemens de Dieu plus manifestes ? par lesquelz il punit l'orgueil des meschans, & leur convoitise insatiable de gloire, & leurs vanteries pleines de blasphemes. Et certes il nous faut recognoistre & adorer la providence admirable de Dieu, en cest horrible ennemy du peuple de Dieu, aussi bien qu'en Sobna.

A prefatory note by Nicolas Des Gallars explains that Calvin's commentaries on Isaiah were assembled and edited by him. A further note, probably also by Des Gallars, adds that after the Latin version of the book was published, it was translated into French, but no indication is given as to who the translators were. The Latin version has been published by J.W. Hogan in *Moreana* 45 (1975) p. 37-38, with an English translation published in 1609 by a certain « C.C. » The French follows the Latin so closely that it is not possible to infer from the texts which version the English is derived from.

Fr. Marc'hadour has suggested to me that Calvin may have drawn on John Fox's *Book of martyrs* for the Frith story. This is not possible, however, as Fox's *Commentarii rerum in Ecclesia gestarum* [...], the forerunner of the *Book of martyrs*, did not appear until 1554 (B.L. G 12011) and does not have the Frith story anyway. It first appears in Fox, so far as I know, in the enlarged edition of the *Commentarii,* published in 1559 (B.L. 479 c 13, p. 127-135). It is of course possible, though, that Fox supplied Calvin with material before publishing it himself in the *Book of martyrs*.

I do not know Calvin's source for his statement that More had a magnificent tomb. Perhaps he was embroidering on the fact that More did indeed in 1533 send Erasmus a copy of the epitaph he had written for himself (see M. de la Garanderie, « Sur la publication de l'épitaphe de Thomas More », *Moreana* 17 (1968) p. 15-19).

5. Honorius Dominicus CARAMELLA, *Museum illustriorum Poetarum, qui ad haec usque Latino carmine scripserunt : cum notis Michaelis Foscarini nobilis Veneti,* Venetiis, 1651, B.L. 276 a 23. This edition has a preliminary poem in which Caramella, the author of the collection of the two-line verse verdicts on poets, dedicates his book to cardinal Bernardino Spada, and a short prefatory note in which Michael Foscarenus,

the author of the prose annotations, appeals to readers for information which would enable him to improve his notes in a subsequent edition. Another edition appeared in 1653 (Bibliothèque Nationale, Paris, H 13249 - 13250) but I have not been able to consult it. On p. 277 of the 1651 edition, under the heading « Thomas Morus », is found the following :

Carmina conscripsit Iuvenis divina, senexque
Divinum proprio sanguine scripsit opus.

Thomas Morus Nobilis Anglus dum Iuvenis esset, cecinit Latino carmine, & puritate Italica. Vir omni alia eruditione refertus : Hic cum Regni Angliae Magnus Cancellarius esset, nolletque quoddam diploma Ecclesiae Romanae contrarium subscribere, iussu Henrici Octavi Regis, capite truncatus est.

6. Lancelot CARLE. *Epistre contenant le proces criminel faict à l'encontre de la royne Anne Boullant d'Angleterre,* Lyon, 1545 : the poem, extant in several manuscript versions, was reprinted by G. Ascoli in *La Grande-Bretagne devant l'opinion française depuis la Guerre de Cent Ans jusqu'à la fin du XVIe siècle,* Paris, 1929, p. 231-273. Ascoli based his text on a manuscript dating from 1536 and gave variant readings. Lines 201 - 219, dealing with the passing by Parliament of the Act of Supremacy (18 November 1534) and its enforcement, would read as follows in the more correct 1545 version :

Puys ordonna que le Roy seroit chef
De son Eglise, et que pareil meschef
Seroit, venir contre l'auctorité
Que delinquer en lese majesté.
Ce que depuys fut monstré par effect,
Car pugny fut Morus pour ce meffaict,
Et cinq chartreux mesprisans leurs editz,
Tous vifs ouvers, seullement estourdiz.
Le peuple, esmeu de veoir la nouveaulté
De ceste grande et dure cruaulté,
En murmurant de ce faict devisoit,
Et plus souvent la royne Anne accusoit
D'avoir esté cause d'ung tel erreur.
Pour comprimer du peuple la fureur,
Le roy voulut que qui mediroit d'elle
Seroit pugny d'une peine mortelle,
Dont close fut la bouche aux medisans
Qui bien estoient en nombre suffisans,
En ung besoing, pour remplir une armée [...]

Lines 885-888 of the same poem praise More's eloquence.

7. Jean CHASSANION, *Histoires memorables des grans et merveilleux jugemens et punitions de Dieu avenues au monde, principalement sur les grans, à cause de leurs mesfaits, contrevenans aux Commandemens de la Loy de Dieu,* [Paris,] 1586, B.L. 09004 a 1. Chassanion reproduces part of Calvin's verdict on More (p. 69). Mr Michael Heath kindly drew my attention to Chassanion's allusion to More.

8. Jean CRESPIN, *Histoire des martyrs, persecutez et mis à mort pour la verité de l'Evangile, depuis le temps des Apostres jusques à l'an 1574,* [Genève] 1582, B.L. 487 1 23, 100ro - 102vo, reproduces the story that More was responsible for the execution of John Frith. Crespin follows the account given by John Fox in his *Rerum in Ecclesia gestarum* [...] *Commentarii,* pars prima, 1559, B.L. 479 c 13, p. 127 - 135.

9. Joannes DOBNECK, called Cochlaeus, *Historia de actis et scriptis Martini Lutheri Saxonis* [...], Parisiis, 1565, B.L. 857 c 10, extols and quotes from More's defence of Henry VIII's book on the seven sacraments (60vo - 63ro), records that in martyrdom More displayed the fortitude of Socrates (265vo - 266ro), mentions that Pope Paul III « contra defectionem & crudelitatem Regis Angliae, multis conquestus est epistolis ad Reges & Principes » and cites the complaint made by Erasmus in the *Ecclesiastes* about More's execution (266vo).

10. Jean DOUBLET, *Les elegies,* reproduites d'après l'édition de 1559 [...] par P. Blanchemain, Rouen, 1869, 54vo - 55ro, *Du latin de Morus.* The translation is of the epigram *In episcopum illiteratum* [...] (« Magne pater, clamas : occidit littera [...] », no. 186 in Bradner and Lynch), in which More alludes to St Paul's « The letter kills, but the spirit gives life » (*2 Cor.* 3 : 6) :

> Docte Docteur, toujours tu nous viens dire
> La lettre occit, tu n'as que ce propos,
>   La lettre occit : tant le redire ?
>   Tu nous occis de ces deux mos :
> Mais, quant à toi, tu as donné bon ordre,
> Que nulle lettre occir onq' ne te vint :
>   Lettres n'ont garde de te mordre,
>   Car te voir onq ne leur avint.
> Si n'esse à tort que tu creins, teste sote,
> D'en estre occis : bien t'en dois soucier :
>   Car tu n'as d'esprit une iote,
>   Qui te puisse vivifier.

11. Antoine DU VERDIER, *Les diverses leçons* [...] *suyvans celles de P. Messie,* 1592, B.L. 9007 bbb 12. A survey of « plusieurs hommes lettrez anciens & modernes lesquels moururent miserablement » includes More as the last example (p. 159) : « Et Thomas More Chancelier d'Angleterre fut decapité à Londres, pour avoir repris Henry Roy d'Angleterre du divorce & repudiation de sa femme ».

12. *Elegie de feu maistre Thomas Morus, en son vivant Chancellier d'Angleterre.* This eulogy of More, in 158 lines of verse, extant in two manuscript copies at Soissons, was published by G. Ascoli in *La Grande-Bretagne devant l'opinion française [...], p. 227-231.* As with the Carle item, one is surprised that this poem, published in Ascoli's well-known book, seems to have escaped the attention of More scholars.

13. Girolamo GHILINI, *Teatro d'huomini letterati,* Venetia, 1647, B.L. 617 k 14. This author has no separate entry on More but refers to him in the entry on « Guglielmo Rastallo » (II, 168) :

> Nacque in Londra Metropoli famosa dell'Isola d'Inghilterra, da Elisabeth sorella di quel Tomaso Moro, che per la bonta di vita, e per l'eccellente dottrina fu in ogni parte conosciuto, & ammirato [...] con gran diligenza, e molta fatica cerco tutte le *Opere di Tomaso Moro suo scritte in lingua Inglese,* le quali mise insieme, e ridotte in un Volume, procuro, che fossero ad utilita de· studiosi ingegni stampate.

14. Simon GOULART, *Discours des jugemens de Dieu sur les perse-cuteurs de l'Eglise* (published with Pietro Martire Vermigli's *Epistre à quelques fideles touchant leur abjuration* [...] [Geneva ?], 1574, B.L. 3902 a 52), p. 121 :

> Roffense [i.e. Fisher] Evesque de Rochestre & Thomas Morus chancelier du Royaume, auteurs de la mort de Jean Frith docte & singulier tesmoin de la verité, furent envoyez au gibet, & tous deux decapitez.

Goulart then (p. 121-123) cites Calvin's verdict on More.

15. Claude LE MAISTRE, *Elegie prise du Latin de Thomas Morus, qui se commence Cum tumida horrissonis & c.* (« Estant en mer un navire agité [...] ») : printed by Estienne Groulleau in Paris in 1550 in *Traduc-*

tions de latin en françoys, imitations, et inventions nouvelles, tant de Clement Marot, que d'autres des plus excellens Poetes de ce temps and reprinted, with More's original text, by E. Droz in *Chemins de l'hérésie*, III, Genève, 1974, p. 108 - 111. The statement there that More's epigram influenced chapter xix of Rabelais's *Quart livre* seems questionable. The epigram is no. 157 in Bradner and Lynch.

16. Claude MIGNAULT, in his commentary on Alciati (*Omnia Andreae Alciati V.C. Emblemata,* Antuerpiae, 1581, B.L. 12305 bb 37), cites epigrams by More against misers (« Os canis implet anas [...] », p. 254, emblem 66 : no. 116 in Bradner and Lynch) and against astrologers (« Saturnus procul est [...] », p. 368, emblem 104 : no. 47 in Bradner and Lynch). Mignault's excellent annotated editions of Alciati's emblem book were frequently reprinted and must have contributed significantly to the fame of More's epigrams.

17. Florimond de RAEMOND, *L'histoire de la naissance, progrez et decadence de l'heresie de ce siecle,* Paris, 2 t., 1605, B.L. 860 1 8, II, 21ro - 22ro (an account of the trial and execution of More) and 90vo - 91ro (the « miracle », also related in Stapleton's *Tres Thomae,* whereby More's daughter Margaret mysteriously found money for his burial). The equivalent passages in the Latin version of Raemond's book (*Synopsis omnium huius temporis controversiarum* [...], Coloniae Agrippinae, 1717, B.L. 4571 e 2) are at pages 540 - 542 and 612 - 613.

18. René RAPIN, *Les réflexions sur la poétique de ce temps et sur les ouvrages des poètes anciens et modernes,* ed. E.T. Dubois (Textes Littéraires Français), Genève, 1970 (first edition 1674). In the third edition (1684), the following is added at the end of the section on satire ([II] xxviii ; p. 126) :

> Thomas Morus qui fit une satire contre les Allemans, contenta tellement Charles IX, qu'il commenda à Ronsart d'en composer une pareille contre les dérèglements de la Cour, qui ne réussit pas, manque de délicatesse.

Dubois was unable to identify any such poem by Ronsard. Fr. Marc'hadour suggested that Rapin's allusion to Germans may evoke More's epigrams against Germanus Brixius, but none of these epigrams seems to have served as a model for Ronsard (see Bradner and Lynch, p. 78 - 82, 88, 112 - 114). It is possible that Ronsard did write such a poem, however, and that it is among his lost satires (see the edition of Ronsard by Laumonier, Silver and Lebègue, XVIII, 522-523).

19. Charles de SAINTE-MARTHE, *In Psalmum Septimum et Psalmum xxxiii, Paraphrasis,* quoted by C. Ruutz-Rees, *Charles de Sainte-Marthe (1512-1555),* New York, 1910, p. 582 [More is not named but, as Ruutz-Rees points out (p. 150, n. 1), appears to be alluded to] :

> Quod scribo de Principibus, qui malo consilio acquiescentes, saeviunt in bonos et pios, intellego de iis, quorum mores facta satis ostendunt, quales experta est Italia saepe multos, & non ita pridem Anglia. Sed nominatim illos exprimere non placuit, cum periculosum sit de Principibus huius modi etiam vera scribere.

20. Albertus Henricus de SALLENGRE, *Novus thesaurus antiquitatum Romanarum,* 3v., Hagae-Comitum, 1718, B.L. 588 1 14 - 16. In a discussion of whether the death penalty is appropriate for theft, this author cites *Utopia,* extolling « Thomas Morus, illustre illud Angliae sidus, (quo ab Henrico VIII. Angliae Rege capite mulctato Carolus V. Imperator dixisse fertur, Rex Henricus toti Angliae caput amputavit, cum Morum sustulit, referente Drexelio in *Tobia* part. I. cap. 11. § 2. lib. 1.) » (II, col. 864). Sallengre's reference is to *Tobias morali doctrina illustratus,* by Hieremias Drexelius (see F. and M.P. Sullivan, *Moreana, Materials for the study of Saint Thomas More,* I, 295).

21. Lope de VEGA's epitaph on More, full of puns on More and (miscreant) Moor and Muro (wall), was quoted from the 1623 edition of *Rimas* by Professor Francisco López Estrada, « Santo Tomás Moro en España y en la América Hispana », *Moreana* 5 (1965), 36, and again by Germain Marc'hadour, « A Name for All Seasons », *Essential Articles for the Study of Thomas More* (Hamden 1977), 544-46. In the same year 1623 it appeared, anonymously, in *Epitaphia iocoseria, Latina, Gallica, Hispanica, Lusitanica, Belgica,* a collection made by Franciscus Sweertius, Coloniae, M.DC.XXIII, B.L. 1213 d 32. The epitaph *De Tomas Moro Ingles* is to be found in the section *Epitaphia hispanica,* on p. 302-303.

Bedford College, University of London.   Malcolm C. Smith

Bibliothèque d'Humanisme et Renaissance - Tome XLVII - n° 3, pp. 609-611.

NOTES ET DOCUMENTS

TWO UNKNOWN POEMS BY RONSARD

In 1586, a pamphlet containing principally work by Pontus de Tyard (or Thyard) was published as an act of homage to Ronsard, who had died on 28 December in the previous year. This pamphlet includes two poems which it attributes to Ronsard. These poems have not hitherto been published among his works, and I am reproducing them here.

The title of the pamphlet, which is in the John Rylands Library, Manchester University, is *Ponti Thyardaei Bissiani, Ad Petrum Ronsardum, De Cœlestibus Asterismis Poematium. Gallicis versibus expressum ab Antonio Bletonnierœo* (Parisiis, Apud Ioannem Richerium, via D. Ioannis Lateranensis, sub Arbore Virescenti, 1586). There is another copy in the Houghton Library of Harvard University. Its contents are as follows:

> *Francisci Ambosii Parisini* (verso of title page; a poem in praise of Ronsard beginning «Debebat Phœbus Ronsardo præmia vati [...]»);
>
> *Pontus Tyardeus Bissianus Petro Ronsardo, S.* (A ii r°; a letter dedicating to Ronsard the poem about the stars which is found later in the pamphlet);
>
> *Ronsardus ad suos encomiastas*, A ii v°; one of the two poems published in this article;
>
> *Epit [aphium]* (A ii v°; two lines signed P[ontus] D[e] T[yard]: «Petrus Ronsardus iacet hic: si cetera nescis, / Nescis quid Phœbus, Musa, Minerva, Charis»);
>
> *Ponti Thyardei, Bissiani, Ad Petrum Ronsardum: De Cœlestibus Asterismis, Poematium* (also numbered A ii r°; beginning «Dum fera discordes agitat discordia mentes [...]»);
>
> *Reverendo D. Ponto Tyardaeo Bissiano, Episcopo Cabilonensi, Mœcenati suo, Antonius Bletonnieraeus* (B r°; a letter explaining that the moment of mourning for Ronsard's death was a fitting one to translate into French and publish the Latin poem which Tyard had previously dedicated to Ronsard);
>
> *Traduit du latin de P. de Tyard par Antoine de la Bletonniere* (B v°; a translation of *De cœlestibus asterismis*, beginning «Tandis que nous voyons nos esprits discordans [...]»);
>
> *Priere à Dieu par Monsieur de Ronsard estant malade*, B iv v°; the second of the two poems published here.

The poem by François d'Amboise and the main Latin poem with its dedicatory epistle were published by John C. Lapp in his edition of Tyard's *Œuvres poétiques complètes* (S.T.F.M., Paris, 1966, 292-300). Lapp's edition is unfortunately none too correct: in the first line of Tyard's dedicatory epistle, read *ederem*, not *ederent*; l. 2, read *utrique*, not *verique*; l. 5, comma after *collegi*; l. 13, read *fiet*, not *siet*, and *Poëtae*, not *Poëte*; and in the poem on the stars: l. 17, *quid*, not *qui*; l. 79, *stulta*, not *stula*; l. 87, *quae*, not *qua*; l. 105, *pudeat*, not *pedeat*.

There is a close parallel in content between the *Priere à Dieu* reproduced here and the other edifying poems which Ronsard was writing in his last days, and which were published, also in 1586, in the *Derniers vers* (see the edition of Ronsard's *Œuvres complètes* by P. Laumonier, I. Silver and R. Lebègue, XVIII, 173-182). It is interesting that Ronsard, who in the first years of his career as a poet was the object of innumerable criticisms of his allegedly «pagan» poetry, should have ended his life on such a devout note, actually denouncing «Mille Dieux abuseurs que feint la Poësie».

La Bletonnière, who was probably responsible for the compilation and publication of this pamphlet, does not explain how the poems attributed to Ronsard came into his possession. One might be happier about this attribution had he done so, especially as the poems do not figure in the edition of the collected works published by Binet and Galland the following year. At the same time, the Latin poem is very typical of Ronsard's assessments of his achievement, and the French one is very close in theme and content to the certainly-authentic *Derniers vers*. The fact that the pamphlet was published as an act of homage to Ronsard and under the auspices of Tyard also argues for the authenticity of the two poems. On balance, it seems safe to add them to the Ronsard canon.

London.   Malcolm C. SMITH.

RONSARDUS AD SUOS ENCOMIASTAS

Lustrali tepidos cineres aspergite lympha,
    Et precibus manes rite piate meos:
Nostraque nec vobis tantæ sit gloria curæ,
    Nam peperi laudis satque superque mihi.

PRIERE A DIEU FAICTE
PAR MONSIEUR DE RONSARD ESTANT MALADE

Dieu, vray Dieu, et Seigneur de nous pauvres humains,
Dieu, qui nous baillas être, et nous fis de tes mains,
Dieu, Dieu, qui es seul Dieu, Dieu de qui la facture
C'est la Terre et le Ciel, c'est toute creature,
C'est tout, tout ce qui est, et tout ce qui sera —
Lors qu'il faudra qu'il soit, lors ta main le fera;
Dieu, qui de tous nos faits comme il te plaist disposes,
Dieu, qui d'un seul clin d'œil peux faire toutes choses,
Dieu, sans qui ni le Ciel, ni l'homme terrien,
N'ici bas, ne là haut, n'ont puissance de rien,
Dieu, que seul Dieu je tien, Dieu en qui seul j'espere,
Dieu, que je recognoi pour mon Seigneur et pere,

Dieu, mon Roy, Dieu mon tout, Dieu en qui j'ay ma foy,
Dieu en qui je m'atten, Dieu en qui seul je croy:
Las mon Dieu, si tu vois qu'en toy je me confie,
Guery moy, ô Seigneur, de ceste maladie.
S'il est ainsi, mon Dieu, que je n'aye attenté
Autre moyen que toy pour r'avoir ma santé,
Si je n'ay point forgé dedans ma fantasie
Mille Dieux abuseurs que feint la Poësie,
Si d'autre que de toy je n'ay cherché secours,
Si seulement à toy j'ay tousjours eu recours,
Gueri moy, ô Seigneur, et de ton Ciel m'envoye
Le jour tant desiré, que sain je me revoye.
Lors, mon Dieu, s'il te plait me remettre en santé,
Le bien que m'auras fait sera par moy chanté;
Lors ayant dans le cœur emprainte la memoire
Du bien qu'auray receu, j'exalteray ta gloire,
Et par tout où j'yray, je diray que c'est toy
Qui seul m'as delivré de la peine où j'estoy.

Malcolm Smith on a cycling-club outing, Kent, 1968/69

[155]

Bibliothèque d'Humanisme et Renaissance - Tome XLVIII - 1986 - n° 2, pp. 421-430.

A REFORMER'S REPLY TO RONSARD'S
DISCOURS A LA ROYNE

In 1973, Jacques Pineaux published the extant pamphlets against Ronsard written by Reformers during and after the first civil war[1]. In 1975, I presented a tract in this series which Pineaux had been unable to locate, the *Remonstrance sur la diversité des Poëtes* (1563)[2]. My purpose here is to publish a further pamphlet against Ronsard, the *Contrediscours des miseres* of 1562.

This *Contrediscours* — which is in the Bibliothèque Mazarine, shelf-mark 18824 A 3 (15) — is mentioned by Jean-François Gilmont in his very useful recent article on Eloi Gibier, of Orléans, who printed it[3]. Gilmont mentions the pamphlet in a discussion of anti-Ronsard polemic, but his very brief treatment does not reflect the importance of the work. The *Contrediscours* was unknown to Pineaux, and unknown to Charbonnier who, many years ago, compiled what is still the best bibliography of pamphlets against Ronsard of the civil war period[4]. It was also unknown to Ronsard himself, who did not include it in his own admittedly hasty list of writings against himself, and did not reply to material in it in his *Responce aux injures* of 1563[5].

The *Contrediscours* is a close parody, in its title, arguments and language, of Ronsard's 1562 pamphlet titled *Discours des miseres de ce temps à la Royne mere du Roy*. I shall refer to Ronsard's pamphlet henceforth as the *Discours à la Royne* (this is to avoid confusion, for he later gave the title *Discours des miseres* to his whole collection of poems against the Reformers)[6]. There are two significant differences between Ronsard's *Discours à la Royne* and the parody. One is that while Ronsard repeatedly appeals to history for lessons applicable to the present, his adversary does

---

[1] See *La polémique protestante contre Ronsard* (S.T.F.M.), Paris, 1973.

[2] See «A 'lost' Protestant pamphlet against Ronsard», *B.H.R.*, XXXVII, 1975, 73-86. I pointed out in this article that the polemic between Ronsard and the Reformers had its origin in hostile criticisms of the poet's early work, and have since then explored this question in greater detail: see «Ronsard et ses critiques contemporains» (to appear in the proceedings of the Colloque Ronsard held at Tours and Paris, September 1985).

[3] See «Eloi Gibier, éditeur de théologie réformée: nouveau complément à la bibliographie de ses éditions», *B.H.R.*, XLVII, 1985, 395-403.

[4] See. F. Charbonnier, *Pamphlets protestants contre Ronsard (1560-1577)*, Paris, 1923.

[5] Ronsard's list of pamphlets against him is in the *Epistre au lecteur* which prefaces the *Trois livres du Recueil des nouvelles poësies* of 1563: see my edition of the *Discours des miseres*, T.L.F., Genève, 1979, 223. For the *Responce aux injures*, see the same edition, 149-215.

[6] The *Discours à la Royne* is in the *Discours*, éd. cit., 61-75.

this less often and less cogently. The other is that Ronsard, whilst committed to the Catholic view, sympathised with those humanists who sought to
achieve religious concord by reform of corruption and by scholarly endeavour, and his *Discours à la Royne* is much less partisan than the *Contrediscours*[7].

This rejoinder to Ronsard is of particular interest as being the earliest in
the series of pamphlets against him by Reformers during the civil war
period[8]. Ronsard composed the *Discours à la Royne* in June 1562 and, because of its high topicality, published it very rapidly (rapidly enough for
four more known editions to appear before the end of the year)[9]. The
appeal of the *Contrediscours*, equally, depended largely on topicality.
There are two indications that it appeared very soon indeed after the *Discours à la Royne*. One is that it does not mention Ronsard's next pamphlet,
the *Continuation du discours*, which may have been written as early as the
end of July[10]. The other is that the author of the *Contrediscours* was almost
certainly replying to the first of the five 1562 editions of the *Discours à la
Royne*, for he did not know the author of the *Discours* was Ronsard, and
only the first edition omits his name (had he known his adversary was Ronsard, he would have highlighted the fact, as other Reformers did)[11].

The *Contrediscours* is accompanied by a sonnet in praise of the author,
signed «F.C.». This could well be Florent Chrestien, who wrote two other
pamphlets in this series, the *Seconde response de F. de La Baronie à messire Pierre de Ronsard* (1563) and the *Apologie ou deffense d'un homme
chrestien* (1564)[12]. It is quite possible that the *Contrediscours* itself is also
by Chrestien (whose sonnet would then be a commendation of himself).
This would account for the title of his *Seconde response* — and no other
satisfactory explanation of this title has been given[13]. This theory is sup-

---

[7]   On the quest for concord, see Mario Turchetti's monumental *Concordia o tolleranza? François Bauduin (1520-1573) e i «Moyenneurs»*, Genève, 1984. In the late summer of
1562, after the failure of attempts to secure peace, Ronsard became a more militant foe of the
Reformers.

[8]   Charbonnier (*Pamphlets protestants* [...], 3-4) mentions three short poems by Reformers dated 1562, but the earliest pamphlets known until now appeared in the following year.
The 1560 works implied by his title are poems by Ronsard.

[9]   On the 1562 editions of the *Discours à la Royne*, see J.P. Barbier's very useful *Bibliographie des Discours politiques de Ronsard*, Genève, 1984, nos. 24-28.

[10]   For the dates of Ronsard's *Discours* and *Continuation du discours*, see my edition, 67
and 97-98.

[11]   See Barbier, *Bibliographie* [...], no. 24.

[12]   For the texts, see Pineaux, *Polémique protestante* [...], 324-395 and 460-502.

[13]   Pineaux argued (*Polémique protestante* [...], 520) that Chrestien did not write a reply
to Ronsard before the *Seconde response*. This is highly implausible: the title *Seconde response*
strongly implies there had been a first. Pineaux's edition is highly useful, but his historical
material is often questionable (on this, see Kathryn Evans, «Grévin, author of the *Temple de
Ronsard*? », *B.H.R.*, XLVII, 1985, pp. 619-625.

ported by the fact that Chrestien's *Seconde response* and *Apologie ou deffense* were, like the *Contrediscours*, also published by Gibier[14].

London.   Malcolm C. SMITH.

CONTREDISCOURS DES MISERES DE CE TEMS

Depuis le premier tems que la faute premiere
Priva tout en un coup l'univers de lumiere,
Les tenebres et maus succedans en son lieu,
Tout le mal fut en nous, et le bien vint de Dieu.
Nostre mal prit deslors à l'envy sa croissance
De ce bien qui en nous prenoit de Dieu naissance,
Si que depuis on veit d'accroissement egal
De Dieu couler le bien, et sourdre en nous le mal:
Ainsi que chacun sait qu'une chose contraire
10   S'arme pour s'opposer à l'autre, ou la defaire,
Et pour ce en mesme tems on peut bien voir icy
Des gens fort vertueus, et fort meschans aussi.
    Or comme il plaist à Dieu exercer sa justice,
En un lieu la vertu regne en l'autre le vice.
Ainsi change de lieu l'un ou l'autre souvent,
Comme par les saisons on voit changer de vent,
Et celuy-là qui met en main le sceptre aus Princes
Gouverne et eus, et l'âge, et les meurs des Provinces,
Les baisse, les accroist, les maintient, les deffait,
20   Seul cognoist le conseil de tout ce qu'il en fait.

---

[14]   See L. Desgraves, *Eloi Gibier imprimeur à Orléans (1536-1588)*, Genève, 1966, nos. 39 and 85 and, on the attribution to Chrestien of the anonymous *Apologie ou deffense*, F. Charbonnier, *La Poésie française et les guerres de religion (1560-1574)*, Paris, 1920, 110-112 and Pineaux, *Polémique protestante* [...], 462. Gibier also published another work against Ronsard, the *Response aux calomnies* by Antoine de La Roche Chandieu (1563; Desgraves, Gibier, no. 35).

N.B. — Jean Céard has very kindly pointed out to me that the *Priere à Dieu* published in my article «Two unknown poems by Ronsard» (*B.H.R.*, 1985, 609-611) is in the edition of Ronsard prepared by Laumonier and published by Lemerre (1914-1919; VI, 506-507) and that *Ronsardus ad suos encomiastas* is in Nolhac's *Ronsard et l'Humanisme* (1921, 200). Scholars in general, myself included, have relied on the S.T.F.M. edition by Laumonier, Silver and Lebègue (20 v., Paris, 1914-1975) for the complete extant Ronsard, the more readily as it errs on the side of safety by incorporating works of dubious authenticity (in the section «Pièces diverses attribuées à Ronsard»: XVIII, 340-489). This edition does not contain the two works I published, notwithstanding the fact that their authenticity is at least probable. Céard has performed a very useful service to scholarship in signalling the necessity of consulting earlier editions — and, at the same time, has reminded us implicitly of how useful it will be to have the new complete edition on which he is working with Daniel Ménager and Michel Simonin.

Ainsi plaist-il à Dieu, sans qu'homme le merite,
Faire part de ses biens, ou priver qui l'irrite,
Comme un pere à son fils acquiert des biens beaucoup,
Qu'il luy peut, offensé, oster tout en un coup.
    Que s'il nous chaloit plus d'histoires veritables
Que des exemples faus des mensongeres fables,
Par le discours des temps nous connoistrions assez
Que ce siecle n'est pas different des passez,
Esquels on voit les Rois pourchasser à outrance
30 Ceus qui avoient en Christ mise leur esperance.
On les voit par les grans et peuples mutinez,
Par glaive, eau, feu, noyez, bruslez, assassinez,
Si qu'il semble que l'eau, le feu, l'air et la terre,
Aient à l'encontre d'eus juré mortelle guerre.
Mais (après longue attente) on voit Dieu irrité
Du sang des innocens, en son throne monté
Casser en son courrous aus plus braves les testes,
Lors que plus asseurez ils demenent leurs festes.
Pour venger en un coup cent mille iniquitez,
40 On luy voit abismer les superbes citez,
Voire estendre sa main sur les Empires mesmes
Par peste, guerre, faim, et autres maus extresmes,
Ou, tralignant les Rois, leur estat rechanger,
Ou les faisant gibier d'un puissant estranger,
Tant il est important à un Roy qu'il avise
De vivre selon Dieu, et cherir son Eglise,
Et que les gouverneurs establis en un lieu
Mettent le gouvernail entre les mains de Dieu.
    Ce monde corrompu, ce monde miserable,
50 Dedans tout son enclos n'avoit rien agreable
A son facteur. Mais luy, ainsi qu'il luy a pleu,
Du rebut de ce monde a seulement esleu
Peu de gens et espars, où tant sa grace abonde
Que pour le seul amour d'iceus le monde est monde.
Et quoy qu'il semble bien qu'estans à la mercy
De leur haineus, il ait d'eus bien peu de soucy,
Si voit on en cela plus clair son assistance,
Qu'il gourme des meschans la haineuse puissance,
Ainsi que sa bonté fait qu'un petit oiseau
60 Pond, couve, esclost, au sein de la fureur de l'eau.
    Maintenant que l'on voit que la France esperdue
Regrette de son char la conduite perdue,
Les chartiers eslongnez, les chevaus si rebours,
Que la vois ne le mors n'en modere le cours,
Ores que la fureur dont elle est agitée
L'effroye de danger d'estre precipitée,
Il est temps, ou jamais, d'eviter prontement
Le peril trop voisin d'un pire evenement.

Ces pauvres simples gens que par tout on sacage
70 Sont ceus que Dieu a pris icy pour son partage,
Sont ceus qu'il a si chers, que pour eus maintesfois
Il n'a pas espargné nos pays et nos Roys:
N'esperons donques pas voir son ire apaisée
Que leur clameur ne soit premierement cessée.
    O vous donq qui avez commandement sur tous,
Aportez-y la main, que Dieu en son courrous
De vos trop paresseus souspirs ne tienne conte.
Le chommer est nuisant: comme celuy qui monte
Contre le cours d'un eau, s'il relasche les bras,
80 Est soudain emporté par le courant à bas.
Pour Dieu entendez y! La France vous en somme,
Ou pour mieus ce qu'en France à bon droit France on nomme,
Cœurs vrayement françois, que nul mortel efroy
N'empesche de garder ce Royaume à leur Roy.
    Ce Pharamond, du quel nous gardons la memoire,
Pource qu'il a de Dieu premier eu ceste gloire
D'avoir, sage et vaillant, ralié les François,
Qui barbares devant vivoient sans Rois et lois,
Ce Clodion aussi, pensez de quel visage
90 Ils verroient ès François le barbare courage,
Qui repand tant de sang innocent en tout lieu,
Encore que tous deus ne conneussent point Dieu!
Et si Clovis a eu de Dieu la connoissance
Telle qu'un Chrestien doit, las quelle desplaisance
Auroit-il en son cœur de voir ainsi meurtris
Ceus là qu'il connoistroit de son Dieu tant cheris?
Et s'il n'est pas ainsi, son esprit debonnaire
Pourroit-il endurer un peuple sanguinaire?
Nos Pepins, nos Martels, nos Charles, nos Louis,
100 Quoy que l'abus Romain les avoit esblouis,
Si n'auroient-ils jamais enduré que la rage
D'un triple Gerion eust causé tel outrage:
Ils eussent bien gardé que la temerité
D'un peuple eust enjambé sur leur autorité,
Peuple armant ses exces de l'aveu et soufrance
Du Conseil establi pour maintien de la France,
De laquelle jadis tant de chevaliers morts
Ont au pris de leur sang en vain poussé les bors
Jusqu'aus monts et aus mers. Si maintenant leur race
110 Du pays conquesté ingratement on chasse,
La despouillant du bien tesmoin et guerdonneur
Des faits de leurs ayeuls tous morts au lit d'honneur,
Pour estre mis en proye au monstre qui regorge,
Et glouton ne combat que pour ne rendre gorge.
Monstre ingrat et cruel, qui degaste insensé
Le fertile pays, dont il est engraissé:

[160]

Tout ainsi le sanglier, tout ainsi la vipere,
Qui gaste loin les fruits de la terre sa mere,
Qui parricide occit celle qui l'a conceu.
120   Pieça France devoit avoir bien aperceu
Tel inconvenient, si le Royal presage
Et la vois du commun, l'eust peu faire plus sage,
Qui menaçoient et Roy et peuple de dangers
Extremes, par les mains des ingrats estrangers.
Et sans nous arrester à l'efroy des Cometes,
Et aus abus fondés sur le cours des Planetes,
Leurs furieus desseins tant de fois retentés
Nous ont de tems en tems assez amonnestés
Que par ce qu'ils auroient entrepris ceste année
130 Avec son Roy seroit la France ruinée —
De laquelle les grans esblouis n'ont conneu
Ce que de là le Rhin, la mer, les monts, ont veu:
Les pays eslongnez, qui d'une pitié tendre
Nous envoyent icy leurs gens pour la defendre.
       Ces trois freres chenus, trois Nestors, qui tous trois
Souloient reigler l'estat et les Cours de nos Rois
(Venerables vieillars en leurs grans robes blanches
Recamées de lis, ceints au dessus des hanches
D'un baudrier tout pareil, monstrans leur loyauté,
140 Leur franchise, et l'amour à ceste Royauté),
Pieça, bannis des Cours, donnoient par les villages
Des avertissemens certains de nos dommages,
Puis sortans hors des bois passerent aus fausbourgs
Des notables cités, et des villes aus Cours,
Où d'un front asseuré ont fait leur remonstrance
En semblable propos: «O trop heureuse France,
Trois fois heureuse et plus, si une fois ta main
Pardonne au sang de ceus que l'on meurtrit en vain!
Mais malheureuse France, ah France malheureuse,
150 Si tu poursuis tousjours d'une main furieuse
Les pauvres innocens, qui contre tes efforts
Plus drus et plus gaillars renaistront de leurs morts!
Tu seras par les tiens, par les tiens assiegée,
Tu seras par les tiens, par les tiens sacagée,
Et dans toy l'estranger defera l'estranger,
Qui te ruinera pour te vouloir venger.
Retourne toy à Dieu, car l'heure en est venue:
Encontre l'esperon en vain le poulain rue.»
       Or ainsi que l'essueil s'assourdit aus abois
160 De la mer tempestueuse, ainsi à ceste vois
Nos chefs sourds n'ont esgard, que l'on voit avenue
A coup sans y penser telle desconvenue.
Ainsi ceus de Gomorrhe, après un long mespris,
Se trouverent soudain foudroyez et peris.

[161]

Quand donques nous voyons par les cours des années
Les pays ravagés par eaus desordonnées,
Ou brusler les moissons par un chaud furieus,
Ou le vent eslever la mer jusques aus cieus,
Il ne faut pas juger que le Seigneur s'oublie
170 De la teneur qu'il a aus saisons establie,
Ainçois qu'il veult benin par là nous avertir
De recevoir les fruits d'un sage repentir.
Le Ciel tant pluvieus, les eaus noyans les plaines,
Nous avertissoient prou de nos douleurs prochaines:
Mais le peuple est si lourd qu'il n'a jamais pensé
Que par cela il fust du Seigneur menacé,
Et Seine qui troubloit Paris de sa furie
A rougy de l'horreur de sa mutinerie.
Par un tel nonchaloir, et par si fort erreur
180 Nous avons atisé la divine fureur.
        Or jaçoit qu'à bien peu soient ores profitables
Les saints enseignemens d'exemples si notables,
Si est-ce à l'avenir que ceus là qui liront
L'histoire de ce tems (telle que l'escriront
Les Chroniqueurs, desquels la plume non flateuse
Abhorre sur tous maus une histoire menteuse),
En voyant tell'horreur de maus prodigieus
Ils leveront au Ciel et les mains et les yeus
Esbahis de l'erreur seul appuy du faus zele,
190 Qui arme tant de gens à si lasche querelle.
Mais ils detesteront tous ceus là que la peur
Aura faits compaignons à un si grand malheur,
Pardonnant moins à ceus qui d'un lasche courage
Se seront ou soustraits, ou livrés à la rage
De ces loups acharnés, et ceus qui connoissans
Le merite du fait, les vont autorisans,
Hommes tous monstrueus qui de raisons subtiles
Arment le monstre autheur de nos guerres civiles.
        On dit quand Hercules en jeunesse choisit
200 Le train de la Vertu, qu'elle le conduisit
Par la main au milieu d'une libre campagne
Jusqu'à l'empatement d'une haute montagne.
Où elle luy disoit: «Mon fils, à qui j'ay pleu,
Pour mieus te faire voir que tu as bien esleu,
Montons icy dessus. Or regarde et avise
Que ce mont que l'on croit n'estre qu'un, se divise,
De peur qu'à l'avenir, suivant l'erreur commun,
Tu ne cuides, trompé, que les deux ne soient qu'un.»
Puis elle commanda que sa seur, la Sagesse,
210 Luy enseignast du mont les secrets et l'adresse.
Il vit premierement les piés des deus costaus
Tous raportans entre eus, tous pareils, tous esgaus,

Fors que l'herbe et les fleurs de cestuy là fletrissent,
Et de l'autre tousjours verdoyent et fleurissent.
Quand en montant plus haut furent plus apparens
Leurs sommets, il vit mieus qu'ils estoyent differens.
    Sur l'un, à costé droit, seoit une pucelle
Dessus un diamant, plus seante que belle,
De beauté toutesfois telle que sont les traits
220 Qui nous font amirer les antiques portraits.
Son vestement estoit d'une fine tissure,
De lin blanc qui n'avoit aucune autre pareure,
Mais qui, fort delié, faisoit que par dehors
On voyoit à travers la beauté de son cors.
C'estoit la Verité, et les cinq autres filles
Belles esgalement, esgalement gentilles,
Estoyent Science, Foy, Douceur, Simplicité,
Et Consolation, qui suivent Verité.
Tousjours un mesme vent doucement les evente.
230 Ne le froid rigoureus, ne le chaut les tourmente.
Peu de gens estoyent là, tous de mesme propos,
Tout le lieu s'esgayoit en un profond repos.
    Dessus l'autre sommet estoit Hypocrisie,
Qui long vestue en or et soye cramoisie,
Pour la naïve fleur d'une vraye beauté
Abuse les voyans d'un visage emprunté.
Ignorance y estoit, l'Abus, la Tromperie,
Et dessus le chemin s'embuschoit Flaterie,
Qui prenant la couleur des prochaines couleurs,
240 Charme tout sentiment de vices et malheurs
Es gens qu'elle a saisis. La Tarde Repentance
Un peu plus à l'escart avoit sa demourance
Entre mille serpens, qu'elle repaist des cors
D'hommes, qui tous les jours revivent demy morts.
Tout ce sommet noircist d'une brouée espesse,
Et par tous les endroits ront et bruit de la presse,
Laquelle sans raison par un exemple suit
Le chemin des premiers, qui, aisé, la conduit
A la Dame du lieu, laquelle onq n'est esprise
250 De plus forte fureur que quand on la mesprise.
    Or maintenant donq que Dieu par sa seule bonté
Nous veult acheminer au train de Verité,
Elle par le depit de se voir mesprisée
Vomissant le venin de sa haine embrasée
Es chapitres, couvents et cloistres a touché
Les François de Discord, là dedans embusché.
Comme l'on voit soudain l'armée courroucée
Des mousches, en venger une seule offensée,
Ainsi elle qui a gens par toutes les Cours,
260 A tout en un instant pratiqué le secours

De tous ses alliez, et (sous couleur trompeuse)
A mesmes atiré ceste gent belliqueuse,
Laquelle a tant soufert mettant en liberté
Son pays abatu dessous sa cruauté.
      Par elle maintenant France à la France louve,
Dedans le cœur des siens si forte haine couve,
Que l'enfant craignant Dieu par son pere est meurtry,
Le pere par le fils lequel il a nourry.
Au lit de son mary n'est la femme fidele
270   En seureté, ne luy, si sa femme n'est telle.
Le frere Caïnize, et mesme l'estranger
En la chambre de l'hoste est tousjours en danger.
Le païsan est juge, et sa rage effrenée
Execute soudain la sentance donnée.
L'artizan desbauché met son art en oubly,
Esperant par la mort des bons estre anobly.
Le faquin soufreteus, qui de vile pitance
Dontoit, par ses crochets, les abois de sa pance,
Maintenant gentilhomme et riche de butin,
280   N'a plus aucun soucy de se lever matin.
Justice n'a plus lieu, l'impunie licence
Deschire maintenant la miserable France.
Ces saints Temples de Dieu, les cors de ses esleus,
Comment sont-ils par tout ou destruits ou pollus?
Si que Dieu — quel horreur! — en sa propre demeure
Des sanguinaires mains asseuré ne demeure,
Lequel voyant cecy merque tout de ses yeus,
Attendant si la France un jour devers les cieus
Levera le visage en vraye repentance,
290   Pour requerir pardon de si mortelle offense.
      Vous donques qui voulez garder l'autorité
Que Dieu vous y acorde en la minorité
Du Roy, venez à luy, repoussant ceste rage
Des peuples mutinés, et d'un brave courage
Sans esgard punissant (car il le veut ainsi)
Les rebelles auteurs de tous ces maux icy.
Lors en un mesme temps vous verrez destournée
La vengeance de Dieu, et leur rage bornée.
Pour conserver les bons punissez les mutins:
300   Pour sauver les levriers on tue les mastins,
Qui souvent ont chassé par leurs abois fideles
Des troupeaus aguettés maintes bestes cruelles.
Si non, Dieu desdaignant s'aider de vos moyens,
Contre eus et contre vous exploitera les siens,
Punissant leurs forfaits et vostre nonchalance,
Tout en un mesme coup d'exemplaire vengeance.
      O Dieu (que par ton fils en vain prie celuy
Qui ne monstre de fait la foy qu'il a en luy),

Puis qu'en soy l'homme n'a ne pouvoir ny envie
310 De jamais faire bien sans toy, je te suplie
De donner à nos chefs pouvoir et volonté
D'apaiser la fureur de ce monstre indonté,
Et que par leur devoir la discorde enserrée
Ronge en vain les courreaus d'une porte ferrée,
A fin que jouissans d'une fidele pais
Nous puissions haut chanter la grandeur de tes faits.
    Ou bien si, O Seigneur, ta volonté est telle
De chastier les tiens par la verge cruelle
De si forts ennemis, et si à ceste fois
320 Tu veus renouveler tout ce monde François,
Donne nous en nos maus contre la violance
De nos persecuteurs, une telle constance
Dont ils soyent condamnés, et après que leurs mains
T'auront servy, puny leurs exces inhumains.
Noye ces Pharaons dans la mer furieuse,
Frappe ces Philistins de main victorieuse,
Suscitant des Mosés, des Davids, des Sansons,
Et peu de gens choisis aveq leurs Gedeons,
A fin qu'après l'effroy d'une telle tempeste
330 Ton fils victorieus dresse aus nues la teste.

SONNET EN FAVEUR DE L'AUTEUR DE CE DISCOURS

Celuy qui tient la terre sur le port
Prent bien plaisir à voir dessus la mer
La nef d'autruy en profond abysmer
A qui les vents ont denié le bord.

Lors il s'esgaye estant loing de la mort,
Et ne voudroit tout l'or du monde aymer
Pour seulement se voir ainsi pasmer
Par la fureur du Harbin et du North.

Mais s'il advient qu'il soit en ce danger
Il tiendra bon, et se viendra ranger
Au bon conseil du sage gouvernal.

Qui comme toy, ô tres beau discoureur,
Sache si bien entendre le malheur
Pour se sauver du naufrage et du mal.

F.C.

THE LIBRARY

Sixth Series, Volume VIII, No. 2, June 1986

Lost Works by Ronsard

By MALCOLM SMITH

A paper read before the Bibliographical Society on
19 March 1985

IN AN ELOQUENT PASSAGE of one of his *Hymnes*, Ronsard longingly evokes the possibility that some of the lost work of the great Greek poets might be rediscovered. But, he concludes sadly, such is not the will of God:

> Mais Dieu ne le veut pas, qui couvre soubz la terre
> Tant de livres perdus, miseres de la guerre.

Our quest for lost books, Ronsard adds, is subject always to the decrees of Fate, for

> . . . le Sort a puissance
> (O cruauté du Ciel) sur l'humaine science![1]

What Ronsard says of ancient Greek poetry applies also, alas, to his own work, a great deal of which is lost. Four hundred years after the poet's death, twelve works or groups of works are thought by Ronsard scholars to be lost, and I shall here be adding a further eleven to that list.

Why are so many books by Ronsard lost? The answer is that his massive production was highly diverse, and that its intrinsic diversity is reflected in the myriad of places in which he published it, places where scholars often do not think of looking today. The aim of Ronsard and the other Pléiade poets was to achieve success in every poetic genre which mattered to them, and Ronsard was repeatedly praised for having succeeded in this aim.[2] When it came to publishing his vastly heterogeneous output, Ronsard cast his poems to the wind:

---

[1] Ronsard, *Œuvres complètes*, edited by P. Laumonier, I. Silver, and R. Lebègue (STFM), 20 vols (Paris, 1914–75). All references to Ronsard, unless indicated otherwise, are to this edition.

[2] For the aim, see Du Bellay's *Defence et illustration de la langue françoyse*, II, v (which Ronsard helped write: see Ronsard, X (1939), 367 and my edition of the *Discours des miseres de ce temps*, Geneva, 1979, pp. 47–48). Eulogies of the diversity of Ronsard's excellence are found in (for example) Ronsard, VIII (1935), 4 and XVIII (1967), 207 (tributes by Dorat and Pasquier); Claude Binet, *Vie de Ronsard*, edited by P. Laumonier (Paris, 1910), p. 46; and Guillaume Colletet, *Pierre de Ronsard*, edited by F. B. Caldari (Paris, 1983), p. 44; see also p. 41).

. . . ma fureur sans ordre se suivant
Esparpille ses vers comme feuilles au vent.[3]

Thus, while he assembled poems in collections such as the *Odes*, *Amours*, and *Hymnes*, he also scattered a great deal in pamphlets containing individual poems — and some of these pamphlets are anonymous or quasi-anonymous; and he disseminated a great many poems in volumes by other authors — for example, commendatory poems, and circumstantial poems.

But while Ronsard scattered his poems like leaves in the wind, he also gathered most of them together in collected editions of his work, from 1560 onwards. These collected editions are eloquent evidence of his care to preserve his writing: and he seems to have devoted particular attention to his last two collected editions. He spent the winter of 1583–84 working on the sixth such edition, which appeared early in 1584; and he spent the last painful months before his death in December 1585 revising this edition: his revisions are incorporated in the first posthumous edition of 1587. Two well-informed contemporaries stress how important these last two editions were to Ronsard. On the 1584 edition, Jacques Davy Du Perron commented in his funerary oration on Ronsard as follows:

Mais encore ce qui l'acheva de ruiner, ce fut ceste derniere diligence dont il usa pour donner ordre à l'impression de ses escrits. Car estant desja fort indisposé de luy-mesme, le moindre excez qu'il pouvoit faire en un travail si violent, comme est celuy de l'esprit, il n'y a point de doute qu'il ne fust suffisant pour le mettre extremement bas. Ses œuvres doncques furent achevees d'imprimer en une nouvelle forme avecques beaucoup de contentement pour luy, de voir qu'il avoit eu le loisir devant que d'estre prevenu d'aucun accident, de leur dire le dernier à Dieu, & de les disposer en la façon qu'il vouloit qu'elles fussent leuës de la postérité.[4]

And Claude Binet, in the 1587 edition of his *Vie de Ronsard*, said of the first posthumous edition that

cette derniere main de ses Œuvres . . . comme un testament porte sa volonté gravée, ainsi qu'il me l'avait recommandée, inviolable.[5]

These collected editions do not, however, include all he ever wrote. Some poems which he omitted survive because books in which they did appear are extant; many others are lost. To the greatest editor of Ronsard, Paul Laumonier, it did not matter too much that they were lost, since it was

[3] *Responce aux injures*, ll. 849–50 (XI (1946), 159; and my edition of the *Discours*, p. 195). In the way of Montaigne, I have adapted Ronsard's sense to suit my purpose.
[4] Ronsard, XVIII, xx–xxi.
[5] *Vie de Ronsard*, ed. Laumonier, p. 50. The 1597 version of Binet's text, which revises this passage, is equally emphatic. The first posthumous edition of Ronsard is now regarded as thoroughly authentic. See my review (in *Bibliothèque d'Humanisme et Renaissance*, 29 (1967), 734–37) of Isidore Silver's magnificent edition of the 1587 text, and especially Silver's remarks in vol. XVIII (xxxiii–lvii) of the STFM edition.

Ronsard who had taken the decision not to preserve them. For Laumonier, the most important poems were the ones which Ronsard included in the last collected edition he prepared; the next most important were those he had included in earlier collected editions and subsequently dropped; and the least important were those he never included in any collected edition.[6]

On this analysis, Ronsard's lost works are of minor importance, since it is the poet himself who allowed them to become lost. But quite apart from the fact that Ronsard was not necessarily the best judge of his own work, the fact that Ronsard allowed poems to become lost does not necessarily mean he thought relatively little of them. We simply do not know why he dropped these poems. They might have been politically inopportune, or have contained delicate allusions to individuals, or may have duplicated other poems, or have encountered a hostile contemporary reception (as we know many of his poems did).

Some at least of the poetry Ronsard omitted from his collected works certainly is very important, and that is his satire. Ronsard was keen to satirize corruption at the court, and Charles IX encouraged him to do so.[7] But Charles IX died before Ronsard could publish such satire, and Charles's successor Henry III, whose blessing Ronsard sought for satire, was anything but enthusiastic: in March 1577, when satirical poems directed at him and his wife were found in his wife's bedroom, he jailed all poets who could be found.[8] Ronsard wrote much satire which he did not publish and which is lost: it is plausible that he omitted it from his collected works not because he wanted to but because he had to omit it. It is safest to regard any lost work by the greatest French poet as being potentially very important, and to record carefully all that is known about material which has not come down to us.

I. WORKS KNOWN TO BE WHOLLY LOST

The edition of Ronsard's *Œuvres complètes* by Laumonier, Silver, and Lebègue has a list of lost works identified by the editors. I want first to recall what this list contains, before turning to what it omits. I shall also assess the likelihood that each of the items listed by Laumonier and his collaborators actually existed.[9]

---

[6] See Ronsard, XVIII, xix–xx.

[7] See the *Estreines au roy Henry III*, in vol. XVII (1959) of Laumonier's edition, pp. 85–93. Laumonier and his successors were unable to locate the original edition of this poem, and I published it in *Bibliothèque d'Humanisme et Renaissance*, 37 (1975), 213–24. Binet and Colletet both also say Charles IX urged Ronsard to write satire (see respectively *Vie de Ronsard*, ed. Laumonier, p. 26; and *Pierre de Ronsard*, ed. Caldari, p. 143 — a quotation from Colletet's life of Mathurin Régnier).

[8] In July 1575 he had also had Benjamin Jamyn, the brother of Ronsard's secretary Amadis, imprisoned and tortured, though for reasons which are obscure. On these events, see R. J. Sealy, *The Palace Academy of Henry III* (Geneva, 1981), pp. 77–78 and notes. Ronsard's request to Henry III for permission to write satire is in the *Estreines* (XVII, 87–91).

[9] The list of lost works is in Ronsard, XVIII, 522–29: it contains the relevant references which are not repeated in the present survey.

1. *La Luicte de Calaïs et d'Orfée*

Claude Binet mentions this in the 1586 edition of his *Vie de Ronsard* as an unpublished and incomplete work left by Ronsard on his death. But Binet dropped the mention of this work in later editions of his biography of Ronsard, and Ronsard's editors surmise that this is because he realized he had misinterpreted manuscript fragments of Ronsard's elegy titled *Orfée* and of the *Hymne de Calaïs et de Zetes* as being a new poem. This explanation is conceivable: and it seems anyway unlikely that the 'lost' *Luicte de Calaïs et d'Orfée* ever existed.

2. *Satirical work*

This is also mentioned by Binet in his *Vie de Ronsard*. In the 1586 edition, Binet noted that Charles IX had given Ronsard permission to write satire, and in the 1597 edition he mentioned specific satirical works, now lost, which Ronsard had written. One is titled *La Dryade Violée* and is against Charles IX's advisers who had him allow a forest to be cut down, another is titled *La Truelle crossée*, against over-generous payment of masons and architects, and attacking the architect Philibert de Lorme; another deals with the king's own shortcomings, and begins 'Il me desplaist de voir un si grand Roy de France'. These poems almost certainly existed: the information Binet gives is precise, we know Ronsard was vexed by misgovernment and keen to denounce it, and the sensitivity of the material gives a plausible explanation for the loss of the poems.

3. *Letters to Estienne Pasquier*

As Ronsard's editors point out, it is known from Pasquier's extant letters to Ronsard that the poet's letters to Pasquier once existed. I would add that Ronsard's letters to Pasquier are likely to be particularly interesting, for Pasquier's letters to the poet suggest a close friendship and one in which frank exchanges of view were possible: for in a letter of 1555, Pasquier criticizes the poet for being too willing to extol unworthy people.[10]

4. *Epitaphe de Mons. d'Orleans*

This is referred to in Antoine Foclin's *Rhetorique françoise*. Ronsard's editors note that this 'Mons. d'Orléans' must have been Charles d'Orléans, third son of Francis I, whom Ronsard served as a page for five years, and who died of the plague in 1545.[11] It is in my view possible that this work is not lost at all, and that Foclin was thinking of an ode, published in 1550, entitled *A la roine de Navare sur la mort de Charles de Valois, duc d'Orléans*.[12]

[10] See E. Pasquier, *Choix de lettres sur la littérature, la langue et la traduction*, edited by D. Thickett (Genève, 1956), pp. 3–8.

[11] See Ronsard, XVIII, 524. The loss of this work is also mentioned, but without further details, by Marguerite de Schweinitz in *Les épitaphes de Ronsard, étude historique et littéraire* (Paris, 1925), p. 10.

[12] See Ronsard, I, 179–83.

5. *An epitaph of Andrea Navagero*

This is referred to in a sonnet by Jean-Antoine de Baïf dedicated to Navagero:

Ronsard et moy Baïf, qui ta memoire
Solennisons, ce lorier, ce lierre,
Ces fleurs, ce miel, ce lait, ce vin nouveau,
Ronsard soigneux de ta vivante gloire,
Moy ton Baïf né de ta meme terre,
Avec nos pleurs donnons à ton tombeau.

This sonnet is found in Baïf's *Troisieme livre des passetems*.[13] But Baïf's sonnet may well also have appeared in some sixteenth-century edition of Navagero, or a volume commemorating his death, and bearing in mind the wording of Baïf's sonnet one would expect the same publication to contain Ronsard's eulogy of Navagero. Baïf's testimony makes the existence of Ronsard's work on Navagero virtually certain.[14]

6. *Three works mentioned by Brantôme*

These are an epitaph of Thony, the royal Fool; a eulogy of Margaret of Navarre; and what Laumonier coyly describes as 'un quatrain . . . sur le souverain bien de la jouissance en amour'. Brantôme claims to have been an acquaintance of Ronsard, and the likelihood these works existed is high.[15]

7. *A sonnet in praise of 'Sincero'*

This sonnet is referred to by Catherine Des Roches in her *Missives* of 1586: there seems no reason to doubt the sonnet existed. According to Laumonier and Thickett, 'Sincero' may be the pseudonym of Claude Pellejay, a poet and friend of Catherine Des Roches.[16]

8. *The compilation of unpublished Greek poems*

This is referred to by George Crichton (or Creighton) in his funerary oration on Ronsard, and by Colletet in his biography of Ronsard. Crichton says he expected Jean Galland (who, jointly with Binet, was Ronsard's literary executor) would publish this collection, and Colletet says Galland

---

[13] See his *Euvres en rime*, edited by C. Marty-Laveaux, 5 vols (Paris, 1881–90), IV (1887), 331–32.
[14] I have found nothing by Ronsard in Navagero's *Opera omnia* (Venice, 1754). Schweinitz notes the loss of this epitaph (*Les épitaphes de Ronsard*, p. 10).
[15] That Brantôme was acquainted with Ronsard emerges in a remark that Ronsard and he read the famous Casket Letters together (see P. de Bourdeille, seigneur de Brantôme, *Œuvres complètes*, edited by L. Lalanne, 11 vols (Paris, 1864–82), VII (1872), 406–07). It is perfectly plausible that Ronsard wrote an epitaph on Thony: he mentions him several times (see my edition of the *Discours des miseres*, pp. 165, 209–10 and 228). The loss of this epitaph is noted by Schweinitz (*Les épitaphes de Ronsard*, p. 10).
[16] See Ronsard, XVIII, 525–26, and Thickett's edition of Pasquier (*Choix de lettres sur la littérature*, p. 50).

ought to have done. It seems quite conceivable, given Ronsard's profound interest in Greek texts, that the compilation existed.[17] Ronsard's annotations on the Greek texts of Nicander have certainly survived, but have not been published.[18]

9. *Annotations on Bembo*

Colletet, in his biography of Ronsard, cited as evidence of Ronsard's familiarity with Italian literature 'les exemplaires de quelques livres italiens que Ronsard avait lus exactement & qui sont en mille endroits marqués & annotés de sa main propre. Je mets en ce rang les diverses rymes italiennes du cardinal Bembo & [lacune dans le manuscrit] qui sont tombées entre mes mains'. The annotations of Bembo have been lost. Laumonier and his collaborators do not note that Colletet also claims in his *Traitté du sonnet* to have actually owned the volume:

Et puis j'ay encore dans mon Cabinet les Rimes diverses du Cardinal Bembo, marquées de la propre main de Ronsard, et les pieces qu'il avoit imitées, ou qu'il s'estoit proposé d'imiter, ou de traduire.[19]

The book therefore definitely existed.

10, 11 and 12. *Letters by Ronsard*

These comprise respectively letters in praise of Jean-Antoine de Baïf which Guillaume Colletet said he possessed, letters stolen from French public libraries and letters mentioned in auction catalogues. Laumonier's edition gives references to all these documents (XVIII, 527–29), and it seems clear they existed.

II. ADDITIONS TO THE LIST OF LOST WORKS

The list of lost works in Laumonier's edition is therefore a lengthy one: but it is, as I hope now to show, very far from being exhaustive. Other contemporaries of the poet besides those mentioned by Laumonier *et al.* cite now-lost works of Ronsard; further, Laumonier and his collaborators have not, surprisingly, exhausted the information in those contemporaries of the poet they do cite; and, still more surprisingly, they have omitted now-lost works which Ronsard himself says he has written. I propose to arrange these newly identified lost works in approximate chronological order.

---

[17] On this philological work, see P. de Nolhac, *Ronsard et l'humanisme* (Paris, 1966), pp. 132–36. I. Silver does not mention it in his *Ronsard and the Hellenic Renaissance*, I, *Ronsard and the Greek epic* (St Louis, 1961).

[18] See P. Laumonier, 'Sur la bibliothèque de Ronsard', *Revue du seizième siècle*, 14 (1927), 315–35 (pp. 328–33), and I. Silver, *Ronsard and the Hellenic Renaissance*, pp. 77–83 and notes. It is of course highly probable that a great many other books containing annotations by Ronsard are lost.

[19] *Traitté de l'epigramme et Traitté du sonnet*, edited by P. A. Jannini (Geneva and Paris, 1965), p. 198.

1. *The early Latin poems*

These were the first poems Ronsard wrote. One of his earliest French poems, titled *A son luc*, suggests this:

> Si autrefois sous l'ombre de Gâtine
> Avons joué quelque chanson Latine
>   D'Amarille enamouré,
>   Sus, maintenant Luc doré,
> Sus l'honneur mien, dont la vois delectable
> Sçait rejouir les Princes à leur table,
>   Change ton stile, & me sois
>   Sonnant un chant en François.[20]

He is more categorical in an *Elegie* dedicated to Pierre L'Escot:

> Je n'avois pas douze ans qu'au profond des vallées,
> Dans les hautes forets des hommes reculées,
> Dans les antres segrets de frayeur tout couverts,
> Sans avoir soing de rien, je composois des vers . . .
>   Je feu premierement amoureux du Latin:
> Mais cognoissant helas! que mon cruel destin
> Ne m'avoit dextrement pour le Latin fait naistre,
> Je me fiz tout françois, aymant certes mieux estre
> En ma langue, ou second, ou le tiers, ou premier,
> Que d'estre sans honneur à Rome le dernier.[21]

Several Latin works by Ronsard do survive, but these early poems seem all to be lost.[22] Ronsard's Latin poetry was not greatly admired by contemporaries: Binet wrote that his Latin verses 'monstrent par quelque contrainte forcée, ou qu'il n'y estoit point entierement né ou qu'il ne s'y plaisoit pas'.[23] It may be because his Latin work was less admired than his French poetry that Ronsard played it down — conscious, no doubt, of the massive and justified fame of the Latin poetry of his friend and rival Joachim Du Bellay.[24]

2. *The French translation of Aristophanes's* Plutus

Claude Binet attributes to the poet a translation of Aristophanes's *Plutus*, composed during the five years he spent as a pupil of Jean Dorat (i.e. between 1545 and 1550). In the original 1586 edition of the *Vie de Ronsard*, the passage read:

---

[20] Ronsard, II (1914), 155–56.
[21] Ronsard, x, 304.
[22] On the surviving poems, see Ronsard, XVIII, 505–21 and n. 1, p. 505, and for the recently-rediscovered epitaph entitled *Ronsardus ad suos encomiastas*, see my article 'Two lost poems by Ronsard', *Bibliothèque d'Humanisme et Renaissance*, 47 (1985), 609–11.
[23] *Vie de Ronsard*, ed. Laumonier, p. 49.
[24] See my article, 'Joachim Du Bellay's renown as a Latin poet' in P. Tuynmann, G. C. Kuiper and E. Kessler, eds, *Acta Conventus Neo-Latini Amstelodamensis* (Munich, 1979), pp. 928–42.

Il s'adonna des lors souvent à faire quelques Sonnets et tels petits ouvrages, premiers essais d'un si brave ouvrier. Quand Dorat eut veu que son instinct se deceloit à ces petits echantillons, il luy predit qu'il seroit quelque jour l'Homere de France, et pour le nourrir de viande propre luy leut de plain vol le Promethée d'Æschyle, pour le mettre en plus haut goust d'une Poësie, qui n'avoit encor passé la mer de deçà, et en sa faveur traduisit cette Tragedie en François, laquelle si tost que Ronsard eut goustée: Et quoy, dit-il à Dorat, mon maistre, m'avez vous caché si long temps ces richesses? Ce fut ce qui l'incita à tourner en François le Plutus d'Aristophane, et le faire representer en public au college de Cocqueret, qui fut la premiere Comedie Françoise joüé en France.

For his 1597 edition of the biography of Ronsard, Binet more clearly attributed the translation to Ronsard rather than Dorat by amending his text to read: 'Ce fut ce qui l'incita encor, outre le conseil de son precepteur, à tourner en François le Plutus'.[25] A fragment of the work appeared in the 1617 edition of Ronsard, accompanied by the following poem (which the next complete edition of Ronsard, in 1623, ascribes to Claude Garnier):

> A vingt ans le grand Vendomois,
> Sortant de la maison des Roys,
> Mit cette Commedie entiere
> Dessur le Theatre en lumiere.
> Au bout de soixante et douze ans,
> Comme une relique du Temps,
> Ce Fragment que sa dent nous laisse
> Est mis au jour devant les yeux
> Sur le Theatre de la Presse,
> A fin qu'il y reluise mieux.[26]

Further, in 1624, the poet Claude Expilly prefaced a sonnet in praise of Ronsard with the remark, 'Lors que Monsieur de Ronsart commensa de mettre en lumiere les premieres pieces de ces poësies (ce fut la traduction du *Plutus* d'Aristophane) il écrivit Ronsart par un T'.[27] Clearly if Binet's attribution is correct, a major lost work of Ronsard awaits rediscovery, for it seems the whole work, and not just the extant fragment, once existed.[28]

---

[25] Binet, *Vie de Ronsard*, ed. Laumonier, pp. 12–13 and 102–03.

[26] Binet, *Vie de Ronsard*, ed. Laumonier, p. 103. The text of the fragment is in Ronsard, XVIII, 364–89.

[27] See Lino Pertile's excellent article 'Claude Expilly e il "Plutus" di Ronsard', *Studi francesi*, 16 (1972), 232–43 (p. 235). Pertile demonstrates (pp. 238–40) that Expilly's likely source was Nicolas Richelet, the commentator of Ronsard.

[28] Laumonier argued against the authenticity of the fragment published in 1617, and against the translation ever having existed. But had the attribution to Ronsard of such a significant work been erroneous, one would have expected the poet's contemporaries would have told Binet, certainly in time for him to correct the error in the 1597 edition of the *Vie de Ronsard*; and Laumonier was unaware of the testimony of Claude Expilly. Lebègue, who did not know Expilly either, advanced other arguments which counter Laumonier's doubts about this work (see Ronsard, XVIII, 364, n. 2).

3. The Greek verse

Ronsard was a pupil of Jean Dorat, who wrote much Greek verse, he probably (as we have seen) assembled his own collection of Greek manuscripts, his knowledge of Greek was excellent.[29] That he had tried his hand at Greek verse is strongly suggested by a passage in his *Responce aux injures* defying Theodore Beza, the Reformer and professor of Greek literature, to write against him:

> J'ay dequoy me deffendre et dequoy l'irriter
> Au combat, si sa plume il veut exerciter:
> Je sçay que peut la langue et Latine et Gregeoise,
> Je suis maistre joueur de la Muse Françoise.
> Vienne quand il vouldra, il me verra sans peur
> Dur comme un fer tranchant qui s'affine au labeur,
> Vif, ardant et gaillard, sans trembler soubz l'audace
> D'un vanteur qui par aultre au combat me menace.[30]

4. Two love poems dedicated to Cassandre

A source which Laumonier's edition fails to exhaust is Guillaume Colletet's lives of poets. Colletet's manuscript was destroyed in a fire in the Louvre during the Commune in 1871, but biographies of several individual poets had been published by then. Achille de Rochambeau included valuable Colletet material in his *La famille de Ronsart* (Paris, 1868). An extract from Colletet's life of Guy de Tours published by Rochambeau reads as follows:

Ainsy le grand Ronsard parle quelquefois à sa chère Cassandre comme si elle estoit ceste royalle fille de Priam qui portoit le mesme nom dans l'ancienne Troye, etc.:

> Tu conseillois à la germaine Elise etc.[31]

And another extract, from Colletet's life of Muret, reads:

Pierre de Ronsard lui [*sc.*: to Muret] dédia plusieurs de ses poëmes, témoin cette belle élégie des amours de Cassandre qui commence ainsi:

> Non, muses, non, ce n'est pas d'aujourd'huy, etc.[32]

Neither of these poems are found in Laumonier's edition of Ronsard, nor are they mentioned in the list of lost works. Ronsard published his poems to Cassandre in many editions, and it seems on the whole probable that Colletet is mistaken in attributing these two poems to him. But he may well

---

[29] See P. de Nolhac, *Ronsard et l'humanisme* (Paris, 1966), pp. 36–43 and 84–91, and I. Silver, *Ronsard and the Greek epic*, pp. 42–115.
[30] Lines 37–44: p. 157 in my edition of the *Discours des miseres* (Geneva, 1979).
[31] Rochambeau, p. 230. The same passage is found in Caldari's very useful edition of Colletet's *Pierre de Ronsard* (pp. 137–38), but she does not point to the fact that the work mentioned is unknown.
[32] Rochambeau, p. 234; Colletet, ed. Caldari, p. 141.

have had access to material now lost, and it is just conceivable there are new love poems to Cassandre awaiting discovery.[33]

5. *The verse plan of the* Franciade

Olivier de Magny records in his *Gayetez* that a fellow-poet, Lancelot Carle, recited to King Henry II a plan of the *Franciade*. What Carle recited was, says Magny,

> un dessein
> Que fait le Vendomois Cigne,
> Un dessein que, docte, il faict
> De sa docte Franciade,
> Où si bien il contrefaict
> L'escrivain de l'Iliade.[34]

Magny says the recitation took place on the feast of the Epiphany: he does not say which year (the *Gayetez* appeared in 1554). It is conceivable that what Carle recited was one or other of two works which are extant and which summarize the *Franciade* — Ronsard's *Ode de la paix*, or the *Ode* dedicated to Henry II and published at the beginning of the third book of *Odes* in the edition of 1555.[35]

6. *The summaries of the* Franciade

Claude Binet tells us that Ronsard had written the summaries for fourteen books of the *Franciade*:

Charles neufiesme . . . prit Ronsard en telle amitié, admirant l'excellence de son divin exprit, qu'il luy commanda de le suyvre, et de ne le point abandonner . . . De ceste faveur il reprit courage, et plus que jamais s'eschaufa à la poësie, et mit en effect les projects de la *Franciade*, dont il avoit dressé le dessein par arguments de quatorze livres que j'ay veus.[36]

These summaries must be a different work from the verse plan which Magny says Carle recited, for Binet describes this work as *arguments*, thereby inviting a link with the prose summaries by Amadis Jamyn which actually appeared with the four books of the *Franciade* in 1572. Binet is by no means entirely reliable, but what he says is substantially confirmed by Colletet on the strength of what Claude Garnier, commentator of the *Franciade*, told him:

Et il est si vray que Ronsard en nous donnant cet eschantillon d'un poëme épique [*sc.* Books 1–4 of the *Franciade* published in 1572], avoit l'intention de nous donner la

---

[33] The compilers of the list of lost works in Laumonier's edition of course knew Rochambeau's *La famille de Ronsart*: their reference to Ronsard's lost letters to or about Baïf is from Rochambeau. But curiously this reference to the Cassandre poems was missed.
[34] *Les Gayetez*, edited by A. R. Mackay (Geneva, 1968), p. 96.
[35] See Ronsard, III (1921), 8–22 and VII, 24–34 respectively.
[36] *Vie de Ronsard*, ed. Laumonier, p. 25.

pièce entière, que Claude Binet rapporte, en quelque endroict de sa vie, qu'il luy en avoit monstré les argumens des douze [*sic*] premiers livres, ce que Claude Garnier m'a confirmé depuis, lorsque'il me dict que feu Jean Gallandius les gardoit encore parmy ses papiers.[37]

It is extraordinary that whilst Laumonier edited Binet, and whilst these summaries of the *Franciade* are mentioned in the volume of his edition which contains Ronsard's epic, they are not in the list of lost works in his great edition![38]

7. *A poem on the victory of Francis of Guise at Renty*

In a poem addressed to Cardinal Charles de Lorraine, *Le Procès*, published in 1565, Ronsard claimed to have written a poem extolling the military prowess of Charles's brother Francis, duke of Guise. The poem, which he describes as follows, is not among Ronsard's extant poetry in praise of the duke:

> Puis quand par la vertu que l'heur accompagna
> Vostre frere à Ranthy la bataille gaigna,
> Et que tous les Flamans & les peuples d'Espagne
> A son bras foudroyant quitterent la campagne,
> Il [= Ronsard] celebra sa gloire, & par son vers fut mis
> La honte doublement au front des ennemis.

This passage suggests the poem was written shortly after Guise's defeat of the army of Charles V at Renty, which took place on 12 August 1554.[39]

8. *An epitaph of Francis of Guise*

A Latin manuscript in the Bibliothèque Nationale in Paris presents what is claimed to be a translation of an otherwise unknown poem by Ronsard. It is titled *In tumulum cordis Francisci Lothareni Ducis Guisiaci Ex Gallico P. Ronsardi*, and reads as follows:

> Guisiadae iacet hic Francisci cor Lothareni,
>   Illius invicti magnanimique ducis.
> Cor, Gallorum in quo vitae spes omnis, et omnis
>   Spes rebus dubiis certa salutis erat.
> Cor nunquam trepidans ad aequa pericula, et hostes
>   Usque sua cogens vis trepidare metu.

[37] Colletet, *Pierre de Ronsard*, ed. Caldari, p. 64.
[38] See XVI (1950), p. xvii for the reference to the summaries.
[39] The passage is in Laumonier's edition, XIII (1948), 20. Laumonier there notes that the work appears to be lost, 'à moins de ne voir ici qu'une allusion à quelques vers adressés au roi Henry II' (VII, 1934, p. 5; VIII, 1935, p. 38). This latter hypothesis is untenable, since neither passage cited is in praise of Francis of Guise. It is extraordinary that while Laumonier's note points to the loss of this work, it is not included in the list of *Œuvres perdues* in his own edition!

Cor, quod pro patriisque focis dum pugnat et aris
  Vi vincens, victis victima fraude cadit.
Tale cor haud iacet hic breve mole, sed ampla capaxque
  Omnis vertutis consiliique domus.
Denique cor iacet hic centena quod intus habebat
  Corda sua, et populi non numeranda sui.
Hoc quae cuncta uno cum corde sepulta iacerent
  Si possent uno cuncta iacere loco.
Quod quia non licuit, non cor, sed cordis inanis
  Umbra sub hoc vacuo marmore clausa latet.
At cor Guisiaci verum Ducis omnia corda
  Gallorum, vera et viva sepulchra tegunt.

The manuscript does not identify the translator.[40] It is very plausible that Ronsard did indeed compose the epitaph on which this translation is based, for two other epitaphs of Francis of Guise by him are known.[41]

9. *A poem extolling Charles IX and Henry d'Anjou*

In a poem titled *L'hydre deffaict*, written and published in 1569, Ronsard extols the military prowess of Henry, duke of Anjou (the future Henry III). He says Henry has cut off the three heads of the Hydra (the Hydra represents the army of the Reformers), but urges him to destroy what remains of the body of the monster, after which Ronsard will write him a poem extolling him and his brother King Charles IX. The poem will be in the form of the description of a temple in which the exploits of the two brothers are commemorated. Ronsard adds,

> . . . sera dict LE TEMPLE DES DEUX FRERES.
> Ainsi Castor et Pollux n'estant qu'un
> N'avoient aussi qu'un mesme autel commun.[42]

That Ronsard did actually write such a poem is strongly suggested by a passage of the *Discours au Roy après son retour de Pologne*, published in 1575. There, after alluding to the *Hydre deffaict*, Ronsard notes that Charles IX encouraged him one day to write about his brother Henry, and Ronsard adds:

> Admirant tel amour qu'au monde on ne voit plus
> Il bastit de Castor le temple & de Pollux,
> Et le vous dedia, pour remarque immortelle
> D'une si rare & saincte amitié fraternelle.[43]

[40] See 'Manuscrits latins', 8139, fol. 121 for the text.
[41] These are the *Prosopopée de feu François de Lorreine duc de Guise* (XII, 299–300), and an *Epitaphe de François de Lorraine, duc de Guyse* (XVIII, 334–35).
[42] See my edition of the *Discours des miseres*, pp. 260–61, and Ronsard, XV (1953), 385.
[43] Ronsard, XVII, 22–23. This must be a reference to a poem in praise of Henry and Charles, since this passage forms an integral part of a list of the poems Ronsard has written for Henry: Laumonier thought otherwise (see his n. 1, p. 23), but he was mistaken.

Ronsard here says he has 'built the temple of Castor & Pollux', and this precisely echoes what he had said in 1569 about the planned *Temple des deux freres*, brothers who resembled Castor and Pollux. The rivalry between Henry and Charles, or indeed Ronsard's increasing disaffection for Henry, could explain the poet's failure to include this poem in his collected works.

10. *The adaptation of a satire by Thomas More*

In the third edition of *Les reflexions sur la poëtique de ce temps et sur les ouvrages des poëtes anciens et modernes*, published in 1684, René Rapin added the following passage at the end of the section on satire ([II] xxv, iii):

Thomas Morus qui fit une satire contre les Allemans, contenta tellement Charles IX, qu'il commanda à Ronsart d'en composer une pareille contre les dérèglements de la Cour, qui ne réussit pas manque de délicatesse.[44]

The possibility that there exists a work by Ronsard based upon emulation of Thomas More is intriguing: none of his extant poetry seems to correspond to the work described by Rapin. It is of course possible that this work is among the lost satires mentioned above.[45]

11. *The Summary of a projected book on the French army*

Another work to which Binet refers is Ronsard's summary of his projected three books on the French military organization: 'Il avoit aussi desseigné trois livres de la Militie Françoise qu'il adressoit au Roy'. The summary was in verse, for Binet quotes sixteen verse lines of it.[46] The remainder of the summary is lost, and no trace of the work itself is known.[47]

Thus, eleven lost works can be added to the list of twelve in Laumonier's edition. Three more works have been mentioned by scholars as lost Ronsard poems. Pierre Champion, in his edition of Jules Gassot's *Sommaire memorial*, commented that verses which Gassot says Ronsard wrote for the baptism of Charles de Neufville are lost: in fact, these *Stances pour jouyr sur la lyre* were published in the *Sixiesme livre des poëmes* of 1569, and were to appear in the Laumonier edition.[48] Two works are attributed to Ronsard by Robert J. Sealy in his book, *The Palace Academy of Henry III*. One is a lost discourse on the moral virtues (in addition to the one which survives).[49] But Sealy's

---

[44] See the edition by E. T. Dubois (Geneva, 1970), p. 126.
[45] Dubois, the editor of Rapin, was unable to identify the poem in Ronsard's work. Fr Germain Marc'hadour suggested to me that Rapin's allusion to Germans may evoke More's epigrams against Germanus Brixius, but none of these epigrams seems to be a model for any extant poetry by Ronsard. (See *The Latin Epigrams of Thomas More*, edited and translated by L. Bradner and C. A. Lynch, Chicago, 1953).
[46] 'Je chante par quel art la France peut remettre . . .': Ronsard, XVIII, 153–54.
[47] See Binet, *Vie de Ronsard*, ed. Laumonier, p. 49.
[48] See Gassot, ed. Champion (Paris, 1934), pp. 69–70 and Ronsard, XV, 136–41.
[49] See *The Palace Academy* (Geneva, 1981), p. 39 and n. 3.

argument, that a reference by Desportes to 'Les beaux discours de Monsieur de Ronsard' proves the existence of two separate discourses, is untenable, since *discours* can simply mean 'arguments'. The other work which Sealy conjectures Ronsard wrote is a poem celebrating the victory of the duke of Anjou at La Charité on 2 May 1577, but the document he cites does not support the case at all well.[50]

III. WORKS WHICH RONSARD PLANNED TO WRITE

In compiling a list of lost works, one should be attentive also to statements by Ronsard or by contemporaries, about poems which he intended to write. Obviously, his intention may not have been fulfilled: but it is important to be alert to the possible existence of these works. I do not think it is worth taking account of nebulously phrased declarations of intent (for example, to write further poems in praise of patrons he was already extolling), and limit myself to mentions of specific projects upon which the poet appears seriously to have intended working.[51]

1. In the preface to the *Odes*, of 1550, Ronsard says he will not on this occasion explain the meaning of Strophes, Antistrophes or Epodes (the Pindaric form he often uses in his own odes), nor recount the history of the lyre, nor will he recall the status enjoyed by lyric poets in antiquity, and he adds:

Je reserve tout ce discours à un meilleur loisir: si je voi que telles choses meritent quelque breve exposition, ce ne me sera labeur de te les faire entendre, mais plaisir, t'assurant que je m'estimerai fortuné, aiant fait diligence qui te soit agreable.[52]

2. There is a further promise of a tract on poetry in his *Abbregé de l'art poëtique françois* of 1563:

Or, si je cognois que cest abbregé te soit aggreable, & utile à la posterité, je te feray un plus long discours de nostre poësie, comme elle se doibt enrichir, de ses parties plus necessaires, du jugement qu'on en doibt faire, si elle si peult regler aux piedz des vers Latins & Grecz, ou non, comme il fault composer des verbes frequentatifz, incoatifz, des noms comparatifz, superlatifz, & autres telz ornements de nostre langage pauvre & manque de soy.[53]

The promised contents of this discourse and the one mentioned in the preface to the *Odes* do not correspond to any extant treatise by Ronsard, and

---

[50] See *The Palace Academy*, pp. 83–84.
[51] Thus, I exclude most notably the poems of epic dimension for which he sought commissions from the Châtillon and Guise families at the same time as he was seeking royal patronage for the *Franciade* (see VIII, 72–84, 105, and 293–95 for the Châtillons, and V (1928), 218, VIII, 47–49 and IX (1937), 57, 70–71 for the Guise family); also poetry which he promised to write in praise of Charles IX's future conquests (XIII (1948), 139–40); a eulogy of Jean de Monluc (XIII, 246); and a poem in praise of Villeroy's estate (XVIII, 43).
[52] Ronsard, I, 46–47.
[53] Ronsard, XIV (1949), 34.

it is not inconceivable that one or both of these projected works was written and awaits discovery.

3. In *Le Narssis*, dedicated to the poet François Charbonnier and published in the *Bocage* of 1554, Ronsard claimed to be preparing a long poem to be dedicated to Charbonnier and his patron Jean d'Avanson. The passage records Ronsard's indebtedness to Avanson and couples Avanson's name with that of Michel de L'Hospital as an early defender of his poetry. Bearing in mind what Ronsard says about Avanson in this passage, and his undoubted gratitude to those who defended his early poetry, and the wording of his reference to the projected poem ('Que deja je t'apreste . . .'), it is distinctly possible that a lost poem dedicated to Avanson awaits discovery.[54]

4. A further specific promise is found in the opening lines of the *Hymne du Ciel*, in which Ronsard dedicates that poem to Jean de Morel, pending completion of another poem for him:

> Cependant qu'à loysir l'Hymne je te façonne
> Des Muses, pren' en gré ce CIEL que je te donne.

Did Ronsard write an *Hymne des Muses*? It seems unlikely, as none has survived, but Laumonier was being over-bold when he wrote 'Cet hymne n'a jamais été fait'.[55]

5. In the prose *Epistre au lecteur* which precedes his *Recueil des nouvelles poësies* of 1563, Ronsard attacks adversaries who had written pamphlets against him when he defended the Catholic faith. There, probably addressing Florent Chretien, he accuses him of sodomy and adds:

Cet article avecques bon tesmoignage sera traitté plus amplement en ta vie et en celle de l'ignorant Drogueur, que tu voirras bien tost de la main d'un excellent ouvrier.

The 'Drogueur' is the doctor Jacques Grévin, and Ronsard is evidently here threatening to write a satirical life of these two individuals.[56]

6. Finally, Estienne Pasquier gives us information about a projected work by Ronsard. In a letter to Ronsard, he says the poet was 'deliberé de discourir sur nostre poësie Françoise', and offers him information for this purpose. Ronsard is not said by Pasquier to have written the poem on the history of French poetry, but he would hardly have sought detailed information from Pasquier had this not been a fairly firm intention.[57]

---

[54] Ronsard, VI (1930), 82.
[55] See Ronsard, VIII, 141 and n. 3.
[56] See Ronsard, XII (1946), 21 and, in my edition of the *Discours des miseres*, p. 233.
[57] See Laumonier's edition, XVIII, 523 and Pasquier, *Lettres* (Paris, 1586), fols 43–47. Laumonier stated, in his *Ronsard poète lyrique* (second edition, Paris, 1923), that 'tout porte à croire que le projet de Ronsard, qui ne fut jamais exécuté, date de l'époque où il rédigea son *Abbregé de l'art poëtique*' (p. 227, n. 1). This suggestion seems to me to have very little foundation, and it is not reiterated in the list of lost works in Laumonier's edition.

IV. LOST AND NEGLECTED EDITIONS OF KNOWN WORKS

Laumonier's list of lost works is confined to those of which no trace has been found in any edition. But a list of lost editions of works which do survive would be very valuable. I am referring here of course to those editions for which Ronsard himself was responsible: clearly, unauthorized editions cannot strictly be described as Ronsard's lost books. These lost editions are often important historically, for many of the political poems respond closely to contemporary events, and each edition is likely to offer its own particular reflection of those events. They are also important aesthetically, for each state of the same poem is likely to have variant readings which illustrate Ronsard's tireless quest for perfection.

There is information in Laumonier's critical apparatus itself about editions which Ronsard himself prepared and which are lost: the second edition of the *Bocage* of 1554, the first edition of the *Nouvelle continuation des Amours* of 1556, the first, 1560, edition of the prose discourse on music and (possibly) a first, 1563, edition of the *Complainte à la Royne mere*.[58] But it is also possible to make a strong inference in favour of the existence of further lost editions. For example:

1. The *Harangue que fit Monseigneur le duc de Guise aux Soudards de Mez* was published with the fifth book of Ronsard's *Odes* in 1553 — but a separate *privilegium* was issued, which suggests it may have been published separately, as indeed were several other circumstantial poems which Ronsard included in his *Odes*.[59]

2. In 1561, Benoist Rigaud published in Lyons a pamphlet titled *Elegie sur le despart de la royne d'Escosse*, dealing with the return of Mary Queen of Scots from France to Scotland. It was included subsequently in the *Recueil des Nouvelles Poësies* of 1564. Laumonier opined that the manuscript of the poem was communicated without Ronsard's permission to Rigaud, but it seems much more likely that Ronsard commemorated this topical event involving a monarch he admired by publishing this poem in an authorized edition in Paris, and that it is this edition, now lost, on which Rigaud based his own. Such a publication may well have included other related poems, such as the elegy dedicated to Jerome Lhuillier ('L'Huillier, si nous perdons cette belle Princesse . . .') and the *Elegie à la Royne d'Escosse* ('Le jour que vostre voyle aux vagues se courba . . .'), both of which also appeared in the *Recueil des Nouvelles Poësies*.[60]

---

[58] See, respectively, Ronsard, VI (1930), xv; VII, xx–xxiv; XVIII, 480, n. 1, and XIII, v and n. 2.
[59] For the *privilegium*, see Ronsard, V, 202; and for separately-published circumstantial poems in the *Odes*, I, 9–16, 17–23, 24–39; III, 1–38, 39–85.
[60] See Ronsard, XII, 193–99 (for the *Elegie sur le depart*), xiv (for Laumonier's surmise about it), and 189–93 and 277–84 (for the two other poems).

3. In the *Epistre au lecteur* which accompanies his magnificent *Responce aux injures et calomnies de je ne sçay quels Predicans, et Ministres de Geneve*, Ronsard declares that if he knew more about his adversary's personal life, he would have been able to write a whole Iliad about him instead of these 1500 or 1600 lines. The poem in the form we have it is just 1176 lines long: it is quite conceivable that what we have is an abbreviated version of a longer original edition.[61]

4. In 1569, Ronsard published *Le sixiesme livre des poëmes* and *Le septiesme livre des poëmes*. Laumonier explained these two titles by suggesting that the first three books were the three books of poems included in the 1567 collected works, and that the fourth and the fifth were the collections of, respectively, epitaphs and sonnets in that same collected edition. But he was dissatisfied with his own explanation; and rightly so, since for Ronsard a collection of sonnets could not easily be described as a book of *poèmes*. There is, however, an alternative explanation of the title of the sixth and seventh books of poems, and it is that after publishing the first three books of poems in the 1567 *Œuvres*, Ronsard published the fourth and fifth books in an edition or editions now lost. There are several 'new' poems in the 1571 collected edition, and these may have appeared originally in these fourth and fifth books.[62]

5. A poem on the defeat of the Reformers at Montcontour (3 October 1569) has been ascribed to Ronsard. It is titled *Le Charon*, and in its extant state (a manuscript which in 1919 was in the archives of the château de La Bâtie, near Chambéry) the text is marred by omissions. Ronsard wrote circumstantial poems of this kind for immediate publication, and he sometimes published them anonymously: it is conceivable that a printed edition, perhaps anonymous, exists and would restore to us a complete text.[63]

6. In 1569, Ronsard wrote another poem against the Reformers, *Les Elemens ennemis de l'Hydre*, which purports to show how the four elements have joined the struggle against the 'Hydra' of the Reformation. He included it in his collected edition in 1578, but it seems likely that this circumstantial poem was published earlier, whilst it was more topical.[64]

Ronsard, we saw at the outset, attributes to a divine decree the loss of great poetry. One need not despair of some of the lost works being restored to us by the liberality of Fate. Indeed, I am myself indebted to Fate for the

---

[61] See Ronsard, XI, 112 and pp. 150–51 in my edition of the *Discours des miseres*.
[62] See, for the sixth and seventh books, Ronsard, XV, 13–265, and for Laumonier's view on the titles, XV, v–vi.
[63] On this work, see Ronsard, XVIII, 431–38 and 431, n. 1.
[64] See my edition of the *Discours des miseres*, pp. 263–66.

discovery of four lost or forgotten works of Ronsard.[65] This present survey may help scholars to identify hitherto lost works. Indeed, there is certainly a case for pursuing the kind of research which this paper presents, and for ultimately preparing a proper Ronsard bibliography, which would include pirated editions and translations of Ronsard.[66] Bibliographical discoveries, at least where the world's great poets are concerned, are rewarding above all else for the improvement they permit in editing. We ought to be contemplating with an awesome feeling of responsibility — and with exhilaration — the task of producing the new complete edition of Ronsard, which would consign the great Laumonier edition, already almost a century old in its conception, to its honourable place in the history of Ronsard scholarship.

London

[65] See my articles, 'An early edition of a *Discours* by Ronsard' [containing the text of the original edition of the *Priere à Dieu* of 1569], *Bibliothèque d'Humanisme et Renaissance*, 28 (1966), 682–90; 'The first edition of Ronsard's *Recueil des nouvelles poësies*', *Bibliothèque d'Humanisme et Renaissance*, 36 (1974), 613–20; 'The first edition of Ronsard's *Estreines au roy Henry III*', *Bibliothèque d'Humanisme et Renaissance*, 37 (1975), 213–24; and 'Two lost poems by Ronsard' [an epitaph titled *Ronsardus ad suos encomiastas* and a *Priere à Dieu faicte par Monsieur de Ronsard estant malade*], in *Bibliothèque d'Humanisme et Renaissance*, 47 (1985), 609–11.
[66] Laumonier's *Tableau chronologique des œuvres de Ronsard* (second edition, Paris, 1911) and his 'Additions et corrections au *Tableau chronologique des œuvres de Ronsard*' (*Revue du seizième siècle*, 4 (1916), 117–42) have many omissions; and A. Pereire's 'Bibliographie des œuvres de Ronsard' (*Bulletin du Bibliophile*, nouv. sér., 15 (1936), 494–503, 540–46; 16 (1937), 20–26, 68–75, 108–14, 352–60, 447–51, 506–12, 556–60; 17 (1938), 16–18, 54–59, 158–61, 268–71, 304–07, 358–62, 488–92; (1939), 67–75, 104–10, 204–15) covers only the first third of the poet's career, to 1558. An interesting article by L. Salem deals with the 1550 *Odes* ('Quelle est la rareté d'un livre rare? Le cas d'une édition originale de Ronsard', *Bulletin du Bibliophile*, 1 (1978), 8–11). See also J. P. Barbier, *Bibliographie des Discours politiques de Ronsard* (Geneva, 1984).

Montaigne and the Christian Foes of Tacitus

Malcolm Smith

Various writers, from very early times, have expressed hostility towards Tacitus on account of what he says about Jews and Christians. One passage which caused disquiet is the long description of the origins and beliefs and customs of the Jewish nation, in the fifth book of the *Histories* (1–13).[1] Another, and this is the one which mainly concerns us here, is the passage in the fifteenth book of the *Annals* (44) in which Tacitus relates how Nero blamed Christians for the fire in Rome in A.D. 64. Tacitus here describes Christians as "a class of men loathed for their vices," and describes their belief as a "pernicious superstition" and a "disease"; and, while he attacks Nero vigorously for his treatment of Christians, he adds that they "had earned the most exemplary punishment."

Interest in Tacitus appears to have grown rapidly in the second half of the sixteenth century.[2] As this interest grew, his admirers sought to mitigate damage to his reputation caused by his remarks about Christians. One of his defenders was Jean Bodin who, in 1566, in his *Method for easily understanding history,* refuted hostile verdicts on him by Guillaume Budé (1467–1540) and by Tertullian (c. 155–c. 222) and Paulus Orosius (c. 390–after 418).

> Budé (writes Bodin) harshly called Tacitus the most wicked writer of all, since he wrote things against Christians. And it is for this reason, in my view, that Tertullian called him a great liar, and Orosius called him a sycophant. But, just as Marcellus, the lawyer, said that a whore acted repulsively in so far as she was a whore, but did not repulsively choose to be a whore, in the same way Tacitus acted impiously, in so far as he was not a Christian, but did not impiously write against us, since he was bound by a pagan superstition. Indeed, the reason I would not call him impious is that he did hold that there was a religion which was true, and he observed that religion and sought to overthrow those opposed to it. For, at a time when Christians and Jews were being condemned daily, as being sorcerers

and tainted with every crime and scandal, what historian could refrain from
insulting them? If ignorance is an excuse, then Tacitus certainly has to be
excused [...]

The point of the rather unfortunate analogy between Tacitus and a whore seems
to be that Tacitus was not in a position to make a free and conscious choice to
adopt paganism and reject Christianity: his religion was thrust upon him by the
milieu in which he found himself, and his ignorance of Christianity was not his
fault.[3]

Michel de Montaigne was another French Renaissance author who felt that
early Christian attitudes to Tacitus had been unjustly severe. In 1580, in the
chapter of his *Essays* titled "On freedom of conscience" (II.xix) he deplored the
fact that much of Tacitus's work is lost,[4] and blamed this loss on the fanaticism
of early Christians:

> It is common to see good intentions, if pursued immoderately, impel men
> to very evil results. [...] It is certain that when our religion first began to
> flourish and acquire legal authority and power, zeal armed many people
> against all sorts of pagan books and, as a result of this, men of letters have
> suffered an amazing loss. In my view, this disorder wrought more damage
> to literature than all the flames of the barbarians. Cornelius Tacitus is a
> good witness to this: for, though his relative the emperor Tacitus had by
> special decree populated every library in the world with his books,
> nonetheless not one complete copy has survived the meticulous searches of
> those who sought to suppress him for the sake of five or six trivial clauses
> contrary to our faith.[5]

I have conjectured, in my book *Montaigne and the Roman Censors*, that Montaigne
is here referring, allusively and discreetly, to harm caused to literature in his own
day by burning of books by religious authorities.[6]

There is another sense in which Montaigne may in this passage be alluding
to topical events. The third-century emperor Tacitus who, Montaigne recalls,
disseminated the books of his namesake the historian, had initiated another monument to him by having a tomb built for him. Now, just as fanatical early Christians destroyed the books, a zealous Christian contemporary of Montaigne's
destroyed the tomb, and this sixteenth-century foe of Tacitus was no less a person than Pope Pius V, the erstwhile Grand Inquisitor of the Roman Church.[7]
It is not inconceivable that Montaigne's attack on zealous Christians seeking to
stamp out the name of Tacitus is an allusion to Pius V. For Montaigne was well
capable of such oblique allusions to contemporaries, and indeed he seems to have
become increasingly keen that his readers should be alert to such allusions. In
1588, two-thirds of the way through the chapter "On vanity" (*Essays* III.viii), he
wrote that his book contains many discreet topical allusions to contemporary peo-

ple and events, and that some people will see more in these passages than others will. He added:

> I reveal here what my inclinations and feelings are in so far as I decently can; but I do this more freely and readily face to face to anyone who wants to know more.

He reiterated the point in the first posthumous edition of the *Essays* (1595). The examples I cite, he says, "[...] often refer allusively to more delicate matters, for the benefit of myself (for I do not wish to express myself more fully) and of those readers who catch what I am getting at" ("A consideration about Cicero," *Essays* I.xl).

A further indication of hostility towards Tacitus in inquisitorial circles is given in a letter written from Rome by Marcus Antonius Muretus, dated 2 November 1572 and addressed to a lawyer in the Paris *parlement* named Claude Dupuy. The letter, written in a curious mixture of Latin, Greek and French, tells a rather entertaining story:

> I hear you had a good laugh at the criticisms of Tacitus, and the story is worth telling in some detail. Just recently someone who was teaching Latin literature here, in the post which Romulus Amasaeus used to hold, left: and no-one could be found to replace him. The cardinals who are responsible for the teaching besought me, with exquisite courtesy, to take the job on. I declined. In the end, the chief priest himself summoned me. He addressed me with great kindness, and indicated that if I were to undertake that task, he would greatly appreciate it. What could I do? By asking, he compelled me, and you know what happened. I was all the more ready to yield to his request in that instead of the two hundred crowns I was earning, he raised my salary to four hundred. The next question which arose was, what book was I going to lecture on? I told cardinals Sirleto and Alciati, who are responsible for the syllabus, that I would like to lecture on Tacitus. They strongly dissuaded me, for he speaks unfavourably somewhere of Christians, and of Jews, and, in a word, they had it in mind to forbid his works. I gave many reasons why I should be released from the responsibility, but they would not yield. I feel so annoyed about this that I wish I had never started work on this author. But I cannot be frightened off loving him and reading him, and reading him assiduously.

Muretus does not tell us which "chief priest" (that is, pope) he is referring to but given the date of his letter it must be either Pius V (who had died on 1st May that year) or his successor Gregory XIII.[8] The anecdote would of course be all the more amusing if it were about Pius V, the fanatical opponent of Tacitus's renown.

Muretus's account suggests that the passages in *Histories* V and *Annals* XV, dealing respectively with Jews and Christians, formed the basis of the hostility to

Tacitus. Further possible grounds for this hostility in inquisitorial circles are indicated by a Jesuit scholar, Antonius Possevinus, who was closely in touch with these circles at about this time and who some years later was to publish a book titled *Materials for the history of all nations*.[9] Possevinus, besides deploring Tacitus's allegedly "malicious" remarks about Christians, alleges that some of his own sixteenth-century contemporaries were so besotted by Tacitus that they overlooked what Christ says about how to administer affairs (doubtless an allusion to "Machiavellian" politicians who turned to Tacitus for guidance[10]); he attacks what he sees as a denial of divine providence, in the *Histories*;[11] and he objects to Tacitus's proposed derivation for the word *Iudaeos* (from Mount Ida, in Crete: *Histories* V.2) — a curious detail to single out in the long disquisition on Jews.[12] A further possible reason for objection to Tacitus by Roman Catholic theologians, particularly in view of the Reformation controversies on miracles, is that he records the popular belief that the emperor Vespasian wrought miracles (*Histories* IV.81). And a final reason might be that some inquisitors simply felt ill at ease about such an ardent advocate of freedom of thought and of speech: for example, in the *Annals* (IV.35), Tacitus argues firmly against the burning of books and, as one illustrious sixteenth-century Tacitus scholar pointed out, there was a lesson in this for the papists who used the same methods.[13]

Whatever factors may have prompted guardians of orthodoxy to destroy Tacitus's tomb, to forbid Muretus's lectures in 1572, and to contemplate including Tacitus in the *Index of forbidden books*, there existed other considerations militating in favour of liberalism. One was that many of the custodians of orthodoxy were themselves committed scholars. Pope Paul III, who founded the Roman Inquisition in 1542, was himself, according to Muretus, a constant reader of Tacitus, and took more delight in the historian than in any other secular author.[14] And Cardinal Sirleto, one of the two who forbade Muretus to lecture on Tacitus, actually gave considerable help to Muretus himself, and to Justus Lipsius, in ensuring they had access to manuscripts of Tacitus![15] And, as Paul Grendler has shown in his admirable book *The Roman Inquisition and the Venetian Press*, inquisitors were concerned not to alienate by unduly repressive measures those Catholic scholars and printers upon whom the Church depended so much for a restoration of its credibility and prestige in the aftermath of the Reformation. Furthermore, Tacitus had merits which could not be gainsaid even by his Christian foes: Possevinus, in the passage I have already referred to, cited with approval a eulogy by Lipsius of Tacitus's prudence, his moral teaching, his love of truth, his conciseness, and his aphorisms, and acknowledged for his own part Tacitus's discernment and the relevance in his (Possevinus's) own day of Tacitus's judgments on princes.[16] Indeed, these merits of Tacitus must account for the fact that one sixteenth-century Roman Catholic index not of forbidden books but of commended books includes the works of Tacitus![17] And a final factor which could work in favour of liberalism (or, of course, in the opposite direction) was the individual outlook of whoever happened to be pope. For example, the destroyer of Tacitus's tomb, Pius V, was an utterly relentless exponent and supporter of inquisitorial methods[18]—but he was succeeded by Gregory XIII who gradually and unobtrusively relaxed a whole series of repressive measures.[19]

It may well be as a result of the increasing liberalism under Gregory XIII that in November 1580 Muretus was finally let off the leash and given permission to lecture on Tacitus in Rome. Muretus, doubtless confident that the old repressive attitudes towards Tacitus would not return, immediately spoke out freely and vigorously against Tacitus's foes. He declared, in a discourse inaugurating his lectures on Tacitus, "I shall reply to those people who are surprised at my high esteem for Tacitus, and surprised that I sought for so long and so strenuously to secure permission to expound his work publicly." And a little later in the same discourse, he adds, "I shall refute and confound a few of those objections which are rashly flung at him by the ignorant." In a second discourse, he defended Tacitus against five objections which, he said, had been made by those who had sought to prevent him lecturing on him. These five objections are (i) that Tacitus wrote about tyrannical emperors and a period of moral degeneracy, and that Suetonius is a better historian of the imperial period anyway; (ii) that Tacitus's books contain falsehood; (iii) that he was an acknowledged enemy of the Christian faith; (iv) that he is difficult; and (v) that he writes bad Latin.

The second and third of these objections are the ones that concern us here. Broaching the charge that Tacitus's work contains falsehood, Muretus, who does not elaborate on what the alleged falsehoods are, observes that the same has been said of every other illustrious historian, and there is no reason why the charge should be held to be particularly damaging when levelled at Tacitus. He then turns to Tertullian, who described Tacitus as "the most garrulous liar," and says he will answer this charge at the same time as he answers the most serious of the objections, which is that Tacitus was hostile to the Christian faith. This, incidentally, suggests that the alleged lies in Tacitus were pre-eminently his remarks about Christians. The earliest Christians, Muretus says, were so pious ("and would that we were!" he adds parenthetically and perhaps a little disingenuously) that they would hear nothing that was not Christian, and totally rejected everything that was opposed to Christianity. But if we adopted that rule nowadays, Muretus asks, what would happen? We would be obliged to refrain from reading all the ancient Greek and Latin writers. Muretus then gives a very interesting survey of ancient Greek and Latin authors, pointing out those aspects of their work which the kind of Christian who objects to Tacitus would logically be obliged to deplore. If it is argued (said Muretus: and his wording suggests it may well have been argued by some at the time) that pre-Christian Greek and Latin authors can more readily be forgiven than can Tacitus, who lived after the time of Christ, then it will still be necessary to condemn—if you are going to condemn the historian—authors like Suetonius, who refers scornfully to Christians; the younger Pliny, who actually prosecuted Christians; Plutarch, who "has the same fables about Moses and the Jews as Tacitus does"; Quintilian, who writes with scorn about

Moses; Ulpian, who wrote a book on how to punish Christians; and the philosophers Porphyry, Simplicius, and Averroes, as well as Galen; and the historians Ammianus Marcellinus, Eunapius and Zosimus. Muretus concludes:

> If, however, we do not reject them as well, why should we be more severe
> towards Tacitus? Is any of us so weak that there is a danger of him stum-
> bling in his Christian faith if he were to find out that Tacitus was not a
> Christian? Let us rather feel sorry for him, and be grateful to God for bath-
> ing our souls in greater light.[20]

This defence of Tacitus is a shrewd one. If Muretus's argument that Tacitus is
no more harmful to Christianity than other ancient writers is accepted, then the
Church could not forbid him without virtually declaring war on classical literature.
Clearly there was no desire for such a crusade. On the contrary, ancient texts
were generally looked on with indulgence: the rules of the Council of Trent's *Index of forbidden books*, for example, stipulate only that those ancient texts which
are obscene should not be used in schools.

In the same month as Muretus was eventually allowed to lecture on Tacitus,
November 1580, Montaigne, who had been a pupil of Muretus's at the Collège
de Guyenne in Bordeaux, arrived in Rome.[21] One aspect of Rome which interested Montaigne greatly, and which disturbed him, was incursions by the Inquisition on personal and intellectual freedom. It is clear, moreover, from a remark
by Montaigne's secretary recorded in his diary, that this was a favoured topic
of conversation with Montaigne.[22] We know from Montaigne's diary that he met
Muretus in Rome on at least one occasion: in March 1581 he dined with Muretus
and other scholars at the French ambassador's house. It is tempting to conjecture
that, either at this meeting or on other occasions during his visit to Rome, Montaigne sounded Muretus out on the effects of the Inquisition on intellectual
freedom: for Muretus was evidently a veritable mine of information on the subject, as Dejob showed in his book *Marc-Antoine Muret*, and his views on the subject
were very similar to Montaigne's. They might indeed have discussed the specific
case of attitudes to Tacitus, for Montaigne's recently published *Essays* had, as we
have seen, deplored the fanatical suppression of Tacitus by early Christians —
and Muretus had himself been a victim of a similar "fanatical" suppression of
Tacitus.

A few days later, still in March 1581, Montaigne was himself to have the first
of two encounters with the Church's censors, in fact with the two officials in charge
of the censorship, Sisto Fabri and his assistant Joannes Baptista Lancius. I have
described these encounters in *Montaigne and the Roman censors*. The censors were
armed with a list of objections to the *Essays*, and they invited Montaigne to comment on these. Six of these objections are known, for Montaigne lists them in
his diary, but he adds that there were others besides, and I have been unable
to identify them. But it is highly tempting to speculate that his attack on the fourth-
century Christian zealots who destroyed Tacitus's work was on the list: for the

other example of excessive Christian zeal which Montaigne attacks in the very same passage, the over-hasty condemnations of the emperor Julian, was censured. Furthermore, if the passage about Tacitus's enemies was read by the censors as an allusive attack on his enemies in the sixteenth century, and notably his foes among the guardians of orthodoxy—and we have seen it can easily be read that way—this would be additional cause for objection. Whether or not this passage on Tacitus was originally censured, we know that the censors were so satisfied with Montaigne's explanations of the censured passages that they withdrew all objections—and indeed expressed great approval of that intellectual freedom which so intimately characterises Montaigne's book. I have concluded that the encounters of Montaigne and the censors illustrate the relative liberalism of the pontificate of Gregory XIII.

The 1588 edition of the *Essays* contains, for the first time, a great many first-hand borrowings from Tacitus.[23] It also contains a long passage on Tacitus which answers some sixteenth-century Christian objections to him, and this passage may be, like so many others in later editions of the *Essays*, a reply to the censors who momentarily objected to parts of his book in 1581 (though of course it is possible Montaigne encountered these objections elsewhere, e.g., through his reading of Bodin, or his meeting with Muretus[24]). In the chapter "On the art of conversation" (*Essays* III.viii), Montaigne affirms, against those who accused Tacitus of purveying falsehood, that "Those who call into question his honesty are revealing they have some other grievance against him"—and this "other grievance" is almost certainly his anti-Christian sentiment (for, the charges of being a liar and of being anti-Christian are coupled in the defences of Tacitus by Bodin and Muretus). A little further on, Montaigne answers a second objection:

> He does not need any excuse for approving the religion of his time, according to the laws which governed him, and for ignoring the true one. That is his misfortune, not his shortcoming.

We have seen similar versions of this defence of Tacitus in both Bodin and Muretus: it seems to me a fair argument, since the remarks in Tacitus which his Christian foes objected to do indeed show he had no knowledge at all of Christian belief and only heard rumour about the lives of Christians. And a third passage in this chapter "On the art of conversation" seems to rebut objections by some Roman Catholics to Tacitus: Montaigne defends him for giving accounts of apparent miracles. Miracles were being invoked then by Catholic theologians in polemic with the Reformers as a sign of divine truth: clearly it would be hazardous to concede (as Tacitus records some people did) that Vespasian, a pagan, could procure miracles. This must be the point of Montaigne's comment, which is that it is proper for historians to record what is commonly believed about alleged miracles, and that this is all that Tacitus does. Montaigne adds, and pointedly it seems, that the task of the theologian and of the philosopher is to say whether these common beliefs are correct beliefs.[25] He is delineating, judiciously, the territory of respective disciplines and firmly repelling incursions by theologians into the domain of historians.

In defence of Tacitus, Montaigne not only deals with specific issues which preoccupied theologians, he offers a full portrait of the man and his work. Unlike those early Christians whom he had castigated, in the earlier chapter "On freedom of conscience," for condemning Tacitus on the strength of "five or six trivial clauses contrary to our faith," Montaigne intended to make an equitable judgment. He carefully stresses at the beginning of his discussion of Tacitus that he has read the historian's whole extant work, and indeed that it is highly unusual for him to do this sort of thing ("It is twenty years," he says, "since I spent a whole hour on one book"). The verdict which he arrives at is a nuanced one, but as a whole overwhelmingly favourable. He commends (against Tacitus himself) the moral and political usefulness and attraction of history that deals with the lives of individuals, commends the solid arguments Tacitus deploys, his pointed and unaffected style, his sound opinions, his honesty and courage. Interestingly, this approach to an author, in which discussion of individual opinions is placed in the context of an overall appraisal of the man, an approach so characteristic of Montaigne, seems to have been that which the Roman censors themselves adopted, at least in the case of Montaigne himself.[26]

At the beginning of the chapter "On the art of conversation" and (implicitly) at the end, Montaigne stresses that he is no kind of model to be emulated or authority to be believed. Such disclaimers, in the *Essays*, are usually a sign that he is broaching moral or religious issues. The fact that these disclaimers embrace the chapter as a whole suggests that the whole chapter has something to say which might interest theologians. And indeed it has. Montaigne's point is that all intellectual encounter is about free exchange of ideas. We must be receptive to corrections, he says—but at the same time we must retain our freedom of judgment. It is a point which, in the fourth century, the fanatical Christian foes of Tacitus had forgotten: and it is a point which their sixteenth-century successors needed reminding of. This surely is why, in a chapter devoted to conversation, Montaigne includes the otherwise rather incongruous discussion of the character and work of Tacitus. It is no coincidence that the chapter on conversation, which deplores tyranny and domineering assertiveness, is also the chapter which, more fully than the earlier—and possibly censured—one, rehabilitates a historian who had himself advocated freedom of thought and expression, and who had been a posthumous victim of opponents of such freedom.

Bedford College, London

Notes

1. Other material in Tacitus which alludes to Jews is recorded and annotated in M. Stern's formidably erudite book, *Greek and Latin authors on Jews and Judaism*, 2 vols. (Jerusalem, 1976, 1980), II, 1–93.

2. P. Burke has counted four editions of the *Annals* and *Histories* in the second half of the fifteenth century, thirteen in the first half of the sixteenth, and thirty-two in the second half. In the following fifty years Tacitus was to become the most widely-published ancient historian. See "A survey of the popularity of Ancient Historians, 1450–1700," *History and Theory*, 5 (1966), 135–52.

3. The passage is from Bodin's assessment of Tacitus in chapter 4 of his *Methodus ad facilem historiarum cognitionem* (Parisiis, 1566, BL 580 g 2). For Budé on Tacitus ("vaecordium omnium scriptorum perditissimus," etc.), see J. von Stackelberg, *Tacitus in der Romania* (Tübingen, 1960), 160; for Tertullian, see his *Liber apologeticus adversus gentes pro christianis*, ch. xvi; I have not traced the allusion to Tacitus in Orosius which Bodin is referring to, despite the excellent indexes in the edition by C. Zangemeister (*Historiarum adversum paganos libri VII; accedit eiusdem liber apologeticus*, Vindobonae, 1882).

Bodin's *Methodus* was to be included in Roman Catholic lists of prohibited books in and after 1581. See F. H. Reusch, *Die Indices librorum prohibitorum des sechzehnten Jahrhunderts* (Tübingen, 1886), pp. 356, 412, 493–94, 559 (and cf. 537). A Jesuit writer on history (and on many other subjects), Antonius Possevinus, repudiated Bodin's view that Tacitus's defence of his pagan religion shows he was not impious (see Possevinus's *Iudicium de Nuae* [...], *Joannis Bodini, Philippi Mornaei et Nicolai Machiavelli quibusdam scriptis* [...] [Lugduni, 1593, BL 1492 f 56], p. 89).

4. Of the thirty books of history Tacitus is known to have written, only the first four books of the *Histories* and a fragment of the fifth have survived, and the first four books of the *Annals*, a fragment of the fifth, most of the sixth and books eleven to sixteen (though the beginning of the eleventh and the end of the sixteenth are lost).

5. Modern scholars discount the possibility of a family relationship between the historian Tacitus and the emperor. On the emperor disseminating the historian's works ("almost certainly a fabrication of the late fourth century," according to L. D. Reynolds and N. G. Wilson, *Scribes and Scholars* [Oxford, 1975], p. 29), see the life of the emperor by Flavius Vopiscus (*Historia Augusta*, ed. D. Magie, Loeb, *Tacitus* X). I do not know what Montaigne's source is for the statement blaming Christians for the loss of Tacitus's work: other sixteenth-century commentators I have read merely state that the emperor's dissemination of Tacitus's books failed to preserve them (e.g., Bodin, and F. Baudoin, *De institutione historiæ universæ* [...], published in the 1576 Basle edition of Bodin's *Methodus*, BL 580 c 9, p. 654). Nor do I know how Montaigne was able to assert that it was for "five or six trivial clauses" that Tacitus's books were destroyed (for presumably the work now lost may have contained more anti-Christian material).

6. See *Montaigne and the Roman Censors* (Geneva, 1981), pp. 53–55.

7. On Pius V destroying Tacitus's tomb, see Francesco Angeloni, *Historia di Terni* (Roma, 1646, BL 660 e 11), pp. 51–52 (Dr J. F. Killeen of the University of Galway very kindly drew my attention to this book). Contemporary apprehensiveness about Pius V's plans to destroy "pagan" remains in Rome is documented in vol. 17 of L. von Pastor's *History of the Popes* (London and St. Louis, 1951), pp. 113–14, 407.

8. For the text of Muretus's letter, see P. de Nolhac, "Lettres inédites de Muret," *Mélanges Graux* (Paris, 1884), pp. 381–403 (pp. 389–90). Unfortunately Nolhac has no infor-

mation on the nature of the criticisms of Tacitus which amused Dupuy. P. Paschini, in his excellent study "Letterati ed indice nella riforma cattolica in Italia," quotes a letter from Pier Vettori to Sirleto (19 December 1575) acknowledging "la lettera di V.S. R^{ma} sopra quel mio dubbio di Tacito," but does not have the text of Sirleto's probably important letter (see his *Cinquecento romano e riforma cattolica* [Romæ, 1958], pp. 237-73, 241).

9. A letter of Possevinus's to Cardinal Sirleto (undated, but probably written between 1573 and 1580) gives an interesting glimpse of his contact with Sirleto and of his zealous action against condemned books: see C. Dejob, *De l'influence du Concile de Trente sur la littérature et les beaux-arts chez les peuples catholiques* (Paris, 1884), pp. 43-45.

10. One scholar has concluded that in the Renaissance, "condemnation of Tacitus had its genesis in the fact that he was considered as the intellectual parent of the author of the *Prince*, synonym for all that was to be condemned" (J. L. Brown, *The "Methodus ad facilem historiarum cognitionem": a critical study* [Washington, DC, 1939], p. 112). This seems untenable: Tacitus was condemned on other grounds besides. On use of Tacitus by Machiavelli, see J. von Stackelberg, *Tacitus in der Romania* (Tübingen, 1960), especially 4, "Machiavelli und der Tacitismus" pp. 63-93.

11. It seems to me highly unlikely that Tacitus really is denying providence in the passage Possevinus quotes, which reads: "Never did more appalling calamities befall the Roman people, as a clear sign that the gods were concerned not to save us but to punish us" (*Histories* I.3).

12. See Possevinus's *Apparatus ad omnium gentium historium* [...] (Venetiis, BL 580 c 15), III, xiv. On this book, see note 16 below.

13. The scholar is Justus Lipsius, and the occasion was an inaugural discourse on Tacitus at Iena in 1572: see his *Orationes octo* [...] (Francofurti, 1608, BL 1090 c 7), pp. 35-36. Lipsius was later to return to the Roman Catholic faith, which accounts for the cordial tone of an exchange of letters with Possevinus (see note 16 below). Burning of books in the Reformation era was not of course the sole prerogative of Roman Catholic judiciaries: see my *Montaigne and the Roman Censors*, pp. 53-55 and 121-22.

14. See Muretus's *Scripta selecta*, ed. J. Frey, 2 vols. (Lipsiae, 1871, 1873), I, 151.

15. See J. Rysschaert, "Juste Lipse éditeur de Tacite," in *Atti del Colloquio la Fortuna di Tacito dal secolo XV ad oggi*, a cura di F. Gori e C. Questa (Urbino, 1979), pp. 47-61 (pp. 53, 54). Sirleto's tireless dedication to scholarship is chronicled in P. Paschini's excellent monograph, "Guglielmo Sirleto prima del cardinalato," in his *Tre ricerche sulla storia della chiesa nel cinquecento* (Roma, 1945), pp. 153-281.

16. Possevinus's overall verdict on Tacitus is therefore a balanced one. Interestingly, this book was extolled by no less a Tacitus scholar than Justus Lipsius. Lipsius's very cordial letter to Possevinus (29 January 1599) can be read in his *Centuriae* (III, lxii: in his *Epistolarum selectarum chilias* [Lugduni, 1616, BL 1084 h 9], p. 280) and Possevinus's equally cordial reply (24 March 1599) is in Petrus Burmannus's *Sylloges epistolarum a viris illustribus scriptarum* (Leidae, 1727, BL 636 k 16-20), II, 45.

17. The document, published in Munich, contains the tridentine *Index of Forbidden Books* together with a list of books *ex quibus integra Bibliotheca Catholica institui recte possit*, and this latter list contains the name of Tacitus. The year of publication was 1569 — during the pontificate of Pius V, the foe of Tacitus's renown! See F. H. Reusch, *Die Indices librorum prohibitorum*, pp. 329-37.

18. On the activities of Pius V (Michele Ghislieri) as inquisitor, see L. von Pastor, *The History of the Popes*, XVII (London and St. Louis, 1951). His relentless zeal was well described by Muretus in his funerary oration:

Cum autem alia in hoc viro admirabilia fuerunt, tum singulare studium conser-

vandae verae ac catholicae religionis, et adversus eos qui illam ulla ex parte labefac-
tare conarentur, implacabile odium semper eluxit. Quibus cum ille perpetuum bellum
gerens, ne punctum quidem temporis in vita ab eis vexandis et exagitandis conquievit.
[...] Qui ab ecclesia descivissent, nisi aut ipsos erroribus, aut ipsis orbem purgaret,
vitam sibi acerbam atque insuavem esse ducebat (*Oratio habita in funere Pii V. Pont.
Maximi*, Patavii, 1572, BL 4855 bb 25, pages unnumbered).

Muretus's true feelings were less enthusiastic: see the next note.

19. On 2 June 1572, a month after the death of Pius V, Muretus wrote to Claude Dupuy
contrasting the freedom of speech which prevailed in France with the "oppression" in Rome
under Pius V (this part of his letter is written — perhaps prudently — in Greek). He adds
that with the new pope, Gregory XIII, "On se promettoit quelque plus grande liberté,
mais je me doutte, qu'il n'i aura plus grand gaing au change" (Nolhac, "Lettres inédites
[...]," p. 387). But Gregory XIII did turn out to be relatively liberal: see *Montaigne and
the Roman Censors*, pp. 108, 127.

20. See Muretus's *Scripta selecta*, ed. J. Frey (Lipsiae, I, 1871), pp. 158-61.

21. On Muretus's relationship with Montaigne, see R. Trinquet, *La Jeunesse de Montaigne* (Paris, 1972), especially pp. 460-65, 488-91, 503-05 and 548-50.

22. See *Montaigne and the Roman Censors*, pp. 15-16.

23. It appears that whereas the 1580 edition had contained no material directly derived
from Tacitus, the 1588 edition contains three quotations and twenty-three borrowings from
him, and five further quotations and nine borrowings were added to the *Essays* thereafter:
see P. Villey, *Les Livres d'histoire moderne utilisés par Montaigne* [...] (Paris, 1908), p. 241.
One of the quotations from Tacitus in the 1595 edition is presented to elucidate the nature
of Christian faith: "Sanctius est ac reverentius de actis deorum credere quam scire" (*Germania* XXXIV, quoted in *Essays* II.xii).

24. Montaigne was in contact also with Justus Lipsius, who has been described (by Frank
Goodyear in his superb edition of Tacitus's *Annals*) as "First and indisputably first of all
Tacitean scholars." Three of Lipsius's letters to Montaigne have survived, though none
of Montaigne's to Lipsius is extant (they are not listed in the admirable *Inventaire de la correspondance de Juste Lipse, 1564-1606*, by A. Gerlo and H. D. L. Vervliet, Antwerp, 1968).
Montaigne borrowed copiously from Lipsius's *Politica* (a book which draws heavily on
Tacitus), and paid tribute in the *Essays* (I.xxvi) to this "learned and industrious compilation"; and he described Lipsius as "the most learned man still living, endowed with a very
fine and judicious mind" (*Essays* II.xii). Lipsius, for his part, having enjoyed the *Essays*
of the "French Thales," lavishly extolled his wisdom. See P. Villey, *Montaigne devant la postérité*
(Paris, 1935), pp. 24-26, 348-50 and especially G. Abel, "Juste Lipse et Marie de Gournay: autour de l'exemplaire d'Anvers des *Essais* de Montaigne," *BHR*, 35 (1973), 117-29.
There is no echo of the contemporary debate on Tacitus in Lipsius's surviving letters to
Montaigne.

Lipsius and Montaigne had a joint acquaintance in Muretus: on Lipsius's acquaintance
with Muretus, see J. Rysschaert, "Une édition du Tacite de Juste Lipse, avec annotations
de Muret, conservée à la Mazarine," *RBPH*, 23 (1944), pp. 251-54 and especially the same
scholar's article, "Le séjour de Juste Lipse à Rome (1568-70) d'après ses *Antiquae lectiones
et sa correspondance*," *Bulletin de l'Institut historique belge de Rome*, 24 (1947-1948), pp. 139-92.

25. See also the end of chapter xxvi in Book I of the *Essays*, on attitudes of theologians
and philosophers towards reports of miraculous events. Montaigne has several judicious
passages dealing with such reports. See for example *Essays* I.xxvii, where he denounces
the folly of rashly disbelieving accounts of miracles; III.xi, where he attacks the opposite
folly of excessive credulousness; and II.xxxii, where he defends Plutarch against Bodin's

charge that he included incredible things in his history. There is an interesting discussion of Tacitus's account of Vespasian's "miracles" in Innocent Gentillet's *Discours contre Machiavel* (II.ii: pp. 163–64 in the edition by A. d'Andrea and P. D. Stewart, Florence, 1974).

26. See *Montaigne and the Roman Censors*, pp. 20, 105.

Bibliothèque d'Humanisme et Renaissance - Tome XLIX - 1987 - n° 2, pp. 309-318.

LOST WRITINGS BY MONTAIGNE

Montaigne is the author of at least ten lost or unidentifiable works. Curiously, scholars seem unaware that so many works are lost[1]. My purpose here is to draw up a list of Montaigne's lost works. Awareness of what is lost will enhance the prospect of finding some of it: *qui veut guerir de l'ignorance, il faut la confesser*. This public confession of what scholars have failed to discover will be, like Montaigne's own *Essais*, an exercise in humility: *confessio imperitiae summa peritia est*[2].

This discussion of the ten lost writings does not fully expose our ignorance of what is lost. Other works than those discussed here may or may not have existed. Did Montaigne write the chapter of the *Essais* which he promised on the origin of laws of honour? We do not know[3]. Did he write the book on famous deaths which he adumbrated near the end of *De trois bonnes femmes*? We do not know[4]. He thought a treatise on the way politicians exploit religion would be most useful: did he write one? We do not know[5]. And we know no more, obviously, about other possible writings which have left no trace in his extant work.

The lost works, if found, might tell us things about Montaigne which his *Essais* do not. The *Essais*, it is true, reveal the personality of their

---

[1] The article by Roger Trinquet, «La chasse aux inédits de Montaigne» (*Bulletin de la Société des Amis de Montaigne*, 3ᵉ série, 28, 1963, 21-27) deals solely with the circumstances under which Montaigne's letters to Matignon were first published.

[2] I recently conducted a similar investigation on Ronsard: see «Lost works by Ronsard», *The Library*, 6th series, VIII, 109-126.

[3] The promise is at the end of *De la praesomption* (*Essais*, II, xvii):

> Quant aux divers usages de nos dementirs, et les loix de nostre honneur en cela, et les changemens qu'elles ont receu, je remets à une autre-fois d'en dire ce que j'en sçay, et apprendray cependant, si je puis, en quel temps print commencement cette coustume de si exactement poiser et mesurer les parolles et d'y attacher nostre honneur.

[4] He notes there that such a book would be both useful and easy to produce. He may well have started writing one and included the material in the *Essais*.

[5] Montaigne states towards the end of *De la gloire* (*Essais*, II, xvi) that such a treatise would be valuable, and gives there and elsewhere (*Essais*, I, xlii, II, xii and III, viii) indications that he well understood how widespread the misuse of religion by politicians is, and that he strongly deplored it. His views were fully shared by La Boëtie who, in the *Servitude volontaire*, gives ancient and (boldly) topical French examples of this.

author more intimately than any other book reveals its author. But the
Montaigne of the *Essais* was writing for publication, and he revealed only
as much of the truth about himself as he dared, as he tells us in *Du repentir*
(*Essais*, III, ii) and *Des boyteux* (*Essais*, III, ix). The lost works were
written for a closer audience of friends and family, and in one case at least
for Montaigne alone. Such works are complementary to the *Essais*. The
discovery of his diary in 1770 revealed a great deal of new information
about such topics as his health and his religious practice.

I am arranging the ten lost works by Montaigne that I know about in
the ascending order in which they arouse my curiosity. I hope that with this
arrangement the article becomes progressively more interesting, *viresque
acquirit eundo*.

I rank tenth the lost edition of the *Essais*. Editions are known to have
appeared in 1580, 1582 and 1587, and the next known edition, that of 1588,
is described in the title not as the fourth but as the fifth. Nor is this just a
printer's mistake, for Montaigne himself, in preparing the next edition for
the printer, crossed out «Cinquiesme» on the titlepage of his copy of the
1588 edition and wrote «Sixieme»[6]. Corroboration that it existed is
provided by La Croix Du Maine in his *Bibliothèque françoyse* of 1584:

> [...] ce beau Livre, qu'il a intitulé Essais [...] a été imprimé à Bordeaux
> chez Simon de Millanges, l'an 1580, en deux volumes, et depuis encore
> l'an 1582, par lui-même, et à Rouen aussi et autres divers lieux, tant
> cet Ouvrage a été bien reçu de tous hommes de Lettres[7].

Why is this edition lost? Maybe it contained contentious material, not
found in surviving editions, which attracted the attention of censors, but
this seems unlikely, for Montaigne commented in the *Essais* on judicial
destructions of books, and if he had had personal experience of this he
would almost certainly have found some discreet way to intimate, in later
editions, that he had[8].

---

[6] Montaigne's manuscript note seems to me to prove that this lost edition once existed.
Curiously, the note is not mentioned by R.A. Sayce and David Maskell in their «Note on the
missing edition» in *A descriptive bibliography of Montaigne's* Essais *1580-1700* (London,
1983, 11), although they draw attention to it in their entry on the Bordeaux copy. The 1582
edition is described on the titlepage as the second, but the 1587 edition has no indication as to
whether it was the third or the fourth: see Sayce and Maskell, 7, 9.

[7] *Les Bibliothèques françoises de La Croix Du Maine et de Du Verdier* [...], ed. Rigoley
de Juvigny, 6 t., Paris, 1772-1773, B.L. 618 h 8-13, II, 130.

[8] The comment on destruction of books is towards the end of *De l'affection des peres
aux enfans* (*Essais*, II, viii). If the lost edition did contain contentious material, Montaigne
would only with great reluctance have removed that material, for he stressed several times that
the essence of his book was that it recorded all his fluctuating opinions (see *Essais*, II, viii,
near the end; II, xxxvii, beginning; and III, ix — «J'adjouste, mais je ne corrige pas [...], etc.).

In ninth place I put his poetry. What Montaigne says about it goes some way towards reconciling us to its loss. In a discussion of writing in general, in *De la praesomption* (*Essais*, II, xvii), he says that he is a good judge of other people's work, but not good at writing himself. This is especially apparent, he adds, in the case of poetry:

> Je l'ayme infiniment; je me congnois assez aux ouvrages d'autruy; mais je fay, à la verité, l'enfant quand j'y veux mettre la main; je ne me puis souffrir. On peut faire le sot par tout ailleurs, mais non en la Poësie,
>> mediocribus esse poetis
> Non dii, non homines, non concessere columnae.

Montaigne's judgement here of his writing generally is too unfavourable, but he was an excellent judge of poetry and may well have been right to deprecate his own. He suggests in another chapter, *Sur des vers de Virgile*, that his poems were too derivative: «[...] ils accusoient evidemment le poëte que je venois dernierement de lire» (*Essais*, III, v).

In eighth place, his notes on the progress of his disease, the stones which worked their way through his body:

> A faute de memoire naturelle j'en forge de papier, et comme quelque nouveau symptome survient à mon mal, je l'escris. D'où il advient qu'à cette heure, estant quasi passé par toute sorte d'exemples, si quelque estonnement me menace, feuilletant ces petits brevets descousus comme des feuilles sybillines, je ne faux plus de trouver où me consoler de quelque prognostique favorable en mon experience passée (*De l'experience*, *Essais*, III, xiii).

Anything which helps us understand Montaigne's serene acceptance of a very painful disease would be valuable. The only reason for ranking these «Sibylline» pages relatively low among the lost works is that they are unlikely to be entirely unique, as Montaigne's diary records details of his illness and a long passage in *De l'experience* describes how he came to terms with the pain.

Next, the lost fragment of that diary of his journey to Italy. The whole diary was lost, and its existence unsuspected, until 1770 when one abbé Prunis, looking for documents for a history of Périgord, discovered it in Montaigne's house[9]. The opening folio had long since been torn away.

---

[9] The diary was published and, it seems, correctly, by Meunier de Querlon in 1774 — which is fortunate, since the manuscript disappeared from the royal library, where it had been deposited, and all but one of several manuscript copies made shortly after the discovery of the original are also lost. See F. Moureau, «La copie Leydet du Journal de voyage», in *Autour du Journal de voyage de Montaigne, 1580-1980, Actes des Journées Montaigne*, Mulhouse, Bâle, octobre 1980, Genève, Paris, 1982 (107-185), 107-108.

What might it contain? Possibly, some kind of preface, intimating what sort of person Montaigne envisaged might read the diary (if, that is, he wanted anyone else at all to read it): for both the major surviving works, the *Essais* and the translation of Sabunde, begin this way.

In sixth position, I place Montaigne's historical writing — for in my view it is probable he turned his hand to this. To the best of my knowledge, no Montaigne scholar has suggested this possibility. A passage in the *Essais* may have thrown readers off the scent:

> Aucuns me convient d'escrire les affaires de mon temps, estimans que je les voy d'une veuë moins blessée de passion qu'un autre, et de plus près, pour l'accez que fortune m'a donnée aux chefs de divers partis. Mais ils ne disent pas que, pour la gloire de Salluste, je n'en prendroys pas la peine; ennemy juré d'obligation, d'assiduité, de constance; qu'il n'est rien si contraire à mon stile qu'une narration estenduë: je me recouppe si souvent à faute d'haleine, je n'ay ny composition, ny explication qui vaille, ignorant au-delà d'un enfant des frases et vocables qui servent aux choses plus communes; pourtant ay-je prins à dire ce que je sçay dire, accommodant la matiere à ma force; si j'en prenois qui me guidast, ma mesure pourroit faillir à la sienne; qué ma liberté estant si libre, j'eusse publié des jugemens, à mon gré mesme et selon raison, illegitimes et punissables (*De la force de l'imagination*, *Essais*, I, xxi).

But it is conceivable that Montaigne arrived at this perception of the disadvantages by actually trying his hand at the writing of history. And very significantly, the most illustrious French historian of his day acknowledges that Montaigne gave him material. Jacques-Auguste De Thou declared he had received a great deal of material from Montaigne who, he said, had accurate information about public affairs in Guienne. We do not know, unfortunately, whether Montaigne supplied De Thou with material orally or in writing[10].

The material Montaigne gave De Thou is not lost — it is in De Thou's massive history, somewhere! — but is virtually unidentifiable, as De Thou

---

[10]   What De Thou says (in *De vita sua*, II, referring to a stay in Bordeaux in 1582) is as follows:

> Nec interea studia intermittebat Thuanus; et eorum, quorum consuetudine et familiaritate ad opus historicum, quod iam tum animo complectebatur, opus habebat, amicitiam, quacunque ibat, sedulo ambiebat. Ita animatus multa quae aut scripta aut iactata meminerat, quae ab aliis aut in dubium revocabantur aut aliter narrabantur, judicio adhibito didicit [...] multa a Michaele Montano ingenii liberi homine, et a partibus alieno, qui tunc Majoris munere in illa urbe perhonorifica fungebatur, et rerum nostrarum, ac suae praesertim Aquitaniae, multam ac certam notitiam habebat. (*Sylloge scriptorum varii generis et argumenti*, Londini, 1733, iv, 39.)

does not cite Montaigne as his source for individual passages. However, I think it is possible to attribute one passage to Montaigne: the account of events in Bordeaux in August 1548 during the revolt over the imposition of the salt tax. The reasons for attributing this long passage to Montaigne are (i) De Thou's general acknowledgement that Montaigne gave him information about Guienne; (ii) Montaigne intimates in the *Essais* that he was in Bordeaux at the time, and two members of his family had a prominent role in negotiations with the rebels; (iii) the passage has an otherwise rather gratuitous reference to a highly controversial book on tyranny, the *Servitude volontaire*, by Montaigne's close friend Estienne de La Boëtie; and (iv) it contains a defence of the *Servitude volontaire* identical to that given by Montaigne in his *Essais*[11].

It has been suggested that another historical work, the second edition of Florimond de Raemond's book about the mythical pope Joan, titled *Erreur populaire de la papesse Jeanne*, has material by Montaigne not found in the *Essais*. The assertion is an unsupported one, and so would not normally command attention[12]. But the suggestion has a certain plausibility: Raemond, who in 1570 became Montaigne's successor as councillor in the Bordeaux *parlement*, knew Montaigne very well — so well that Montaigne vouchsafed to him confidences about the identity of unnamed individuals in the *Essais*[13]. Moreover, Raemond's work on pope Joan is the sort of book Montaigne could happily have contributed to, for he would have liked both its substance (a refutation of the Reformers) and its style (which, while very lively, is more scholarly than polemical). Now there are passages in Raemond's book which echo parts of Montaigne's *Essais*, but I have found no evidence in it of anything by Montaigne not found in the *Essais*[14].

In fifth place among Montaigne's lost works I place the parts of his *Essais* which he says a secretary of his stole. The context of his reference to

---

[11] The attribution of this passage of De Thou to Montaigne is discussed in my forthcoming edition of La Boëtie's *Servitude volontaire*. The passage in De Thou's *Historia*, is V, xiii (vol. I, pp. 183-188 in the 1733 London edition).

[12] See an unsigned note in the *Bulletin de la Société des Amis de Montaigne*, 2e série, VIII, 1940, 32.

[13] Raemond, happily, conveyed these confidences to posterity: see A.M. Boase, «Montaigne annotated by Florimond de Raemond», *Revue du Seizième Siècle*, XV, 1928, 237-278 and P. Bonnet, «Une nouvelle série d'annotations de Florimond de Raemond aux *Essais* de Montaigne», *Bulletin de la Société des Amis de Montaigne*, 3e série, 10, 1959, 10-23.

[14] Some echoes of Montaigne in this work and in Raemond's *Antichrist* are noted by A.M. Boase in *The fortunes of Montaigne*, London, 1935, 31-34.

these lost parts suggests they were among the earliest parts of the *Essais* to be written:

> Je veux representer le progrez de mes humeurs, et qu'on voye chaque piece en sa naissance. Je prendrois plaisir d'avoir commencé plustost et à reconnoistre le trein de mes mutations. Un valet qui me servoir à les escrire soubs moy pensa faire un grand butin de m'en desrober plusieurs pieces choisies à sa poste. Cela me console, qu'il n'y fera pas plus de gain que j'y ai fait de perte (*Essais*, II, xxxvii, beginning).

Montaigne's early writing is on the whole less interesting than what he wrote later, but the reason he gives for wanting to see this lost early work is a good one: that it would help us trace the evolution of his thought.

In fourth place, a lost book which almost certainly contained material by Montaigne: an edition of the collected works of Estienne de La Boëtie, the scholar, poet, statesman and theologian. To appreciate the full interest of this publication, it is necessary to recall the salient facts about the early publication of La Boëtie's work. The scholarly references for material that follows are in my editions of La Boëtie's *Mémoire sur la pacification des troubles* (the tract formerly — and misleadingly — known as the *Mémoire sur l'Edit de Janvier*) and the *Servitude volontaire* (both in the Textes Littéraires Français series).

Montaigne inherited La Boëtie's books and papers when La Boëtie died in 1563. He prepared an edition of La Boëtie which appeared in 1571, and which is extant, but he left out of this edition two tracts by La Boëtie. One was the *Mémoire sur la pacification des troubles* of 1561 (a memorandum on how to reconcile the Catholic Church and the Reformers). The probable reason Montaigne omitted this document is that La Boëtie argues that the differences between Catholics and Reformers could be bridged if Catholics would make concessions, and within months of La Boëtie writing it the Council of Trent rejected all concessions to the Reformers. The other text Montaigne omitted from the 1571 edition was the *Servitude volontaire*, La Boëtie's attack on monarchy: Montaigne was warned by politicians that it would be dangerous to publish it. But he remained every bit as keen to publish these two tracts as he had been to publish the other works. He seems to have decided to publish the *Mémoire* and the *Servitude volontaire* in Book I of his *Essais*, where chapter xxvii seems to have been conceived as an introduction to the *Mémoire sur la pacification des troubles* and chapter xxviii is presented as an introduction to the *Servitude volontaire*.

But neither the *Mémoire* nor the *Servitude volontaire* ever actually appeared in Montaigne's *Essais*, the first edition of which came out in 1580. Circumstances had made it still more dangerous to publish these treatises than it had been in 1571. After the Saint Bartholomew's Day massacres of 1572, the new and subversive alliance of Reformers and anti-royalist Catholics endeavoured to show that the differences between their two faiths were minimal, and the *Mémoire sur la pacification des troubles* would have served their cause admirably. The *Servitude volontaire*, an analysis of tyranny, was actually exploited by them — they published it to discredit Charles IX and, later, Henri III. One of the Reformers' editions, which probably came out in 1573, has vanished, presumably because it was burned (the evidence that it existed is in my forthcoming edition); another edition (of 1577) is known to have been burned on the orders of the *parlement* of Bordeaux, but copies survived. Montaigne was highly indignant that the Reformers had published the *Servitude volontaire* in a context which suggested La Boëtie was subversive: he declined to assist their cause by publishing either text by La Boëtie himself (he expounds his position on this in *De l'amitié*).

But about the time of Montaigne's death, a new edition of the works of La Boëtie appeared. This edition is lost. But it was very probably prepared by Montaigne: it was published in Bordeaux by Simon Millanges, who had been Montaigne's own printer for the first two editions of the *Essais*. In my view, Montaigne prepared this edition because he knew his life was drawing to a close and his last chance to restore fully the reputation of a friend whose work had been traduced was at hand. What did he say in this edition about the *Mémoire sur la pacification des troubles* and the *Servitude volontaire*? We do not know. But these two texts would have been every bit as contentious in the early 1590s as in the 1570s. The *Mémoire*, which advocated concessions to the Reformers which had since been ruled out by the Council of Trent, would have incensed the Catholic League. The *Servitude volontaire* would have outraged the royalists. It is very probable that this lost edition contained remarks by Montaigne about these two tracts, and his remarks may have ruffled authoritarian feathers sufficiently to get the work suppressed. I personally feel the loss of this edition of La Boëtie keenly, since Fortune allotted to me the task of producing scholarly editions of those two texts Montaigne felt unable to publish[15].

---

[15]   I would not rule out the possibility that Montaigne included in this lost edition of La Boëtie the text either of the *Servitude volontaire* or the *Mémoire sur la pacification des troubles*, or both. He was committed to freedom of expression (he deplored the burning of books, in *De l'affection des peres aux enfans*, and may well have been moved to this by the burning of the *Servitude volontaire*); he felt that even if a book has dangerous opinions, it is sufficient to alert the reader to this fact, as he did with Sabunde's *Theologia naturalis* in the

Now, my top three lost works. In third place, the judgements on authors which Montaigne wrote in his copies of their works. He explains in *Des livres* (*Essais*, II, x) that he put these judgements down in writing because his memory was bad, and gives in that chapter examples of these verdicts — on Guicciardini, Philippe de Comines and Martin Du Bellay. Fortune has preserved a small number of books by other authors containing Montaigne's verdicts. One is his Caesar, with a page commending the soldier and historian for his conscientiousness, generosity and modesty[16]. Another is his copy of Nicole Gilles's *Annales et chroniques de France*: Montaigne's very copious annotations reveal a superbly scholarly and judicious mind at work[17]. Another surviving book is his Quintus Curtius, which has a very eulogious verdict on the historian[18].

The common feature of Montaigne's verdicts on authors, and the main reason for lamenting the loss of his annotations, is that his special gift was to see beyond a writer's words into his very soul. He read books not for what the author had to say, but to know the mind and heart of the author: «[...] je poursuy la communication de quelque esprit fameux, non pour qu'il m'enseigne, mais pour que je le cognoisse» (*Essais*, III, viii). And of his favourite author, Plutarch, he wrote, «Je pense le connoistre jusques dans l'ame» (*Essais*, II, xxxi). This, to Montaigne, was the key to correct understanding of literary authors.

The few surviving books annotated by Montaigne afford a most tantalising glimpse of the treasures we have lost. He tells us he had a thousand books, and whether or not that is an accurate figure, it is plain that many books annotated by him have been lost. But some may be recovered. Reinhold Dezeimeris found Montaigne's Nicole Gilles in 1891 in a bookshop in Bordeaux in a pile of books which were so dilapidated they were about to be taken away to be pulped[19].

---

preface to his translation and with La Boëtie's *Mémoire sur la pacification* in his *Essais* (I, xxvii); and he felt an obligation to make La Boëtie known by publishing his works, as La Boëtie was «le plus grand homme de nostre siecle». But on balance it is unlikely the lost edition contains these works.

[16]   See Armaingaud's edition of Montaigne's *Œuvres complètes* (12 t., Paris, 1924-1941), XI, 297-306.

[17]   See the Armaingaud edition, XII, 9-222.

[18]   See the Armaingaud edition, XII, 223-411. Other books annotated by Montaigne are Jan Herburt's *Histoire des rois de Pologne*, translated by François Baudoin (1573) and Denis Sauvage's *Chronique de Flandres* (1562): see G. Richou's *Inventaire de la collection des ouvrages et documents réunis par J.F. Payen et J.B. Bastide sur Michel de Montaigne*, Paris, 1878 for these (xi-xii) and other annotated books (29-35).

[19]   See the Armaingaud edition, XII, 11-12.

In second place, Montaigne's letters and papers on affairs of state. Again, the pain of the loss is mitigated by the fact that some of this material survives. Two surviving letters interestingly bear out something Montaigne tells us several times in the *Essais* (notably II, xvii, III, i and III, xiii): that he involved himself in affairs of state only on the basis that his independence of the monarch was never to be compromised[20]. This freedom of expression doubtless explains the loss of what must be the overwhelming mass of Montaigne's official documents. He declined to write history, as we have seen, through fear that his freedom would lead him to express views which were best kept quiet. He refrained from publishing his official documents for the same reason — and because he was a most scrupulous respecter of confidentiality. And there is doubtless another reason they are lost: he felt it demeaning for politicians to seek renown as mere writers (see *Essais*, I, xl, beginning). If he kept his official papers at all, he committed them to Fortuna who, in her mysterious way, has so far denied almost all of them to us.

What could be more interesting than Montaigne's public letters? If we follow his own inclination, and I do, then his private letters would be more interesting. And it is these that I put in pride of place among his lost works. «Les mouvemens publics dependent plus de la conduicte de la fortune, les privez de la nostre» (*Essais*, III, viii). We can point to people who received now-lost letters from Montaigne. Justus Lipsius is one: although three letters from Lipsius to Montaigne survive, Montaigne's to Lipsius do not[21]. He wrote to some of the people he encountered on his travels in Germany and Italy: the diary summarizes a letter written from Bolzano (27 October 1580) to François Hotman and mentions a letter to a friend called Saminiati[22]. He wrote love letters which he says were lost (and which he also suggests were rather good)[23]. Letters to his adopted daughter, Marie de Gournay, are lost[24].

---

[20]   See his *Œuvres complètes*, ed. A. Thibaudet and M. Rat, Paris, 1962, 1397-1399 and 1399-1400.

[21]   Lipsius's letters are dated 15 April 1588, 30 August 1588 and 17 September 1589. For early editions of Lipsius which contain them, see G. Abel, «Juste Lipse et Marie de Gournay: autour de l'exemplaire d'Anvers des *Essais* de Montaigne», *BHR*, XXXV, 1975 (117-129), 117, n. 2.

[22]   See Montaigne, *Œuvres complètes*, ed. A. Thibaudet and M. Rat, Paris, 1962, 1173, 1277.

[23]   «Si tout le papier que j'ay autresfois barbouillé pour les dames estoit en nature, lorsque ma main estoit veritablement emportée par ma passion, il s'en trouveroit à l'adventure

318   M.C. SMITH

It seems possible that Justus Lipsius, who greatly admired Montaigne, tried to ensure that personal letters of Montaigne were published. For Lipsius tells us that he sent copies of letters Montaigne wrote him to Francis Raphelengius, the printer and son-in-law of the celebrated Christopher Plantin. Moreover, Lipsius may well have asked Marie de Gournay for letters Montaigne had written her, since in a letter to Lipsius dated 2 May 1596 she told him she intended to publish Montaigne's letters to her[25]. Alas, neither Lipsius's project nor Gournay's seems to have come to fruition[26].

London.   Malcolm C. SMITH.

---

quelque page digne d'estre communiquée à la jeunesse oysive, embabouinée de ceste fureur» (*Essais*, I, xl).

[24]   Marie de Gournay bequeathed «[...] her vast correspondence and other papers and books to La Mothe Le Vayer»: see M.H. Ilsley, *A daughter of the Renaissance, Marie le Jars de Gournay, her life and works*, The Hague, 1963, 263. There is no further information on the fate of this bequest in F.L. Wickelgren's monograph, *La Mothe Le Vayer, sa vie et son œuvre*, Paris, 1934. Particularly interesting would be the message Montaigne sent to Marie de Gournay as he was dying (see Ilsley, 43).

[25]   She planned to include them in the second edition of *Le proumenoir de Monsieur de Montaigne*: see her letter of 2 May 1596 to Lipsius, cited in «A.S.», «Quelques lettres de Montaigne perdues», *Bulletin de la Société des Amis de Montaigne*, 2e série, X, 1941, 16.

[26]   No trace of the correspondence between Lipsius and Montaigne is found in the catalogue of Raphelengius's books and manuscripts auctioned in 1626 (*Catalogus variorum librorum e bibliothecis Francisci Raphelengii* [...] *eiusque filiorum* [et aliorum] [...], *quorum auctio habebitur in bibliopolio Elzeviriano die 5 octobris*, Lugduni Batavorum, 1626, B.L. S.C. 883), or in J. Denucé, *Musaeum Plantin-Moretus, Catalogue des manuscrits*, Anvers, 1927.

[205]

Bibliothèque d'Humanisme et Renaissance - Tome L - 1988 - n° 1, pp. 95-100.

A SOURCE OF MONTAIGNE'S UNCERTAINTY

In *De l'incertitude de nostre jugement* (*Essais*, I, xlvii), Montaigne discusses six dilemmas which can arise in warfare:

(i)   Should you pursue the remnants of a defeated army, or let them escape?
(ii)   Should your soldiers be given rich apparel?
(iii)   Should you allow your soldiers to insult the enemy?
(iv)   Should the general be disguised when battle is joined?
(v)   Should you charge the enemy or wait for the enemy to charge you?
(vi)   Should you, given the choice, fight in the enemy's lands or your own?

In each case, Montaigne shows that whilst formidable arguments and precedents support a particular answer, equally weighty arguments and examples justify the opposite course. And (more importantly) he draws the general conclusion that the outcome of human affairs depends not upon our calculations but upon the will of Fortune. It is characteristic of Montaigne both to move from the particular to the universal, and to acknowledge human fallibility as he does so: «Je ne regarde pas l'espece et l'individu comme une pierre où j'aye bronché; j'apprens à craindre mon alleure par tout, et m'attends à la reigler» (*De l'experience*: *Essais*, III, xiii). *De l'incertitude* thus refutes the type of dogmatist who imagines that by study of history and use of reason we can usurp the role of Fortune.

While Montaigne's interest lies in the universal, the target of *De l'incertitude* is in my veiw not just a type but also an individual: the Machiavelli of the *Discorsi sopra la prima deca di Tito Livio*[1]. We know Montaigne

---

[1] Parallels between the *Discorsi* and *De l'incertitude* are not pointed out in any of the studies of Montaigne's reactions to Machiavelli which I have looked at (such studies are listed in P. Bonnet's *Bibliographie méthodique et analytique des ouvrages et documents relatifs à Montaigne (jusqu'en 1975)*, Genève, Paris, 1983 and in R.A. Brooks, *A critical bibliography of French literature*, vol. II, revised, *The sixteenth century*, ed. R.C. La Charité, Syracuse, N.Y., 1985). Nor are they mentioned in any of the following studies on the fortuna of Machiavelli: L. Firpo, «Le origini dell'antimachiavellismo», *Il pensiero politico*, II, 1969, 337-367; S. Mastellone, «Antimachiavelismo, machiavellismo, tacitismo», *Culture e scuola*, IX, 1970, 132-136; R. de Mattei, *Dal premachiavelismo all' antimachiavellismo*, Firenze, 1969 and «Distinzioni in sede di antimachiavelismo», *Il pensiero politico*, II, 1969, 368-375; G. Procacci, *Studi sulla Fortuna del Machiavelli*, Roma, 1965; and articles by A. M. Battista, «Sull' antimachiavellismo francese del secolo XVI», *Storia e politica*, I, 1962, 413-417; «La penetrazione del Machiavelli in Francia nel secolo XVI», *Rassegna di politica e di storia*, 67-68, 1960, 1-16, and «Direzione di ricerca per una storia di Machiavelli in Francia», *Atti del convegno internazionale su il pensiero politico di Machiavelli e la sua fortuna nel mondo*, Sancasciano-Firenze, 28-29 settembre 1969, Firenze, 1972, 37-66.

read Machiavelli. He does not say why he found him worth reading, but it is easy to see what drew him to this author. He liked writers who write about public affairs on the strength of personal experience; he liked authors who go straight to the point, without academic preambles, and those who present material in short fragments; and, perhaps most important of all, he enjoyed contact with those with whom he disagreed[2].

In the *Discorsi*, Machiavelli deals explicitly or implicitly with all the six dilemmas in *De l'incertitude*:

(i)   Should you follow up a victory? No, says Machiavelli in the chapter of the *Discorsi* titled «Ai principi e republiche prudenti debbe bastare vincere; perché il più delle volte quando e' non basta si perde» (II, xxvii): one ought not to put at risk a gain in the uncertain hope of further gain[3]. This proposition, Machiavelli says, is best demonstrated by *esempli* rather than by *ragioni*. He gives three examples. Hanno advised the Carthaginians to make an advantageous treaty with the Romans after defeating them at Cannae. The citizens of Tyre wore down Alexander for four months — but were not content with an honourable peace treaty, and defied him, to their cost, in 332. The Florentines lost the chance of a favourable deal with Spanish forces seeking to restore the Medici, in 1512 — and paid for their pride. Machiavelli, then, has a clear answer to a question which Montaigne feels cannot be answered[4].

(ii)   Should your soldiers be given sumptuous apparel? This is one of only two of Montaigne's dilemmas which Machiavelli had not tackled in identical form in the *Discorsi*. But he had touched on it incidentally in the chapter titled «I danari non sono il nervo della guerra, secondo che è la comune opinione» (*Discorsi*, II, x), where the theme is that brave soldiers matter more to a state at war than money does. Machiavelli goes on to make the point Montaigne underlines — that ostentatious wealth can stimulate an enemy's greed: «I danari non solo non ti difendono, ma ti fanno predare più presto» — and he gives historical examples. Montaigne's dilemma is slightly different (Whether a display of wealth by soldiers will stimulate their pride more than it does the enemy's greed), but the similarity between the two authors is close. Machiavelli's answer to Montaigne's dilemma would clearly have been: do not risk arousing the enemy's greed[5].

---

[2]   All of these points are discussed in *Des livres* (*Essais*, II, x), except the last (about preferring those who disagree), which is dealt with in *De l'art de conferer* (*Essais*, III, viii).

[3]   The edition of the *Discorsi* I used is Machiavelli's *Opere*, a cura di Ezio Raimondi (I Classici Italiani, 5), Milano, 1973. There is an excellent commentary in L.J. Walker's volume of notes accompanying his translation, *The Discourses*, London, 1950.

[4]   His answer is found also in Book 7 of *Dell'Arte della guerra*: «Colui che seguita con disordine il nimico poi ch' egli à rotto, non vuole fare altro che diventare di vittorioso perdente» (*Opere*, ed. Raimondi, 429).

[5]   That this inference is correct is confirmed by a precept in Book 7 of *Dell'Arte della guerra*: «Avezza i tuoi soldati a spregiare il vivere delicato e il vestire lussurioso» (*Opere*, ed. Raimondi, 430).

(iii)   Should you let your soldiers insult the enemy? No, says Machiavelli, in his chapter «Il vilipendio e l'improperio genera odio contro a coloro che l'usano, sanza alcuna loro utilità» (*Discorsi*, II, xxvi). Reason tells us that people you insult will hate you more deeply and try harder to harm you. And experience confirms this. The Veii provoked the enemy soldiers to defeat them by insulting them. And a demoralised Persian army was abandoning the siege of Amida when the defenders came to the city walls and hurled derision at them: this goaded them to a successful assault on the city.

(iv)   Should the general be disguised when battle is joined? Machiavelli does not tackle this directly, but in the chapter «Como debbe essere fatto uno capitano nel quale lo esercito suo possa confidare» (*Discorsi*, III, xxxviii) he cites with approval the words attributed to Valerius Corvinus on the need for a general to give an example of bravery in battle. His answer to Montaigne's dilemma must have been that the general must be recognizable.

(v)   Should you charge the enemy or let him attack? Machiavelli has the answer in «Quale sia migliore partito nelle giornate, o sostenere l'impeto de' nemici e, sostenuto, urtargli; o vero da prima con furia assaltargli» (*Discorsi*, III, xlv). Experience, he declares, indicates the path to follow. The two consuls Decius and Fabius each faced the Samnites and Tuscans, and each had charge of a Roman army. Decius led his forces in charging the enemy, Fabius waited for the enemy to attack. Decius was defeated, Fabius was victorious. And reason confirms what experience illustrates: for those who charge the enemy are dissipating their ardour and their energy before they even come to blows.

(vi)   Should you invade your enemy's lands, or fight at home? In the chapter «S'egli è meglio, temendo di essere assaltato, inferire o aspettare la guerra» (*Discorsi*, II, xii), Machiavelli acknowledges that experience can support either option. Croesus advised Cyrus to fight queen Tomyris in her lands, since to defeat her elsewhere would not rob her of her kingdom; and Hannibal saw that to fight the Romans outside Italy would leave intact their source of reinforcements. Agathocles sought out the Carthaginians in their own lands and had them sue for peace, and Scipio too attacked them in Africa. On the other hand, Machiavelli notes, the Athenians were victorious fighting near home — and were defeated in Sicily. Antaeus, king of Libya, was unconquerable so long as he fought Hercules the Egyptian within his own kingdom, but was slain when lured away. And Ferdinand, king of Naples, advised his son Alphonso to let Charles VIII of France come and attack him — advice which his son ignored to his cost. And reason appears equally ambivalent. If you invade your enemy's lands you gain momentum and confidence, you can cut off your enemy from his own resources, and force him to cripple his subjects with taxation to support a war at home; and your soldiers will be stirred to bravery to survive in a foreign land. But reason also says that if you let your enemy invade, you

can easily disrupt his supplies, you have the better knowledge of the ter-
rain, you can assemble your forces readily, and recover more quickly from
defeat. Ultimately, however, Machiavelli has the answer. If you do not
have a standing army, fight away from home: you can use national revenue
to fight foreign wars, whereas war at home disrupts tax collection. But a
state which is already militarily strong ought to fight at home — its forces
will be irresistible when concentrated. And Machiavelli supports this view
by appealing to experience.

Thus, Montaigne's six dilemmas have in common the fact that they are
ones to which Machiavelli had found answers. There is thus a case for the
hypothesis that *De l'incertitude* was written as a rejoinder to Machiavelli —
but, so far, only a *prima facie* case: many other authors had touched on
one or more of the dilemmas which Montaigne discussed, and indeed his
examples show how ancient the dilemmas are[6].
But the case is strengthened by two considerations. The first is that
Montaigne closely parodies Machiavelli in his treatment of the dilemmas.
Like the Italian author, he appeals to experience and to reason; he discusses the issues at similar length; his culminating example, and the one to
which he accords longest treatment, is an issue which Machiavelli himself
discussed at length and intimated was finely balanced; and he playfully
echoes Machiavelli's own assertive language. Anyone who reads the parts
of the *Discorsi* mentioned here and then turns to *De l'incertitude* is likely to
come to the view that Montaigne is affably refuting Machiavelli — and to
see a hitherto unsuspected geniality and wit in *De l'incertitude*.
The second, and stronger, reason for concluding that *De l'incertitude* is
a rejoinder to Machiavelli is to be found in remarks in *De la praesomption*
(*Essais*, II, xvii) which illustrate what Montaigne there calls (perhaps
echoing the title of the chapter we are considering) «L'incertitude de mon
jugement»:

> [...] Notamment aux affaires politiques, il y a beau champ ouvert au bransle et
> à la contestation:

---

[6] Plutarch recorded (in *Sayings of the Romans*, 206 D, E) Caesar's criticisms of Pom-
pey for not pursuing a defeated foe and for waiting for the enemy to attack him. The dilemmas were often touched on in the Renaissance. Thomas More's Utopians had a policy not to
pursue a defeated enemy (see *The complete works*, vol. 4 (*Utopia*), ed. E. Surtz and J.H.
Hexter, New Haven and London, 1965, 212). That was the view also of Rabelais's strategists,
Gymnaste, Gargantua and Frère Jean (see *Gargantua*, ed. R. Calder and M.A Screech (Textes
Littéraires Français), Genève, 1970, 208, 244, 267). Jean de La Taille looked at four of the
dilemmas in *Le Prince necessaire*, a political poem presented to Henri de Bourbon (the future
Henri IV) in 1573 (see R. Pintard, «Une adaptation de Machiavel au XVIe siècle», *Revue de
Littérature Comparée*, XIII, 1933, 385 — 402: the dilemmas La Taille touches on are (i), (iii),
(v) and (vi)). And René de Lucinge, in his essay on how to defeat the Turks, *De la naissance,
durée et chute des estats*, probably written in 1586, urges the view that the enemy should be
attacked in his own land (see the edition by Michael Heath, Textes Littéraires Français,
Genève, 1984, I, 2). It would doubtless be easy to multiply such references, perhaps by looking in the thirty-three French works on the art of war (almost all of the sixteenth century) discussed by G. Dickinson in her edition of the *Instructions sur le faict de la guerre* by Raymond
de Beccarie de Pavie, sieur de Fourquevaux (London, 1954, xcii-cix).

Iusta pari premitur veluti cum pondere libra
Prona, nec hac plus parte sedet, nec surgit ab illa.

Les discours de Machiavel, pour exemple, estoient assez solides pour le subject; si, y a-il eu grand aisance à les combattre; et ceux qui l'ont faict, n'ont pas laissé moins de facilité à combatre les leurs. Il s'y trouveroit tousjours, à un tel argument, dequoy y fournir responses, dupliques, repliques, tripliques, quadrupliques, et cette infinie contexture de debats que notre chicane a alongé tant qu'elle a peu en faveur des procez,

Caedimur, et totidem plagis consumimus hostem,

Les raisons n'y ayant guere autre fondement que l'experience, et la diversité des evenements humains nous presentant infinis exemples à toute sorte de formes.

This passage exactly reproduces the thought of *De l'incertitude de nostre jugement* — and, this time, Montaigne explicitly presents the thought as being a refutation of Machiavelli's *Discourses* (for the phrase «Les discours de Machiavel» must, in context, be a reference to that book). Incidentally, Montaigne's observation that those who have refuted the *Discorsi* can as easily be refuted themselves does not apply to his own attack on Machiavelli, which avoids the dogmatism he denounces.

This part of *De la praesomption* echoes *De l'incertitude* also in stressing our reliance upon Fortune:

L'incertitude de mon jugement est si egalement balancée en la pluspart des occurences, que je compromettrois volontiers à la decision du sort et des dets; et remarque avec grande consideration de nostre foiblesse humaine les exemples que l'histoire divine mesme nous a laissez de cet usage de remettre à la fortune et au hazard la determination des elections ès choses doubteuses: «Sors cecidit super Matthiam».

De la praesomption has the same message about our dependence on Fortune as *De l'incertitude* — and projects it more pointedly. The apostles of Christ, Montaigne recalls, appealed to Fortune to choose for them a successor to Judas. The recurrent theme of *De la praesomption* is that an awareness of how dependent we are on Fortune is the one sure antidote to presumption. Fortuna here, as often in Montaigne (and he himself indicates the fact), is simply a poetic synonym for divine Providence. To seek to usurp the role of Fortuna was not merely overweening dogmatism, it was impious[7].

Machiavelli may be the target of similar passages in other chapters. In *Divers evenemens de mesme conseil* (*Essais*, I, xxiv), Montaigne contrasts Augustus, who benefited by pardoning a would-be assassin, and the duke of Guise, who did not, concluding, «[...] c'est chose vaine et frivole que l'humaine prudence; et au travers de tous nos projets, de nos conseils et precautions, la fortune maintient tousjours la possession des evenemens». In *Nous ne goustons rien de pur* (*Essais*, II, xx), he writes, «Il faut manier

---

[7]   Fortuna is presented as a synonym for divine providence in the following chapters in addition to *De la praesomption*: I, xxviii, lvi; III, x and xii. I have argued that these reflections were prompted by criticism, in Rome, of his use of the word «Fortune»: see *Montaigne and the Roman censors* (Genève, 1981), 27-34.

les entreprises humaines plus grossierement et plus superficiellement, et en laisser bonne et grande part pour les droicts de la fortune. Il n'est pas besoin d'esclaircir les affaires si profondement et si subtilement. On s'y perd, à la consideration de tant de lustres contraires et formes diverses». And in *De l'art de conferer* (*Essais*), III, viii): «C'est imprudence d'estimer que l'humaine prudence puisse remplir le rolle de la fortune. Et vaine est l'entreprise de celuy qui presume d'embrasser et causes et consequences, et mener par la main le progrez de son faict; vaine surtout aux deliberations guerrieres.» *De l'incertitude* is far from Montaigne's only word on this subject; and a common feature of these attacks on machiavellian calcula- tion is a pious respect for the prerogatives of Fortune[8].

Had Montaigne looked beyond the *Discorsi* for Machiavelli's views on Fortune, as several modern scholars have, he would probably have found the Italian author's treatment of the concept more diverse and intriguing, for Machiavelli, like Montaigne himself, looks at issues from different angles at different times — and uses the same word in various ways. But Montaigne's objection to Machiavelli — that in striving for certainty in the *Discorsi* he usurps the role of Fortune — remains a strong one[9].

If Machiavelli presents certainty, why have I titled this note, «A source of Montaigne's uncertainty»? Because the assertive tone of the *Discorsi* would have more effectively strengthened Montaigne's scepticism than would the reasonings of Socrates himself: «[Je] m'instruis mieux par contrarieté que par exemple, et par fuite que par suite» (*De l'art de confe- rer*: *Essais*, III, viii).

London.   Malcolm C. SMITH.

---

[8] Montaigne had other disagreements with Machiavelli besides the one discussed here. He deplored the view (cf. *Discorsi*, I, xi-xv) that religion should be exploited to buttress the power of the ruler (see notably *Essais*, II, xvi), and he rejected Machiavelli's opinion (cf. *Il Principe*, 18) that lying can be politically useful (see *Essais*, I, ix and II, xvii).

[9] On Fortune in Machiavelli, see (among many studies) S. Anglo, *Machiavelli: a dissec- tion*, London, 1969, 216-237; T. Flanagan, «The concept of Fortuna in Machiavelli', in A. Parel, ed., *The political calculus: essays on Machiavelli's philosophy*, Toronto and Buffalo, 1972, 127-156; and M. Santoro, «Machiavelli e il tema della Fortuna», in his *Fortuna, ragione e prudenza nella civiltà letteraria del Cinquecento*, Napoli, 1966, 179-231.

Latin Translations of Ronsard

Malcolm C. Smith

From the outset of his career, Ronsard repeatedly claimed that he would enjoy worldwide renown for his poems.[1] However, he was sufficiently realistic to acknowledge that Latin translations of these poems contributed significantly to his fame. He took a pride in these translations, as can be seen from remarks he addressed to Henry III about translations of *L'Hydre deffaict*, a 1569 poem in praise of victories over the Reformers:

> [Ronsard] vous fit un tel hymne,
> Que l'arrogance Grecque, et la grandeur Latine,
> Le voulurent tourner, et sema par ses vers
> Vostre nom admirable en ce grand univers.[2]

While he does not appear to have produced Latin translations of his own poems (curiously, as he did write a fair amount of Latin poetry), he at least once expressed delight at the efforts of a translator of his poems.[3]

Ian McFarlane has established a very valuable checklist of Latin translations of Ronsard which comprises 41 items published between 1555 and 1596 in the works of Ronsard and in sixteen other publications. He lists also a further 32 translations extant in manuscript, all but two of them in the British Library's manuscript of translations by François de Thoor.[4] I shall be mentioning eighteen more translations of poems or parts of poems which I have seen in six separate publications, another publication (which I have not seen) containing a number of translations of passages of the *Franciade*, an unknown manuscript translation, and finally two more translations which could well have been printed but which no-one seems to have located. My survey, like McFarlane's, is chronological by date of publication.

In 1558, there appeared Jean Dorat's translation, into 164 lines of Latin verse, of Ronsard's *Exhortation au camp du roy*. The pamphlet in which it appeared is titled *Ronsardi exhortatio ad milites Gallos*. This translation is not unknown, for Ronsard's most famous editor, Paul Laumonier, referred to it, but McFarlane only mentions the 1586 edition in Dorat's *Poematia*. The 1558 edition is important in that it appeared while the material in the poem was still topical. Laumonier observed that the French poem was composed in the last week of August 1558, when a decisive battle between the French and the Spanish was anticipated, and he surmised, very plausibly, that the Latin translation was composed for the benefit of foreign troops in the French army.[5]

Another political poem translated into Latin was the *Priere à Dieu pour la victoire* (1569). In this case, the French text and the Latin translation (which is in 147 lines by Antoine Valet) were published on facing pages of the same pamphlet. Here, again, the material is topical, dealing with an imminent battle in the third civil war. The importance of topicality is illustrated by the fact that by the time this prayer for victory was printed, the victory itself had materialised (at Montcontour on 3rd October), and so the astute printer, Gervais Mallot, altered the title to *Chant triumphal sur la victoire!*[6]

Another 1569 publication containing a Latin translation of Ronsard is Scévole de Sainte-Marthe's *Les premieres oeuvres [. . .] qui contienent ses Imitations et Traductions recueillies de divers Poëtes Grecs et Latins,* wherein Sainte-Marthe translates a sonnet by Ronsard dedicated to Jodelle.[7] According to Claude Faisant, Sainte-Marthe also translated several passages of Ronsard's *Franciade.* Faisant does not give details of these translations other than that they appeared in a volume titled *Poetica paraphrasis [. . .] Sylvarum libri II,* and that they were prefaced by a poem titled *In versos aliquot ex P. Ronsardi Franciade latinos a se factos,* of which he cites an extract.[8] The relationship between Sainte-Marthe and Ronsard was clearly a very cordial and mutually admiring one.[9]

In 1571, there appeared Barthélemy Faye's *Energumenicus* and *Alexicacus,* two books on exorcism published in one volume. Faye's purpose was to refute the claims of the Reformers. The *Alexicacus* contains a Latin translation from Ronsard's *Continuation du Discours des miseres.* The passage is cited to make the point that if Catholic pastors had cared for their flocks, the heretical "wolves" would not have wreaked such havoc. The same work contains, as part of the peroration, a translation from the *Remonstrance au peuple de France.* Ronsard is cited, I would think, not just because his material is apposite, but also because his renown as a Catholic controversialist lent impact to Faye's case. Faye himself is the translator of the extracts.[10]

The next Latin translation offers a further example of the use of Ronsard's text to make an ideological point—and a particularly interesting example, for it concerns use of his text by his political and religious adversaries, the Reformers. The unidentified author of a compilation published in 1574 and titled *Dialogi ab Eusebio Philadelpho cosmopolita in Gallorum et caeterorum nationum gratiam compositi* cites, in a total of 109 lines of Latin verse, seven extracts from Ronsard's *Franciade.*[11] The author presents Ronsard's denunciations of Childeric and Chilperic as though these passages had been intended to be attacks upon Charles IX, and he presents Ronsard's indictment of Brunhilda as though his

[213]

"real" target had been Catherine de Médicis.[12] The translator is not named: he might well be the unidentified author of the rest of the book. This book — a French version also appeared — was issued by the Reformers in the aftermath of the St. Bartholomew's Day massacres. It is virtually inconceivable that Ronsard intended the passages of the *Franciade* to be read as attacks on the court, even though he almost certainly deplored the massacres and was also capable of conveying political messages allusively.[13]

In 1614, a Latin translation of Florimond de Raemond's history of the Reformation appeared in Cologne. Raemond, like his friend Michel de Montaigne, read Ronsard's poems against the Reformers and, like Montaigne, cited them in his own work. Raemond had cited six extracts from Ronsard in his *Histoire de l'heresie,* and they are rendered into rather laborious Latin by an unnamed translator. Four of the six translated passages are from poems by Ronsard against the Reformers, and there is again a highly apposite integration of Ronsard's own defence of the Catholic faith into the work of another polemicist.[14] The total length of the Latin text is 41 lines.

I can add just one more item to McFarlane's list of manuscript translations. It is a highly interesting one, since the poem by Ronsard upon which it is based is lost. It is titled *In tumulum cordis Francisci Lothareni Ducis Guisiaci Ex Gallico P. Ronsardi,* and reads as follows:

> Guisiade iacet hic Francisci cor Lothareni,
>   Illius invicti magnanimique ducis.
> Cor, Gallorum in quo vitae spes omnis, et omnis
>   Spes rebus dubiis certa salutis erat.
> Cor nunquam trepidans ad aliqua pericula, et hostes
>   Usque sua cogens vis trepidare metu.
> Cor, quod pro patriisque focis dum pugnat et aris
>   Vi vincens, victis victima fraude cadit.
> Tale cor haud iacet hic breve mole, sed ampla capaxque
>   Omnis vertutis consiliiique domus.
> Denique cor iacet hic centena quod intus habebat
>   Corda sua, et populi non numeranda sui,
> Hoc quae cuncta uno cum corde sepulta iacerent
>   Si possent uno cuncta iacere loco.
> Quod quia non licuit, non cor, sed cordis inanis
>   Umbra sub hoc vacuo marmore clausa latet.
> At cor Guisiaci verum Ducis omnia corda
>   Gallorum, vera et viva sepulchra tegunt.

The manuscript, which is in the Bibliothèque Nationale in Paris, does not identify the translator.[15] It is very plausible that Ronsard did indeed compose the epitaph on which this translation is based, for two other epitaphs of François de Guise by him are known.[16] The assassination of Guise in 1563 was an important political event (he had been a member of the Catholic "Triumvirate" which opposed the Reformers in the Civil War of 1562), and so we have here another politically-motivated translation.

The texts we have reviewed are "new" translations of Ronsard which I have been able to locate. Two others can be shown to have existed, but have so far eluded me. A first, a translation of *L'Hydre deffaict,* is mentioned by McFarlane, but he refers only to a footnote in Laumonier's *Ronsard poète lyrique* where the trail ends, since no source is cited there for the existence of the translation.[17] However, there is evidence that this translation existed, and it is the passage in Ronsard, mentioned earlier, expressing pride in Latin and Greek versions of the poem. The obvious place to look for these translations is the collection of Greek, Latin and French poems in which the *Hydre* itself was first published, but it does not contain them.[18]

A second translation of Ronsard which undoubtedly existed is Charles Utenhove's version of Ronsard's elegy dedicated to Paul de Foix. Evidence that it existed is threefold. Firstly, in a sonnet in his *Xenia* of 1568, Utenhove suggests the immortality of Ronsard's elegy to Foix would be assured by Greek and Latin versions (though, conscious no doubt of Ronsard's feelings, he hastily added that Ronsard's French would be immortal anyway).[19] Secondly, Ronsard published the elegy in his *Elegies, Mascarades et Bergerie* (1565), a book designed to improve relations between France and England (Foix was an ambassador in England), and Utenhove, who lived in England, undertook a similar assignment in his *Xenia* (1568): nothing is more plausible than that Utenhove should have translated Ronsard's praise of the ambassador for an English audience.[20] Thirdly, and conclusively, a letter from Utenhove to Ronsard says he is sending him a translation of an elegy dedicated to Foix.[21] It is very curious that it was not published in the 1568 *Xenia.*

Among the reasons why so many contemporaries translated Ronsard, two are highly significant.[22] One is that the content of Ronsard's poems was very often felt to be sufficiently important, on political or religious grounds, to require translation. Indeed, this paper, by drawing attention to many new translations of political and religious works, has significantly altered McFarlane's profile of the *corpus* of translations—especially when one bears in mind that many of the new translations mentioned here are of very long poems. And the second motivation for translations is the fascination with the poet's own excellence, the desire to emulate an acknowledged master, the feeling that translation of such a gifted poet could only extend and refine one's own talents. One of the translators we have looked at, Scévole de Sainte-Marthe, develops this thought in a poem about his translations of Ronsard:

Ad Petrum Ronsardum

Aemula dum Latiis Ronsardi Gallica nostri
    Conor ego in Latios vertere scripta modos,

> Me vis maior agit solito, ignotasque per aeres
>   Abripit hinc tanti spiritus ille viri.
> Quique prius proprio cum plectra furore moverem,
>   Vix bene sum notae serpere visus humi,
> Summa feror super astra: iuvat quoscunque poëtas
>   Despicere, & sacri pectinis esse patrem.
> Sic olim aetheriis aquilae dum Regulus alis
>   Suscipitur, reliquas despicit altus aves.[23]

Thus, while Latin translations contributed powerfully to the international renown of Ronsard, they did no less for the renown of his translators.

Royal Holloway and Bedford New College, London

Notes

1. See Ronsard, *Oeuvres complètes,* ed. P. Laumonier, I. Silver, and R. Lebèque (S.T.F.M.), 20 vols. (Paris, 1914–1975), 1:73 (cf. 77), 204; 2:99–100; and cf. 1:165, 3:161 (references to Ronsard here, unless otherwise indicated, are to this edition), and my edition of his *Discours des miseres* (T.L.F., Genève, 1979), pp. 203–4, note to line 1022.

2. Ronsard 17:22.

3. See I. D. McFarlane, "Pierre de Ronsard and the Neo-Latin Poetry of His Time," *Res Publica Litterarum,* 1 (1978):192, who notes a contemporary comment on a translation of Ronsard by Antoine de Gouvea: ". . . in qua vel Ronsardo iudice Gallicas elegantias salesque non aequavit modo, sed superavit." Coming from Ronsard, that is praise indeed. The translation is titled *Antrum Maedonium ex Gallico Ronsardi expressum.*

4. McFarlane, 203–5; see also P. Bergman, "Les poésies manuscrites de François et Raphaël Thorius," *Mélanges Paul Thomas* (Bruges, 1930), pp. 29–38.

5. The pamphlet (published in Paris by André Wechel) also contains a poem by Dorat titled *Ad Ronsardum et eius Musas* ("Vestrum erat, ô Musae, pacem suadere, nec arma [. . .]." The copy I used is in the Bibliothèque Nationale, Paris (Ye 494); others are mentioned in A. Pereire's "Bibliographie des oeuvres de Ronsard," *Bulletin du Bibliophile,* nouv. sér. (1939), 18:211, n. 3, and there is one at Harvard University. The translation begins, "Quod dudum optastis contingere tempus, id ultro [. . .]." For the French text, see Ronsard, 9:1–11 and cf. ix–x.

6. Copies are in the Bibliothèque Nationale, Paris (Rés. Ye 1136 and Inv. Yc. 1759) and British Library (11474 h 27 [12]); see my article, "An Early Edition of a *Discours* by Ronsard," *Bibliothèque d'Humanisme et Renaissance,* 28 (1966): 682–84.

7. The book was published in Paris. I used the British Library's copy (241 k 27 [1]). The translation of Ronsard is at 101vo; the original is in Ronsard, 10:80 (*Second livre des meslanges,* 1559). The translation is mentioned by Guillaume Colletet: see his *Traitté de l'épigramme et Traitté du sonnet,* ed. P. A. Jannini (Genève and Paris, 1965), pp. 237 and 241–42 (the page reference in Sainte-Marthe which Jannini gives is erroneous).

8. See C. Faisant, "Un des aspects de la réaction humaniste à la fin du XVIe siècle: la paraphrase latine des poètes français," in P. Tuynman, G. C. Kuiper and E. Kess-

ler, eds., *Acta Coventus neo-Latini Amstelodamensis* (München, 1979), p. 365 and notes 19 and 20. Faisant does not give the date of publication of Sainte-Marthe's *Poetica paraphrasis* (where, he notes, the *Franciade* translations are at 37vo). The poem which prefaced the *Franciade* translations (*In versos aliquot . . .*), and of which he cites a short passage, is the one published in collected editions of Sainte-Marthe with the title *Ad Petrum Ronsardum* (see note 23). The *Franciade* translations are not in the later editions of Sainte-Marthe that I have consulted (*Les oeuvres,* Paris, 1579, B.L. 640 k 3 [2]; *Poemata,* Augustoriti Pictonum, 1596, Bibliothèque Nationale Yc 1698; *Poemata et Elogia,* Augustoriti Pictonum, 1606, B.L. C 65 bb15; and *Opera latina et gallica,* Lutetiae Parisiorum, 1633, B.L. C 108 e3).

9. See Ronsard, 15:85; 18:489-90 and, for Sainte-Marthe's admiration for Ronsard, P. de Nolhac, *Ronsard et l'humanisme* (Paris, 1966), pp. 194-96 and 240-42.

10. He points this out when introducing the first translation, and in a manuscript not at the beginning of the British Library's copy. On Faye's book (Lutetiae, 1571, B.L. C 46 c 7), see the late D. P. Walker's excellent book, *Unclean Spirits: Possession and Exorcism in France and England in the late sixteenth and early seventeenth centuries* (London 1981), pp. 19-28. It was Professor Walker who drew my attention to Faye's translations of Ronsard. They are found respectively on pages 172-73 and 396 of Faye's book, and they are of lines 351-68 of the *Continuation* and 185-90 of the *Remonstrance* (pages 99-100 and 114 respectively in my edition of Ronsard's *Discours*).

11. The publication appeared under an Edinburgh imprint and in two parts. I used the British Library's copy (1059 a 11 [1]); the translation of Ronsard, with a commentary on the supposed meaning of the passages, is in t.I, 75-81. The tract has been attributed to F. Hotman and H. Daneau jointly (see an article by M. Ishigami in *Bulletin de la Société des amis de Montaigne,* 1976) and to N. Barnaud (see Haag, *La France protestante,* 2e éd., I, 844). A French version also appeared (*Le resveille-matin des François et de leurs voisins, composé par Eusèbe philadelphe cosmopolite en forme de dialogues,* 2t. [Edimbourg, 1574], B.L. 1059 b 18 [1]); it contains Ronsard's original French (109-14).

12. The passages are from the fourth book of the *Franciade,* successively lines 1557-68; 1599-1626; 1633-50; 1324-68; 1379-82; 1423-32 and 1439-46 (all in vol. 16 of Laumonier's S.T.F.M. edition). On the interpretation of these passages as satire of Charles IX and Catherine, see F. Charbonnier, *La Poésie française et les guerres de religion (1560-1574)* (Paris, 1920), pp. 353-59; K. Cameron, "Ronsard and Book IV of the *Franciade,*" *Bibliothèque d'Humanisme et Renaissance,* 32 (1970): 395-406; and N. Cazauran, "La 'tragique peinture' du premier dialogue du *Réveille-matin*" in *Etudes seiziémistes offertes à V. L. Saulnier* (Genève, 1980): 336-38.

13. On Ronsard's allusiveness, see my article, "The Hidden Meaning of Ronsard's *Hymne de l'Hyver,*" in *French Renaissance Studies in Honor of Isidore Silver* (Lexington, 1974), pp. 85-97 and studies mentioned there.

14. See *Historia de ortu, progressu et ruina haereseon huius saeculi,* 2 t. (Coloniae, 1614), B.L. 4571 b 10. The translations of Ronsard are as folllows: 1:127, a translation of Ronsard, 11:172; 2:197, translation of Ronsard, 12:180, lines 155-65 (ending at "Vivent après leur mort"); 2:209, translation of 12:181, lines 179-84; 2:378, translation of 11:84, lines 397-400; 2:380, translation of 11:23, lines 79-80; and 2:419-20, translation of 11:47-48, lines 201-8. The original passages from Ronsard's *Discours* are found also in my edition, pages 208, 125, 66 and 90. The translations of Ronsard were doubtless done by the translator of the whole book, whom I cannot identify (the publisher, in a prefatory note, simply says "totum hoc opus in Latinam linguam [. . .] ut converteretur atque hac forma excuderetur curavi"). The undeserved neglect from which Raemond suffers will in due course be rectified by Lionel Swain's London Ph.D. thesis.

[217]

15. Manuscrits latins, 8139,121^{vo}.

16. See the *Prosopopée de feu François de Lorreine duc de Guise* (13:299–300) and an *Epitaphe de François de Lorraine, duc de Guyse* (18:334–35).

17. See McFarlane, 204, footnote, and P. Laumonier, *Ronsard poète lyrique*, 2e éd. (Paris, 1923), p. 243, n. 3. These scholars attribute the translation to Dorat, but I do not know on what evidence.

18. The work is *Paeanes Sive Hymni in triplicem victoriam, felicitate Caroli IX. Galliarum Regis invictissimi, et Henrici fratris, Ducis Andegavensis virtute partam*, Ioanne Aurato et aliis doctis poëtis auctoribus (Lutetiae, 1569), Houghton Library, Harvard, FC5. D 7267. 569 p.

19. See his *Xenia, seu Ad illustrium aliquot Europae hominum nomina, Allusionum liber primus* (Basiliae Rauracorum, 1568), B.L. 11475 b 44, p. 85.

20. On the diplomatic role of the *Elegies, Mascarades et Bergerie,* see my "Ronsard and Queen Elizabeth I," *Bibliothèque d'Humanisme et Renaissance,* 29 (1967): 93–119.

21. See Nolhac, *Ronsard et L'humanisme,* 217–18. The relationship between Ronsard and Utenhove is discussed by W. Janssen in *Charles Utenhove, sa vie et son oeuvre (1536–1600)* (Maastricht, 1939), 31–35, but although he declares (32) that Ronsard translated the elegy to Foix into Latin, he gives no source for this, and none of the manuscripts he cites in his bibliography (75–79) appears to contain it. Utenhove's translation of part of Ronsard's *Discours à Monseigneur le Duc de Savoie* (9:157), published in the *Xenia,* is in McFarlane's list.

22. Scholars have pointed to other reasons for translating Ronsard: the desire to make his poetry available to foreigners, to put his poetry into a "durable" language and help make it immortal, the feeling that Latin was a more appropriate medium for serious subjects, and the simple desire to "show off" (see McFarlane, "Pierre de Ronsard . . .," 197, and cf. G. Demerson, *Dorat et son temps, culture classique et présence au monde* [Paris, 1983], pp. 28–29).

23. *Poemata,* Augustoriti Pictonum (1596), B.Nat. Yc 1698, 230.

RONSARD ET SES CRITIQUES CONTEMPORAINS

par

Malcolm SMITH

Dans la préface de ses *Odes*, de 1550, Ronsard évoque l'accueil déjà réservé à ces poèmes : on prétend qu'il est « vanteur, et glouton de louanges », qu'il ne fait qu'imiter d'autres poètes français, que sa poésie est trop variée, que son orthographe est nouvelle, qu'il flatte les personnalités puissantes, qu'il se sert de mots de dialecte (Lm, I, 43-50 et voir 55). Il donnera une nouvelle liste d'objections dans une ode *A Madame Marguerite*, sœur du roi Henri II, publiée en 1552 (Lm, III, 107). L'Hospital et Muret recensent diverses objections à ses œuvres [1] comme le fera Claude Binet [2]. Il importe de mieux connaître les critiques contemporains de Ronsard, aujourd'hui assez mal connus [3]. J'examine ici trois de leurs plus fréquentes objections.

I. La 'Muse Flatteresse' de Ronsard

Une première objection à Ronsard, c'est qu'il flatte des personnages illustres. Ne va-t-il pas jusqu'à « déifier » les personnes qu'il loue ? Henri II est le « dieu » invoqué au début des *Odes* — et ailleurs [4]. Ce langage, qui est le reflet d'ambitions nationales [5], déplaît au réformateur Théodore de Bèze, qui le dénonce dans la préface de son *Abraham sacrifiant* (1550) [6] et dans un poème de 1551 :

---

[1] Pour L'Hospital, v. *Elegia nomine P. Ronsardi adversus eius obtrectatores et invidos* (Lm, XVIII, 257-262), et pour Muret, v. la préface de son commentaire sur les *Amours* de Ronsard (Lm, V, XXIV).

[2] *La vie de P. de Ronsard (1586)*, éd. P. Laumonier, Paris, 1910, 17-21 et voir un passage de la *Vie de Ronsard* de Colletet (v. F.B. Caldari, *Pierre de Ronsard, ses juges et ses imitateurs*, Paris, 1983, 42-44).

[3] Voir P. Laumonier, *Ronsard poète lyrique*, 2ᵉ éd., Paris, 1923, 70-119 ; M. Raymond, *L'influence de Ronsard sur la poésie française (1550-1585)*, nouv. éd., Genève, 1965, I, 329-357 et, du même auteur, *Bibliographie critique de Ronsard en France (1550-1585)*, Paris, 1927 ; J. Pineaux, *La polémique protestante contre Ronsard*, Paris, 1973 ; M.C. Smith, « A lost Protestant pamphlet against Ronsard », *BHR*, XXXVII, 1975, 73-86.

[4] Lm, I, 63 ; cf. III, 97 ; IX, 50-51 ; X, 43, 66, 339 ; XII, 293, variante ; XIII, 13, 18, 345 ; et H. Chamard, *Histoire de la Pléiade*, 4 v., Paris, 1939-1940, 272-279 ; D. Ménager, *Ronsard : le roi, le poète et les hommes*, Genève, 1979, 156-161.

[5] Françoise Joukovsky, *La Gloire dans la poésie française et néo-latine du XVIᵉ siècle*, Genève, 1969, 197-218 et 177-188.

[6] Bèze, *Correspondance*, éd. H. Aubert, H. Aubert et H. Meylan, I, Genève, 1960, 200-201.

Flattez, mentez, faites du diable un ange :
Vos dieux mourront, vous et votre louange [7].

C'est un écho d'un avertissement biblique [8].

Vers 1560, un réformé anonyme adresse une ode au prince de Condé,
où il déclare :

Strophe 1 :

Je ne veux point que mes vers
Soyent flatteusement couvers
Du manteau de voz louanges :
Et moins veux j'avoir le soing
De les envoyer bien loing
Vers les nations estranges.
Pour un fardeau si pesant,
Mon dos n'est point suffisant :
Et quand bien la suffisance
Le ciel m'auroit octroyé,
Tel bien seroit employé
A plus utile despence. [...]

Strophe 2 :

Car les louanges de Dieu
Obtiendront le premier lieu
Et marcheront les premieres [...] [9].

C'est Ronsard qu'il attaque (il fait écho à l'ode à L'Hospital : Lm, III, 161).

Les catholiques aussi sont offensés par la « flatterie » ronsardienne. Dans
la *Servitude volontaire*, écrit en 1548 et révisée vers 1554, La Boëtie déplore
que les rois de France se soient efforcés « d'accoustumer le peuple envers
eus, non seulement à obeissance et servitude, mais encore à devotion ».
Ces remarques s'accompagnent d'observations sur Ronsard : La Boëtie
l'admire, mais déplore ses louanges hyperboliques [10].

Un autre catholique, Estienne Pasquier, s'adresse au poète en 1555 :

[...] je souhaiterois que ne fissiez si bon marché de vostre plume à hault-
loüer quelques-uns que nous sçavons notoirement n'en estre dignes. Car en
ce faisant, vous me direz qu'estes contraint par leurs importunitez de ce
faire, ores que n'en ayez envie. Je le croy : mais la plume d'un bon poëte
n'est pas telle que l'oreille d'un juge, qui doit donner de mesme balance
audience au mauvais, tout ainsi qu'au bon. Car quant à la plume du poëte,
elle doit estre seulement voüee à la celebration de ceux qui le meritent [11].

Dans la préface des *Odes*, Ronsard anticipait ces objections : « [...] c'est
le vrai but d'un poëte Liriq de celebrer jusques à l'extremité celui qu'il
entreprend de louer » (Lm, I, 48). Pour lui, la louange est un portrait conven-

---

[7] Bèze, *Correspondance, éd. cit.*, I, 210. Sur la date du poème, qui parut avec les
traductions des *Psaumes* à partir de l'édition de 1553, voir les remarques des éditeurs, p. 207.
[8] Voir la *Deuxième épître aux Corinthiens*, XI, 12-15.
[9] Cette *Ode* parut dans l'*Hymne à Dieu, pour la delivrance des Françoys de la plus
que Egyptienne servitude* [...] (s.l.n.d.), B. Nat. Ye 24330, B v r°.
[10] Voir *Œuvres complètes*, éd. P. Bonnefon, Bordeaux et Paris, 1892, 41-44, et cf. un
poème de La Boëtie *In adulatores poetas* (éd. cit., 219).
[11] *Les Lettres*, Paris, 1586, 14 r°.

84

tionnel et idéaliste — où on souligne les qualités que le sujet ne possède pas, et qu'il devrait cultiver. Quand Ronsard affirme que Henri II ne jure pas, c'est pour l'inviter à corriger un vice qu'il possédait notoirement [12]. Sa « louange » de Charles de Lorraine laisse entrevoir un homme irrésolu, évasif, déloyal et peu judicieux [13]. C'est donc en bonne conscience que Ronsard dénonce la flatterie dans une *Elégie au cardinal de Châtillon* (Lm, X, 5-9), de 1559. Et vers ce moment, le thème du châtiment de l'orgueil du prince devient fréquent chez lui [14]...

Dans sa grande polémique avec les réformés (1562 à 1564), Ronsard affecte de croire que les critiques de sa « flatterie » sont uniquement des réformés :

> Voyant cette escriture ils diront en courroux
> Et quoy, ce gentil sot escrit doncq contre nous !
> Il flatte les Seigneurs, il fait d'un diable un ange (Lm, XI, 94).

Plus précisément, c'est une réplique à Bèze, qui avait invoqué le passage biblique sur le diable et l'ange. Ronsard répond ailleurs à l'accusation (Lm, XI, 151-152 ; XII, 6-7), et souligne son refus de flatter Catherine de Médicis et Charles de Lorraine (Lm, XII, 172-188 ; XIII, 3-14 et 15-29). Les réformés dénonçaient sa flatterie avec virulence dans les pamphlets de la première guerre civile — mais ils ne disaient rien de neuf [15].

II. Le poète « païen »

Une deuxième objection à Ronsard : il est « païen » [16]. Là encore, le poète s'est exposé à cette critique dès ses débuts. Il veut passer pour l'inventeur de l'ode (il est « le premier auteur Lirique François » : Lm, I, 44-45) — mais les traductions des *Psaumes* par Marot étaient considérées comme les premières odes écrites en français [17]. Ronsard insiste donc sur ce qui sépare ses *Odes* des *Psaumes* de Marot. Marot avait rejeté le modèle païen, Horace [18] ; Ronsard, « prenant stile apart », suit ostensiblement Horace — et il décida de le faire, dit-il, « dès le même tens que Clement Marot [...] se travailloit à la poursuite de son Psautier » (Lm, I, 44) [19].

---

[12] V. VIII, 14. Sur l'élément de convention dans les louanges, v. Alex Gordon, *Ronsard et la rhétorique*, Genève, 1970, 49-72. Voir aussi Erasme, épîtres 179 et 180 (II, 79, 81-83 dans la traduction de l'Université de Toronto), et cf. V.-L. Saulnier, « Une œuvre inédite de Jacques Peletier du Mans (L'Oraison Funèbre de Henri VIII, 1547) », *BHR*, XI, 1941, 7-27, et J.M. Weiss, « The technique of faint praise : Johann Sturm's *Life of Beatus Rhenanus* », *BHR*, XLIII, 1981, 289-302.

[13] Voir mon livre, *Joachim Du Bellay's veiled victim*, Genève, 1974, 64.

[14] F. Joukovsky, *La gloire* [...], 224.

[15] Voir Pineaux, *Polémique protestante* [...], 4, 108-109, 294, 389-390.

[16] Voir Raymond, *L'influence de Ronsard* [...], I, 329-357 et Guy Demerson, *La Mythologie classique dans l'œuvre lyrique de la Pléiade*, Genève, 1972, 253-274 et 395-453.

[17] Voir Peletier, *L'art poetique* (1555), éd. A. Boulanger, Paris, 1930, 176.

[18] Marot, *Œuvres complètes*, éd. C.A. Mayer, VI, Genève, 1980, 313 :
> Pas ne fault doncq qu'aupres de lui Orace
> Ce mette en jeu s'il ne veult perdre grace.

[19] Sur les rapports entre les *Odes* de Ronsard et les *Psaumes* de Marot, voir M. Jeanneret, *Poésie et tradition biblique au XVIᵉ siècle*, Paris, 1969, 71-76. On opposait volontiers David à Horace (ou à Orphée) : voir Guy Demerson, *La mythologie classique* [...], 253-256.

85

Voilà la carrière de Ronsard lancée sous l'enseigne d'un poète païen. La critique contemporaine s'en ressent. Théodore de Bèze déclare dans la préface de l'*Abraham sacrifiant* que Ronsard aurait dû « chanter un cantique à Dieu » plutôt que de « contrefaire ces fureurs poétiques à l'antique »[20]. Bèze sera suivi par d'autres réformés — Albert Babinot et Jean Tagaut, connus déjà[21], et Yves Rouspeau, auteur d'un *De pace et bello carmen elegiacum* (1556), où un poème liminaire se situe dans le courant antironsardien :

AD PRISCOS ET HUIUS TEMPORIS POËTAS, MENDACIA SCRIBERE SOLITOS

Scribite vaniloqui mendacia vana poëtae,
    Scribite cum fictis somnia ficta diis :
Nil mihi cum vobis, nos vera referre paramus,
    Nullus et in nostra carmine fucus erit.
Non ego Pieridum, nec Phoebi numen adoro,
    Non ego Parnassi numina montis amo.
Qui tenebras noctemque meo de pectore pellet,
    Verus opem nobis Christus Apollo dabit :
Hunc sitio fontem, procul hinc, procul este poëtae
    Qui miseri latices quaerite Aonios.
Solus hic etenim fons, unde poëta repente
    Esse queam, sine quo sudor inanis erit[22].

D'autres réformés, amis du poète, s'opposent à sa muse païenne. Charles Utenhove :

Si tu me crois Ronsard, des poetes la gloire,
Des plus sçavans Ronsard, le plus noble du sang,
Des plus nobles du sang, justement mis au rang
Des plus sçavans aussi par tu vertu notoire.

Si tu me crois Ronsard, tu changeras la Muse
De ton divin esprit à chanter desormais
Les louanges de Dieu plus que ne fis jamais,
A chanter ce grand Roy personne ne s'abuse.

L'ung chantera la Paix, l'ung les champs & les bois,
L'ung sonnera le loz du grand Roy des François,
Ou quelque demi-Dieu de ceste terre basse.

Mais toy favorisé sur tous aultres des Cieulx,
Chanteras desormais le plus grand Dieu des Dieux,
Qui tous Dieux, qui tous Roys, seul Dieu, seul Roy surpasse[23].

[20] Voir sa *Correspondance, éd. cit.,* I, 201.

[21] Voir Raymond, *op. cit.,* I, 333 et 341-342. Raymond range Babinot parmi les auteurs catholiques (I, 329), mais le poète fut converti à la Réforme par Calvin dès 1534 (v. N. W[eiss], « La Christiade d'Albert Babinot », *B.S.H.P.F.,* 37, 1888, 112).

[22] Parisiis, B.L. C 39 f. 24(2), 2. Le thème revient dans deux épigrammes de Rouspeau dans la même plaquette (39). Je remercie David Hartley de m'avoir signalé ce livre.

[23] Voir G. Buchanan, *Franciscanus et fratres, quibus accessere varia eiusdem et aliorum Poëmata* [...], 3 v., Basiliae Rauracorum [1568], B.L. 1213 g 10, III, 84. Sur la religion d'Utenhove, voir W. Janssen, *Charles Utenhove, sa vie et son œuvre (1536-1600),* Maastricht, 1939, 10-14 22, 35, 46-49, 53-55 et 60-61 ; sur ses relations avec Ronsard, v. Janssen, 31-35.

Et Louis Des Masures :

Sus ma muse entonne, & commence
A chanter la haute clemence
Du tout-puissant, du Roy des Rois,
Qui par sa bonté qui abonde
M'a fait (s'il est heur en ce monde)
Par deux fois heureux, voire trois.
Cesse à conter la destinée,
Les erreurs, les guerres d'Enée,
De Dido, l'amour & la mort :
Laisse moy ces fabuleux songes,
L'ondoyante mer de mensonges,
Et tire au plus asseuré port.
L'eternel seul est veritable,
De qui la bonté charitable
Demeure à perpetuité.
Si tost que gemissans nous sommes,
Noz maux il remet à grans sommes,
De sa pure gratuité [24].

Mais des catholiques aussi s'opposent au Ronsard « païen » — Denisot, Jodelle, Muret, Jean Macer [25] et, notamment, Michel de L'Hospital, dans une épître dédiée à Claude Despence :

AD CLAUD[IUM] ESPENCIUM,
NOBILISSIMUM ET DOCTISSIMUM THEOLOGUM, DE POESI CHRISTIANA JUDICIUM ET EXEMPLUM.

Qui, pater ESPENCI, qui fit res carmine sacras
Ut pauci tractent hodie, vix unus et alter,
Vatibus innumeris quum regia perstrepat aula ?
An genus hoc hominum nullos (Epicurus ut olim)
Autumat esse Deos, et rident sacra profani ?
An duram et sterilem fugiunt, neque versibus aptam
Materiem, in qua vix florens et nobile sese
Jactare ingenium, famamque adquirere possit ? [...] [26]

Quelle est la réaction de Ronsard ? Il tâche de désarmer les adversaires. L'*Hercule chrestien* (1553) prétend contenter les « chrestiennes oreilles » [27]. Les *Hymnes* offrent des apologies discrètes des dieux et des mythes païens [28]. Et dans les *Hymnes*, et les poèmes de 1558 à 1560, Ronsard multiplie les échos bibliques [29]. Mais vers 1560, sa patience s'épuise. Dans l'*Elegie à Des*

---

[24] *Œuvres poetiques*, Lion, 1557, B.N. Rés. Ye 366, 43. Des Masures rejette l'inspiration profane aussi dans ses *Vingt Psaumes* [...] (Lion, 1557, B.N. Rés. Ye 368, 3-4) et dans *Babylone ou la Ruine de la Grande Cité* [...] (Genève, 1563, B.L. 698 c 4 (8), A ii v°).
[25] Voir Raymond, *op. cit.*, I, 335-336 et, pour Macer, l'article de Raymond, « Deux pamphlets inconnus contre Ronsard et la Pléiade », *R.S.S.*, 13, 1926, 243-264. Cet article reproduit aussi (255-264) la préface par André de Rivaudeau à la *Christiade* de Babinot, où Rivaudeau attaque la poésie païenne.
[26] *Ad Claud*[ium] *Espencium, nobilissimum et doctissimum theologum, de poesi christiana judicium et exemplum*, dans les *Œuvres complètes* de L'Hospital, éd. P. J. S. Duféy (3 t., Paris, 1724-1825), III, 41.
[27] Voir Ronsard, Lm, VIII, 207-208 et, pour la date de composition, 207, n. 1.
[28] Voir Ronsard, Lm, VIII, 69, 100 et 291-292. Sur la dimension théologique et édifiante des *Hymnes*, voir Guy Demerson, *La Mythologie classique* [...], 404-453.
[29] Voir J. Frappier, « L'inspiration biblique et théologique de Ronsard dans l'*Hymne de la justice* », *Mélanges Chamard*, Paris, 1951, 97-108 et J. Hanks, *Ronsard and biblical tradition*, Tübingen et Paris, 1982, 179.

Masures, il attaque « ceulx de la nouvelle foy » qui l'exhortent à « chanter de Jesuchrist » (Lm, X, 364). En 1563, dans la *Response aux injures*, il dénonce la poésie biblique des réformés, les « chansons » pour « valets de boutique » (Lm, XI, 168 ; cf. 98-99 et XV, 153). Et il multiplie les explications du sens moral des mythes païens [30]. Les réformés, pour leur part, dénoncent avec vigueur son « paganisme » en 1563 et 1564 [31] — mais, là encore, sans rien dire de neuf...

III. Le poète licencieux

Une troisième objection à Ronsard, c'est qu'il écrit des poèmes licencieux — ou simplement, qu'il écrit des poèmes d'amour. Là encore, il est vulnérable, notamment pour avoir publié en 1553 un *Livret de Folastries* qui encourut des objections de la part de Robert de La Haye, Nicholas Denisot et Michel de L'Hospital [32].

Mais Théodore de Bèze n'avait pas attendu les *Folastries* pour critiquer la poésie d'amour. Dans la préface de l'*Abraham sacrifiant* (1550) il attaque la pratique de « petrarquiser un sonnet, et faire l'amoureux transy » [33]. Il vise Peletier et Du Bellay, mais savait sans doute que Ronsard préparait les *Amours* de 1552 [34]. Bèze, auteur d'un recueil célèbre de poèmes érotiques, dénonce fréquemment la poésie d'amour et, nous le verrons, on est parfois sûr qu'il vise Ronsard [35].

Une curieuse lettre datée du 26 août 1559, adressée à Catherine de Médicis et signée D.V. (de Villemadon ?), dénonce Charles de Lorraine, qui aurait détourné Catherine des *Psaumes* de Marot et propagé les « infâmes amours » des « beaux Poëtes du Diable » qui engouffrent leurs lecteurs « [...] en abysme de toute iniquité & désordre, voire de toute impiété ». Cet auteur, un réformé, semble attaquer Ronsard [36].

Mais l'opposition à l'érotisme de Ronsard vient des deux familles religieuses. Jacques Peletier dénonce la poésie d'amour en 1550, dans une *Apologie à Louis Meigret* qui sert de préface au *Dialogue de l'ortografe et prononciation françoise* : il savait certainement que *L'Olive* venait de paraître

[30] Voir mon article, « The hidden meaning of Ronsard's *Hymne de l'Hyver* », dans *Studies in honor of Isidore Silver*, Lexington, Ky., 1947, 85-86.

[31] C'est le thème de la *Remonstrance sur la diversité des Poëtes de nostre temps* [...] (1563 : v. mon édition dans *BHR*, XXXVII, 1975, 73-86), et voir Pineaux, *Polémique protestante* [...], 23, 43-44, 82, 137, 140, 215, 216, 367.

[32] Voir Laumonier, *Ronsard poète lyrique*, 104-105. Mais ce *Livret* fut admiré par Baïf, Muret, Tahureau, Magny et Pasquier (*ibid.*).

[33] *Correspondance*, éd. cit., I, 200-201.

[34] Sur l'amitié de Peletier et Bèze, voir N. Z. Davis, « Peletier and Beza part company », *Studies in the Renaissance*, XI, 1964, 188-222. Peletier publia des traductions de douze sonnets de Pétrarque : voir ses *Œuvres poétiques*, éd. L. Séché et P. Laumonier, Paris, 1904, 74-79. Le recueil pétrarquiste de Du Bellay, *L'Olive*, parut en 1549.

[35] Voir un poème écrit pendant ses années d'études à Orléans (v. F. Aubert, J. Broussard et H. Meylan, « Un premier recueil de poésies latines de Théodore de Bèze », *BHR*, XV, 1953, 170) et un *Double sonnet à Pierre de Courcelles*, écrit entre 1561 et 1564 (*Correspondance*, éd. H. Aubert, H. Meyland, A. Dufour et A. Tripet, t. IV (1562-1563), 295). Voir aussi note 45 de cette communication.

[36] Voir V.-L. Saulnier, « Autour de la lettre dite de Villemadon », *BHR*, XXXVIII, 1975, 349-376. J'ai utilisé l'édition dans les *Mémoires de Condé*, 6 v., Londres, 1743, I, 620-629.

88

et que Ronsard préparait les *Amours* [37] ... Et en 1554, l'auteur d'un recueil de *Chansons tressalutaires et catholiques* déclare :

> Armes ou amours descrire
> N'est pas mon intention.
> Je veux louer sur ma lyre
> L'eternel dieu de Sion
> Qui des cieux où il reside
> Tire à mon esprit la bride
> Et me dit que desormais
> Il ne faut plus que je chante
> Chose lascive ou meschante
> Mais sa louange à jamais.

Son but, déclare-t-il dans son *Epitre aux lecteurs*, est de « [...] donner entrée aux excellentz poetes d'immiter son entreprinse, et de vous degouster des chansons pleines d'impudicitéz, qui corrumpent bonnes mœurs ». Dans une de ses chansons, l'auteur anonyme déclare :

> Changeons propos, c'est trop chanté d'amours ;
> C'est pour gens lourds, qui n'ont sens en la teste,
> Nuls bons chrestiens n'ont à Venus recours
> Ains avec pleurs font à dieu leur requeste.

Parmi les « excellents poètes », cet auteur a dû songer à Ronsard, le plus « excellent » de tous, qui venait justement de publier ses *Folastries* [38].

Et la réaction de Ronsard ? Dans la *Continuation des Amours* (1555), il évoque la réception accordée aux *Folastries* : « chacun dit [...] que je me dements parlant trop bassement » (Lm, VII, 115). Dans la *Nouvelle Continuation des Amours* (1556), il a l'air de chanter la palinodie pour les *Folastries* (Lm, VII, 229-230 ; cf. 315-316). Dans un *Chant pastoral* (1559), il rapporte des reproches que L'Hospital lui aurait adressés (Lm, IX, 88). Dans la polémique de la première guerre civile, Ronsard prétend que les adversaires de sa poésie d'amour étaient uniquement des réformés (Lm, X, 364) ; et les pamphlétaires réformés, pour leur part, poursuivent avec vigueur l'accusation [39].

IV. Conclusion

Après 1564, Ronsard continue à faire des concessions à la critique. Le poète « flatteur » émet l'opinion que l'élégie doit être courte (Lm, XVIII, 246), il attaque la vie abjecte du courtisan (Lm, XV, 78-82 et XVIII, 100-101),

---

[37] Voir I. Silver, *The intellectual evolution of Ronsard*, I, *The formative influences*, St. Louis, 1969, 165. Silver se trompe (165, n. 1) sur la date de publication, qui est du 5 janvier 1550 n.s. Une amitié étroite lia Peletier et Bèze avant la conversion de Bèze à la réforme (v. Davis, « Peletier and Beza [...] », 188).

[38] Rouen, 1554, B.L. 11475 a 8, verso de la page de titre, A iii r° et 21 v°. D'autres catholiques s'opposent au Ronsard érotique : Denisot et Robert de La Haye (cf. P. Laumonier, *Ronsard poète lyrique*, éd. cit., 105 et n. 2) ; Jean Macer (v. Raymond, « Deux pamphlets inconnus [...] », 245-254) ; sans doute aussi Michel Fouqué (voir *La vie [...] de nostre Seigneur Jesus Christ* [...], Paris, 1574, B.L. 850 c 1, 11, 12, première éd. 1561). Voir aussi les *Discours non plus melancoliques que divers*, Poitiers, 1557, B.L. Hirsch I, 593, p. 66).

[39] Voir Pineaux, *Polémique protestante* [...], 109, 111, 149, et cf. 23, 108, 167, 178, 181, 311, 508-511.

et surtout se transforme en poète satirique[40]. Le poëte « païen », vers la fin de sa vie, veut « escrire plusieurs œuvres Chrestiennes », il laisse un fragment d'un poème de la *Loy divine* (Lm, XVIII, 293-295), et meurt en dictant des méditations chrétiennes (Lm, XVIII, 173-182). Le poète « licencieux » opère de nombreuses suppressions dans ses éditions collectives, par exemple dans les *Folastries*.

Après 1564, les adversaires du poète sont presque uniquement des réformés. Innocent Gentillet[41] et Théodore Agrippa d'Aubigné[42] semblent dénoncer sa flatterie. Henri Estienne attaque dans ses *Deux dialogues du nouveau langage françois italianizé* (1578) le langage païen de la Pléiade[43], et en 1579 un polémiste réformé, François de L'Isle, reprend le grief de « Villemadon » pour attaquer « Ronsard, Jodelle, Baïf et autres vilains poëtes » qui auraient supplanté les *Psaumes* de Marot avec leurs « vilaines chansons et lascive musique »[44]. Bèze, dans la préface de l'édition de 1569 de *ses Poemata* — édition expurgée, bien sûr —, dénonce les poètes lascifs, y compris Ronsard[45]. Du côté catholique, Ronsard ne trouve désormais que des admirateurs : Paul de Foix trouve en lui un adversaire de la flatterie[46] ; Montaigne suit Ronsard en condamnant la poésie des réformés, les chansons pour « garçons de boutique » (*Essais*, I, lvi) et il défend la poésie d'amour (*Essais*, III, ix) ; et les auteurs des oraisons funèbres de Ronsard le présentent comme un héros de la réforme catholique[47]. Après la première guerre civile, donc, les réactions à Ronsard reflètent la divergence religieuse.

Concluons : 1) ces controverses engagent des auteurs de grande importance ; 2) la polémique de Ronsard avec les réformés des années 1560 à 1564 se situe dans un contexte historique qui, largement, l'explique et d'où on ne devrait plus la séparer ; 3) on connaît un peu mieux la personnalité de Ronsard — souple, intègre, alerte, judicieux, spirituel... Surtout, on connaît sa sensibilité à la critique, et la combativité qui le poussait à vaincre des adversaires vaillants et, ce faisant, à triompher des siècles.

Université de Londres.

[40] Il obtient de Charles IX la permission d'écrite des satires de la Cour (Lm, XVII, 90), et il dénonce la sodomie d'Henri III (Lm, XVIII, 415-417). Beaucoup de ses satires sont perdues : voir mon article, « Lost works by Ronsard' », dans *The Library*, 6th series, VIII, 1986, 109-126.

[41] Voir *Discours contre Machiavel*, éd. A. D'Andrea et P.D. Stewart, Firenze, 1974, 78.

[42] Voir *Les Tragiques*, II, *Princes*, notamment 85-120 et 949-956, où Aubigné reprend l'accusation que les flatteurs transforment le diable en ange, et où il semble faire allusion au *Discours des vertus intellectuelles et morales*, de Ronsard, prononcé en présence du roi Henri III (Lm, XVIII, 451-460).

[43] Voir Silver, *Intellectual evolution* [...], 95-96.

[44] Voir *La legende de Charles cardinal de Lorraine*, Reims, 1579, B.L. 804 a 2 (1), 20 v°-21 r°. Selon Saulnier, L'Isle « se contente de recopier à peu près un bon passage de la lettre de Villemadon » (*art. cit.*, 369).

[45] Voir sa *Correspondance*, éd. H. Aubert, A. Dufour, C. Chimelli et B. Nicollier, t. X (1569), Genève, 1980, 92. Un poème *In quosdam poetas* publié avec les *Poemata* en 1582 (Genève, B.L. 1213, f. 5) semble viser Ronsard (a v r°-v°) ; cf. le début de la *Sylva III* (p. 74 dans cette même édition).

[46] Voir sa lettre au secrétaire de la reine Elizabeth d'Angleterre, que j'ai publiée dans « Ronsard and queen Elizabeth I » (*BHR*, XXIX, 1967, 96, n. 18).

[47] Voir J. Velliardus, *Petri Ronsardi Poetae Gallici laudatio funebris* [...], Parisiis, 1586, B. Nat. Ln 27 17840, 16 r°-v° ; G. Crittonius *Laudatio funebris habitat in exequiis Petri Ronsardi* [...], Lutetiae, 1586, B. Nat. Ln 27 17841, 7 ; et cf. F.A. Yates, *The French Academies in the sixteenth century*, London, 1947, IX, 177-198.

90

NOTES ET DOCUMENTS

JANUS VITALIS REVISITED

In 1977, I published in *Revue de Littérature Comparée* an article on the very famous epigram by Janus Vitalis which observes that Rome cannot be found in Rome, since the great ancient city is now but ruins – and which invites the reader to reflect that while the monuments of Rome have perished, the Tiber alone remains. The article gave the text and twelve variant versions of the epigram, and cited a further eighteen poems written in emulation of it (or of the adaptation by Joachim Du Bellay) in the sixteenth and seventeenth centuries in Latin, French, English, Spanish and Polish. My purpose here is to bring to light further derivatives of Vitalis's poem which date from that period, taking the known total of poems in this remarkable tradition to twenty-eight and adding Greek, German and Italian to the languages represented [1].

1. See " Looking for Rome in Rome : Janus Vitalis and his disciples ", *Revue de Littérature Comparée*, 51, 1977, p. 510-527. G.H. Tucker has recently published the earliest known version of Vitalis's epigram, which appeared in 1552 in his *Romanae Ecclesiae Elogia* :

ROMA PRISCA

Qui Romam in media quaeris novus advena Roma,
   Et Romam in Roma vix reperis media,
Aspice murorum moles, praeruptaque saxa,
   Obrutaque horrenti vasta Theatra situ,
Haec sunt Roma, viden velut ipsa cadavera tantae
   Urbis, adhuc spirent imperiosa minas ?
Vicit ut haec mundum, nisa est se vincere, vicit,
   A se non victum ne quid in orbe foret,
Nunc victa in Roma Roma illa invicta sepulta est,
   Atque eadem victrix, victaque Roma fuit,
Albula Romani restabat nominis index,
   Quin etiam fugit ille citis non rediturus aquis ;
Disce hinc quid possit Fortuna, immota labascunt
   Et quae perpetuo sunt agitata, manent.

Tucker argued that this text is superior to the one which appeared the following year in Venice (see *R.L.C.*, 1977, p. 513, n. 6), but in my view he mistakenly dwells on the latter's misprints at the expense of important variants which were retained by subsequent editors. An interesting fact Tucker draws attention to is that in the 1553 publication, *Roma prisca* is the first half of a diptych, the other half being a poem titled *Roma instaurata*. See " Sur les *Elogia* (1553) de Janus Vitalis et les *Antiquitez de Rome* de Joachim Du Bellay ", *Bibliothèque d'Humanisme et Renaissance*, XLVII, 1985, p. 103-112.

1. JOANNES METELLUS. The following poem is attributed to
" Joannes Metellus Sequanus " in the anthology by Franciscus Sweertius,
*Selectae christianae orbis Deliciae ex Urbibus, Templis, Bibliothecis, et
aliunde* (Coloniae Agrippinae, 1625, British Library, London, 604 b 18,
p. 15) :

> Mors venit et saxis, tacitisque senescitur annis :
>   Sic venit et claris urbibus atra dies.
> Quis Romam in media iam quaereret, en ego Roma !
>   Haec vetus in nostra tota sepulta iacet.
> Nec quicquam superest, quam quas mirere ruinas,
>   Tempore quodque mori vivere morte queat.
> Scilicet annosa ut quercus celsissima crevit,
>   Postque cadit, victa haec tempore Roma fuit.
> Urbibus at certis, post funera vita resurgit,
>   Sedibus aut migrant omine forte suo.

Metellus's immediate source is probably Du Bellay rather than Vitalis,
for the second part of the poem employs the comparison found in Du
Bellay's *Antiquitez* (sonnet 28) between Rome and an ageing oak tree[1].

2. LAURENT LE BRUN. The following adaptation appeared in Nico-
laus Mercier's *De conscribendo epigrammate* (Paris, 1653, B.L. 11405 bb
25, p. 246-247) :

CUR ROMA EVERSA FUERIT, ET FLUVIUS ALBULA SIVE TIBERIS
PERMANSERIT
> Quid veterem Romam Roma in praesente requiris ?
>   In media Roma Roma sepulta iacet.
> Palluit extinctum signis tabentibus aurum,
>   Romam multa dies fecerat, una tulit.
> Romani Imperii solus manet Albula testis :
>   Mobilibus favit mobile tempus aquis.
> Firma ruunt, dum fluxa manent, et dispare sorte
>   Lapsa est urbs stabilis, labilis unda stetit.
> Quid non aequales ambo traxere ruinas ?
>   Est Saturnus edax, sed fugit esse bibax.

Le Brun uses the tradition freely, but his point about Rome being
buried in Rome points to Vitalis rather than Du Bellay as his source[2].

3. JACQUES GRÉVIN. My earlier article reproduced one of Jacques
Grévin's *Sonnets sur Rome* written in Vitalis's tradition. Another collection by Grévin, the second book of the *Gelodacrye* of 1561, has a sonnet
developing the Vitalian theme that while great cities die, their rivers flow
on perennially (*Théâtre complet et poésies choisies*, ed. L. Pinvert, Paris,
1922, p. 341) :

---

1. I have not been able to identify Metellus : the epithet " Sequanus " indicates he
was a Frenchman. Sweertius's anthology contains also Vitalis's epigram and the adaptation
by Andreas Frusius which I published in 1977 (and which has also been attributed to
Fulvius Cardulus : see *R.L.C.*, 1977, p. 515).
2. On Le Brun (1608-1663), a jesuit poet, see A. and A. de Backer and A. Carayon,
Bibliothèque de la Compagnie de Jésus, nouv. éd. par C. Sommervogel, 9 v., Bruxelles,
Paris, 1890-1909, IV, 1629-32.

O mélange du monde ! ô mondaine inconstance !
  O monde, mais immonde ! ô grand tout, mais un rien !
  O le monde nouveau ! ô le monde ancien !
  O tous deux parangons de certaine impuissance !
Que tien-tu dedans toy qui tienne une constance
  Sinon cest élément, qui ha moins de moyen
  De garder entre tous l'accoustumé maintien,
  Et qui semble de soy faire moins résistance ?
Troye, le grand tombeau de la Grèce féconde,
  Et Romme, la tremeur du demeurant du monde,
  D'eux-mesmes ont esté en la fin le tombeau.
Le Xante est demouré, le Tybre coule encore :
  Voylà pourquoy, BORDAT, maintenant, je déplore
  Ce monde, ne voyant qu'asseurance dans l'eau.

As with the poem in the *Sonnets sur Rome,* it is difficult to say whether Grévin's source is Vitalis or Du Bellay. The formula, " Romme, la tremeur du demeurant du monde ", is closer to Vitalis's " Vicit ut haec mundum... " than to Du Bellay ; and the expression of the idea that Rome lies buried is closer to Vitalis. On the other hand, the exclamation, " ô mondaine inconstance " and the phrase " faire résistance " look like textual echoes of Du Bellay. That Grévin did borrow very heavily from Du Bellay is now well documented in a recent study by Kathryn Evans, and it seems on balance that his model here is the French poet[1].

4. LUIS MARTIN DE LA PLAZA. This poem, found in a manuscript dated 1611, is in *Segunda parte de las Flores de poetas ilustres de España,* ordenada por D. Juan Antonio Calderón, anotada por D. Juan Quirós de los Ríos y D. Francisco Rodríguez Marín, Sevilla, 1896, p. 129 (n° 78) :

A ROMA

  Peregrino, que, en medio della, á tiento
Buscas á Roma, y de la ya señora
Del orbe, no hallas rastro : mira y llora
De sus muros por tierra el fundamento.
  Arcos, termas, teatros, cuyo asiento
Cubre yerba, esto es Roma. ¿Ves ahora
Cómo, aun muerta, respira vencedora
Las amenazas de su antiguo aliento ?
  Triunfó del mundo ; y porque no quedara
Algo en él por vencer, vencióse, y yace,
Quedando el Tibre, que su gloria hereda.
  De la fortuna en el poder repara :
Aquélla, que era firme, se deshace ;
Y aquéste, que se mueve, firme queda.

This sonnet is based on Vitalis rather than Du Bellay, for it has Vitalis's image, not found in Du Bellay, of the dead Rome breathing threats.

---

1. See K. J. Evans, *A study of the life and literary works of Jacques Grévin with special reference to his relationship with the Pléiade poets* (London University Ph. D., 1983). Kathryn Evans is at present working on the much-needed edition of Grévin's complete poetry.

5. LUÍS VÉLEZ DE GUEVARA. This sonnet is also in *Segunda parte de las Flores de poetas ilustres de España,* p. 200 (n° 134) :

> Turbias aquas del Tíber, que habéis sido
> De puentes y arcos mármoles triunfales
> Para mirarse espejos y cristales,
> Donde como Narcisos han caído :
> Ya vuestras aguas son las del olvido,
> Pues destos edificios principales
> Las piedras, los cimientos, las señales
> Habéis en las arenas escondido.
> Y sólo una señal, sólo un cimiento
> En un ramanso escasamente asoma
> De aquella puente que os sirvió de yugo.
> Por vos quedó en el mundo el sentimiento ;
> Mucho ayudáis al tiempo contra Roma,
> Pues que sois de sus fábricas verdugo.

This poem uses the tradition so freely that one cannot identify the direct source.

6. GIROLAMO PRETI. This sonnet is in his *Poesie,* Bologna, 1644 (B.L. 11429 aa 44 (1), p. 128) :

ROVINE DI ROMA ANTICA
> Qui fu quella d'Imperio antica Sede,
> Temuta in pace, e trionfante in guerra.
> Fu : perch'altro, che il loco hor non si vede.
> Quella, che Roma fu, giace sotterra.
> Queste, cui l'herba copre, e calca il piede,
> Fur Moli al Ciel vicine, ed hor son terra.
> Roma, ch'il Mondo vinse, al Tempo cede,
> Che i piani inalza, e che l'altezze atterra.
> Roma in Roma non è. Vulcano, e Marte
> La grandezza di Roma a Roma han tolta,
> Struggendo l'opre e di Natura, e d'Arte.
> Voltò sossopra il Mondo, e'n polve è volta :
> E trà queste ruine a terra sparte
> In sè stessa cadeo morta, e sepolta.

This is a free use of the tradition and it does not seem possible to identify the direct source [1].

7. MARTIN OPITZ. The following poem is found in a compilation titled *Florilegium variorum epigrammatum Martinus Opitius ex vetustis ac recentioribus poetis congessit et versibus Germanisticis reddidit* (Francofurti, 1634, B.L. 11517 e 18 (2), p. 34) :

AUSS DIE VERWÜRSTETE STADT ROM
> Rom der du Rom in Rom jetzt suchst O neuer Gast
> Und mitten doch in Rom Rom nicht zu finden hast !

---

1. The sonnet by Preti (1582-1626) also appears in *Il Sonetto, Cinquecento sonetti dal Duecento al Novecento,* a cura di G. Getto e di E. Sanguineti, Milano, 1980, p. 322. No echo of Vitalis's epigram is found in another prospective Italian " quarry ", the *Sonetti romani* of Bernardino Baldi (1553-1617).

Schaue an der Maueren Werck die ungeheueren Steine
Die Lustspielhäuser hier so bloss noch stehn im Scheine :
  Diss ist Rom. Sihst du nicht wie noch diss Aass der Stadt
  Der Abraum gleichsam dreuet und leben in sich hat ?
Die Welt war nun erlegt Rom wolt' auch sich erlegen
Damit nichts vuerlegt zu sehn sei allerwegen.
  Ach ! Das die Siegerinn in der besiegten ligt !
  Rom ein Rom ist es nur das hat und war besiegt.
Die Tiber die noch Rom von Namen zeiget bleibet
Der Fluss so diesen Tag sein Wasser Seewerts treibet.
  Was tan dess Glückes macht ! Was standhaft ist vergeht ;
  Und was ohn unterlass bewegt wird das besteht.

This is a translation of Vitalis and was published with the text of the original.

8 and 9 JOANNES COTTUNIUS. The following Greek and Latin versions appeared in
'Ελληνικῶν ἐπιγραμμάτων βιβλία δύο, *Graecorum epigrammatum libri duo cum eiusdem versione latina,* Patavii, B.L. 11405 bbb 19, p. 63-64 :

Περὶ τῆς ἀρχαίας Ῥώμης

Πῆ κεδνα σεῦ πολίεθρα ; πῆ ἔνδιον ἔσκεν ἀνάκτων ;
  Πῆ σοβαροῦ κόσμου κάλλεα ἀμφεχύθη ;
Τοῦτο θέατρον ἔη, τῆδ' ἔτρεχε φῦλα λατίνων,
  Τῆ χρυσους κονίη αμφεκάλυψε δόμους.
'Εγγυτερον τῆ δέρκε πελωριος ἄστρα κολοσσος
  Νυν σαφα νητριεκέως οὐκ ἐδαην ἐνεπειν
Τῆδ', ἤ τῆ καπιτώλιον, ἄ τί Νέρωνος ἐνιψω
  'Ευδμήτων λοετρῶν τείχεα, καί λιβάδας ;
Τῶνδ' ἐν σῶον ὀρόω, ἕλκειν Θιμβριν ῥοον. ἔρρει
  'Εμπεδα, ὅς δὲ ῥεει, ἔμπεδος αὐθι μένει.

DE ANTIQUA ROMA

Ubi praeclara tua civica aedificia ? ubi palatium Regum ?
  Ubi superborum ornamentorum pulchritudo dispersa est ?
Hoc erat theatrum, hic gentes cursitabant Latinorum,
  Hic aureas domos pulvis usquequaque obtexit.
Hic ingens Colossus propius cernebat astra,
  Nunc re ipsa vera indicare haud scio
Hic, aut hic (erat) Capitolium. Heu quid Neronis recenseam
  Bene extructarum balnearum moles, et amoenas humiditates ?
Horum (omnium) unum cerno superstes, Tybrim (videl.) fluere.
  Fluunt quae stabilia sunt : qui vero fluit, stabilis perseverat.

The direct source cannot be ascertained.
Two of the poems derived from Vitalis and cited in my previous article were published in other places besides those mentioned there. The attractive poem " Languentem gressum paulisper siste viator... " appeared, appositely, in an archaeological manual on Rome by Alexander

Donatus, published in Rome in 1665[1]. And Edmund Spenser's translation of the sonnet in Du Bellay's *Antiquitez de Rome* appeared also in 1631 in John Weever's *Ancient funerall monuments*[2].

My earlier article listed thirteen editions of Vitalis's Latin text, and three more have since been added to the list[3]. Two further versions are in manuscripts in the Bibliothèque Nationale in Paris. One manuscript simply gives the text[4]. The other presents the text with the following rather amusing though doubtless apocryphal anecdote :

Regnant François I, un Gentilhomme revenant d'Italie venant saluer le Roy, après l'avoir courtoisement receu, le Roy luy dict : Vous avez la reputation d'estre bon Poëte, faictes nous veoir quelque chose de vostre ouvrage. Le Gentilhomme supplia le Roy de luy donner quelque subject. Le Roy luy dict, " Prenez-le tel que vous vouldrez. Et bien, vous venez d'Italie, faictes quelque chose sur Rome. " Le Gentilhomme donc fit les vers qui ensuyvent, et ne se trouvent point imprimez :

> Qui Romam in media quaeris, novus advena, Roma
>   Et Romae in Roma nil reperis media :
> Aspice murorum moles, praeruptaque saxa,
>   Obrutaque ingenti vasta theatra situ.
> Haec sunt Roma : Viden velut ipsa cadentia, tantae
>   Molis, adhuc spirent imperiosa minas ?
> Vicit ut haec mundum, nisa est se vincere, vicit ;
>   A se non victum ne quid in orbe foret.
> Nunc victa in Roma, Roma illa invicta sepulta est,
>   Atque eadem victrix, victaque Roma fuit.
> Albula Romani restat nunc nominis index,
>   Quin etiam rapidis fertur in aequor aquis.
> Disce quid hinc [sic] possit fortuna, immota labascunt,
>   Et quae perpetuo sunt agitata manent.

Quelques jours après ce Gentilhomme presenta cest Epigramme au Roy comme il se mettoit à table pour disner. Le Roy se le fit lire, et luy pleust fort, tellement qu'en disnant, et mangeant de fort bon appetit il repeta souvent ces mots : Voila un bon Epigramme, voilà un Epigramme qui est bien faict. Un autre Gentilhomme qui estoit au disner du Roy estimant que la viande à laquelle le Roy prenoit goust s'appelloit Epigramme, descendit aussi tost à la cuisine, et dist au Maistre Cuisinier, " Je vous prie me dire quelle viande que c'est qu'un Epigramme, et comme il la faut apprester : par ce que j'ay veu maintenant que le Roy y a prins un grand goust ". Le Cuisinier, que n'entendoit point ce jargon, luy dist : " Je n'entends

1. The work is *Roma vetus ac recens...* (B.L. 140 c 18) : the poem, titled *In urbem Romam,* is in unnumbered pages at the end. The text is that given by Sweertius and Labbé (see *R.L.C.,* 1977, p. 515, n. 8), and the poem is attributed in this publication to Andreas Frusius.

2. See *Ancient funerall monuments within the united Monarchie of Great Britaine, Ireland, and the Ilands adjacent...,* London, 1631, B.L. 577 k 1, p. 3. Spenser's translation of Du Bellay is found also in the 1767 edition (London ; B.L. 209 c 6, p. iii). Weever, an antiquarian, was moved to compile this record of surviving monuments by anguish at contemporary vandalism – an anguish which was widespread in England after Henry VIII destroyed the monasteries. See Margaret Aston, " English ruins and English history : the Dissolution and sense of the past ", *Journal of the Warburg and Courtauld Institutes,* 36, 1973, p. 231-255.

3. Vitalis's text is on p. 34 of the *Florilegium* and follows the 1554 edition (see *R.L.C.,* 1977, p. 513, n. 2, (a)).

4. This is ms. lat. 8139, 113ro. The text follows the 1554 version, except : line 7, Vicit ut haec mundum, *voluit se* vincere, vicit ; line 9, Nunc *Roma invicta,* Roma illa invicta sepulta est ; line 13, Albula Romani *solus stat* nominis index ; line 14, *Quinetiam instabili fertur in aequor aqua.*

point ce que vous me dictes, il le faut demander au Maistre d'Hostel " ; lequel Maistre d'Hostel estant venu en mesme temps à la cuisine, le Gentilhomme luy fist la mesme demande qu'il avoit faicte au Cuisinier. Le Maistre d'Hostel, recognoissant l'ignorance et stupidité du Gentilhomme, respondit qu'il n'en estoit bien memoratif, mais qu'il le demanderoit au Roy, auquel faict le conte, y en eust grande risée. Depuis, le Cardinal Du Bellay a traduict en françois le susdit Epigramme, comme appert par le sonnet suivant qui est imprimé avec ses œuvres.

There follows the text of sonnet 3 of the *Antiquitez* (which is of course by Joachim Du Bellay and not, as the writer thought, by his father's cousin) [1].

Although the focus of my earlier article and of this one is sixteenth – and seventeenth-century derivatives of Vitalis, the tradition lives on in more recent adaptations. Fourteen of these are cited in my previous article [2]. Additionally, a Russian translation by V. Lyevika of Du Bellay's sonnet has appeared in a very attractive anthology of Pléiade poetry and Russian translations [3]. And the phrase " Rome n'est plus dans Rome ", which encapsulates Vitalis's basic paradox, has had a life of its own : Harry Cockerham has pointed out to me that it is in one of Edmond Texier's *Lettres sur l'Angleterre* [4], in the title of a play by Gabriel Marcel (who took the phrase from Pierre Corneille [5]), and in Marguerite Yourcenar's *Mémoires d'Hadrien* [6].

For Vitalis and many of his followers, the eternal city is emblematic of humanity at large. " Rome fut tout le monde, et tout le monde est Rome ", as Du Bellay put it (*Antiquitez*, 18). Vitalis's message about Rome has a universal relevance : the more strenuously a nation aspires to military supremacy, the more assuredly it consigns itself to ruin. Vitalis's disciples have disseminated his message in European nations which are only too well able to recognize it as a truism [7].

Malcolm C. SMITH
London

1. This material is in the Dupuy Collection, no. 844, 29vo.
2. See *R.L.C.*, 1977, p. 525-526 and notes 15-17.
3. See *Poésies de la Pléiade*, Moscou, 1984, p. 257-259.
4. On foreigners flocking to London for the Great Exhibition of 1851, Texier wrote : " Rome n'est plus dans Rome, elle est à Hyde-Park, à Regent-Street, à Belgrave-Square, à Hay-market, et aussi à Greenwich... " (Lettre sixième, Londres, 9 mai [1851], in *Lettres sur l'Angleterre (Souvenirs de l'Exposition universelle)*, Paris, 1851, p. 77).
5. Marcel's *Rome n'est plus dans Rome* appeared in 1951. The source of his title, as he indicates at the end, is Corneille's *Sertorius* (III, i).
6. See the edition published by Gallimard (1974), p. 116-117.
7. Germain Marc'hadour has also recently discussed the fortuna of Vitalis, pointing out that in the sixteenth and seventeenth centuries he enjoyed fame for another epigram, on the execution of Thomas More :
Dum Morus immeritae submittit colla securi,
Et flent occasum pignora cara suum :
Immo, ait, infandi vitam deflete tyranni,
Non moritur, facinus qui grave morte fugit.
He has also surmised that a poem titled *Ioannis Vitalli Londinensis Carmen in Lutherum*, published at the end of More's *Responsio ad Lutherum*, was written by More and that the Joannes Vitalis to whom More playfully attributes the poem is our poet, whose Christian name, before he changed it to Janus, had been Joannes (see " Janus Vitalis ", *Moreana*, XIX, 74, 1982, p. 104 and cf. A. Blanchard, " Poèmes du XVIᵉ siècle à la mémoire de Thomas More et de John Fisher ", *Moreana*, 41, p. 93-99). I should be delighted if More had a reason to regard Vitalis as a Londoner, but do not know of any !

Bibliothèque d'Humanisme et Renaissance - Tome LII - 1990 - n° 1, pp. 7-21

OPIUM OF THE PEOPLE:
NUMA POMPILIUS IN THE FRENCH RENAISSANCE[1]

1. INTRODUCTION

This is the essay which Montaigne did not get round to writing — on political benefits which princes could derive from religion, or thought they could. By «religion» I mean what Montaigne did in this context, the veneration which accompanies the supernatural. Why did Montaigne not write that study which he adumbrates at the end of *De la gloire*? Almost certainly because an essay on the political exploitation of religion would inevitably have included (at least implicitly) critical scrutiny of his own monarch. He was prepared, in the interests of the state, to place limits on his freedom of expression[2].

Renaissance commentators were acutely conscious of the political advantages of religion. Religious belief generates fear of God and socially desirable behaviour — for divine and eternal punishment in the life to come is a powerful disincentive to vice. This view, which is ancient[3], was often advanced in the Renaissance[4]; and it has been said, though not entirely

---

[1] This article is an abridged version of the George Clapton Memorial Lecture given at the University of Leeds in 1988.

[2] The risk that his freedom of thought would lead him to express politically-damaging views deterred Montaigne from writing history (see *Essais*, I, xxi).

[3] The view is found in Cicero's *Laws* (for example II, vii (15-16), and cf. *De natura deorum*, 1, 2, 4) and in Polybius's *History* (VI, 56; C. Vivanti argues in his edition of Machiavelli's *Discorsi* (Torino, 1983, p. 65, n. 1) that this is a source for Machiavelli's views on the political advantages of belief in divine sanctions). Ancient philosophers accepted immortality of the soul, Montaigne noted, for two reasons: «[...] l'une, que, sans l'immortalité des ames, il n'y auroit plus dequoy asseoir les vaines esperances de la gloire [...] l'autre, que c'est une très-utile impression, comme dict Platon, que les vices, quand ils se desroberont à la veue obscure et incerteine de l'humaine justice, demeurent tousjours en butte à la divine, qui les poursuivra, voire après la mort des coupables» (*Essais*, II, xii; ed. J. Plattard, Les Textes Français, Paris, 1946-1948, p. 325).

[4] See, for example, Pierre Du Val:

> Qui faict sinon la divine science,
> D'horrible peur trembler la conscience
> D'un homicide et parjure menteur,
> D'un sacrilege et faulx blasphemateur?

From *De la grandeur de Dieu, et de la cognoissance qu'on peult avoir de luy par ses œuvres*,

accurately, that the political need for God and immortality led to complete intolerance of atheists[5]. And other political advantages of worship of God were put forward. The Almighty would reward the pious monarch in this life by favours to his nation[6] — and would reward kings who foster the religion he himself ordains[7], or who introduce ordinances guided by divine law[8]. Also religion can be a focal point of state unity[9]. And a pious prince more readily secures the loyalty of his people[10].

Paris, 1557, B.L. C. 46 c 1 (1), 21 r°. Other exponents of this view: Ronsard, *Œuvres complètes*, ed. P. Laumonier, révisées et complétées par I. Silver et R. Lebègue, 20 vol., Paris, 1914-1975, VIII, p. 168; Louis Le Caron, *Des differens et troubles advenans entre les hommes pour la diversité des opinions en la religion*, Paris, 1562, B.N. D 41510, a ii r°-a ii v°; Pierre Viret, *De la Providence divine, touchant tous les estats du monde, et tous les biens et les maux qui y peuvent advenir* [...], Lyon, B.L. 850 d 4, pp. 20-21; Jean Bodin, *Les six livres de la Republique*, Paris, 1576, B.L. C 115 h 1 (1), p. 611.

[5] Joseph Lecler reached this conclusion in his *Histoire de la tolérance au siècle de la réforme*, 2 vol., Paris, 1955, II, p. 155. But Thomas More's Utopians tolerated atheists, «quod persuasum habeant, nulli hoc in manu esse, ut quicquid libet, sentiat»: see *The Complete Works*, vol. 4, ed. E. Surtz and J.H. Hexter, New Haven and London, 1965, pp. 220-223, and notes. And Montaigne noted newly-discovered societies «[...] où l'on vit soubs cette opinion si rare et incivile de la mortalité des ames» (*Essais*, I, xxiii; *ed. cit.*, p. 157): in context, he is saying belief in immortality is not, as is thought, essential to the survival of a society.

[6] As Montaigne put it:

> Les histoires payennes reconnoissent de la dignité, ordre, justice et des prodiges et oracles employez à leur profit et instruction en leurs religions fabuleuses: Dieu, par sa misericorde, daignant à l'avanture fomenter par ces benefices temporels les tendres principes d'une telle quelle brute connoissance que la raison naturelle nous a donné de luy au travers des fausses images de nos songes.

Les Essais, II, xii (*ed. cit.*, p. 265). Just as God rewards the virtuous monarch (it was thought), he punishes the wicked. In Ronsard's *Hymne de Castor et de Pollux*, the tyrant Amycus makes an atheist profession of faith (for atheism is a faith), and is promptly, and edifyingly, slain (ed. Laumonier, VIII, p. 306).

[7] French kings have had the assistance of God (argues François de Belleforest) — and they have all been Catholics: «[...] il n'y a nation qui aye plus dequoy louer Dieu que la nostre, veu que jamais Roy de France ne fust sans sentir l'evidence de la faveur divine, pour-ce aussi que nul d'eux ne se forvoya onc de la foy, et ne laissa l'union de l'Eglise» (*Discours des presages*, 1568, B.L. 1193 h 30 (5), 11 r°-v°). Conversely, God's approval (argue the Reformers) requires suppression of blasphemy — which means suppression of papistry: see C.M.N. Eire, *War against the idols: the reformation of worship from Erasmus to Calvin*, Cambridge (England), etc., 1986.

[8] Ronsard has an excellent non-sectarian statement of this belief in his *Hymne de la Justice*: ed. Laumonier, VIII, pp. 69-71 and cf. IX, pp. 108-113.

[9] Machiavelli urges this in his *Discorsi sopra la prima deca di Tito Livio*, I, xii, as does Ronsard in his *Remonstrance au peuple de France*, lines 397-400 (see the notes on this passage in my edition of the *Discours des miseres*, Genève, 1979, p. 125). Montaigne, while conscious of the political pressure for religious unity, insisted that unity should not be imposed: the English, who had changed divine truths three or four times, show the fatuousness of state religions (see *Essais*, II, xii, *ed. cit.*, pp. 365-366). La Boëtie, likewise, denied to the monarch a right to impose a religion (see his *Mémoire sur la pacification des troubles*, ed. M. Smith, Genève, 1983, p. 36).

[10] Jamyn argued that pious observance of the Christian religion would be more politically effective even than the piety of Sertorius and Numa in a false one:

2. THE DIVINE KING

But my principal subject is not the worship of God but worship of the king. Claims which have been made for the monarch range from actual divinity to (more modestly) a God-given entitlement to respect. An intermediate position is that God has indicated his favour for an individual monarch or dynasty by miracles, or has endowed a monarch with supernatural therapeutic powers. But propagandists who advance royal claims tend not to make such distinctions: their aim is not to engage the critical faculties of their readers by opening up a discussion of the degree of veneration the monarch commands, but to anaesthetize those faculties; that is the whole point of surrounding the monarch with a religious aura[11].

Biblical texts can be invoked to support the whole range of such claims[12]. And there are numerous pagan examples of the «divine» king. Of these ancient examples, the most famous one in the Renaissance was probably Numa Pompilius, the second king of Rome (said to have reigned from 715 to 673BC, though his historical existence is in doubt). He was a man of

---

Comment ne serviroit la vraye conscience
Et la certaine foy, quand la faulse apparence
Et l'ombre seulement de quelque deïté
A Sertore et Numa jadis ont proffité,
Soit pour planter des loix en diverses murailles,
Soit pour conduire un camp au meurtre des batailles?

From a poem titled *Que prier Dieu est œuvre tres-necessaire et digne d'un vray Chrestien*: see his *Premières poésies et livre premier*, ed. S.M. Carrington, Genève, 1973, p. 182.

[11] For an excellent introduction to the notion of the «divine» king in very diverse societies, see the essays in D. Cannadine and S. Price, eds., *Rituals of royalty: power and ceremonial in traditional societies*, Cambridge (England), 1987 and studies cited there, especially in the Introduction by David Cannadine, pp. 1-19 and notes.

[12] *Exodus* declares (VII, 1) that the Lord appointed Moses to be the «God» of Pharaoh; and the psalmist describes judges and men of power as «Gods, and sons of the most high» (LXXXII (LXXXI), 6). At the other end of the spectrum of claims, the book of *Wisdom* declares (VI, 3) that power is given to kings by the Lord and St. Paul urges that everyone be subject to governing authorities, for there is no authority but from God, and to resist authorities is to resist God, who will pass judgement (*Romans*, XIII, 1-7). And biblical texts support the intermediate position, that a particular monarch enjoys direct divine favour: David was chosen by God to be king, and so was his son Solomon; and God actually appeared to Solomon and offered him any gift (and Solomon chose wisdom, most fitting for a king; see *1 Chronicles* XXVIII and *2 Chronicles*, I; on kings as Solomon, see M.M. McGowan, *Ideal forms in the age of Ronsard*, Berkeley, Los Angeles and London, 1985, pp. 14, 17, 19 and notes). Biblical, classical and medieval texts supporting the analogy between the king and God were deployed by many authors, for example Maurice Poncet in his *Remonstrance à la noblesse de France de l'utilité et repos que le roy apporte à son peuple*, Paris, 1572, B.L. 1193 h 30 (4). There are of course biblical texts which argue against monarchy altogether — for example, chapter VIII of the *First book of Samuel*, invoked by La Boëtie, supports the anti-monarchical view (see my edition of La Boëtie's *De la Servitude volontaire*, Textes Littéraires Français, Genève, 1987, p. 45 and n. 13).

great virtue, wisdom and piety who, after the death of his wife, became
wedded to the goddess Egeria. The divine assistance which this relationship
gave him was most useful: Numa pacified a warlike nation by religious
ceremonies, and by intimating that deities had appeared to him and had
uttered warnings. On one occasion, when Rome was suffering from a
pestilence, a bronze shield fell from heaven, and Egeria and the Muses told
Numa that it was sent for the salvation of the city, and must be carefully
preserved, and the spot where it fell consecrated to the Muses: and the plague
immediately ended. Indeed, thanks to the popular perception that he was a
quasi-divine ruler, Numa was consummately successful. «The city became
so tractable» (Plutarch records) «and stood in such awe of Numa's power,
that they accepted his stories, though fabulously strange, and thought
nothing incredible or impossible which he wished them to believe or do»;
and in the forty-three years of his reign, Rome and the neighbouring cities
knew not one day of war[13]. Was it because Numa was pious that he enjoyed
the favour of the gods and ruled successfully? Or was it rather that Numa
was politically astute, and so claimed to enjoy the favour of the gods, and
subdued the masses by exploiting their superstition? Plutarch suggests it was
a little of both: Numa was genuinely pious — *and* his converse with a deity
was a legitimate deceit, facilitating great political innovations. But a scholar
might observe that genuinely pious people are unlikely to manipulate
religion for political ends[14].

Some Renaissance commentators stress (approvingly) his success, others
(disapprovingly) his use of deception. Machiavelli was full of admiration for
him. He noted that Numa turned to religion «come cosa al tutto necessaria
a volere mantenere una civiltà»: he instilled fear of God in the people, and
this produced a disciplined army, maintained virtue and shamed the wicked;
and to alter the constitution of the state, he wisely pretended to be the recipient of divine messages — an excellent way of getting innovations accepted.
Any good prince, according to Machiavelli, ensures that his laws have the

---

[13] Plutarch's *Life of Numa* can be read in Bernadotte Perrin's edition of the *Lives*, with
a translation (from which I have quoted here), in the Loeb Classical Library (11 vol., Cambridge, Mass. and London, 1967; I, pp. 305-401).

[14] This observation was also made in the sixteenth century. Noël Du Fail denounced those
atheists who had no use for religion except in so far as it keeps people obedient: see *Propos
rustiques, baliverneries, contes et discours d'Eutrapel*, Paris, 1842, pp. 379-398. Pierre de La
Primaudaye reported that many atheists felt that the only advantage of religion was that it kept
fools in their place, and that religions are based solely on fear and have no substance, but are
socially useful: see his *Suite de l'Academie françoise*, Paris, 1580, ch. 95, 97. See also the next
note (for Campanella's denunciation of Machiavelli).

sanction of religion behind them[15]. French commentators, too, noted the advantage of «deifying» the monarch. Claude Cottereau, a friend of Rabelais and Dolet, commended techniques like those of Numa[16]. Jacques Tahureau, in his *Dialogues* of 1555 (first published posthumously in 1556), exposed Numa's practice as fraudulent — but at the same time endorsed it as politically desirable[17]. Louis Le Roy, in 1576, noted Numa's success — and remarked that almost all ancient lawgivers had claimed to enjoy divine assistance[18].

---

[15] See *Discorsi sopra la prima deca di Tito Livio*, I, xi (*ed. cit.*, pp. 153-155). The miracles of Numa had been endorsed as genuine by Dante in his *De monarchia*, II, iv: see *Tutte le opere*, ed. F. Chiappelli, Milano, 1965, pp. 750-751. Machiavelli's praise of Numa as an astute manipulator of religion for political ends was to be echoed by Girolamo Cardano and noted by Gabriel Naudé: see G. Procacci, *Studi sulla fortuna del Machiavelli*, Roma, 1965, p. 105. There is a useful discussion of Machiavelli's views on the political uses of religion in Bernard Guillemain's *Machiavel, l'anthropologie politique* (Genève, 1977), pp. 326-337: he notes (p. 328) that Campanella denounced Machiavelli as an atheist for reducing religion to an instrument of government.

[16] Cottereau wrote:

> Hic proderit imperatori, fingere se oraculo admonitum: iis enim terriculamentis, et commentis facile incenduntur homines. Hoc modo Sylla sibi a Diis futura prædici simulavit. Notumque est illud de cerva Sertorii. Sic Archidamus Lacedæmoniis contra Archadas pugnaturus finxit Castorem, et Pollucem sibi pugnam consulisse. Omnino pugnaturus imperator exercitum suum non solum viribus armisque propriis tutum, sed etiam quibusvis numinibus maxime confidentem reddere debet. Pulchre quidem Ap. Claudius apud Livium loquitur: Eludant nunc licet religionem: quid enim est, si pulli non pascentur? se ex cavea tardius exierint? si occinerit avis? Parva hæc sunt: sed parva ista non contemnendo Maiores nostri maximam hanc Republicam fecerunt.

In his *De officio imperatoris liber* (published with his *De iure ac privilegiis militum libri tres*), Lugduni, 1539, John Rylands Library, Manchester, 4 h 4, p. 241.

[17] See the excellent edition by Max Gauna (Genève, 1981), pp. 223-224, 231-232.

[18] Le Roy observed that Numa's relationship with Egeria was the basis of his authority, and that the long period of peace enabled Rome to become established: see *De la vicissitude ou varieté des choses en l'univers* [...], Paris, 1576, B.L. C 115 h 1 (2), 65 v°. He noted later (90 v°) that tactics like Numa's were well-nigh universally used:

> Presque tous les anciens legislateurs qui baillerent loix et manieres de vivre aux peuples en divers pays et temps, faignirent qu'elles estoyent envoyées par le commandement de Dieu, pensans leur donner par ce moyen plus d'authorité, et les faire plus aiseement recevoir: et icelles attribuerent à la divinité soubs noms differens, selon les opinions des pays où ils estoient, comme Zoroastre legislateur des Bactriens et des Perses à Horosmadis, Trimegiste des Egyptiens à Mercure, Zamolsis des Scythes à Veste, Charondas des Calcides à Saturne, Minos des Cretes à Iuppiter, Numa des Romains à Egerie, et autres semblables personnages, lesquels ayans à manier des peuples rudes et farouches, et voulans introduire de grandes nouvelletez és gouvernemens de leur pays, ils faignirent avoir communication avec les dieux, comme si celle fiction eust esté utile à ceux mesmes ausquels la faisoient accroire. Ainsi Mahumed voulant donner loix aux Arabes rudes et grossiers, vivans la pluspart de briganderies par les montaignes, leur feit accroire qu'il les recevoit de Dieu par l'Ange Gabriel, à fin qu'ils y obeissent plus volontiers.

But other commentators stressed the fraudulence of techniques used by Numa rather than his success. Etienne Jodelle deplored the exploitation of religion by the Romans after the manner of Numa, though without naming him, implicitly criticizing the practice of French kings; Agrippa d'Aubigné, again without naming Numa, attacked his technique:

> Nos Rois qui ont appris à machiaveliser,
> Au temps et à l'estat leur ame desguiser,
> Ployans la pieté au joug de leur service
> Gardent religion pour arme de police.

The author (perhaps Aubigné again) of a *Libre discours sur l'estat present des Eglises Reformées en France* deplored the fact that the earliest legislators had reduced religion to «un instrument de police», and had not cared whether people believed in God so long as what they did believe kept them in their place; he described Numa as «le premier autheur de leurs malices»[19].

3. RONSARD AND THE DIVINE KING

In all the massive scholarly literature on the «divine» king, relatively little attention seems to have been paid to the individuals who, pre-eminently, diffused that notion in Renaissance France, namely poets[20]. Foremost among these is Pierre de Ronsard. The central message of his single most important poem, the ode dedicated to his friend, patron and defender, Michel de L'Hospital (1553), is that the pre-eminent role of the Muses is to confer divine status on monarchs and thus help them carry out their political function. This is seen in the request which Calliope makes to her father Jupiter:

---

[19]   My source for the material in this paragraph is the immensely rich Ph. D. thesis by Heather Ingman, *A study in ambivalence: the influence of Machiavelli on poetry and drama of the French Renaissance* (University of London, 1982). See pp. 124-125 (on Jodelle, referring to his *Œuvres complètes*, ed. E. Balmas, II, Paris, 1968, p. 211), 279 (on Aubigné, cf. *Princes*, ll. 651-654; I have altered the reading «ame de police») and 280-281 (on the *Libre discours* [...], [s.l.], 1619, B.N. Lb 36 1264, pp. 127-128). Ingman refers to other French Renaissance authors who commented on Numa's use of religion: Gentillet, Pasquier, Hurault, Lucinge and Naudé: see pp. 614-615.

[20]   This subject has however been admirably explored by Margaret McGowan in her *Ideal forms in the age of Ronsard* (see note 12 above). The most important part of her book for our subject is ch. 1, «The perfect prince», pp. 9-50. The pioneering study of E. Bourciez (*Les mœurs polies et la littérature de cour sous Henri II*, Paris, 1886) is still relevant. See also Geneviève Demerson, *Dorat en son temps: culture classique et présence au monde*, Clermont-Ferrand, 1983, pp. 313-317, «Caractère divin du pouvoir royal».

> Donne nous que les Seigneurs,
> Les Empereurs, et les Princes,
> Soyent veuz Dieux en leurs provinces
> S'ilz reverent noz honneurs.
> Fay, que les Roys decorez
> De noz presentz honorez,
> Soyent aux hommes admirables,
> Lors qu'ilz vont par leur cité,
> Ou lors que plains d'equité
> Donnent des loix venerables[21].

And so it was to Ronsard that Henri II turned for the divine image which would buttress his position. As Henri II entered Paris in 1549, Ronsard exclaimed, in a pamphlet commemorating the event,

> Sus donq Paris, regarde quel doit estre
> Ton heur futur, en adorant ton maistre,
> Ton nouveau Dieu, dont la divinité
> T'enrichira d'une immortalité[22].

The first lines of the *Odes* of 1550 recall that the ancients began their poems by invoking Jupiter, but (Ronsard adds),

> HENRI sera le Dieu
> Qui commencera mon mettre
> Et que j'ay voué de mettre
> A la fin et au milieu[23].

In the Olympus which Ronsard creates in his *Odes*, the king is the new Jupiter, his wife Catherine de' Medici is the new Juno, his sister Marguerite is Pallas[24]. Often, the conception of the divine king is encapsulated in aphorisms: «Mais du grand Jupiter les Roys tiennent leur estre»; and «Et bref,

---

[21]   Ronsard, ed. Laumonier, III, pp. 139-140. This is the culmination of a passage in which Ronsard has the Muses put to Jupiter requests which reveal his view of the role of a poet. To hazard an interpretation of a difficult passage (lines 341-364 of this poem), he sees the functions of the Muses as being to adore the Creator, to bring the created universe to life in their poems, to utter divine prophecies, to cure diseases, to confer immortality on subjects of their verse, to be astrologers, and to guide people's souls from worldly thoughts to eternal ones — and, more importantly than any of these, to secure veneration for the monarch. There are interesting reflections on the symbiotic relationship between poet and monarch in D. Ménager's *Ronsard: Le Roi, le Poète et les hommes*, Genève, 1979.

[22]   Ronsard, ed. Laumonier, I, 18. The poem was published as a pamphlet in 1549 but never included in sixteenth-century collected editions. On the ceremonial of royal entries, in which kings were commonly linked with ancient deities, see L.M. Bryant, *The king and the city in Parisian royal entry ceremony: politics, ritual and art in the Renaissance*, Genève, 1986.

[23]   Ronsard, ed. Laumonier, I, 63.

[24]   See Bourciez, *Les mœurs polies* [...] (cf. note 20 above), Livre II, ch. ii, «L'Olympe nouveau», pp. 176-202.

c'est presque un Dieu que le Roy des François»; and «Qui fait honneur aux Roys, il fait honneur à Dieu»[25].

A helpful adjunct to kings is tangible evidence of divine endorsement of the claims they advance. Just as a shield fell from heaven in front of Numa, divine gifts supposedly came the way of the first Christian king of France, Clovis. On the occasion of his baptism, he was anointed with oil delivered from heaven in a vase by a dove, or by angels; and angels also delivered an oriflamme which displayed the cross of Christ, and an armorial shield displaying three *fleurs-de-lys*, to replace his pagan insignia of three fat toads. Since the late Middle Ages, «Saint» Clovis had become in patriotic propaganda the emblem of God's providential design for France, a man of exemplary virtue enjoying divine support in the form of miracles, and ruling his kingdom in justice and peace[26]. Ronsard makes Clovis and the miracles accompanying his conversion the centrepiece of his patriotic epic, the *Franciade*; and he places Clovis in a dynasty which traces its origins to Francus, the son of Hector and Andromache — Hector himself being a descendant of Jupiter[27]. In Ronsard's poem, as in French propaganda generally, French kings, the *roys treschrestiens*, bathed in the divine aura of the miracles of Clovis[28]. In Ronsard's day, and earlier, French kings claimed a further divine gift, the power of healing: curiously, Ronsard says nothing about it[29].

---

[25] The three quotations are from Ronsard, ed. Laumonier, VIII, pp. 25, 33 and X, 38. Other examples: I, pp.18, 63, 67; III, pp. 96-97; VII, pp. 9, 41, 47, 52, 54, 67, 69, 71, 77, 80; VIII, pp. 5-6, 9, 24, 26, 34; IX, p. 61; X, pp. 66, 78-79, 142, 296; XI, p. 5; XIII, pp. 100, 130, 132, 163-169, 231-232, 240; XIV, p. 133.

[26] See the excellent book by Anne-Marie Lecoq, *François Ier imaginaire, Symbolique et politique à l'aube de la Renaissance française*, Paris, 1987, especially pp. 199-201. The legend of the phial of sacred oil was thought to enjoy the endorsement of Thomas Aquinas, for a fourteenth-century continuation of Aquinas's *De Regimine principum* (probably by the polygraph Fra Tolomeo of Lucca) was often attributed to him, and it endorses the miracle in a passage on the sanctity of French kings: see M. Bloch, *Les Rois thaumaturges: étude sur le caractère surnaturel attribué à la puissance royale particulièrement en France et en Angleterre*, Strasbourg, 1924, pp. 133-134. On the political use of these legends in the Middle Ages, see J.L. Nelson, «The Lord's anointed and the people's choice: Carolingian royal ritual», in Cannadine and Price, *Rituals of royalty* (see above, note 11), pp. 137-180.

[27] On the «Trojan» ancestry of French kings, see for example Ronsard, ed. Laumonier, I, p. 30; III, pp. 8-22; V, p. 209; VI, p. 57; VII, pp. 9-10, 25-30, 33, 300-301, 347; X, pp. 74-75.

[28] *Franciade*, Livre IV, 1143-1156; Ronsard, ed. Laumonier, XVI, p. 298.

[29] On the therapeutic powers of French kings, see Bloch, *Les Rois thaumaturges* (see note 26 above). The first known case of a French monarch touching sick persons is Charles VIII, in 1484 (Bloch, pp. 283-284). Henri II's Book of Hours contains «Les oraisons qu'ont accoustumé de dire les Roys de France quand ils veulent toucher les malades des escrouelles» (p. 286). Under Henri II and Charles IX, the ceremonies had become so important that foreigners were given payments to make the trip to France to be touched by the king (pp. 311-312). The memorialist Claude Haton has an interesting account of the ceremony, which he saw performed by Henri II in 1556:

Ronsard encountered resistance to his «deifications» of Henri II and other French monarchs[30]. Probably as a result, he toned down his statements[31]. But he still cast a divine aura around the person of the king. Towards the end of his life he advocated a monarchy modelled on Numa's. This is in the *Panegyrique de la Renommée*, dedicated to Henri III and first published as a pamphlet in 1579. In this poem, an allegorical figure, «Renommée» or Renown, declares that the French civil wars were a punish-

---

> Durant le temps de la gésine de la royne dame Katherine de Médicis, le roy fut adverty qu'audit lieu de Fontainebleau y avoit grande multitude de malades des escrouelles qu'on appelle de monsieur St. Marcoul, qui, par une requeste qu'ils présentèrent à sa majesté le prièrent que, pour l'honneur de Dieu, de la vierge Marie et monsieur St. Marcoul, il luy pleust de les toucher, affin d'estre guaris. A laquelle requeste voluntiers s'inclina, leur faisant assavoir qu'ilz se disposassent tous pour la feste de mons. St. Jehan-Baptiste, et que pour ce faire de sa part se disposeroit, ce qu'il feit. Le dit jour, au sortir de la messe de la chapelle du chasteau, les malades en assez grand nombre furent mis en ordre sur la chaussée de l'estang dudit Fontainebleau, qui est ung beau, grand et large chemin qui conduist du chasteau du roy au chasteau de chenis du roy au chasteau de chenis, couvert de l'ombre de plusieurs gros arbres, qui sont plantez par rottes dedans ledit chemin, et soubz cette umbre estoient à genoux lesdits malades, en attendant sa majesté sortir de la messe pour les toucher. Ce qu'il feit mout humblement, ne desdignant point les pauvres malades, quelque gastez qu'ilz fussent, touchant de sa main dextre le visage d'iceux, en leur disant: «Je te touche, Dieu te guarisse!» Mons. le grand aulmosnier, Loys de Brézé, estoit derrière lesdits malades. Par le commandement du roy, il donna à chascun d'eux une pièce d'argent pour aulmosne, leur disant: «Priez bien pour le roy.» Sa majesté les admonesta, quand ce fut faict, d'estre tousjours bons chrestiens, fidelles et catholicques, servans dévostement à Dieu, à la vierge Marie et à mons. St. Marcoul, ainsi que nous-mesmes le vismes de noz yeux, estant présens audit lieu de Fontainebleau.

Bloch evidently did not know of this account, since he stated (p. 315) that the words «Le roi te touche et Dieu te guérit» are first attested in 1577. Guillaume Budé, among others, endorsed French kings' claims to cure: see McGowan, *Ideal forms* [...] (see above, note 12), p. 14 and n. 20.

[30] Ronsard anticipated such resistance in the preface to his *Odes*, and argued that the task of the poet is to «[...] celebrer jusques à l'extremité celui qu'il entreprend de louer» (ed. Laumonier, I, p. 48). The passage suggests that Ronsard may have encountered criticisms when circulating his *Odes* in manuscript. Jacques Tahureau, too, observed that hyperbolic praise was conventional: «[...] à l'imitation des anciens poëtes, je donne le titre de Dieu et de divin aux personnes excellens, ce qui est fort commun en la poësie, aussi que les choses grandes et belles semblent avoir je ne sçay quoy de divinité» (*Premieres poësies*, 1554: ed. Blanchemain, I, p. 7). Again, the fact he gave the explanation perhaps indicates opposition to his language. Erasmus had warned against such verbal flattery: a young king «hears the terms 'sacred majesty', 'divinity', 'god on earth', and other such superb titles» and «while he is yet a boy, all he learns to play at is being a tyrant»: see M.M. Phillips, *The Adages of Erasmus, a study with translations*, Cambridge (England), 1964, p. 223 (*Adages*, I, III, I, *Aut fatuum aut regem nasci oportere*).

[31] He balanced his eulogies with warnings about the vices of kings and the dangers of flattery — and insisted that he would never indulge in flattery: ed. Laumonier, III, pp. 30-33; VI, p. 8; VIII, pp. 291, 328; IX, pp. 114, 157-159; X, pp. 5-9, 47-48; XI, pp. 3-4, 10; XIII, p. 277. I have studied contemporary criticisms of Ronsard's «flattery», and his responses to them, in «Ronsard et ses critiques contemporains», in *Ronsard en son IVe centenaire, Ronsard hier et aujourd'hui*, Actes du Colloque international Pierre de Ronsard, publiés par Yvonne Bellenger *et al.*, Genève, 1988, pp. 83-90.

ment for impiety but that Henri III has now atoned for this on behalf of the
nation by his zeal for the Catholic faith and by virtues which inspire veneration:

> Seul entre les humains il a peint au visage
> De Dieu le venerable et redoutable image.

The king is the holy image of God, and to decry him in any way is to impugn
God's «sainct simulacre». Henri III is a latter-day Numa Pompilius:

> Tels estoient les bons Roys de l'âge plus fleurie,
> Numa le sacerdote instruit par Egerie; [...]
> Dont les sceptres estoient des peuples redoutez
> Par la loy, que portoient leurs glaives espoinctez,
> Ayant en lieu du fer la douceur pour leur marque[32].

It matters little whether the people believe the king is literally divine —
though Ronsard himself patently did not[33]. Let them but revere him, and he
will reign as effectively as Numa. Henri III, who was tutored in politics by
disciples of Machiavelli[34], was perhaps consciously emulating that ancient
«divine» king when he so ostentatiously put himself at the head of novel
pious confraternities, prompting the derision of Reformers like Aubigné and
the concern of Catholics like Montaigne[35].

---

[32]   The *Panegyrique de la Renommée* is in Ronsard, ed. Laumonier, XVIII, pp. 1-17; my
quotations are from pages 15-17. Guy de Bruès, in his *Dialogues*, shows Ronsard advocating
this paternalistic fraud: «[...] il a esté necessaire que les législateurs ayent persüadé maintes
choses, combien qu'elles ne fussent pas vrayes, à celle fin que le populasse (qui n'est comme
Horace dit qu'une beste ayant plusieurs testes) se contint en quelque devoir. Tout ainsi que les
meres nourrices espouvantent leurs petits enfans, et les menassent qu'ils seront devorez de quelques horribles bestes, s'ils se despartent d'elles: car autrement ils se mettroient inconsiderement
en mille dangers de leurs vies»: cited (from the edition by P.P. Morphos, Baltimore, 1953, p.279)
by D. Ménager, *Ronsard* [...] (see above, note 21), p. 32, n. 24.
[33]   While using poetic fiction and hyperbole to enhance the status of the king, Ronsard
had no illusions about the all-too-palpably human Valois monarchs. Daniel Ménager, usually
so perceptive, thinks Ronsard believed his own propaganda: see *Ronsard* [...] (cf. note 21
above), pp. 158, 197, 355.
[34]   See Procacci, *Studi alla fortuna* [...] (see note 15 above), pp. 174-175.
[35]   Aubigné's attack is in *Les Tragiques*, Princes, 949-996. Montaigne's remark near the
beginning of *De la moderation* almost certainly alludes to Henri III: «J'ay veu tel grand blesser
la reputation de sa religion pour se montrer religieux outre tout exemple des hommes de sa
sorte.» Likewise, a comment in *De l'experience* about a king's fickleness seems to refer to Henri
III's oscillations between debauchery and piety: «[...] nulle assiette moyenne, s'emportant tousjours de l'un à l'autre extreme par occasions indivinables», etc.: *ed. cit.*, III, xiii, p.197. These
passages both appeared for the first time in the posthumous edition of Montaigne, after the
assassination of Henri III: Montaigne, scrupulous as always about avoidance of subversion,
would not have published either during the lifetime of the monarch. On the penitential frater-
nities, see R.A. Schneider, «Mortification on parade: penitential processions in sixteenth- and
seventeenth-century France», *Renaissance and Reformation*, New series, X, 1986, pp. 123-146.

4. LA BOËTIE

The young La Boëtie, writing his *Servitude volontaire* at the same time as Ronsard was composing his *Odes*, inverts the notion of the divine king. His argument runs, «Kingship is repugnant to Nature; Nature is the minister of God; therefore kingship is repugnant to God»; thus, for La Boëtie, kingship is a «blasphème», liberty is «sacré» — and God punishes kings in hell: the theological resonance to his political discourse, though discreet, is firm. And since, for him, kingship is abhorrent to true piety, it follows that the exploitation of religion is, among all those machinations by which kings impose their will, peculiarly pernicious[36]. Kings' claims to possess therapeutic powers are a fraud: and when he attacks the miracle-worker Vespasian, his real target is almost certainly Henri II, who was ostentatiously reviving the ancient claim of French monarchs to cure scrofula[37]. La Boëtie demolishes even the venerable patriotic legends (the sacred oil, the oriflamme and the *fleur-de-lys*), though he does this indirectly: he draws a parallel between ancient «miracles» and French ones but, whereas he explicitly derides ancient miracles, he merely says of the French ones that they belong not in his tract but in poetry (that is, in fiction, for the etymology of «poetry» was well known). Thus, he says, Ronsard will extol the French equivalent of the shield which fell from heaven at the feet of Numa[38].

And so at virtually the same moment as Ronsard was disseminating patriotic legends about the divine king, La Boëtie was debunking them — though, so far as is known, only in a manuscript intended for discreet circulation[39]. La Boëtie had a great admiration for Ronsard and his closest associates: French poetry, he declared, had been «faite tout à neuf par nostre Ronsard, nostre Baïf, nostre Du Bellay», and he defended Ronsard when he

---

[36] La Boëtie describes four ways in which tyrants impose their will: (a) they exploit the power of custom, so that subjugated peoples imagine that servitude is their natural state; (b) they pander to people's base instincts to distract them from love of freedom; (c) they claim to have divine powers; and (d) where all else fails, they cow their subjects into submission. See my edition (cf. note 12 above). I have also published an English translation (*Slaves by choice*, Runnymede Books, Egham, 1988).

[37] On Vespasian and Henri II, see *ed. cit.*, pp. 61-62. The reason for seeing remarks about Vespasian as an allusion to Henri II is (apart from the stark topicality of La Boëtie's material) that the author implicitly invites readers to use his historical anecdotes to judge the present: see my edition, p. 52.

[38] See *ed. cit.*, pp. 63-65.

[39] Ronsard started publicising the legend of Francus in 1549 in an attempt to interest Henri II in commissioning the *Franciade*, and the *Servitude volontaire* was probably written in the latter part of 1548 and revised around 1553 (see my edition of the *Servitude volontaire*, p. 64, n. 48 and 7-12).

was attacked for not writing pious poetry[40]. But the differences between the two on politics in the early years of Henri II could hardly be greater. Ronsard had praised Henri II for crushing the revolt over the salt tax in 1548 — and it was precisely this brutal exercise of power which led the outraged La Boëtie to write the *Servitude volontaire*[41]. Ronsard intended to rehearse patriotic legends about divine support for French kings — let him do that if he must, says La Boëtie, so long as we remember that these legends are fraudulent nonsense designed to exploit the gullibility and superstition of the masses. The *Servitude volontaire* is the thinking man's antidote to the beguiling chauvinistic fictions of Ronsard. And La Boëtie's attack in the *Servitude volontaire* on kings who claim to be Jupiter may be directed at Ronsard's *Odes*, where Henri II is often given this epithet; and Ronsard may not have been far from his thoughts when he penned an attack on adulatory poets[42].

But just as Ronsard modified his more extreme views, La Boëtie learned from his political experience. When the south-west of France plunged towards civil war in 1561, La Boëtie personally was given an important role in pacifying the region and was defeated by the task. In that *Mémoire sur la pacification des troubles* which is the fruit of his experience, he declared that the king's authority must be restored: «Et maintenant, ce qu'on a principallement à faire, c'est d'enseigner les subjectz du roy à le reverer et les remectre en ce chemin de luy porter honneur»: yes, the king must now be not just accepted, not just respected, by «revered»[43]! Montaigne was entitled to insist, as he did in *De l'amitié*, that La Boëtie was not seditious[44]. La

---

[40]   La Boëtie pays glowing tribute to Ronsard in the *Servitude volontaire* (see pp. 64-65 of my edition). His defence of Ronsard is in his poem *In Lavianum, qui Petrum Ronsardum monuerat, ut non amplius amores, sed Dei laudes caneret* (in his *Œuvres complètes*, ed. P. Bonnefon, p. 217).

[41]   Ronsard's poem on the revolt is titled *Prophetie du Dieu de la Charante aux mutins de la Guienne* (ed. Laumonier, I, pp. 192-196). On the *Servitude volontaire* as a protest against the government's response to the revolt, see my edition, pp. 7-11.

[42]   La Boëtie's attack on kings who claim to be Jupiter is on pp. 62-63 of my edition. The attack on flattering poets (*In adulatores poetas*) is in his *Œuvres complètes*, ed. Bonnefon, p. 219.

[43]   The quotation is from my edition of the *Mémoire sur la pacification des troubles*, p. 63. On the previous page, La Boëtie advocates exemplary punishments for the worst disorders, and that the people should see «la terible fasse de la justice courroussee». Also in this essay, La Boëtie underlines the political desirability of religious union: a consequence of division was «une hayne et malveillance quasi universelle entre les subjects du Roy» (*ed. cit.*, p. 36) — though he rules out coercion to achieve unity.

[44]   At the end of this chapter (*Essais*, I, xxviii), Montaigne declares that La Boëtie believed what he wrote, but that «[...] il avoit un'autre maxime souveraine empreinte en son ame, d'obeyr et de se soubmettre très-religieusement aux loix sous lesquelles il estoit nay. Il ne fut jamais un meilleur citoyen, ny plus affectionné au repos de son païs, ny plus ennemy des remuements et nouvelletez de son temps».

Boëtie's desire to avoid subversion (along with his casual approach to all his writings) must account for the fact he did not have the *Servitude volontaire* printed; and Montaigne, who inherited the manuscript, was (it seems) advised against including it in his 1571 edition of La Boëtie, and left it out of his *Essais* because it had by then been published to subversive ends by Reformers[45].

5. MONTAIGNE

Like La Boëtie, Montaigne looked upon kings with independence of judgement. In *De la gloire*, he challenges the Machiavellian use of the divinity of kings. Numa, he says, used counterfeit currency — and, he audaciously notes, so does every other legislator:

> [...] n'est police où il n'y ait quelque meslange ou de vanité ceremonieuse, ou d'opinion mensongere, qui serve de bride à tenir le peuple en office. C'est pour cela que la pluspart ont leurs origines et commencemens fabuleux et enrichis de mysteres surnaturels. C'est cela qui a donné credit aux religions bastardes et les a faites favorir aux gens d'entendement; et pour cela que Numa et Sertorius, pour rendre leurs hommes de meilleure creance, les paissoyent de cette sottise, l'un que la nymphe Egeria, l'autre que sa biche blanche luy apportoit de la part des dieux tous les conseils qu'il prenoit.

Montaigne goes on to quote other examples of legislators who claimed to have received their laws from a god, concluding that «[...] toute police a un dieu à sa teste, faucement les autres, veritablement celle que Moïse dressa au peuple de Judée sorty d'Ægypte»[46].

---

[45] On Montaigne's attitude towards the text, see my edition, pp. 21-23, 27-28 and 30-31. On the publication of the *Servitude volontaire* by Reformers, see my edition, pp. 23-24 (for the lost 1572 or 1573 edition), 24-25 (for the extract in the *Reveille-matin* of 1574), 25-26 (for the edition in Goulart's *Memoires de l'estat* of 1577) and C. Barmann, «Exemplaires uniques ou rarissimes conservés à la B.M. de Grenoble», *Bibliothèque d'Humanisme et Renaissance*, LI, 1989, pp. 139-141 (for the recently-discovered *Vive description de la tyrannie et des Tyrans, avec les moyens de se garentir de leur joug* of 1577, which contains the text). In the aftermath of the St. Bartholomew's Day Massacre, Reformers had particular reason to deplore the notion of a divine king: in 1579, Henri Estienne, not the most outspoken Reformer, denounced the «dieux terrestres jupitrizans» and the «blasphemy» of deifying the royal family (*Apologie pour Herodote*, ed. Ristelhuber, Paris, 1879, I, p. 195, quoted by Bourciez, *Les mœurs polies* [...] (see note 20 above), p. 179). In 1584, when the Reformer Henri of Navarre became heir to the throne, the Catholic League adopted La Boëtie's tract against divine kings as readily as Reformers had done: see my edition, pp. 28-29.

[46] See *Essais*, II, xvi (*ed. cit.*, pp. 44-45).

And in *De l'art de conferer*, Montaigne again stresses that in venerating powerful people, notably kings, we are mesmerised by their decorative attributes: «Ce que j'adore moy-mesmes aus Roys, c'est la foule de leurs adorateurs. Toute inclination et soubmission leur est deuë, sauf celle de l'entendement. Ma raison n'est pas duite à se courber, ce sont mes genoux.» He then denounces all those nations who «[...] canonizent le Roy qu'ils ont faict d'entre eux, et ne se contentent point de l'honnorer s'ils ne l'adorent». The subjects of the kings of Mexico, Montaigne observes, do not dare look him in the face once they have crowned him but, «[...] comme s'ils l'avoyent deifié par sa royauté», make him swear to make the sun shine, the rains fall, the rivers run their course and the earth bear its fruit[47]. Outspoken reflections such as these, so characteristic of the later Montaigne, may help account for the disclaimer with which the chapter begins — Montaigne does not expect (he says) that anyone should follow his example on anything.

6. CONCLUSION

To conclude by parodying Montaigne, «chaque societé porte la forme entiere de l'humaine condition». The notion of the divine king goes back at least to the semi-legendary origins of Rome, and it thrived in Renaissance France. And it is far from dead. In many nations, contenders for high office court the electors with trappings of religion. The divine king (or state) does not even require a culture of theism: the state itself can be a surrogate deity (requiring, often, faith as defined in the *Letter to the Hebrews*, XI, 1 — the ability to believe things which one's eyes have not seen). Ancient and Renaissance apologists of the «divine» king thus have spiritual heirs today in political systems of the utmost diversity. It behoves us to look with some comprehension upon the eulogists of Henri II.

Indeed, one is moved to ask: is it possible, or indeed desirable, to eliminate the notion of the divine king? If Plutarch is to be believed — and who will argue with Plutarch? — Numa was a consummately successful monarch. And the French civil wars could be seen at least in part as the

---

[47]   See *Essais*, III, viii (*ed. cit.*, pp. 216-218). In *De l'inequalité qui est entre nous*, possibly based on Xenophon's *Hiero*, Montaigne argues that the difference between kings and the rest of us is merely decorative and that kings are purely human — and he quotes a blunt anecdote, previously used by Rabelais, about Antigonus I acknowledging his own humanity in the face of a flattering poet: see *Essais*, I, xlii (*ed. cit.*, p. 168) and Rabelais, *Quart Livre*, ch. 60. Quite apart from his attacks on the «divine» king, Montaigne abhorred the casual use of the language of divinity: see his *Essais*, I, xl (*ed. cit.*, p. 156) and II, xii (*ed. cit.*, p.228).

price of a demystification of royal authority. Before even a fraction of that price had been paid, the alert and enlightened La Boëtie saw that royal authority had to be «venerated». It is a fact of experience that many citizens are angered at reports of wrongdoing by people in authority — angered not at the wrongdoing, but at the report; they yearn for the simplicity and the comfort of blind reverence. The spirit of Numa walks the earth and will not readily be gainsaid.

London.   Malcolm C. SMITH.

Bibliothèque d'Humanisme et Renaissance - Tome LII - 1990 - n° 2, pp. 345-353

THÉODORE DE BÈZE AND «PHILÆNUS»

Around the beginning of 1544, a manuscript copy of Bèze's poems was produced. The manuscript contains six poems which attack a certain «Philænus»; three of these poems were retained in the 1548 edition of Bèze's *Poemata*[1]. None of the numerous studies of the *Poemata*, to my knowledge, has identified Philænus, and this is what I aim to do in this article[2]. In the process, I hope to add to the little that is known of the Paris years (1539-1548) of the great Reformer[3]. It will also be possible to add to what is known about our «Philænus» himself — a very important figure, and far more frequently referred to in the sixteenth century than scholars realize (many of the references to him, like Bèze's, are allusive).

(i) Bèze attacks Floridus and «Philænus»

«Philænus» makes his first appearance in the 1544 manuscript in the third of three epigrams which attack Franciscus Floridus, known (after his birthplace) as Sabinus. The three epigrams read as follows:

---

[1] The manuscript was probably produced at the initiative of Bèze's friend Germain Audebert (to whom it belonged): it is now in the library at Orléans — ms. 1674. See F. Aubert, J. Boussard and H. Meylan, «Un premier recueil de poésies latines de Théodore de Bèze», *BHR*, XV, 1953, pp. 164-191, 258-294 and, for a description of the content of the whole manuscript, J. Boussard, «Le ms. 1674 de la Bibliothèque Municipale d'Orléans», *BHR*, V, 1944, pp. 346-360.

[2] The most useful recent studies of the *Poemata* are A.L. Prescott, «English writers and Beza's Latin epigrams», *Studies in the Renaissance*, XXI, 1974, pp. 83-117 and Thomas Thomson, «The *Poemata* of Théodore de Bèze», *Acta Conventus Neo-Latini Sanctandreani*, ed. I.D. McFarlane, Binghamton, 1986, pp. 409-415. Both these articles cite other important studies. Henry Meylan surveyed Bèze's early poetry in «La conversion de Bèze ou Les longues hésitations d'un humaniste chrétien» (in his *D'Erasme à Théodore de Bèze*, Genève, 1987, pp. 145-167; originally published 1959), but without noting the historical significance of the poems discussed here.

[3] On Bèze's time in Paris, see E. Droz, «Deux notes sur Théodore de Bèze», *BHR*, XXIV, 1962, pp. 392-412, 589-610.

In Sabinum Floridum, doctorum omnium calumniatorem:

> Quum nec sis cerebro senex, Sabine,
> Nec ætate senex, tamen reprendis
> Vivos, Floride, mortuosque cunctos,
> Sabinam referens severitatem.
> At cave tibi nunc, miselle censor,
> Nam se Gallia tota scire dicit
> Qualis, Floride, gens sit Italorum.

[Against Floridus Sabinus, the slanderer of all learned men: «*Though you are not mature in mind, Sabinus, nor mature in years, you reproach all men, living and dead, with truly Sabine severity. But watch out, wretched censor, for the whole of France is saying it knows what sort of people Italians are*»]

In eundem:

> Nullus, Floride, vir tibi eruditus,
> Unum præter et alterum probatur.
> Nulli de numero eruditiorum
> Unum præter et alterum probaris.

[Against the same man: «*According to you, Sabinus, no man is learned, except one or two who meet with your approval. Among the ranks of the learned, Sabinus, no man thinks you learned, except that you meet with the approval of one or two*»]

In eundem et Philænum:

> Carpit Philænum Floridus malus malum,
> Juvenem juvenis; uter alteri cedet, rogo?
> Uno Sabino criminosius nihil,
> Uno Philæno est impotentius nihil[4].

[Against the same man and Philænus: «*The evil young man Floridus censures the evil young man Philænus. The question is, will he yield to him? Nothing is more slanderous than Sabinus, and nothing more violent than Philænus*»]

The third epigram, presenting «Philænus» as the foe of Floridus, provides a very substantial clue to his identity. For Franciscus Floridus had one very public adversary, and that was Estienne Dolet. Two chapters of Floridus's *Lectiones succisivæ*, published at Basle in 1540, attack Dolet's *De imitatione ciceroniana* (1535), accusing him of plagiarism, triviality and denial of the immortality of the soul; Dolet retaliated in his *De imitatione ciceroniana adversus Floridum Sabinum* (the dedicatory letter, to Guillaume Bigot, is dated 1 October 1540), and Floridus returned to the attack in the following year with a *Liber adversus calumnias Doleti*, published in Rome[5]. Bèze's whole point is to juxtapose Floridus and his notorious foe, and so there is a good *prima facie* case for regarding «Philænus» as a pseudonym for Dolet. Moreover, the last line, describing «Philænus» as *impotens* («headstrong», «furious», «violent»), applies exactly to Dolet, the killer of Compaing. And

---

[4]   The texts of all the epigrams from the 1544 manuscript cited in this article are from Aubert, Boussard and Meylan, art. cit.

[5]   On this controversy, see E.V. Telle's edition of Dolet's *De imitatione ciceroniana* (Genève, 1974), pp. 79-88.

the name «Philænus» suggests «Lover of praise» — a far from unsuitable epithet for the conceited Dolet[6].

(ii) The Ciceronian from Orléans

Other epigrams in this collection attack «Philænus» and confirm that the epithet represents Dolet. One epigram takes up Dolet's well-known boast that he is another Cicero:

In Philænum:

Philænus Cicero videtur alter
Et est: quippe superbus est peræque.

[Against Philænus: «*Philænus seems to be another Cicero — and indeed he is: for he is every bit as haughty as him*»][7]

Another epigram alludes to Dolet's love of praise of his poetry:

In Philænum:

Omnes excellis vates, te teste, Philæne,
  Et peream si non credo, Philæne, tibi.
Nam cum te dicis vates excellere cunctos,
  Te quoque credibile est dicere velle malos.

[Against Philænus: « *You outrank all poets, Philænus — we have your word that you do. Let me perish, Philænus, if I should fail to take your word for it. For when you say you outrank all poets, what you must mean is all bad ones*»]

These two epigrams together invert the claim of Dolet's eulogists that he has credibly rivalled the greatest ancient Latin prose (Cicero's) and verse (Virgil's)[8]. All clues to the identity of Bèze's target point inexorably to Dolet.

---

[6] A historical Philænus is known: Philænus Lunardus, the joint addressee (with Joannes Angelus Odonus) of a letter from Sebastian Gryphius about Ortensio Lando: see P. Grendler, *Critics of the Italian world*, Madison, etc., 1969, p. 23, n. 12. To test my hypothesis that «Philænus» is Dolet, I kept open the alternative possibility that he is this Philænus, or one no longer known. But I have concluded that this alternative explanation is untenable. I know of no reason why Bèze should have linked Philænus Lunardus or any other historical Philænus with Floridus; neither «Philænus» nor «Lunardus» occur in Bèze's *Correspondance*, ed. H. Aubert, F. Aubert, H. Meylan, A. Dufour, A. Tripet, Genève, 1960 onwards, or in P.-F. Geisendorf's *Théodore de Bèze* (Genève, 1949); and the case for identifying «Philænus» as Dolet finally seemed watertight.

[7] Dolet's claim to be the new Cicero was derided by (among others) Julius Cæsar Scaliger in an epigram titled *Doletus iactabat se habere Ciceronis animam* (in his *Poemata*, 3 pts., [Heidelberg,] 1574, B.L. 1213 1 2, I, p. 197). The claim rests upon Dolet's *De imitatione ciceroniana*.

[8] Godefroy Béringier commended Dolet's twin achievement:

Inter Latinos est poëtas maximus
Vergilius: inter rhetores est Tullius.
Lumen Doletus universæ Galliæ
Utrunque si non vincit, exæquat tamen.

[« *Virgil is pre-eminent among Latin poets, and Cicero among orators. Dolet, the light of all France, though not superior to them, is the equal of both*»]

From Dolet's *Carminum libri quatuor*, Lugduni, 1538, B.L. G 9713 (1), Z 2vo. His status as an emulator of Virgil rested on his *Fata Francisci regis*.

If corroboration were needed, it is supplied by the three other epigrams attacking «Philænus» in the 1544 manuscript, the ones which Bèze retained in the 1548 printed *Poemata*[9]. The first refers to Philænus's conceit. If you want someone to testify to Philænus's outstanding achievements, Bèze remarks, Philænus himself will readily do that:

In Philænum

Nil non egregie facit Philænus —
Tersus, integer, elegans Philænus.
Testem si petis, en tibi: Philæno
Teste, hæc omnia perficit Philænus.

[Against Philænus: «*Philænus is without peer in all he does — Philænus the pure, the blameless, the tasteful. If you require a witness to that, here he is — Philænus is our witness that he is perfect in all these respects*»]

In the second 1544 epigram reproduced in 1548, the phrase *Aurelium fucum* tells us that Philænus comes from Orléans, which is where Dolet was born, and the poem alludes also to his readiness to criticise, an attribute which won Dolet innumerable enemies:

In Philænum:

Aurelias vocare vespas suevimus
Ut dicere olim mos erat nasum Atticum:
At te, Philæne, Aurelium vocabimus
Fucum, quod omnes adeo pungas frigide,
Aculeum ut interim relinquas nemini.

[Against Philænus: «*Orléans has become a by-word for its wasps just as Attica was for its wit. But, Philænus, we shall call you the drone of Orléans, because your attacks on people are so feeble that you never leave your sting behind in anyone*»]

The third evokes Philænus's hostility to Erasmus (Dolet's *De imitatione ciceroniana adversus Desiderium Erasmum* enjoyed a *succès de scandale* throughout Europe):

In Philænum:

Erasmus ille, quo fatentur plurimi
Nihil fuisse, vel futurum doctius,
Tibi Philæne stupidus est et plumbeus:
Et quicquid uspiam ab omnibus fingi potest
Calumniarum, stulte in illum congeris.
Latra Philæne quandiu et quantum voles,
Hunc scire constat plura, quam tu nescias.

[Against Philænus: «*Many people acknowledge that there never was, nor will be, anyone more learned than Erasmus. But according to you, Philænus, he is dull and worthless and, in your folly, you heap up against him every kind of calumny ever imagined. Carry on barking, Philænus, as long and as much as you like: it is clear that his knowledge exceeds even your ignorance*»]

---

[9]   I used the copy in the British Library (Lutetiæ, 11403 aaa 35); the poems are respectively at pp. 61, 71 and 74-75. For their fate in later editions of the *Poemata*, see below, note 22.

Thus, this group of poems concerns the notorious foe of Floridus, a man who (as the name suggests) loved fame, who claimed to be a latter-day Cicero *and* Virgil, who came from Orléans, who was a detractor of Erasmus and a carping critic of others: beyond any doubt, Estienne Dolet — who, incidentally, seems to have been attacked by others as «Philænus»[10].

(iii) The letter to Maclou Popon

These epigrams must date from the time of the confrontation between Dolet and Floridus (1540-1541) or a little after. But it is very likely that the paths of Bèze and Dolet had crossed before then, for the two had close acquaintances in common in Orléans (many of the poems in Bèze's 1544 manuscript are dedicated to these friends)[11]. A letter written by Bèze in mid-December 1539 to a friend in Orléans, Maclou Popon, is of interest to us. A remark in that letter reads: «Stephanus mecum agit, sed capite minutus.» The editors were unable fully to explain the phrase «capite minutus», but wrote: «Est-ce une plaisanterie de juriste, ou faut-il penser à l'une des sortes de 'capitis deminutio' (perte de la 'civitas' ou de la 'libertas' ou de la 'familia') que le droit romain connaissait?»[12] The editors did not identify the man Bèze refers to — but (a) he was called Stephanus or Estienne, (b) quite possibly, since the letter is to Popon in Orléans, he had some connection with Orléans, and (c), he seems to have been in trouble. Our Estienne Dolet of Orléans qualifies in every respect for, as is well known, he obtained the royal pardon on 19 February 1537 following his killing of Compaing, but the charges remained on the file and returned to haunt him in the last months of his life. It seems likely, then, that the «Stephanus» of the letter to Popon is Dolet[13]. Why does Bèze refer to him solely by his Christian name? Conceivably because prudence dictated discretion when writing about one's relationship with a man who faced murder charges[14].

---

[10] See Antonio Gouveia, *Epigrammata*, Lugduni, 1540, B.L. G 17437 (2), p. 13 and Simon Vallambert, *Epigrammaton somnia*, Lugduni, 1541, John Rylands Library, Manchester, 21 g 13, p. 51. Both these humanists also denounced Dolet in other poems.

[11] Friends of Bèze in Orléans who knew Dolet include Jean Truchon and Jean Dampierre. On these and other acquaintances of Bèze in Orléans, see H. Meylan, «Bèze et les *sodales* d'Orléans», in his *D'Erasme à Théodore de Bèze*, Genève, 1976, pp. 139-144 (Dolet is not mentioned in this article).

[12] See Bèze's *Correspondance*, ed. cit., I, pp. 37, 38. The reference to «Stephanus», interestingly, comes immediately after a mention of «Beraldus noster», whom the editors identify as Nicolas Bérauld: Bérauld was another scholar from Orléans who was acquainted both with Dolet (who had been a pupil of his in Paris) and Bèze.

[13] Bèze was writing from Paris: it is not known that Dolet was in Paris at the time, but nor is it known that he was not.

[14] The editors of the *Correspondance*, in their annotation on the Popon letter, note that a letter of January 1540 from Jacques Joubert to Maclou Popon sends him greetings from Bèze and from «Stephanus», who is plausibly the same man as Popon refers to.

There is another possible reason for Bèze's coyness about his link with Dolet. From the mid-1530s onwards, scholars started denouncing Dolet (often under pseudonyms) as an atheist[15]. If the letter of 1539 to Popon is about Dolet, Bèze was at that time prepared to tell a close friend, discreetly, that he associated with him. But some time between then and the compiling of the 1544 manuscript, Bèze decided to distance himself unequivocally from Dolet. Perhaps he had got word of those uninhibited speculations on theology which Dolet seems to have vouchsafed to scholars who met him personally; just possibly, given that he and Dolet had friends in common, he had met him and heard these speculations himself. At all events, he knew Floridus's book — which accuses Dolet of denying the immortality of the soul. Moreover, in referring to Dolet, Bèze now moves from the Christian name to the more opaque «Philænus». Even when attacking atheists, you did not make it too obvious that you knew such people. As a further precaution, you refrained from attacking their views on religion (lest it be thought you had engaged in dialogue with them on the subject). Calvin's Geneva and the Portuguese Inquisition looked with equally critical eyes on people who had associated with Dolet, and no doubt other authorities did as well[16].

(iv) Dolet the martyr

In the early 1540s, Dolet made strenuous efforts to dissipate his dangerous reputation for impiety by publishing evangelical tracts. These did not impress the Sorbonne, which had them burned, but Dolet's image among Reformers momentarily improved. Even Calvin, who had a strong dislike for Dolet[17], acknowledged that it was good news that he was publishing the *Psalms* and that he planned to issue the Bible in Olivétan's translation; Satan, Calvin noted in a sardonic echo of the first chapter of

---

[15]   I have assembled a substantial dossier of contemporary statements on Dolet. The dossier goes beyond the material in the section of the *Bibliotheca dissidentium* devoted to Dolet (IV, Baden-Baden, 1984, pp. 53-98; by Claude Longeon). I hope to use this material to produce a study of the *fortuna* of Dolet, giving prominence to the many intriguing statements about his opinions.

[16]   Jacques Gruet confessed under torture in Geneva in 1547 to knowing Dolet (see H. Fazy, *Procédures et documents du XVIe siècle (1546-1547)*, Genève, 1886, pp.95, 98). For Calvin, anyone who had been close to Dolet was strongly suspect: see his letter of 23 September 1544 to Pierre Viret, in H.L. Herminjard, ed., *Correspondance des Réformateurs dans les pays de langue française*, 9 t., Genève, etc., 1866-1897, IX, pp. 331-332. Diogo de Teive had to account for his acquaintance with Dolet at his trial by the Portuguese Inquisition in 1550-1551 (see I.D. McFarlane, *Buchanan*, London, 1981, p. 133).

[17]   Calvin's distaste for Dolet may be due to the latter's derisive remarks in *De imitatione ciceroniana* about theologians in general and Reformers in particular; and he could have learned of the reputation of Dolet from Mathurin Cordier, who was employed by Andrea Gouveia as a professor at the Collège de Guyenne from January 1535 to late in 1536, where he had known many of Dolet's close associates, and from where he went directly to Geneva: see E. Gaullieur, *Histoire du Collège de Guyenne*, Paris, 1874, pp. 95-99, 127-130.

Job, can be the minister of God[18]. Another Reformer, Jean L'Archer, enthusiastically commended Dolet's evangelical books[19]. And in 1544, an anti-monastic epigram by Dolet, which had appeared originally in the *Carminum libri quatuor* of 1538 (I, 17), was published in Geneva («Eleutheropolis»)[20].

This improvement in Dolet's image, coupled with his execution on 3 August 1546, may account for the next twist in Bèze's attitude towards him. For, in his *Poemata* of 1548, Bèze suppressed all of the three poems about Floridus, one of which provided the clue which identified Philænus for us (it doubtless also identified him for contemporaries — and much more readily). Bèze also sacrificed those two further poems on Philænus as the new Cicero and as the conceited poet which confirm his identification as Dolet. The other three poems on Philænus were retained — but the suppressions make it much more difficult to identify Dolet.

That these suppressions are not fortuitous is confirmed by inclusion of the following poem (p. 51) which is explicitly about Dolet and which unequivocally extols him for the manner of his death.

Stephani Doleti Aurelii:

> Ardentem medio rogo Doletum
> Cernens Aonidum chorus sororum,
> Charus ille diu chorus Doleto,
> Totus ingemuit, nec ulla prorsus
> E sororibus est reperta cunctis,
> Naias ulla, Dryasve, Nereisve,
> Quæ non vel lachrymis suis, vel hausta
> Fontis Pegasei studeret unda
> Crudeles adeo domare flammas.
> Et iam totus erat sepultus ignis,
> Iam largo madidus Doletus imbre,
> Exemptus poterat neci videri,
> Quum cælo intonuit severus alto
> Divorum pater, et velut peraegre

---

[18]   Calvin and Viret wrote to Farel around 4 December 1541 as follows: «Lugduni hoc boni est, quod Doletus nunc Psalterium excudit: mox biblia incipiet, ac versionem Olivetani sequetur. Eant nunc qui negant Sathanam esse Dei ministrum» (Herminjard, *op. cit.,* VII, p. 374). Calvin thus reconciled with a jest his dislike of Dolet («Satan»: he evidently saw Dolet as an atheist by 1541) and the news that he was about to publish the *Psalms* and Olivétan's Bible (so far as is known, Dolet did not actually publish the latter).

[19]   L'Archer wrote to Farel on 27 March 1542 as follows:

> Doletus multos egregios et utiles libellos gallice impressit, nempe: *Novum Testamentum, Præcationes Biblicas, Fontem Vitæ, Adhortationem ad studium sacrarum literarum ex patribus excerptam, Enchiridion militis christiani, Præparationem ad mortem,* et alios multos, qui quantum audivi, fructum multum fecerunt. Tandem in carcerem conjectus et hæreseos accusatus, Luteciam ductus est. Quid illo factum sit nescimus.

In Herminjard, *op. cit.,* VIII, p. 303. For condemnations of works printed by Dolet, see F.M. Higman, *Censorship and the Sorbonne,* Genève, 1979, pp. 58, 81, 89, 96-100.

[20]   Dolet's poem is found in an anthology titled *Pasquillorum tomi duo,* p. 72: the title, *De Cucullatis, St[ephani] Dol[eti]* suggests that at that date there was no problem in issuing material by Dolet in Geneva. See E.V. Telle, «L'épître liminaire de Dolet à son édition des *Tusculanes* (1543)», *BHR,* XLI, 1979 (pp. 99-107), p. 104, n. 12.

Hoc tantum studium ferens sororum,
At cessate, ait, et novum colonum
Ne diutius invidete cælo,
Cælum sic meus Hercules petivit.

[Concerning Estienne Dolet of Orléans: « *The choir of sisters from Aonia, whom Dolet had for so long cherished, seeing him ablaze on the pyre, sighed in unison. And every single one of those sisters, and every Naiad, and every Dryad, strove to extinguish the cruel flames with her tears and with water drawn from the fountain of Pegasus. And now the flame was entirely extinguished, and Dolet seemed already to be saved from death, when the stern father of the gods thundered aloft and, as though angered by the zealous exertions of the sisters, said: 'Enough! Stop preventing this man from coming into heaven. My Hercules entered heaven in the same way as he is'* »]

What are we to conclude from this latest change of attitude by Bèze? Firstly, that scholars could forgive each other much when one of them paid the ultimate price for intellectual liberty. Secondly, and more importantly, that this poem perhaps illuminates the genesis of Bèze's conversion to the Reformed faith. As a humanist, he deplored the execution of Dolet; as an incipient Reformer, he was prepared to set aside his earlier criticisms and commend the publisher of evangelical tracts who had paid with his life for his opposition to the clerical establishment. Others, too, saw Dolet in a similar light: he had a tenacious *fortuna*, albeit a very ill-founded one, as a martyr of the Reformation[21]. The first edition of Bèze's *Poemata* is not yet the work of a Reformer (witness the subsequent expurgations), but the poem on Dolet perhaps indicates where his heart lay. Dolet had Catholic admirers also (to whom I hope to devote a separate study): but whilst they extolled his philology, they did not place him in heaven as Bèze does.

(v) Bèze drops his praise of Dolet

There was a final vicissitude in Bèze's attitude to Dolet. Very soon after publishing the first edition of his *Poemata*, he seems to have been disabused about Dolet, for the sympathetic epitaph is not found in the 1549 edition of the *Poemata* or in subsequent editions[22]. Nor does Bèze seem to have referred to Dolet in later years: there is no mention of him in the texts published so far in the *Correspondance* of Bèze[23]. Perhaps Calvin showed him that

---

[21]   On Dolet as a Reformed martyr, see for example a letter of 5 August 1546 from Michel Bäris to Boniface Amerbach and a letter of 10 August 1546 from Johann Heinrich Ryhiner to Oswald Myconius in *Die Amerbachkorrespondenz*, ed. A. Hartmann (Basel, 9 Bd., 1942-1983), respectively VI, p. 298 and VI, p. 20. Telle misattributes the second of these letters in his edition of Dolet's *De imitatione ciceroniana*, p. 90, n. 30.

[22]   See F. Gardy, *Bibliographie des œuvres théologiques, littéraires, historiques et juridiques de Théodore de Bèze*, Genève, 1960, p. 5.

[23]   In the 1569 edition of his poems (*Poematum editio secunda* [Geneva], B.L. 677 b 23 (1)), Bèze omitted the first of the three «Philænus» poems which had appeared in 1548 (the remaining two are on pp. 140 and 143). None of these poems remained in the 1597 edition (*Poemata varia* [Geneva], B.L. 837 i 3). This 1597 edition has, interestingly, a section titled *Cato censorius Christianus*, which consists in a series of individual poems deploring various vices (pp. 234-235; repeated, certainly in error, pp. 270-281). Could Bèze have got the idea for his title from Dolet's *Cato Christianus*?

Dolet's challenge to the establishment was a very different one from that of the Reformers: Calvin's intense dislike of Dolet manifests itself not only in the denunciation of him as «Satan» in 1544, but also, and with equal vigour, in the *Traitté des scandales* of 1550[24]. It is understandable that Bèze suppressed the epitaph, which praises a man whom Calvin regarded as an atheist. Subsequent compilers of anthologies and historical compendia, however, had no such inhibitions, and reproduced Bèze's attractive epigram[25].

London.   Malcolm C. SMITH.

---

[24] The famous passage reads:

> Chacun sçait qu'Agrippa, Villeneuve, Dolet, et leurs semblables ont tousjours orgueilleusement contemné l'Evangile: en la fin, ils sont tombez en telle rage, que non seulement ilz ont desgorgé leurs blasphemes execrables contre Jesus Christ et sa doctrine, mais ils ont estimé, quant à leurs ames, qu'ils ne differoient en rien des chiens et des pourceaux.

From the edition by O. Fatio, Genève, 1984, pp. 136-138 (Calvin seems here to suggest that Dolet's supposed denial of immortality was more reprehensible than his «blasphemies» against Christ). Many passages in Calvin's *Institution de la religion chrestienne* could be seen as applying to Dolet, for example his attacks on practical atheism (I, iv) and formal atheism (I, v, 11); but I have found no passage which appears to be directed at Dolet specifically. See the edition by J.-D. Benoît (5 v., Paris, 1957-1963).

[25] The epitaph appeared in R. Gherus [i.e. Janus Gruterus], *Delitiæ poetarum Gallorum*,1606, III, pp. 596-597, in Jean Le Laboureur's edition of Michel de Castelnau's *Mémoires* (5 t., Bruxelles, 1731), I, p. 348 (where line 6 reads «Nyas *n*ulla» and line 14 «secu*r*us») and in Estienne Baluze's annotation in his edition of Pierre Galland's *Petri Castellani magni Franciæ Eleemosynarii Vita* (Parisiis, 1674, John Rylands Library, Manchester, 43 c 8, p. 157).

Latin Epigrams on Etienne Dolet

MALCOLM C. SMITH

French Neo-Latin poets exchanged epigrams in the 1530s (and later) on any and every pretext.[1] It is not surprising, therefore, that many epigrams are dedicated to Dolet, or have him as their subject. But the epigrams on Dolet are of particular interest. For one thing, they seem to be exceptionally numerous: I have discovered well over twenty people who wrote Latin epigrams on Dolet, and a total of about one hundred poems.[2] Many of them give insight into the particularly complex and intriguing personality of Dolet. Many have historical interest, for Dolet is impor-

---

[1] As Lucien Febvre showed in his admirable portrait of this scholarly milieu in *Le problème de l'incroyance au seizième siècle, La religion de Rabelais* ("L'évolution de l'humanité"), éd. revue, Paris, 1962, I, i, 18–104.

[2] The genre of the epigram is not rigidly defined. J. C. Scaliger, in the section of his *Poetices libri septem* dealing with the epigram ([Lyon,] 1561, B.L. 833 1.24, 169–71), notes that epigrams are of varied lengths, and adds: "Recipit autem omne genus Poeseos, διαλογικον, sive δραματικον, et διηγηματικον, et μικτον. Epigrammatum autem genera tot sunt, quot rerum. Tot versuum generibus explicantur, quot sunt versuum genera. Tot versibus verborumque generibus, speciebus, formis, figuris, modis componuntur, quot sunt in quocunque linguæ, nationis, populi, gentis ambitu genera, species, formæ, figuræ, modi verborum" (170). Guillaume Colletet, in his *Traitté de l'épigramme et traitté du sonnet*, defines the epigram as "Tout Poëme succinct, qui désigne et qui marque naïfvement, ou une personne, ou une action, ou une parole notable; ou qui infere agreablement une chose surprenante de quelque proposition advancée, soit extraordinaire, ou commune," and adds that "la jurisdiction de l'Epigramme s'estend sur toutes les matieres, et sur toutes les choses morales, naturelles, feintes, et imaginaires" (ed. P. A. Jannini, Genève, 1965, 31). Colletet's treatise is an excellent introduction to the genre, especially in the scholarly edition by Jannini. I have accepted as an epigram any poem which its author described as such, or which is succinct, witty and pointed in the conclusion, especially if it offers a verdict upon a person. I have included one poem (that by Beza on Dolet's death) which the author classifies in a different genre.

tant for the history of scholarship and printing, as well as for his eventful life (which included five spells in prison, mostly on religious charges) and momentous death (he was executed in 1546, supposedly for denying the immortality of the soul).[3] Often, these epigrams say as much about the people who wrote them as they do about Dolet. This is to the best of my knowledge the first attempt to list them, and I hope in due course to publish them.[4] Since the poems are by definition short, it seems sufficient to give the author's name in references: the sources are cited in an appendix.

Dolet was distinctive (and hence an appropriate subject for epigrams) in three ways. Firstly for his scholarship and prowess as a writer. Many of the epigrams on Dolet deal with this. For some commentators, his *Fata Francisci regis* qualified him as the new Virgil and his *De Imitatione Ciceroniana* as the new Cicero. For Godefroy Béringier, Dolet is the equal of both Cicero and Virgil.[5] Guillaume Durand declares that his Latin poetry is the equal of that of the ancient Greeks and Romans. Nicholas Bourbon,

---

[3] Dolet was imprisoned (a) in Toulouse, in March 1534, on a charge of exciting a riot and contempt for the *Parlement*; (b) after the murder of the painter Henri Guillot (or Guillaume), known as Compaing, 31 December 1536; (c) in July or August 1542, on suspicion of heresy, probably at the instigation of printers at Lyons; (d) on 6 January 1544, after two packets of heretical books addressed to Dolet had been seized on entry into Paris, and an order for his arrest sent to Lyons (he escaped two days later to Piedmont); and (e) after publishing his *Second Enfer* with his translations of *Axiochus* and *Hipparchus*. See R. C. Christie, *Etienne Dolet, the martyr of the Renaissance, a biography*, London, 1880, respectively 131; 296–313; 401–3, where the charges are related (he was released in October 1543); 425; 431–61. He was arrested for the last time either at Lyons or at Troyes by 7 September 1544, condemned principally for his translation of a passage of the *Axiochus* which taken in isolation denies the immortality of the soul, and condemned to death on 2 August 1546. Nor were these his only unfriendly encounters with authority: see Christie, 154–55 (his retreat from Toulouse to avoid a second arrest there), 157–58 (his banishment from Toulouse) and 385 (trouble over *Cato Christianus* and epigrams).

[4] Michael Maittaire compiled a collection of biographical statements on Dolet, including some epigrams, in his *Annales typographici*, 5t., Hagæ Comitum, 1715 (B.L. 823 h), III, i, 9–113, which I have drawn on. Another very useful source is Claude Longeon's *Bibliographie des œuvres d'Etienne Dolet*, Genève, 1980.

[5] On Dolet as a latter-day Virgil and Cicero, see the flattering comment of Béringier in the epigram cited above, and the sardonic remark of Scaliger in his *Poetices libri septem*, cited by Maittaire (III, i, 16): "[...] suo arbitratu Vergilianas gemmas suæ inserit pici, ut videri velit sua. Ignavus loquutulejus, qui ex tessellis Ciceronis febriculosas quasdam conferruminavit (ut ipse vocat) orationes; ut docti iudicant, latrationes: putavit tantum licere sibi in divinis operibus Virgilianis." On echoes of Virgil in Dolet, see V. J. Worth, "Etienne Dolet: from a neo-Latin epic poem to a chronicle in French prose," in I. D. McFarlane, ed., *Acta Conventus Neo-Latini Sanctandreani* (Binghamton, 1986), 423–29.

commenting on Dolet's oratory, applies to it successively the terms *flumina, lumina, fulmina* and *numina*. Aneau commented that Francis I would be an Augustus to Dolet and Dolet a Virgil to Francis. Several, including Bourbon, Macrin and (curiously) the illustrious Catholic scholar and controversialist Gentian Hervet (whose epigrams glowingly praise Thomas More and John Fisher as well as Dolet) gratify his insatiable thirst for eternal renown. But not all the epigrams on Dolet as a scholar and author are eulogious. George Buchanan tartly comments that it is small wonder that Dolet's poems lack meaning, as their author lacks a mind; and, in another epigram, that Dolet (as no-one can deny) offers splendid words, but that that is all he offers. Several mock Dolet's supposed claim to be Cicero incarnate: Ducher claimed that he had the soul not of Cicero but of Villanovanus, whose Ciceronian scholarship he had stolen (*De Cloaco et Duro*). Gouvea noted that Cicero's soul had lost its power when spread through Dolet's colossal body. And some (Ducher, Gouvea, Scaliger) criticize his versification.[6]

Dolet was egregious secondly for his personality. To put it mildly, several contemporaries found him difficult to get along with—and the epigram is an ideal medium for those with scores to settle. Thus, epigrammatists focused on his ingratitude, his unsociability, his austerity, his treachery, his conceit.[7] From the outset of his career as orator and writer he manifested a tendency to antagonize authority, and this immediately worried even his friends, many of whom, as we shall see, later distanced themselves from Dolet by writing hostile epigrams. And Dolet, who had no mean opinion of himself, had a propensity to belittle others—notably Erasmus, whose friends (Ducher, Binet . . .) retaliated in epigrams directed at Dolet.

The third interesting thing about Dolet is his views on religion, which are presented—perhaps caricatured—by epigrammatists. In order to understand what preoccupied them, it is necessary to examine briefly Dolet's religious views. He cavalierly dismissed dogmatic theology, and

---

[6] Dolet was sensitive to this criticism and replied to it in a prefatory letter in his *Carminum libri quatuor*, 1538.

[7] Even those modern scholars who feel drawn to Dolet have noted these negative aspects. See notably the studies by Claude Longeon: "Cohérences d'Etienne Dolet," in I. D. McFarlane, ed., *Acta Conventus Neo-latini Sanctandreani* (Binghamton, 1986), 363–69; and the introductions to his editions of Dolet's *Le Second Enfer* (Genève, 1978) (11) and *Correspondance* (Genève, 1982) (7) and to his *Bibliographie d'Etienne Dolet* (Genève, 1980) (xx–xxii, xxiv). Among the characteristics which Longeon notes are his instability, irascibility, conceit, intransigence, self-justification, naivety, vindictiveness, suspiciousness and recklessness. On his love of fame, see especially F. Joukovsky, *La gloire dans la poésie Française et latine du XVIe siècle* (Genève, 1969), 191–92.

notably that of Erasmus.[8] He did not profess atheism in any extant document,[9] but we have reliable witnesses to his utterance of such views orally. One is Joannes Angelus Odonus, who visited Dolet in Lyons when Dolet was working at Sebastian Gryphius's printing house: Odonus declared, in a letter to Gilbertus Cognatus dated October 29, 1535, that the University or *Parlement* of Paris might be preparing to have him executed for his atheism—which was public knowledge, for Dolet's own words declared him to be an "impious fellow, without God, without faith, without religion." Dolet, he wrote, perceptively and prophetically, is "For the sake of a slight breath of applause, [...] rushing to certain destruction both of body and soul."[10] Another commentator on Dolet's religious views is Bonaventure Des Périers who worked with Dolet from the summer of 1535 until May 1536 correcting the first volume of Dolet's massive *Commentarii Linguæ Latinæ* [11] and who, in his *Cymbalum mundi* of 1537, implicitly accuses

---

[8] Dolet felt particular scorn for theologians: his *De imitatione Ciceroniana* of 1535 rails against "the insolence, the intolerable conceit and the lunacy not just of Erasmus but of the whole sect of Lutherans." Ranking Erasmus among the Lutherans was a solecism, and an intentionally offensive one, insinuating that Erasmus's refutations were counterproductive—and that dogmatic theologians are all indistinguishable, and all equally noxious. Religion, Dolet urges, "consists entirely in an inner stirring of the soul, in religious awe, in reverence—and is not brought about by words: if you debate about it, or write freely and verbosely about it, then reverence will wither, religious awe will gradually be removed, belief in God will be destroyed and religion will decline into mere commonplace and be dissipated." The *De imitatione Ciceroniana*, though ostensibly philological, is a work of theology, or anti-theology—and highly readable. See the edition by E. V. Telle: *L'Erasmianus sive Ciceronianus d'Etienne Dolet (1535)* (Genève, 1974), especially p. 34–37 of the facsimile, where the passages I have translated here are found. Dolet's cavalier dismissal of Erasmus amounts, needless to say, to caricature: Erasmus, too, saw the need for silence in the face of the divine (see J. C. Margolin, "Erasme et le silence," *Mélanges Saulnier* (Genève, 1984), 163–78). Dolet's abrasive attack on theology recalls another adversary of Erasmus, the renegade Carthusian Otto Brunfels, the founder of modern Nicodemism: the links between the two are explored in my forthcoming study of contemporary views on Dolet.

[9] Scholars have frequently pointed this out, from Maittaire onwards: "At invisum 'αθεον nomen, quod Doleto inurit Scaliger, illi convenire nondum mihi fuit satis compertum. Quantum ex aliquibus eiusdem operibus conjicio, non tantum Deum esse aperte professus est, sed a religione Christiana minime alienum et generalioribus ejusdem dogmatibus imbutum esse se indicavit" (III, i, 17; cf. 101 and notes there). But it is meaningless to say that there is no atheism in Dolet's writing. To consign such thought to print was to write one's own death sentence.

[10] See Christie, *op. cit.*, 216–20. Odonus's attack may have been known to Dolet: see Dolet's *Correspondance*, ed. Longeon, 1982, 62 and n. 4. On Odonus's visit to Dolet, see Longeon, *Bibliographie*, xxv–xxviii.

[11] See Longeon, *Bibliographie*, xxvi and notes 42 and 43 there; see also E. Droz,

Dolet of militant atheism.[12] By 1538, denunciations of Dolet's atheism come thick and fast—and from former friends.[13]

This is the background to epigrams on Dolet published by his close friend and fellow-epigrammatist Joannes Vulteius. Vulteius published some thirty epigrams in praise of Dolet in 1536 and 1537. In 1538, in poems clearly alluding to Dolet though not by name, he accuses him of being a covert atheist—and says he took singularly little trouble to conceal his views.[14] Vulteius's *In quendam irreligiosum Luciani sectatorem* fits absolutely the portrait given in the *Cymbalum mundi*. Nor was Vulteius the only epigrammatist to castigate Dolet for atheist views. The reason why Vulteius and others publicly distanced themselves was that Dolet's reputation made him a dangerous man to know. Friendship with radical thinkers aroused suspicion: at least one humanist was questioned by the Inquisition for his friendship with Dolet.[15] Dolet was an especially dangerous friend for those who had themselves come under suspicion for their religion, as many of Dolet's friends had.

Was Dolet really an atheist? Might one argue that his "real" position is better represented by his work in publishing edifying biblical books? Witnesses like Odonus, Des Périers and Vulteius, who all knew Dolet, leave little or no room for such speculation. Their presentation of Dolet

"Pierre de Vingle, l'imprimeur de Farel," in G. Berthoud *et al.*, *Aspects de la propagande religieuse* (Genève, 1957), 74.

[12] I accept the traditional attribution of the *Cymbalum mundi* to Des Périers: see L. Sozzi, *Les contes de Bonaventure Des Périers*, Torino, 1965, 36. It is in my view inconceivable that during the many months that Des Périers and Dolet worked together, and in Lyons in the 1530s, they failed to discuss religion; I propose to examine Des Péziers's attack on Dolet's atheism elsewhere.

[13] Clément Marot is one, assuming his epigram *Contre l'inique*, written around 1538, is, as has been supposed, directed at Dolet—cf. Chassaigne, *op, cit.*, 195-97. But Lionello Sozzi surmised that the epigram was directed at Des Périers—see "Marot, Dolet, Des Périers e l'epigramma *Contre l'inique*," *Studi francesi*, V, 1961, 83-88. A mysterious attack on Dolet by Jean Binet may refer to his atheism: see J. Dupèbe, "Un poète néo-latin: Jean Binet de Beauvais," *Mélanges V. L. Saulnier* (Genève, 1984), 613-28, 625 n. 82.

[14] That the enemy denounced by Vulteius is Dolet has been argued before, notably by Lucien Febvre in *Le Problème de l'incroyance au seizième siècle, la religion de Rabelais* (Paris, 1942), 48-60. My reading of the *Cymbalum mundi* strongly corroborates this interpretation. Dolet's religion (or lack of it) was attracting increasingly frequent comment.

[15] Diogo de Teive's friendship with Dolet was held against him at his trial by the Inquisition in Portugal: see R. Trinquet, *La Jeunesse de Montaigne*, Paris, 1972, 500 n. 99.

is borne out by Cardinal Philibert Babou de La Bourdaisière, who apparently also knew Dolet: "[...] Dolet un des premiers, [...] commençant par assez legeres opinions et de peu d'importance, tomba en peu de temps es plus execrables blasphemes que j'ouys jamais."[16] Dolet had a public and cosmetic position represented by his pious publications and by his (nebulous) declarations of belief, and a semi-public and real position which was atheism. Having been guided to this conclusion by people who can be trusted, one can say that it is borne out by contemporary polemicists (from both sides of the religious divide) whose testimony one is more inclined to treat with caution.[17]

Dolet's obsession for self-justification and fame led him to a mistake which was to prove fatal: instead of playing down the allegations of atheism, he denied them—thus keeping alive the question, "Is Dolet an atheist?" In a dedicatory letter to Jacopo Sadoleto in his *Cato Christianus* of 1538, he drew attention to the fact that his enemies alleged he was an atheist but claimed that the *Cato Christianus* would itself dispel that charge. Guillaume Durand, in an involuntarily revealing epigram published in this work, urged Dolet's detractors to stop describing him as "void of religion" and to conclude from his book that he is a "learned teacher of religion." These claims availed nothing: the book was condemned.[18] Dolet added a further profession of faith in his *Genethliacum* of 1539 and, in a tract against Floridus Sabinus published in 1540, refuted the allegation (which Sabinus had made the year before) that he had denied the immortality of the soul.[19] However, the manner of Dolet's protests of orthodoxy remains truculent. And their content remains nebulous. The same contempt for dogmatic theology which made the *De Imitatione Ciceroniana* such an electrifying document pervades or underlies his subsequent statements on religion. None of these statements silenced his foes: Sabinus attacked him for irrelig-

---

[16] Cited from Michel de Castelnau's *Mémoires*, 1660, I, 355–56 by Maittaire, III, i, 111, note.

[17] Calvin declared, in his *Traitté des scandales*: "Chacun sçait qu'Agrippa, Villeneuve, Dolet, et leurs semblables ont tousjours orgueilleusement contemné l'Evangile: en la fin, ils sont tombez en telle rage, que non seulement ilz ont desgorgé leurs blasphemes execrables contre Jesus Christ et sa doctrine, mais ils ont estimé, quant à leurs ames, qu'ils ne differoient en rien des chiens et des pourceaux" (ed. O. Fatio, Genève, 1984, 136–38). Cf. the verdict of Proteolus [Gabriel Du Préau?] cited by Maittaire, III, i, 106, note (m), from Bayle, *Dict.*, II, 1012.

[18] See C. Longeon, *Documents d'archives sur Etienne Dolet* (Saint-Etienne, 1977), 27.

[19] See Christie, *op. cit.*, 336–38 and 273–75.

ion again in 1541.[20] Dolet's uncompromising attitude towards powerful foes remained with him until the end—and doubtless hastened the end: shortly before his death he published a virulent denunciation of the Inquisitor Matthieu Orry.[21]

That Dolet's erstwhile friends had reason to distance themselves was soon to become graphically apparent.... And his death, like his life, inspired epigrammatists, some writing long after his death. One epigram is friendly to Dolet: Théodore de Bèze, in his *Poemata* of 1548, has a picture of the Muses dampening with their tears the flames which are consuming Dolet—until Jupiter instructs them to stop delaying his entry into heaven (the poem was not reprinted in later editions).[22] But most are hostile. Jean Binet noted that Dolet, who had written of the destiny of Francis I, has not foretold his own, and ought rather to have followed Christ than adopted atheism and the fate that went with it. Andreas Frusius commented gruesomely that Dolet's desire to shine brightly had been met in the manner of his death and, in another epigram, that Dolet used to rejoice in his belief that the soul is mortal but now grieves at the fact that it is not. Estienne Pasquier commented that the flames had failed to purify Dolet and that he had sullied the flames; Jacques Servert, author of a work titled *L'Anti-martyrologe* published in Lyons in 1622, attributed to Dolet an epigram at the moment of his execution: "Dolet is not grieving (*Non dolet ipse Dolet*), but the pious crowd is"—and attributed to a bystander the cruel rejoinder, "The pious crowd is not grieving, but *dolet ipse Dolet.*"

A good epigram moves swiftly and inevitably towards a conclusion which is startling but which on reflection seems inevitable. Dolet's life—brief, unpredictable, striking, memorable—has the qualities of the epigram. And it resembles the epigram most intimately and poignantly in that the most disconcerting, moving and memorable point comes at the end: the epigram, wrote Guillaume Colletet, must have a "conclusion artificieuse, surprenante, et dont la pointe vive et aiguë soit capable d'émouvoir et d'enlever l'esprit du Lecteur."[23] And just as the good

---

[20] See Christie, *op. cit.*, 275-76.

[21] Dolet described Orry in the following terms: "soy disant Inquisiteur de la foy (je ne sçay si plus tost se debvroit appeller inquietateur d'ycelle [...] je n'en cogneus jamais ung plus ignorant, ung plus maling et plus appetant la mort et destruction d'ung Chrestien" (Dolet, *Préfaces françaises*, ed. C. Longeon, Genève, 1979, 169).

[22] On this, and other epigrams by Bèze which I have recently proved have Dolet as their (unnamed) subject, see my "Théodore de Bèze and Philaenus, *Bibliothèque d'Humanisme et Renaissance*," LII, 1990, 345-353.

[23] Colletet, *op. cit.*, 83.

epigram carries throughout the seeds of its own ineluctable conclusion, the life of Dolet prepares the end: the rootless youth, the precarious livelihood, the defiance of the system, the disparagement of privileged but untalented colleagues, the unbridled love of intellectual freedom in a society which limited its exercise, the idealism which ultimately would not bow to expediency—these characteristics stirred friend and foe into action and, ultimately, into action which cost Dolet his life. His life and his death were an epigram: doubtless subconsciously, his contemporaries discerned just how apposite the epigram is as a vehicle for their verdicts upon him.

Royal Holloway and Bedford New College
(University of London)

Bibliography

Barthélemy Aneau, in Dolet's *Francisci Valesii Gallorum regis Fata*, Lugduni, apud Doletum, 1539, B.L. G9713 (3), 78.

Godefroy Béringier, in Dolet's *Carminum libri quatuor*, Lugduni, 1538, B.L. G9713 (1), Z2vo.

Théodore de Bèze, *Poemata*, 1548, B.L. 11403 aaa 35, 51.

Jean Binet, B.Nat. ms. n.a. lat. 2070 (two poems; cf. *Mélanges sur la littérature de la Renaissance à la mémoire de V.-L. Saulnier*, Genève, 1984, 621, n. 52); manuscript verse in the B.Nat. copy of Dolet's *Francisci Valesii Fata* (see Christie, *op. cit.*, 466).

Nicolas Bourbon, Παιδαγωγειον, Lugduni, 1536, B.L. 11403 aaa 14, 26 (two poems), 33 and 45; also Dolet, *Carminum libri quatuor*, 1538, Zro (two poems).

Jean Boyssoné, Latin poems in defence of Dolet: see H. Jacoubet, *Les Poésies latines de Jehan de Boyssoné*, Toulouse, 1931.

George Buchanan, *Franciscanus et fratres* [s.l.], 1584, 160–61 and 166; and another poem cited by Christie, *op. cit.*, 478, n. 1.

Claude Cottereau, in Dolet's *Genethliacum Claudii Doleti*, Lugduni, apud Doletum, 1539, B.L. G9713 (2), C2ro (two poems).

Estienne Dolet, poem on his own impending execution: in Jacques Severt, *L'Anti-Martyrologe*, Lyon, 1622, cited by Christie, *op. cit.*, 458–59.

Gilbert Ducher, *Epigrammaton libri duo*, Lugduni, 1538, B.L. 11409 aa 23, 12, 38, 90, 96, 104, 104–5 and 105.

Guillaume Durand, in Dolet's *Cato Christianus*, Lugduni, apud Doletum, 1538, John Rylands Library, 3 d 1, 7; another epigram in Dolet's *Francisci Valesii Fata*, 78.

Andreas Frusius, *Epigrammata in haereticos*, Antuerpiæ, 1606, B.L. 11408 a 41 (two poems).

Joannes Gigas, four epigrams against Dolet in *Sylvarum liber*, Vitebergæ, 1540 according to Christie, *op. cit.*, 466.

Antonius Gouvea, *Epigrammata*, Lugduni, 1540, B.L. G17437 (2), 16; this and three others on Dolet in Leodegarius a Quercu, *Flores Epigrammatum ex optimis quibusque authoribus excerpti*, t.1, 1555, B.L. 11403 a 29, 313vo, 314vo, 315vo and 316vo; and another in Dos Reys, *Corpus illustrium Poetarum Lusitanorum*, Lisbonæ, 7v, 1745-48, VII, 454.

Janus Guttanus, in Dolet's *Genethliacum Claudii Doleti*, C2vo.

Gentian Hervet, *Epigrammata*, Lugduni, apud Doletum, 1541, B.L. 8411 aa 24, 72.

Jean Salmon Macrin, in Dolet's *Carminum libri quatuor*, Y4vo.

Estienne Pasquier, *Poemata*, 1585, B.L. 11408 aaa 58 (2), 5ro; and a poem from his *Tumuli* cited by F. Berriot, *Athéismes et athéistes*, Lille, 1976, 392.

François Rabelais, in Dolet's *Carminum libri quatuor*, 75-76.

Georgius Sabinus, in *Delitiæ poetarum Germanorum huius superiorisque ævi illustrium*, Pars V, collectore A.F.G.G. [Janus Gruterus], Francofurti, 1612, B.L. 238 i 21-22, 1138 (two poems).

Julius Caesar Scaliger, *Poemata omnia*, 1600, B.L. 1213 1 4, 182, 184 (three poems), 330, 377, 382, 401 and 588.

Maurice Scève, in Dolet's *Genethliacum Claudii Doleti*, C2vo.

Hubert Sussaneau, *Ludorum libri*, Parisiis, 1538, B.L. 1070 d 14, 16ro-vo, 16vo, 25vo-26ro, 27vo and 34ro-vo.

Pierre Tolet, in Dolet's *Genethliacum Claudii Doleti*, C4vo.

Simon Vallambertus, in Leodegarus a Quercu, *Flores*, 129vo.

Joannes Vulteius, *Epigrammatum libri duo*, Lugduni, 1536, B.L. 1213 k 5 (1), 8 (two poems), 11, 12 (two poems), 13, 16, 25, 26, 29, 48, 73-74, 100, 102, 106, 110, 134, 152, 158, 161, 173; further poems are found in the 1547 edition (B.L. 1213 f 1), 31, 190, 206, 220-22, 230, 230-33, 248-49, 250 (two poems) and 254; more poems in his *Hendecasyllaborum libri quatuor*, Parisiis, 1538, B.L. 11405 a 52, 9ro-10ro, 10ro, 10ro-11ro, 22ro-vo, 28ro (two poems), 30vo-32vo, 42ro-vo, 47vo-48ro, 71vo-72vo, 81vo, 84ro-vo, 92ro and 96vo (two poems).

A SIXTEENTH-CENTURY ANTI-THEIST
(on the *Cymbalum mundi*)

This article presents a discovery about the meaning of eight lines in the mysterious *Cymbalum mundi*. The initial discovery led to others, and unless I am mistaken the article puts together several pieces in the jigsaw of French sixteenth-century radical thought.

I. WHY IS THE «CYMBALUM MUNDI» DIFFICULT TO UNDERSTAND?

The *Cymbalum mundi*, a collection of four Lucianic dialogues, was published anonymously in Paris towards the end of 1537 or early in 1538[1]. It is full of allusive commentary on contemporary events. Fiction often was at the time: readers were invited, implicitly or (as in the case of Rabelais's prologue to *Gargantua*) explicitly, to detect the underlying message — which, because it was an underlying one, the author could usually repudiate if necessary.

But though the sense of the *Cymbalum mundi* is veiled, the book was immediately denounced — both by Catholics (the Sorbonne condemned it as pernicious and had it burned) and by Reformers; and commentators continued to attack it for the remainder of the century[2]. Very understandably, sixteenth-century readers did not spell out the «scandalous» meanings they had discerned: that would have given currency to views they abhorred; so it is difficult for the modern reader to see what shocked them. And recent scholars, and excellent ones, see nothing anti-religious in the book at all, and

---

[1] The date is 1537, old style. The publisher was Jean Morin, and the book was also issued very soon after in Lyons by Benoist Bonnyn. See L. Febvre, «Une histoire obscure: la publication du *Cymbalum mundi*», *Revue du seizième siècle*, XVII, 1930, pp. 1-41.

[2] These condemnations are rehearsed below: see section (IX). Some scholars since the sixteenth century have seen this work as irreligious (see note 46), but the consensus of the most recent commentators is that it is not.

describe it as a work of mysticism which piously deprecates dissensions of theologians[3].

The reason modern readers have been able to interpret the book as pious is that no-one, either in the sixteenth century or more recently, has identified a single passage which would incontrovertibly have shocked a reader at the time the work was published. This article identifies one such passage — and will enable us to see the sense of sixteenth-century verdicts on the book. First, though, it will be helpful to recall the meaning of the title and to discuss the authorship of these enigmatic dialogues.

II. WHAT DOES THE TITLE «CYMBALUM MUNDI» MEAN?

It has been said that the title of the *Cymbalum mundi*, «cymbal of the world», is an echo of St. Paul and thus reflects a pious intent. «If I speak in the tongues of men and angels, but have not love», declares the Apostle in the *First letter to the Corinthians*, «I am a noisy gong or a clanging cymbal» (XIII, 1). Thus, the title *Cymbalum mundi* (according to this theory) designates the idle and resounding chatter which Paul castigates — and which is indeed denounced in the dialogues themselves[4]. The problem about this interpretation of the title is that St. Paul did not refer to a «cymbal of the world» but to a «clanging cymbal», so the match between the title of the satire and the epistle to the Corinthians is far from perfect.

Indeed, it has been well argued that the title *Cymbalum mundi* is an echo not of St. Paul but of the Elder Pliny's preface to his *Historia naturalis*. There, we find the precise phrase *Cymbalum mundi*. Erasmus explained the phrase in his *Adagia*, drawing on Pliny: «cymbal of the world» is what the emperor Tiberius called the grammarian Apion (since Apion, the emperor

---

[3]   See especially the fundamental article by V.L. Saulnier, «Le sens du *Cymbalum mundi* de Bonaventure Des Périers», *Bibliothèque d'Humanisme et Renaissance*, XIII, 1951, pp. 43-69, 137-171. P.H. Nurse, in the introduction to his standard edition (*Cymbalum mundi*, texte établi et présenté par P.H. Nurse, préface de M.A. Screech, Textes littéraires français, Genève, 1983), maintains that the author of the *Cymbalum mundi* presents a mystic religion of divine love, a religion shorn of «human» doctrine: «Si, pour le fond, sa morale est d'inspiration chrétienne, sa théologie contredit toutes les 'orthodoxies'» (pp. xxxviii-xxxix). For surveys of interpretations of the *Cymbalum mundi*, see the first part of the article by Saulnier mentioned above and W. Boerner, *Das «Cymbalum mundi» des Bonaventure des Périers: Eine Satire auf die Redepraxis im Seitalter der Glaubensspaltung*, München, 1980, pp. 9-39.

[4]   See Nurse's introduction: «Le *cymbalum mundi* désigne bien ce 'monde-cymbale' où chacun 'parle langages des hommes', mais où personne n'entend la vraie Charité, ressemblant par là à 'l'airain qui résonne, ou la cymbale qui tinte'» (p. xxxii; cf. p. xiv).

thought, had the ability to confer great fame upon those whom he extolled). But, Erasmus adds, again echoing Pliny, Apion ought rather to be called a *tympanum publicæ famæ*, a «drum» conferring vulgar notoriety — for (Erasmus explains) drums were made from asses' skins, and Pliny was alluding to the «asinine» noise of Apion's rhetoric[5]. A *cymbalum mundi*, then, is a rhetorician who, like Apion, fills the world with noise and beguiles powerful people like emperors, but who is «rumbled» by alert scholars like Pliny.

This interpretation of the term *Cymbalum mundi*, a strident orator acclaimed by the mighty, fits the content of the work — for it is about people who fill the world with noise. The author was thus writing under the aegis, as it were, of Pliny, not St. Paul. Indeed, as our examination of the book unfolds, we shall see that the title cannot be a pious echo of St. Paul.

III. WHO WROTE THE «CYMBALUM MUNDI»?

But who wrote the anonymous *Cymbalum mundi*? This article will shed light on that issue; but first, I want to summarize the best contemporary testimony (which some recent writers have overlooked); that of Andrée Zébédée. Zébédée, a native of Brabant, had taken a teaching post at the Collège de Guyenne in Bordeaux towards the end of 1533. He had had to flee Bordeaux early in 1538 in the face of measures against Reformers and had become pastor at Orbe, near Lausanne. His comment on the authorship of the *Cymbalum mundi* is in a letter written in Geneva on 31 July 1538 to «de Cande» in Bordeaux (Charles de Candely). The letter was intercepted in Lyons with seven others by Reformers and was sent to the Chancellor of France, Antoine Du Bourg, with a covering letter dated 8 August.

Zébédée's letter does not survive, but a contemporary summary does. The relevant part of the summary reads as follows:

> ... L'article suyvant dit que France est par grans espritz tirée à l'enseigne d'Epicure et que celluy qui a faict *Cymbalum mundi* ne tendit jamais à aultre chose. Lequel (ce dit) estoit sorty de eulx et avoit esté clerc de Olivetain à mettre la bible en françoys. Le IIIIᵉ article contient ce propos: «Il me souvient bien de *Dolet, Rabelez*, et *Marot* et je m'estonne quant je rememorre ce qu'on m'en a dit à Lyon.»

---

[5] See H. Busson, *Le rationalisme dans la littérature française de la Renaissance, 1553-1601*, nouv. éd., Paris, 1957, p. 182 and n. 3 (Busson refers to Adrien Turnèbe's *Lucubrationes*, 1597, p. 30) and M.A. Screech, «The meaning of the title *Cymbalum mundi*», *Bibliothèque d'Humanisme et Renaissance*, XXXI, 1969, pp. 343-345 (drawing on Erasmus's *Adagia*, IV, X, LXXXII).

The author of the *Cymbalum mundi* had thus been a Reformer and had worked as the *clerc* or editorial assistant on Olivétain's translation of the Bible; and he had abandoned his Reformed faith (he was «sorty de eulx»)[6].

Olivétain (or Olivétan; his real name was Pierre Robert) had published his French Bible in June 1535. It contains several indications that the editorial assistant had been Jean Bonaventure Des Périers. A preliminary Latin poem bears the title *Io. Eutychi Deperii amanuensis interpretis de Gallica hac Bibliorum versione carmen* («*A poem of Jean Bonaventure Des Périers, secretary of the translator, concerning the present translation of the Bible*»). In an *Apologie du translateur*, Olivétan attributes to Des Périers the compilation of the summaries and index of meanings of proper names. And the latter index bears a heading crediting it to Des Périers and «Rosa» (probably Hugues Sureau Du Rosier)[7]. Thus, when Zébédée attributed the *Cymbalum mundi* to Olivétan's editorial assistant, he was attributing it to Des Périers.

Although only a summary of Zébédée's letter survives, there is reason to believe it is a faithful one. This is because the seven other letters by Reformers which were seized at the same time were also summarized, and the seven summaries are extant, and are accurate; it would be extraordinary if the eighth, that of the letter by Zébédée, were inaccurate. Furthermore, Zébédée is probably a good source: he had worked for several years at the Collège de Guyenne in Bordeaux, which was an intellectual crossroads[8]; and the summary of his letter shows he also had acquaintances among scholars in Lyons, where Des Périers worked. Zébédée's attribution was, as will be seen later, backed by others.

Des Périers (?1510—?1543), «le talent le plus naïf, le plus original et le plus piquant de son époque»[9], is surrounded in mystery. So, too, is the

---

[6]   On this letter, see G. Berthoud, «Lettres de réformés saisies à Lyon en août 1538», *Revue de Théologie et de Philosophie*, nouv. sér., XXIV, 1936 (pp. 154-178), p. 177. Berthoud supposes (p. 161) that Zébédée's source on Dolet, Rabelais and Marot was Visagier, his former colleague at the Collège de Guyenne in Bordeaux.

[7]   See Sozzi, *Les contes de Bonaventure Des Périers*, Torino, 1965, p. 17 and n. 42. Sozzi is incorrect in saying (p. 17) that Zébédée «affirme explicitement que Des Périers 'avoit été clerc de Olivétain à mectre la Bible en françois'»: what Zébédée affirms it that the author of the *Cymbalum mundi*, whom he does not name, had been Olivétan's «clerc». But though Zébédée does not name him, it seems certain that he was pointing to Des Périers. On Olivétan's Bible, see G. Casalis *et al.*, *Olivétan, traducteur de la Bible*, Paris, 1987 (none of the studies in this symposium is devoted to the role of Des Périers).

[8]   On the Collège de Guyenne, see E. Gaullieur, *Histoire du Collège de Guyenne*, Paris, 1874.

[9]   The phrase is Charles Nodier's: quoted by Sozzi (*Les Contes* [...], p. 9) from *Bonaventure Des Périers, Cyrano de Bergerac*, Paris, 1841, p. 3.

Cymbalum mundi: «L'homme est un inconnu, l'œuvre une énigme»[10]. He was probably born in Burgundy, and became a pupil around 1530 of Robert Hurault, *abbé* of Saint-Martin (who, according to the authors of the Reformers' *Histoire ecclésiastique* of 1580, believed «[...] beaucoup de choses des rêveries des libertins»). He seems to have had a peripatetic and indigent existence. After his editorial work on Olivétan's Bible, he worked in Lyons for eleven months with Estienne Dolet on the latter's *Commentarii Linguæ Latinæ*, and knew several scholars and poets there. In 1536, he began to dedicate works to Marguerite de Navarre and was appointed a *valet de chambre* in her household, probably working as a scribe. He was the first poet to defend Marot in the latter's quarrel with François Sagon. Very little is known about his last years; on 31 August 1544, Antoine Du Moulin published the *Œuvres de feu Bonaventure Des Périers*. According to Henri Estienne (in his *Apologie pour Herodote* of 1566), Des Périers committed suicide[11].

That, then, is the man usually credited with the *Cymbalum mundi*. However, I intend for the time being to treat the authorship as an open issue, and to return to it towards the end of this article.

IV. WHAT IS THE MEANING OF HYLACTOR'S MISCHIEF?

The fourth dialogue of the *Cymbalum mundi* is between Hylactor and Pamphagus, two of the dogs who, in the fable recorded by Ovid (*Metamorphoses*, III, 138-252), devoured their master Actaeon when Diana turned him into a stag. To Ovid's account, the author adds the notion that these two hounds devoured Actaeon's tongue, and can therefore talk. In an opening monologue, Hylactor, who has been separated from Pamphagus, deplores the fact that no other dog can talk. Hylactor here admits to being a mischief-maker. He wanders the streets at night and calls the names of residents — who rush to their windows in alarm. Or he yells «Murder!» or «Thieves!» or «Fire!» He spreads alarm wherever he goes: he is a thoroughly anti-social creature.

---

[10] Quoted by Sozzi (*ibid.*) from L. Febvre's *Origène et Des Périers, ou l'énigme du Cymbalum mundi*, Paris, 1942, p. 11.

[11] Sozzi accepted that Des Périers committed suicide on the grounds (tenuous, in my view) that «l'accent du malheur n'est pas absent de ses poèmes» (*Les Contes*, p. 46). Sozzi is my source for the biography of Des Périers. He discusses the authorship of the *Cymbalum mundi* on p. 36.

Much worse is to come:

> ... Puis, quant j'ay bien faict toutes les follies de mes nuictz attiques,
> jusques au chapitre *Qui sunt leves et importuni loquutores*, pour
> mieulx passer le demourant de mes phantasies, ung peu devant que le
> jour vienne, je me transporte au parc de noz ouailles faire le loup en
> la paille; ou je m'en voys desraciner quelque arbre mal planté, ou
> brouiller et mesler les filetz de ces pescheurs, ou mettre des os et des
> pierres au lieu du tresor que Pygargus l'usurier a caché en son champ;
> ou je voys pisser aux potz du potier et chier en ses beaulx vases. Et si
> d'aventure je rencontre le guet, j'en mors trois ou quatre pour mon
> plaisir, et puis je m'en fuy tant que je puis, cryant: «Qui me pourra
> prendre, si me prenne!»

The phrase «nuictz attiques» echoes the title of the famous compilation
by Aulus Gellius, and the Latin words are from the beginning of a chapter
which consists in quotations from ancient authors on the theme of idle
speech (*Noctes Attiæ*, I, xv); more on that later. More important is Hylactor's list of mischievous acts. All five are carried out furtively, under cover
of darkness. And all evoke the Bible — and to make the same point. The
Church of Christ is a sheepfold, threatened by ravening wolves — like Hylactor. The Church is a tree in which birds find a home — a tree which Hylactor
uproots. The apostles are fishers of men — and Hylactor entangles their
nets. The kingdom of heaven is a treasure buried in a field — but Hylactor
substitutes rubbish for the treasure. And we creatures are the vessels
fashioned by the Creator — vessels in which Hylactor relieves himself[12].

The presence of five successive phrases with biblical resonance cannot be
fortuitous, for the book is full of theological comment (and if Des Périers
wrote it, it is by a man who had just finished annotating the Bible). These
allusions are likely to have been discerned at the time. And to discern them
is to capture the meaning — that Hylactor, on his own confession, mocks
the Creator and is an atheist. Indeed, worse: he is an unremitting foe of the
Creator, an anti-theist who sabotages the design of the Creator. And he
cynically employs the sacred word itself to describe his sacrilegious deeds.

---

[12]   The sheepfold: *John* X (and many other texts). The tree: *Matthew* XIII, 31-32; *Mark*
IV, 30-32; *Luke* XIII, 18-19. The nets: *Matthew* XIII, 47-50. The treasure: *Matthew* XIII, 44.
The pots: *Romans* IX, 20-24. W. Boerner saw the source of the remark about the pots, and
linked the tree with *Matthew* XV, 13, which could be correct; he traced the nets to *Luke* V, 1-4,
which seems a less good parallel than the one I have suggested. However, he missed the fact
that all Hylactor's five acts of mischief echo the New Testament (and that all allude to the Christian Church, and show Hylactor undermining it). See *Das «Cymbalum mundi» des Bonaventure des Périers: Eine Satire auf die Redepraxis im Zeitalter der Glaubensspaltung*, München,
1980, pp. 269-270 and notes.

Immediately after listing his mischievous deeds, Hylactor tells how he bites those in authority and flees, crying «Qui me pourra prendre, si me prenne!» This is another biblical echo and, in the light of what we now know, a clever one. The text in question (*Matthew* XIX, 12) runs, in the form in which it would have been recognized then, *Qui potest capire, capiat*: it means, indeed, «Let whoever can, capture me» — and also means «Let whoever can understand, understand». Hylactor is thus playfully and impiously echoing Christ's instruction to his disciples to listen receptively to his message. Hylactor's own discourse is the anti-parable of an anti-theist[13].

The damage Hylactor does to the Church is shown as part of an anti-social way of life. He spreads alarm in the community at night; and, when he has done his best to subvert the Church, he defies the authorities to do anything about his activities — biting them and fleeing with a derisively impious challenge. We see here a characteristic sixteenth-century presentation of atheism — which, it was thought, abolished fear of divine and eternal sanctions for vice and virtue, and therefore unleashed all manner of anti-social behaviour in this life[14].

V. WHAT IS HYLACTOR'S MESSAGE?

In that opening monologue, Hylactor says he longs to speak in the presence of men, since a talking dog will immediately gain great fame, prestige and wealth. Indeed he declares (a little contradictorily) that he has spoken to a select group: «Si j'en avoye tant seulement dict autant que j'en vien de dire en quelque compagnie de gens, le bruyt en seroit desja jusques aux Indes, et diroit-l'on partout: 'Il y a, en ung tel lieu, ung chien qui parle!'» But he leaves us with the impression that apart from this occasion he has yet to show men he can speak, and that before doing so he wants to meet another talking dog like himself. Just as he is losing hope of finding another talking dog, Pamphagus appears and in the remainder of the dialogue they debate whether to use their gift of speech in the presence of men. Pamphagus tries

---

[13]   I am indebted to Boerner (Das «Cymbalum mundi [...]», p. 369) for the source of «Qui me pourra prendre».

[14]   So anti-social was atheism held to be that virtually everybody regarded it as impossible to tolerate (see my «Opium of the people: Numa Pompilius in the French Renaissance», *Bibliothèque d'Humanisme et Renaissance*, LII, 1990, pp. 7-8 and n. 5).

to restrain Hylactor's desire to acquire notoriety by untimely speech, eventually admitting his efforts are likely to have been fruitless.

What is the author getting at? Hylactor must represent someone who is about to attack the Church of Christ in public. Before he does so, however, he hopes to find kindred spirits, and so he whispers in the ears of others in the hope of finding «dogs» like him. Indeed, there is a small group to whom he has spoken, and the author is implicitly indicating that he is part of that group. Why, incidentally, represent this anti-theist as a dog? Perhaps the author was thinking of Diogenes who, on account of his shameless rejection of convention, was known as a «dog» (κυων — hence the epithet «cynic» bestowed on his followers). In the sixteenth century, cynics and atheists were frequently denounced as «dogs»[15].

The author presents Hylactor's message as a dangerous one and hence an alluring one. Hylactor has to impart it furtively and allusively. He has so far only divulged it to a fellow-dog and a small group of intimates: when he utters it openly, it will give him instant notoriety. The cynical mischief which accompanies his dangerous opinion (and which was thought at the time to be the invariable concomitant of atheism) is perpetrated under cover of darkness. A similar aura of furtiveness surrounds the *Cymbalum mundi* itself: the ostensible editor professes to have found the manuscript in the ancient library of a remote monastery, and strictly adjures the unnamed dedicatee to allow no copy to circulate, lest the text fall into the hands of printers. The author is presenting the work itself, as well as the veiled message of Hylactor, as a kind of «forbidden fruit».

VI. WHO IS HYLACTOR?

Many of the «fictitious» characters in the *Cymbalum mundi* would have been recognizable at the time. In the first dialogue, Curtalius represents a hunchback (for that is what the name κυρτάλιος means), and his name and his actions suggest the theologian Noël Béda. In the second dialogue, the odious Rhetulus is an anagram of Lutherus, and Cubercus an anagram of

---

[15] Agrippa von Nettesheim, for example, in his *De vanitate* (written 1526, published 1531), declared that Celsus, Porphyry, Lucian, Pelagius and Arius «barked like dogs» against Christ (chapter 53); and Calvin, in a famous passage of *Des scandales* of 1550, referred to Agrippa, Villeneuve, Dolet, Rabelais, Gouvea and Des Périers as «chiens» (Genève, 1550, p. 73). On these passages, see C. Lauvergnat-Gagnière, *Lucien de Samosate et le lucianisme en France au XVIᵉ siècle, athéisme et polémique*, Genève, 1988, respectively pp. 170 and 152-153.

Buccerus (i.e. Martin Bucer). Contemporaries must have delighted in seeking to identify other characters, as modern readers do.

It would be of particular interest to identify Hylactor, this anti-theist in a culture which held «mere» atheism in horror. The author provides several clues. He wanted contemporaries to identify Hylactor.

a) Hylactor possessed a reputation for impiety — or was acquiring one.

b) The name Hylactor derives from ὑλακτέω, «I bark» — and Ovid describes Hylactor as having a shrill tongue (*Metamorphoses*, III, 224), so Hylactor was noted for stridency.

c) Hylactor craves notoriety.

d) Hylactor is a mischief-maker — who, so far at least, has evaded retribution from the authorities.

e) Hylactor has been in a fight — he is so disfigured by a cut ear and a scarred brow that Pamphagus fails to recognize him. And the incident is one which he adamantly refuses to discuss.

f) The title *Cymbalum mundi* designates, as we have seen, a rhetorician who impresses the powerful by his ability to confer renown — and it is possible that Hylactor illustrates that title.

g) The author of the *Cymbalum mundi* must have been a close associate of the individual whom Hylactor represents — for atheists at that time would only have confided in close associates. In all probability, the author was close to this atheist immediately prior to the publication of the *Cymbalum mundi* — for much of the point of the book is its topicality.

One contemporary perfectly fits all these elements — Estienne Dolet[16]:

a) Dolet had a growing reputation for atheism. He did not record atheist views in any extant document. But, as we shall see, he had already published a cavalier dismissal of dogmatic theology. And a contemporary, Joannes Angelus Odonus, tells us (in a letter to Gilbert Cousin) that Dolet professed atheism orally[17]. By 1538, denunciations of Dolet's

---

[16] Reasons for identifying Hylactor as Dolet were presented by Peter Nurse in his edition, pp. 48-49. The present discussion develops some of those reasons, and adds others.

[17] R.C. Christie published a translation of Odonus's letter in *Etienne Dolet, the martyr of the Renaissance, 1508-1546, a biography*, new ed., London, 1899, pp. 224-228. Odonus's

atheism come thick and fast — and from former close associates who were in a position to know[18].

b) Ovid's epithet for Hylactor, «acutæ vocis», perfectly fits the strident Dolet, whose speeches at Toulouse had provoked student riots and whose caustic tongue and abrasive pen so readily won him enemies. Incidentally, when Ovid describes Actaeon's pack of hounds (*Metamorphoses*, III, 206-225), he names no fewer than thirty-one dogs. The author of the *Cymbalum munti* chosen the two names which fitted his purpose (for we shall see that the name «Pamphagus» is significant, too).

c) Dolet's love of fame was legendary. Odonus, in the letter referred to above, declares that Dolet is «For the sake of a slight breath of applause [...] rushing to certain destruction both of body and soul».

d) Dolet, like the anti-social Hylactor, had stirred up trouble — and, for the time being had escaped relatively unscathed[19].

e) Hylactor is scarred — and on 31 December 1536, only months before the appearance of the *Cymbalum mundi*, Dolet had been in a brawl with the painter Compaing and slain him. Dolet had then had to flee from Lyons to Paris where, thanks to the intervention of his friends, he secured on 19 February 1537 a royal pardon[20].

f) Of all contemporaries, no-one better deserved the epithet *Cymbalum mundi* than Estienne Dolet. For, like Apion, the original *Cymbalum mundi*, Dolet rejoiced in his fame as a rhetorician (indeed, as the new Cicero). And, just as Apion had been admired by Tiberius, Dolet was

---

attack may have been known to Dolet: see Dolet's *Correspondance*, ed. C. Longeon, Genève, 1982, p. 62 and n. 4.

[18] See my «Latin epigrams on Estienne Dolet» (forthcoming, in the *Acta* of the Seventh International Congress of the International Association for Neo-latin Studies). Since writing that paper I have collected further contemporary and near-contemporary denunciations of Dolet's atheism which I hope eventually to make into a book on the world of Estienne Dolet. Calvin declared (in *Des scandales* — see below) that Dolet, Agrippa and Villeneuve «ont desgorgé leurs blasphemes execrables contre Jesus Christ et sa doctrine» — which is reminiscent of Hylactor's avowal in the *Cymbalum mundi*.

[19] Dolet had been imprisoned twice before the publication of the *Cymbalum mundi*, in March 1534 (for inciting a riot in Toulouse: see Christie, *Etienne Dolet*, pp. 135-139) and after the murder, on 31 December 1536, of the painter Henri Compaing, known as Guillot (see the next note). He was to be imprisoned three more times.

[20] The Compaing event was well-known among scholars — many (named by Dolet in a poem in his *Carmina* of 1538) were present at a banquet in Paris celebrating the pardon. The banquet took place shortly after the royal pardon. On the Compaing episode, see Christie, *Etienne Dolet*, pp. 306-313.

securing the admiration of the king — and at the very time when the *Cymbalum mundi* was published[21].

The above six elements add up to a weighty case for the identification of Hylactor as Dolet. In the event that the author of the *Cymbalum mundi* is Des Périers, we have a seventh:

g) In the summer of 1535, immediately on completion of his work on the Bible, Des Périers had come to Sebastian Gryphius's printing shop in Lyons where, until May 1536, he helped Dolet correct the first volume of his *Commentarii Linguæ Latinæ* (1536); Dolet refers in the second volume (published in February 1538) to Des Périers's assistance[22]. Des Périers had thus worked side-by-side with Dolet for eleven months and was uniquely well-able to offer up-to-date and informed comment on the rapidly-emerging scandal of Dolet's atheism.

Finally, Hylactor says that in alarming the townsfolk, he is carrying out the «follies of [his] Attic nights, as far as the chapter *Those who are frivolous and importunate speakers*». The jesting allusion to the chapter in Aulus Gellius's *Attic nights* seems to be parenthetical and to allude to Hylactor's garrulousness. But to describe the nocturnal activities of Hylactor as «Attic» is singularly appropriate if he is Dolet, for Dolet prided himself on being a latter-day Cicero (a claim which was mocked by his contemporary enemies)[23]: the author of the *Cymbalum mundi* may well be jestingly associating Dolet with Cicero's famous friend Atticus.

If Dolet read the *Cymbalum mundi*, how did he react to the presentation of Hylactor, who almost certainly represents him? For if we can see the

---

[21] In the first volume of his *Commentarii Linguæ Latinæ*, published in 1536, Dolet seeks in an epistle to Francis I (*2 r°) to interest the king in his project of writing history, and returns to this project in the second volume of this work (1538), *2 r°-v° and col. 1385. He presented the *Commentarii* to Francis at Moulins in March 1538, and this led the king to grant him the famous *privilegium* to operate as a printer (see Dolet's *Préfaces françaises*, ed. C. Longeon, Genève, 1979, pp. 167 and 168, n. 3). In August 1539, Dolet was to dedicate to the king his *Francisci Valesii Gallorum regis Fata*, which summarizes foreign policy in the reign of the monarch.

[22] See *Commentariorum Linguæ Latinæ tomus secundus*, Lugduni, 1538, B.L. 69 g 13, col. 535, where, under the entry «Superbus», Dolet refers to «Ioannes Euthychus Deperius Heduus, cuius opera, fidelia ea quidem et accurata, in primo Commentariorum nostrorum tomo describendo usi sumus». Dolet later planned to publish Olivétan's translation of the Bible, on which Des Périers had worked: see my «Théodore de Bèze and Philænus», *Bibliothèque d'Humanisme et Renaissance*, LII, 1990, pp. 345-353, n. 18.

[23] Claude Ducher and Antonió Gouvea ridiculed Dolet's notion that he was Cicero incarnate: their attacks on him are mentioned in «Latin epigrams on Etienne Dolet» (see above, note 18).

meaning of Hylactor's mischief and can identify him, contemporaries must have been able to. Dolet would therefore have known that he was portrayed as an anti-theist. Understandably, he left no published reaction to the *Cymbalum mundi*. After 1538, he had to play down his alleged atheism: to comment on a book which facetiously divulged that atheism would not have been politic. All he said about Des Périers in print is in that passage in the second volume of his commentaries on the Latin Language to which I have just referred: there, he pays tribute to the «faithful and accurate scholarship» of Des Périers, which (Dolet says) he made use of in publishing the first volume of his commentaries.

VII. WHO IS PAMPHAGUS?

Who is the other talking dog who ate part of Actaeon's tongue, the «Pamphagus» whom the author associates with Hylactor? It has been said that it is the author, casting himself in the role of the prudent counsellor[24]. But if one of the talking dogs is an anti-theist, the author would hardly present himself as a fellow-dog, or fellow-cynic. Pamphagus was a fairly widely-used pseudonym for anyone «omnivorous», which is what the word means[25]. We are looking for a known associate of Dolet, someone who was either gluttonous or an «omnivorous» reader, who relished semi-clandestine discussion of religion — and who, unlike the iconoclastic Dolet, drew back from dangerous confrontation with authorities.

One candidate is Ortensio Lando (or Landi), who had a great deal in common with Dolet. They both worked for Gryphius in Lyons — in 1534, Lando was a proof-reader there. They were both interested in the «Ciceronian» debate (Lando's first work, *Cicero relegatus et Cicero revocatus*, a satirical commentary on debates in Italy prompted by Erasmus's *Ciceronianus*, was published by Gryphius). According to contemporaries, Dolet and Lando shared a volatile temperament and the ability to intrigue people and to repel them; and both had an unprepossessing physical appearance. Each had an iconoclastic attitude towards authorities; they seem both to have held radically heterodox religious views. According to Joannes Angelus

---

[24]   This is the view of Nurse: see his edition, p. 48.
[25]   See H. Busson, «Pamphagus», *Bibliothèque d'Humanisme et Renaissance*, XIV, 1952, pp. 289-293. There is another example in Simon Vallambert's *Epigrammatum somnia*, Lugduni, 1541, John Rylands Library 21 g 13, p. 18.

Odonus, Dolet and Lando were close associates; and Lando mentions Dolet several times[26].

Another candidate, and a better one, is François Rabelais. He was at one time a close associate of Dolet[27]. He was linked with Dolet in several denunciations of atheists[28]. He makes an excellent Pamphagus to Dolet's Hylactor for, while he shared a taste for audacious intellectual speculation, he was less incautious: and the Pamphagus who recoils at Hylactor's determination to utter his scandalous message corresponds well to the historical Rabelais who, in 1538 precisely, was backing away from Dolet[29]. It is not difficult to see why contemporaries might have applied a name which means «omnivorous» to Rabelais[30]. If the author of the *Cymbalum mundi* is Des Périers, this may

---

[26]   On Lando, see especially S.S. Menchi's «Spiritualismo radicale nelle opere di Ortensio Lando attorno al 1550», *Archiv für Reformationsgeschichte*, LXV, 1974, pp. 210-277; Paul F. Grendler, *Critics of the Italian world*, Madison and London, 1969.

[27]   Dolet and Rabelais may have met in the circle of Gryphius (who in 1532 published Rabelais's edition of the letters of the Ferrarese doctor Jean Manardi). Rabelais had been present at the banquet in 1537 celebrating Dolet's release (see above, n. 20). And Rabelais dedicated to Dolet a poem concerning the recipe for the ancient sauce known as *garum*, which Dolet published, together with a reply to Rabelais, in his *Carminum libri quatuor* of 1538: *Ad Franciscum Rabelæsum de Garo salsamento*, pp. 75-76. Dolet dedicated several other poems to Rabelais: *Ad Franciscum Rabelæsum, De mutua inter se, et Clementum Marotum amicitia* (p. 30); *Ad Franciscum Rabelæsum de medico quodam indocto* (pp. 55-56); *Ad Cardinalem Turonium, Cædis a se factæ, et sui deinde exilii descriptio* (pp. 62-63); *Cuiusdam epitaphium*, inspired by Rabelais's dissection in Lyons of the corpse of a strangled criminal (pp. 164-165). In the *Commentarii Linguæ Latinæ*, also of 1538 (I, col. 1158), Dolet mentions Rabelais in a list of the six most illustrious French doctors.

[28]   For example, the letter by Zébédée which attributes the *Cymbalum mundi* to Olivétan's clerk. Also, texts by Postel (1543), Calvin (1550) and Henri Estienne (1566) cited by Grève in *L'Interprétation de Rabelais au XVIe siècle*, Genève, 1961, respectively pp. 55-56, 77 and 125-127.

[29]   So far as is known, the poem on the garum (see note 27 above) is Rabelais's only reference to Dolet — and the poem does not actually praise him, and it was published by Dolet, not Rabelais. After participating in the banquet which celebrated Dolet's pardon, Rabelais seems to have distanced himself from Dolet, though Dolet was showering commendations upon him. Rabelais doubtless deplored Dolet's 1535 attack on Erasmus, but this had not prevented him consorting with him; plausibly, the latter's reputed atheism did. Rabelais's hostility to Dolet seems at a later date to have been intense. In 1542, Dolet published an edition of *Pantagruel* and *Gargantua* which retained contentious theological passages and contemptuous references to the Sorbonne which Rabelais removed in the edition published by François Juste at Lyons that same year — and Dolet claimed on the titlepage of *Gargantua* that his unauthorized edition was «reveue et de beaucoup augmentée par l'Autheur mesme». Rabelais was doubtless highly alarmed, for his next edition, titled *Grandes annales*, was accompanied by a note, by the printer or by Rabelais, deploring «la bastarde et adulterine edition du present œuvre» issued by «un plagiaire, homme incliné à tout mal» — that is, Dolet. The note adds that «tel monstre est né pour l'ennuy et injure des gens de bien». See S. Rawles, M.A. Screech *et al.*, *A new Rabelais bibliography: editions of Rabelais before 1626*, Genève, 1987, n°s 13 and 24 (Dolet's editions of Rabelais) and 25 (the rejoinder to Dolet, where the diatribe against him is reproduced in facsimile).

[30]   Joachim Du Bellay's epitaph *Pamphagi medici* seems to be about Rabelais (see his *Œuvres poétiques*, ed. H. Chamard and G. Dermerson, Société des textes français modernes,

strengthen the theory that he is alluding to Rabelais, as Des Périers seems to have known Rabelais's work (another work attributed to Des Périers contains echoes of Rabelais)[31]. There is a further reason for seeing Rabelais as Pamphagus, and the key to it is the identity of Actaeon.

VIII. WHO IS ACTAEON?

Hylactor and Pamphagus gained the ability to speak by eating the tongue of their master Actaeon; and in the fourth dialogue, they lavish praise upon this worthy man, «who loved dogs». Who is Actaeon? It has been suggested that he represents Christ, who brought the divine word to men and who was killed by his own people. Citing praise of Actaeon by Hylactor and Pamphagus, one commentator concludes: «[...] ce portrait se présente comme le pendant du Bon Pasteur de l'Evangile, il témoigne de toute la vénération que Des Périers portait à la personne de Jésus.»[32]

But Actaeon is praised by two dogs, one of which is an out-and-out mischief-maker and the other his complaisant companion; and dogs, we have seen, often represented cynics. So the Actaeon they are extolling is unlikely to be Christ. Actaeon in my view represents a very different historical figure, an ancient writer who was often denounced as an atheist and who, according to a legend recorded by Suidas and frequently reiterated in the sixteenth century, was punished for his impiety precisely by being devoured by dogs: the satirist Lucian[33]. Hylactor and Pamphagus are thus contemporary

---

VII, p. 207 and notes). I came to the conclusion that the Pamphagus of the *Cymbalum mundi* is Rabelais independently of Abel Lefranc (see his edition of Rabelais, t. 3, Paris, 1922, pp. lxv-lxvi). The issue is not discussed by M. de Grève in his *L'Interprétation de Rabelais au XVIe siècle* (Genève, 1961).

[31] On echoes of Rabelais in the *Nouvelles récréations et joyeux devis*, see Krystyna Kasprzyk's introduction to her edition (Paris, 1980), pp. xxix-xxx. The *Nouvelles récréations* were attributed to Des Périers by Robert Granjon when first published in 1558 but there is in my view far more doubt over that attribution, which was contested in the sixteenth century, than over the attribution of the *Cymbalum mundi* (see Kasprzyk's discussion in her edition, pp. vii-xx). Nothing in these short stories, incidentally, seems to shed light on the issues discussed in this article (one of these stories, n° 17, contains a not unfriendly allusion to Pierre Lizet, the President of the Paris *Parlement*, who had been involved in proceedings against Jean Morin, printer of the *Cymbalum mundi*).

[32] This is the verdict of Nurse, who links this part of the fourth dialogue with the episode of Celia (whom he sees as the representation of divine love) in the third dialogue (p. 48 of his edition). A parallel between Ovid's Actaeon and Christ was drawn by Pierre Bersuire in his *Ovidius moralizatus* of 1509: see A. Moss, *Ovid in Renaissance France*, London, 1982, p. 25.

[33] C. Lauvergnat-Gagnière has a list of authors who recalled the story: see *Lucien de Samosate et le lucianisme en France au XVIe siècle, athéisme et polémique*, Genève, 1988, pp. 12-13, 187 and n. 198.

authors who acquired Lucian's voice — that is, the ability to express impious views.

Pamphagus, if he is Rabelais, could certainly be described as «Lucianic»: Joachim Du Bellay called him just that[34]. Rabelais offers that blend of philosophy and facetious dialogue which distinguished Lucian and, like Lucian, his targets are commonly abuses of religion; and several of his episodes seem to be derived from Lucian[35]. Identification of Actaeon as Lucian would thus strengthen the case for seeing Pamphagus, one of the two dogs who devoured Lucian's tongue and acquired Lucianic speech, as Rabelais.

But is it possible to describe the second dog, Hylactor/Dolet, as Lucianic? On the face of it, no, because Dolet castigated Lucianic writing (of Erasmus; in the *De imitatione ciceroniana*, of 1535)[36]. But the term «Lucianic» was readily applied in polemical literature to anyone thought to be a mocker of religion, and particularly to anyone thought to deny the immortality of the soul, as Lucian had supposedly done[37]. And, whether Dolet liked it or not, others saw him as «Lucianic». Floridus Sabinus, in a rejoinder published in 1541 to Dolet's *De imitatione ciceroniana*, compares Dolet to Lucian for his alleged impiety[38]. And Jean Visagier (Vulteius), a one-time close friend and tireless eulogist of Dolet who turned against him, seems to have had Dolet as his target in a poem titled *In quendam irreligiosum Luciani sectatorem*, published in 1538: Visagier's «Lucianist» corresponds absolutely to the Hylactor of the *Cymbalum mundi*: «Vixi non homo, sed *canis*», he admits, and, «nec hominem sapis, nec ipse es!», he is told[39].

---

[34]   See *Deffence et illustration de la langue francoyse*, ed. H. Chamard, S.T.F.M., 1948, p. 191 and note.

[35]   On Rabelais as a «Lucianist», see Lauvergnat-Gagnière, *Lucien de Samosate*, pp. 235-261.

[36]   See the facsimile edition published by E.V. Telle: *L'Erasmianus sive Ciceronianus d'Etienne Dolet (1535)*, Genève, 1974, pp. 18-19, 40, 89.

[37]   Lauvergnat-Gagnière shows (*Lucien de Samosate*, pp. 135-144) how, following Luther's denunciation of the «Lucianic» Erasmus in 1525, the name of Lucian came to be used freely as a synonym for «atheist». There is little evidence that Lucian denied immortality of the soul (see Lauvergnat-Gagnière, pp. 7-8), but he was frequently accused of having done so.

[38]   See Lauvergnat-Gagnière, *Lucien de Samosate*, pp. 145-146.

[39]   The poem is in Visagier's *Hendecasyllaborum libri quatuor*, Parisiis, 1538, B.L. 11405 a 52, 10 r°-11 r°. Sozzi (*Les Contes de Bonaventure Des Périers*, pp. 61-64) maintains that the «Lucianist» of this poem in Des Périers, but there is no evidence that Visagier ever had hostile feelings towards Des Périers, and it is known that he came to despise Dolet.

The culminating dialogue of the *Cymbalum mundi*, then, is a veiled commentary on the deeds of a self-confessed anti-theist; that anti-theist is almost certainly Dolet; his companion, who is something of a kindred spirit but deplores his recklessness, is probably Rabelais. Dolet and Rabelais are two dogs who devoured the tongue of Actaeon, who probably represents the reputed atheist Lucian. The *Cymbalum mundi* thus reveals the existence of latter-day «Lucianists», atheists who facetiously mock religion, and warns that the most fearsome of them, an as-yet-furtive foe of the Christian Church, is about to disseminate his views in public. That, in a nutshell, is the meaning of the last dialogue in the *Cymbalum mundi*. Interestingly, the author uses the Lucianic genre, the satirical dialogue, to expose these Lucianists. But this fact is less paradoxical than it may seem: his attitude towards them is (as we shall see) largely one of connivance. Which leads to our next point.

IX. HOW DID CONTEMPORARIES REACT?

Significantly, Reformers and Catholics attacked the book with equal vigour (and attacked Des Périers). The first hostile Reformer appears to have been Zébédée who, identifying the author as Olivétan's clerk, that is as Des Périers, noted that he had become an «Epicurean» (perhaps significantly, Zébédée speaks of Dolet and Olivétan's clerk virtually in the same breath, condemning both). Calvin declared in his *Des scandales* of 1550 that Des Périers, like Rabelais and Gouvea, had tasted the gospel but had then been blinded (and that Agrippa, Villeneuve and Dolet had always despised the gospel): the only work attributable to Des Périers that could, and certainly would, have elicited this response is the *Cymbalum mundi*. Also in 1550, Guillaume Farel attacked the «erreurs des Libertins [et] du tresméchant Deperius et des Atheistes»; again, the only text attributable to Des Périers to which Farel could have been referring is the *Cymbalum mundi*. Henri Estienne, in his *Apologie pour Herodote* of 1566, described Des Périers as the «auteur du détestable livre intitulé *Cymbalum mundi*» and as a «contempteur et mocqueur de Dieu». Jean Chassanion, in 1581, referred to «ce malheureux Bonaventure [...] auteur du detestable livre intitulé *Cymbalum mundi*, où il se moque ouvertement de Dieu et de toute religion»; and Simon Goulart repeated Estienne's verdict[40].

---

[40]   See Sozzi, *Les Contes*, pp. 59-60 (Calvin) and p. 43 and 67 (Estienne); Lauvergnat-Gagnière, *Lucien de Samosate*, p. 268 (Farel and Chassanion). According to Nurse (in his edi-

Catholics also saw the book as dangerous. The Sorbonne, on 19 July 1538, declared it was «perniciosus» and should be suppressed, and in 1545 and 1551 included it in lists of censured books[41]. Guillaume Postel, in his *Alcorani seu legis Mahometi et evengelistarum concordiæ liber* of 1543, attacked it as an atheist work. Estienne Pasquier declared, probably in 1583 or 1584, that the *Cymbalum mundi* is Lucianic and deserves to be burned — with the author, were he alive. The Catholic bibliographer La Croix Du Maine, notwithstanding his remarkable open-mindedness, was also hostile to Des Périers. And the owner of the copy now in the Bibliothèque Nationale, Paris (whose religion cannot be ascertained), wrote on it, «L'aucteur Bonaventure Des Périers, homme meschant et athée comme il apparait par ce detestable livre. *Dixit insipiens in corde suo non est Deus*» [*Ps.* X, 3-4; XIV (XIII), 1; LIII (LII), 2] — a later hand, perhaps that of Pierre de l'Estoile, added «Telle vie, telle fin. Avéré par la mort de ce misérable indigne de porter le nom d'homme» — possibly an allusion to the story (which is impossible to substantiate) that Des Périers committed suicide[42].

Scholars have been baffled by the chorus of denunciation — and especially baffled that the Sorbonne condemned a work so hostile to the Reformers. But we can now see exactly why the theologians felt the work «contains no explicit doctrinal errors, but is pernicious». On the one hand, the allusion to anti-theism is veiled (and the author does not endorse anti-theism anyway); but on the other, the author intimates that the theist consensus is breaking down, that a small number of «dogs» are exchanging anti-theist views and that one of them is seeking out kindred spirits and awaiting the right moment to unleash his impious views openly on the flock of Christ. Even if the portrayal of the anti-theist had been a disapproving one, that would have mattered little: a mere allusion to the existence of a «reprehensible» opinion could be condemned[43].

tion, p. viii), Estienne attributes the *Cymbalum mundi* to Des Périers in the *Introduction au Traité de la conformité des Merveilles anciennes avec les modernes* (1566, p. 309).

[41] See F.M. Higman, *Censorship and the Sorbonne*, Genève, 1979, pp. 85-86, 121, 149.

[42] See Sozzi, *Les Contes*, p. 59 (Postel), p. 67 (La Croix Du Maine and Pasquier), pp. 66-67 and n. 199 (the copy now in the Bibliothèque Nationale). According to H. Busson (*Le rationalisme dans la littérature française de la Renaissance (1533-1601)*, Paris, 1957, p. 188), François Sagon called Des Périers an atheist; Sozzi refers to Sagon's attack on Des Périers (pp. 29-31 and 57), but gives no indication of what Sagon said.

[43] Montaigne noted that the Roman Inquisition went so far as to prohibit in Italy books by German Catholics which rehearsed the opinions of Reformers in order to refute them (*Journal de voyage*, ed. C. Dédéyan, Paris, 1946, p. 201).

And the portrayal of the atheist Hylactor is far from being a disapproving one. Hylactor's furtively-expressed views (we have seen) have the allure
of forbidden fruit. And Hylactor's imprudence is criticised — not his views:
propagation of atheism is presented merely as untimely. And the situation
is presented as a laughing matter — and in terms plundered from holy writ.
To any sixteenth-century Christian able to discern the veiled message, the
book was pernicious: the theologians needed no persuading to have the book
suppressed[44].

Reformed and Catholic readers alike had another reason for hostility
towards the author: whoever he was, he was an associate of his impious
Hylactor. Those readers who attributed the text to Des Périers and who
recognized Dolet in Hylactor, might have known that the two had been
closely linked: eleven months of close collaboration in such a Mecca as
Gryphius's printing shop in Lyons could not pass unnoticed. Association
with radical thinkers aroused suspicion — and was referred to with
metaphors about contagious diseases[45]. It may be because the *Cymbalum
mundi* contained an implicit admission of association with an atheist that
the author published it anonymously.

There would have been further grounds for condemnation of the book
if, as now seems probable, it contains impieties beyond the one I have
elucidated. Scholars have in the past discerned such sentiment, but because
nobody has been able to point hitherto to a single passage which must have
an impious meaning, their views have not got beyond mere conjecture. It

---

[44]   Scholars have been hard put to it to explain the Sorbonne's verdict. Abel Lefranc
argued that the Sorbonne either realized that the book is impious but pretended not to so as
not to draw attention to it or was unable to see the impiety; both explanations seem implausible
(see «Rabelais et les Estienne. Le procès du *Cymbalum* de Bonaventure Des Périers», *Revue du
Seizième Siècle*, 1928, pp. 356-366). Screech (*Cymbalum mundi*, pp. 4-9) felt the theologians
must have liked the book's attacks on Reformers; they condemned it at the behest of the king
(who deplored an attack on Girard Roussel, a protégé of his sister Marguerite), but resisted
pressure from the King to some extent by saying it contains no explicit doctrinal errors. For
Higman, similarly, the weak terms of the Sorbonne's condemnation suggest deference to the
King (*Censorship and the Sorbonne*, pp. 35, 85-86, 121, 149). My hypothesis obviates the need
to posit pressure on the theologians and suggests that the verdict they gave exactly corresponded
to their views of the book. Lauvergnat-Gagnière described the judgements of contemporaries
on the *Cymbalum mundi* as «aussi péremptoires que dépourvus de toute justification» (*Lucien
de Samosate*, p. 268). I think it hazardous to dismiss sixteenth-century interpretations of allusive
texts of that period, especially when they all point the same way.

[45]   Catholic and Reformed judiciaries alike interrogated people about their links with
Dolet. Diogo de Teive was interrogated by the Inquisition in Portugal and Jacques Gruet was
questioned in Geneva: see my «Théodore de Bèze and Philænus», *Bibliothèque d'Humanisme
et Renaissance*, LII, 1990 (pp. 345-353), p. 350, n. 16. Dolet was an especially dangerous friend
for those who had themselves come under suspicion for their religion, as many of his friends
had: see Christie, *Etienne Dolet*, pp. 398-399.

now seems distinctly possible that some passages signalled by earlier commentators as impious actually are[46].

Another reason for hostility towards the *Cymbalum mundi* could be that
the second dialogue seems to attack theologians[47]. Satire of individuals
would not necessarily have been regarded as dangerous; indeed, some commentators regard the scene in which three theologians bicker as to which of
them has found the truth (for Mercury has ground the philosopher's stone
into powder) as a pious deprecation of disputes about the word of God. But
we now know the author as someone who makes light of the dissemination
of atheism (and uses the sacred text to do so): it seems highly likely that here,
he is not simply deriding individuals, he is debunking dogmatic theology.

X. WAS THE AUTHOR A NICODEMITE?

There is an intriguing possible source for that scene in the second
dialogue where identifiable theologians bicker over grains of sand which
they mistake for the philosopher's stone. In a work titled *Loci omnium
ferme capitum evangelium* [...] *Actorum item Apostolorum* published in
1527, the renegade Carthusian monk Otto Brunfels declared that the gospel

---

[46] In 1732, La Monnoye argued that the disreputable Mercury of the *Cymbalum mundi*
represents Christ (see Nurse's edition, p. xxxiii). Among others to present the book as anti-
Christian was Abel Lefranc: «Il est hors de doute qu'il doit être considéré, d'un bout à l'autre,
comme l'attaque la moins déguisée et la plus violente qui ait été dirigée, au cours du XVIᵉ siècle,
contre l'essence même du christianisme» (introduction to his edition of the *Œuvres de François
Rabelais*, III, Paris, 1922, p. lxi) — but Lefranc did not say very clearly on what this judgement
rests. It has been suggested that Des Périers rehearses in the *Cymbalum mundi* the anti-
Christian ideas of Celsus recorded by Origen (see L. Febvre, «Origène et Des Périers ou l'énigme
du *Cymbalum mundi*», *Bibliothèque d'Humanisme et Renaissance*, II, 1942, pp. 7-131, ch. III,
«De la Bible à Dolet», pp. 41-59), but any echo of Celsus's views in the text is in my opinion
at best tenuous. Two modern scholars who see the book as irreligious (but without touching
on the essential argument advanced here) are H. Busson (*Le rationalisme dans la littérature
française de la Renaissance, 1533-1601*, Paris, 1957, pp. 178-190) and M. de Grève (*L'Interprétation de Rabelais au XVIᵉ siècle*, Genève, 1961, p. 53).

[47] «Cubercus» and «Rhetulus» in that dialogue are, as noted above, anagrams of «Buccerus» and «Lutherus». Screech has argued that the author's third target in that dialogue,
«Drarig», is not Erasmus as has been thought, but the bishop and Reformer Girard Roussel,
and that the author is thus not attacking (incongruously) two Reformers and a Roman Catholic,
but three Reformers (see pp. 11-14 of his *Préface*; the theory had previously been advanced by
L. Delaruelle in «Etude sur le problème du *Cymbalum mundi*», *Revue d'Histoire littéraire de
la France*, XXXII, 1925 [pp. 1-23], p. 8).

was «crumbling» and that not a single grain of it was left[48]. And the hallmark of Brunfels's work generally is a contempt for theology[49].

Otto Brunfels is famous as the founder of Nicodemism — the opinion that the secret beliefs in one's heart matter more than the words which one utters in the presence of men. The appellation «Nicodemite» derives from the disciple who saw Christ furtively, at night, for fear of persecution (cf. *John*, III). Though it is paradoxical to propagate the Nicodemite position, Brunfels did just this. At the very least, there is an intellectual kinship between Brunfels and the author of the *Cymbalum mundi*: both tend to undermine dogmatism through allusive discourse which makes use of biblical texts; both seem to have held that the nucleus of religious truth is tiny; that religious rites are unimportant since religion is an «internal» matter; that acts of charity are primordial; that theologians are redundant. And both seek, somewhat contradictorily, to shelter themselves from authority by veiling their meaning, whilst at the same time displaying a dismissive and provocative attitude to authority.

Further research may well demonstrate an intellectual relationship between Brunfels and the author of the *Cymbalum mundi*. The *Cymbalum mundi* is presented in the dedicatory letter as the translation of a tract which was discovered eight years previously in a monastery library — which takes us back to the time when the ex-Carthusian Brunfels was issuing his Nicodemite tracts... Interestingly, Brunfels was the author of a mock-almanach denouncing astrology — and so too was Des Périers, the possible author of the *Cymbalum mundi*[50]. And the most implacable anti-Nicodemite, Calvin, was also a biting critic of Des Périers[51].

---

[48] On the «crumbling» gospel, see C. Ginzburg, *Il Nicodemismo, Simulazione e dissimulazione religiosa nell'Europa del' 500*, Torino, 1970, p. 47. Ginzburg is my principal source on Nicodemism.

[49] Brunfels expressed contempt for theology in his *De corrigendis studiis severioribus* of 1519 and in his *Confutatio sophistices et quæstionum curiosarum* of 1520, the latter being a collection of passages from Greek and Latin Fathers of the Church deprecating theological curiosity. In his *Loci omnium ferme capitum evangelium* [...] *Actorum item Apostolorum* of 1527, he presented a series of judicious extracts from the New Testament indicating that the intellect cannot comprehend divine truths. And in a 1529 edition of his *Pandectæ*, a collection of biblical passages arranged under headings (a work originally published in 1527), he attacked the biblical commentaries of Erasmus. The *Pandectæ* were translated into German, Dutch, English, Italian and French. A pharmacist in Toulon was executed for writing his name in a copy of the French translation. An English translation of Brunfels's *Precationes biblicæ* was owned, less dangerously, by Queen Elizabeth of England.

[50] Like Brunfels's, which appeared in 1526, Des Periers's almanach professes with deliberate absurdity to be valid for ever; and also like Brunfels's, it uses biblical quotations to

A possible intermediary between Brunfels and the author of the *Cymbalum mundi* is Estienne Dolet. Dolet published Brunfels's *Precationes biblicæ* in French translation (though, so far as is known, not until 1542)[52]. And Dolet, who may have drawn on Brunfels, could be a source of the attack on dogmatic theology in the second dialogue of the *Cymbalum mundi*. For in 1535, in his *De imitatione ciceroniana*, Dolet had heaped derision on those «Lutherans» (among whom he maliciously included Erasmus) who claim to be in possession of the truth and to be making good the deficiencies of the holy Spirit by elucidating obscurities in the Bible. The analogy between Dolet's diatribe and the second dialogue of the *Cymbalum mundi*, which has often been noted, is a close one[53]. It is distinctly possible that the *Cymbalum mundi* (if its author is Des Périers) echoes discussions between Dolet and Des Périers in that period of collaboration in Lyons in 1535-1536[54].

---

confute astrologers. See Des Périers's *Œuvres françoises*, ed. L. Lacour, 2 v., Paris, 1586, I, pp. 130-138.

[51] Calvin denounced Nicodemism notably in his *Epistolæ duæ de rebus hoc sæculo apprime necessariis* of 1537, in his *Petit traicté monstrant que c'est que doit faire un homme fidele congnoissant la verité de l'Evangile quand it est entre les papistes* of 1543 and in his *Excuse à Messieurs les Nicodemites* of 1544. See Ginzburg, *Nicodemismo*, respectively pp. 121-124, 153-154 and 154-158, and C.M.N. Eire, «Prelude to sedition? Calvin's attack on Nicodemism and religious compromise», *Archiv für Reformationsgeschichte*, 76, 1985, pp. 120-145.

[52] See C. Longeon, *Bibliographie des œuvres d'Etienne Dolet, écrivain, éditeur et imprimeur*, Genève, 1980, n° 223. The work was condemned by the Sorbonne in 1544: see Higman, *Censorship and the Sorbonne*, pp. 99, 127. The translation had originally been published in 1530 by Pierre de Vingle; Dolet added a preface of his own (see his *Préfaces françaises*, ed. C. Longeon, Genève, 1979, pp. 151-154).

[53] The *De imitatione ciceroniana*, though ostensibly philological, is a work of theology (or anti-theology) — and highly readable. See the edition by E.V. Telle referred to above (n. 36). The essence of the attack on dogmatic theology is on pp. 34-37 of the facsimile. The possible influence of Dolet's *De imitatione ciceroniana* upon Des Périers has been noted by Nurse (see his edition, xix-xx), following J. Bohatec («Calvin et l'humanisme», *Revue historique* [183, 1938, pp. 207-241; 185, 1939, pp. 71-104], pp. 72-79). See also L. Febvre's «Origène et Des Périers ou l'énigme du *Cymbalum mundi*», *Bibliothèque d'Humanisme et Renaissance*, II, 1942, pp. 7-131, ch. III, «De la Bible à Dolet», pp. 41-59.

[54] V.L. Saulnier argued that Des Périers had an influence upon Dolet, persuading him to take religion seriously. But Saulnier missed the biblical allusions in Hylactor's monologue, and his thesis also requires us to ignore overwhelming contemporary evidence for Dolet's radical heterodoxy (see «Le sens du *Cymbalum mundi*», *Bibliothèque d'Humanisme et Renaissance*, XIII, 1951, pp. 158-159). Dolet's «edifying» publications have sometimes been invoked to prove his piety, but in my view their nebulous content points rather to him having been a cynical Nicodemite who was also commercially astute. One of these publications, the *Cato Christianus* of 1538, contains the preposterous claim that Dolet is a good teacher of religion: the book was censured by the Sorbonne, and Dolet was ordered to withdraw it from sale (see Christie, *Etienne Dolet*, pp. 389-392).

XI. WHAT HAVE WE LEARNED ABOUT THE AUTHORSHIP
OF THE DIALOGUES?

We saw that the attribution of the *Cymbalum mundi* to Des Périers rests primarily upon the testimony of André Zébédée which is close to the date of publication, that Zébédée probably had access to good sources and that the attribution is confirmed by later sixteenth-century writers[55]. But in conducting this enquiry into the sense of the book, I refrained from endorsing that attribution.

However, that attribution now seems to me robust, and for the following reasons:

(i) If Hylactor is Dolet (and we have seen good evidence for this, independently of the hypothesis that Des Périers wrote the work), then the author of the *Cymbalum mundi* has to be someone who was close enough to Dolet immediately prior to publication of the *Cymbalum mundi* to have been privy to his «atheistical» utterances. Des Périers qualifies in virtue of the eleven months he spent at Gryphius's workshop in Lyons helping Dolet correct the proofs of his *Commentarii Linguæ Latinæ*.

(ii) The *Cymbalum mundi*, a satirical attack on dogmatic theology, curiously echoes ideas published by Dolet in the *De imitatione ciceroniana*: the author thus seems to be familiar with the thought of Dolet — and nobody was better placed than Des Périers to know Dolet's thought.

(iii) If the *Cymbalum mundi* is, as I suggest, an audacious work with jesting allusions to anti-theism, and if it is by Des Périers, then these facts account for the chorus of denunciations of him — denunciations which are otherwise highly baffling, for his other work is singularly innocuous, even pious.

---

[55] Screech argues, in his edition (p. 15; cf. p. 9), that «L'attribution du *Cymbalum mundi* repose sur l'autorité d'Henri Estienne dans son *Apologie pour Hérodote*», and that neither Estienne nor subsequent writers who attribute the book to Des Périers had seen a copy, for the work had been burned. However, the attribution does also (and mainly) rest on Zébédée; and while it is true that apart from Zébédée, none of the earlier attacks on either the *Cymbalum mundi* or on Des Périers attributes the work to him, it is hard to see what else in the *œuvre* of Des Périers could have given rise to these attacks. And it seems bold to say that those who mentioned the book had not seen it, for we do not know how many copies Jehan Morel sold before he was arrested, nor how many copies of Benoist Bonnyn's Lyons edition survived. But Screech's scholarly investigation should not be cavalierly dismissed (as T. Peach does in «Bonaventure Des Périers: *La prognostication des prognostications* (1537), Texte et notes», *Bibliothèque d'Humanisme et Renaissance*, LII, 1990 [pp. 109-121], p. 109).

(iv) The Nicodemite resonance in the work is consistent with the cultural milieu in which Des Périers circulated.

(v) Many people were keenly interested in knowing the identity of the author (and the name was divulged by the printer, Jean Morin, to agents of the *Parlement*), but none of those texts which attribute the work to Des Périers was, so far as is known, ever challenged, and no other name than that of Des Périers was put forward as the author.

(vi) There is no record of the author of the *Cymbalum mundi* having been molested by the authorities even though they knew (from Morin) his identity; a reasonable inference would be that he had powerful protectors — and Des Périers was a protégé of Marguerite de Navarre. Which leads to our next question.

XII. WHAT WAS DES PÉRIERS'S RELATIONSHIP WITH MARGUERITE DE NAVARRE?

It has been argued, against the attribution of the *Cymbalum mundi* to Des Périers, that as a protégé of Marguerite de Navarre he would have been unlikely to attack Reformers in the way the *Cymbalum mundi* does[56]. Des Périers's early sympathy for the Reformation may indeed have helped him secure employment at Marguerite's court[57]. But the *Cymbalum mundi* represents a later stance: Reformers like Zébédée and Calvin regarded him as «sorty de eulx». Moreover, Marguerite was tolerant of a wide range of religious opinion — including possibly Nicodemism[58].

Any reputation for piety which Des Périers gained on the strength of his poetry quickly withered. And there are indications that relations between Marguerite and Des Périers became strained, and the two facts may be linked. At an unknown date, Des Périers had to request to be restored to the

---

[56]   See Screech, *Préface* to *Cymbalum mundi*, p. 14. Nurse, on the contrary, argues (pp. x, xii) that Marguerite must have approved of the *Cymbalum mundi*: this seems very unlikely in view of what we now know about that text.

[57]   Some of his religious poetry is based on Olivétan's Bible: see L. Sozzi, «Remarques sur la poésie religieuse de Des Périers», in *Etudes seiziémistes offertes à V.L. Saulnier*, Genève, 1980, pp. 205-222. Sozzi suggests (pp. 217-218) that one of the poems based on Olivétan's translation, *Le cri touchant de trouver la bonne femme* (based on *Proverbs*, XXXI, 10-31), was intended as a tribute to Marguerite.

[58]   On Nicodemites in the entourage of Marguerite de Navarre, see Ginzburg, *Nicodemismo*, pp. 86-90, 102, 123 and 182 (but I am not convinced by Ginzburg's presentation of Lefèvre d'Etaples as a Nicodemite).

royal payroll[59]. In October 1541, he was belatedly paid for a year when he had been omitted from the salary list — whether by error or by design is not known[60]. And it has been suggested that significant passages in Charles de Sainte-Marthe's *Oraison funebre de Marguerite de Navarre* refer to Des Périers: Sainte-Marthe notes that Marguerite patronized people of suspect religion but expelled the obdurately impious from her house[61]. If Marguerite knew the *Cymbalum mundi* at all, she may well have felt that Des Périers's opinions had become unacceptably radical. Interestingly, when Antoine Du Moulin published the posthumous edition of Des Périers's work in 1544, he indicated that Des Périers had several times declared that his intention was to dedicate his complete works to Marguerite; and Du Moulin also mentioned that Marguerite possessed unpublished work by Des Périers[62]: perhaps he was trying to rehabilitate the late Des Périers in the eyes of his patron. At all events, Des Périers's status as a protégé of Marguerite de Navarre does not preclude his authorship of the *Cymbalum mundi*. My conclusion is that he is almost certainly the author[63].

XIII. **HAVE WE DISCOVERED AN ATHEIST?**

In my view, it would not be accurate to describe the author of the *Cymbalum mundi* as an atheist. «Pernicious» in the Sorbonne's terms, yes; but his book (again in their terms) contains no explicit doctrinal errors. Yet here is a book which shows the author as part of a very small group to which «Hylactor» has divulged his virulently anti-Christian views and who (albeit covertly) is disseminating those views (whilst affecting to disapprove of their being divulged by Hylactor himself). So, while the author of the *Cymbalum*

---

[59] See Des Périers's *Œuvres françoises*, ed. L. Lacour (2 t., Paris, 1856, I, p. 153, *A Monsieur le Chancelier d'Alençon).*

[60] See Sozzi, *Les Contes*, p. 42 and n. 123.

[61] See Sozzi, pp. 64-65 and n. 193.

[62] See Des Périers's *Œuvres françoises*, ed. L. Lacour, 2 t., Paris, 1856, I, p. 3, 4.

[63] Screech notes a denunciation by Guillaume Postel of «nefarius tractatus Villanovani de tribus prophetis, Cymbalum Mundi, Pantagruellus et novæ insulæ» and suggests the *Tractatus de tribus prophetis* is itself the *Cymbalum mundi*, which would thus be by a Villanovanus or Neufville. This interpretation of Postel's syntax, though possible, seems unlikely, for only the second dialogue in the *Cymbalum mundi*, not the work as a whole, deals with «three prophets»; and a seemingly mythical book of «three impostors» has been attributed to a great many authors since the thirteenth century (see F. Berriot, *Athéismes et athéistes au XVIe siècle en France*, Lille, 1976, chap. III, «Les trois imposteurs», pp. 303-590). Or Postel may have been thinking of Simon Villanovanus, professor of Latin composition at Padua (a teacher of Estienne Dolet and, like him, often accused of holding subversive views).

mundi cannot be called an atheist, he can be called irreligious, for he is cavalier in his dismissal of dogmatic theology and complaisant in the presentation of his mischievous atheist Hylactor.

And Hylactor, as presented by Des Périers, patently is an atheist — on his own admission, which is couched in a biblical language used with sacrilegious intent. We have here no mere banal denunciation in which words like «atheist» are losely used as terms of opprobrium: we have a case of someone who admits not only that he rejects the Christian revelation but that he does his best to undermine it, and who in his jesting echoes of the Bible mocks Christianity. If Hylactor designates a real person, and if Des Périers's portrait of him is authentic, then atheism existed.

Hylactor does seem to designate an identifiable individual, as other characters in the *Cymbalum mundi* do; and that individual is almost certainly Estienne Dolet. There is (unsurprisingly) no extant published profession of atheism by Dolet, but there is overwhelming circumstantial evidence that he uttered views which reliable contemporaries regarded as atheistical. And since I have argued that great weight should be attached to contemporary verdicts on the *Cymbalum mundi* on the grounds that sixteenth-century authors were best placed to comment on it, I doubtless ought logically to accept that Dolet was an atheist on the grounds that so many of his contemporaries said he was.

But two considerations make me hesitate. One is that Dolet could have acquired his reputation without being a committed atheist. All he needed to do was what the *Cymbalum mundi* presents him as doing: mischievously whispering subversive views into people's ears, cocking a snook at the clerical and political establishment, engaging in the violence which earned him the cut ear and scarred brow which made him unrecognizable (for anti-social behaviour was interpreted as a mark of atheism), and all the time defying the authorities to catch him. He may, in other words, simply have been a reckless young scholar who never outgrew a desire to defy an establishment which he saw as corrupt and oppressive; and, ultimately, a victim of his wounded pride rather than a martyr to atheism. Montaigne showed, with remarkable perception, that once pride became an issue in confrontation between scholars and authority, individuals with perfectly innocuous views found their way to the stake[64]. The hypothesis of a Dolet more anxious to

---

[64]   See my *Montaigne and religious freedom* (Genève, 1991), Chapter VI, (i), «Freedom and the nature of man», pp. 121-126.

shock the establishment than to destroy Christianity is compatible (just) with the chorus of denunciations of him.

The second reason I hesitate to call Dolet an atheist lies in the curious and hitherto unnoticed fact that in the years after his death, several scholars (interestingly, all of them Catholics) praised him and paid tribute to his scholarship though they must certainly have known of his reputed views and that he had been condemned to death on charges related to those views. They may have felt that the line which separates the pious anti-dogmatism of *The imitation of Christ* (which, incidentally, Dolet published) and the apparently impious antidogmatism of the *De imitatione ciceroniana* cannot be discerned with certainty. Those as-yet-unsung defenders of Dolet form a chapter in the history of thought which has yet to be written and to which I shall perhaps return.

XIV. CONCLUSION

Il y a prou loy de parler par tout et pour et contre. The enigmatic nature of the *Cymbalum mundi* enables scholars to advance the most contradictory interpretations: «par ceste varieté et instabilité d'opinions il nous meinent tacitement, comme par la main, à ceste resolution de leur irresolution». Heather Ingman has just presented an opposite hypothesis to mine: that the author of the *Cymbalum mundi* contrasts the God-given Catholic religion with the human squabbling of Reformers, and that the dogs of the fourth dialogue are persecuted for their knowledge of spiritual things[65]. This is but the most recent statement (and one of the most intelligent) of a view of the *Cymbalum mundi* which is gaining ground — that the book presents committed Christian views of one kind or another. It is with trepidation that I part company with scholars of the stature of Saulnier, Nurse, Screech and Ingman in coming down on the side of the «irreligious» *Cymbalum mundi*. But my interpretation does seem to make sense of key passages — and to account fully for the otherwise baffling contemporary verdicts.

London   Malcolm C. SMITH.

---

[65]   See her «Silence, Harpocrates and the *Cymbalum mundi*», *Bibliothèque d'Humanisme et Renaissance*, LI, 1989, pp. 569-577.

Bibliothèque d'Humanisme et Renaissance - Tome LV - 1993 - n° 2, pp. 301-315

PAUL DE FOIX AND FREEDOM OF CONSCIENCE

In 1561, the young scholar and politician Paul de Foix wrote a memorandum on the state of religion in France[1]. With impressive scholarship and incisiveness, he analyses the history of attitudes of Christians towards permission of cults with which they disagree and then, in the light of this analysis, discusses whether it is desirable in the France of his day to accord freedom of religion to Reformers. The fascination of this document lies in the fact that it is at once a thoroughly documented historical essay and a piece of acutely topical political comment (indeed, like other contemporary memoranda with which it can be compared, it was an attempt to influence the legislators); and it sheds important light on the genesis of religious freedom in Europe in modern times. It is also, as we shall see, one of four known attempts by Foix to sway religious policy at critical historical moments. The main purpose of this article is to recall the context of the memorandum of 1561, and to reproduce the text[2].

Foix (1528-1584) was an aristocrat, related to the Valois and d'Albret families. He learned Greek from Toussaint and Strazel, and Hebrew from Vatable, and then pursued studies in law at Toulouse and mathematics and philosophy in Paris. In 1555, he was appointed *conseiller-clerc* in the *Parlement*, having been dispensed, on the recommendation of Catherine de Médicis, from the usual requirement of being an ordained cleric. But his main career was as a diplomat: he was to become Ambassador in Scotland (1561), England (1562-1566), Venice (1567-1570) and Rome (1573-1574 and 1581-1584). In 1571, on the resignation of Jean de Morvilliers, he was offered

---

[1] The most important sources on Foix are two studies by Noël Didier, «Paul de Foix à la mercuriale de 1559, son procès, ses idées religieuses», *Mélanges d'archéologie et d'histoire, Ecole française de Rome*, LVI, 1939, pp. 396-435 (henceforth «Didier, 1939»), and «Paul de Foix et Grégoire XIII, 1572-1584: une suite à la mercuriale de 1559», *Annales de l'Université de Grenoble*, Section lettres-droit, XVI, 1939, pp. 93-245 (reissued as a book in Grenoble, 1941; henceforth «Didier, 1941»). Didier's studies are my sources for the life of Foix.

[2] The memorandum is in the Bibliothèque Nationale, Paris (ms. fr. 4766, 24 r°-33 v°). Didier drew attention to it, and published short extracts from it, in his two studies: 1939, p. 433, n. 2 and 1941, p. 15, n. 41. It is not mentioned in Joseph Lecler's *Histoire de la tolérance au siècle de la Réforme* (2 vol., Paris, 1955). Mario Turchetti mentions Foix, notably as a protector of the *moyenneur* François Bauduin (*Concordia o tolleranza? François Bauduin e i «Moyenneurs»*, Genève, 1984, p. 211, n. 30 and 343), but does not mention Foix's memorandum. It is possible that Foix's source for the views of early Christian theologians is his protégé François Bauduin, who told his friend Georg Cassander in a letter of 1 April 1558 that he hoped shortly to publish the «leges et iudicia veterum Christianorum de coërcitione hereticorum»; and he added, «nam et in Gallia desiderantur» (see M. Erbe, «François Bauduin and Georg Cassander: Dokumente einer Humanistenfreundschaft», *Bibliothèque d'Humanisme et Renaissance*, XL, 1978 (pp. 537-560), p. 543). No such work however appears in the list of Bauduin's publications in Turchetti, pp. 599-602.

the post of Chancellor of France, but refused, probably on the grounds that it was widely expected that Michel de L'Hospital, the illustrious previous holder of the post (and a close friend of Foix) would be recalled[3]. In August 1571, he returned to England for what turned out to be abortive negotiations for a marriage between the Duke of Anjou and Queen Elizabeth; the following year, in June, he was back in England to negotiate another prospective marriage of a French prince, this time the Duke of Alençon, and Elizabeth: these negotiations, which continued over many years, also came to nothing. In 1574, Charles IX agreed to his nomination as Archbishop of Toulouse — which led to very protracted negotiations to convince Gregory XIII of his orthodoxy: it was not until 1582 that Foix finally succeeded — only to die in Rome in 1584 without having been able to take up the post.

Foix's first known intervention in debates on the treatment of religious dissidents was in the *mercuriale* of 1559, the famous series of meetings of the *Parlement* when magistrates were invited to give their views. The impetus for the *mercuriale*, which was held in the late spring and early summer, came from the King, who was determined that all magistrates should enforce the Edict of Compiègne, of 1557, which required the death penalty for convicted *sacramentaires* (i.e. for those who denied the Catholic doctrine on the Eucharist). The texts of the interventions are not extant, but it is known that Foix attempted to circumvent the draconian zeal of certain magistrates (and indeed of the King). He urged a distinction between Reformers who denied the form of the sacrament of the Eucharist but accepted the Real Presence, and those who denied the substance as well as the form: this distinction would have spared Lutherans the death penalty, for they could not be charged as «sacramentaires» under the Compiègne Edict; and the great majority of French Protestants at the time would thus have been spared. Foix added that the question of the treatment of heresy, and indeed all controversial theological issues, should be judged by a council of the Church, and he almost certainly also urged that pending the outcome of such a council, procedures against Reformers should cease. For advancing these propositions, he was arrested following the session of 10 June and imprisoned in the Bastille, along with others who had expressed liberal views. The death of Henri II did not prevent his trial by members of the *Parlement*. He was found guilty by the narrowest of majorities: it seems that a determining factor in his conviction was a desire to avoid making the late King look stupid. On 8 January 1560, Foix was condemned to retract and was banned from the *Parlement* for one year[4].

His intervention in 1559 in favour of leniency towards Reformers and his imprisonment seems to have contributed to a belief in some circles that Foix

---

[3]   On the friendship of Foix and L'Hospital, see Didier, 1939, p. 429; 1941, p. 19 and n. 63.

[4]   Didier was able to reconstruct the main elements in Foix's speech (which spanned two successive days) on the basis of a collection of testimonials to Foix assembled in 1574 by the Archbishop of Paris (see below, note 16). See Didier, 1939, which also covers Foix's arrest and his subsequent trial. The other *parlementaires* pursued in 1559 with Foix were Louis Du Faur, Anne Du Bourg, Eustache de la Porte and Antoine Fumée; three others who were due to be arrested, Nicolas Du Val, Claud Viol and Arnaud Du Ferrier, took flight before they could be apprehended (see Didier, 1939, pp. 415-416).

was a covert Reformer, or sympathetic to the Reformation, and it is worth digressing momentarily to examine his religious opinions. The belief that he was a Reformer seems to have been particularly prevalent in diplomatic circles. On 18 March 1561, Nicholas Throckmorton, English Ambassador in France, wrote to Elizabeth to report that Foix would be nominated as Ambassador and that he had been in trouble in 1559 for religion; on 6 March 1562, he reported to Elizabeth the view of Coligny that «Foix, the French ambassador in England, is inclined to advance religion»; and on 24 March he told Elizabeth that another Ambassador was to be sent to England because «M. de Foix is suspected to be too well affected to the Admiral [Coligny] and the Protestants»[5]. On 2 August 1562, the Spanish Ambassador in Paris, Chantonnay, described Foix as a Reformer[6]. Once an individual acquired a reputation as a sympathiser with the Reformation, it tended to stick. Thus, on 12 May 1568, Sir Henry Norris, English Ambassador in France, wrote to the Earl of Leicester that he «Understands that Mons. de Foix, late ambassador in England, is commanded home [from Venice], being suspected to be of the religion»[7]. And the mere fact that Foix had once had this reputation seriously preoccupied Gregory XIII, and impeded his nomination as Archbishop of Toulouse.

It certainly seems that Foix's conciliatory temperament, together with his function as a diplomat in Scotland and England, dictated gestures which were at the very least ambivalent. In a letter of 7 December 1561, the English ambassador in Scotland, Thomas Randolph, reported to Queen Elizabeth's Secretary, William Cecil, that Foix had been introduced to him and had «commended the religion» to him. Thereupon Randolph had told Foix «what men thought of hym for that he had indured for Chrystes sake»; the last remark indicates that Randolph ascribed Foix's imprisonment to sympathy for the Reformation rather than to a belief in leniency *per se*; there is no indication that Foix did anything to disabuse him. Randolph's satisfaction with Foix's religion was rapidly marred, however, since his letter continues: «The nexte daye after, notwithstondynge, he [Foix] was with the Quene [Mary] at the Masse!» Foix had afterwards «repented hym self» and had not attended Mass on the previous Friday and Saturday, «to the great myslykynge of the Quene»[8]. Foix's conciliatory outlook emerges also in a letter of 10 December 1561 from Randolph to Cecil: Foix is inclined to peace between all princes, «which well agrethe unto all those that professethe Chryste, for whose cawse your honour knowethe what he hathe indured» — again, an allusion to the *mercuriale* and Foix's imprisonment[9]. Another wit-

---

[5]   See J. Stevenson, ed., *Calendar of State Papers, Foreign Series, Elizabeth, 1561-1562*, London, 1866, respectively nos. 49 (para. 2), 924 (3) and 1043 (3).

[6]   «L'ambassadeur d'Espagne Chantonnay s'avançait beaucoup en écrivant alors que M. de Foix était de la religion nouvelle» (Didier, 1941, p. 16, referring to *Mémoires de Condé*, 1743, II, p. 53).

[7]   A.J. Crosby, ed., *Calendar of State papers, Foreign Series, Elizabeth, 1566-1568*, London, 1871, no. 21279.

[8]   See J. Bain, *Calendar of the State papers relating to Scotland and Mary, Queen of Scots, 1547-1603*, I, 1547-1563, Edinburgh, 1898, no. 1049 (p. 577).

[9]   See Bain, no. 1050 (p. 579).

ness to Foix's conciliatory spirit — or, conceivably, temporising spirit — is Nicholas Throckmorton, English Ambassador in Paris. On 8 January 1562, he reported that Foix, on his return from England, had visited him and commended Queen Elizabeth and spoken well of the form of religion used in England; it was Foix's intention to show a French translation of the Book of Common Prayer to the Queen Mother, the King of Navarre and the Chancellor[10]. His conciliatory attitude towards the Anglican religious settlement contrasts strongly with that of another commentator, Estienne de La Boëtie, who saw it as heretical[11]. Foix's religious position at this time has been characterised by the best scholar to write about him as «vacillating»[12].

Foix's position seems to have evolved, however, in the direction of unequivocal Catholic orthodoxy[13]. During his principal period as Ambassador in England (1562-1566), he assisted English Catholics and allowed them to hear Mass at the embassy; some were imprisoned for this, and he secured their release[14]. A further indication of his orthodoxy is that one day in Holy

---

[10]   See Stevenson, no. 789, para. 7; also H.O. Evennett, *The Cardinal of Lorraine and the Council of Trent*, Cambridge (England), 1930, pp. 403-404.

[11]   See my edition of La Boëtie's *Mémoire sur la pacification des troubles*, Genève, 1983, pp. 55 and 94.

[12]   Didier concluded, on the strength of Foix's 1561 memorandum, that his religious thought was «singulièrement vacillante», and he added, «Bien que, par la forme de son langage, il se range parmi les catholiques, il ne sait pas qui a raison dans le grand débat en cours. Peut-être n'est-il pas loin d'admettre que la Réforme l'emportera un jour. En attendant, les affirmations tranchantes, les attitudes raides lui déplaisent. Cet humaniste est-il un sceptique? Il est plutôt de ceux que la Réforme a profondément ébranlés en plusieurs articles de leur foi, mais qui n'ont pas encore, en leur for intérieur, pris un parti définitif» (1939, p. 434; and see also Didier, 1941, p. 146 and n. 54). This verdict is highly consistent with the impression Foix made upon contemporary English diplomats (Didier did not exploit the English and Scottish material in either of his two studies).

[13]   Didier considered that during the reign of Franci II, Foix «[...] paraît s'être détourné de plus en plus du protestantisme, devenu calviniste, dogmatisant et séditieux, pour s'enfermer dans un catholicisme fortement gallican» — while remaining a friend of prominent Reformers such as Duplessis-Mornay and Hubert Languet (1941, pp. 25-26 and notes). It seems to me that the change came slightly later than the reign of Francis II, for Foix seems to have been making ambivalent statements to English diplomats in 1562. It should also be said that while his commitment to the Catholic faith became more unequivocal, his conciliatory outlook remained, as is shown by the advice he gave in 1574 to Henry III (discussed later).

[14]   «En déjouant les machinations des huguenots, en secourant de ses conseils, de son argent et de son influence les catholiques anglais ou étrangers persécutés par 'Jésabel', en leur permettant de venir chez lui entendre la messe au grand mécontentement de la reine, à qui il répondit que les portes des ambassadeurs étaient ouvertes à tous et qu'il ne pouvoit interdire l'assistance à une action aussi bonne que le saint sacrifice de la messe, Paul de Foix avait donné des signes non équivoques de son catholicisme» (Didier, 1941, p. 17, who refers to statements made on behalf of Foix to the Archbishop of Paris in 1574; see also Didier, 1939, p. 430, n. 2). Marc-Antoine Muret also noted Foix's assistance to English Catholics in a Latin funerary oration (see *Orationes quattuor*, Ingolstadii, 1585, B.L. 1090 i 8 (6), pp. 31-32), which was published in translation with the 1628 edition of Foix's *Lettres au Roy Henry III* (Paris, B.L. 831 b 15, i iii v°-i iv r°). In *Montaigne and religious freedom* (p. 211), I cited Ronsard as a witness to Foix's defence of English Catholics, but mistakenly: what Ronsard praises Foix for is brave endurance of hardship inflected on him during his embassy at the time of civil war in France (see Ronsard's *Elegie à Monsieur de Foyx*, published in the *Elegies, Mascarades et Bergerie* of 1565: vol. XIII, p. 154, in Paul Laumonier's edition of Ronsard's *Œuvres complètes*).

Week, in 1581, he and Michel de Montaigne spent five hours together visiting seven churches in Rome (a Catholic devotional practice of the time); if Foix had any sympathy for the Reformation, Montaigne would almost certainly have noted the fact (as he did in the case of the French Ambassador in Venice, Arnaud Du Ferrier, with whom he had attended Mass a few weeks earlier)[15]. Perhaps the most telling indication of Foix's orthodoxy lies in the testimonies assembled in 1574 by Pierre de Gondi, Archbishop of Paris, at the instigation of Gregory XIII, and in the fact that Foix was able to persuade Gregory XIII of his orthodoxy — so successfully, it seems, that Gregory XIII would have nominated Foix as a cardinal but for his untimely death[16].

On 8 February 1561, the conviction against Foix arising from the *mercuriale* of 1559 was revoked. Thereafter, he continued to participate in debates on religious freedom. His characteristic view is found in a speech delivered to the Paris *Parlement* on 23 June 1561. This speech is his second known intervention in the debate (assuming, as seems to me reasonably safe, that the speech is by Foix)[17]. In this speech, the options open to the government are appraised: repressive measures against Reformers (execution or banishment) are ruled out, liberty of religion is presented as a policy of last resort (since diversity of cults will dissipate ecclesiastical discipline), and conciliation in the form of a national council of the Church is strongly advocated. The speech is extant: it was published in the *Mémoires de Condé*[18]. As he probably knew, Foix was pushing at an open door: the national council was to materialize in the following September and October in the form of the celebrated Colloquy of Poissy.

The sentiments in the speech of 23 June are echoed and developed in the memorandum which I am presenting here, which is Foix's third known intervention. The memorandum, which is ascribed to Foix in the manuscript in which it is found, is again an attempt to influence the legislators. It was writ-

---

[15] For Montaigne and Foix in Rome, see Montaigne's *Journal de voyage en Italie*, ed. C. Dédéyan, Paris, 1946, p. 233; for his comments on Du Ferrier, *Journal*, p. 172. After the death of Foix in 1584, Montaigne included a glowing tribute to him in *De la vanité*.

[16] Gondi collected the testimonies at the time when Foix was a candidate for the archbishopric of Toulouse, to satisfy the Pope of his orthodoxy. There are thirty-six of them, mainly by participants in the 1559 *mercuriale*. The manuscript in the Vatican Library containing them was discovered by Didier, and is the principal source for his 1939 article on Foix and the *mercuriale*. On Foix's orthodoxy, see especially p. 420, n. 2 and 430, n. 2 of that article; also Didier, 1941, pp. 86-88 and notes 31 and 32.

[17] I pointed out that it is by someone who had denounced persecution in the *mercuriale* of 1559, and that its ideas are echoed in the memorandum published here, which is known to be by Foix (see *Montaigne and religious freedom: the dawn of pluralism*, Genève, 1991, pp. 193-194). The case is stronger than the one I made out, since Foix states in this memorandum that he had given a view to the *Parlement* in July, and that he had declared his commitment to religious unity in the *Parlement*, a commitment which is indeed found in the July speech; also, he states in the memorandum that he had already urged a national council on the *Parlement*, again a view found in the speech.

[18] For the text, see *Advis donné au roy en l'assemblée tenue en la Cour de Parlement à Paris sur le faict de la religion, le vint-troisieme jour de Juin, MDLXI*, in *Mémoires de Condé, ou Recueil pour servir à l'histoire de France* [by D.F. Secousse], 6 t., Londres, 1743, II, pp. 409-423.

ten after the Colloquy of Poissy, to which it refers. More specifically, it was
written late in 1561 for Catherine de Médicis, who had convened an assembly
of privy councillors and *parlementaires* which was to determine the policy to
be pursued in the face of Reformers' claims for freedom to practise their
religion. This is what Foix is alluding to when, addressing Catherine de
Médicis, he refers to «la deliberation qu'il vous a pleu nous faire proposer».
The meetings, which were held early in January 1562, were to lead later that
month to publication of the famous Edict which, for the first time in Europe
in modern times, legitimised the nationwide practice of a minority religion.
Other politicians were to write memoranda at this time in the hope of
influencing the assembly of *parlementaires*, for example Estienne de La
Boëtie[19] and Arnaud Du Ferrier[20]. These texts, and others of the kind, give
fascinating insight into the genesis of religious freedom in Europe, and I hope
to publish elsewhere a more detailed survey of the most important of them.

Foix's memorandum draws on a wealth of historical precedents, and is
very well-structured and succinct. The opening paragraphs make it clear that
Foix (like La Boëtie) felt uneasy about seeking political solutions to religious
strife when the underlying cause, the religious division itself, remained unad-
dressed. He argues (again, as La Boëtie did) that part of the problem is that
Reformers have a high profile as religious dissidents, unlike long-established
religious minorities elsewhere (he cites the examples of Christians in Turkey
or Jews in Italy and Germany). He then demonstrates that the problem of
legislating for the presence of dissidents will vary according to their relationship with the majority. Thus, when the Christians in ancient Rome were a
persecuted minority, they sought equal rights with the Roman pagan
religion: they knew there was only one true religion, but they advocated freedom in the expectation that if the true religion could be freely preached, it
would prevail. Then, when freedom was accorded to Christians and the
Church found itself at the mercy of the Arian sect which enjoyed political
power, orthodox Christians called for «liberté de religion» for both Christian groups. However, when orthodox Christianity prevailed, the Catholic
bishops argued that the civil authorities should uphold true religion. This
analysis shows that Christians of whatever persuasion have tended to seek
support for their religious mission from the secular authorities.

---

[19]   See my edition of his *Mémoire sur la pacification des troubles* (Genève, 1983) and, for
a discussion of the issues it raises, *Montaigne and religious freedom*, chapter III, «La Boëtie's
formula for peace», pp. 51-74. It is possible that Foix knew La Boëtie: in a letter of 1 September
1570 dedicating to Foix the French poetry of La Boëtie, Montaigne wrote «[...] pouvez avoir
eu quelque cognoissance de luy pendant sa vie, mais certes bien legiere pour en discourir la grandeur de son entiere valeur» (see La Boëtie's *Œuvres complètes*, ed. L. Desgraves, 2 vol., Bordeaux, 1991, II, p. 100).

[20]   Du Ferrier's 1561 memorandum on the treatment of religious dissidents is in the same
manuscript in the Bibliothèque Nationale, Paris, as Foix's (ms. fr. 4766, 24 v°-29 r°); I have
transcribed Du Ferrier's memorandum, and hope to publish it. According to Didier (1941, p. 9),
Foix had known Du Ferrier from his time as a student of law at Toulouse. Like Foix, Du Ferrier
expressed contentious views in the *mercuriale* of 1559 (see above, note 4). In June 1567, Foix
succeeded Du Ferrier as Ambassador in Venice (and was succeeded by him in 1570, when Du
Ferrier began a second term of office).

Foix then applies this analysis to the present situation — and sees merit in liberty of religion. The Reformers seek «liberté d'ung costé et d'autre» because they know that that is the most they can hope to get in the present circumstances — and they cite Christians who argued for liberty. Catholics on the other hand feel that their side has greater political strength, and they resist this. However, Foix adds, there have been Catholic emperors who, though they held political power, have accorded «liberté de religion». In drawing attention to this fact, Foix is implicitly challenging the prevailing wisdom. Indeed, his use of the positive term «liberté de religion» as distinct from the negative term of «tolerance» is significant: the latter term was used to imply that permission of the Reformed faith was something intrinsically undesirable, something to be endured[21]. Foix appears to be one of the first, if not the first, to use the term «liberté de religion» in France[22]. And his support for freedom was, as we have seen, no mere academic position: he has the rare distinction of having defended the freedom both of Reformers (in France) and of Catholics (in England) — and at his peril in each case.

However, as in the speech of 23 June, religious liberty is presented as an imperfect solution: it does not tackle the underlying problem of religious disunity (here, too, Foix's thought mirrors that of La Boëtie). His preferred solution is that the King will select a group of dispassionate theologians of both sides who will confer, «comme juges chercheans la seule verité par les escriptures». There are excellent historical precedents, he argues, for the success of this method. The recent attempt at conciliation, the Colloquy of Poissy, has failed (he argues) because participants displayed a partisan spirit and because they were more preoccupied with recognition of their rank than they were with the truth. This seems to be a veiled attack on Catholic dignitaries — probably either Cardinal Tournon or the Cardinal of Lorraine or both[23]. The task of conciliation, Foix argues, must be entrusted, instead, to people of integrity and erudition. One senses, in reading the memorandum, that Foix felt he had a role to play in such an initiative. His preferred option is thus conciliation, the policy which has come to be known as «concord».

---

[21]   Religious liberty (or freedom of conscience) and tolerance are sometimes used as synonyms, but the terms had different inferences: see *Montaigne and religious freedom*, pp. 47-50. The distinction between freedom and tolerance seems to be gaining ground: see, for example, the papers by Bernard Cottret and Mario Turchetti in H.R. Guggisberg, F. Lestringant, J.-C. Margolin, eds., *La Liberté de conscience (XVIe-XVIIe siècles)*, Actes du Colloque de Mulhouse et de Bâle (1989), Genève, 1991; also A. Rotondò, *Europe et Pays-Bas: évolution, réélaboration et diffusion de la tolérance aux XVIIe et XVIIIe siècles*, Firenze, Università degli studi, 1992, especially section 5.

[22]   See *Montaigne and religious freedom*, pp. 35-36 and 59-60.

[23]   Didier suggested, though without stating his grounds, that Foix is attacking either Tournon or Este (1939, p. 433, n. 2). Tournon is a possible target of Foix's remarks because he insisted that the Reformers should not be accorded equal status to the bishops (see L. Romier, *Catholiques et Huguenots à la Cour de Charles IX*, Paris, 1924, p. 219-220). Lorraine may be the object of attack, with Tournon, because the two of them held the title of Papal Legate and were (it seems) offended by the nomination of Este to this title without consultation with them (see Romier, *Catholiques et Huguenots*, p. 225).

If conciliation is not to be pursued, then the King must, Foix argues, permit the practice of the Reformed faith. The alternative is that Reformers will hold surreptitious assemblies, which is dangerous — or that they will not hold religious services at all, and so will fall into atheism. To banish them would be impractical in view of their numbers — and would anyway be damaging to France, and a source of strength to neighbouring nations; and there is no-one (he rather optimistically says) so cruel and barbaric as to want to kill them. It is desirable that they be reunited with the Roman Church, but they will refuse this as long as the abuses in the Roman Church remain uncorrected — and one cannot in good conscience require them to join an unreformed Church (again, a view identical to that of La Boëtie). Foix adds that he is the more ready to allow assemblies of Reformers in that their belief accords with that of Catholics on many essential points.

Foix was to become a still more convinced defender of religious liberty as the prospects for conciliation receded. In 1574, in his fourth known contribution to the debate, he urged the new King, Henry III, to abandon the repression associated with his predecessor and make a binding peace with Reformers based on liberty of conscience: «[...] What is it that the Protestants have sought from the very beginning? The answer is obvious: that care should be taken to protect freedom of consciences.» Freedom had been granted them in the Edict of January 1562 — but violated in the massacre at Vassy, which had precipitated the first civil war. Peace was made by a new edict, but four years later the Reformers again feared loss of freedom and took up arms. After the St. Bartholomew's Day massacre, the Reformers were emboldened by despair, recovered their strength and renewed their demands for liberty. «They have been terrified and driven to distraction, and you must dispel the dark clouds of suspicion and fear. You must grant them liberty according to the provisions of earlier edicts. This will give them grounds to hope that their liberty will be more secure in future; and you will gradually bring alienated souls to obedience by gentle government [...] You will not be abandoning any part of your authority if you grant liberty of conscience: you will be seen as exercising the only form of legitimate authority there is, and will be ruling over free men rather than slaves.» Foix ended his speech in tears, for he knew that a secret decision had already been taken to wage war on Reformers[24].

In most countries, the transition from religious unity to pluralism was fraught and costly. Foix's memorandum helps us see how the transition was accomplished. Any attempt to secure religious unity by coercion will be (he says) impracticable as well as inhuman. Conciliation is thus the only way to unity — but it may not work: the Colloquy of Poissy has been aborted by human weakness (and religious leaders on all sides were becoming increasingly hostile to conciliation). Thus, purely pragmatic considerations invited

---

[24]   His speech, given at an assembly in Lyons, was recorded by Jacques-Auguste de Thou: see *Historiarum sui temporis tomus primus [-septimus]*, Londini, 1733, III, pp. 353-358 or, in the French translation (*Histoire universelle depuis 1543 jusqu'en 1607*, Londres, 1734), t. VII (1573-1578), pp. 138-149. The passage is near the beginning of Book 59 of the *Historia*.

people to think of pluralism, however reluctantly. For Paul de Foix and a few other scholars and statesmen, principle points in the same direction as pragmatism: religious liberty has intrinsic merit, and it is unthinkable to compel dissidents to subscribe to a religion which lacks moral authority.

London.   Malcolm C. SMITH.

De Monsieur de Foix à la Royne mere du roy sur le mesme subject

C'est une chose très certaine, Madame, que la source et origine de touttes les calamitez et miseres humaines a proceddé du mespris et contemnement de la loy de Dieu. Et mesmes la corruption de nostre nature, qui est nostre plus grand malheur, a proceddé de ce que nostre premier pere auroit mesprisé le commandement de son seigneur. David, Roy, ayant en brief recité au pseaume lxe les miseres et afflictions desquelles Dieu a travaillé le peuple d'Israel, en attribuë la cause à l'ingrat mespris du commandement et volonté de Dieu, et de là mesme sont yssus entre les hommes les controverses de la religion tant du temps passé que present, qui sont tresdommageables et dangereuses, non seulement parce qu'elles desplaisent à Dieu, duquel tout bien nous vient, et provoque[nt] son ire contre nous, mais aussy parce qu'elles engendrent noyse, contention et sedition, je dis sedition procedant d'une opinion qui est en nostre entendement sy vehemente que mesmes elle faict oublier tout debvoir de pieté, provocquant le filz contre le pere, et mespriser ce que les hommes ont plus cher, comme les biens et la vye.

Ce qui rend la deliberation qu'il vous a pleu nous faire proposer très difficile, comme aussy de ce qu'il semble que l'on veuille regler et ordonner la police, la religion demeurant desreglée et desordonnée, chose à mon jugement impossible et indigne du nom que nous portons: car estant Chrestiens, nous debvons detester la sagesse mondaine des anciens Romains qui n'ont eu esgard à la religion que pour servir à leur police; et nous, au contraire, voyons que la republicque plustost doibt servir à la religion, nous proposans pour dernier but et fin le service de Dieu, ayant soing de la police afin qu'en paix et tranquilité il y puisse estre honoré premier. Davantage, la difficulté qui se presente est d'autant plus grande qu'il n'est point question s'il faut endurer les Mahometistes comme ils nous endurent, ou les Juifz comme ils sont endurez en Allemagne et Italie, ne aussy s'il fault endurer les antiens heretiques, Arriens, Manicheans et autres, desquelz l'assemblée pouvoit estre aucunement endurée sy l'on n'eust eu esgard qu'à la republicque, d'autant qu'il n'y avoit aulcune difference d'eux avecq les Catholiques en l'apparance exterieur et en ceremonies, mais seulement en quelques pointz de la doctrine. Mais ceux qui font aujourd'huy nouvelles assemblées sont du tout separez de l'Eglise romaine en la forme exterieure, ceremonies et disciplines, ce qui accroist les seditions, mesmement du populaire ignorant, grossier et sensuel, qui s'arreste plus à l'apparance exterieur et à ce qui se presente à l'œil qu'à la doctrine.

Madame, cette difficulté n'est point nouvelle, ains a esté souventesfois proposée par les antiens, lesquelz, s'il vous plaist ouyr, ils vous pourront ayder de conseil et d'authorité. Et pour mieux descouvrir leur advis, nous considererons trois temps, le premier celuy auquel l'Esglise de Dieu a esté soubz la servitude et tirannie des payens, le second celuy auquel ils ont esté persecutez par les Arriens, et finalement quand les Chrestiens ont esté par la grace de Dieu en plus grand pouvoir et force que les autres.

En premier lieu, quand ils ont esté soubz la servitude des payens ils ont requis qu'il fust loysible et entier à ung chascun de suivre la religion qu'il voudroit, remonstrant qu'il estoit juste de permettre la chrestienne comme la romaine, et autres. Telle fut la remonstrance de Justin Martir et de Athenagoras en son apologitique addressée aux empereurs Anthonius pere et filz. Peu après, Tertulian, personnage de grande authorité en l'Esglise, s'addressant au senat romain, en dist aultant, usant de ces motz: *Videte ne et hoc ad irreligiositatis elogium concurat, admire* [*sic*: for «*adimere*»] *libertatem religionis et interdicere optionem divinitatis, ut non liceat mihi colere quem velim, sed cogar colere quem nolim.* Telle aussy a esté la remonstrance de Lactance, parlant du temps de Diocletian. Ce que ces grands et saints personnages demandoient, non qu'ilz ne sceussent tresbien qu'il n'y avoit qu'une seulle et vraye religion à laquelle tous se debvoient soubmettre, mais d'autant qu'ilz cognoissoient que c'estoit le plus qu'on pourroit obtenir, et esperoient que la vraye doctrine preschée appelleroit après soy et convaincroit touttes les faulces.

Or après que Constantin eut mis l'Esglise chrestienne en liberté, les Arriens ayant gaigné son fils Constance et ayans par son moyen le dessus, les bons et saints evesques requeroient liberté de religion d'ung costé et d'autre, comme St. Hilaire tesmoigne: *Permitat (inquit) lenitas tua populis ut quos voluerint, quos putaverint, quos elegerint audiant docentes.* De mesme demandoit ce grand evesque St. Athanase en quelque sienne lettre apologicque en rendant raison et disant: *piæ religionis proprium est non cogere sed suadere* (c'est à dire, que le propre de la sainte religion est de non contraindre mais persuader).

Or se trouvans les Catholicques en plus grand nombre, et assez puissans pour contraindre et donner loy aux autres, les bons evesques catholicques ont changé de propos et ont dit, tant pour le regard des heretiques qu'autres religions, que l'on ne les debvoit souffrir ne endurer, comme dispute longuement St. Ambroise contre Auxence, Arrien, et Simmache envoyé ambassadeur par le Senat romain devers les empereurs Valentin et Gratian, estant lors à Milan, pour les requerir de leur rendre et restituter les temples des antiens dieux (l'histoire en est amplement escrit en son V^e livre, epistres XXX, XXXII, XXXIIIe). Aussy Gregoire Nazianzene, comme il est escript en Socrates, Livre VIe, en mesme temps reprit Nectare, evesque de Constantinople, de ce qu'il permettoit les hereticques (et nommément les Apolinaires) faire leurs assemblées. Et le Concile, qui pour lors estoit assemblée à Constantinople, escripvit une lettre aux evesques d'Italye assemblez à Rome, inserée en l'histoire ecclesiasticque, se plaignant de ce que l'on enduroit des assemblées d'heretiques à Constantinople. Sainct Augustin aussy et St. Chrisostome ne veulent pas que l'on permette lesdictes assemblées.

Voilà, Madame, comment les saints personnages ont diversement escrit, eu esgard à la diversité du temps. Et de mesme cause procedde la diversité d'oppinions que vous avez ja ouyes: car ceux qui cuident la religion nouvelle estre la vraye, demandent liberté d'ung costé et d'autre, cognoissans que c'est le plus qu'ilz pourroient obtenir, pour n'estre pareilz ne en nombre ne en force aux autres. Et pour ce, se servent des exemples de Justin, Athenagoras, Tertulian, Lactance, St. Hilaire et Athanase. Au contraire, ceux qui s'arrestent en la religion de leurs peres, en laquelle ils ont esté nourriz et eslevez, cuydans leur party estre la plus forte, insistent à ce que l'on ne permette de s'assembler à ceux de la nouvelle doctrine, usans de l'authorité de St. Ambroise, Gregoire Nazianzene, St. Augustin et St. Chrisostome.

Toutesfois les empereurs chrestiens et catoliques, encores qu'ilz usassent volontiers du conseil de ces saints personnages, pourvoyans au repos de la republique ont souventesfois permis liberté de religion. Constantin premier en publia ung edict lequel puis après revoqua, se congnoissant avoir la commodité et pouvoir de ce faire, comme escrit Eusebe en livres premier et IIIe de la Vye de Constantin. Peu après, l'empereur Jovianus, voulant restablir l'Esglise que Julien l'Apostat avoit renversée au commancement de son regne, publia une autre ordonnance de liberté, comme il est escript en l'histoire eclesiastique tripartite et de Nicephorus. Depuis, Valentin premier en occident fit mesme loy, [et] en est loué par Amien Marcelin, historien de son temps, au Livre XXXe. Son filz Gratien en feit autant, exceptans les Phociniens, Manicheens et Eunomiens; depuis, toutesfois, à l'exemple de Constantin, revocqua ladicte loy (Socrates, Livre V^e; Sozom., Livre VIIe). Et en mesme temps Theodose en orient en fit autant, revoquant ladicte loy de liberté après l'avoir auparavant publiée. Nicephorius, Honorius et Arcadius, filz et successeurs dudict Theodoze, meirent et osterent par plusieurs fois et en mesme année ladicte loy de liberté, dequoy nous en avons quelque marque au code Theodozien, Livre XVIe, titre IIIe. Après la mort de cet empereur, et l'Esglise catolique estant destituée de bons evesques, l'empereur Zeno, et depuis Anastaze, et finalement Heraclius, voyans que les ungs suivans [sic] le Concile de Calchedoine, les autres non, pensans qu'il estoit expedient de laisser l'une et l'autre partye en liberté, publierent une ordonnance à ces fins qu'ilz appellerent [there is a gap in the manuscript: is the allusion to the «Henotikon» of Zeno (482 A.D.) and the «Ecthesis» of Heraclius I (638 A.D.)?], pensans que ce feust le moyen d'unyon et paix civile.

Voilà, Madame, les advis, loix et jugemens des antiens, tant ecclesiastiques que politiques.

Il pleut au roy au mois de Juillet dernier faire mettre la mesme chose en deliberation en la cour du Parlement, et je dis ce que je desirois et esperois, comme encore je desire, et ne desespere pas et veux desirer toutte ma vye. C'est que nous ayons une seulle religion vraye et entiere, conforme à la parole de Dieu, qui induise les hommes à l'honorer, rendre au roy très prompte obeissance et demeurer avecq son prochain en fraternelle paix, amitié et dilection, d'autant qu'en nostre confession de foy, que nous appellons le simbole, nous ne recognoissons qu'une seulle Esglise Catolicque, qui estoit acause de ce appellée par les antiens d'ung nom d'unité, comme St. Cyprian, et St. Augustin en ses livres De unitate adversus Donatistas, tesmoignent. L'Apostre aussy nous commande de n'endurer des schismes entre nous, et veut que nous n'ayons qu'ung Dieu, une foy, ung baptesme, et proteste que notre Dieu n'est point Dieu de division.

Doncques n'y ayant qu'une seulle et vraye religion, estant baptisez d'ung seul baptesme, appellez d'ung seul nom de Chrestiens, ayans ung seul sauveur, nous devons estre unis à ung seul Jesus Christ et à une seule et sienne Esglise. Et sy nous estions unis par une seule bonne et saincte religion, cela engendreroit une grande amitié en nous, detant que nous nous suporterions plus facillement les ungs et les autres, et nous garderions de nous entr'offenser, estant la paix de Dieu entre nous qui nous entretiendroit en unyon et concorde. Aultrement je prevois une terrible confusion, tant acause que nous irriterons Dieu que parce que nous aurons noyses et contentions entre nous. Nous en avons l'exemple des Samaritains, qui habitoient au milieu des Juifz entre la Judée et la Galilée, lesquelz exercerent une sy grande inimitié contre lesdictz Juifz, principalement acause du differend de la religion, qu'il s'esleva entre eux une telle sedition, et sy furieuse, que la cause fut appellée devant Alexandre le Grand et son conseil, à la charge et sur telle peyne que les advocatz de la partye vaincuë seroient punis de mort, comme Josephe en son 13e Livre des Antiquitez, Chapitre VIe, racompte. Et en Egypte il y a eu tousjours des divisions et seditions qui proceddoient acause de la division des religions, comme le mesme Josephe tesmoigne en l'epistre Domas à Ptolomée et Cleopatra. Je pourrois poursuivre ce propos par infinis exemples des histoires et beaucoup de sages sentences des antiens. Mais pour cette heure je me contanteray à reprendre ce que j'ay desja dit et ma conscience me contrainct de redire, c'est que je desire qu'il n'y ayt qu'une seulle religion qui nous unisse avecq Dieu et entre nous, à quoy, Madame, le roy se doibt principallement employer. Et pour ce, Esaye appelle les roys pere[s] nourisseurs de l'Esglise de Dieu. Et s'il est ainsy que les roys soient justement appellez peres de leurs subjects et que le pere, par ordonnance de Dieu, doibt soigneusement prendre garde que ses enfans soient institutez et nourris en vraye et sainte religion, il s'ensuit que Dieu, ayant faict le roy pere de son peuple, luy a imposé cette charge de prendre garde qu'il soit repeu de la vraye viande spirituelle, à l'exemple de Moyse, Josué, Samuel, David, Esechias, Josias. Ce que sy le roy faict, Dieu fera indubitablement suivant ses promesses, et comme il a fait à ces bons princes, prosperer ses affaires, et se rendra protecteur de luy et de son estat.

L'on me dira, «Quel moyen y a il de parvenir à cette unyon?» J'en proposé à la cour de Parlement ung qui a esté pratiqué heureusement par les antiens, et a mis en paix et repos de nostre temps tous noz voisins. C'est, Madame, qu'il plaise au roy faire choix de certain nombre de personnes, tant d'ung costé que d'autre, ayans bon tesmoignage de leur bonne vye, non partiaux ny factieux, versez en saincte escripture et livres des anciens docteurs, hors d'interest, ne cherchans leur gloire ny proffict, mais aymans l'unyon de l'Esglise et repos de voz subjects, lesquelz conferent ensemble des debatz qui sont aujourd'huy, tant acause de la doctrine que des ceremonies, comme juges chercheans la seule verité par les escriptures. Il est à esperer qu'ilz tomberont à ung bon et sainct accord. Nous lisons de deux grandz personnages, l'ung nommé Cyrille, evesque d'Alexandrie, l'autre Jehan evesque d'Antioch, avoir esté en grand differand pour ung point de la religion, d'où sortoient de grandes factions. Et y eut plusieurs escritz d'ung costé et d'autre, plains d'injures et amertume, de sorte que l'Asie et l'Afrique en furent grandement troublez, et ne sceut on par autre moyen les accorder que par une honneste conferance de ces deux personnages, lesquelz, parlans ensemble et cherchans seullement le service de Dieu, tomberent d'accord et apporterent la paix et unyon à toutte la Syrie et Egypte. Il est aussy escript en l'histoire tripartite qu'en Argnoide il y avoit grandes sectes et divisions acause d'une heresie prise des livres d'ung nommé Nepos, pour laquelle appaiser Clement Alexandrin, par l'espace de trois jours, soir et matin, confera en publicq avecq le principal deffenseur de cette heresie, nommé Coracion. A la fin, ayans conferé raisons avecq raisons, escriptures avecq escriptures, tomberent d'accord, et dist cet excellent personnage qu'il avoit affaire avecq personnes qui interrogeoient et respondoient appropos, et ne cherchoient qu'estre instruictz et trouver la verité, ce qui apporta l'unyon en ce pays.

Ce mesme chemin a esté tenu l'an V^c xli à Ratisbonne par l'empereur Charles V^e (prince, certes, de bonne memoire), lequel après avoir faict dresser un livre par gens sçavans, contenant certaine instruction des pointz qui estoient en difficulté, il le proposa à six personnages qu'il avoit esleuz, trois d'un costé et trois d'autre, pour l'examiner et arrester ce à quoy ils se trouveroient d'accord et, où il y auroit different, mettre par escript les causes et raisons. Et se trouverent d'accord en xviii articles, et eussent achevé (à mon jugement) l'accord, n'eust esté les empeschemens qui leur furent donnez tant par ceux de leur pays que par les estrangers. De cette conference ont aussy usé les princes eslecteurs en leurs terres, Suisses, et Anglois, et veoid mesme que les Saxons et Anglois, qui de leur nature ont tousjours esté plains de factions et seditions, vivent en grande unyon et accord.

De mesme, Madame, s'il plaisoit au roy faire dresser ung livre par quelque personnage sçavant, contenant moderation des points qui sont en difficulté, tant sur la doctrine que ceremonies, et le proposer pour estre examiné par certains personnages esleuz par le roy tant d'ung costé que d'autre, il y auroit grande esperance d'unyon et accord. Je sçay bien que l'on me dira que cette voye a esté essayé dernierement à Poissy sans certain fruict. Mais veritablement, à mon grand regret, je ne puis taire ce que j'y ay veu, c'est que je les ay veu debattre comme advocatz, ou plustost comme partyes cherchans chascun de gaigner sa cause et d'en rapporter la victoire, non comme juges estimans honnorable d'estre vaincus en trouvant la verité, mesmement pour l'unité de l'Esglise, et appaiser les consciences des hommes. J'y ay veu encores quelques vains tiltres d'honneur et dignité avoir eu plus de lieu que la probité et doctrine. Je croy qu'il n'y a personne qui, deliberant faire ung long et dangereux voyage sur mer, ne cherchast ung bon pilote, entendu et experimenté au navigage; ny, tombé en griefve maladie, un medecin docte et praticien; un accusé de quelque grand crime, quelque advocat sçavant en droictz et longuement versé en jugement. Et en chose de plus grande consequence, et où il est question du service de Dieu et de la vie eternelle, l'on y debvroit aller plus soigneusement. Je croy qu'il n'y a personne qui ne trouvast estrange sy les piedz ou les mains ou autres partyes de l'homme vouloient juger de la lumiere, estant cela le propre office de l'œil. Et l'on a beau revestir un asne de la peau d'un lion, jamais n'en fera il l'office.

[305]

A cause de quoy, Madame, si au lieu des partyes affectionnées et de ces vains tiltres vous appellez des juges entiers, de bonne doctrine, en conscience, pour conferer comme j'ay dict cy-dessus, j'aurois grande esperence de l'unyon, laquelle (Dieu m'en est tesmoing) je desire sur touttes choses. Ce qu'il plaisoit au Roy, Madame, pourroit estre promptement executé, et ne seroit besoing d'autre provision. Et c'est mon premier advis, auquel maintenant encores j'inciste.

Et où le vouloir de sa Majesté ne seroit d'user de ce moyen, et que le temps et la necessité presseroit, il me semble que vous ne debvez endurer les assemblées privées et nocturnes, plaines de soupçon et danger, lesquelles tous bons politiques ont tousjours empesché, et nos loix ont compris soubz les mots de colloques et assemblées illicites. Et d'ailleurs, elles apporteroient plusieurs et diverses sectes en la religion, comme nous voyons mesmes au Pays bas où, acause de ce, les heresies des Arriens et Anabaptistes se sont secretement renouvellées. Moings devez vous endurer qu'aucun de voz subjects vivre sans aucune religion, ce qu'ilz feront s'ilz ne sont retenuz en la crainte de Dieu par predications ordinaires, prieres publiques, administrations des saints sacremens, lesquelles choses ostées, ilz tomberont en impieté et toutte maniere de vices, et seront trespernicieux et dommag[e]ables au roy et à ses subjects. De les bannir et exterminer, pour le grand et excessif nombre il est tresdificile, et peut estre impossible, et d'ailleurs tresdommageable au Roy de diminuer d'autant de personnes son royaulme et en accroistre la force de ses voisins d'autant. Car à mon advis il n'y a personne sy inhumain et cruel et de telle barbarie qui voulsist les faire mourir. De les ramener soubz l'obeissance de l'Esglise romaine, à la mienne volonté qu'il se peust faire, et que l'on les peust reduire à une mesme bergerie et troupeau, et soubz ung mesme pasteur. Mais ceux qui cognoissent la diversité et contrarieté de leurs opinions et essayent combien la religion a de force en noz entendemens, jugeront cela estre du tout impossible. Davantage, pour ne rien dissimuler, et dire la verité, les abuz sont tels et tant intolerables en l'Esglise romaine que s'ilz ne sont par grande diligence corrigez et refformez je ne puis en bonne conscience estre d'advis de contraindre ceux qui s'en sont retirez à y revenir.

Ainsy, Madame, non de mon gré mais par la necessité, et m'arrestant principalement à ma premiere oppinion de la conference, je suis contraint en second lieu d'estre d'advis de leur permettre leurs assemblées publicques affin que les magistratz leur esclairent et que l'on voyt à l'œil s'ilz font quelque chose contre le service du Roy, à l'utilité publicque et honnesteté commune. Et ce à l'exemple du medecin, lequel a ung malade qui, pour la grande et longue maladie, est forcé luy permettre de manger des viandes moings bonnes, estant meilleur qu'il soit repeu de quelque chose que de ne manger du tout rien. Et n'eusse esté toutesfois de cet advis n'eust esté qu'ilz sont d'accord avecq nous au simbole des apostres et abregé de nostre foy, et font confession semblable à celle des quatre conciles generaux, parlent sainctement de la foy et des œuvres et en ont grand honneur, et reverent les saints sacremens de Baptesme et de la Cene (estant d'accord avecq nous de l'effect et fruict d'icelle, encores qu'ilz soient differentz avecq nous en la forme et nature), se rendent du tout subjectz et obeissans au roy et à ses loix politiques.

Sy est-ce que je desirerois en premier lieu qu'ilz retinssent toutes les ceremonies et disciplines de l'Esglise romaine qu'ilz pourroient en bonne conscience, à ce qu'ilz rendissent l'honneur qui est deu à l'antiquité, et qu'ilz pensent à l'infirmité de leur prochain, qui moins se scandalizera d'eux les voyans aprochans de l'Esglise romaine, et donneront ouverture à quelque accord doux et gratieux, d'autant qu'il est tresmalaisé de passer d'une extremité à autre, comme du froid en chaud, de blanc en noir: aultrement ilz augmenteront les extremitez de division et osteront l'esperance d'unyon à l'advenir, et certes ilz ne peuvent justement reffuser que l'on ne nous represente les ceremonies qui estoient au temps de ces grandz personnages St Augustin, St Ambroise, St Chrisostome. Et sy les apostres, qui avoient receu l'esprit de Dieu à grande mesure et accompagnoient leur predication de vertu et miracles, pour servir à l'infirmité des Juifz et ne donner empeschement à l'advancement de Christianisme, ont retenu touttes les ceremonies Mosaïques jusques au temps de l'eversion de Herusalem, ceux cy, à leur exemple et ayans esté marquez de la marque de Chrestien en cette nostre Esglise, ne doibvent faire difficulté de leur rendre cet honneur et observance de retenir d'ycelles ce qu'ilz peuvent en bonne conscience et sans idolastrie et superstition. En second lieu, je desire qu'ilz se rendent subjectz du tout à noz loix, j'entendz de mariages, divorces, difference des jours et viandes, comme choses arrestées et ordonnées par le magistrat. Tiercement, qu'ilz ne facent aulcun statut, mesme pour la discipline eclesiastique, sans l'autorisation du Roy. Et en dernier lieu, qu'ayans deposé les armes, ils baillent bonne asseurance des malefices et crimes qui se pourroient perpetrer par ceux de la compagnie.

Voila, Madame, ce qu'en mon ignorance et peu d'experiance, en bonne conscience toutesfois et soubz la crainte de Dieu, j'ay peu apporter en cette deliberation.

Sixteenth Century Journal
XXV/1 (1994)

Early French Advocates of Religious Freedom

Malcolm C. Smith
Royal Holloway and Bedford New College, London

This article presents eight sixteenth-century French politicians who shared the unusual conviction that practice of a dissident religious cult should be permitted, at least in certain circumstances. They are Pierre Du Chastel, Michel de L'Hôpital, the anonymous author of an *Exhortation aux Princes*, Estienne de La Boëtie, Arnaud Du Ferrier, Paul de Foix, Jean de Monluc, and Antoine Loisel. They arrived at their common liberalism by different routes. Some were advocates of religious liberty; others supported the less radical position of tolerance. The former group based permission of dissidence upon a right; the latter saw such permission as merely a concession to expediency. Most of these thinkers are little known, and the article throws new light on the genesis of the famous "tolerance" Edict of January 1562, the first piece of legislation in Europe that permitted nationwide religious dissidence.

FROM THE BEGINNING OF THE REFORMATION until 1561, practice of the Reformed faith was prohibited in France. The prohibition cost many hundreds (possibly thousands) of lives. Henry II sought to exterminate the "infamous Lutheran mob." After his death in 1559, the policy of repression was continued for some months, one of the last victims being Anne Du Bourg, the famous *parlementaire* who had had the temerity to denounce the persecutions. But a series of edicts issued in 1560 and 1561 abated the repression, and after April 1561 the practice of the Reformed faith was tacitly condoned, before being legalized in the Edict of January 17, 1562. Seven of the eight authors presented here were writing before the 1562 edict was issued. They sought to change the prevailing social attitudes, and in most cases they specifically argued for change in the law. The arguments they advanced helped bring about the end of judicial religious oppression in France. That fact alone would commend them to the attention of scholars, but what commends them still more is the urgency and cogency of their interventions in a debate which was at once acutely topical and perennial in its implications.

Most of the authors presented here are advocates of religious freedom, as opposed to tolerance; the exceptions are included to illustrate the distinction. These two positions admit of nuances; essentially, however, religious freedom designates the right of individuals and of groups to hold any belief and express that belief publicly, while tolerance is a merely provisional permission to hold and express beliefs regarded by the state as dissident or reprehensible. According to this distinction, religious freedom is a right; tolerance is a temporary concession. Strictly speaking, the two are mutually exclusive: religious freedom obviates the need for mere tolerance; tolerance implies that there is no entitlement to hold and practice the religion of one's choice. Sixteenth-century French usage reflects that distinction: "liberté" had positive connotations, suggesting respect for the individual conscience, and "tolérance" designated the temporary acceptance of something intrinsically undesirable.[1] The distinction is a useful one, and it seems to be gaining ground in modern scholarship.[2]

It is not always simple to determine whether an individual sixteenth-century writer supports freedom or mere tolerance. For one thing, linguistic usage itself varies, as we shall see. And other nuances besides linguistic ones are important. It is possible, for example, for an author to support freedom of belief for the individual but to refuse it to a group—to distinguish, that is, between private belief and institutional (and thus visible) dissidence. Again, it can happen that legislators will claim to be conceding freedom of religion when what they are really granting is mere tolerance; they are thus using the language of principle to cloak expediency, as legislators are wont to do. Equally, it is possible for an individual to see the virtues of religious freedom, but to balk at its radical implications, and to settle, in the pragmatic world of politics, for mere tolerance. A variant of this view is the position that endorses religious freedom as a desirable principle, but denies it to adversaries on the grounds that they do not accord liberty in countries in which they are in control. Moreover, it is possible for a given commentator to evolve intellectually, to move from support of tolerance to advocacy of freedom (it is theoretically possible to move in the

---

[1]See W.H. Huseman, "L'idea di tolleranza in Francia nel XVI secolo," *Intersezioni, Rivista di Storia delle Idee* 3 (1983): 521–45. Huseman cites examples of the word *tolérer* in 1562 that establish my point, but regrettably he does not usually give precise references.

[2]The distinction is made in Hans R. Guggisberg, "Wandel der Argumente für religiöse Toleranz und Glaubensfreiheit im 16. Jahrhundert," in H. Lutz, *Zur Geschichte der Toleranz und Religionsfreiheit* (Darmstadt: Wissenschaftlicher Buchgesellschaft, 1977), 455–81; B. Plongeron, "De la Réforme aux Lumières: Tolérance et liberté, autour d'une fausse idée claire," *Recherches de Science Religieuse* 78 (1990): 41–72; Bernard Cottret, "La tolérance et la liberté de conscience à l'épreuve: l'Europe du Nord-Est entre Révocation et glorieuse Révolution (vers 1685–vers 1688)," in Hans R. Guggisberg, Frank Lestringant, and Jean-Claude Margolin, eds., *La liberté de conscience (XVIe–XVIIe siècles): Actes de Colloque du Mulhouse et Bâle (1989)*, Etudes de Philologie et d'Histoire, vol. 44 (Geneva: Droz, 1991), 269–87. This distinction is also present in Mario Turchetti, "La liberté de conscience et l'autorité du magistrat au lendemain de la Révocation," ibid., 289–367. Incidentally, Turchetti offers some interesting definitions in that article (302–5, 364–67); he distinguishes (and so far as I know, is the only scholar who has done so) between "liberté de conscience" (the Pauline freedom from the requirements of the law, a freedom claimed by the Reformers) and "liberté de religion" (permission to choose what religion you want). This distinction corresponds to that between the original use by French Reformers of the term "liberté de conscience" (freedom from the requirements of the law) and their use of that same term, from 1562, in its modern sense; see Joseph Lecler, "Liberté de conscience: origines et sens de l'expression," *Recherches de Science Religieuse* 54 (1966): 370–406.

opposite direction, though I know of none who did). Awareness of these nuances helps us determine whether a particular writer who advocates permission of a dissident cult is a supporter of tolerance or, much more radically, of freedom. The distinction between freedom and tolerance not only helps us understand important sixteenth-century texts, but it invites us to identify rational bases for a right that is now often taken for granted.

A further complication is the development of skepticism in the latter half of the sixteenth century. The impact of skepticism on sixteenth-century religious debates in France was multifaceted.[3] On the precise question of permission of a dissident religion, skepticism can be invoked in favor of liberalism in two ways. First, a skeptical nonbeliever might say that since it cannot be ascertained what is true, it cannot be ascertained what is erroneous either, and we must therefore refrain from coercion. I do not know of anyone who advanced this position in so many words, but it is strongly implicit in certain statements by people who adopted a supposedly neutral stance on religion.[4] Second, a believer might invoke skepticism to say that possession of truth belongs to God and to those on whom God has conferred the gift of faith: one should not punish an individual for not having what only the Creator can give. The latter thought is present in two of the authors considered here.[5] A variant of that position, and we shall see an example, is that the area of undisputed truth is so small that in practice only a tiny handful of people can be convicted as

[3]Skepticism can be used to undermine a dogmatic position on religion; e.g., Cicero's famous presentation of skeptical arguments may well have inclined Estienne Dolet towards those reputedly atheistic views which were to cost him his life. On skeptical arguments, see especially Charles B. Schmitt, *Cicero Scepticus* (The Hague: Martinus Nijhoff, 1972). Conversely, skepticism could support dogmatism by undermining the claims of philosophy and pointing to dependence upon faith. Thus, Catholic writers turned to skepticism to refute Reformers; two notable examples are Pierre de Ronsard, *Remonstrance au peuple de France* (1562), and Michel de Montaigne, *C'est follie de rapporter le vray et la faux à nostre suffisance* and *Apologie de Raimond Sebond*. On the use of skepticism in religious controversies, see especially Richard H. Popkin, *The History of Skepticism from Erasmus to Spinoza*, rev. ed. (Berkeley: University of California Press, 1979), chap. 1.

[4]The violence associated with religious unrest in France seems to have engendered some indifference to religion. Jean-Antoine Brusquet, the royal fool, alluded to neutralism and endorsed it: "Je voy et oy ce que dit le pauvre peuple: Que diable avons-nous affaire, ne nous, ne nos biens, si l'un ne veut aller à la messe, ou si l'autre ne veut aller au presche? Qui voudra aller au diable y aille, le chemin est assez grand. Ce pendant nous sommes ruynez, corps et biens"; (*Advertissement de Brusquet au roy de France, touchant les troubles qui sont de present en France pour le fait de la religion*, s.l., (1568), British Library 114 k 3, A2v–A3r).

[5]It is seen in Thomas More's *Utopia*; see Thomas More, *Complete Works*, vol. 4, ed. Edward Surtz and Jack H. Hexter (New Haven: Yale University Press, 1965), 222–23. A version of this idea is found (curiously, and only momentarily) in Calvin; see Olivier Millet, "Le thème de la conscience libre chez Calvin," in Guggisberg, et al., *La liberté de conscience*, 34–35. The idea is also present in Montaigne, explicitly in *De la punition de la couardise* (*Essais*, 1: chap. 16), and implicitly in *De l'art de conferer* ("Nous sommes nés à quester la verité: il appartient de la posseder à une plus haute puissance"; *Essais*, 1: chap. 8).

heretics.[6] The positions both of nonbelieving skeptics and believing skeptics are probably closer to freedom of religion than to tolerance as I have defined those terms, since these are positions of principle rather than expediency, and (in theory at least) are not dependent upon, or vulnerable to, the pressures of circumstance.

The texts presented here are mentioned only cursorily or not at all in the standard studies. One of the most important of these studies is Joseph Lecler's *Histoire de la tolérance au siècle de la Réforme*. This work presents biblical and patristic texts commonly cited by advocates of tolerance and freedom, and analyzes the work of the main advocates of permission of dissident cults in various European countries. The other principal study on which I draw is Mario Turchetti's *Concordia o tolleranza? François Bauduin e i "Moyenneurs,"* a meticulous scrutiny of the *fortuna* of irenist thought at the time of the Colloquy of Poissy of 1561.[7] Most of the authors presented here were writing in the latter part of that year, a crucial moment, when French debates on whether to permit the Reformed faith came to a head. The material is presented roughly in chronological order; to give perspective, I begin with an individual who intervened twenty years before this date, and end with one who wrote twenty years later.

Pierre Du Chastel

Pierre Du Chastel (ca. 1504–1552), scholar, bishop, and intimate of Francis I, was educated at Langres and Dijon; by 1527 he was working at the press of Johann Froben in Basel. He lived for some months in Erasmus's household (and remained in touch with him); he left Basel after the city adopted the Reformation in 1529. At Bourges, Du Chastel followed

[6]Castellio narrowed the definition of a heretic by confining it to those who are either obstinately immoral or obstinately in error; see Hans R. Guggisberg, "Haïr ou instruire les hérétiques La notion d'hérétique chez Sébastien Castellion et sa situation dans l'exil bâlois," in Guggisberg, et al., *La liberté de conscience*, 65–81. That idea, which is similar to the thought of Peter Abelard and Thomas Aquinas, was adopted also by Catholic theologians of the seventeenth and eighteenth centuries; see J.-P. Massaut, "Les droits de la conscience erronée dans la théologie catholique moderne," in *La liberté de conscience (XVIe–XVIIe siècles), Actes du Colloque de Mulhouse et Bâle (1989)*, Etudes de Philologie et d'Histoire, vol. 44 (Geneva: Droz, 1991), 237–55.

[7]Joseph Lecler, *Histoire* (Paris: Auber, 1955); for France, see 2:5–160. Mario Turchetti, *Concordia o Tolleranza?*, Travaux d'Humanisme et Renaissance, 200 (Geneva: Droz, 1984). Other important studies include Joseph Lecler and Marius Valkhoff, *Les premiers défenseurs de la liberté de conscience* (Paris: Les éditions du Cerf, 1969), an anthology of texts with succinct historical commentary; see also Mario Turchetti, "Religious Concord and Political Tolerance in Sixteenth- and Seventeenth-Century France," *Sixteenth Century Journal* 22 (1991): 15–25, and idem, "Concorde ou tolérance de 1562 à 1598," *Revue Historique* 274 (1986): 341–55; and several of the essays in Guggisberg, et al., *La liberté de conscience*. This latter symposium and the books by Lecler and Turchetti have additional bibliographical information, which can be supplemented by the bibliography in Malcolm C. Smith, *Montaigne and Religious Freedom: The Dawn of Pluralism*, Etudes de Philologie et d'Histoire, 45 (Geneva: Droz, 1991).

lectures on law given by Andrea Alciati; on completion of his studies, in 1531, he became secretary to the French Ambassador in Rome. After a few months there, he taught in Venice, then visited the Holy Land, and returned to the French court by the beginning of 1537. As Bishop of Tulle (1539) and of Macon (1544), and royal librarian, he had great influence upon Francis I; under Henri II, in 1548, he was appointed Grand Almoner (1548) and Bishop of Orléans (1551).[8] It has been said that he was sympathetic to the Reformation, but it seems likely that his loyalty lay with the Catholic Church: he argued that it was better to tolerate appalling abuses in the Catholic Church than embrace the Reformation, a course which he said tended to lead to atheism and denial of personal immortality.[9]

Du Chastel's intervention in 1543 to save the radical thinker Estienne Dolet gives insights into his views on religious dissidence (though Dolet's alleged offence was impiety rather than heresy). Du Chastel was reproached for being soft on dissidents, and according to his biographer Pierre Galland, gave a very spirited reply:

> Du Chastel was vehemently denounced by those who seemed all-powerful with the King. One among them was a cardinal of great renown. This man approached Du Chastel and took him to task for the fact that he — an orthodox bishop in the true Church! — opposed all those who had at heart the cause of religion and piety, and had dared to intervene with the King on behalf of people who were not only infected with the Lutheran disease, but were actually atheists. I recall that Du Chastel, when he had recovered his composure somewhat, replied with some emotion and feeling that he could with justice turn the accusation against his accuser: he, for his part, had done what was proper to a man of the Church and to a bishop, but the other man was expecting bishops to carry out the function of veritable executioners. For the task of the bishops and priests was to follow the example of Christ and the Apostles and the saints, who made the Church holy for us by shedding their blood, and to turn the King from harshness and cruelty to gentleness, mercy and pity, to take an erring sheep on their shoulders and bring

[8]My main source for the life of Du Chastel is Franz Bierlaire's entry in Peter G. Bietenhoz, Thomas B. Deutscher, et al., *Contemporaries of Erasmus: A Biographical Register of the Renaissance and Reformation*, 3 vols. (Toronto: University of Toronto Press, 1985–87), 1: 409–10.

[9]For Du Chastel's view that the Reformation tended to atheism, see Pierre Galland, *Petri Castellani magni Franciae Eleemosynarii Vita* (Paris: Estienne Baluze, 1674), chap. 36, pp. 56–58, in the John Rylands Library, Manchester. R. Doucet, "Pierre Du Chastel, Grand Aumônier de France," *Revue Historique* 133 (1920): 212–37; and idem, 134 (1920): 1–57, maintains that Du Chastel, notwithstanding his indulgence towards Reformers, was an orthodox Catholic. For the suggestion Du Chastel was a Reformer, see Frederic J. Baumgartner, *Change and Continuity in the French Episcopate, the Bishops and the Wars of Religion, 1547–1610* (Durham: Duke University Press, 1986), 136 and n. 11.

it back to the sheepfold, and to triumph joyfully in the return of that sheep as one would in capturing an enemy's fort, especially when there were good grounds for hope that the individual would lead a better life. He had in no way offered the King any defense of Dolet's crimes and offences; what he had done was put to the King a request worthy of a Christian on behalf of a man who promised to live a more virtuous life. His view was that if anyone discerned any desire for repentance at any time in someone who had plunged headlong into error, then the womb of the Church should be expanded to embrace that person. Christ our protector does not delight in the shedding of human blood as Diana in Cherronesus once did, for we find in the sacred scriptures that God does not seek the death of the sinner but his life, and his conversion to better conduct. Those who took the opposite view and urged the King to punish penitents who sought to be reintegrated in the body of the Church, ought rather to be called executioners than bishops.[10]

Du Chastel thus offers a humane argument for tolerance, expressed in evangelical language. Many French bishops in the reign of Francis I sought to play down the existence of dissident thought in order to deny it publicity, and they were reluctant to invoke against it laws which were potentially draconian and whose application created martyrs. For them, tolerance of dissidence was a means first of limiting it, then of dissipating it.[11]

In his sermon on the death of Francis I, Du Chastel went further. He declared that no one should be executed for heresy, "since no mortal man, whoever he may be, can through any human argument or reasoning judge with certainty what is true."[12] Within this latter statement is the germ of an argument for religious freedom, for it is implicit that the only certain source of religious truth is the Creator, and one cannot punish an individual for not having what only the Creator can give (the position of the believing

---

[10]According to Doucet, "Pierre Du Chastel," 212, Galland's *Petri Castellani Vita* was written in 1552, the year of Du Chastel's death. The passage I have translated is from chap. 39. Galland, a celebrated defender of Aristotle, was immortalized in Rabelais' prologue to the *Quart livre*: see the edition by Michael Heath (Egham: Runnymede Books, 1990), 38.

[11]On French bishops playing down the existence of heresy, see Pierre Imbart de La Tour, *Les origines de la Réforme*, vol. 3, *L'évangélisme, 1521–1538* (Paris: Hachette, 1914), 525–32. Inquisitors in Italy, similarly, refrained from molesting heretics who did not flaunt their faith; see John Tedeschi, *The Prosecution of Heresy: Collected Studies on the Inquisition in Early Modern Italy* (Binghamton, N.Y.: MRTS, 1991), 32.

[12]The *Sermon*, in John Rylands Library, Manchester, 5 e 2, was published, with Du Chastel's funerary orations for the king, *Le trespas, obseques, et enterrement de . . . François . . . roy de France . . . premier de ce nom . . . Les deux sermons funebres pronouncés esdictes obseques* (Paris, 1547), and with Galland's *Vita*. The relevant passage is cited in Emile V. Telle, ed., *L'Erasmianus sive Ciceronianus d'Estienne Dolet, 1535*, Travaux d'Humanisme et Renaissance, 138 (Geneva: Droz, 1974), 455. Doucet, "Pierre Du Chastel," 28–34, maintains that Du Chastel's attitude towards dissidents hardened under Henry II.

skeptic). Du Chastel is thus important to the history of religious freedom, though he has escaped the attention of historians of tolerance and freedom. Indeed, he is important not just for his own views, but also as a close friend and mentor of Michel de L'Hôpital, whose historical role was primordial.

The influence of Du Chastel and people like him seems to have been at first limited and spasmodic: Francis I, and after him Henry II, sent hundreds of Reformers to the stake. But by 1561, it had become apparent that coercive measures were counterproductive. Two options remained: remove religious divisions by conciliation, or accept them as a fact and legally sanction them, at least temporarily. The perception of Mario Turchetti, enshrined in his title *Concordia o tolleranza*, is right: concord (understood as unity of religion, achieved either by conciliation or by coercion) was quite distinct from tolerance. Indeed, the two were mutually exclusive policies; concord obviated the need for tolerance, and tolerance postponed concord.[13] The failure of the government to achieve concord through conciliation at the Colloquy of Poissy in September and October 1561 inclined it towards the alternative policy, permission of the dissident cult, a measure that was to be enshrined in the Edict of January 1562.[14]

Michel de L'Hôpital

The principal architect of the Edict of January, Michel de L'Hôpital (ca. 1504–1573), shared the humanity and vision of his friend Du Chastel.[15] Of all the thinkers presented here, L'Hôpital is by far the best known. It has been argued well that his speeches and actions in 1560 and 1561 show a strong commitment to unity of religion, and that while he adopted a conciliatory stance at the famous Colloquy of Poissy, and felt that the Reformers should be heard, his goal remained at all times to secure their return to the old faith.[16] While that is certainly the case, I would add a

[13]While I agree with Turchetti that in a divided society tolerance and concord are mutually exclusive, I have reservations about his use of the word "concord," which he applies to any policy seeking religious unity, whether through conciliation or through coercion (see, for example, Turchetti, "Religious Concord and Political Tolerance," 15–19). I would apply it only to unity by conciliation. There is all the difference in the world between Henry II and Calvin on the one hand, and La Boëtie and the author of *Exhortation aux princes* on the other. Since the word "concord" clearly has a future, it would be helpful if historians could agree on the sense to give it.

[14]The best contemporary analysis of the situation is in my view found in La Boëtie, *Mémoire sur la pacification des troubles*, discussed below; see my edition of this work, Textes Littéraires Français, 317 (Geneva: Droz, 1983), which includes the text of the Edict of January 1562.

[15]On their friendship, see Jean Héritier, *Michel de L'Hôpital* (Paris: Flammarion, 1943), 46, 61. L'Hôpital dedicated poems to Du Chastel; see Michel de L'Hôpital, *Oeuvres complètes*, ed. P. J. S. Duféy (Paris, 1824–25), 3: 99–109, 517.

[16]This is the view of Turchetti, for whom L'Hôpital had an "intima convinzione della impossibile convivenza di due religioni in uno stato": see Turchetti, *Concordia o tolleranza?* 229, and n. 65; also, and especially, 251–259 and notes (particularly n. 44, reviewing previous verdicts on L'Hôpital, though curiously omitting Lecler).

nuance: in the latter part of 1561, his position seems to have evolved in the direction of liberalism, perhaps in response to the changing political situation, for it was becoming manifest that concord was not possible in the short term. And while he retained the desire for unity, L'Hôpital was to argue that it could only be brought about through respect for consciences, that is, through religious freedom.

One important text, which I think is by L'Hôpital (though it does not appear to have been attributed to him before, or indeed discussed at all by historians), is a letter in the name of the king to the French ambassador in Rome, dated August 3, 1561. The letter attempts to meet Pope Pius IV's objections to increasing French leniency towards Reformers by observing that the pope does not understand the depth of the problem in France when he calls for executions of Reformers: French people obey the King, "but where their consciences are concerned I have always found that they are all amazingly stubborn." Where one remedy does not work, it is the practice of doctors to try another—which is why France is trying gentler remedies; and lenient legislation is "pur politique," that is, a political measure that implies nothing about the king's personal view of religion. The intention of the author of the letter remains the restoration of religious unity, but he acknowledges that consciences cannot be constrained. The letter thus dovetails a consideration of principle (consciences must be free) with a consideration of expediency (coercion has not worked).[17] The use of the word "politique" in the sense it has here, incidentally, is much earlier than any other hitherto traced.[18]

A further statement in favor of religious freedom, this one known to be by L'Hôpital, has also received less attention than it deserves: a speech to the French bishops of September 1, 1561.[19] The use of force, he declares, is contrary to the goal of resolving religious differences. "Conscience, by its nature, cannot be constrained; it must be persuaded by true and cogent

[17]The letter is found in *Instructions et lettres des rois tres-chrestiens et de leurs ambassadeurs, et autres actes concernant le Concile de Trente*, 4th ed. (Paris, 1654), 90–95, British Library 702 k 7. The letter certainly was not written by the eleven-year-old Charles IX, and my reasons for attributing it to L'Hôpital are (apart from the fact that as chancellor he is an obvious person to have written it) that it presents the religious problem as one of conscience, and that it distinguishes political decisions from theological opinions, thereby making a distinction which L'Hôpital perceived. It also uses the "body politic" metaphor, which was dear to L'Hôpital (though admittedly a cliché).

[18]The word is also found in this sense in instructions to Louis de Saint-Gelais (sieur de Lansac), who was sent to Rome with the text of the Edict of January 1562, and in a letter to the Ambassador in Rome, André Guillard (sieur de L'Isle) concerning the same edict (the latter two dated January 20, 1562; both in *Instructions et lettres des rois tres-chrestiens*). Use of "politique" in this sense has usually been dated from 1564. Lecler's earliest example is a comment by Cardinal Granvelle on Gaspard de Coligny made in 1564; see Lecler, *Histoire de la tolérance*, 2: 74; see also Noël Didier, "Paul de Foix et Grégoire XIII, 1572–1584: une suite à la mercuriale de 1559," *Annales de l'Université de Grenoble*, Section lettres-droit, 16 (1939): 100, and n. 37.

[19]Lecler did not mention it in his *Histoire de la tolérance*, but he included a resumé in *Les premiers défenseurs de la liberté de conscience* (1: 72–73). It is not mentioned by Turchetti.

reasons; if faith is the subject of force, it is no longer faith." Reformers had died serenely, invoking the name of Christ as they were consumed by the flames: "these people are utterly persuaded that the doctrine to which they subscribe is a good one." Reformers must on no account be prevented from holding assemblies, for "they believe that the word of God strictly obliges them to hear the gospel preached and to receive the sacraments, and they hold this as an article of faith." They cannot be stopped—and to do so would cut them off from the discipline of religion, and make atheists and subversives of them.[20] In another speech, on January 3, 1562, opening that assembly of *parlementaires* which was to lead to the famous Edict of tolerance on January 17, L'Hôpital sums up his view with the memorable phrase, "L'excommunié ne cesse pas d'estre citoyen."[21] Four decades later (and countless deaths over religion later), the framers of the Edict of Nantes were unable to match this vision.

The "Exhortation aux princes"

The famous *Exhortation aux princes* of 1561 is an important and attractive work. It has rightly received attention from scholars, and the text is easily available, so little need be said about it here. Indeed, my only new observation is that it forms part of an intensive intellectual and political debate that preceded promulgation of the Edict of January, and that for its vision and integrity it can be compared favorably with the other perceptive texts presented here. Tantalizingly, the book carries the initials S.P.P., which were soon interpreted as Stephanus Paschasius Parisiensis, that is, the famous jurist and letter writer Estienne Pasquier. This seductive attribution has many supporters, but it seems safe to conclude that Pasquier could not have written it, as he was a strong foe of conciliatory measures. A difficulty in identifying S.P.P. is that we cannot be totally sure of his religious position: his concern is to appeal to the judgment of his contemporaries and to defuse sectarian passions, so he takes meticulous care to avoid revealing his personal view.[22] I am inclined to link this tract

[20]The text of this speech is in L'Hôpital, *Oeuvres complètes*, ed. Duféy, 1: 459–79.

[21]See L'Hôpital, *Oeuvres complètes*, ed. Duféy, 1: 441–53. According to Seong-Hak Kim, "Michel de L'Hôpital: The Political Vision of a Reformist Chancellor, 1560–1568" (Ph.D. thesis, University of Minnesota, 1991), 102; cf. 109, this remark is uncharacteristic of L'Hôpital: "Nowhere else did L'Hôpital suggest toleration of differing religious beliefs within the community. This particular statement thus appears to be a result of his efforts to stress the need for the legalization of Protestant worship, rather than a manifesto for universal freedom of conscience." It is difficult to disentangle the vision of L'Hôpital the thinker from the pragmatism of L'Hôpital the politician, but the texts I evoke can be seen as indicating an evolution towards liberalism. Incidentally, Duféy presents this speech (in his introduction) as having been made to the States-General at Saint-Germain-en-Laye on August 26, but this is an error.

[22]On the authorship of the tract, see Malcolm C. Smith, *Montaigne and Religious Freedom*, 196. Turchetti, *Concordia o Tolleranza?* 423, n. 71, maintains that the author of *Exhortation aux princes* was a Reformer ("dichiara piu volte il suo crede protestante"). There is no evidence for this.

with the debates of December 1561 and January 1562, which preceded the famous Edict, though Lecler thinks otherwise.

The work is a full-blooded defense of freedom of conscience. It is the will of God (declares the author) that we live "in peace of conscience, without threatening other people's lives, and in the religion to which we consider we have been called." While the existence of two religions cannot be inherently right, the quickest way to pacification is to permit their practice. Banishment of Reformers would be unjust, and persecution has failed. Gamaliel, in Acts 5:34–39, was right: we must trust God to resolve this issue. The main source of heresy has been the popes, who, by granting dispensations to clerics, have deprived the flock of pastors. (The implicit recognition that it is the pope's clerics who are the legitimate pastors suggests the author was a Catholic.) The author notes that the Jews are given freedom in the papal states, and pleads eloquently with the privy councillors: "For God's sake, do not force our consciences at the point of a sword. All of us, Romans and Protestants, are united in one body through the holy sacrament of baptism. All of us adore the same God, not in the same way, perhaps, but with equal fervor."[23] *Exhortation aux princes* is a consummately humane and incisive document, and one yearns to know the identity of S.P.P.

My remaining authors are all much less well known for their views on freedom and tolerance than they deserve to be. The next three were all participants in the consultation exercise launched by the government late in 1561, which led to a meeting of *parlementaires* and of privy councillors at Saint-Germain-en-Laye early in January 1562, and in turn, to the famous Edict of that month.

Estienne de La Boëtie

Lecler and Turchetti both mention Estienne de La Boëtie (1530–1563), but cursorily. Famous as the friend and colleague of Michel de Montaigne, La Boëtie's personal claims to fame have never received their full due. At the age of seventeen, inspired equally by his admiration for the Greeks' resistance to the Persians and by revulsion at Henry II's "tyrannical" revenge for insurrection in Bordeaux in 1548, he penned his brilliant

---

The passages Turchetti refers to simply say that he has a religious faith (without further specification); in one other passage cited by Turchetti (60–61 in Thickett's edition; see n. 23 below), the author of the tract uses a rhetorical artifice and attributes words to an imaginary Reformer, but Turchetti has taken these words as representing the author's belief. Joseph Lecler, "Liberté de conscience," *Recherches de science religieuse* 54 (1966): 387, describes the author as a Catholic, but without saying on what grounds. See also Malcolm C. Smith, *Montaigne and Religous Freedom*, 197, note to p. 37, where I support Lecler's view about the author's religion.

[23]The text of *Exhortation aux Princes* is in *Lettres historiques pour les années 1556–1594 [par] Estienne Pasquir*, ed. Dorothy Thickett, Textes littéraires français, 123 (Geneva, Droz, 1966), 33–90. Lecler, *Histoire de la tolérance*, 2: 43–48 discusses the piece.

diatribe against monarchy, *Servitude volontaire* (he probably revised it a few years later, since it has what appear to be veiled allusions to policies of Henry II of the early 1550s).[24] He was made a member of the Bordeaux *Parlement* at the early age of twenty-three, and had a career as a magistrate and politician. Almost the only significant thing known about his career is that in September and October 1561, along with the king's governor, he was entrusted with the dangerous task of attempting to pacify Guienne; this experience provided material for *Mémoire sur la pacification des troubles*, his blueprint for the restoration of religious and civil peace. La Boëtie died in 1563, apparently of the plague; Montaigne left a poignant description of his death. Like so many others in our story, La Boëtie was acquainted with (and admired) Michel de L'Hôpital.[25]

La Boëtie's *Mémoire sur la pacification des troubles* offers an excellent illustration of the difference between tolerance and freedom.[26] He rejects tolerance, partly for political reasons: tolerance of religious differences leads to the creation of a state within the state; tacit tolerance actually exists in France (as it did, since April 1561), and has led to anarchy; a nation divided is prey to its external foes (meaning Spain); and tolerance will be an irrational concession to force of numbers—and to violence. And he rejects tolerance partly for religious reasons: two conflicting religions cannot both be true; simple folk will imagine the king approves the Reformation if he tolerates it; holy writ seems to rule out tolerance; new religions drive out the old, so tolerance is worse than neutrality; and it may lead to impiety or atheism. His solution is conciliation: concessions to the Reformers where possible, accompanied by elimination of the corruption that had precipitated the Reformation.

But La Boëtie is a strong defender of religious freedom. To anyone familiar with his more famous *Servitude volontaire*, this will come as no surprise. La Boëtie was a pupil at Orléans of the professor, jurist, and *parlementaire* Anne Du Bourg, who had paid with his life in 1560 for

[24]See Malcolm C. Smith, ed., *De la servitude volontaire*, Textes Littéraires Français, 351 (Geneva: Droz, 1987); for veiled allusions to Henry II, see ibid., 12–14, and English translation: Estienne de La Boëtie, *Slaves by Choice*, introduction, translation, and commentary by Malcolm C. Smith (Egham: Runnymede, 1988).

[25]In March 1561, he reported to the Bordeaux Parlement the advice L'Hôpital had given on how to handle the religious strife: to adopt a middle way between severity and license; see La Boëtie, *Oeuvres complètes*, ed. Paul Bonnefon, (Paris, 1892), xxiii–xxiv. For La Boëtie's admiration of L'Hôpital, see Montaigne's letter to L'Hôpital dedicating to him La Boëtie's Latin poem in ibid., 205.

[26]Prior to my edition, this text was known under the title of *Mémoire sur l'Edit de Janvier*, which was misleading, for the text is not a memorandum on the Edict, but a contribution to the consultation exercise which preceded it; see Malcolm Smith, ed., *Memoire sur la pacification des troubles*, by Estienne de La Boëtie, Textes littéraires français, 317 (Genève: Droz, 1983), 12, and nn. 1, 2, 21, 24, 60, 63.

advocating leniency towards the Reformers.[27] La Boëtie declares in his *Mémoire* of 1561 that the conscience of the individual transcends the will of the monarch. The rule which says that people "are under no obligation to obey their legitimate monarch in matters of religion" is "by no means a bad one." It had been wrong to "constrain men's minds and to seek to make oneself a master of their thoughts and opinions." He also defends freedom on pragmatic grounds: constraint had been a failure, and it had been quite right to abandon it; all should have "freedom to live according to their conscience." In presenting his blueprint for conciliation, he seeks, as he puts it, "reunion without offence to consciences." Courts should punish violence, but "in no manner whatsoever inquire into people's religion." Here we have unequivocal and eloquent defense of liberty of conscience.

La Boëtie puts limits upon freedom, however. For him, liberty is without question an entitlement of the individual conscience. However, when individuals form a visible community publicly expressing dissident views, La Boëtie no longer speaks of liberty, but asks whether such public dissidence can be tolerated, thereby illustrating the distinction between freedom and tolerance. Freedom of belief for the individual poses no problems; public manifestations of disunity are a different matter. Interestingly, however, he does not endorse liberty of public cult for Reformers in the present situation, but he is ready to concede total freedom to them if they reciprocate towards Catholics in areas where they are in control, such as England and the southwest of France. But Reformers cannot claim freedom of conscience and of cult so long as they deny it to others. "What kind of hearing," he asks, "would Catholics get from Calvin? What kind of hearing would they get from Queen Elizabeth?"[28] La Boëtie, in short, limits freedom strictly unless it can be made universal. Public dissident worship threatens that visible unity of the nation upon which its political security largely rests; but we can safely extend freedom from the individual to the group provided our religious antagonists and prospective political antagonists do likewise.

Arnaud Du Ferrier

Du Ferrier (ca. 1505–1585) was one of several councillors in the Paris *Parlement* who participated in the celebrated meetings held in 1559 to

---

[27]On Anne Du Bourg, see M. Lelièvre, "Le procès et le supplice d'Anne Du Bourg" and "Les derniers jours d'Anne Du Bourg," *Bulletin de la Société de l'Histoire du Protestantisme Français* 37 (1888): 281–95, 337–55, and 506–529. On La Boëtie as his student, see Bonnefon, ed., *Oeuvres complètes*, xvi–xvii.

[28]La Boëtie's position, although he was almost certainly unaware of the fact, interestingly echoes that of Thomas More, who had favored the creation by Christians and Muslims of pluralist societies in which their faiths could be freely practiced; see Raymond Wilson Chambers, *Thomas More* (London: Jonathan Cape, 1948), 264–65.

discuss policy towards religious dissidents (the *mercuriales*). He incurred the wrath of Henry II by urging leniency. Du Ferrier's arrest was ordered, but he took flight; shortly after, he was rehabilitated.[29] He was a close associate of Michel de L'Hôpital, whom he apparently first met as a student in Padua. According to his biographer, it was L'Hôpital who extricated him from his difficulty in 1559.[30]

At the end of 1561, when the climate was altogether more accommodating to dissidents, he wrote an intriguing memorandum for the meeting of *parlementaires* and privy councillors that was to decide what to do about the Reformers' demands for freedom of cult. He maintains that the period since Francis I has been the happiest for France since the coming of the Christian religion, for people are now concerned about the honor and service of God and are reading the holy scripture. True, there are sects and there is sedition, but this was the case in the early centuries of the Church. People are misguidedly saying that the Reformation is a new religion. What has happened is that in the absence of good pastors over the past thousand years, abuses in morals and in doctrine have been spawned—and not surprisingly, since the Hebrews fell into idolatry when deprived of the presence of Moses for just forty days. National religious unity (*Une roy, une foy, une loy*) has never existed; indeed, every individual is unorthodox in one way or another. We have here an interesting implicit argument for liberty, one which is based upon skepticism: definitive religious truth is thoroughly elusive, and in a society genuinely interested in religion there will necessarily be diverse views on the subject.

Curiously, and perhaps contradictorily, this perception of the omnipresence of religious diversity is accompanied by an assertion that in France at the present time, the two sides are in essence united in religion, as they have the same creed, the same sacraments, and the same scripture (a highly sanguine statement regarding sacraments, and one that skates over controversies on the creeds and on scripture). Thus, having argued for leniency on the ground that dissidence is universal, Du Ferrier argues also for leniency on the opposite ground: that there is no real dissidence. Underlying both positions is an impatience with the niceties of theological debate. In resting his liberal view both upon skepticism about the possibility of doctrinal unity ever being achieved and upon skepticism about the actual existence of

[29]See Edouard Frémy, *Un ambassadeur libéral sous Charles IX et Henri III: ambassades à Venise d'Arnaud Du Ferrier (1563–1567; 1570–1582)* (Paris, 1880), 5–7. On his taking flight to evade capture in 1559, see Noël Didier, "Paul de Foix à la mercuriale de 1559, son procès, ses idées religieuses," *Mélanges d'archéologie et d'histoire, Ecole française de Rome* 56 (1939): 396–435, 416. According to Frémy (p. 4), Du Ferrier was born "vers 1508," but it is possible to be more precise. Montaigne wrote on November 6, 1580, "Ce vieillard . . . a passé septante cinq ans, à ce qu'il dit," which means he was born at the latest in 1505; see *Journal de voyage en Italie par la Suisse et l'Allemagne en 1580 et 1581*, ed. Charles Dédéyan (Paris: Les Belles Lettres, 1946), 172.

[30]Frémy, *Un ambassadeur libéral*, 4, 6. L'Hôpital dedicated Latin poems to Du Ferrier (ibid., 74–77, 110–11), and thought him worthy of the office of Chancellor of France (ibid., 376).

any meaningful doctrinal disunity, Du Ferrier recalls a more famous liberal, Sebastian Castellio. It seems that the only way in which Du Ferrier might have resolved the apparent contradiction in his thought would have been to distinguish between adiaphora and essential beliefs, but his memorandum does not do this, at least not explicitly.

Alongside these two skeptical arguments, which are theoretical, Du Ferrier presents historical and pragmatic considerations. The prospects for conciliation through a general council are illusory: the pope is dragging his feet in calling it, and the Reformers (rightly) refuse to attend. That leaves the options of exterminating Reformers or accepting them. Religion can neither be imposed nor removed forcibly: persuasion alone is effective. The Egyptians and Babylonians were unable to stamp out the Jews, the Romans could not suppress Christians, Charles V could not extirpate the Lutherans. In any case, can the king afford to lose his most able and loyal subjects? So the Reformers must be preserved. And to deny the practice of their religion would make atheists of them. Experience shows that coexistence of two religions in one nation is possible. His conclusion is that the king should permit the Reformers to preach and administer the sacraments.

Du Ferrier's memorandum illustrates the subtlety of the issue of religious freedom, and the difficulty in identifying whether it is freedom or tolerance that an individual is advocating. On the one hand, he declares that religion cannot be introduced or removed by force—and this is the kind of statement frequently made by advocates of freedom. On the other hand, however, he rests this assertion not upon a vindication of the rights of the individual conscience (as one would expect from an advocate of religious freedom), but upon a historical demonstration that coercion does not work. Moreover, his arguments for permission of the minority cult in France are ones of expediency (that France must not drive out people who are valuable to the nation, and that the alternative to permission of their cult is atheism). Du Ferrier adds that the aim of the Council of Constance to suppress heretics was a good one, and that only the means were at fault.

Thus, Du Ferrier's position seems to be: If possible, the state should bring about unity of religion; however, unity is hard to achieve, so the state must be prepared to make concessions. I said at the outset that with two exceptions I present advocates of freedom as distinct from tolerance. Du Ferrier is my first exception, for his advocacy of freedom of conscience seems merely verbal and largely undermined by the content of his analysis. Moreover, the thrust of some of the biblical examples towards the end of his memorandum seems to be that the regent ought not to allow "idolatry," which in context seems to mean the Roman religion. If I were a holder of a minority religion in a prepluralist society, I should be wary of Arnaud Du Ferrier.[31]

---

[31]Du Ferrier's memorandum, like Foix's, is in the Bibliothèque Nationale, Paris, ms. fr. 4766 (24v–29r). I have transcribed it and hope to publish it as part of a separate study of Du Ferrier. The

Incidentally, Du Ferrier's memorandum seems to shed light on the question of his religious beliefs. He presents himself here as a Catholic: the Reformers, he says, profess the same creed, sacraments, and scripture "as we do." Elsewhere in this memorandum he defends a Gallican position; but the document also shows great affinity with the Reformers. He links them, as they themselves did, with the persecuted Hebrews; he denies that the Reformation is a new religion; the corruption within the Church (he says) is not just moral (as Catholics conceded) but doctrinal; the Reformers' religion (he says) seems to be of divine origin, and the most learned men have adopted it. Towards the end of his first period as Venetian Ambassador (1563–1567), rumors were spread to the effect that his religion was suspect; he had undoubtedly given cause for such rumors.[32] Years later, in 1580, Montaigne visited him in Venice (where he was again the French ambassador). Montaigne went to Mass with him, but noted that his opinions "inclined heavily towards the Calvinist innovations."[33] According to some historians, Du Ferrier openly professed the Reformed faith two years later.[34]

Paul de Foix

Paul de Foix (1528–1584) was an aristocrat, related to the houses of Valois and d'Albret, and was a profoundly learned scholar, who had learned his

---

only substantial study of him that I know of is Frémy, *Un ambassadeur libéral*, which only cursorily covers Du Ferrier's career prior to 1563, and does not mention the 1561 memorandum.

[32]On these rumors, see Frémy, *Un ambassadeur libéral*, 73. Frémy describes them as "perfides insinuations," but the 1561 memorandum would have provided some substantiation. Moreover, Du Ferrier seems to have had a reputation as a crypto-Reformer among Reformers themselves. He supplied Théodore de Bèze with commentaries on Job, which a Hebrew scholar, Jean Mercier, had given him in Venice; see Bèze's preface to Mercier, *Commentarii in librum Job* (1573), in Bèze, *Correspondance*, 15:296. When, in 1582, Philippe Du Plessis-Mornay urged Du Ferrier to embrace the Reformed faith, he wrote: "Considerez, Monsieur, combien il y a que vous cachez ce talent: il en faut payer les arrerages tout en un coup. Dieu vous a attendu en ses misericordes, dont je suis temoing, il y a plus de quinze ans. Depuis tout ce temps, il frappe à vostre porte et crie à vostre oreille" (cited by Frémy, *Un ambassadeur libéral*, 373). See also nn. 33, 34 below.

[33]See Montaigne, *Journal de voyage*, ed. Dédéyan, 172: "Ses opinions panchent fort evidamment, en matiere de nos affaires, vers les innovations Calviniennes."

[34]Frémy, *Un ambassadeur libéral*, 369–79, notes that Du Ferrier, on his return from Venice in 1582, was offered employment by Du Plessis-Mornay on behalf of Henry of Navarre on condition he embrace the Reformed faith. Mornay states in his memoirs (Frémy adds) that Du Ferrier did become a Reformer, but Frémy argues that Mornay is not a disinterested commentator, since he had endeavored to convert Du Ferrier; moreover, Frémy adds, Mornay is not entirely reliable; he had said that Du Ferrier had been a crypto-Reformer for fifteen years, a statement for which Frémy sees no justification. However, Du Ferrier's 1561 memorandum and Montaigne's remark (neither of which Frémy knew) support the view that Du Ferrier was indeed a dissimulator. There seems therefore no need to doubt Mornay, either when he says that Du Ferrier was a crypto-Reformer or when he says that he became a professing Reformer. In *Des prieres* (*Essais*, 1: 56), Montaigne refers to a person who confessed to him that he had for a lifetime professed and practiced a religion contrary to the one he believed so as not to lose esteem and public office, and commentators of Montaigne have seen this (plausibly) as an allusion to Du Ferrier.

Greek from Toussaint and his Hebrew from Vatable. He had studied law at Toulouse before becoming, in 1552, the *Aumônier* of Catherine de Médicis. He had been appointed *Conseiller-clerc* in the *Parlement* (1555), and was to serve as Ambassador in Scotland (1561) and England (1562–1566). Charles IX then attempted to appoint him as ambassador to Rome, but Pius V vetoed the nomination on the grounds that his religion was suspect, and he was appointed as ambassador in Venice from 1567, in succession to Arnaud Du Ferrier, whom he had met while a student at Toulouse.[35] He was offered the post of chancellor in 1571, but he turned it down, apparently in the expectation that Michel de L'Hôpital would be restored to the post (from which he had retired—or been dismissed—in 1568). Foix eventually became Archbishop of Toulouse, after protracted negotiations with Gregory XIII, who at first doubted his orthodoxy, and he died in 1584—to a chorus of praise for his integrity.[36] Like Du Ferrier, Foix was suspected of being a crypto-Reformer;[37] however, in his case the suspicions were probably unfounded.[38] He was a friend and confidant of L'Hôpital, and may have been acquainted with La Boëtie.[39]

Like Du Ferrier, Foix was one of the Paris councillors who, at the 1559 sessions of the Paris *Parlement* to debate the treatment of Reformers, urged leniency. He argued that to deny the real presence of Christ in the Eucharist—and thus deny the matter of the sacrament—is worse than merely to argue for communion under both kinds; the two positions should be distinguished, and holders of the latter treated more leniently. Foix's

[35]See Frémy, *Un ambassadeur libéral*, 74. Foix was also succeeded as Ambassador in Venice by Du Ferrier in 1570, when Du Ferrier began a second period in this office; see ibid., 95–96.

[36]My principal source for the life of Foix is Didier, "Paul de Foix et Grégoire XIII." A funerary oration on Foix was published in Marc-Antoine Muret, *Orationes quattuor* (Ingolstad, 1585), 23–38 (British Library 1090 i 8).

[37]The sources of the suspicion are probably (1) his arrest for expressing liberal views on the treatment of dissidents, and (2) the fact that his job as ambassador in Scotland and England required a conciliatory approach and led him to make accommodating statements about the Reformation; see Joseph Bain, ed., *Calendar of State Papers relating to Scotland and Mary, Queen of Scots, 1547–1603*, preserved in the Public Record Office, the British Museum, and elsewhere in England, vol. 1, 1547–1563 (Edinburgh, 1898), letters dated December 7 and 10, 1561. In 1562, the Spanish ambassador in Paris, Chantonnay, described Foix as a Reformer; see Didier, "Paul de Foix et Grégoire XIII," 102, and n. 52. It is easy to see why Gregory XIII was reticent about making him archbishop of Toulouse.

[38]In defense of his orthodoxy, he cited to Gregory XIII his tenacious defense of Catholics in England; see Didier, "Paul de Foix et Grégoire XIII," 145. More especially, his appointment as archbishop was preceded by meticulous scrutiny of his religious views, as Didier shows. Interestingly, Montaigne participated with Foix (as with Du Ferrier) in a religious rite in Rome, spending five hours with him, visiting seven churches one day in Holy Week in 1581, but Montaigne expressed no doubts about Foix's orthodoxy; see *Journal de voyage*, ed. Dédéyan, 233.

[39]On Foix and L'Hôpital, see Didier, "Paul de Foix à la mercuriale," 427. On Foix and La Boëtie, see the letter Montaigne wrote Foix when dedicating La Boëtie's French poems to him (in La Boëtie, *Oeuvres complètes*, ed. Bonnefon, 249).

distinction was designed, it seems, to secure mitigation of the punishment of most dissidents. He was not at this stage arguing for freedom of conscience or anything like it, but simply for a form of tolerance based on considerations that were humanitarian or pragmatic (the failure of persecution was becoming widely acknowledged). For these views, he was arrested following the session of June 10, and imprisoned in the Bastille. On January 8, 1560, he was ordered to retract, and was banned from the *Parlement* for one year. Early in 1561, his conviction was revoked, a sign of the more liberal climate.[40]

On June 23, 1561, a speech of high historical interest was delivered to the *Parlement*, and Paul de Foix is in my view its almost certain author. The nation, he said, had three options. First, it could attempt to secure religious unity by executing Reformers or by banishing them—a policy which, given the vast numbers of Reformers, was impractical. Second, it could permit liberty of religion, including liberty to assemble for religious services. Third, it could secure restoration of unity through a council of the Church. He strongly preferred the third option, but the reference to liberty of religion is in positive terms, and it is his second choice. He is, as far as I know, the first person to use the term liberty of religion in its modern sense in France. This speech has not previously been mentioned in histories of tolerance (or freedom).[41] Indeed, nobody, so far as I know, has attributed it to Paul de Foix. My grounds for the attribution are circumstantial: (1) the author says in the speech that he had denounced executions at the meetings of the *Parlement* in 1559, and Foix is known to have done this; and (2) the ideas in the speech recur in a memorandum known to be by Foix and written for the regent, Catherine de Médicis, towards the end of 1561.

In this latter memorandum, which begins with a succinct and fascinating history of Christians' attitudes towards permission of dissident cults, Foix argues that the best course would be to obviate dissension by restoration of religious unity. But, he adds, if Her Majesty were not to adopt that course, then the alternative would be permission of the Reformed cult—which would be necessary, since to prohibit it would lead to atheism, which would be worse. Further, the Reformed religion must enjoy open permission (as distinct from surreptitious connivance), since clandestine meetings would favor the development of still more radical heterodoxies. It is none too easy to say whether Foix's fallback position (assuming his preferred option of conciliation is not adopted) is freedom or tolerance, as I have defined those terms. On the one hand, he refers

[40]The minutes of the relevant meetings of the *Parlement* are lost, and Didier reconstituted these events brilliantly, making use of the record of an inquiry, instigated in 1574 by Gregory XIII, into Paul de Foix's role; see Didier, "Paul de Foix à la mercuriale."

[41]This speech, titled *Advis donné au roy en l'assemblée tenue en la Cour de Parlement à Paris sur le faict de la religion, le vint-troisieme jour de Juin, MDLXI,* is in Denis François Secousse, *Mémoires de Condé, ou Recueil pour servir à l'histoire de France,* 6 vols. (London, 1743), 2: 409–23; esp. 411, 416.

positively in this memorandum to religious freedom, as he had done in the speech of June 23 (assuming he is the author of the latter); on the other, the justification he gives for permitting practice of the Reformed faith in France is a pragmatic one rather than one of principle. What can be safely said, however, is that Foix is a scholar who knows and likes religious freedom, and whose appreciation of it is informed by wide reading of history.

Paul de Foix impresses us as a politician of humanity and integrity, the very qualities which provoked his arrest. His place in the history of religious freedom in France seems an important one—and a neglected one, since the memorandum, like the speech, escaped the attention of Lecler and Turchetti.[42] His concern for conciliation seems to have been profound, and to have transcended national and confessional boundaries. For, while he calls for a national council of the Church, he stresses that a universal council would be preferable. Interestingly, just as he suffered for calling for liberty for Reformers in France, he was to suffer as ambassador in England for seeking to protect the liberty of Catholics.[43] Like Du Chastel, he is far too little known, though he has been immortalized by compliments from Ronsard and Montaigne.[44]

Jean de Monluc

Jean de Monluc, or Montluc (?–1579), the liberal Bishop of Valence and counselor of Catherine de Médicis, is another politician who interests us.[45] Monluc has been described as a "loose-living, skeptical, and secularized Dominican, whose connivance had made possible the growth and public emergence of the Huguenot community in Valence"; and his loyalty to the Catholic faith was indeed suspect.[46] In a speech to the Privy Council on

[42]The manuscript is in the Bibliothèque Nationale, Paris, ms. fr. 4766, 29r–33r. Extracts were published in Didier, "Paul de Foix à la mercuriale," 431–35, and idem, "Paul de Foix et Grégoire XIII," 101, n. 41. There is a translation of part of it in Smith, *Montaigne and Religious Freedom*, 31–32; it is also mentioned by Linda L. Taber, "Religious Dissent within the Parlement of Paris in the Mid-Sixteenth Century: A Reassessment," *French Historical Studies* 16 (1990): 684–99. I have transcribed the document in Malcolm C. Smith, "Paul de Foix and Freedom of Conscience," *Bibliothèque d'Humanisme et Renaissance* 55 (1993): 301–5.

[43]On Foix's intervention on behalf of English Catholics, see Didier, "Paul de Foix à la mercuriale," 430, n. 2, and Muret, *Orationes quattuor*, 31–32.

[44]See Ronsard, *Elegie à Monsieur de Foyx*, in Paul Laumonier, ed., *Oeuvres complètes*, 20 vols., Société des Textes Français Modernes (Paris: Didier, 1914–75), 13: 150–58, and Montaigne, *De la vanité* (*Essais*, 3: chap. 9).

[45]His date of birth is unknown, but was in the first years of the sixteenth century; see H. Reynaud, *Jean de Monluc, évêque de Valence et de Die* (Paris, 1893), 14.

[46]My quotation is from Henry Outram Evennett, *The Cardinal of Lorraine and the Council of Trent, A Study in the Counter-Reformation* (Cambridge: Cambridge University Press, 1930), 146; Evennett also notes that he was "denounced as a heretic by the dean of his own Chapter," ibid. He was one of eight French bishops ordered by the Roman Inquisition in 1563 to come to Rome and

August 23, 1560, he argued eloquently that the Reformed ministers were diligent and scholarly and appeared to be holy men—and they had no fear of dying for their beliefs. They had secured a hearing because the Catholic clerics were negligent; the only concern of the popes had been to sow discord between nations and make war. Monluc's remedy for division and strife is prayer (including daily sermons in the royal household and the singing of psalms), and a general council of the Church, or failing that, a national one to which Reformers should be invited. The government had to draw a careful distinction between subversive Reformers and those whose actions showed that their sole motivation was religious, for experience and history alike demonstrate that punishments of heretics are ineffectual.[47]

The document by Monluc which most interests us is a later one, in which he speaks positively of liberty of conscience. The text, which is anonymous, is *Apologie contre certaines calomnies mises sus à la desfaveur et desavantage de l'Estat des affaires de ce Roiaume*.[48] I attribute it to Monluc because on January 26, 1562, the English ambassador in Paris sent to Elizabeth's secretary a book which he called "the Bishop of Valence's Apology."[49] That the *Apologie* we are considering is the "Apology" attributed by the ambassador to Monluc is suggested by its title, by its content (an uncritical defense of royal policy consistent with the position of Monluc), and by its date of publication, for the *Apologie* places the Colloquy of Poissy (September and October 1561) in the past, and refers to an assembly the queen hopes to convene in January to resolve the religious issue (evidently an allusion to the assembly at Saint-Germain-en-Laye, which produced the Edict of January 1562). It is likely that the *Apologie* was written to present the view of the government to the January assembly, and that it was published in January in order to help secure acceptance of the edict.

Monluc declares that Reformers "submit to subjection of every kind, and even to ill treatment, provided they are allowed freedom of conscience." But the Bishop of Valence does not explore the nature of liberty of conscience; he simply presents it as something axiomatically good—not because it is a human right, but because it buys the Reformers' abstention from sedition. In fact, notwithstanding his use of the phrase, I do not think

---

answer charges of heresy; see the fascinating article by A. Degert, "Procès de huit évêques français suspects de calvinisme," *Revue des Questions historiques* 76, new ser., 32 (1904): 61–108. Degert summarizes (68–71) the abundant grounds for suspecting Monluc of unorthodoxy. See also Baumgartner, *Change and Continuity*, 132–38.

[47]Jean de Monluc, *Harangue faicte devant le Roy Françoys second* in *Mémoires de Condé*, 1: 555–68; for the date, see 556, note.

[48]The *Apologie* was published in 1562 (s.l.; British Library 8050 bb 4); it is also found in *Mémoires de Condé*, 2: 579–600. It is not mentioned by Reynaud, Lecler, or Turchetti.

[49]See Joseph Stevenson, ed., *Calendar of State Papers, Foreign Series, Elizabeth, 1561–1562* (London, 1866), no. 839.

Monluc is defending freedom of conscience as I have defined the term; rather, he is defending tolerance (a concession to expediency), and presenting it in terms of principle. It is clear from the tract as a whole that the Bishop of Valence was adept at putting a politically opportune gloss on events. His analysis of the contemporary situation is hopelessly optimistic: he recalls those bishops who, in the 1530s, had endeavored to palliate and dissipate the religious division and attendant social ills by pretending they did not exist — and with much less plausibility than they, since the division had seriously deepened since the 1530s. His tract is light years away from the incisive and forthright analyses of Foix and La Boëtie. It is the work of a courtier — the courtier who, ten years later, was to act as apologist for the St. Bartholomew's Day massacres.[50]

Antoine Loisel

Finally, I jump forward twenty years, to another climate and another approach to the issue. Antoine Loisel (1536–1617) is another historical figure who deserves greater attention than he has received. He was the chairman of a special tribunal inaugurated in Bordeaux in January 1582 to deal with infringements of edicts of pacification. These successive edicts were enacted at the end of each civil war, and invariably proved simply to be prologues to the next war. At the first session of the tribunal, in Bordeaux on March 31, 1582, a large crowd assembled to air their grievances. Loisel promised dispassionate application of the edicts. The Mayor of Bordeaux, Michel de Montaigne, heard the speech with which Loisel concluded his hearings in Bordeaux, and congratulated him on it. Loisel's tribunal moved from town to town in the southwest of France, and he pronounced an opening speech each time. These speeches, which were published in 1605, are masterpieces of political eloquence. Like so many others of his time, Loisel wedded scholarship to the business of government.[51]

The speech that Loisel delivered at Saintes deals with religious differences. His aim is to win the confidence of individuals on opposing sides by appeals to common sense and by tenacious evenhandedness. What should the state do, he asks, about dissident religions? There are arguments in favor of permission of a dissident religion, and there are arguments against — and he summarizes both sets of arguments. But, he concludes, verbal debate has secured no benefit, nor has religious war. The key to peace

---

[50]See Reynaud, *Monluc*, 132–48. The historian Jacques-Auguste de Thou deplored the fact that men like Monluc (and Guy du Faur de Pibrac, Jean de Morvilliers, and his own father, Christophe) extolled or condoned the massacres; these men detested the government's action in their hearts, he wrote, but thought the good of the state obliged them to defend it; see Frances Amelia Yates, *The French Academies of the Sixteenth Century* (London: Routledge, 1988), 212.

[51]Loisel's speeches are in *La Guyenne, qui sont huict remontrances faictes en la chambre de justice de Guyenne sur le subject des Edicts de pacification* (Paris, 1605), British Library 1059 c 24.

is in the lives of individuals, and Reformers and Catholics alike are in sore need of real reform. The early Christians refused to bear arms even for a just cause, let alone against a legitimate ruler—a barb against Reformers; and there has been no removal of corruption in the Catholic Church.

We see in this speech of Loisel's a development from the 1561 contributions to this debate. The quest in 1561 had been for the formula that would solve the problem of religious division and the social problems it brought. In quick succession, legislators and administrators sought to persecute the Reformers out of existence, then to reunite them with Catholics by conciliatory measures, then to tolerate them (or, in the case of some bolder minds, to afford them freedom). None of these approaches had produced the desired effect. Since 1562, France had been plunged into a series of wars which, with attendant famine and disease, were in the process of claiming vast numbers of lives. Loisel has no panacea, no blueprint for nationwide peace. The question of permission of dissidents is academic. Progress will only be achieved by moral reform—and the restoration, by determinedly evenhanded action, of political institutions which command confidence and respect.

Loisel's approach to the issue is reminiscent of that of his friend and admirer Montaigne. Montaigne had followed the debates with close interest. It is quite possible that back in 1561 he had helped La Boétie write that *Mémoire* which, as we have seen, deplored tolerance while defending freedom. At any rate, there is reason to believe that Montaigne had shared La Boétie's views at that time. It is clear that Montaigne regarded tolerance as unsatisfactory; it had been introduced because (as he memorably put it) French kings had been unable to attain the desirable (unity of religion) and so had pretended to desire the attainable (tolerance). At the same time, however, Montaigne was as keenly committed to freedom as La Boétie had been, and like him, saw coercion as counterproductive. In 1580, he included in the first edition of his *Essais* many other reflections on tolerance and freedom, some of them allusive (later editions have copious elaboration on some of these passages). At the end of 1580, he traveled to Germany, where he noted a wide degree of effective freedom, and observed that peace prevailed there among people divided in religion. It is easy to see why, immediately on his return from this trip, he was ready to endorse the pragmatism of an enlightened politician such as Loisel.[52]

The International Dimension

One after the other, various states in Europe were confronted in the sixteenth century with the problem of religious dissidence. Comparative

---

[52]For a fuller discussion of points in this paragraph, see Malcolm C. Smith, *Montaigne and Religious Freedom: the Dawn of Pluralism* (Geneva: Droz, 1991).

study of national policies would be a productive area for future research. The range of options was limited, and this meant that several countries trod a similar path. For example, it seems that the evolution from persecution of dissidents to quest for conciliation to a provisional tolerance (and from there, over long decades, to a de facto acceptance of a right to freedom) occurred repeatedly. It seems also that the catalytic moment came in any given country not when the intellectuals were ready for change, but when the persecuted minority was sufficiently numerous to insist on it, where-upon the intellectual justifications for change became politically respect-able (and were disseminated by the government, at least in the case of Monluc's tract). Thus, the year 1561 was critical in France, just as the year 1531 had been in Germany.[53]

Lecler shows that the thought of writers such as Erasmus and Castellio crossed national frontiers, and he draws attention to recurrent topoi in liberal literature, such as the appeal to the example of Gamaliel in Acts 5:34–39 or to the papal tolerance of Jews (both of which are in *Exhortation aux princes*). There is ample scope for further exploration of international influences. In 1561, the French government studied English and German religious settlements to see what, if anything, could be learned from them; La Boëtie alluded to the Elizabethan settlement (albeit to reject it); later, Montaigne was to learn from his experience in Germany. Conversely, French thought was exported: the admirable *Exhortation aux princes* was translated into Latin and German, Monluc's tract was sent to England by the ambassador in Paris, and it would be surprising if Paul de Foix did not discuss his ideas on freedom with kindred spirits during his four years as ambassador in England.

The most graphic illustration that I have found of the transnational nature of the issue is the fact that the earliest French use of the term "liberté de conscience" in something like its modern sense occurs not in France, but in Scotland. It is in a document dated July 24, 1559, recording a truce between Scottish Reformers and Marie de Guise: both sides undertook to

---

[53]The counsellors of Charles V had given him the same advice that Foix and Monluc gave Catherine: to seek to conciliate dissidents, and if that failed, to permit their religion. See Henry Kamen, "Toleration and Dissent in Sixteenth-Century Spain: The Alternative Tradition," *Sixteenth Century Journal* 19 (1988): 3–23, esp. 10–16. On the situation in Germany, see also Heinz Schilling, "Alternatives to the Lutheran Reformation and the Rise of Lutheran Identity," in Andrew C. Fix and Susan C. Karant-Nunn, eds., *Germania Illustrata: Essays on Early Modern Germany presented to Gerald Strauss*, Sixteenth Century Essays and Studies, 28 (Kirksville, Mo.: Sixteenth Century Journal Publishers, 1992), 99–120. Schilling shows (114–15) that individuals in Germany were prepared to argue that "a community could flourish even if its members did not share the same belief and did not belong to the same church," but the prevailing view was that uniformity of religion was a prerequisite for political stability. Nonetheless, confessional diversity flourished widely in German towns and villages, as is clear from Montaigne's observations; and see R. Po-chia Hsia, "Between State and Community: Religious and Ethnic Minorities in Early Modern Germany," in Fix and Karant-Nunn, *Germania Illustrata*, 169–80, esp. 174–77.

coexist in "liberté de conscience" until a definitive settlement was arranged. The phrase, incidentally, illustrates the fact that linguistic usage was at first not always precise: it here designates a policy of "freezing" the issue. Future scholarship might usefully explore the extent to which discussions in France on religious freedom between 1559 and 1561 were influenced by the experience of the French in handling religious dissidence in Scotland.[54]

Most of the authors touched on deserve a biography, or better still, an edition. Most have not been mentioned before in the context of the history of religious freedom. The attractions of embarking on scholarship in this area are considerable: the interest and importance of the subject; the wealth of almost untouched primary sources; the exhilaration and pleasure of encounter with the writers, who, for the most part, are incisive, humane, and visionary people who applied scholarship to the business of living. What they wrote has a haunting topicality today. The presence of Muslims in a nominally Christian society poses similar challenges to that of Reformers in a nominally Catholic society. And denial of religious freedom in various countries in our time has been a precondition of political oppression (and its restoration has been the prelude to, or accompaniment of, retrieval of political freedoms). Another article could be written on the present-day issues on which these writers shed light.

---

[54]See Smith, *Montaigne and Religious Freedom*, 36, 195–96. This truce was a fragile one indeed, and the understanding of "liberty of conscience" only rudimentary; indeed, the term may just have been a decorative description of a stalemate. See David Calderwood, *The History of the Kirk of Scotland*, ed. Thomas Thomson, 8 vols. (Edinburgh: Woodrow Society, Edinburgh, 1842–49), 1: 483–89, and Bain, *Calendar of State Papers*, especially nos. 500, 503–8. For a detailed discussion of events in Scotland, see Volker Roeser, *Politik und religiöse Toleranz vor dem ersten Hugenottenkrieg in Frankreich* (Basel: Helbing & Lichtenhahn, 1985), 17–54. Roeser perceived the high relevance of the Scottish experience to subsequent developments in France.

CITIZEN OF THE WORLD:
MONTAIGNE'S TRAVELS

On the morning of the interview for the chair of French here, I asked myself what questions might be put. The most interesting I could think of was, 'Why do you want the job of Head of the French Department at the New College?' 'That', I would have had to say, 'is a very good question'. But my answer would have been, 'So as to give an inaugural lecture'. For what could be more delightful than to share with friends and colleagues the exhilaration of being a scholar, and to air some views about our role in the rapidly-changing academic world?

All sorts of topics for an inaugural immediately came to mind. A basic one: finding the texts of the great Renaissance authors. For the invention of printing only partially preserved their writing. In my first days as a researcher my supervisor, Mike Screech, had me work through the British Museum Catalogue of sixteenth-century French books. 'Do it thoroughly' he said, 'or you will have to do it again' (thank you Mike: academic standards began on day one). I looked at hundreds of French and Latin books and one turned out to be an unknown book by Ronsard. Fortune has since led me to several other lost books by Ronsard, who

1

is surely the greatest of the French poets (for details of these, see the notes which follow the text of this lecture). So one possible subject for an inaugural was how you determine which Renaissance books have been lost, how you go about finding them and which of the lost Renaissance books I would most like to discover. (If you are wondering which one this is, see the notes!)

Or, a lecture on how you publish these texts: the lecture would discuss problems in establishing the texts, and in annotating them. The texts which gave me greatest pleasure to publish were two by La Boétie, the scholar and statesman. One was his attack on tyranny, the *Servitude volontaire*, a work banned and burned in the sixteenth century and so incisive and humane as to send shivers down the spine of any autocrat anywhere, anytime. The other was his essay on how to pacify a nation consumed by sectarian strife, the *Mémoire sur la pacification des troubles* (*see Illustration 1*). La Boétie's friend and editor Montaigne was unable to include them in his 1571 edition of La Boétie because they are so outspoken. So my editions completed Montaigne's work. I would be minded to include some reflections on how you market these texts. Most of my books have been published by a Swiss firm at anti-social prices. However, the Computer Centre has taught us to use new technology (a cordial 'Thank you!' to Phil Taylor and Lewis Nodes) and so the complete La Boétie which I am working on will be published at a very modest price by Runnymede Books, provided it is acceptable to our outside referees. In case anyone has not heard, Runnymede Books is the firm we set up in the French Department to make scholarly books available at student-friendly prices.

2

In publishing editions of sixteenth-century texts you have to work out what they mean, and the lecture could be about how you discover the meanings of texts written in a different culture. The poets are a particular challenge. Any great poet, whether he writes in verse or prose, is a creator (that is what the word 'poet' means), a creator of a fictional universe; and the reader of great poetry, of any epoch, is invited to reflect about every moral, political and theological issue there is. But in the sixteenth century the poet had additional specific messages about contemporary issues. These topical messages seem to be so utterly lost that few modern critics even know they were ever there. Sometimes (if I am correct) the contemporary messages were highly audacious — for example, that Henri II of France was autocratic and a warmonger, and that his principal minister was duplicitous, vacillating and conceited. These veiled messages to contemporaries are of profound historical significance. The lecture might be about how we may discern them.

Or, a lecture on another allusive genre, the emblem. An emblem consists of an enigmatic picture complemented by an explanatory epigram. The inventor of the genre was Alciati. His emblems helped young people learn Latin — and (principally) moral philosophy, the art of living. My mind went back to a public lecture I gave in March 1974 for the Classics Department at Cornell University in New York State, titled 'Integrity in politics: the emblems of Alciati'. The lecture presented, in a series of pictures, Alciati's views on the need for political leaders to be altruistic, truthful, accessible and so forth — and what you do about political leaders who do not have these virtues. This was the most successful lecture I shall ever give: the audience assumed the

3

lecture was a very clever allusive commentary on the supposed misdemeanours of the current U.S. President — as though I were capable of such subtlety. Whilst the emblem lends itself to timeless adaptations, my lecture would be on the specific meanings of emblems at the time they were composed, and how you find these meanings (*see Illustration 2*).

Another Italian had equally profound influence in France: Machiavelli. The scope for new lectures on Machiavelli is endless. One precept of his I find particularly interesting: that the ruler should use religion as an instrument of state. This practice goes back at least as far as Numa Pompilius, the second king of Rome, whom Machiavelli warmly commends. Numa convinced the people that he enjoyed divine favour and, having done that, was able to have them accept any policy he wished. French political theorists, notably the incomparable La Boëtie, made short shrift of ancient rulers like Numa who prey on the superstition of their subjects — and then turned to French kings and denounced legends about the divine favour they supposedly enjoy, legends about the *fleur de lys*, the phial of sacred oil and the oriflamme. His immediate target was Henri II, but his strictures were to be even more applicable to Henri III, who was thoroughly schooled in Machiavellian precepts. Political practitioners still exploit religion — everywhere. The lecture could be titled 'Opium of the people: religion as a political tool from Numa Pompilius to ...' (and you can supply almost any name including many from nominally atheist states — *quem vis, media elige turba*). Montaigne felt, rightly, that this subject would make a very good book.

4

Machiavelli's attitude towards religion led many to call him an atheist. What about a lecture on an even more intriguing atheist? 'Etienne Dolet, the first French atheist' (*see Illustration 3*). That title has a ring to it. 'But', you will say, 'scholars are not agreed that Dolet was an atheist, let alone that he was the first in France'. 'Indeed', is my answer, 'but let's look at my dossier of new documents'. The lecture would present the material, discuss the pitfalls in interpreting it, and show how I conclude that Dolet was an atheist and (especially) how I tried to demolish my hypothesis in order to test it. The Dolet dossier would present views regarded then as atheistical or quasi-atheistical: epicureanism — both cosmological and moral; denial of the immortality of the soul; Lucianism; Nicodemism; determinism. The lecture could look at Dolet's fame as scholar and publisher, the charges he faced of murder and of heresy, the attitudes of his few friends and many foes, his death at the stake in 1546; it could explore his motives in sacrificing his life for his opinions and offer comparative profiles of other martyrs — Thomas More, Michael Servetus, Anne Du Bourg, Giordano Bruno... Above all, you, the audience, would be invited to judge my hypothesis about the atheism of Dolet. For this is what happens in lectures: students learn to assemble information and, especially, to judge it. (If you are interested in our work, buy our Runnymede book, *The Right angle, your degree in French*, now in its second edition and available in the French Department and from any reputable bookseller!)

One idea, as you see, immediately led to another. But as I was musing on topics for an inaugural lecture *if* I got the job (for, you will recall, we are talking about the morning of the interview for the New College Chair

5

of French), the phone rang and brought me abruptly down to earth. A very businesslike woman on the other end said 'Is that Malcolm Smith? It's the Jimmy Young programme here. Are you willing to talk to Jimmy about today's government report on language teaching in schools?' I said 'Certainly' — and asked the Departmental Secretary, Cathy Hewson, to go and buy the papers so as to read up on this before Jimmy phoned back. No sooner had I finished reading than the phone rang and another businesslike woman said 'We want to get your introduction right. You are Dr. Malcolm Smith?' 'Yes.' 'And you are the Head of the French Department?' 'Yes.' 'At...?' She paused expectantly so I said, 'Royal Holloway and Bedford New College University of London' (giving equal emphasis to each word). 'I see', she said, having doubtless made a mental note to tell Jimmy to take a very deep breath. 'Okay, you're on when the next record ends. He'll call you Malcolm and you must call him Jim or Jimmy. Goodbye'. She left me listening to an excruciating pop record.

After what seemed an eternity, Jimmy came on, summarised the report and said, 'Now Malcolm, is it true that British people are very bad at languages?' 'Well, Jim, there is a lot in that. However, if they come to the French Department at the New College...' He spotted the plug a mile off, and interrupted: 'Malcolm, is British business at a disadvantage because of our problem with languages?' 'Jim, you have to communicate to do business with people. Of course, there are additional reasons for learning languages...' 'Malcolm' (he interrupted) 'what can we do about this?' 'Jim, the nation must accept that language learning is good

6

business and is an excellent intellectual discipline. And we must make the necessary investment. The latest round of cuts...' I think Jim interrupted that one too. He was probing at the nation's provision of a functional service — I was hinting there might be deeper benefits in language learning.

This anecdote illustrates a tension. The aim of the scholar is to give rein to intellectual curiosity, to pursue issues wherever they lead, and to whatever conclusions they lead. And a vital part of the role of the holder of a university chair in the humanities — in my view, *the* vital part — is to encourage and lead a community of scholars in historical and literary research. For the hallmark of a university has to be intellectual vitality: without it, we would be an Ealing comedy, and not a very funny one. The part of my work which gives me keenest pleasure is discussion with students of their essays and discussion with colleagues of their research. But the wider community, in the shape of Jimmy Young and his several million listeners, was coming to me not for scholarship but for views on the training of sharper entrepreneurs. And when the wider community engages in dialogue with us about our work, it behoves us to listen most carefully: they are the people we serve. A tension, without a doubt. Back to Jimmy later. First, Montaigne.

You probably already know Michel de Montaigne (1533-1592) as the founder of modern scepticism, and as a theologian — the scepticism served the theology, unsurprisingly since theology is about mystery (*see Illustration 4*). He was also a political theorist and practitioner, mayor of Bordeaux, diplomat and adviser

7

of Henri IV (he describes politics as the most honourable of occupations). Above all, perhaps, he is a moral philosopher — and (to be bold) a more appealing moral philosopher than any other I have encountered and that includes Socrates. His moral philosophy is presented in his *Essais*, first published in 1580: by the word 'essay' (which in its present application he invented) he meant a personal exercise in intellectual speculation (*not* a rehash of what other people have said). I mention his view of what an essay is in case it is of relevance to anyone here!

The main source for this lecture on Montaigne the traveller is his diary, that *Journal de voyage* which records his journey through France, Germany, Switzerland, Austria and Italy in 1580 and 1581 (perhaps diaries of his other journeys remain to be discovered). Montaigne travelled, as he tells us in his essay *On vanity*, to discover new things, to avoid the hassles of running his estate, to escape from the French civil wars and for the exercise of body (for he travelled on horseback) and of mind. And travel was therapeutic: admittedly the spa waters had little effect upon the stones that tormented him, but travel distracted him from the pain (p. 252: references are to the Dédéyan edition). For everything interested him — industry and commerce; economics and politics; history and archaeology; architecture and building methods; art and literature; food and drink; sexual *mores*; the roads, the landscape; everything.

A hallmark of the diary, as of the *Essais*, is Montaigne's candour. Germans, Montaigne says, are conceited, irascible and drunk: but they are not treacherous and they are not thieves (p. 125), and Germany is a

8

land of comfort, of courtesy, of justice and the rule of law (p. 159) and of impeccable cleanliness (unlike Italy where, to avoid the lice, he slept on the table: p. 340, 404). The candour becomes particularly interesting when he turns to politics. He feels at ease in cities where social distinctions are of least account (for example, Mulhouse, p. 99). He is particularly sensitive to the degree of freedom in any given place (p. 276, 232), records what people said about those who governed them (p. 268), and has incisive judgements of his own about political and religious leaders, many of whom he met: his candour on this borders on indiscretion and in my view this fact explains why he did not publish the diary. This candour contributes massively to the historical interest of the text.

The principal characteristic of Montaigne the traveller is his curiosity. He was keen to learn of strange events, for example of the girl from Chaumont-en-Bassigny who passed herself off as a man, and got married, and was convicted of using fraud to disguise her sex and executed (p. 87-88). In Rome, he witnessed an exorcism and gave a fascinating account of it (p. 220). Also in Rome he learned of eight Portuguese homosexuals who had had their union blessed in the church to legitimize it but had been quickly disabused — and executed (p. 231). On another journey outside France, a prince (whom he unfortunately does not identify) showed him convicted witches, which may have prompted his audacious and witty essay on the burning of witches. Miracles, too, attracted him. At Loreto, miraculous misadventures befell those who stole from the shrine (p. 259): so Montaigne felt safe in leaving there a tableau with silver figures of the Virgin Mary, himself,

9

his wife and daughter (if it is still there that certainly will be a miracle). Also at Loreto, he closely questioned a man who claimed to have been miraculously cured of a serious leg injury and fever; he found his story plausible (though in general, Montaigne says, 'the only miracles I believe are the ones my faith requires me to'). He was less convinced by an altar at Pisa with bloodstains of St. Clement, the fourth pope: the bloodstains, he remarks, look about three days old (p. 358). He mentions relics, including the heads of St. Peter and St. Paul (p. 239) and the famous shroud now in Turin (p. 238) — always with open-mindedness, great care about facts and sharp judiciousness.

Nothing better illustrates that open-mindedness than Montaigne's encounters with people with whom he disagreed. *Qui me contredit, m'instruit.* Let us look at two cases. First, his encounters with German Reformers. He sought their company, invited them to dine with him and to expound their beliefs, and attended their services. They opened their hearts to him, and his diary is an intimate record of the state of religion in the towns through which he passed. Most remarkably, these dialogues changed Montaigne's views on tolerance. Twenty years earlier, in 1561, he had reflected on this issue. He was then a member of the *parlement* of Bordeaux, the sovereign court, the French legislature: so was his close friend Estienne de La Boëtie. He almost certainly helped La Boëtie write that *Mémoire sur la pacification des troubles* in which La Boëtie argues against tolerance. Why did two such enlightened people oppose something as sensible as tolerance? For several reasons: theological (for rival churches cannot be the will of God), social (division is disruptive), political (national divisions

10

invite foreign meddling) — and above all moral (the corruption which had caused the Reformation should be cleaned up, not palliated). La Boëtie and Montaigne advocated instead conciliation: reforms which would meet every reasonable aspiration of Reformers without sacrificing essentials. Their arguments were unavailing and in January 1562 France became the first country in Europe in modern times to permit nationwide religious dissidence.

By 1580, however, when Montaigne first published his *Essais* and just before he set out for Germany and Italy, his views had evolved. Conciliation had failed, and twenty years of war supposedly over religion had crystallised the division. At several points in that first edition of the book, he alludes to the tolerance legislation of 1562. 'What do you do (he asks) when principle requires one thing (like unity of religion) but circumstances make that unattainable?' Montaigne acknowledges in the 1580 edition of the *Essais*, but reluctantly, that the law must yield to necessity: what you cannot change, you tolerate ('tolerance' has negative connotations in sixteenth-century French). He was painfully discovering what the process of legislation is perennially about: the framing of laws which offer the best attainable combination of the ideal and the expedient (with the balance weighted towards the latter). There are many allusions to the 1562 tolerance legislation in the *Essais* of 1580 but they are almost never explicit and you need some knowledge of history to appreciate what Montaigne is referring to.

But now, in Germany, encounters with Lutherans, Zwinglians, Calvinists and others (for every village had

11

its own variety of the Reformed faith) brought about a further evolution in Montaigne's views. To his fascination, Germans no longer fought wars over religion, there were no sectarian assassins of the kind who on at least one occasion very nearly killed him, and people of differing religions lived in peace and cordiality and indeed (to Montaigne's stupefaction) married each other. Nor was this through indifference to religion. On the contrary: the presence of opposing faiths sharpened people's commitment. Montaigne, the opponent of tolerance in 1561 and the grudging acceptor of tolerance in 1580 becomes, through his experience of Germany, Switzerland and Austria, the advocate of religious liberty: you can see this evolution in the expanded editions of his *Essais* published later in life. Montaigne's diary and the successive states of his *Essais* provide engrossing — and unexploited — material on the development of modern pluralism. This is what the College has given me sabbatical leave to write a book about.

The second historical and intellectual issue I want to invite you to reflect on is Montaigne's encounter with the Roman Inquisition, on which I have some new thoughts. The story so far, as told in my book *Montaigne and the Roman censors*: when Montaigne entered Rome in November 1580, a copy of his *Essais*, which had just appeared, was taken from him by agents of the Inquisition. Four months later, Montaigne was invited to meet Sisto Fabri, personal theologian of pope Gregory XIII and adviser to the Congregation of the Inquisition, and Joannes Baptista Lancius, the secretary to the Congregation of the Index (which compiled the list of prohibited books). They asked him to comment on various objections which their reader had raised to

12

his *Essais*: that he had used the word 'fortune', named heretic poets, defended the so-called 'apostate' emperor Julian, said that when you pray you should be free of vicious inclination, argued that people who are being executed ought not to be tortured and declared that a child should be brought up to be capable of doing anything. On hearing Montaigne's explanations, the theologians withdrew their objections. At a second meeting, the same two officials told Montaigne they had no quarrel with him and that he should make whatever use he wanted to of their censure, and they conveyed their embarrassment at the ineptitude of much of it, and apologized for it. When Montaigne was back in France, he elaborated copiously on the points which had been called into question.

But the intellectual encounter of the greatest French philosopher and the Inquisition still has secrets to yield. Montaigne lists the six objections in his diary, then adds 'et autres telles choses', 'and other such things'. What were these things? There are lines of enquiry which I shall pursue, for there are no insoluble problems, just some which take longer than others. Meantime, see what you think about these three guesses about what the lost objections might have been.

One is the view we have just seen Montaigne express, that laws must yield to necessity, and that the French legislation of 1562, tolerating religious dissidents, illustrates this. The reasons which lead me to conclude the censors may have objected to this: (i) Rome had strongly opposed the French tolerance legislation of 1562; (ii) Montaigne returned to this proposition in post-1580 editions of the *Essais* in ways which suggest

13

he was replying to criticism of his earlier statements; and (iii), he observes in a 1588 passage in his essay *On vanity* that the conscientious rectitude of clerics is out of place in the business of legislating: *exeat aula / Qui vult esse pius.* Of course, no-one knew better than the inquisitors that you have to make tactical concessions. But Montaigne was actually saying you have to do this.

A second lost objection may be to Montaigne's criticism of the use of torture in judicial investigations. The reasons: (i) he was criticising a judicial practice current in Rome (and, I think, everywhere else in Europe); (ii) one of the six known censures of Montaigne was of his analogous view that use of torture in executions is deplorable; and (iii) after his meeting with the Inquisition, he amplified and strengthened the relevant passage in later editions of the *Essais*, in precisely the same way as he did with passages known to have been censured.

A third opinion is the one which I am most confident was criticised, and it is by far the most interesting. It is the view, advanced in the chapter *On freedom of conscience*, that zeal can be misplaced and that fourth-century Christians illustrate this:

> *It is common to see good intentions, if pursued immoderately, impel men to action which has very evil results. [...] When our religion first acquired legal authority and power, many zealous people were up in arms against pagan books of every kind and, as a result of this, literature has suffered grievous loss. In my view, this disorder wrought more damage than all the flames of the barbarians. Cornelius Tacitus is a good witness to this: for, though his relative the emperor Tacitus had by special decree populated every library*

14

in the world with his books, not one single complete copy has survived the meticulous searches of those who sought to suppress him for the sake of five or six trivial clauses contrary to our faith. And they were too ready to praise all emperors who were on our side and to condemn globally all the actions of our adversaries, as can easily be seen in the case of Julian, the so-called 'Apostate'.

The reasons for suggesting Montaigne was criticised for this are (i) that the remarks about Julian were censured and it would make little sense not to have objected also to the accompanying and essentially identical comment on Tacitus; (ii) the Inquisition was hostile to Tacitus on account of his derogatory remarks about Christians and Jews, and had kept Tacitus off the university syllabus in Rome for many years — so Montaigne's attack upon people for seeking to suppress Tacitus could be construed as an attack upon the Inquisition itself; (iii) pope Pius V, whose pontificate ended only in 1580, had ordered the destruction of Tacitus's tomb, and the remarks about excessive Christian zeal against Tacitus might easily have been construed as an allusion to this; (iv) Montaigne responded to the six known criticisms with a thorough re-evaluation of each censured view — and after his return from Italy, he read Tacitus's complete surviving works from beginning to end (and, he says, 'it is twenty years since I spent more than an hour on a book'); (v) in 1588, he recalled telling the 'magistrate' (by which in context he means the Inquisition) that you do not have to approve someone's religion to commend his qualities, and in the next breath and in this same context referred to his earlier passage on Tacitus; and (vi) especially, Montaigne added after 1580 a long defence of Tacitus which refutes

15

known inquisitorial objections to him. For example, meeting head-on the question of Tacitus's disparagement of Christians and Jews, Montaigne writes, 'He does not need any excuse for approving the religion of his time, according to the laws which governed him, and for ignoring the true one. That is his misfortune, not his shortcoming'. This detailed defence of Tacitus comes at the end of the chapter *De l'art de conferer*, which in the light of what I am going to say next, I would be tempted to translate as 'On the art of dialogue'.

If the detailed appraisal of Tacitus at the end of *De l'art de conferer* was at least in part a considered rebuttal of a censure, then this permits some interesting new conclusions about this essay, which is in my view the most readable and spirited Montaigne wrote. The essay, which shows that humanity thrives on open-minded intellectual dialogue and shuns the dead hand of authoritarianism, may have been largely a message for the Inquisition. Passages which support this conclusion include the one in which Montaigne argues that we are born to seek truth and that possession of it belongs to a higher power (and the world itself is an *escole d'inquisition*), and another in which he warns of the danger of misuse of *authorité magistrale*. The attractions about the hypothesis that the chapter was partly inspired by his experience in Rome are that it is consistent with Montaigne's intellectual audacity and with his calm, firm and judicious reaction to the inquisitors, and that it provides a perfect explanation of three otherwise strange facts: (i) that the chapter begins with one of those disclaimers which Montaigne always introduces when he broaches contentious moral or theological issues — a disclaimer which is quite unnecessary if his subject

16

is simply the art of conversation; (ii) that Montaigne read the complete extant Tacitus twenty years after he had lost the habit of systematic study; and (iii) that this chapter on intellectual dialogue ends with an otherwise incongruous appraisal of an ancient author, an appraisal which on the face of it belongs not here but in his chapter on reading, *Des livres*. If *De l'art de conferer* is, as I suspect, a manifesto in favour of the free exchange of ideas, and a manifesto partly triggered by dialogue with the Inquisition, then the chapter has an altogether unsuspected profundity and historical significance.

It was not until almost a century after the first appearance of the *Essais* that Montaigne's boldness finally proved too much for the Roman authorities. I am now going to stray momentarily from Montaigne's travels and indeed from his own lifetime, partly because Montaigne himself encourages digression, partly because this is an interesting footnote to his encounter with the inquisitors Fabri and Lancius, but above all because this provides you with a chance to exercise your judgement and work out what triggered the ultimate condemnation of Montaigne. In 1640, Montaigne's book of *Essais* was banned by the Spanish Inquisition, *hasta que se expurgue*. A Spanish manuscript obligingly points to the two suspect pages, but without specifying the precise passage. So this is your chance to don the mantle of an inquisitor, and spot the incriminating clauses. The first passage is in the chapter *On custom*. There are societies, Montaigne says, and now I quote:

[...] in which husbands can repudiate their wives without citing a reason, and without there being a reason. In which they can sell their wives, if they are sterile. In which they

17

cook the corpses and grind them into a pulp which they mix with their wine and then drink. Where the most desirable form of burial is to be eaten by dogs, and elsewhere by birds. Where they believe that the souls of the blessed live in complete freedom, in beautiful fields provided with all that they could desire, and that these souls produce the echoes we hear. [...] Where the eunuchs who guard women devoted to religion have their noses and lips cut off, so that they cannot be loved. Where each person makes his own god, and a hunter's god will be a lion or a fox, and the fisherman's a particular fish, where they make idols of human passions, where the sun, the moon and the earth are the principal gods, where they swear by putting a hand on the ground while gazing at the sun; and in that society, they eat meat and fish raw. Where their great oath is to swear by the name of some dead man of great repute, with a hand placed upon his tomb. [...] Where the system of government is changed when political circumstances make that necessary, and they depose the king when it seems expedient to do so, entrusting the government to one of the elders or sometimes to the people. Where men and women are circumcised and also baptised. Where they hold that very rare and anti-social opinion that souls are mortal.

One of these propositions the Spanish Inquisition found disquieting, and quite possibly more than one. Deposing the king and accepting mortality of the soul seem especially dangerous. *Something* on this page was more sensitive than anything on the previous page, which points among other things to societies where abortion could be had on demand, and more sensitive than anything on the following page, which points to societies in which incest was normal. Interestingly, it was not for endorsing these customs that Montaigne was

18

prohibited (for he does not endorse them). All he does is mention them — and, in his preamble, invite the reader to reflect that our society has customs as barbaric as any we condemn in others. Before Montaigne, Thomas More in his *Utopia* had also mentioned alien customs (in his case, euthanasia, a communist society and legalising of atheism) and had gone much further than Montaigne and suggested there are rational arguments for these customs. No doubt *Utopia* would have been condemned eventually had More not earned permanent immunity to inquisitorial scrutiny by the manner of his death.

And the other passage which disturbed the Spanish Inquisition? It is about how to write, and is in the chapter *On the education of children*. Spot the incriminating clause here:

What matters is substance, which should so grip the listener that he simply forgets the words. The kind of communication I like is simple and natural, the same on paper as in speech, succulent, sinewy, concise and cogent, not so much refined and ordered as vigorous and lively: **Hæc demum sapiet dictio, quæ feriet** *['The right style is the one which has impact'], difficult maybe but boring never, with no affectation, unbridled, unordered and daring; each element self-sufficient; quite unlike the utterances of academics, preachers and lawyers, more like a soldier's, which is how Suetonius describes Julius Cæsar's style, and I do not know why he criticises him for it. [...] Eloquence undermines substance, by drawing attention to itself. Just as it is a sign of faint-heartedness to seek to stand out by wearing unusual clothes, so with speech, the quest for novel phrases and unfamiliar words derives from a puerile ambition of the kind that academics have. I would be quite happy with*

19

the vocabulary of the markets in Paris! Aristophanes the grammarian did not know what he was talking about when he reproached Epicurus for the simplicity of his language and for saying that lucidity is the goal of rhetoric. It is easy enough to imitate words — anyone can do that. To imitate judgement and creativity, that takes a little longer. [...] Most people I meet speak the way my **Essais** *do; but I'm not sure whether they think the same way.*

What is objectionable there? Surely not the fact that Montaigne criticises preachers as well as academics and lawyers for waffling? Or could it be for defending the simple speech of Epicurus? That, I am afraid, is the issue: Epicurus denied the immortality of the soul, and you were not supposed to acknowledge any merit in people whose views conflict with your religion. There is something anti-climactic about the founder of modern scepticism being condemned for reasons as trivial. Some years later, in 1676, the Roman Inquisition also included Montaigne in its Index, possibly for the same reason, for compilers of Indexes often took over each other's prohibitions.

Three concluding remarks which bring us back to Montaigne the traveller. Firstly, the ease with which he handled encounters with Reformers and inquisitors, encounters which could readily have become dangerously charged, is symptomatic of his cosmopolitanism: he was a citizen of the world, receptive to all opinions and shocked by none, keen to evaluate and learn. In the university we, too, are citizens of the world. Our interest in ideas and in people transcends boundaries of space and of time — and transcends disciplines, which was the point of my initial remarks about the range of possible

20

topics for an inaugural lecture. Like Montaigne, we can profitably draw upon universal human experience. On tolerance, Montaigne moved from 'No surrender' to pluralism — a lesson not without relevance in the British Isles, the last part of the world where these sixteenth-century controversies still cost lives. In his encounter with the Inquisition, he courteously and firmly resisted what he saw as unjustified incursions upon freedom of the media — that too may be topical. The student of Renaissance literature, and of any literature, discovers all the time that the link between literature and life is an intimate one. *Nulla ars in se versatur.* Without some awareness of that link, our studies could become introverted, narcissistic and trivial.

Secondly, the original citizen of the world, Socrates, concluded from his dialogue with his contemporaries that he was wiser than them simply because he acknowledged his ignorance. And Montaigne, whose dialogue with the world was as intimate and discerning as that of Socrates, echoes him in acknowledgement of ignorance — indeed, the title of his book, 'Essais', declares he could only offer 'attempts' at finding truth, even about himself. And the Roman inquisitor who acknowledged the deficiencies of his censure of Montaigne shares something of this spirit. Encouraged by these examples we shall always be prepared to admit our ignorance (and shall never take refuge in that obscurity which in the university is the last refuge of the scoundrel). In the university what matters is not to be right (though we shall spare no effort to be), but to think. In the rest of the world, it is the other way round. The lecture you have just heard is historical as much as it is literary, and doubtless my historian friends will now tell me my

21

mistakes. I shall be delighted to listen (but I could have written a very interesting inaugural lecture about errors made by historians who have misunderstood documents written in sixteenth-century French!). Acknowledgement of ignorance is the starting point of scholarship: *Qui veut quérir de l'ignorance, il faut la confesser.* In that same spirit of open-mindedness, we welcome — indeed, we require — informed challenge by students to our ideas, and informed suggestions about how our service to students, to scholarship and to the community may be enhanced.

Which leads to my final point, which is that Montaigne, the lover of scholarly investigation, was also a politician who got useful things done. Jimmy Young, in his inimitably cogent and courteous manner, put it to me that the wider community expects us to perform a functional service, which is teach people French so they can do business with the world. Fine Jim, we'll do it. And a few other things. You want us to be entrepreneurial? Buy a Runnymede book. You want us to help industry? Join our PICKUP classes. You want us to attract outside earnings? Take a look at our balance sheet. What about performance indicators? The students and staff of the French Department have turned the record round on all of them. Would you like us to cost less? Jim, we do. And achieve more? Read our annual report, research profile and submission to the UGC that Harry Cockerham has just produced. And do ask us about accountability. You ask, we deliver. By now, Jim, you are probably asking whether it is because university people are scholars that they achieve so much. Yes, Jim, it is: for encounter with lively minds of past and present enhances open-mindedness, sharpens

22

the intellect, broadens vision, develops resilience and humanity and reminds us to get on with it because we are all mortal and tomorrow will be too late. Of course, Jim, our students will speak impeccable French to the country's clients in the single market — or any market. But it will not just be their French that clinches the deal: they too, like Montaigne, will be citizens of the world and people whom the world will do business with, and with pleasure.

ILLUSTRATIONS

ILLUSTRATION 1: LA BOËTIE'S *MÉMOIRE*

La Boëtie wrote this memorandum on the Reformation controversies very rapidly at the end of 1561 in an attempt to persuade legislators that conciliation was still possible and that there was no need to introduce tolerance (which would consolidate sectarianism and leave fundamental abuses untouched). The manuscript is in the public library in Aix-en-Provence. La Boëtie seems to have dictated the text to a secretary — whose handwriting gets progressively worse! The text below is a transcription of the first page (from the edition by Malcolm Smith, in the 'Textes Littéraires Français' series, Genève, 1983); the illustration opposite shows that same page in the manuscript.

Memoire touchant l'Edit de Janvier 1562 concernant ceux de la Religion P[rétendue] R[éformée]

Le subject de la deliberation est la pacification·des troubles . Il faut doncques entendre premierement en quel estat est à present Je mal qu'on veut guerir; après, recognoistre l'origine et la source pour savoir comment il est nai, comme il s'est nourry et a prins acroisement. Si on doibt trouver quelque remede, il se verra plus à cler après avoir consideré ces deux choses.

Tout le mal est la diversité de religion qui a passé si avant, qu'ung mesme peuple, vivant soubz mesme prince, s'est clerement divisé en deux pars, et ne faut doubter que ceux d'un costé n'estiment leurs adversaires ceux qui sont de l'autre. Non seulement les opinions sont differantes, mais desja ont diverses esglizes, divers chefz, contraires observations, divers ordre, contraire police en religion: bref, pour ce regard, aucunement deux diverses republicques opposées de front l'une à l'autre.

De ce mal en sortent deux autres: l'ung est une hayne et malveillance quasi universelle entre les subjects du Roy, laquelle en quelques endroitz se nourrit plus secretement, en autres se declaire plus ouvertement, mais par tout elle produict assez de tristes effectz.

L'autre est que peu à peu le peuple s'acoutume à une irreverance envers le magistrat, et avecques le temps aprend à desobeyr voluntiers et se laisse mener aux apastz de la liberté, ou plustost licence, qui est la plus douce et la plus friande poison du monde .

MEMOIRE touchant l'Edict de Janvier
1562 concernant ceux de la
Religion P.R.

Le Subiect de la deliberacion s'est la pacificacion des troubles Je suis
doncques entendre premierement en quoi est ce est a present le mal
qu'on veult guerir : apres recognoistre l'origine et la source pour savoir
comment il est nai : comme il s'est nourry et a prins accroissement
et ou doibt trouver quelque remede Je se verra plus a clair apres avoir
considere ces deux choses

Tout le mal est la diversité de religion qui a passé si avant qu'ong
mesme peuple, vivant soubz mesme prince s'est debatu ne dire en deux
parts et ne fault doubter que ceux d'une part ne s'honnent l'autre admissions
ceux qui sont de l'autre. Oloy, seullement les opinions sont differentes.
mais desia ont diverses eglises divers chefz ou l'autres obstinacion
divers ordre et haine police en religion : tres pour ce regard aurons
deux diverses republicques opposees de front l'une a l'autre

De ce mal en sortent deux autres L'ung est une hayne et
malveillance grande immediatte entre les subietz du Roy laquelle
en quelque endroit se nourrie plus l'honteusement en intens se
declaire plus ouvertement mais par tous elle produict assés de tres mauvais
effectz.

L'autre est la peu a peu le peuple s'acoustume a une irreverence
envers le magistrat et avecques le temps a prend esprit & desobeyr volontaire
et se laisse mener aux armes, si ce le bon ou plustost l'heure

[355]

ILLUSTRATION 2: ALCIATI'S EMBLEMS

The reproductions opposite are from the annotated edition of Alciati's *Emblemata* prepared by Claude Mignault and published by Plantin in Antwerp in 1581.

Emblem XXI: *The person who has been caught:* 'Wherever you flee, I shall follow you; and now finally you have been caught in my snare. You will no longer be able to escape from me. I have the eel trapped by a fig leaf'. This emblem teaches us (Mignault explains) that wrongdoers are usually slippery and must be pinned down with good evidence, in the same way as an eel-catcher grips his prey with fig leaves.

Emblem CXX: *Poverty prevents the best minds from making progress:* 'My right hand holds a rock, the other has wings: the wings are a help to me, but the heavy burden drags me down. My mind could soar if the burden of poverty were not weighing me down'. The wings, according to Mignault, symbolise the intellect, which longs to soar aloft through study of the liberal arts; the rock symbolizes the poverty which oppresses students.

40

In deprehensum.

EMBLEMA XXI.

IAMDVDVM *quacunque fugis, te perſequor: at nunc*
Caſsibus in noſtris denique captus ades.
Amplius hand poteris vires eludere noſtras:
Ficulno anguillam ſtrinximus in folio.

EMBLEMATA.　　　435

Paupertatem ſummis ingeniis obeſſe ne
prouehantur.

EMBLEMA CXI.

DEXTRA *tenet lapidem, manus altera ſuſtinet alas:*
Vt me pluma leuat, ſic graue mergit onus.
Ingenio poteram ſuperas volitare per arces,
Me niſi paupertas inuida deprimeret.

ILLUSTRATION 3: ESTIENNE DOLET

The illustration opposite is the only known likeness of
Dolet, the scholar, poet, printer and reputed atheist
who was executed in Paris in 1546. It is from
a work by Antoine Du Verdier, *La Prosopographie
ou description des personnes insignes,* published in
Lyons in 1573. Dolet here features among scholars of
the calibre of Thomas More and Desiderius Erasmus;
books by him are listed and his execution is noted.
Du Verdier praised Dolet again later, in his major
bibliographical work, *La Bibliotheque* (1585), noting his
contribution to French literature but this time without
recording the circumstances of his death. Du Verdier,
a committed defender of freedom of expression, was
courageously dispassionate in his appraisals of books
which others condemned.

42

ſoit en diligence & labeur. Ceſt Eraſme, natif de Rote-
rodam, duquel l'aſſiduité de l'eſtude, & l'infinité de liures qu'il a publié ſoubs ſon nom le rendent admirable
& digne d'eſtre nommé le grand orateur & philoſophe
auſsi bien que Ciceron : car à grand peine pourra vn
homme lire en ſa vie toutes les œuures de ce grand per
ſonnage, qui ſont foy comme il a eſté eloquent & combien luy ſont obligez tous les ſtudieux des bonnes lettres. Leſquels œuures en partie, ont eſté imprimez par
Froben en dix grands tomes in ſolio, & couſtent 26
liures tourn. en blanc. Il mourut à Baſle vn peu apres
qu'il fuſt party de Friburg, aagé de ſoixante dix ans.

Epitaphium Eraſmi a G. Bucchanano.

Ingens ingentem quem perſonat orbis Eraſmus
　Hæc tibi dimidium picta tabella refert.
At cur non totum? mirari deſine lector,
　Integra nam totum terra nec ipſa capit.

DOLET.

 STIENNE Dolet, natif d'Orleans, hô-
me docte & imprimeur à Lyon, a eſcrit en
peu d'annees pluſieurs liures pour l'inſtitu-
tion de la langue Latine, imprimez partie
par

ILLUSTRATION 4: MONTAIGNE AND SCEPTICISM

The page opposite, from a copy of the 1595 edition of Montaigne's *Essais* in the British Library, contains a 'sceptical' passage of *De l'experience* (*Essais*, III, xiii). Each time he discovers that he has made an individual mistake, Montaigne says, he draws the general conclusion, which is that he is fallible — and he thus advances in self-knowledge, in obedience to the precept of Apollo, 'Know thyself'. But, he adds, even in the subject closest to him, which is himself, he discovers such infinite depth that all he can do is acknowledge the frailty of his understanding. This acknowledgement saves him from the scourge of dogmatism, which is the hallmark of a beast. The contemporary owner of this copy has embellished the text with illustrations — of the temple of Apollo (with the inscription *Nosce teipsum*, 'Know thyself'), and of a wolf bearing the inscription 'bestise', which is the word with which the last sentence on the page is completed.

44

train: & la haine & l'amitié, voire & celle que ie me porte à
moy-mesme, sans s'en alterer & corrompre. S'il ne peut reformer les autres parties selõ soy, au moins ne se laisse-il pas
difformer à elles : il fait son jeu à part. L'aduertissement à
chacun de se cognoistre, doit estre d'vn important effect,
puisque ce Dieu de science & de lumiere le fit plâter au frõt
de son temple : comme comprenant tout ce qu'il auoit
à nous conseiller. Platon dit aussi , que prudence n'est
autre chose, que l'execution de cette ordonnáce : & Socrates le verifie par le menu en Xenophon. Les difficultez &
l'obscurité, ne s'apperçoiuent en chacune science, que par
ceux qui y ont entree. Car encore fault-il quelque degré
d'intelligence, à pouuoir remarquer qu'on ignore : & faut
pousser à vne porte, pour sçauoir qu'elle nous est close. D'où
naist cette Platonique subtilité, que ny ceux qui sçauent,
n'ont à s'enquerir, dautant qu'ils sçauét: ny ceux qui ne sçauent, dautant que pour s'enquerir, il fault sçauoir, dequoy
on s'enquiert. Ainsi, en cette cy de se cognoistre soy-mes-
me: ce que chacun se void si resolu & satisfait, ce que chacũ
y pense estre suffisamment entendu, signifie que chacun n'y
entend rien du tout, comme Socrates apprend à Euthyde-
me. Moy, qui ne fais autre profession, y trouue vne profon-
deur & varieté si infinie, que mon apprentissage n'a autre
fruict, que de me faire sentir, combien il me reste à apprendre. A ma foiblesse si souuét recogneuë, ie dois l'inclination
que i'ay à la modestie: à l'obeïssance des creáces qui me sõt
prescrites : à vne constante froideur & moderation d'opinions: & la haine de cette arrogance importune & querel-
leuse, se croyant & fiant tout à soy, ennemie capitale de discipline & de verité. Oyez les regenter. Les premieres sotti-
ses qu'ils mettent en auant, c'est au style qu'on establit les
religions & les loix. *Nihil est turpius, quam cognitioni & perce-
ptioni, assertionem approbationémque præcurrere.* Aristarchus disoit,
qu'anciennement, à peine se trouua-il sept sages au monde,
& que de son temps à peine se trouua-il sept ignorans. Au-
rions nous pas plus de raison que luy, de le dire en nostre
temps ? L'affirmation & l'opiniastreté, sont signes exprez de

MALCOLM SMITH:
BIBLIOGRAPHY OF STUDIES AND EDITIONS

Joachim Du Bellay's Veiled Victim, with an edition of the 'Xenia, seu, illustrium quo-rundam nominum allusiones', Etudes de Philologie et d'Histoire, Genève, Droz, 1974.

Montaigne and the Roman Censors, Etudes de Philologie et d'Histoire, Genève, Droz, 1981.

Montaigne and Religious Freedom: the Dawn of Pluralism, Etudes de Philologie et d'Histoire, Genève, Droz, 1991.

Ronsard and Du Bellay versus Bèze: Allusiveness in Renaissance Literary Texts, Etudes de Philologie et d'Histoire, Genève, Droz, 1995.

Chapters in *The Right Angle: your degree in French*, Egham, Runnymede Books, 1987.

Study Guides to the degree in French, Malcolm Smith and J.D. Barron, eds., five volumes published by the External Division of London University, 1987-1988.

Chapters on La Boëtie, Du Bellay, Ronsard and Montaigne in vol. 3 of *Study Guides to the degree in French*, 1987.

P. de Ronsard *Sonnets pour Helene*, Textes Littéraires Français, Genève et Paris, Droz/Minard, 1970.

P. de Ronsard *Discours des misères de ce temps*, Textes Littéraires Français, Genève, Droz, 1979.

E. de La Boëtie *Memoire sur la pacification des troubles*, Textes Littéraires Français, Genève, Droz, 1983.

E. de La Boëtie *De la Servitude volontaire ou Contr'Un*, Textes Littéraires Français, Genève, Droz, 1987.

E. de La Boëtie *Slaves by Choice* [a translation of the *Servitude volontaire*], Egham, Runnymede Books, 1988.

J. Du Bellay *Les Antiquitez de Rome*, translated by Edmund Spenser as *Ruines of Rome*, Medieval and Renaissance Texts and Studies, Binghamton, NY, 1994.

E. de La Boëtie *Œuvres* (with Richard Cooper), in *Œuvres complètes de Michel de Montaigne et d'Etienne de La Boëtie*, vol. I, Bibliothèque de la Pléiade, Gallimard (forthcoming).

INDEX

Jodelle, Etienne: 51, 100n, 213, 223, 226, 239
John Rylands Library, Manchester: 46, 152, 238n, 253n, 257n, 265n, 278n, 312n, 313n
Johnson, Samuel: 114n, 123
Joubert, Jacques: 253n
Judas Iscariot: 210
Julian, Emperor, the Apostate: 190, 303, 343, 345
Juste, François, printer: 279n
Juvenal: 96

Kitchin, Anthony, Bishop: 17n
Knox, John: 19

Labbé, Philippe: 114n, 115n, 142n, 144, 232n
La Baronie, F. de (*pseud.*): 13n, 74n, 157
La Bletonnière, Antoine de: 152-153
La Boëtie, Etienne de: 196n, 200-202, 203n, 220, 235n, 236n, 244-246, 248, 296, 298-300, 308, 314n, 317-319, 323, 327-329, 332, 334, 340-341, 354
La Croix du Maine, François Grudé de: 112, 197, 283
La Haye, Robert de: 224, 225n
La Jessée, Jean de: 121-122
La Mothe Le Vayer, François de: 205n
Lancius, Joannes Baptista: 189, 342, 347
Lando, Ortensio: 251, 278-279
Languet, Hubert: 296n
La Porte, Eustache de: 294n
La Primaudaye, Pierre de: 237n
L'Archer, Jean: 255
La Roche Chandieu, Antoine: 119-120, 158n
La Taille, Jean de: 209n
La Tour, Ysabeau de: 52
Launoy, Matthieu de: 28n, 29n
League, Catholic: 143, 202, 246n
Le Brun, Laurent: 228
Le Caron, Louis: 61n, 235n
Le Fèvre d'Etaples, Jacques: 289n
Le Laboureur, Jean: 257n
Le Loyer, Pierre: 50n
Le Maistre, Claude: 149
Leo X, Pope: 112
Le Roy, Adrien: 44
Le Roy, Louis: 132, 238
Le Sage, Pierre, printer: 29n
L'Escot, Pierre: 172
Leslie, John, Bishop: 24n, 29n

L'Estoile, Pierre de: 283
L'Hospital, Michel de, Chancellor of France: 11n, 22, 99, 130, 144-145, 180, 219-220, 223-225, 239, 294, 296, 308, 314-316, 318, 320, 323
Lhuillier, Jérôme: 52, 181
Lioult de Chênedollé, Charles-Julien: 126
Lipsius, Justus: 187, 193n, 194n, 204-205
L'Isle, François de: 226
Lizet, Pierre: 280n
Loisel, Antoine: 308, 327-328
Lorme, Philibert de: 169
Lorraine, Cardinal de: *see* Charles de Guise, Cardinal of Lorraine
Loynes, Antoinette de: 140n
Lucian of Samosata: 262, 267, 274n, 280-283, 284n, 335
Lucinge, René de: 209n, 239n
Lucretius: 62n
Lunardus, Philænus: 251n
Luther, Martin: 68-69, 85, 148, 233n, 274, 281n, 285n
Lutheran(s): 19, 49-50, 146, 261n, 287, 294, 308, 312, 321, 329n, 341

Macer, Jean: 223, 225n
Machiavelli, Niccolo: 25n (addendum), 187, 192n, 193n, 195n, 206-211, 226n, 234n, 235n, 237, 238n, 239n, 243, 246, 334-335
Macrin, Jean Salmon: 260, 266n
Madur, Pierre: 30n
Magny, Olivier de: 175, 224n
Mailly, Louise de: 132
Maisonfleur, Etienne de: 24n, 42
Maittaire, Michael: 259n, 261n, 263n
Mallot, Gervais, printer: 2, 4, 31n, 213
Manardi, Jean: 279n
Mangnier, Robert, printer: 39
Marcellinus, Ammianus: 189
Margaret of France, sister of Henry II: 11n, 16n, 88, 90, 132, 134, 219, 240
Margaret, Queen of Navarre: 169-170, 271, 284n, 289-290
Margaret Tudor: 10n
Marot, Clément: 150, 221, 224, 226, 262n, 269, 270n, 271, 279n
Martin de la Plaza, Luis: 229
Mary I, Queen of England: 10n, 17n
Mary of Guise, mother of Mary Stuart: 329
Mary Stuart, Queen of Scots: 10-11, 15-16, 17n, 19, 21-28, 29n, 32, 35-36, 51n, 144, 181, 295, 323n

Throckmorton, Nicholas: 17n, 20n, 29n, 295-296
Tolet, Pierre: 266n
Tournon, François de, Cardinal: 299
Toussaint, Jacques: 293, 323
Trent, Council of (1545-1563): 18n, 20n, 70n, 189, 193n, 201-202, 296n, 315n, 325n
Truchon, Jean: 253n
Turnèbe, Adrien: 24n, 132, 134, 139n, 141n, 269n
Tyard, Pontus de: 152-153

Ulpian: 189
Utenhove, Charles: 99, 132-133, 140n, 215, 218n, 222

Valerianus, Joannes Pierius: 112
Valet, Antoine: 2-4, 9, 213
Vallambert, Simon: 253n, 266n, 278n
Vassy, massacre of (1562): 300
Vatable, François: 293, 322
Vatican Library: 297n
Vauquelin de la Fresnaye, Jean: 135, 141n
Vega, Lope de: 151
Velez de Guevara, Luis: 230
Velliardus, Jacobus: 226n
Vermigli, Pietro Martire: 149
Vespasian, Emperor: 187, 190, 195n, 244
Vettori, Pier: 193n

Villanovanus, Simon: 260, 290n
'Villeneuve' (*i.e.* S. Villanovanus?): 257n, 263n, 274n, 276n, 282
'Villemadon, de' ('D.V.'): 224, 226
Vingle, Pierre de, printer: 262n, 287n
Viol, Claude: 294n
Viret, Pierre: 85, 235n, 254n, 255n
Virgil: 130, 198, 251, 253, 259-260
Vitalis, Janus: 110-121, 123-127, 144, 227-233
Vopiscus, Flavius: 192n
Vulteius, Joannes (Jean Visagier): 262, 266n, 270n, 281

Wargocki, Andrzej: 114n
Wechel, André, printer: 216n
Weever, John: 232
Wilson, Thomas: 24

Xenophon: 247n, 361

Young, Jimmy: 336-337, 352-353
Yourcenar, Marguerite: 233

Zamariel, A (*pseud.*): 13n, 74n
Zanchius, Basilius: 137n
Zébédée, André: 269-270, 279n, 282, 288-289
Zosimus the Historian: 189

[370]